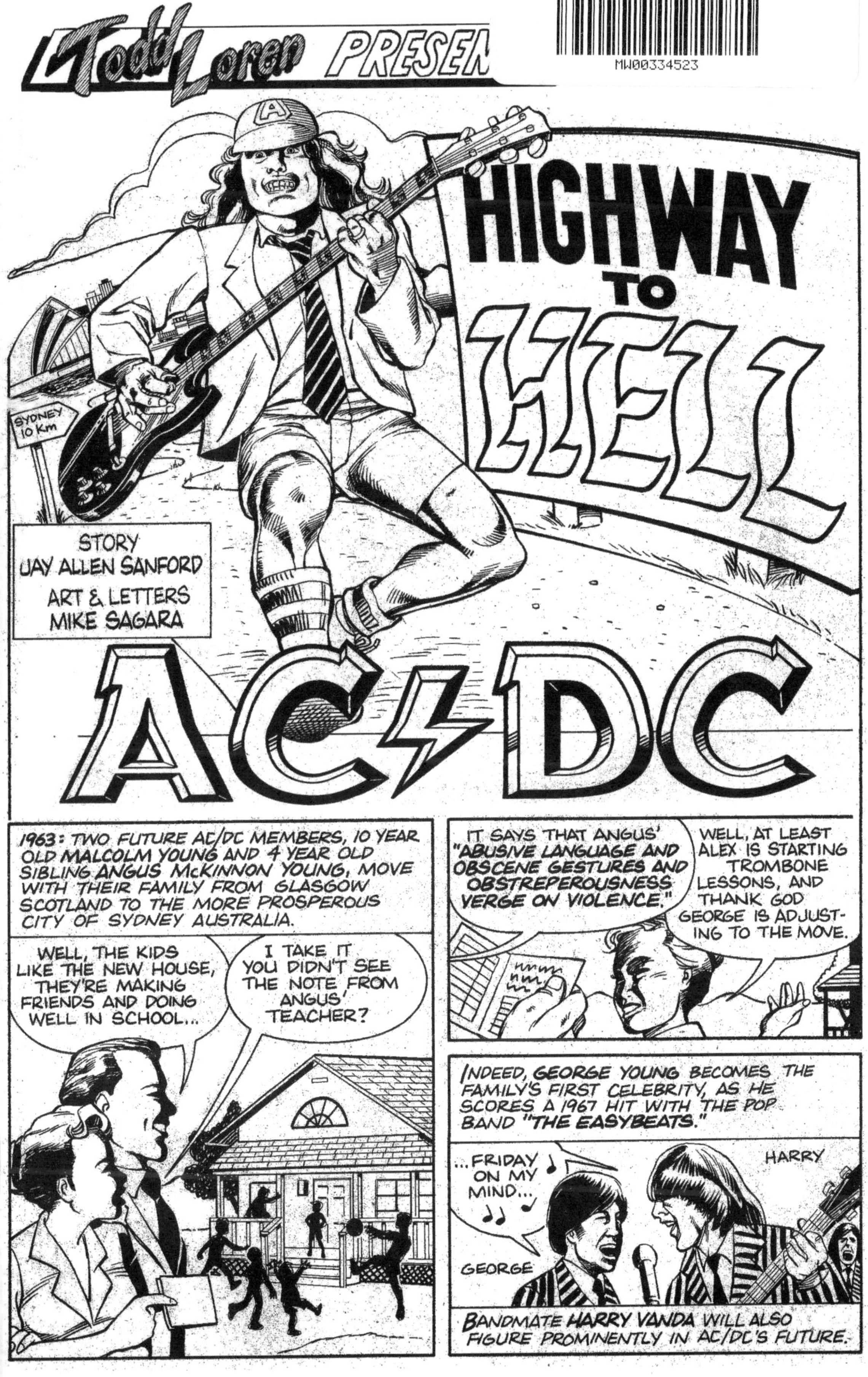

Todd Loren PRESENTS
HIGHWAY TO HELL
SYDNEY 10 Km
STORY
JAY ALLEN SANFORD
ART & LETTERS
MIKE SAGARA
AC/DC
1963: TWO FUTURE AC/DC MEMBERS, 10 YEAR OLD MALCOLM YOUNG AND 4 YEAR OLD SIBLING ANGUS McKINNON YOUNG, MOVE WITH THEIR FAMILY FROM GLASGOW SCOTLAND TO THE MORE PROSPEROUS CITY OF SYDNEY AUSTRALIA.
WELL, THE KIDS LIKE THE NEW HOUSE, THEY'RE MAKING FRIENDS AND DOING WELL IN SCHOOL...
I TAKE IT YOU DIDN'T SEE THE NOTE FROM ANGUS' TEACHER?
IT SAYS THAT ANGUS' "ABUSIVE LANGUAGE AND OBSCENE GESTURES AND OBSTREPEROUSNESS VERGE ON VIOLENCE."
WELL, AT LEAST ALEX IS STARTING TROMBONE LESSONS, AND THANK GOD GEORGE IS ADJUSTING TO THE MOVE.
INDEED, GEORGE YOUNG BECOMES THE FAMILY'S FIRST CELEBRITY, AS HE SCORES A 1967 HIT WITH THE POP BAND "THE EASYBEATS."
...FRIDAY ON MY MIND...
HARRY
GEORGE
BANDMATE HARRY VANDA WILL ALSO FIGURE PROMINENTLY IN AC/DC'S FUTURE.

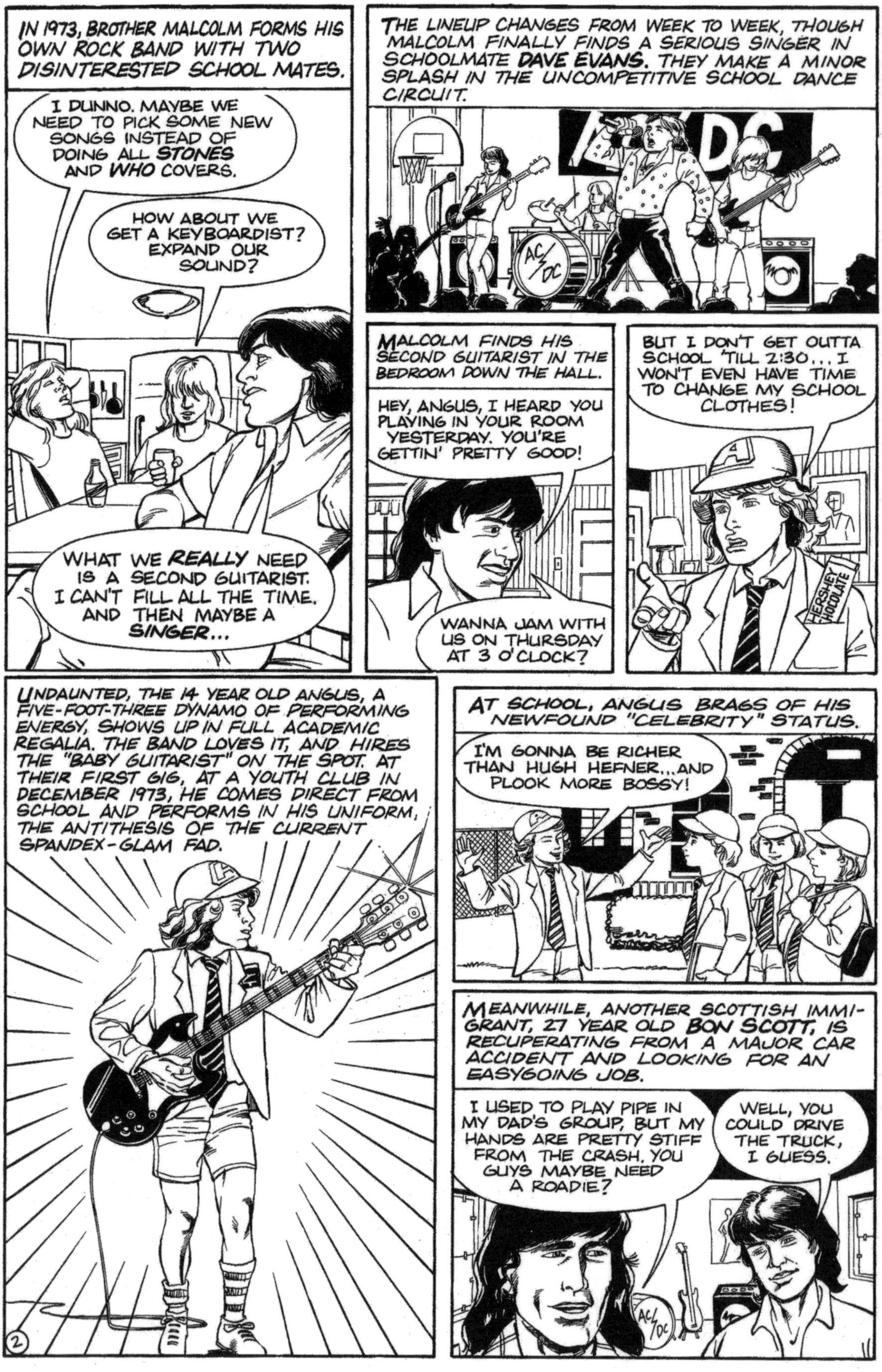

IN 1973, BROTHER MALCOLM FORMS HIS OWN ROCK BAND WITH TWO DISINTERESTED SCHOOL MATES.
I DUNNO. MAYBE WE NEED TO PICK SOME NEW SONGS INSTEAD OF DOING ALL STONES AND WHO COVERS.
HOW ABOUT WE GET A KEYBOARDIST? EXPAND OUR SOUND?
WHAT WE REALLY NEED IS A SECOND GUITARIST. I CAN'T FILL ALL THE TIME. AND THEN MAYBE A SINGER...
THE LINEUP CHANGES FROM WEEK TO WEEK, THOUGH MALCOLM FINALLY FINDS A SERIOUS SINGER IN SCHOOLMATE DAVE EVANS. THEY MAKE A MINOR SPLASH IN THE UNCOMPETITIVE SCHOOL DANCE CIRCUIT.
AC/DC
MALCOLM FINDS HIS SECOND GUITARIST IN THE BEDROOM DOWN THE HALL.
HEY, ANGUS, I HEARD YOU PLAYING IN YOUR ROOM YESTERDAY. YOU'RE GETTIN' PRETTY GOOD!
WANNA JAM WITH US ON THURSDAY AT 3 O'CLOCK?
BUT I DON'T GET OUTTA SCHOOL 'TILL 2:30... I WON'T EVEN HAVE TIME TO CHANGE MY SCHOOL CLOTHES!
HERSHEY CHOCOLATE
UNDAUNTED, THE 14 YEAR OLD ANGUS, A FIVE-FOOT-THREE DYNAMO OF PERFORMING ENERGY, SHOWS UP IN FULL ACADEMIC REGALIA. THE BAND LOVES IT, AND HIRES THE "BABY GUITARIST" ON THE SPOT. AT THEIR FIRST GIG, AT A YOUTH CLUB IN DECEMBER 1973, HE COMES DIRECT FROM SCHOOL AND PERFORMS IN HIS UNIFORM, THE ANTITHESIS OF THE CURRENT SPANDEX-GLAM FAD.
AT SCHOOL, ANGUS BRAGS OF HIS NEWFOUND "CELEBRITY" STATUS.
I'M GONNA BE RICHER THAN HUGH HEFNER...AND PLOOK MORE BOSSY!
MEANWHILE, ANOTHER SCOTTISH IMMIGRANT, 27 YEAR OLD BON SCOTT, IS RECUPERATING FROM A MAJOR CAR ACCIDENT AND LOOKING FOR AN EASYGOING JOB.
I USED TO PLAY PIPE IN MY DAD'S GROUP, BUT MY HANDS ARE PRETTY STIFF FROM THE CRASH. YOU GUYS MAYBE NEED A ROADIE?
WELL, YOU COULD DRIVE THE TRUCK, I GUESS.
AC/DC

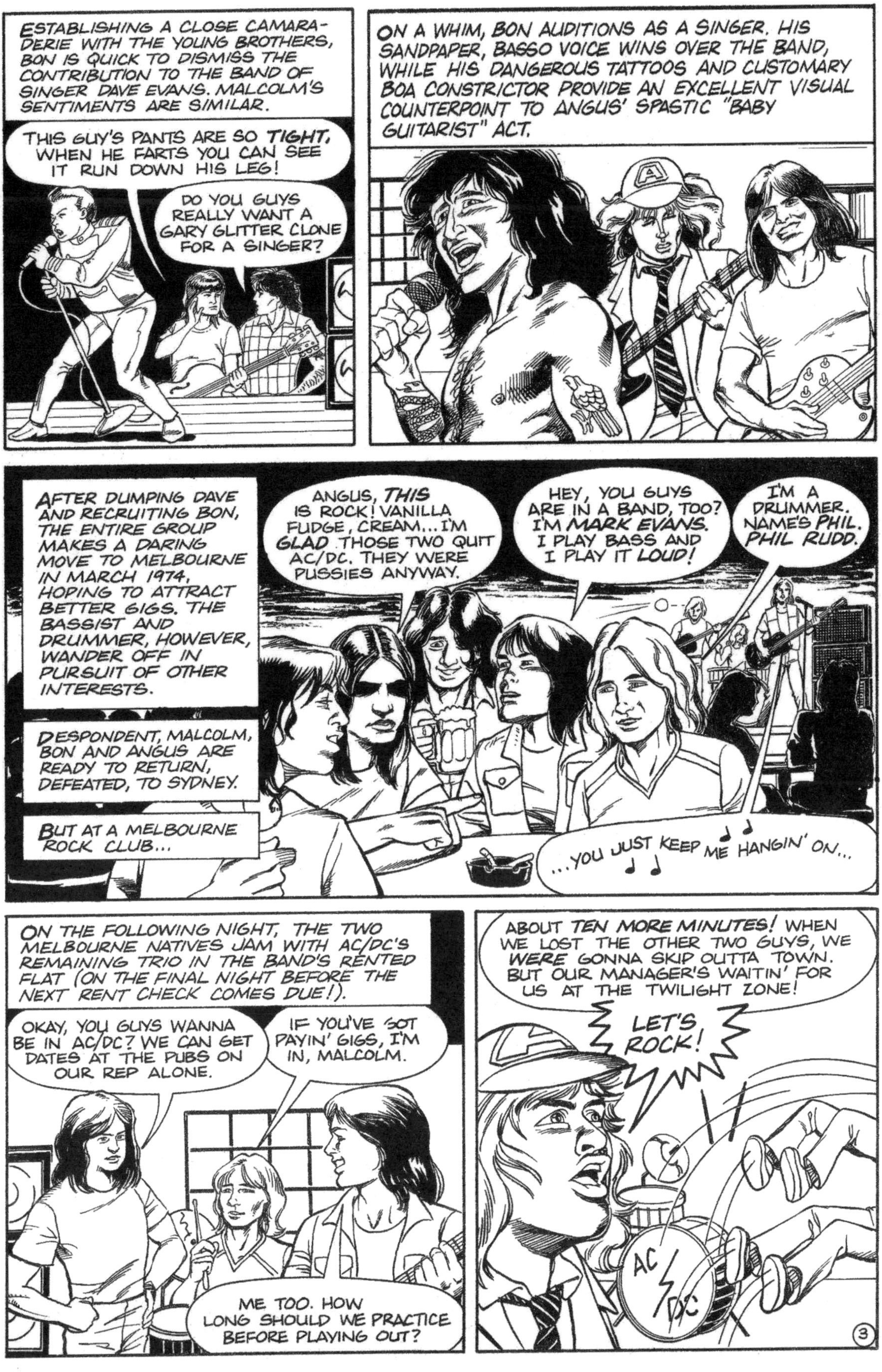
ESTABLISHING A CLOSE CAMARADERIE WITH THE YOUNG BROTHERS, BON IS QUICK TO DISMISS THE CONTRIBUTION TO THE BAND OF SINGER DAVE EVANS. MALCOLM'S SENTIMENTS ARE SIMILAR.
THIS GUY'S PANTS ARE SO TIGHT, WHEN HE FARTS YOU CAN SEE IT RUN DOWN HIS LEG!
DO YOU GUYS REALLY WANT A GARY GLITTER CLONE FOR A SINGER?
ON A WHIM, BON AUDITIONS AS A SINGER. HIS SANDPAPER, BASSO VOICE WINS OVER THE BAND, WHILE HIS DANGEROUS TATTOOS AND CUSTOMARY BOA CONSTRICTOR PROVIDE AN EXCELLENT VISUAL COUNTERPOINT TO ANGUS' SPASTIC "BABY GUITARIST" ACT.
AFTER DUMPING DAVE AND RECRUITING BON, THE ENTIRE GROUP MAKES A DARING MOVE TO MELBOURNE IN MARCH 1974, HOPING TO ATTRACT BETTER GIGS. THE BASSIST AND DRUMMER, HOWEVER, WANDER OFF IN PURSUIT OF OTHER INTERESTS.
DESPONDENT, MALCOLM, BON AND ANGUS ARE READY TO RETURN, DEFEATED, TO SYDNEY.
BUT AT A MELBOURNE ROCK CLUB...
ANGUS, THIS IS ROCK! VANILLA FUDGE, CREAM... I'M GLAD THOSE TWO QUIT AC/DC. THEY WERE PUSSIES ANYWAY.
HEY, YOU GUYS ARE IN A BAND, TOO? I'M MARK EVANS. I PLAY BASS AND I PLAY IT LOUD!
I'M A DRUMMER. NAME'S PHIL. PHIL RUDD.
...YOU JUST KEEP ME HANGIN' ON...
ON THE FOLLOWING NIGHT, THE TWO MELBOURNE NATIVES JAM WITH AC/DC'S REMAINING TRIO IN THE BAND'S RENTED FLAT (ON THE FINAL NIGHT BEFORE THE NEXT RENT CHECK COMES DUE!).
OKAY, YOU GUYS WANNA BE IN AC/DC? WE CAN GET DATES AT THE PUBS ON OUR REP ALONE.
IF YOU'VE GOT PAYIN' GIGS, I'M IN, MALCOLM.
ME TOO. HOW LONG SHOULD WE PRACTICE BEFORE PLAYING OUT?
ABOUT TEN MORE MINUTES! WHEN WE LOST THE OTHER TWO GUYS, WE WERE GONNA SKIP OUTTA TOWN. BUT OUR MANAGER'S WAITIN' FOR US AT THE TWILIGHT ZONE!
LET'S ROCK!
AC/DC
3

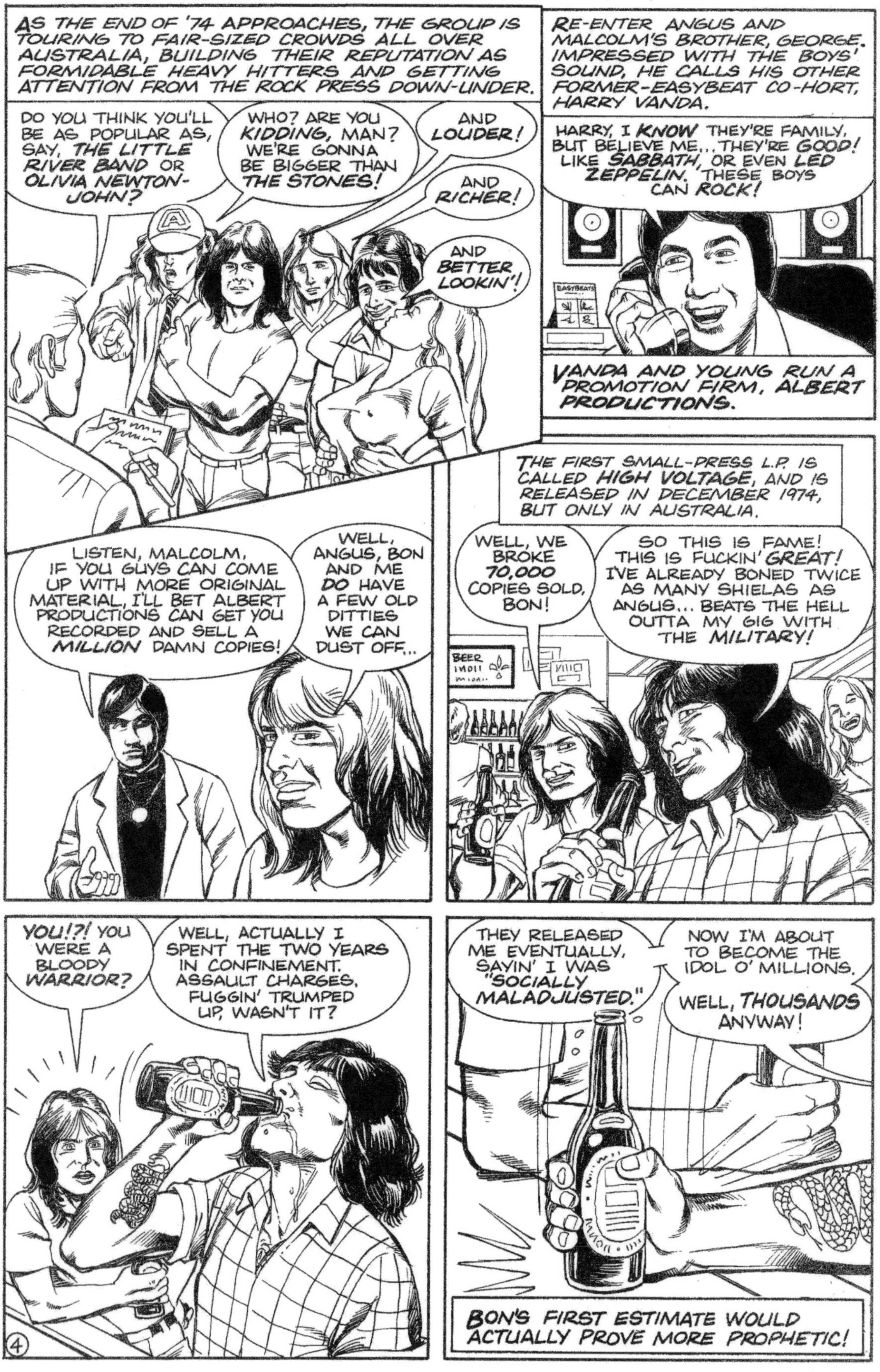

AS THE END OF '74 APPROACHES, THE GROUP IS TOURING TO FAIR-SIZED CROWDS ALL OVER AUSTRALIA, BUILDING THEIR REPUTATION AS FORMIDABLE HEAVY HITTERS AND GETTING ATTENTION FROM THE ROCK PRESS DOWN-UNDER.
DO YOU THINK YOU'LL BE AS POPULAR AS, SAY, THE LITTLE RIVER BAND OR OLIVIA NEWTON-JOHN?
WHO? ARE YOU KIDDING, MAN? WE'RE GONNA BE BIGGER THAN THE STONES!
AND LOUDER!
AND RICHER!
AND BETTER LOOKIN'!
RE-ENTER ANGUS AND MALCOLM'S BROTHER, GEORGE. IMPRESSED WITH THE BOYS' SOUND, HE CALLS HIS OTHER FORMER-EASYBEAT CO-HORT, HARRY VANDA.
HARRY, I KNOW THEY'RE FAMILY, BUT BELIEVE ME... THEY'RE GOOD! LIKE SABBATH, OR EVEN LED ZEPPELIN. THESE BOYS CAN ROCK!
EASYBEATS
VANDA AND YOUNG RUN A PROMOTION FIRM, ALBERT PRODUCTIONS.
LISTEN, MALCOLM, IF YOU GUYS CAN COME UP WITH MORE ORIGINAL MATERIAL, I'LL BET ALBERT PRODUCTIONS CAN GET YOU RECORDED AND SELL A MILLION DAMN COPIES!
WELL, ANGUS, BON AND ME DO HAVE A FEW OLD DITTIES WE CAN DUST OFF...
THE FIRST SMALL-PRESS L.P. IS CALLED HIGH VOLTAGE, AND IS RELEASED IN DECEMBER 1974, BUT ONLY IN AUSTRALIA.
WELL, WE BROKE 70,000 COPIES SOLD, BON!
SO THIS IS FAME! THIS IS FUCKIN' GREAT! I'VE ALREADY BONED TWICE AS MANY SHIELAS AS ANGUS... BEATS THE HELL OUTTA MY GIG WITH THE MILITARY!
BEER
YOU!?! YOU WERE A BLOODY WARRIOR?
WELL, ACTUALLY I SPENT THE TWO YEARS IN CONFINEMENT. ASSAULT CHARGES, FUGGIN' TRUMPED UP, WASN'T IT?
THEY RELEASED ME EVENTUALLY, SAYIN' I WAS "SOCIALLY MALADJUSTED."
NOW I'M ABOUT TO BECOME THE IDOL O' MILLIONS.
WELL, THOUSANDS ANYWAY!
BON'S FIRST ESTIMATE WOULD ACTUALLY PROVE MORE PROPHETIC!

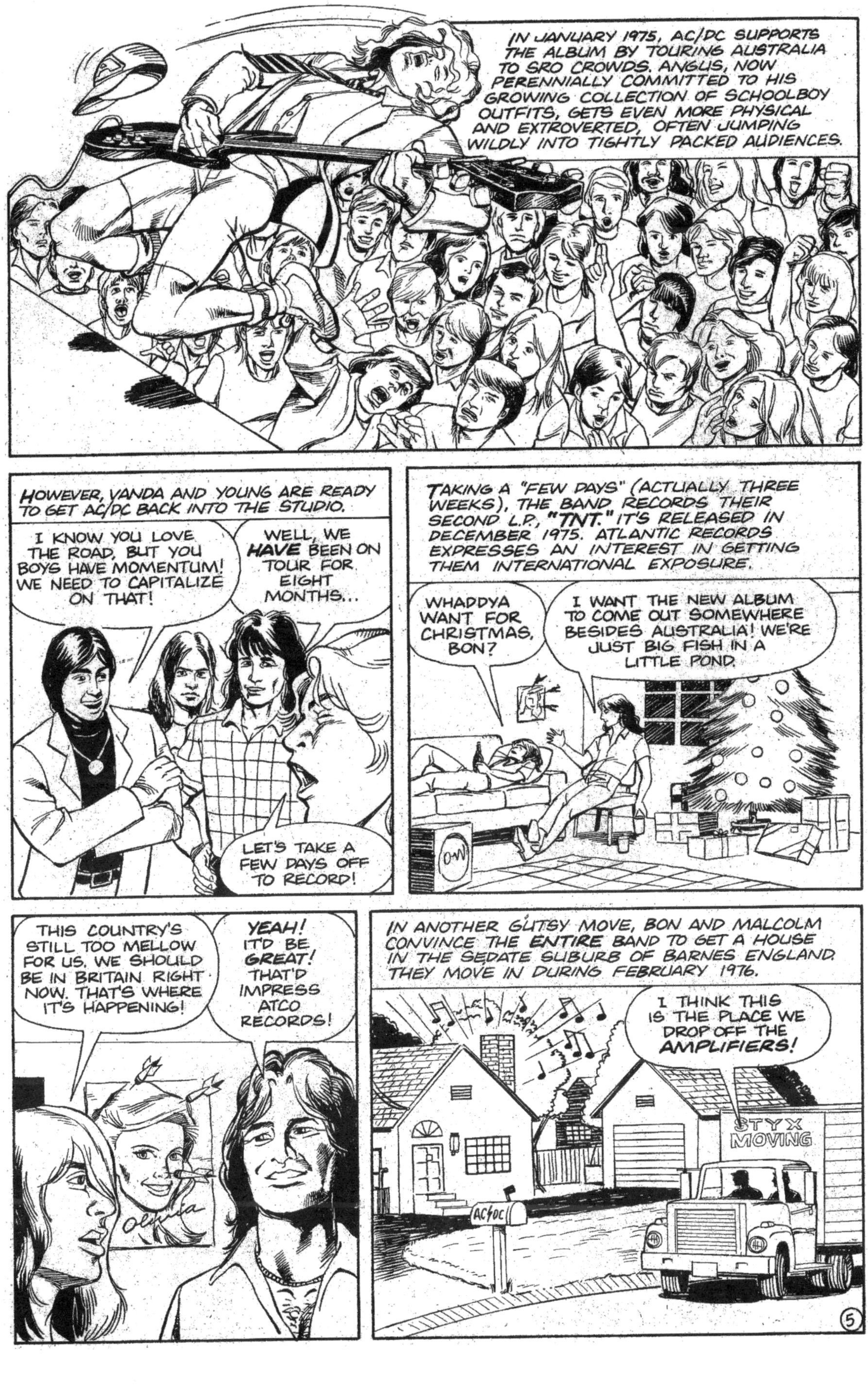
IN JANUARY 1975, AC/DC SUPPORTS THE ALBUM BY TOURING AUSTRALIA TO SRO CROWDS. ANGUS, NOW PERENNIALLY COMMITTED TO HIS GROWING COLLECTION OF SCHOOLBOY OUTFITS, GETS EVEN MORE PHYSICAL AND EXTROVERTED, OFTEN JUMPING WILDLY INTO TIGHTLY PACKED AUDIENCES.
HOWEVER, VANDA AND YOUNG ARE READY TO GET AC/DC BACK INTO THE STUDIO.
I KNOW YOU LOVE THE ROAD, BUT YOU BOYS HAVE MOMENTUM! WE NEED TO CAPITALIZE ON THAT!
WELL, WE HAVE BEEN ON TOUR FOR EIGHT MONTHS...
LET'S TAKE A FEW DAYS OFF TO RECORD!
TAKING A "FEW DAYS" (ACTUALLY THREE WEEKS), THE BAND RECORDS THEIR SECOND L.P., "TNT." IT'S RELEASED IN DECEMBER 1975. ATLANTIC RECORDS EXPRESSES AN INTEREST IN GETTING THEM INTERNATIONAL EXPOSURE.
WHADDYA WANT FOR CHRISTMAS, BON?
I WANT THE NEW ALBUM TO COME OUT SOMEWHERE BESIDES AUSTRALIA! WE'RE JUST BIG FISH IN A LITTLE POND.
THIS COUNTRY'S STILL TOO MELLOW FOR US. WE SHOULD BE IN BRITAIN RIGHT NOW. THAT'S WHERE IT'S HAPPENING!
YEAH! IT'D BE GREAT! THAT'D IMPRESS ATCO RECORDS!
Olivia
IN ANOTHER GUTSY MOVE, BON AND MALCOLM CONVINCE THE ENTIRE BAND TO GET A HOUSE IN THE SEDATE SUBURB OF BARNES ENGLAND. THEY MOVE IN DURING FEBRUARY 1976.
I THINK THIS IS THE PLACE WE DROP OFF THE AMPLIFIERS!
STYX MOVING
AC/DC

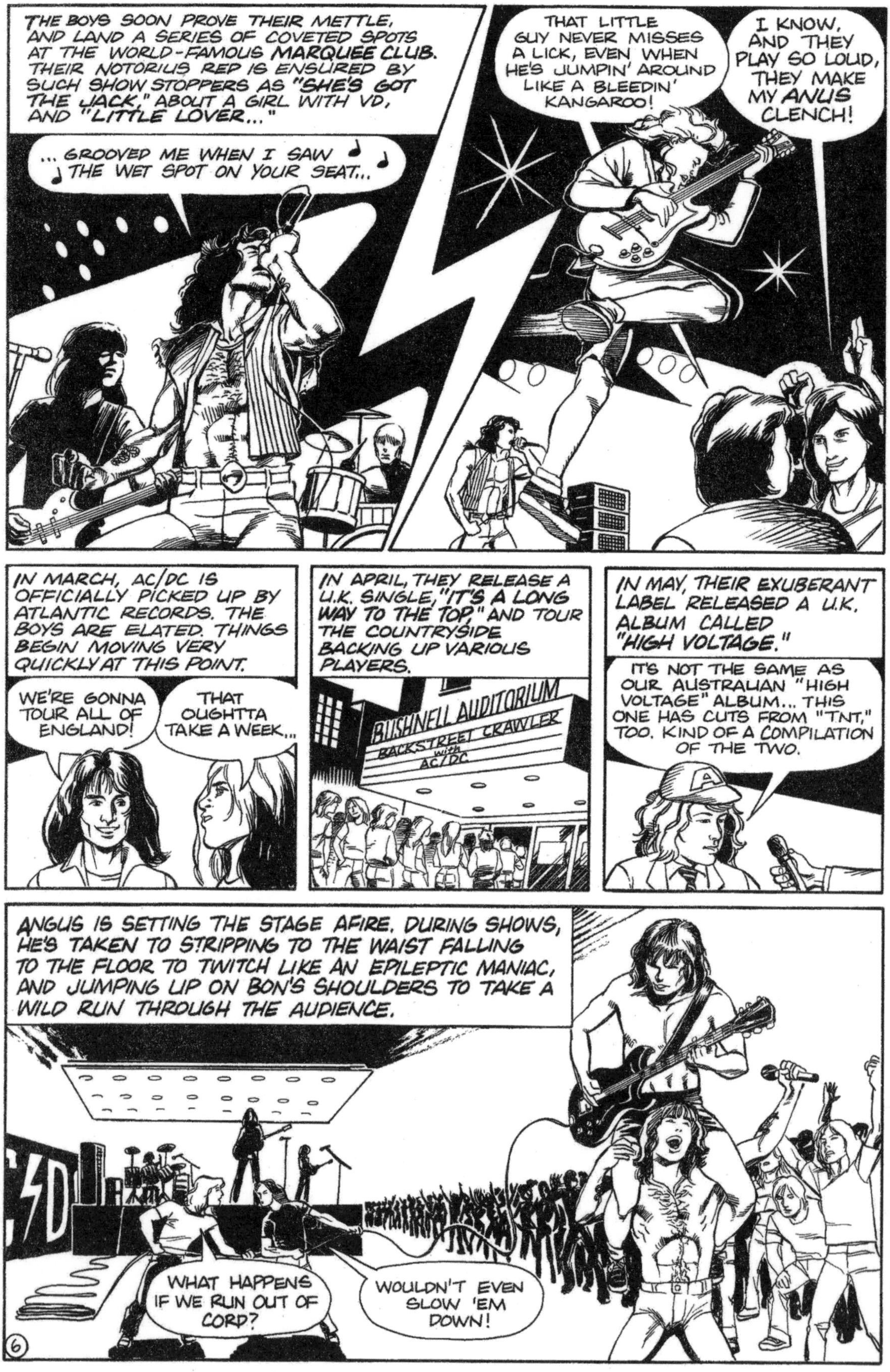
THE BOYS SOON PROVE THEIR METTLE, AND LAND A SERIES OF COVETED SPOTS AT THE WORLD-FAMOUS MARQUEE CLUB. THEIR NOTORIUS REP IS ENSURED BY SUCH SHOW STOPPERS AS "SHE'S GOT THE JACK," ABOUT A GIRL WITH VD, AND "LITTLE LOVER..."
... GROOVED ME WHEN I SAW THE WET SPOT ON YOUR SEAT...
THAT LITTLE GUY NEVER MISSES A LICK, EVEN WHEN HE'S JUMPIN' AROUND LIKE A BLEEDIN' KANGAROO!
I KNOW, AND THEY PLAY SO LOUD, THEY MAKE MY ANUS CLENCH!
IN MARCH, AC/DC IS OFFICIALLY PICKED UP BY ATLANTIC RECORDS. THE BOYS ARE ELATED. THINGS BEGIN MOVING VERY QUICKLY AT THIS POINT.
WE'RE GONNA TOUR ALL OF ENGLAND!
THAT OUGHTTA TAKE A WEEK...
IN APRIL, THEY RELEASE A U.K. SINGLE, "IT'S A LONG WAY TO THE TOP," AND TOUR THE COUNTRYSIDE BACKING UP VARIOUS PLAYERS.
BUSHNELL AUDITORIUM
BACKSTREET CRAWLER
with
AC/DC
IN MAY, THEIR EXUBERANT LABEL RELEASED A U.K. ALBUM CALLED "HIGH VOLTAGE."
IT'S NOT THE SAME AS OUR AUSTRALIAN "HIGH VOLTAGE" ALBUM... THIS ONE HAS CUTS FROM "TNT," TOO. KIND OF A COMPILATION OF THE TWO.
A
ANGUS IS SETTING THE STAGE AFIRE. DURING SHOWS, HE'S TAKEN TO STRIPPING TO THE WAIST FALLING TO THE FLOOR TO TWITCH LIKE AN EPILEPTIC MANIAC, AND JUMPING UP ON BON'S SHOULDERS TO TAKE A WILD RUN THROUGH THE AUDIENCE.
WHAT HAPPENS IF WE RUN OUT OF CORD?
WOULDN'T EVEN SLOW 'EM DOWN!

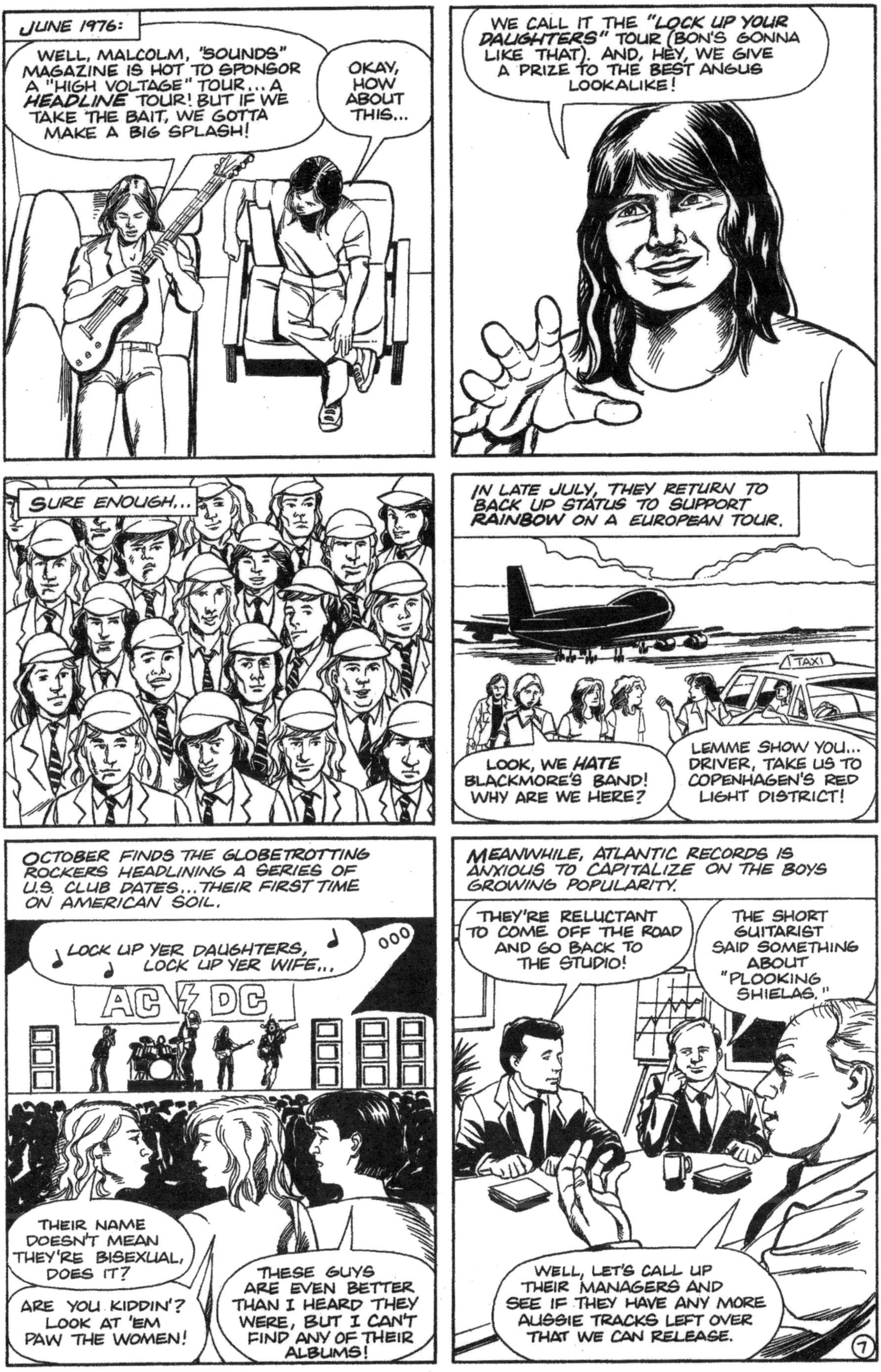
JUNE 1976:
WELL, MALCOLM, "SOUNDS" MAGAZINE IS HOT TO SPONSOR A "HIGH VOLTAGE" TOUR... A HEADLINE TOUR! BUT IF WE TAKE THE BAIT, WE GOTTA MAKE A BIG SPLASH!
OKAY, HOW ABOUT THIS...
WE CALL IT THE "LOCK UP YOUR DAUGHTERS" TOUR (BON'S GONNA LIKE THAT). AND, HEY, WE GIVE A PRIZE TO THE BEST ANGUS LOOKALIKE!
SURE ENOUGH...
IN LATE JULY, THEY RETURN TO BACK UP STATUS TO SUPPORT RAINBOW ON A EUROPEAN TOUR.
TAXI
LOOK, WE HATE BLACKMORE'S BAND! WHY ARE WE HERE?
LEMME SHOW YOU... DRIVER, TAKE US TO COPENHAGEN'S RED LIGHT DISTRICT!
OCTOBER FINDS THE GLOBETROTTING ROCKERS HEADLINING A SERIES OF U.S. CLUB DATES... THEIR FIRST TIME ON AMERICAN SOIL.
LOCK UP YER DAUGHTERS, LOCK UP YER WIFE...
AC DC
THEIR NAME DOESN'T MEAN THEY'RE BISEXUAL, DOES IT?
ARE YOU KIDDIN'? LOOK AT 'EM PAW THE WOMEN!
THESE GUYS ARE EVEN BETTER THAN I HEARD THEY WERE, BUT I CAN'T FIND ANY OF THEIR ALBUMS!
MEANWHILE, ATLANTIC RECORDS IS ANXIOUS TO CAPITALIZE ON THE BOYS GROWING POPULARITY.
THEY'RE RELUCTANT TO COME OFF THE ROAD AND GO BACK TO THE STUDIO!
THE SHORT GUITARIST SAID SOMETHING ABOUT "PLOOKING SHIELAS."
WELL, LET'S CALL UP THEIR MANAGERS AND SEE IF THEY HAVE ANY MORE AUSSIE TRACKS LEFT OVER THAT WE CAN RELEASE.

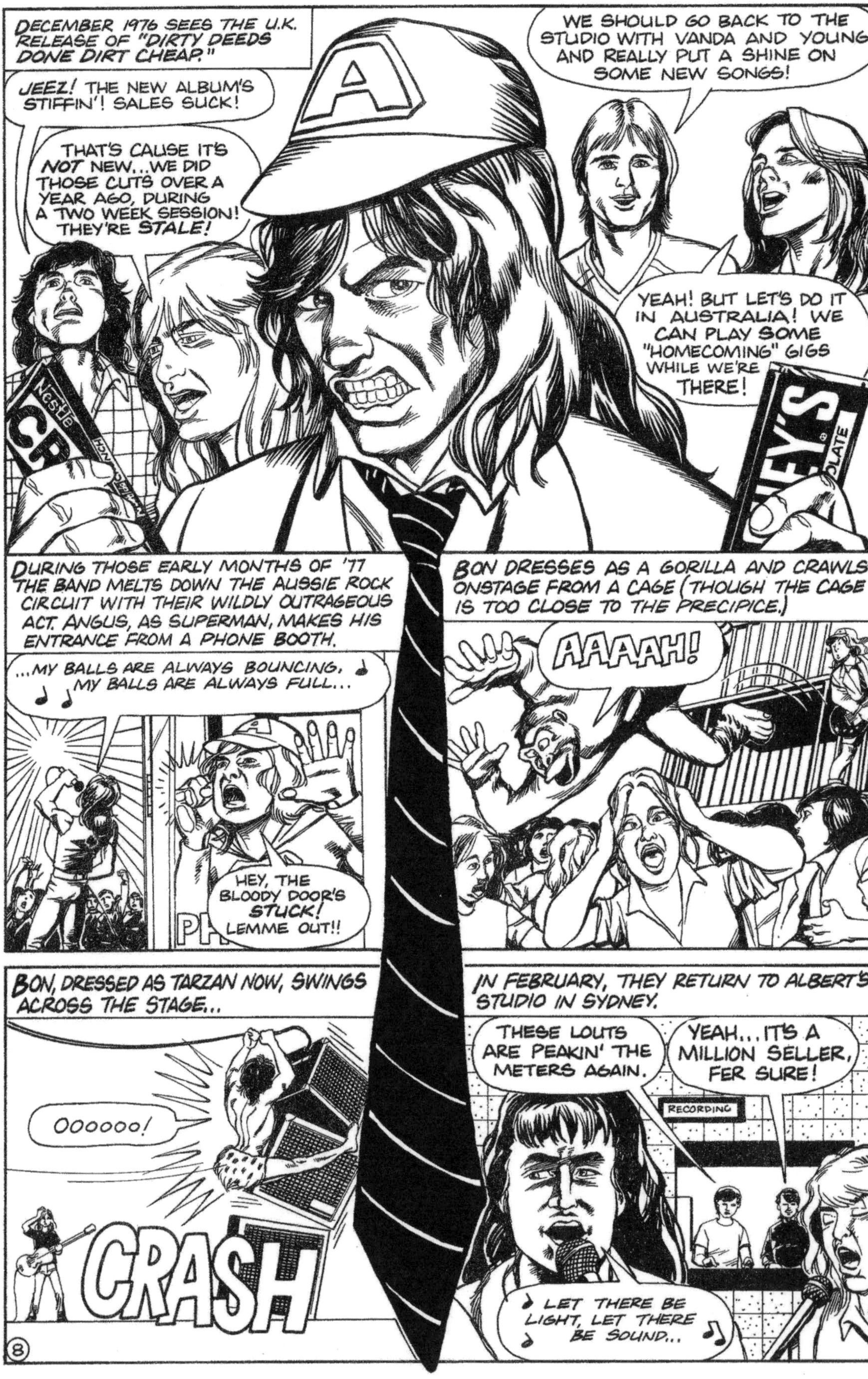
DECEMBER 1976 SEES THE U.K. RELEASE OF "DIRTY DEEDS DONE DIRT CHEAP."
JEEZ! THE NEW ALBUM'S STIFFIN'! SALES SUCK!
THAT'S CAUSE IT'S NOT NEW...WE DID THOSE CUTS OVER A YEAR AGO, DURING A TWO WEEK SESSION! THEY'RE STALE!
WE SHOULD GO BACK TO THE STUDIO WITH VANDA AND YOUNG AND REALLY PUT A SHINE ON SOME NEW SONGS!
YEAH! BUT LET'S DO IT IN AUSTRALIA! WE CAN PLAY SOME "HOMECOMING" GIGS WHILE WE'RE THERE!
Nestlé
DURING THOSE EARLY MONTHS OF '77 THE BAND MELTS DOWN THE AUSSIE ROCK CIRCUIT WITH THEIR WILDLY OUTRAGEOUS ACT. ANGUS, AS SUPERMAN, MAKES HIS ENTRANCE FROM A PHONE BOOTH.
...MY BALLS ARE ALWAYS BOUNCING, MY BALLS ARE ALWAYS FULL...
HEY, THE BLOODY DOOR'S STUCK! LEMME OUT!!
BON DRESSES AS A GORILLA AND CRAWLS ONSTAGE FROM A CAGE (THOUGH THE CAGE IS TOO CLOSE TO THE PRECIPICE.)
AAAAH!
BON, DRESSED AS TARZAN NOW, SWINGS ACROSS THE STAGE...
OOOOOO!
CRASH
IN FEBRUARY, THEY RETURN TO ALBERT'S STUDIO IN SYDNEY.
THESE LOUTS ARE PEAKIN' THE METERS AGAIN.
YEAH...IT'S A MILLION SELLER, FER SURE!
RECORDING
LET THERE BE LIGHT, LET THERE BE SOUND...

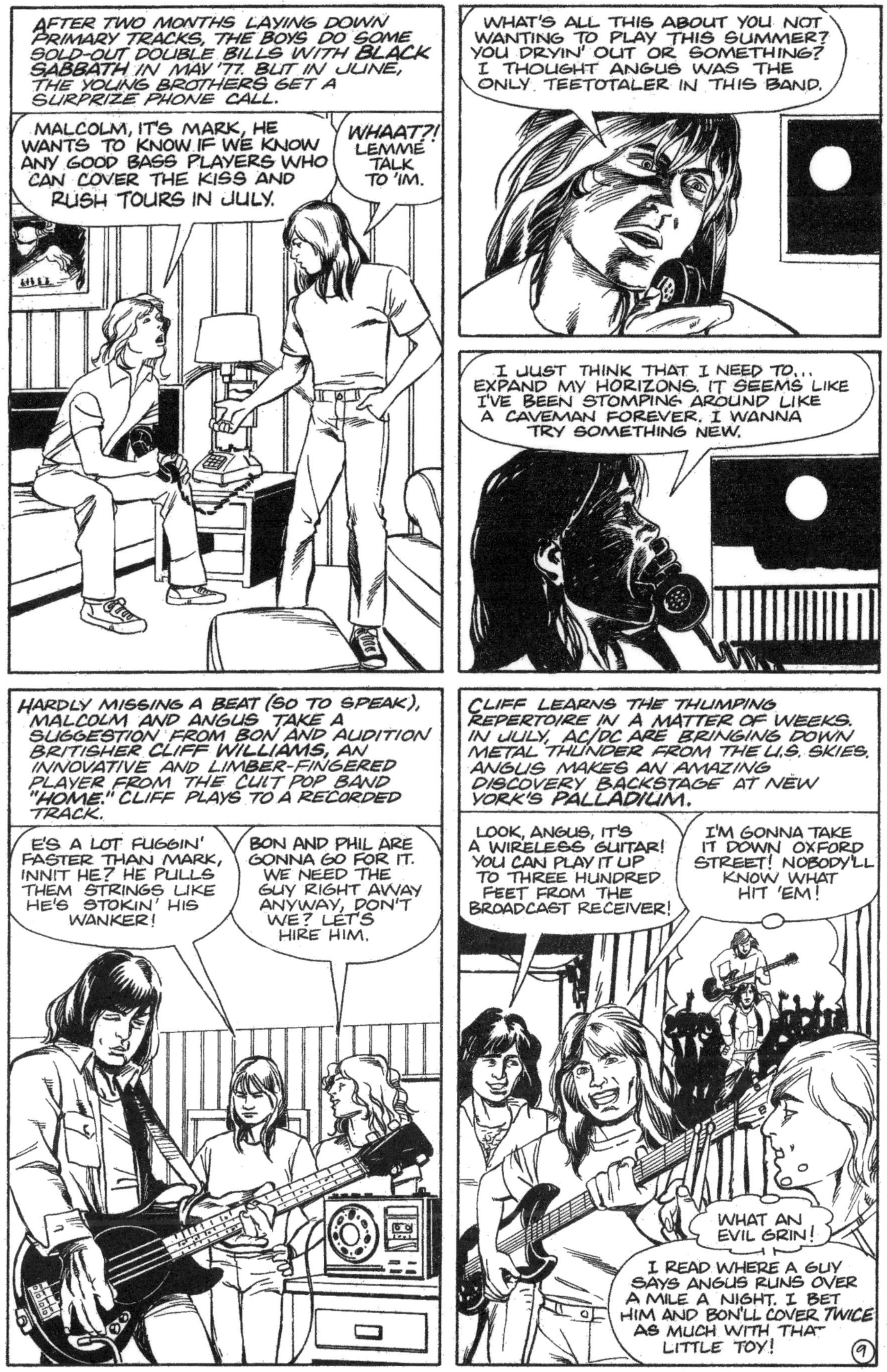

AFTER TWO MONTHS LAYING DOWN PRIMARY TRACKS, THE BOYS DO SOME SOLD-OUT DOUBLE BILLS WITH BLACK SABBATH IN MAY '77. BUT IN JUNE, THE YOUNG BROTHERS GET A SURPRIZE PHONE CALL.
MALCOLM, IT'S MARK, HE WANTS TO KNOW IF WE KNOW ANY GOOD BASS PLAYERS WHO CAN COVER THE KISS AND RUSH TOURS IN JULY.
WHAAT?! LEMME TALK TO 'IM.
WHAT'S ALL THIS ABOUT YOU NOT WANTING TO PLAY THIS SUMMER? YOU DRYIN' OUT OR SOMETHING? I THOUGHT ANGUS WAS THE ONLY TEETOTALER IN THIS BAND.
I JUST THINK THAT I NEED TO... EXPAND MY HORIZONS. IT SEEMS LIKE I'VE BEEN STOMPING AROUND LIKE A CAVEMAN FOREVER. I WANNA TRY SOMETHING NEW.
HARDLY MISSING A BEAT (SO TO SPEAK), MALCOLM AND ANGUS TAKE A SUGGESTION FROM BON AND AUDITION BRITISHER CLIFF WILLIAMS, AN INNOVATIVE AND LIMBER-FINGERED PLAYER FROM THE CULT POP BAND "HOME." CLIFF PLAYS TO A RECORDED TRACK.
'E'S A LOT FUGGIN' FASTER THAN MARK, INNIT HE? HE PULLS THEM STRINGS LIKE HE'S STOKIN' HIS WANKER!
BON AND PHIL ARE GONNA GO FOR IT. WE NEED THE GUY RIGHT AWAY ANYWAY, DON'T WE? LET'S HIRE HIM.
CLIFF LEARNS THE THUMPING REPERTOIRE IN A MATTER OF WEEKS. IN JULY, AC/DC ARE BRINGING DOWN METAL THUNDER FROM THE U.S. SKIES. ANGUS MAKES AN AMAZING DISCOVERY BACKSTAGE AT NEW YORK'S PALLADIUM.
LOOK, ANGUS, IT'S A WIRELESS GUITAR! YOU CAN PLAY IT UP TO THREE HUNDRED FEET FROM THE BROADCAST RECEIVER!
I'M GONNA TAKE IT DOWN OXFORD STREET! NOBODY'LL KNOW WHAT HIT 'EM!
WHAT AN EVIL GRIN!
I READ WHERE A GUY SAYS ANGUS RUNS OVER A MILE A NIGHT. I BET HIM AND BON'LL COVER TWICE AS MUCH WITH THAT LITTLE TOY!

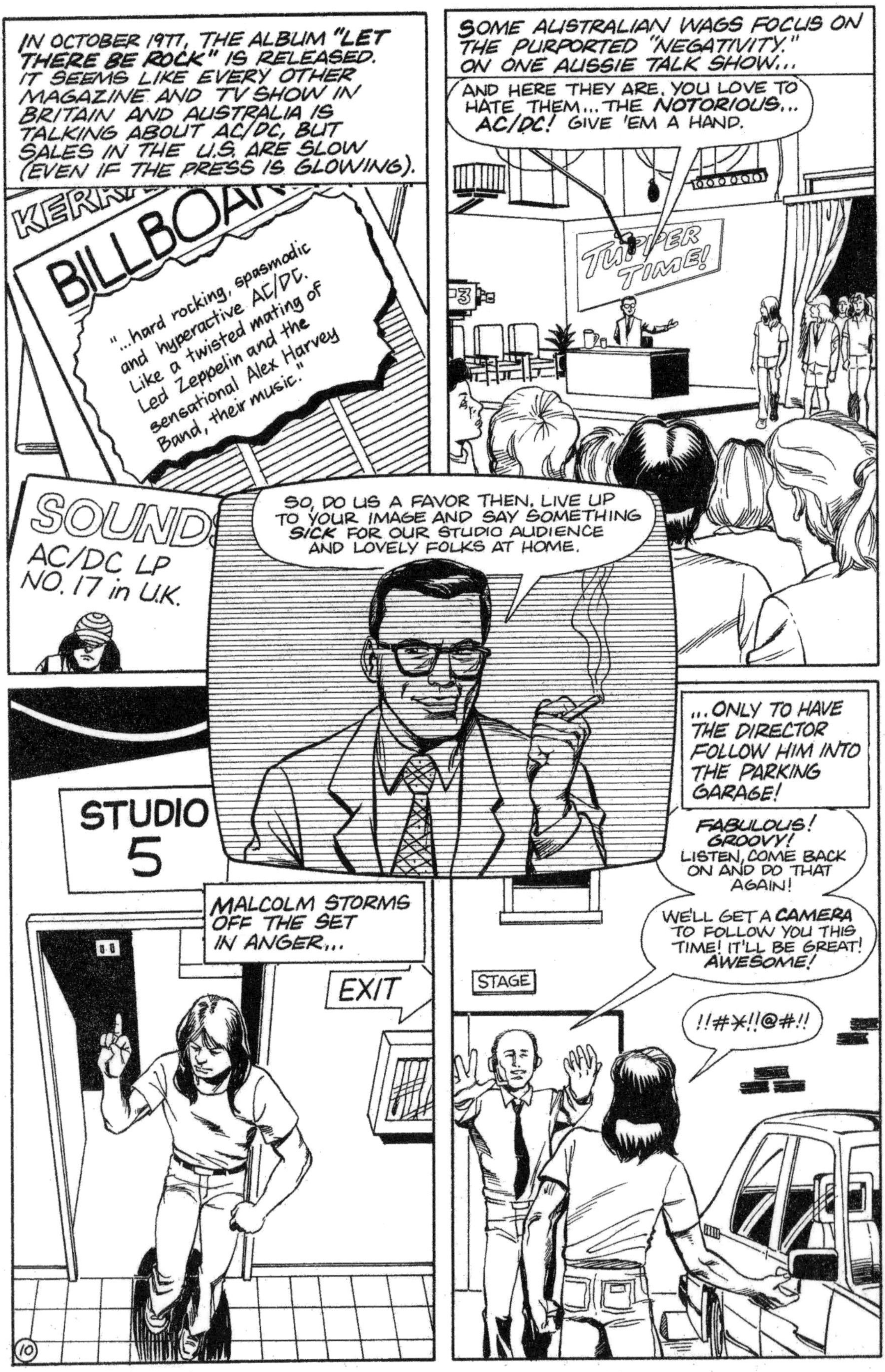

IN OCTOBER 1977, THE ALBUM "LET THERE BE ROCK" IS RELEASED. IT SEEMS LIKE EVERY OTHER MAGAZINE AND TV SHOW IN BRITAIN AND AUSTRALIA IS TALKING ABOUT AC/DC, BUT SALES IN THE U.S. ARE SLOW (EVEN IF THE PRESS IS GLOWING).
BILLBOARD
"...hard rocking, spasmodic and hyperactive AC/DC. Like a twisted mating of Led Zeppelin and the sensational Alex Harvey Band, their music."
SOUNDS
AC/DC LP NO. 17 in U.K.
SOME AUSTRALIAN WAGS FOCUS ON THE PURPORTED "NEGATIVITY." ON ONE AUSSIE TALK SHOW...
AND HERE THEY ARE. YOU LOVE TO HATE THEM... THE NOTORIOUS... AC/DC! GIVE 'EM A HAND.
TUPPER TIME!
SO, DO US A FAVOR THEN. LIVE UP TO YOUR IMAGE AND SAY SOMETHING SICK FOR OUR STUDIO AUDIENCE AND LOVELY FOLKS AT HOME.
STUDIO 5
MALCOLM STORMS OFF THE SET IN ANGER...
EXIT
...ONLY TO HAVE THE DIRECTOR FOLLOW HIM INTO THE PARKING GARAGE!
FABULOUS! GROOVY! LISTEN, COME BACK ON AND DO THAT AGAIN!
WE'LL GET A CAMERA TO FOLLOW YOU THIS TIME! IT'LL BE GREAT! AWESOME!
STAGE
!!#*!!@#!!

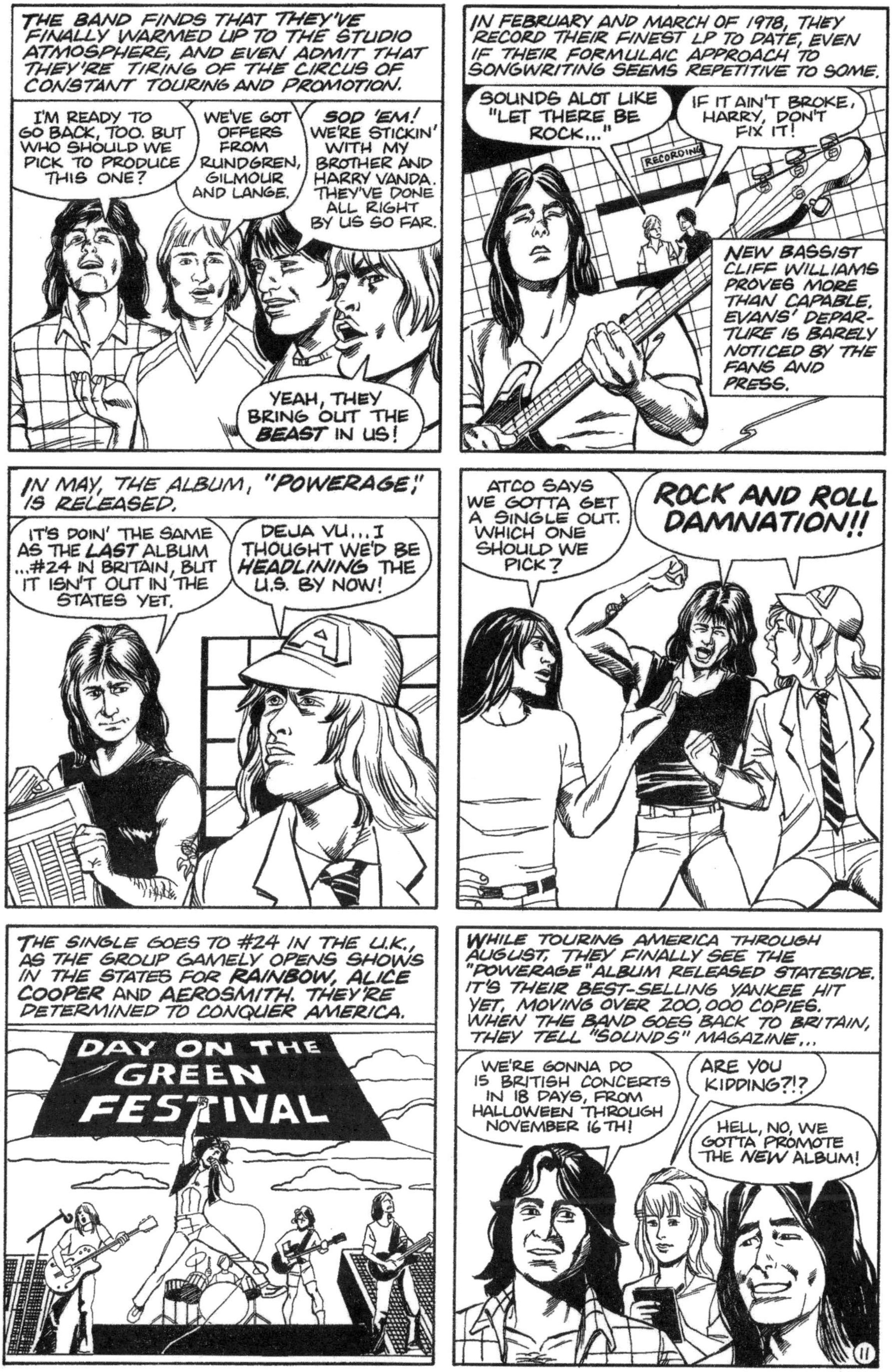
THE BAND FINDS THAT THEY'VE FINALLY WARMED UP TO THE STUDIO ATMOSPHERE, AND EVEN ADMIT THAT THEY'RE TIRING OF THE CIRCUS OF CONSTANT TOURING AND PROMOTION.
I'M READY TO GO BACK, TOO. BUT WHO SHOULD WE PICK TO PRODUCE THIS ONE?
WE'VE GOT OFFERS FROM RUNDGREN, GILMOUR AND LANGE.
SOD 'EM! WE'RE STICKIN' WITH MY BROTHER AND HARRY VANDA. THEY'VE DONE ALL RIGHT BY US SO FAR.
YEAH, THEY BRING OUT THE BEAST IN US!
IN FEBRUARY AND MARCH OF 1978, THEY RECORD THEIR FINEST LP TO DATE, EVEN IF THEIR FORMULAIC APPROACH TO SONGWRITING SEEMS REPETITIVE TO SOME.
SOUNDS ALOT LIKE "LET THERE BE ROCK..."
IF IT AIN'T BROKE, HARRY, DON'T FIX IT!
RECORDING
NEW BASSIST CLIFF WILLIAMS PROVES MORE THAN CAPABLE. EVANS' DEPARTURE IS BARELY NOTICED BY THE FANS AND PRESS.
IN MAY, THE ALBUM, "POWERAGE," IS RELEASED.
IT'S DOIN' THE SAME AS THE LAST ALBUM ...#24 IN BRITAIN, BUT IT ISN'T OUT IN THE STATES YET.
DEJA VU... I THOUGHT WE'D BE HEADLINING THE U.S. BY NOW!
ATCO SAYS WE GOTTA GET A SINGLE OUT. WHICH ONE SHOULD WE PICK?
ROCK AND ROLL DAMNATION!!
THE SINGLE GOES TO #24 IN THE U.K., AS THE GROUP GAMELY OPENS SHOWS IN THE STATES FOR RAINBOW, ALICE COOPER AND AEROSMITH. THEY'RE DETERMINED TO CONQUER AMERICA.
DAY ON THE GREEN FESTIVAL
WHILE TOURING AMERICA THROUGH AUGUST, THEY FINALLY SEE THE "POWERAGE" ALBUM RELEASED STATESIDE. IT'S THEIR BEST-SELLING YANKEE HIT YET, MOVING OVER 200,000 COPIES. WHEN THE BAND GOES BACK TO BRITAIN, THEY TELL "SOUNDS" MAGAZINE...
WE'RE GONNA DO 15 BRITISH CONCERTS IN 18 DAYS, FROM HALLOWEEN THROUGH NOVEMBER 16TH!
ARE YOU KIDDING?!?
HELL, NO, WE GOTTA PROMOTE THE NEW ALBUM!
11

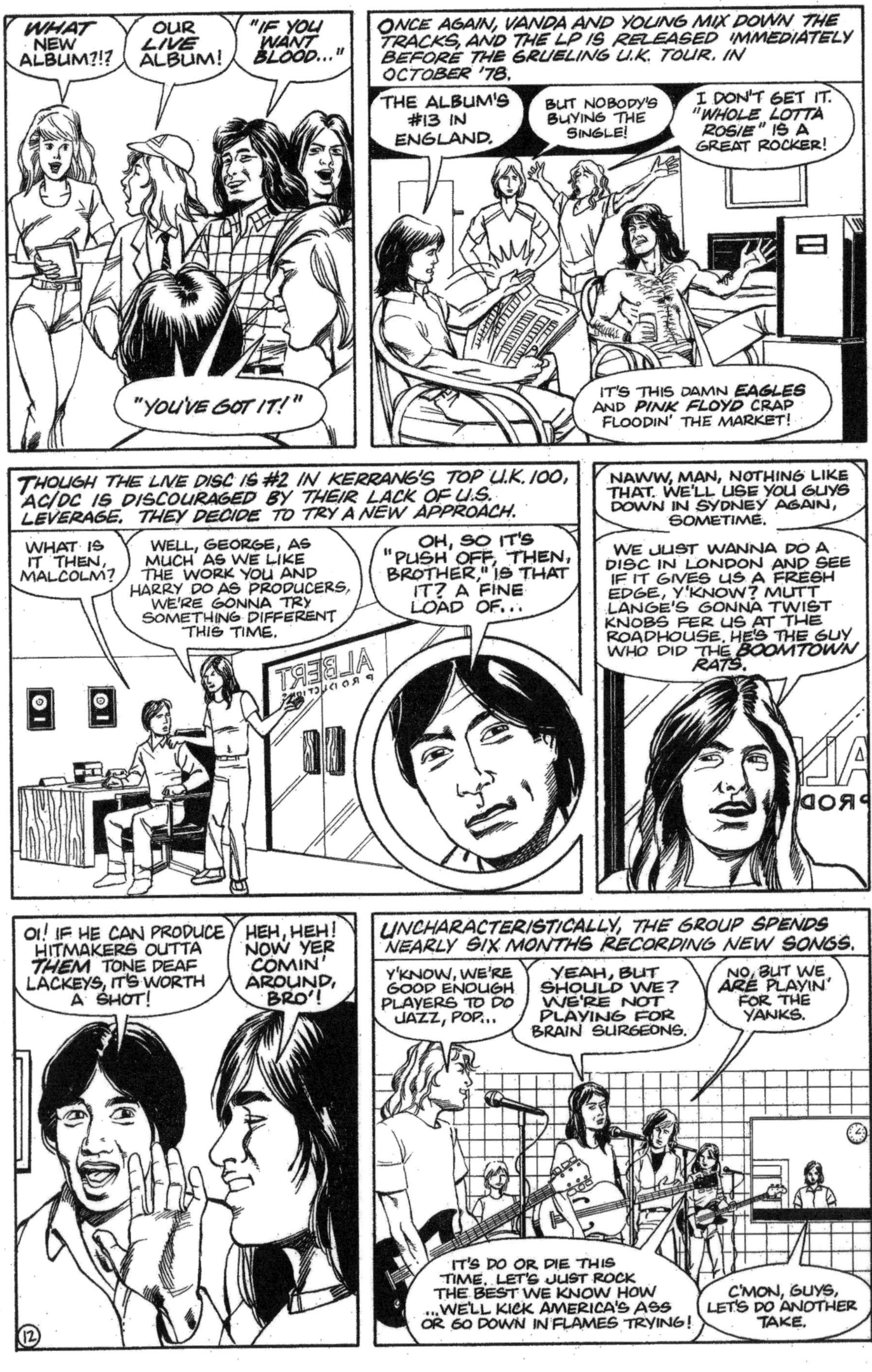
WHAT NEW ALBUM?!?
OUR LIVE ALBUM!
"IF YOU WANT BLOOD..."
"YOU'VE GOT IT!"
ONCE AGAIN, VANDA AND YOUNG MIX DOWN THE TRACKS, AND THE LP IS RELEASED IMMEDIATELY BEFORE THE GRUELING U.K. TOUR, IN OCTOBER '78.
THE ALBUM'S #13 IN ENGLAND.
BUT NOBODY'S BUYING THE SINGLE!
I DON'T GET IT. "WHOLE LOTTA ROSIE" IS A GREAT ROCKER!
IT'S THIS DAMN EAGLES AND PINK FLOYD CRAP FLOODIN' THE MARKET!
THOUGH THE LIVE DISC IS #2 IN KERRANG'S TOP U.K. 100, AC/DC IS DISCOURAGED BY THEIR LACK OF U.S. LEVERAGE. THEY DECIDE TO TRY A NEW APPROACH.
WHAT IS IT THEN, MALCOLM?
WELL, GEORGE, AS MUCH AS WE LIKE THE WORK YOU AND HARRY DO AS PRODUCERS, WE'RE GONNA TRY SOMETHING DIFFERENT THIS TIME.
ALBERT PRODUCTIONS
OH, SO IT'S "PUSH OFF, THEN, BROTHER," IS THAT IT? A FINE LOAD OF...
NAWW, MAN, NOTHING LIKE THAT. WE'LL USE YOU GUYS DOWN IN SYDNEY AGAIN, SOMETIME.
WE JUST WANNA DO A DISC IN LONDON AND SEE IF IT GIVES US A FRESH EDGE, Y'KNOW? MUTT LANGE'S GONNA TWIST KNOBS FER US AT THE ROADHOUSE. HE'S THE GUY WHO DID THE BOOMTOWN RATS.
OI! IF HE CAN PRODUCE HITMAKERS OUTTA THEM TONE DEAF LACKEYS, IT'S WORTH A SHOT!
HEH, HEH! NOW YER COMIN' AROUND, BRO'!
UNCHARACTERISTICALLY, THE GROUP SPENDS NEARLY SIX MONTHS RECORDING NEW SONGS.
Y'KNOW, WE'RE GOOD ENOUGH PLAYERS TO DO JAZZ, POP...
YEAH, BUT SHOULD WE? WE'RE NOT PLAYING FOR BRAIN SURGEONS.
NO, BUT WE ARE PLAYIN' FOR THE YANKS.
IT'S DO OR DIE THIS TIME. LET'S JUST ROCK THE BEST WE KNOW HOW ...WE'LL KICK AMERICA'S ASS OR GO DOWN IN FLAMES TRYING!
C'MON, GUYS, LET'S DO ANOTHER TAKE.

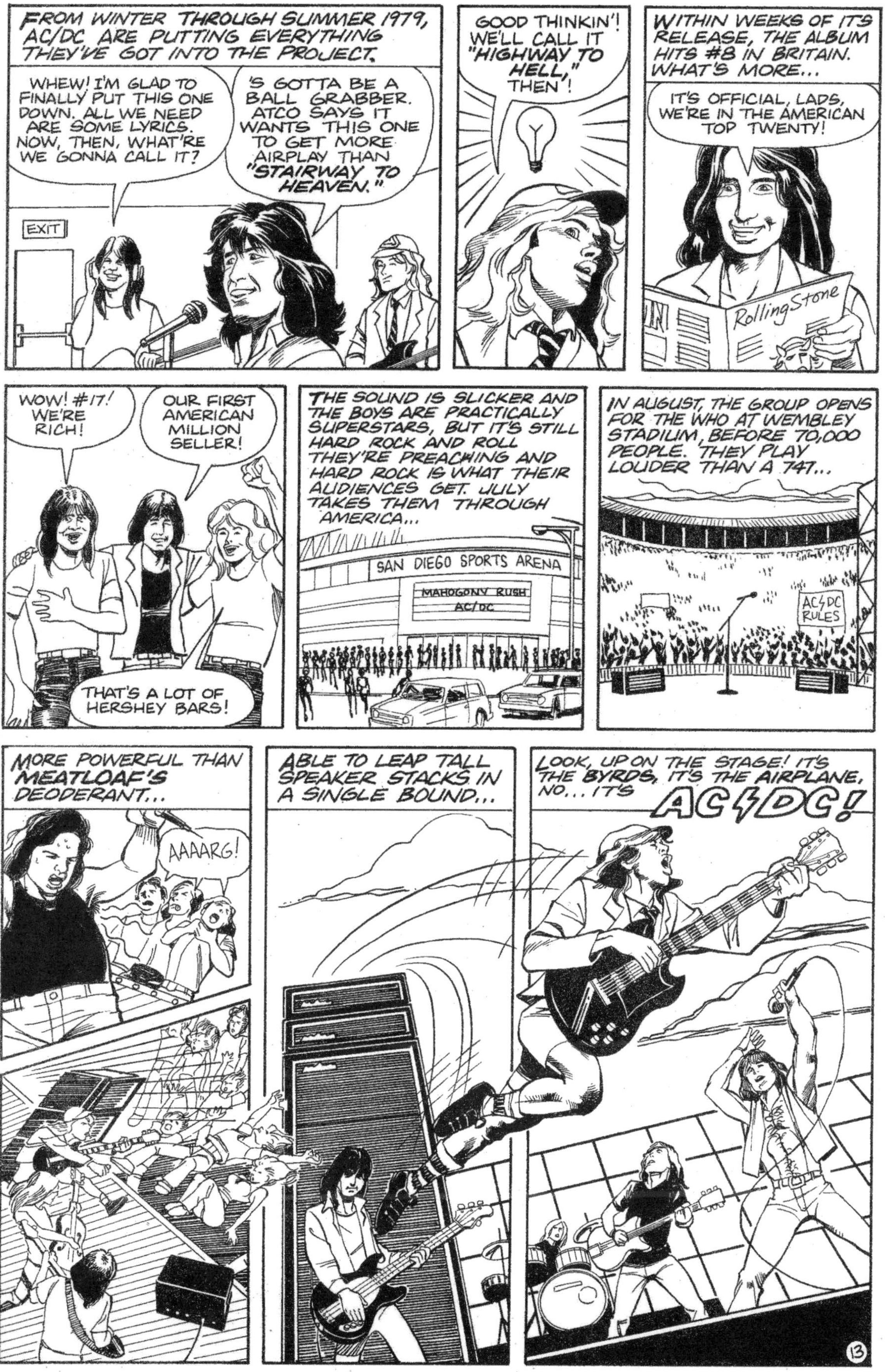
FROM WINTER THROUGH SUMMER 1979, AC/DC ARE PUTTING EVERYTHING THEY'VE GOT INTO THE PROJECT.
WHEW! I'M GLAD TO FINALLY PUT THIS ONE DOWN. ALL WE NEED ARE SOME LYRICS. NOW, THEN, WHAT'RE WE GONNA CALL IT?
'S GOTTA BE A BALL GRABBER. ATCO SAYS IT WANTS THIS ONE TO GET MORE AIRPLAY THAN "STAIRWAY TO HEAVEN."
EXIT
GOOD THINKIN'! WE'LL CALL IT "HIGHWAY TO HELL," THEN'!
WITHIN WEEKS OF IT'S RELEASE, THE ALBUM HITS #8 IN BRITAIN. WHAT'S MORE...
IT'S OFFICIAL, LADS, WE'RE IN THE AMERICAN TOP TWENTY!
Rolling Stone
WOW! #17! WE'RE RICH!
OUR FIRST AMERICAN MILLION SELLER!
THAT'S A LOT OF HERSHEY BARS!
THE SOUND IS SLICKER AND THE BOYS ARE PRACTICALLY SUPERSTARS, BUT IT'S STILL HARD ROCK AND ROLL THEY'RE PREACHING AND HARD ROCK IS WHAT THEIR AUDIENCES GET. JULY TAKES THEM THROUGH AMERICA...
SAN DIEGO SPORTS ARENA
MAHOGONY RUSH
AC/DC
IN AUGUST, THE GROUP OPENS FOR THE WHO AT WEMBLEY STADIUM, BEFORE 70,000 PEOPLE. THEY PLAY LOUDER THAN A 747...
AC/DC RULES
MORE POWERFUL THAN MEATLOAF'S DEODERANT...
AAAARG!
ABLE TO LEAP TALL SPEAKER STACKS IN A SINGLE BOUND...
LOOK, UP ON THE STAGE! IT'S THE BYRDS, IT'S THE AIRPLANE. NO... IT'S
AC/DC!

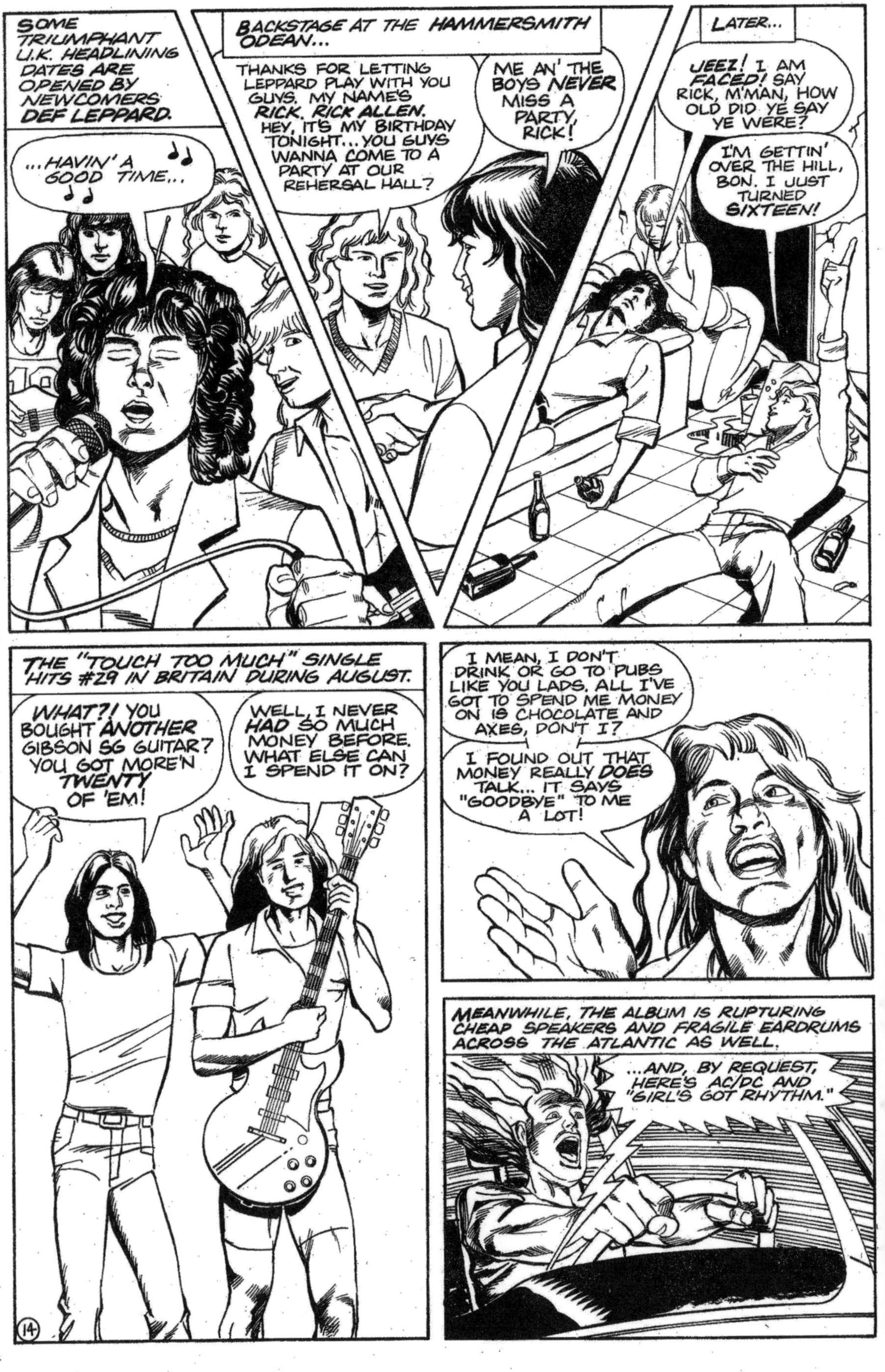
SOME TRIUMPHANT U.K. HEADLINING DATES ARE OPENED BY NEWCOMERS DEF LEPPARD.
...HAVIN' A GOOD TIME...
BACKSTAGE AT THE HAMMERSMITH ODEAN...
THANKS FOR LETTING LEPPARD PLAY WITH YOU GUYS. MY NAME'S RICK. RICK ALLEN. HEY, IT'S MY BIRTHDAY TONIGHT... YOU GUYS WANNA COME TO A PARTY AT OUR REHERSAL HALL?
ME AN' THE BOYS NEVER MISS A PARTY, RICK!
LATER...
JEEZ! I AM FACED! SAY RICK, M'MAN, HOW OLD DID YE SAY YE WERE?
I'M GETTIN' OVER THE HILL, BON. I JUST TURNED SIXTEEN!
THE "TOUCH TOO MUCH" SINGLE HITS #29 IN BRITAIN DURING AUGUST.
WHAT?! YOU BOUGHT ANOTHER GIBSON SG GUITAR? YOU GOT MORE'N TWENTY OF 'EM!
WELL, I NEVER HAD SO MUCH MONEY BEFORE. WHAT ELSE CAN I SPEND IT ON?
I MEAN, I DON'T DRINK OR GO TO PUBS LIKE YOU LADS. ALL I'VE GOT TO SPEND ME MONEY ON IS CHOCOLATE AND AXES, DON'T I?
I FOUND OUT THAT MONEY REALLY DOES TALK... IT SAYS "GOODBYE" TO ME A LOT!
MEANWHILE, THE ALBUM IS RUPTURING CHEAP SPEAKERS AND FRAGILE EARDRUMS ACROSS THE ATLANTIC AS WELL.
...AND, BY REQUEST, HERE'S AC/DC AND "GIRL'S GOT RHYTHM."

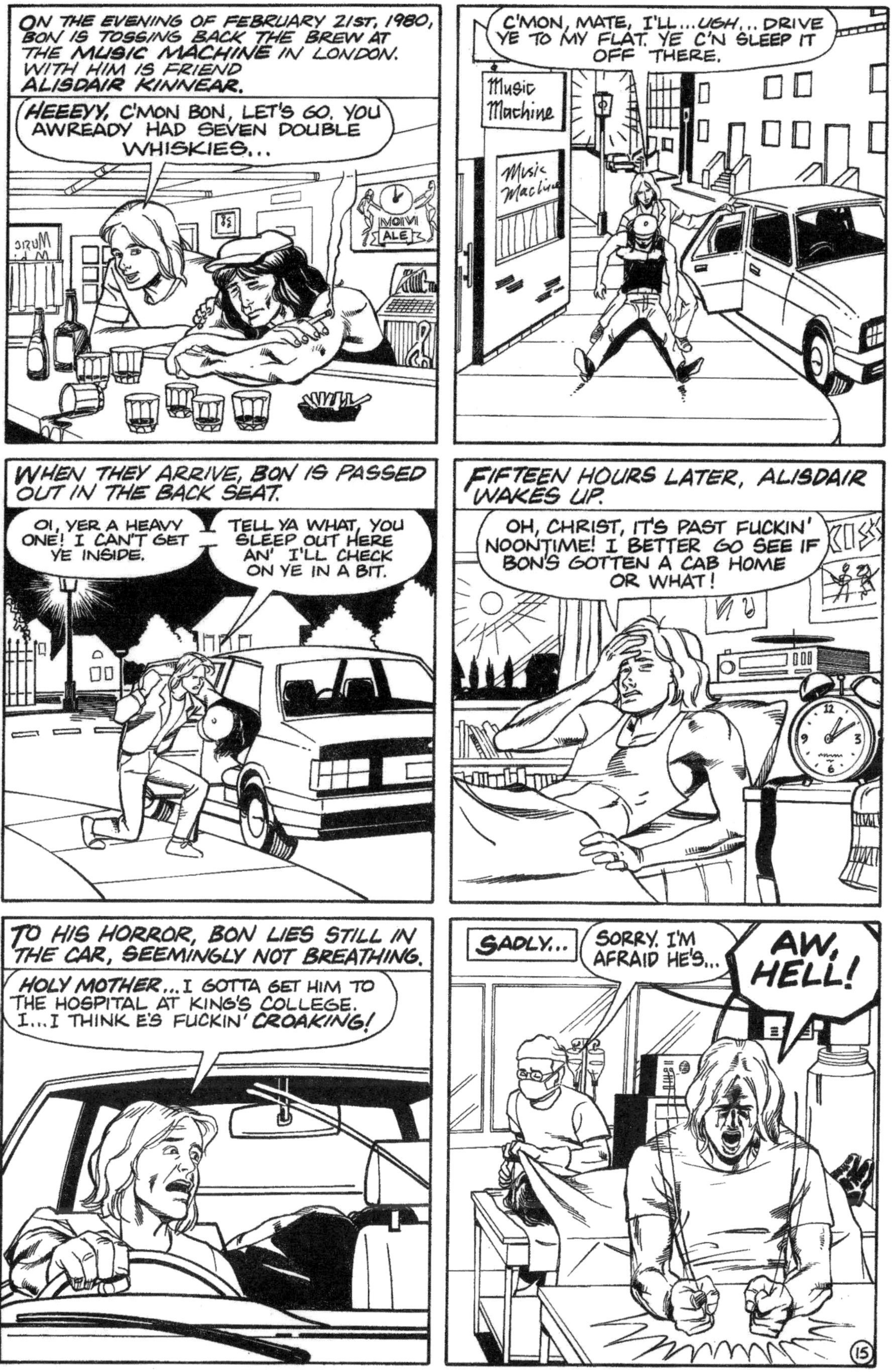
ON THE EVENING OF FEBRUARY 21ST, 1980, BON IS TOSSING BACK THE BREW AT THE MUSIC MACHINE IN LONDON. WITH HIM IS FRIEND ALISDAIR KINNEAR.
HEEEYY, C'MON BON, LET'S GO. YOU AWREADY HAD SEVEN DOUBLE WHISKIES...
ALE
C'MON, MATE, I'LL...UGH... DRIVE YE TO MY FLAT. YE C'N SLEEP IT OFF THERE.
Music Machine
Music Machine
WHEN THEY ARRIVE, BON IS PASSED OUT IN THE BACK SEAT.
OI, YER A HEAVY ONE! I CAN'T GET YE INSIDE.
TELL YA WHAT, YOU SLEEP OUT HERE AN' I'LL CHECK ON YE IN A BIT.
FIFTEEN HOURS LATER, ALISDAIR WAKES UP.
OH, CHRIST, IT'S PAST FUCKIN' NOONTIME! I BETTER GO SEE IF BON'S GOTTEN A CAB HOME OR WHAT!
TO HIS HORROR, BON LIES STILL IN THE CAR, SEEMINGLY NOT BREATHING.
HOLY MOTHER... I GOTTA GET HIM TO THE HOSPITAL AT KING'S COLLEGE. I... I THINK E'S FUCKIN' CROAKING!
SADLY...
SORRY. I'M AFRAID HE'S...
AW, HELL!

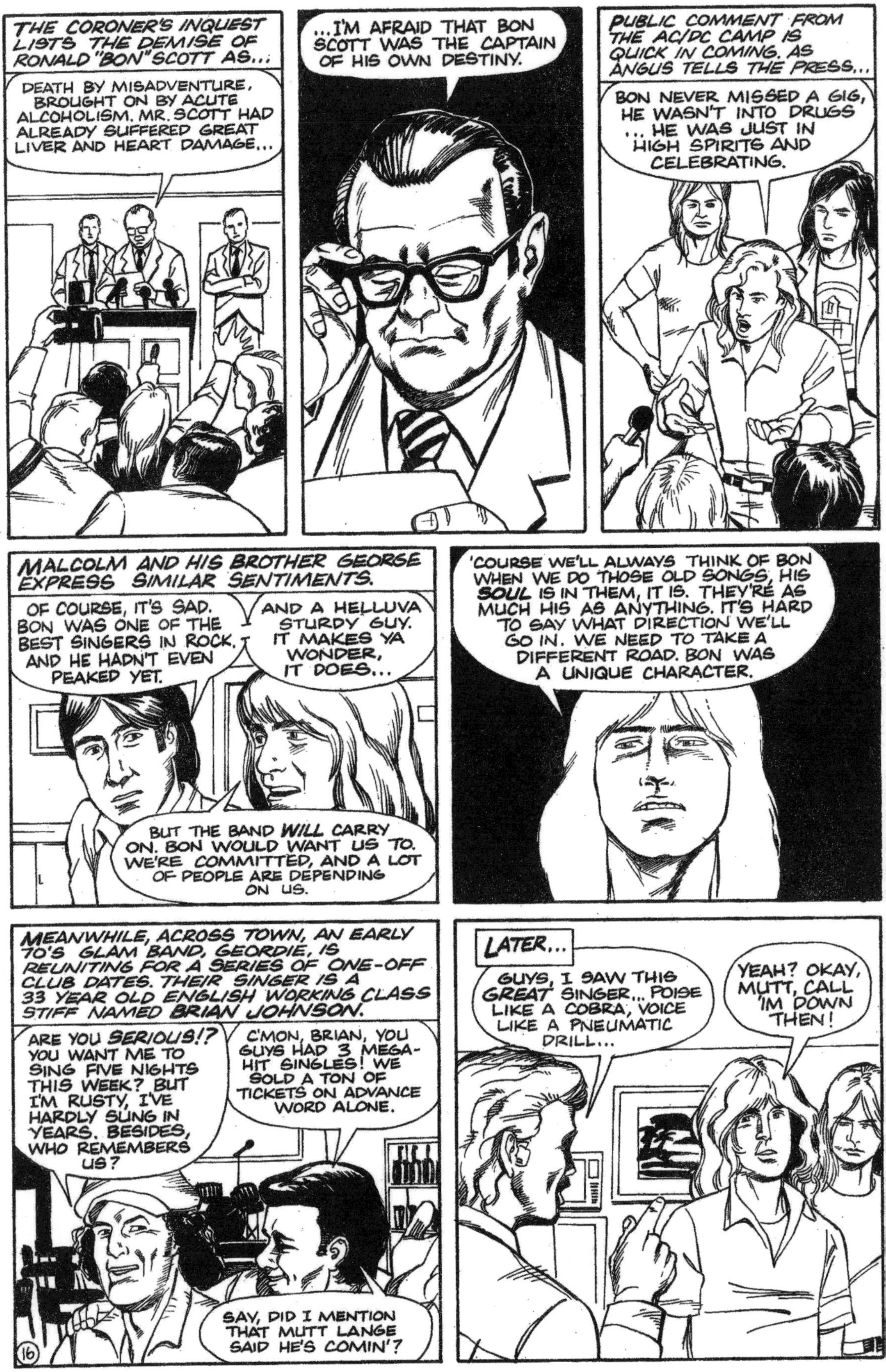

THE CORONER'S INQUEST LISTS THE DEMISE OF RONALD "BON" SCOTT AS...
DEATH BY MISADVENTURE, BROUGHT ON BY ACUTE ALCOHOLISM. MR. SCOTT HAD ALREADY SUFFERED GREAT LIVER AND HEART DAMAGE...
...I'M AFRAID THAT BON SCOTT WAS THE CAPTAIN OF HIS OWN DESTINY.
PUBLIC COMMENT FROM THE AC/DC CAMP IS QUICK IN COMING, AS ANGUS TELLS THE PRESS...
BON NEVER MISSED A GIG, HE WASN'T INTO DRUGS ... HE WAS JUST IN HIGH SPIRITS AND CELEBRATING.
MALCOLM AND HIS BROTHER GEORGE EXPRESS SIMILAR SENTIMENTS.
OF COURSE, IT'S SAD. BON WAS ONE OF THE BEST SINGERS IN ROCK, AND HE HADN'T EVEN PEAKED YET.
AND A HELLUVA STURDY GUY. IT MAKES YA WONDER, IT DOES...
BUT THE BAND WILL CARRY ON. BON WOULD WANT US TO. WE'RE COMMITTED, AND A LOT OF PEOPLE ARE DEPENDING ON US.
'COURSE WE'LL ALWAYS THINK OF BON WHEN WE DO THOSE OLD SONGS, HIS SOUL IS IN THEM, IT IS. THEY'RE AS MUCH HIS AS ANYTHING. IT'S HARD TO SAY WHAT DIRECTION WE'LL GO IN. WE NEED TO TAKE A DIFFERENT ROAD. BON WAS A UNIQUE CHARACTER.
MEANWHILE, ACROSS TOWN, AN EARLY 70'S GLAM BAND, GEORDIE, IS REUNITING FOR A SERIES OF ONE-OFF CLUB DATES. THEIR SINGER IS A 33 YEAR OLD ENGLISH WORKING CLASS STIFF NAMED BRIAN JOHNSON.
ARE YOU SERIOUS!? YOU WANT ME TO SING FIVE NIGHTS THIS WEEK? BUT I'M RUSTY, I'VE HARDLY SUNG IN YEARS. BESIDES, WHO REMEMBERS US?
C'MON, BRIAN, YOU GUYS HAD 3 MEGA-HIT SINGLES! WE SOLD A TON OF TICKETS ON ADVANCE WORD ALONE.
SAY, DID I MENTION THAT MUTT LANGE SAID HE'S COMIN'?
LATER...
GUYS, I SAW THIS GREAT SINGER... POISE LIKE A COBRA, VOICE LIKE A PNEUMATIC DRILL...
YEAH? OKAY, MUTT, CALL 'IM DOWN THEN!

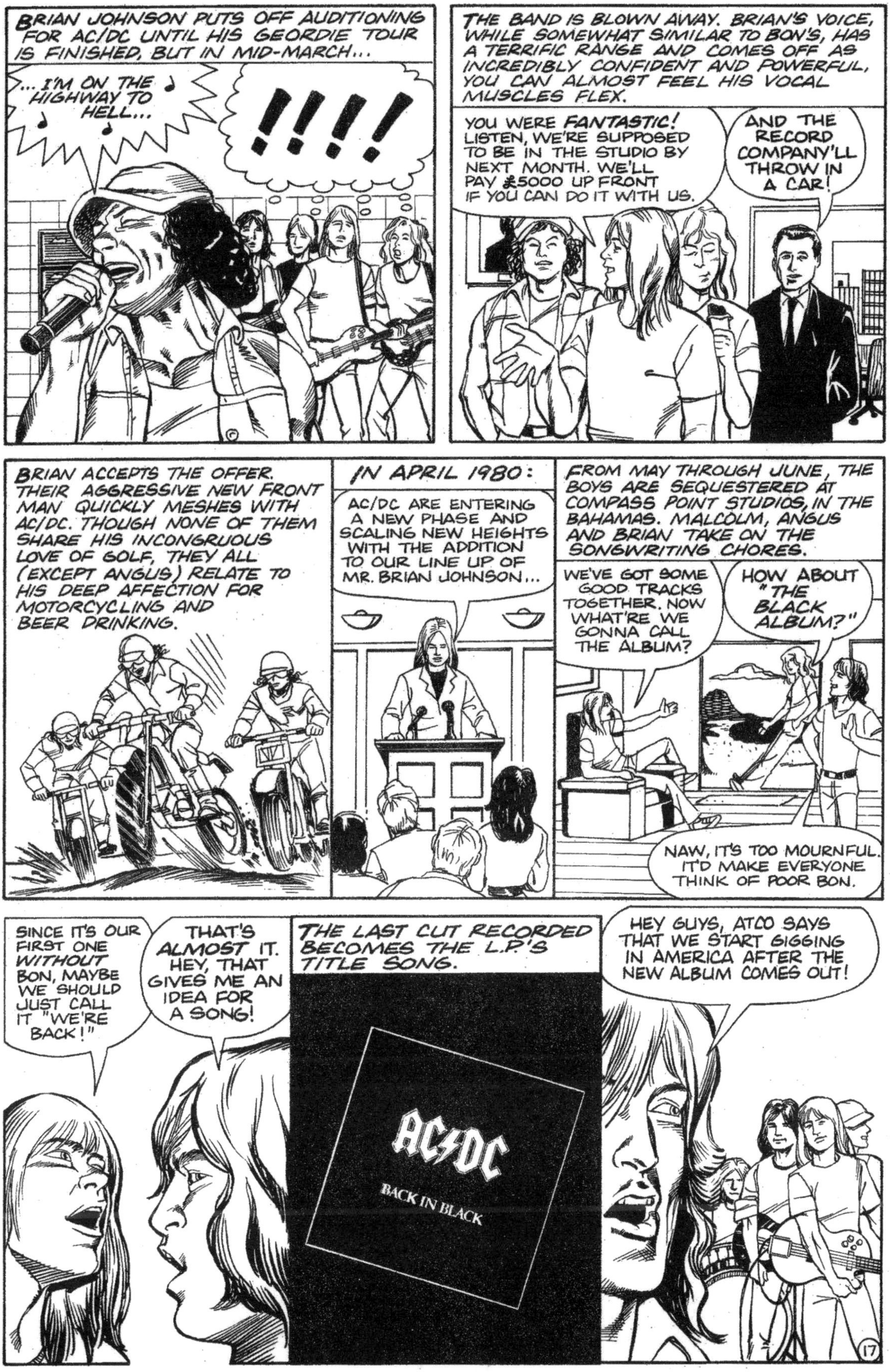
BRIAN JOHNSON PUTS OFF AUDITIONING FOR AC/DC UNTIL HIS GEORDIE TOUR IS FINISHED, BUT IN MID-MARCH...
... I'M ON THE HIGHWAY TO HELL...
!!!!
THE BAND IS BLOWN AWAY. BRIAN'S VOICE, WHILE SOMEWHAT SIMILAR TO BON'S, HAS A TERRIFIC RANGE AND COMES OFF AS INCREDIBLY CONFIDENT AND POWERFUL, YOU CAN ALMOST FEEL HIS VOCAL MUSCLES FLEX.
YOU WERE FANTASTIC! LISTEN, WE'RE SUPPOSED TO BE IN THE STUDIO BY NEXT MONTH. WE'LL PAY £5000 UP FRONT IF YOU CAN DO IT WITH US.
AND THE RECORD COMPANY'LL THROW IN A CAR!
BRIAN ACCEPTS THE OFFER. THEIR AGGRESSIVE NEW FRONT MAN QUICKLY MESHES WITH AC/DC. THOUGH NONE OF THEM SHARE HIS INCONGRUOUS LOVE OF GOLF, THEY ALL (EXCEPT ANGUS) RELATE TO HIS DEEP AFFECTION FOR MOTORCYCLING AND BEER DRINKING.
IN APRIL 1980:
AC/DC ARE ENTERING A NEW PHASE AND SCALING NEW HEIGHTS WITH THE ADDITION TO OUR LINE UP OF MR. BRIAN JOHNSON...
FROM MAY THROUGH JUNE, THE BOYS ARE SEQUESTERED AT COMPASS POINT STUDIOS, IN THE BAHAMAS. MALCOLM, ANGUS AND BRIAN TAKE ON THE SONGWRITING CHORES.
WE'VE GOT SOME GOOD TRACKS TOGETHER. NOW WHAT'RE WE GONNA CALL THE ALBUM?
HOW ABOUT "THE BLACK ALBUM?"
NAW, IT'S TOO MOURNFUL. IT'D MAKE EVERYONE THINK OF POOR BON.
SINCE IT'S OUR FIRST ONE WITHOUT BON, MAYBE WE SHOULD JUST CALL IT "WE'RE BACK!"
THAT'S ALMOST IT. HEY, THAT GIVES ME AN IDEA FOR A SONG!
THE LAST CUT RECORDED BECOMES THE L.P.'S TITLE SONG.
AC/DC
BACK IN BLACK
HEY GUYS, ATCO SAYS THAT WE START GIGGING IN AMERICA AFTER THE NEW ALBUM COMES OUT!

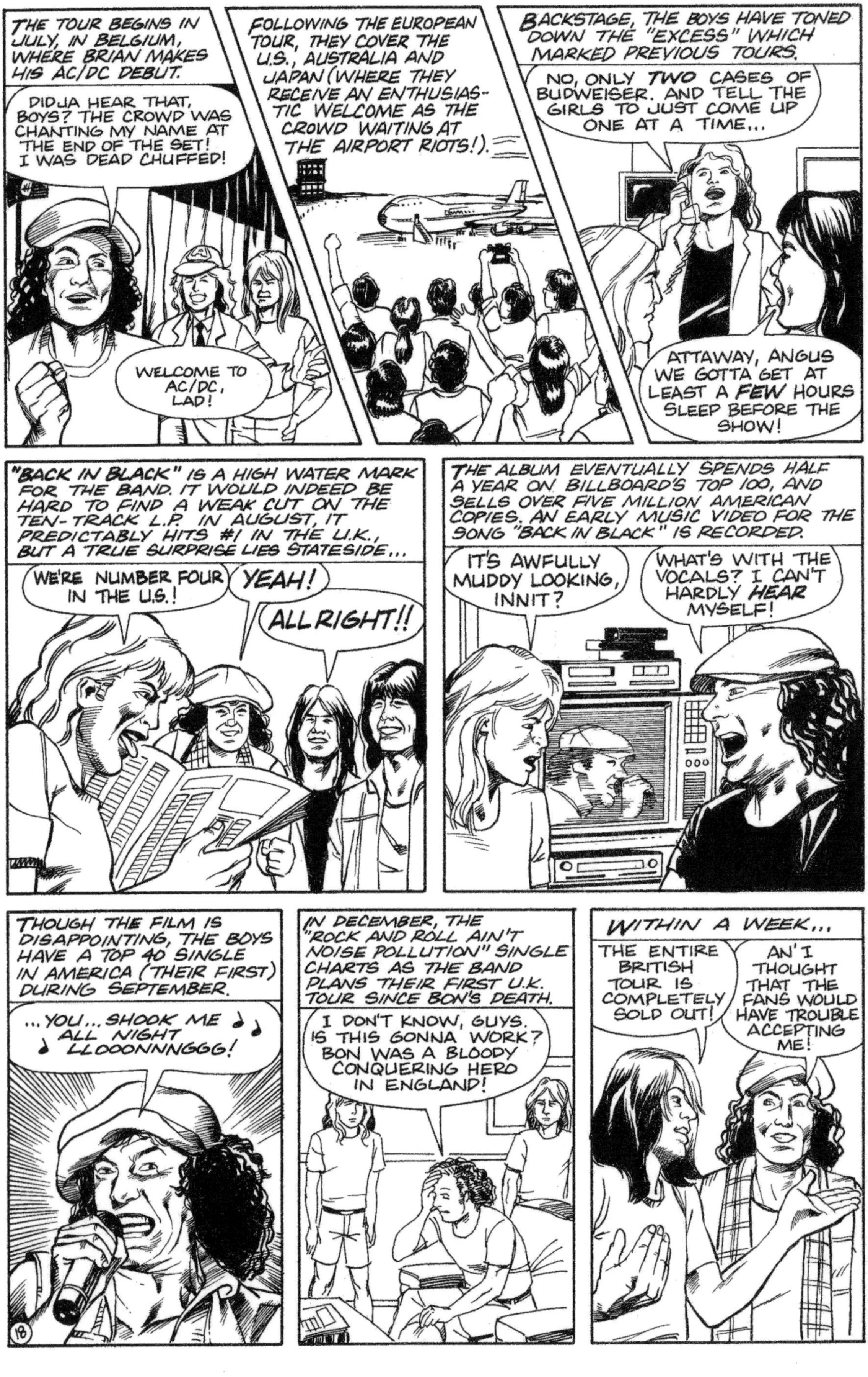
THE TOUR BEGINS IN JULY, IN BELGIUM, WHERE BRIAN MAKES HIS AC/DC DEBUT.
DIDJA HEAR THAT, BOYS? THE CROWD WAS CHANTING MY NAME AT THE END OF THE SET! I WAS DEAD CHUFFED!
WELCOME TO AC/DC, LAD!
FOLLOWING THE EUROPEAN TOUR, THEY COVER THE U.S., AUSTRALIA AND JAPAN (WHERE THEY RECEIVE AN ENTHUSIASTIC WELCOME AS THE CROWD WAITING AT THE AIRPORT RIOTS!).
BACKSTAGE, THE BOYS HAVE TONED DOWN THE "EXCESS" WHICH MARKED PREVIOUS TOURS.
NO, ONLY TWO CASES OF BUDWEISER. AND TELL THE GIRLS TO JUST COME UP ONE AT A TIME...
ATTAWAY, ANGUS WE GOTTA GET AT LEAST A FEW HOURS SLEEP BEFORE THE SHOW!
"BACK IN BLACK" IS A HIGH WATER MARK FOR THE BAND. IT WOULD INDEED BE HARD TO FIND A WEAK CUT ON THE TEN-TRACK L.P. IN AUGUST, IT PREDICTABLY HITS #1 IN THE U.K., BUT A TRUE SURPRISE LIES STATESIDE...
WE'RE NUMBER FOUR IN THE U.S.!
YEAH!
ALL RIGHT!!
THE ALBUM EVENTUALLY SPENDS HALF A YEAR ON BILLBOARD'S TOP 100, AND SELLS OVER FIVE MILLION AMERICAN COPIES. AN EARLY MUSIC VIDEO FOR THE SONG "BACK IN BLACK" IS RECORDED.
IT'S AWFULLY MUDDY LOOKING, INNIT?
WHAT'S WITH THE VOCALS? I CAN'T HARDLY HEAR MYSELF!
THOUGH THE FILM IS DISAPPOINTING, THE BOYS HAVE A TOP 40 SINGLE IN AMERICA (THEIR FIRST) DURING SEPTEMBER.
...YOU...SHOOK ME ♪♪ ALL NIGHT ♪ LLOOONNNGGG!
IN DECEMBER, THE "ROCK AND ROLL AIN'T NOISE POLLUTION" SINGLE CHARTS AS THE BAND PLANS THEIR FIRST U.K. TOUR SINCE BON'S DEATH.
I DON'T KNOW, GUYS. IS THIS GONNA WORK? BON WAS A BLOODY CONQUERING HERO IN ENGLAND!
WITHIN A WEEK...
THE ENTIRE BRITISH TOUR IS COMPLETELY SOLD OUT!
AN' I THOUGHT THAT THE FANS WOULD HAVE TROUBLE ACCEPTING ME!
18

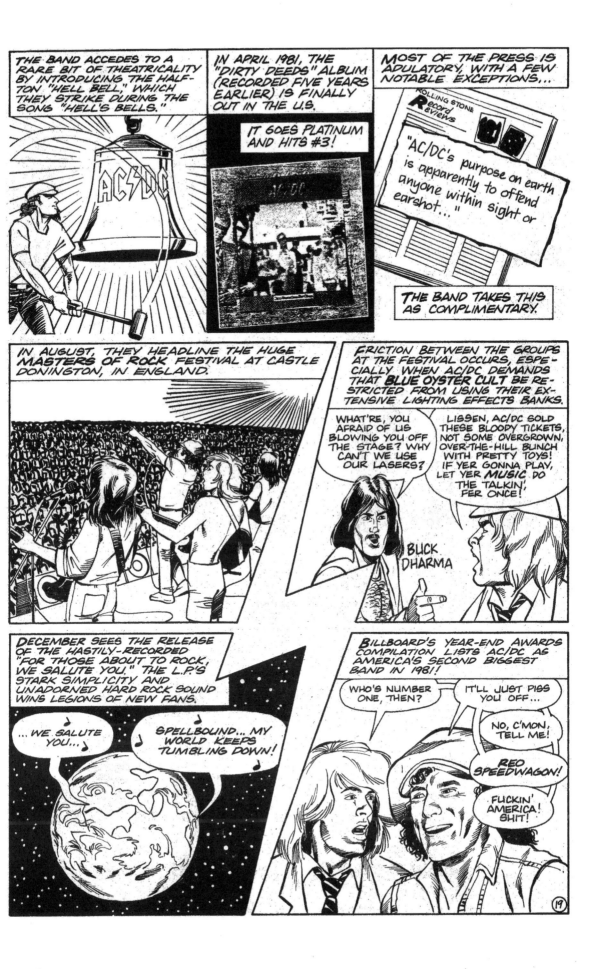

THE BAND ACCEDES TO A RARE BIT OF THEATRICALITY BY INTRODUCING THE HALF-TON "HELL BELL," WHICH THEY STRIKE DURING THE SONG "HELL'S BELLS."

IN APRIL 1981, THE "DIRTY DEEDS" ALBUM (RECORDED FIVE YEARS EARLIER) IS FINALLY OUT IN THE U.S.

IT GOES PLATINUM AND HITS #3!

MOST OF THE PRESS IS ADULATORY, WITH A FEW NOTABLE EXCEPTIONS...

ROLLING STONE Record Reviews

"AC/DC's purpose on earth is apparently to offend anyone within sight or earshot..."

THE BAND TAKES THIS AS COMPLIMENTARY.

IN AUGUST, THEY HEADLINE THE HUGE MASTERS OF ROCK FESTIVAL AT CASTLE DONINGTON, IN ENGLAND.

FRICTION BETWEEN THE GROUPS AT THE FESTIVAL OCCURS, ESPECIALLY WHEN AC/DC DEMANDS THAT BLUE OYSTER CULT BE RESTRICTED FROM USING THEIR EXTENSIVE LIGHTING EFFECTS BANKS.

WHAT'RE, YOU AFRAID OF US BLOWING YOU OFF THE STAGE? WHY CAN'T WE USE OUR LASERS?

LISSEN, AC/DC SOLD THESE BLOODY TICKETS, NOT SOME OVERGROWN, OVER-THE-HILL BUNCH WITH PRETTY TOYS! IF YER GONNA PLAY, LET YER MUSIC DO THE TALKIN', FER ONCE!

BUCK DHARMA

DECEMBER SEES THE RELEASE OF THE HASTILY-RECORDED "FOR THOSE ABOUT TO ROCK, WE SALUTE YOU." THE L.P.'S STARK SIMPLICITY AND UNADORNED HARD ROCK SOUND WINS LEGIONS OF NEW FANS.

... WE SALUTE YOU...♪

♪SPELLBOUND... MY WORLD KEEPS TUMBLING DOWN!♪

BILLBOARD'S YEAR-END AWARDS COMPILATION LISTS AC/DC AS AMERICA'S SECOND BIGGEST BAND IN 1981!

WHO'S NUMBER ONE, THEN?

IT'LL JUST PISS YOU OFF...

NO, C'MON, TELL ME!

REO SPEEDWAGON!

FUCKIN' AMERICA! SHIT!

19

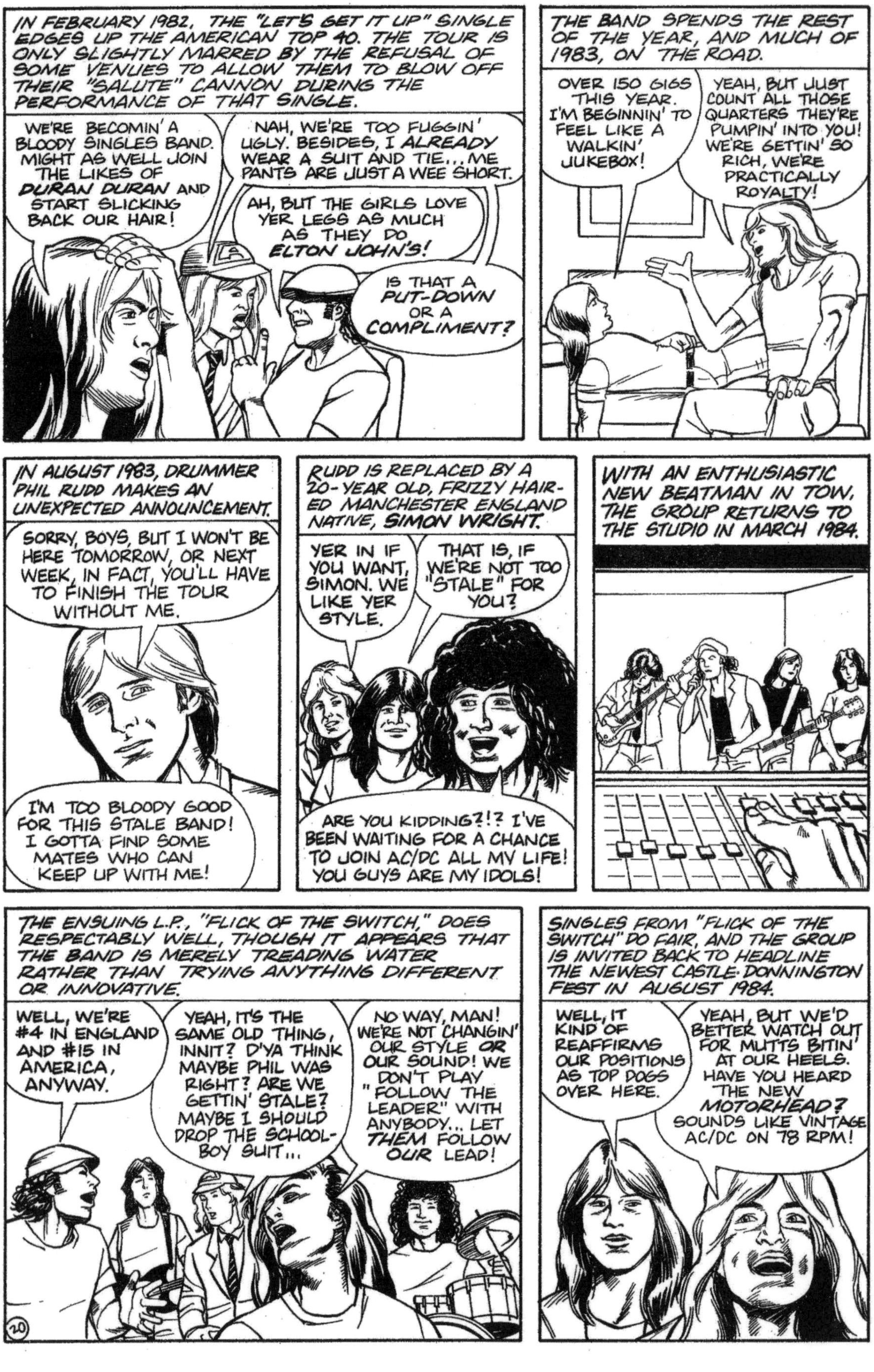
IN FEBRUARY 1982, THE "LET'S GET IT UP" SINGLE EDGES UP THE AMERICAN TOP 40. THE TOUR IS ONLY SLIGHTLY MARRED BY THE REFUSAL OF SOME VENUES TO ALLOW THEM TO BLOW OFF THEIR "SALUTE" CANNON DURING THE PERFORMANCE OF THAT SINGLE.
WE'RE BECOMIN' A BLOODY SINGLES BAND. MIGHT AS WELL JOIN THE LIKES OF DURAN DURAN AND START SLICKING BACK OUR HAIR!
NAH, WE'RE TOO FUGGIN' UGLY. BESIDES, I ALREADY WEAR A SUIT AND TIE... ME PANTS ARE JUST A WEE SHORT.
AH, BUT THE GIRLS LOVE YER LEGS AS MUCH AS THEY DO ELTON JOHN'S!
IS THAT A PUT-DOWN OR A COMPLIMENT?
THE BAND SPENDS THE REST OF THE YEAR, AND MUCH OF 1983, ON THE ROAD.
OVER 150 GIGS THIS YEAR. I'M BEGINNIN' TO FEEL LIKE A WALKIN' JUKEBOX!
YEAH, BUT JUST COUNT ALL THOSE QUARTERS THEY'RE PUMPIN' INTO YOU! WE'RE GETTIN' SO RICH, WE'RE PRACTICALLY ROYALTY!
IN AUGUST 1983, DRUMMER PHIL RUDD MAKES AN UNEXPECTED ANNOUNCEMENT.
SORRY, BOYS, BUT I WON'T BE HERE TOMORROW, OR NEXT WEEK, IN FACT, YOU'LL HAVE TO FINISH THE TOUR WITHOUT ME.
I'M TOO BLOODY GOOD FOR THIS STALE BAND! I GOTTA FIND SOME MATES WHO CAN KEEP UP WITH ME!
RUDD IS REPLACED BY A 20-YEAR OLD, FRIZZY HAIRED MANCHESTER ENGLAND NATIVE, SIMON WRIGHT.
YER IN IF YOU WANT, SIMON. WE LIKE YER STYLE.
THAT IS, IF WE'RE NOT TOO "STALE" FOR YOU?
ARE YOU KIDDING?!? I'VE BEEN WAITING FOR A CHANCE TO JOIN AC/DC ALL MY LIFE! YOU GUYS ARE MY IDOLS!
WITH AN ENTHUSIASTIC NEW BEATMAN IN TOW, THE GROUP RETURNS TO THE STUDIO IN MARCH 1984.
THE ENSUING L.P., "FLICK OF THE SWITCH," DOES RESPECTABLY WELL, THOUGH IT APPEARS THAT THE BAND IS MERELY TREADING WATER RATHER THAN TRYING ANYTHING DIFFERENT OR INNOVATIVE.
WELL, WE'RE #4 IN ENGLAND AND #15 IN AMERICA, ANYWAY.
YEAH, IT'S THE SAME OLD THING, INNIT? D'YA THINK MAYBE PHIL WAS RIGHT? ARE WE GETTIN' STALE? MAYBE I SHOULD DROP THE SCHOOL-BOY SUIT...
NO WAY, MAN! WE'RE NOT CHANGIN' OUR STYLE OR OUR SOUND! WE DON'T PLAY "FOLLOW THE LEADER" WITH ANYBODY... LET THEM FOLLOW OUR LEAD!
SINGLES FROM "FLICK OF THE SWITCH" DO FAIR, AND THE GROUP IS INVITED BACK TO HEADLINE THE NEWEST CASTLE DONNINGTON FEST IN AUGUST 1984.
WELL, IT KIND OF REAFFIRMS OUR POSITIONS AS TOP DOGS OVER HERE.
YEAH, BUT WE'D BETTER WATCH OUT FOR MUTTS BITIN' AT OUR HEELS. HAVE YOU HEARD THE NEW MOTORHEAD? SOUNDS LIKE VINTAGE AC/DC ON 78 RPM!
20

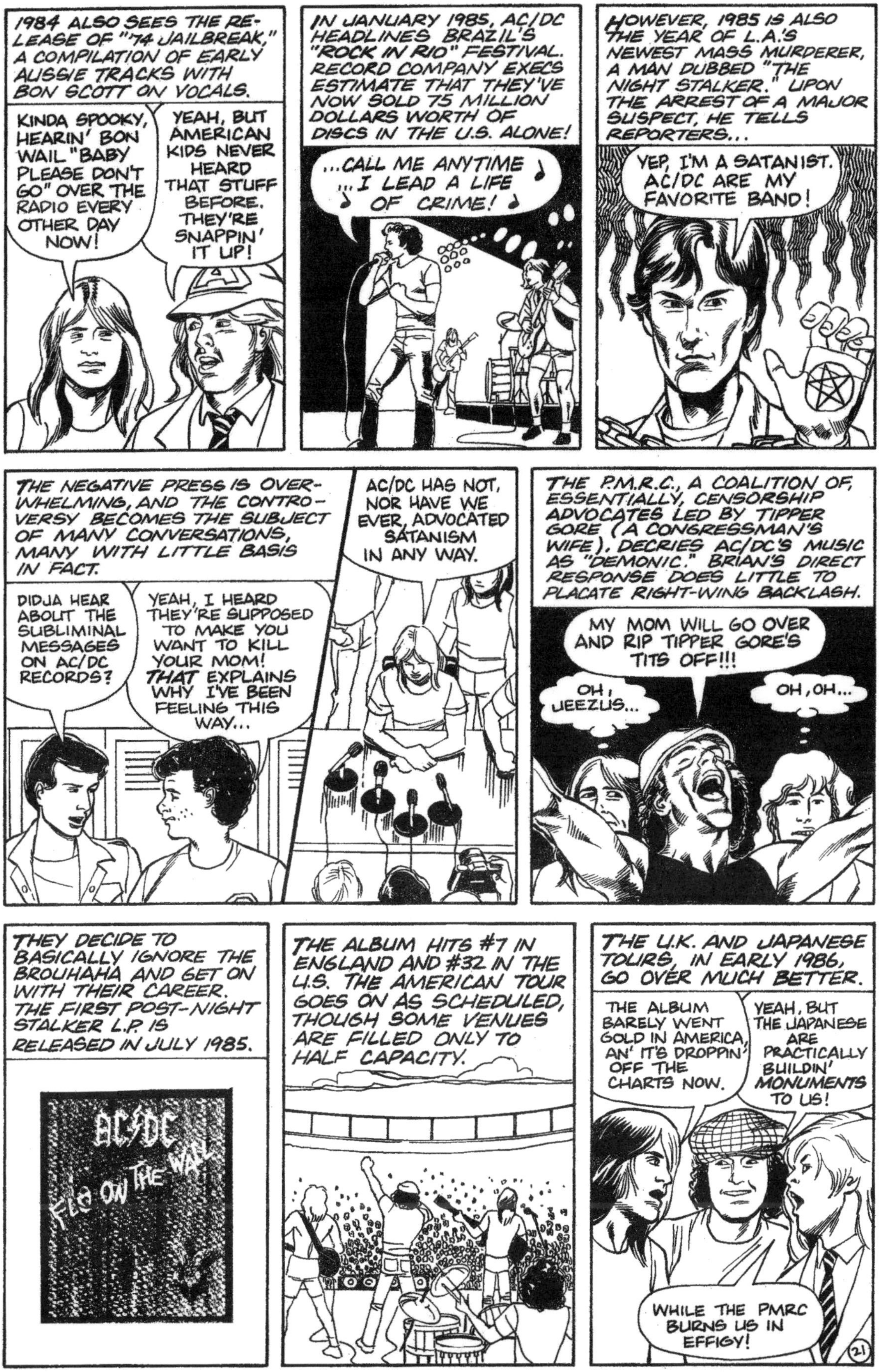
1984 ALSO SEES THE RELEASE OF "'74 JAILBREAK," A COMPILATION OF EARLY AUSSIE TRACKS WITH BON SCOTT ON VOCALS.
KINDA SPOOKY, HEARIN' BON WAIL "BABY PLEASE DON'T GO" OVER THE RADIO EVERY OTHER DAY NOW!
YEAH, BUT AMERICAN KIDS NEVER HEARD THAT STUFF BEFORE. THEY'RE SNAPPIN' IT UP!
IN JANUARY 1985, AC/DC HEADLINES BRAZIL'S "ROCK IN RIO" FESTIVAL. RECORD COMPANY EXECS ESTIMATE THAT THEY'VE NOW SOLD 75 MILLION DOLLARS WORTH OF DISCS IN THE U.S. ALONE!
...CALL ME ANYTIME ♪ ...I LEAD A LIFE ♪ OF CRIME! ♪
HOWEVER, 1985 IS ALSO THE YEAR OF L.A.'S NEWEST MASS MURDERER, A MAN DUBBED "THE NIGHT STALKER." UPON THE ARREST OF A MAJOR SUSPECT, HE TELLS REPORTERS...
YEP, I'M A SATANIST. AC/DC ARE MY FAVORITE BAND!
THE NEGATIVE PRESS IS OVERWHELMING, AND THE CONTROVERSY BECOMES THE SUBJECT OF MANY CONVERSATIONS, MANY WITH LITTLE BASIS IN FACT.
DIDJA HEAR ABOUT THE SUBLIMINAL MESSAGES ON AC/DC RECORDS?
YEAH, I HEARD THEY'RE SUPPOSED TO MAKE YOU WANT TO KILL YOUR MOM! THAT EXPLAINS WHY I'VE BEEN FEELING THIS WAY...
AC/DC HAS NOT, NOR HAVE WE EVER, ADVOCATED SATANISM IN ANY WAY.
THE P.M.R.C., A COALITION OF, ESSENTIALLY, CENSORSHIP ADVOCATES LED BY TIPPER GORE (A CONGRESSMAN'S WIFE), DECRIES AC/DC'S MUSIC AS "DEMONIC." BRIAN'S DIRECT RESPONSE DOES LITTLE TO PLACATE RIGHT-WING BACKLASH.
MY MOM WILL GO OVER AND RIP TIPPER GORE'S TITS OFF!!!
OH, JEEZUS...
OH, OH...
THEY DECIDE TO BASICALLY IGNORE THE BROUHAHA AND GET ON WITH THEIR CAREER. THE FIRST POST-NIGHT STALKER L.P. IS RELEASED IN JULY 1985.
AC/DC
FLY ON THE WALL
THE ALBUM HITS #7 IN ENGLAND AND #32 IN THE U.S. THE AMERICAN TOUR GOES ON AS SCHEDULED, THOUGH SOME VENUES ARE FILLED ONLY TO HALF CAPACITY.
THE U.K. AND JAPANESE TOURS, IN EARLY 1986, GO OVER MUCH BETTER.
THE ALBUM BARELY WENT GOLD IN AMERICA, AN' IT'S DROPPIN' OFF THE CHARTS NOW.
YEAH, BUT THE JAPANESE ARE PRACTICALLY BUILDIN' MONUMENTS TO US!
WHILE THE PMRC BURNS US IN EFFIGY!

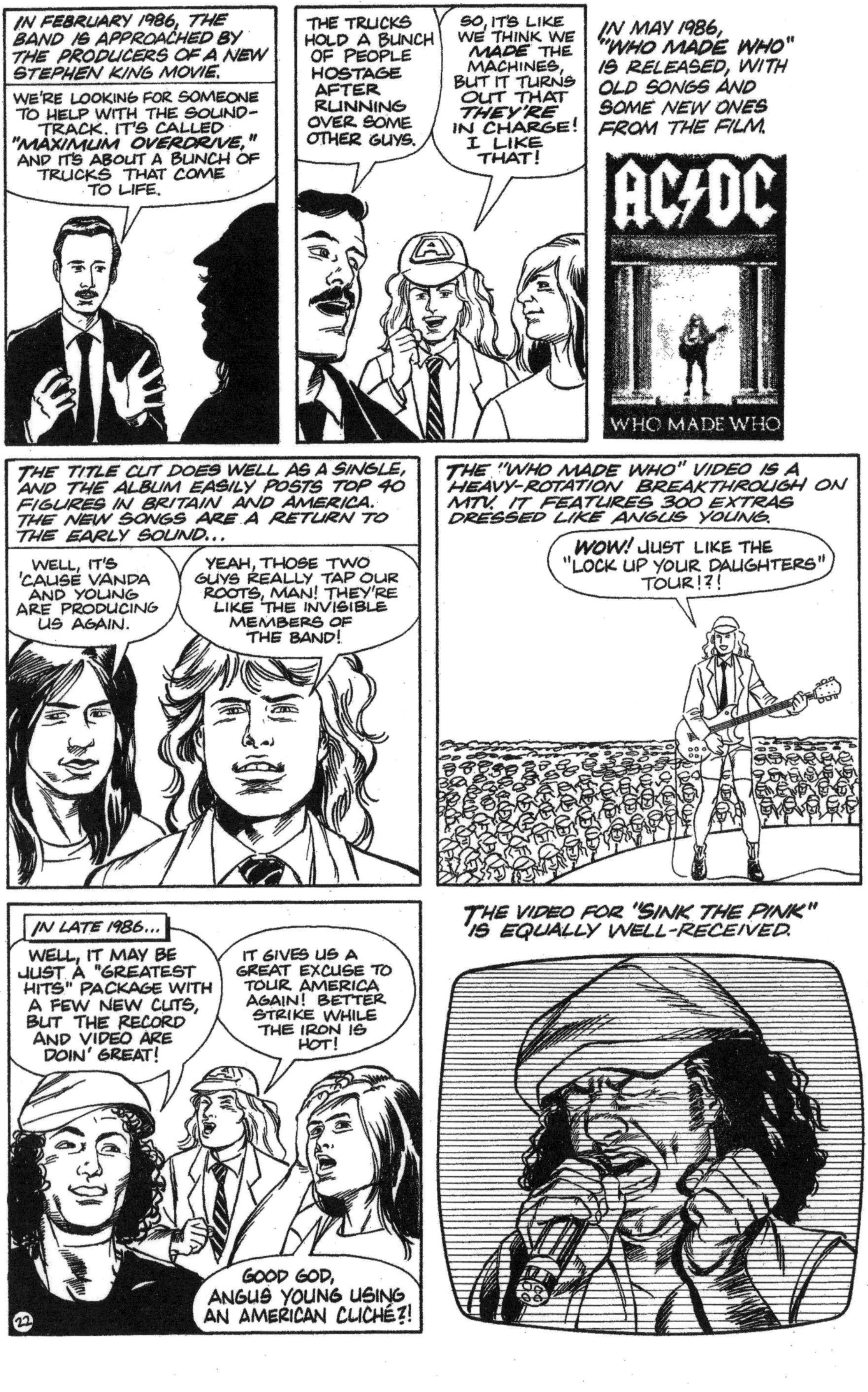

IN FEBRUARY 1986, THE BAND IS APPROACHED BY THE PRODUCERS OF A NEW STEPHEN KING MOVIE.
WE'RE LOOKING FOR SOMEONE TO HELP WITH THE SOUND-TRACK. IT'S CALLED "MAXIMUM OVERDRIVE," AND IT'S ABOUT A BUNCH OF TRUCKS THAT COME TO LIFE.
THE TRUCKS HOLD A BUNCH OF PEOPLE HOSTAGE AFTER RUNNING OVER SOME OTHER GUYS.
SO, IT'S LIKE WE THINK WE MADE THE MACHINES, BUT IT TURNS OUT THAT THEY'RE IN CHARGE! I LIKE THAT!
IN MAY 1986, "WHO MADE WHO" IS RELEASED, WITH OLD SONGS AND SOME NEW ONES FROM THE FILM.
AC/DC
WHO MADE WHO
THE TITLE CUT DOES WELL AS A SINGLE, AND THE ALBUM EASILY POSTS TOP 40 FIGURES IN BRITAIN AND AMERICA. THE NEW SONGS ARE A RETURN TO THE EARLY SOUND...
WELL, IT'S 'CAUSE VANDA AND YOUNG ARE PRODUCING US AGAIN.
YEAH, THOSE TWO GUYS REALLY TAP OUR ROOTS, MAN! THEY'RE LIKE THE INVISIBLE MEMBERS OF THE BAND!
THE "WHO MADE WHO" VIDEO IS A HEAVY-ROTATION BREAKTHROUGH ON MTV. IT FEATURES 300 EXTRAS DRESSED LIKE ANGUS YOUNG.
WOW! JUST LIKE THE "LOCK UP YOUR DAUGHTERS" TOUR!?!
IN LATE 1986...
WELL, IT MAY BE JUST A "GREATEST HITS" PACKAGE WITH A FEW NEW CUTS, BUT THE RECORD AND VIDEO ARE DOIN' GREAT!
IT GIVES US A GREAT EXCUSE TO TOUR AMERICA AGAIN! BETTER STRIKE WHILE THE IRON IS HOT!
GOOD GOD, ANGUS YOUNG USING AN AMERICAN CLICHÉ?!
THE VIDEO FOR "SINK THE PINK" IS EQUALLY WELL-RECEIVED.

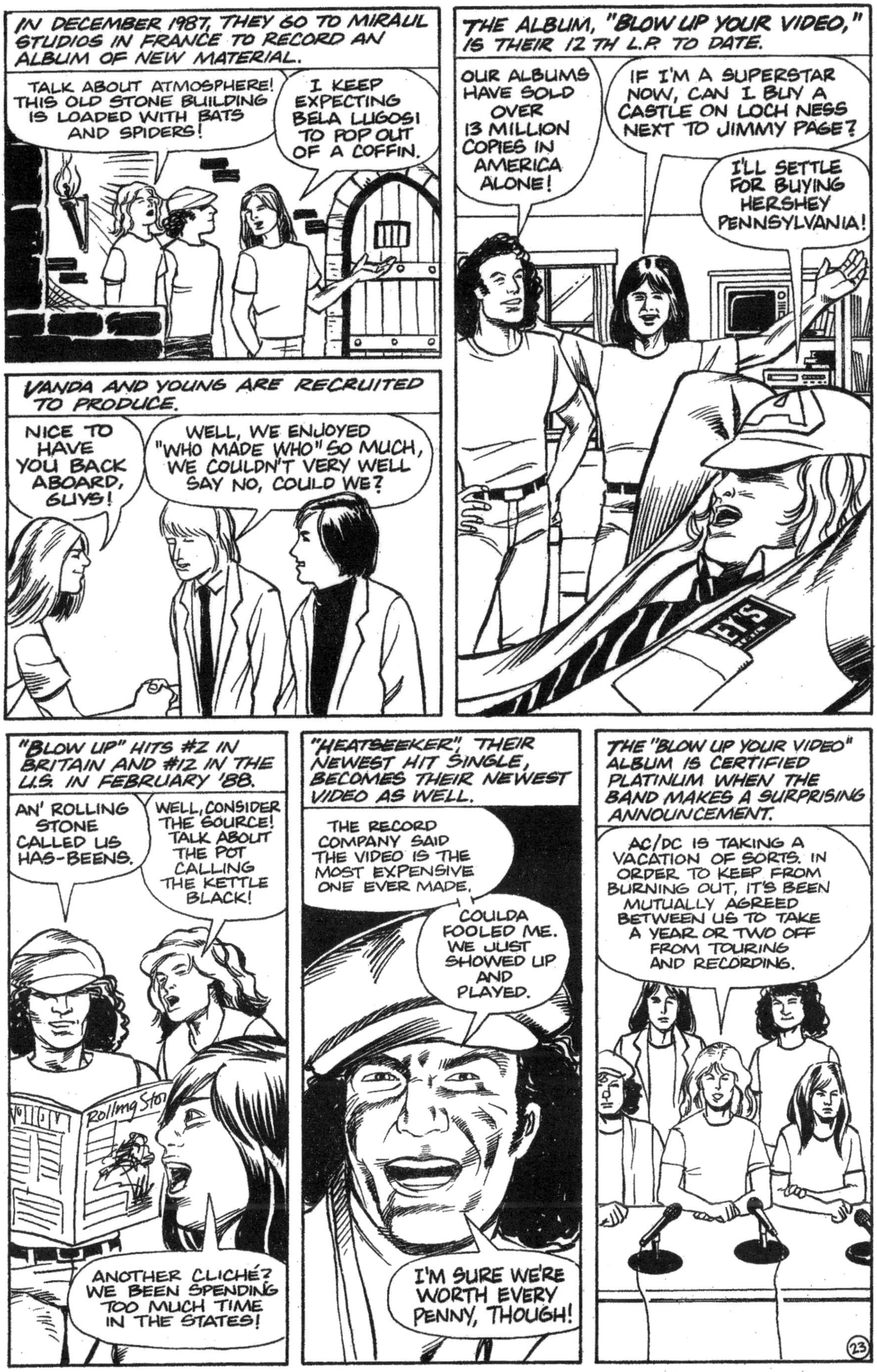
IN DECEMBER 1987, THEY GO TO MIRAUL STUDIOS IN FRANCE TO RECORD AN ALBUM OF NEW MATERIAL.
TALK ABOUT ATMOSPHERE! THIS OLD STONE BUILDING IS LOADED WITH BATS AND SPIDERS!
I KEEP EXPECTING BELA LUGOSI TO POP OUT OF A COFFIN.
THE ALBUM, "BLOW UP YOUR VIDEO," IS THEIR 12 TH L.P. TO DATE.
OUR ALBUMS HAVE SOLD OVER 13 MILLION COPIES IN AMERICA ALONE!
IF I'M A SUPERSTAR NOW, CAN I BUY A CASTLE ON LOCH NESS NEXT TO JIMMY PAGE?
I'LL SETTLE FOR BUYING HERSHEY PENNSYLVANIA!
VANDA AND YOUNG ARE RECRUITED TO PRODUCE.
NICE TO HAVE YOU BACK ABOARD, GUYS!
WELL, WE ENJOYED "WHO MADE WHO" SO MUCH, WE COULDN'T VERY WELL SAY NO, COULD WE?
"BLOW UP" HITS #2 IN BRITAIN AND #12 IN THE U.S. IN FEBRUARY '88.
AN' ROLLING STONE CALLED US HAS-BEENS.
WELL, CONSIDER THE SOURCE! TALK ABOUT THE POT CALLING THE KETTLE BLACK!
Rolling Sto
ANOTHER CLICHÉ? WE BEEN SPENDING TOO MUCH TIME IN THE STATES!
"HEATSEEKER", THEIR NEWEST HIT SINGLE, BECOMES THEIR NEWEST VIDEO AS WELL.
THE RECORD COMPANY SAID THE VIDEO IS THE MOST EXPENSIVE ONE EVER MADE.
COULDA FOOLED ME. WE JUST SHOWED UP AND PLAYED.
I'M SURE WE'RE WORTH EVERY PENNY, THOUGH!
THE "BLOW UP YOUR VIDEO" ALBUM IS CERTIFIED PLATINUM WHEN THE BAND MAKES A SURPRISING ANNOUNCEMENT.
AC/DC IS TAKING A VACATION OF SORTS. IN ORDER TO KEEP FROM BURNING OUT, IT'S BEEN MUTUALLY AGREED BETWEEN US TO TAKE A YEAR OR TWO OFF FROM TOURING AND RECORDING.

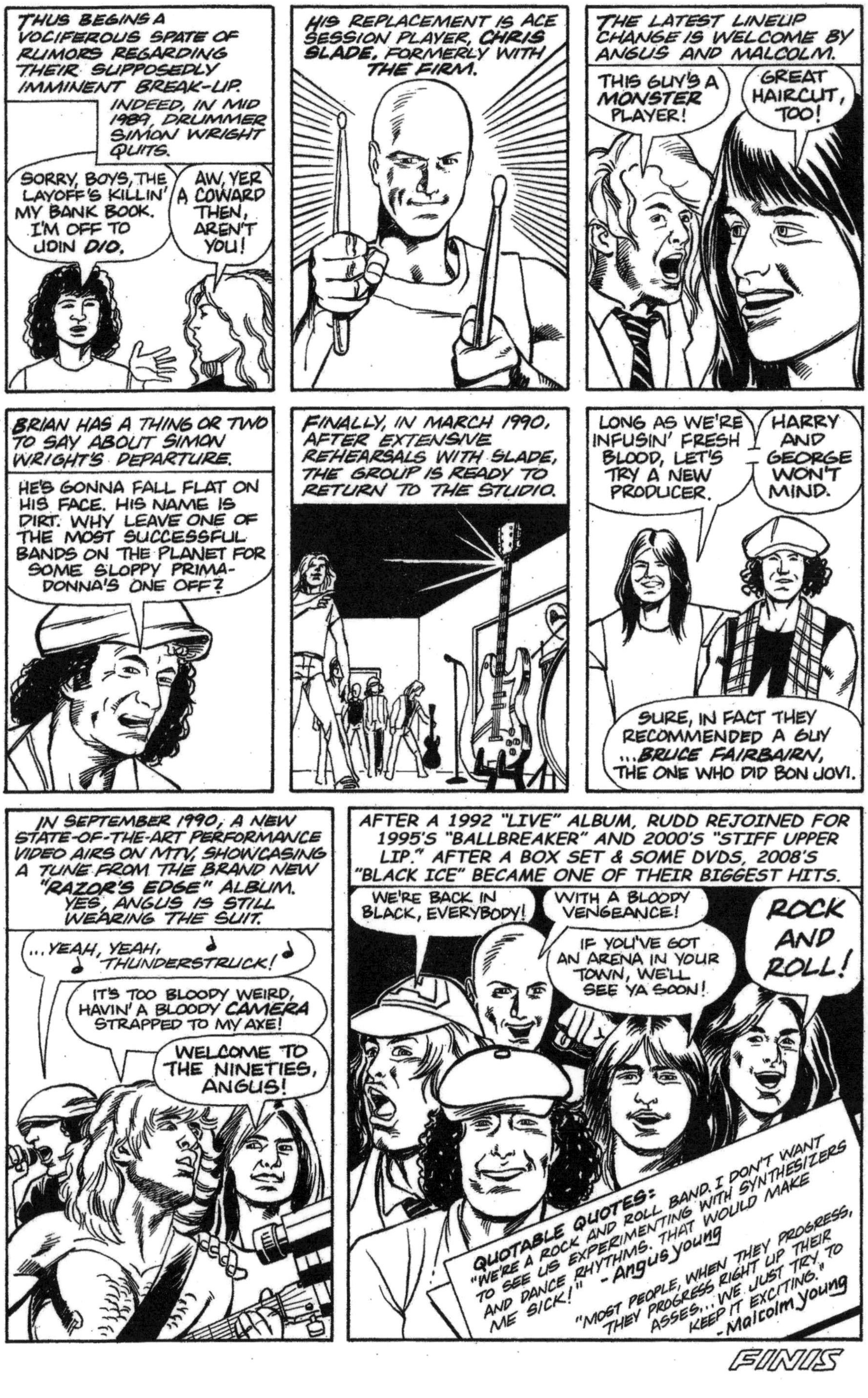
THUS BEGINS A VOCIFEROUS SPATE OF RUMORS REGARDING THEIR SUPPOSEDLY IMMINENT BREAK-UP.
INDEED, IN MID 1989, DRUMMER SIMON WRIGHT QUITS.
SORRY, BOYS, THE LAYOFF'S KILLIN' MY BANK BOOK. I'M OFF TO JOIN DIO.
AW, YER A COWARD THEN, AREN'T YOU!
HIS REPLACEMENT IS ACE SESSION PLAYER, CHRIS SLADE, FORMERLY WITH THE FIRM.
THE LATEST LINEUP CHANGE IS WELCOME BY ANGUS AND MALCOLM.
THIS GUY'S A MONSTER PLAYER!
GREAT HAIRCUT, TOO!
BRIAN HAS A THING OR TWO TO SAY ABOUT SIMON WRIGHT'S DEPARTURE.
HE'S GONNA FALL FLAT ON HIS FACE. HIS NAME IS DIRT. WHY LEAVE ONE OF THE MOST SUCCESSFUL BANDS ON THE PLANET FOR SOME SLOPPY PRIMA-DONNA'S ONE OFF?
FINALLY, IN MARCH 1990, AFTER EXTENSIVE REHEARSALS WITH SLADE, THE GROUP IS READY TO RETURN TO THE STUDIO.
LONG AS WE'RE INFUSIN' FRESH BLOOD, LET'S TRY A NEW PRODUCER.
HARRY AND GEORGE WON'T MIND.
SURE, IN FACT THEY RECOMMENDED A GUY ...BRUCE FAIRBAIRN, THE ONE WHO DID BON JOVI.
IN SEPTEMBER 1990, A NEW STATE-OF-THE-ART PERFORMANCE VIDEO AIRS ON MTV, SHOWCASING A TUNE FROM THE BRAND NEW "RAZOR'S EDGE" ALBUM. YES, ANGUS IS STILL WEARING THE SUIT.
...YEAH, YEAH, THUNDERSTRUCK!
IT'S TOO BLOODY WEIRD, HAVIN' A BLOODY CAMERA STRAPPED TO MY AXE!
WELCOME TO THE NINETIES, ANGUS!
AFTER A 1992 "LIVE" ALBUM, RUDD REJOINED FOR 1995'S "BALLBREAKER" AND 2000'S "STIFF UPPER LIP." AFTER A BOX SET & SOME DVDS, 2008'S "BLACK ICE" BECAME ONE OF THEIR BIGGEST HITS.
WE'RE BACK IN BLACK, EVERYBODY!
WITH A BLOODY VENGEANCE!
IF YOU'VE GOT AN ARENA IN YOUR TOWN, WE'LL SEE YA SOON!
ROCK AND ROLL!
QUOTABLE QUOTES:
"WE'RE A ROCK AND ROLL BAND. I DON'T WANT TO SEE US EXPERIMENTING WITH SYNTHESIZERS AND DANCE RHYTHMS. THAT WOULD MAKE ME SICK!" - Angus Young
"MOST PEOPLE, WHEN THEY PROGRESS, THEY PROGRESS RIGHT UP THEIR ASSES... WE JUST TRY TO KEEP IT EXCITING." - Malcolm Young
FINIS

MEGADETH

Todd Loren PRESENTS

STORY	PENCILS	INKS	EDITS	LETTERS/COVER COLOR
SPIKE STEFFENHAGEN	**DAVE BRIGGS**	**NATHEN ERVING**	**JAY ALLEN SANFORD**	**HEATHER CHENEY**

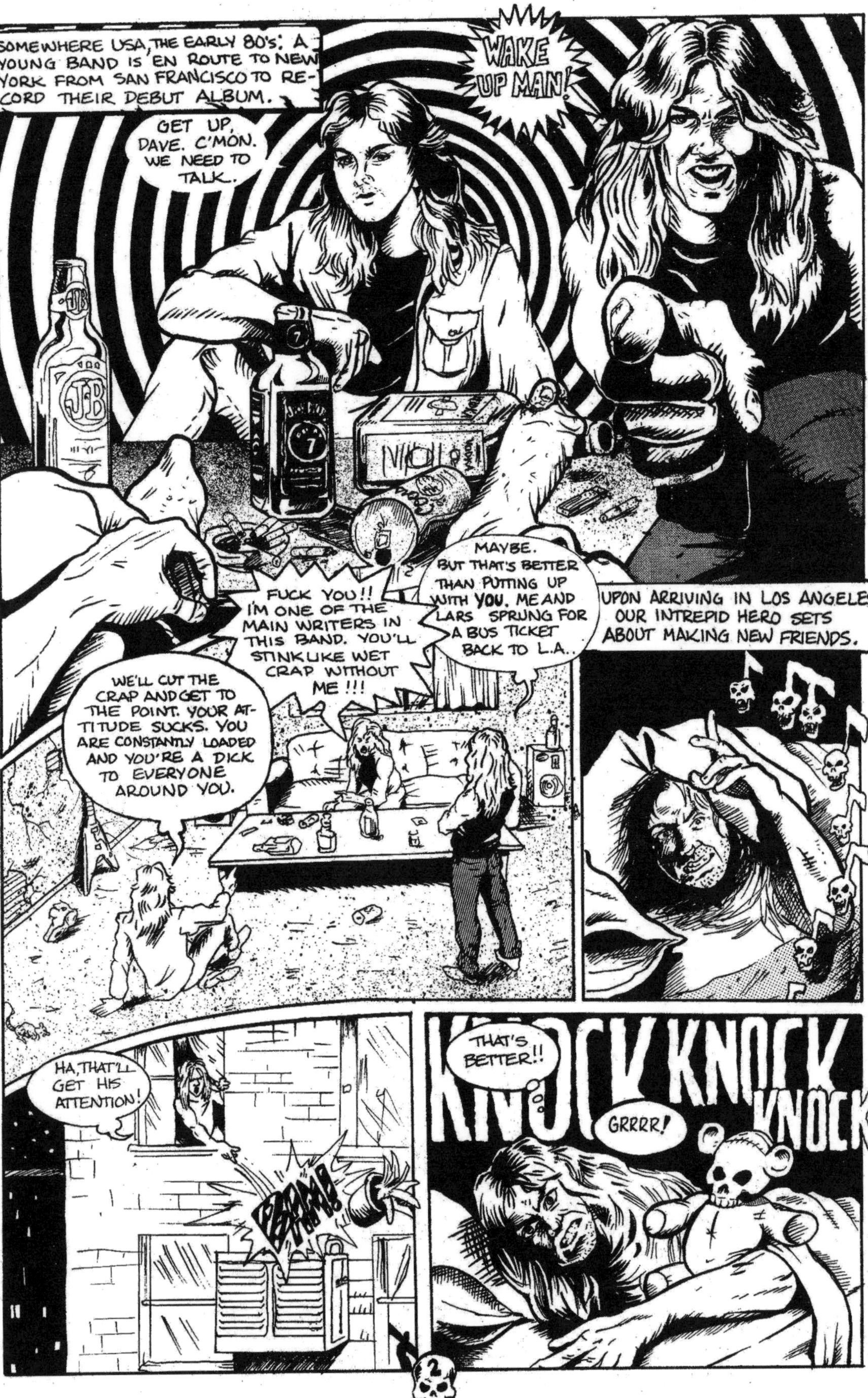
SOMEWHERE USA, THE EARLY 80's: A YOUNG BAND IS EN ROUTE TO NEW YORK FROM SAN FRANCISCO TO RECORD THEIR DEBUT ALBUM.
WAKE UP MAN!
GET UP, DAVE. C'MON. WE NEED TO TALK.
WE'LL CUT THE CRAP AND GET TO THE POINT. YOUR ATTITUDE SUCKS. YOU ARE CONSTANTLY LOADED AND YOU'RE A DICK TO EVERYONE AROUND YOU.
FUCK YOU!! I'M ONE OF THE MAIN WRITERS IN THIS BAND. YOU'LL STINK LIKE WET CRAP WITHOUT ME!!!
MAYBE. BUT THAT'S BETTER THAN PUTTING UP WITH YOU. ME AND LARS SPRUNG FOR A BUS TICKET BACK TO L.A..
UPON ARRIVING IN LOS ANGELES OUR INTREPID HERO SETS ABOUT MAKING NEW FRIENDS.
HA, THAT'LL GET HIS ATTENTION!
KNOCK KNOCK KNOCK
THAT'S BETTER!!
GRRRR!

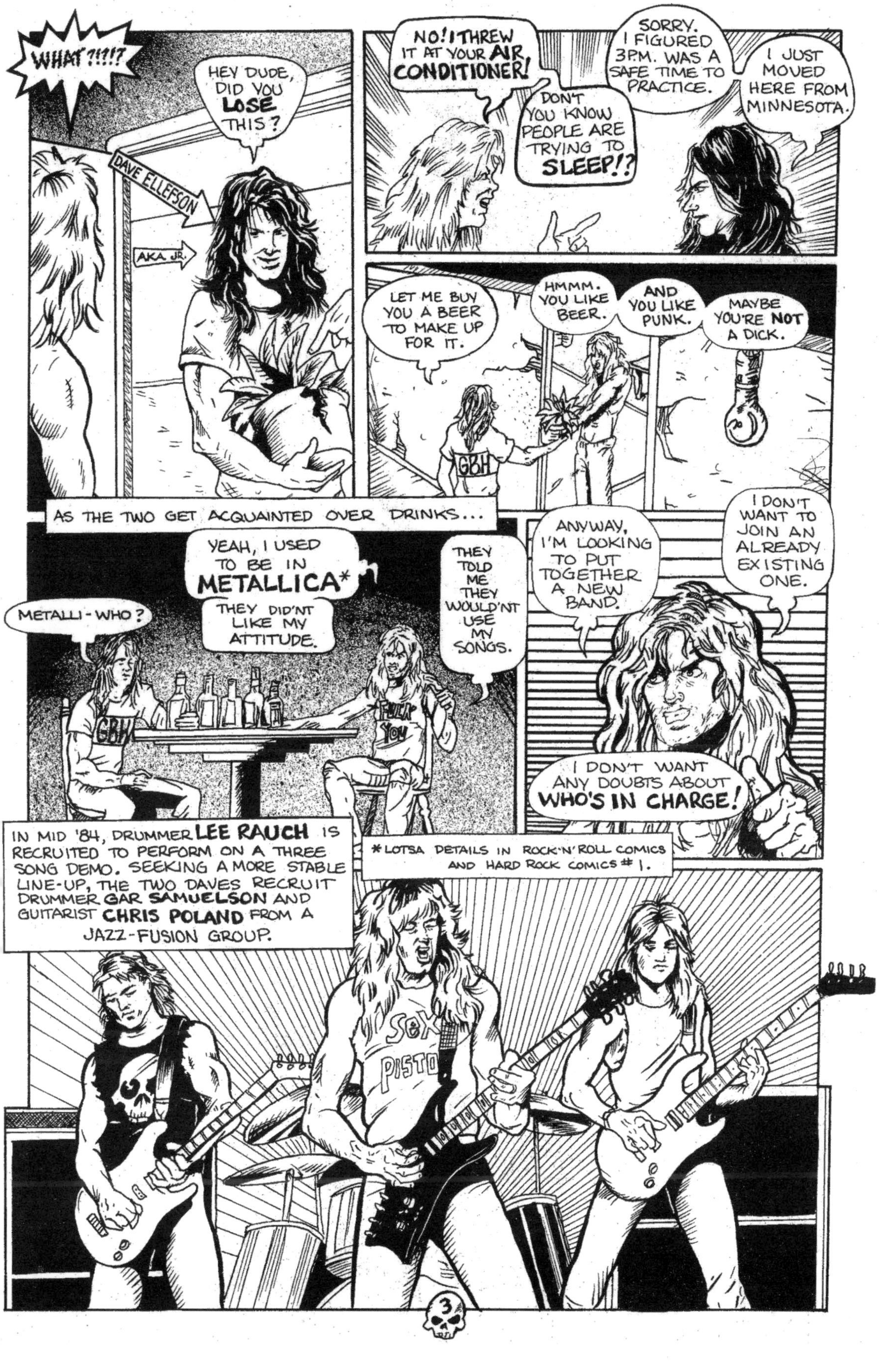
WHAT?!?!?
HEY DUDE, DID YOU LOSE THIS?
DAVE ELLEFSON
AKA JR.
NO! I THREW IT AT YOUR AIR CONDITIONER!
DON'T YOU KNOW PEOPLE ARE TRYING TO SLEEP!?
SORRY. I FIGURED 3P.M. WAS A SAFE TIME TO PRACTICE.
I JUST MOVED HERE FROM MINNESOTA.
LET ME BUY YOU A BEER TO MAKE UP FOR IT.
HMMM. YOU LIKE BEER.
AND YOU LIKE PUNK.
MAYBE YOU'RE NOT A DICK.
AS THE TWO GET ACQUAINTED OVER DRINKS...
YEAH, I USED TO BE IN METALLICA*
THEY DID'NT LIKE MY ATTITUDE.
METALLI-WHO?
THEY TOLD ME THEY WOULD'NT USE MY SONGS.
ANYWAY, I'M LOOKING TO PUT TOGETHER A NEW BAND.
I DON'T WANT TO JOIN AN ALREADY EXISTING ONE.
I DON'T WANT ANY DOUBTS ABOUT WHO'S IN CHARGE!
IN MID '84, DRUMMER LEE RAUCH IS RECRUITED TO PERFORM ON A THREE SONG DEMO. SEEKING A MORE STABLE LINE-UP, THE TWO DAVES RECRUIT DRUMMER GAR SAMUELSON AND GUITARIST CHRIS POLAND FROM A JAZZ-FUSION GROUP.
*LOTSA DETAILS IN ROCK'N'ROLL COMICS AND HARD ROCK COMICS #1.

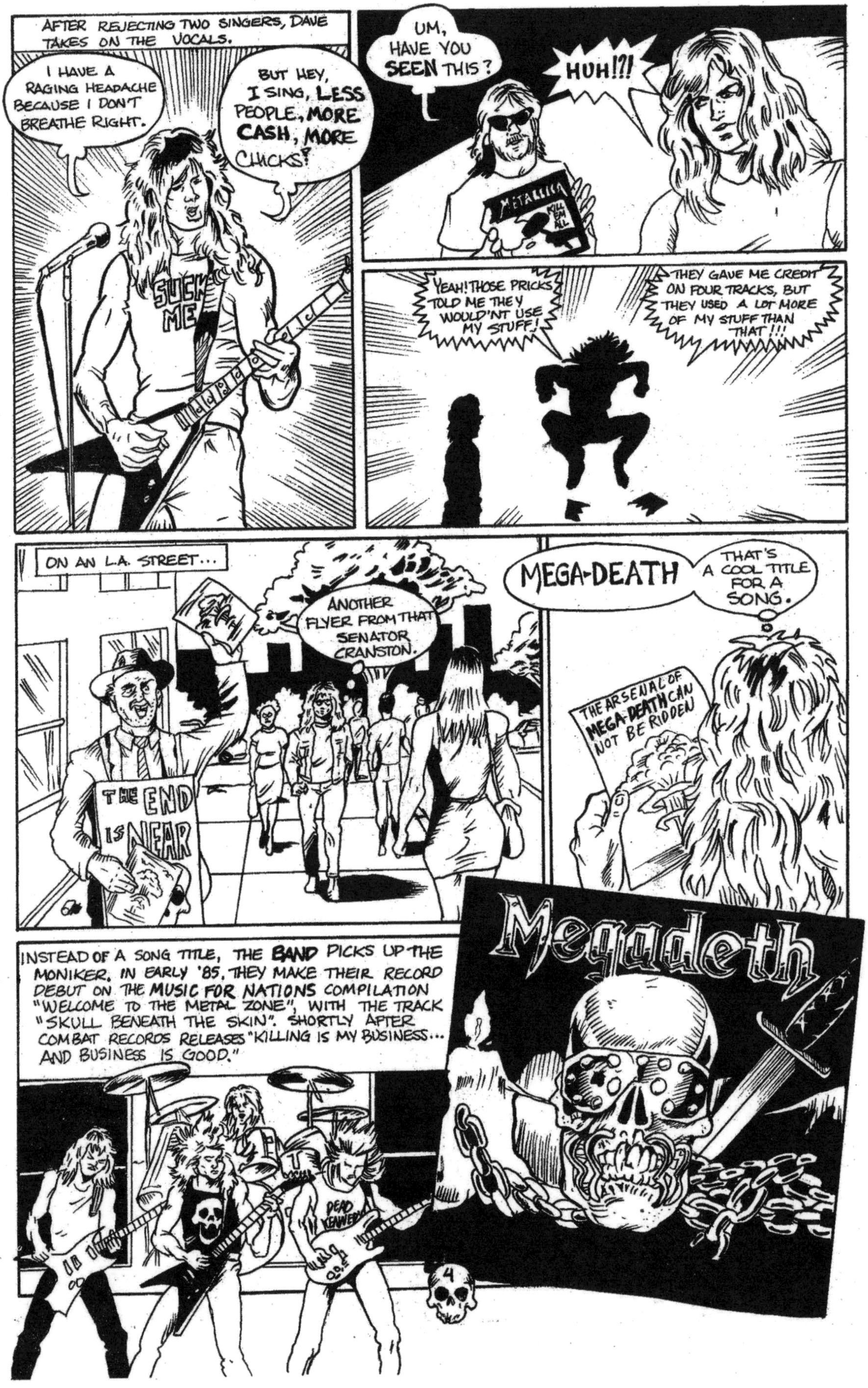

AFTER REJECTING TWO SINGERS, DAVE TAKES ON THE VOCALS.
I HAVE A RAGING HEADACHE BECAUSE I DON'T BREATHE RIGHT.
BUT HEY, I SING, LESS PEOPLE, MORE CASH, MORE CHICKS!
SUCK ME
UM, HAVE YOU SEEN THIS?
HUH!?!
METALLICA
KILL 'EM ALL
YEAH! THOSE PRICKS TOLD ME THEY WOULD'NT USE MY STUFF!
THEY GAVE ME CREDIT ON FOUR TRACKS, BUT THEY USED A LOT MORE OF MY STUFF THAN THAT!!!
ON AN L.A. STREET...
ANOTHER FLYER FROM THAT SENATOR CRANSTON.
THE END IS NEAR
MEGA-DEATH
THAT'S A COOL TITLE FOR A SONG.
THE ARSENAL OF MEGA-DEATH CAN NOT BE RIDDEN
Megadeth
INSTEAD OF A SONG TITLE, THE BAND PICKS UP THE MONIKER. IN EARLY '85, THEY MAKE THEIR RECORD DEBUT ON THE MUSIC FOR NATIONS COMPILATION "WELCOME TO THE METAL ZONE", WITH THE TRACK "SKULL BENEATH THE SKIN". SHORTLY AFTER COMBAT RECORDS RELEASES "KILLING IS MY BUSINESS... AND BUSINESS IS GOOD."
DEAD KENNEDYS

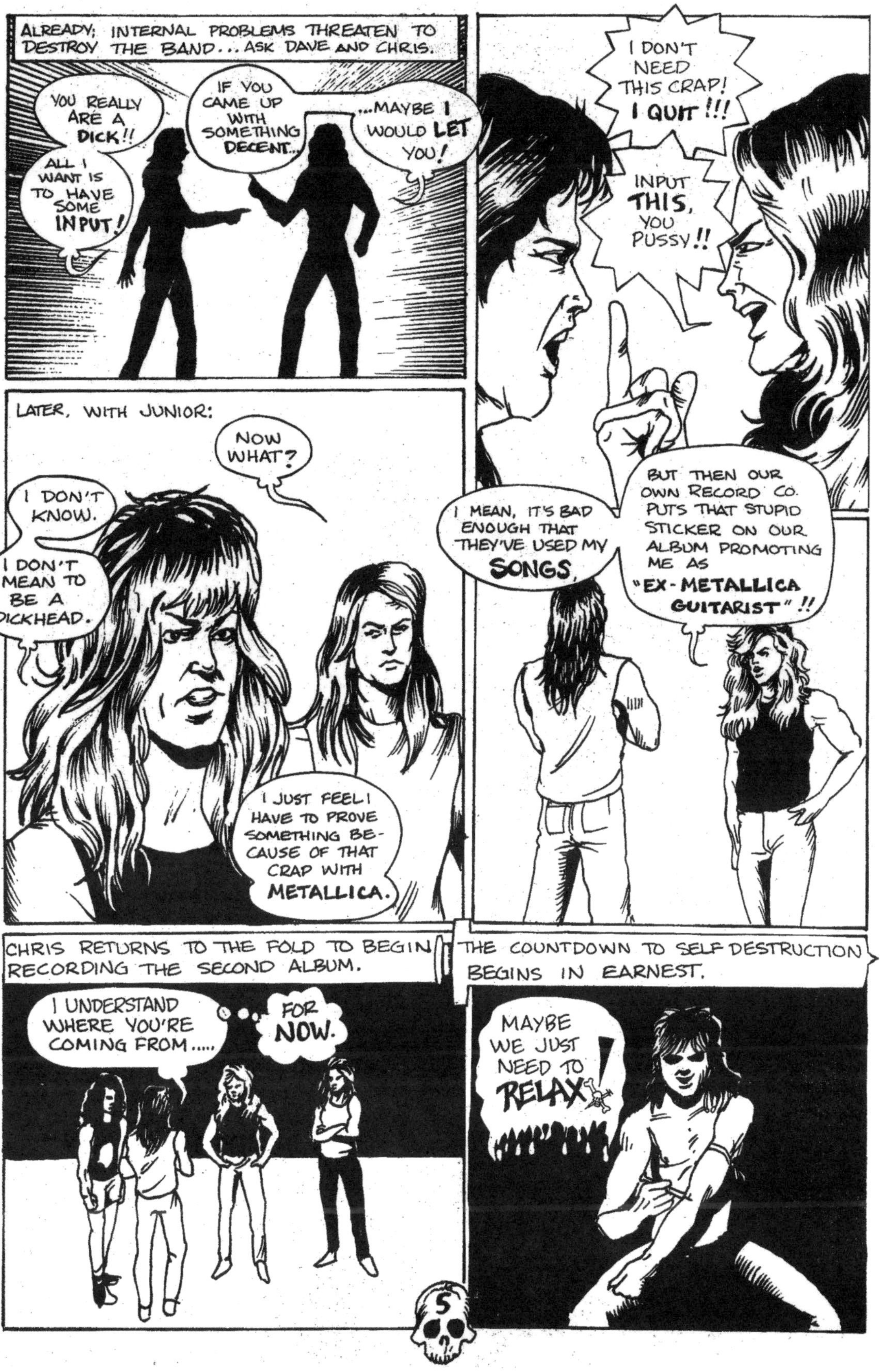
ALREADY, INTERNAL PROBLEMS THREATEN TO DESTROY THE BAND... ASK DAVE AND CHRIS.
YOU REALLY ARE A DICK!!
IF YOU CAME UP WITH SOMETHING DECENT...
...MAYBE I WOULD LET YOU!
ALL I WANT IS TO HAVE SOME INPUT!
I DON'T NEED THIS CRAP! I QUIT!!!
INPUT THIS, YOU PUSSY!!
LATER, WITH JUNIOR:
NOW WHAT?
I DON'T KNOW.
I DON'T MEAN TO BE A DICKHEAD.
I JUST FEEL I HAVE TO PROVE SOMETHING BE-CAUSE OF THAT CRAP WITH METALLICA.
I MEAN, IT'S BAD ENOUGH THAT THEY'VE USED MY SONGS,
BUT THEN OUR OWN RECORD CO. PUTS THAT STUPID STICKER ON OUR ALBUM PROMOTING ME AS "EX-METALLICA GUITARIST"!!
CHRIS RETURNS TO THE FOLD TO BEGIN RECORDING THE SECOND ALBUM.
I UNDERSTAND WHERE YOU'RE COMING FROM.....
FOR NOW.
THE COUNTDOWN TO SELF DESTRUCTION BEGINS IN EARNEST.
MAYBE WE JUST NEED TO RELAX!

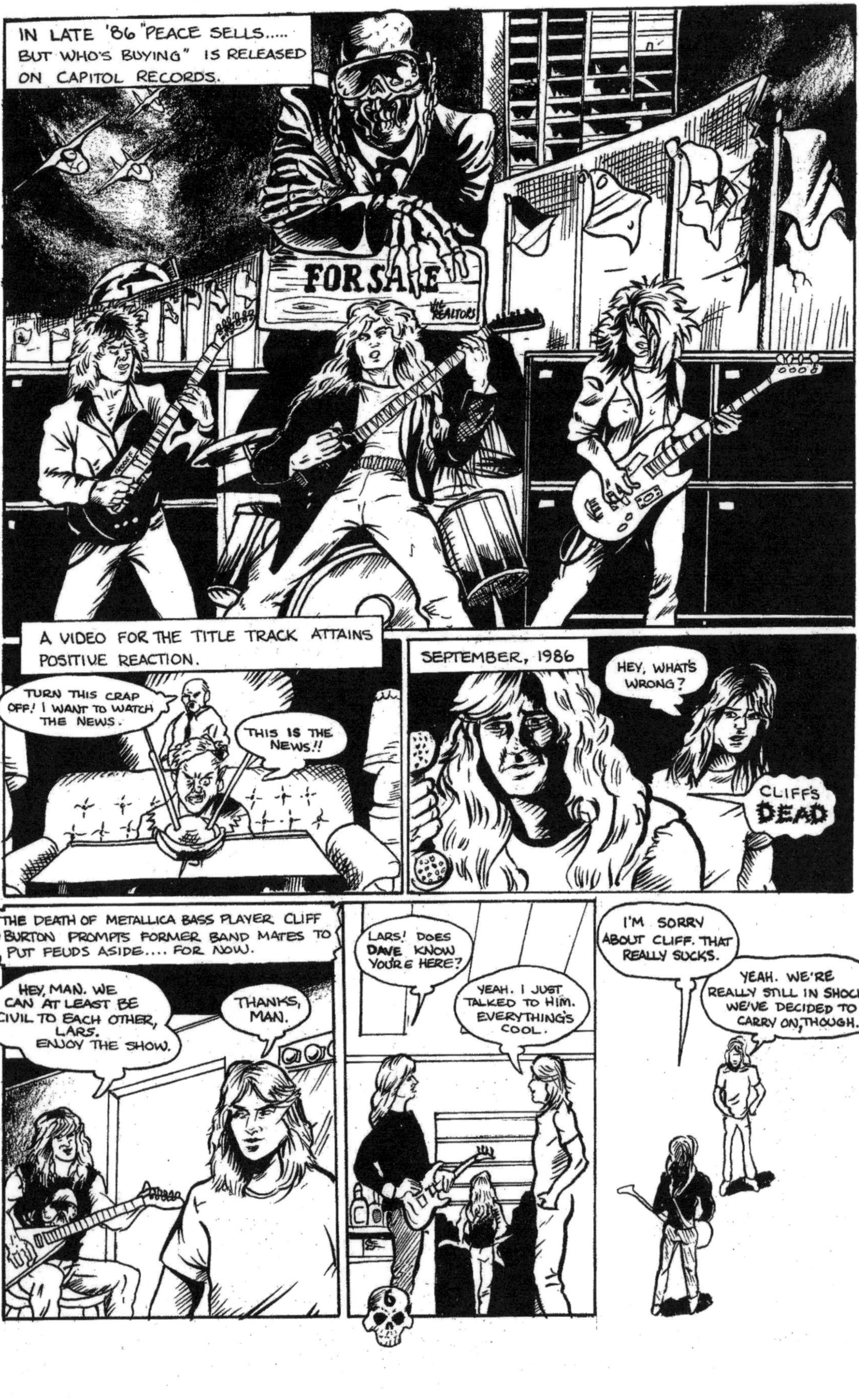

IN LATE '86 "PEACE SELLS..... BUT WHO'S BUYING" IS RELEASED ON CAPITOL RECORDS.
FOR SALE
A VIDEO FOR THE TITLE TRACK ATTAINS POSITIVE REACTION.
TURN THIS CRAP OFF! I WANT TO WATCH THE NEWS.
THIS IS THE NEWS!!
SEPTEMBER, 1986
HEY, WHAT'S WRONG?
CLIFF'S DEAD
THE DEATH OF METALLICA BASS PLAYER CLIFF BURTON PROMPTS FORMER BAND MATES TO PUT FEUDS ASIDE.... FOR NOW.
HEY, MAN. WE CAN AT LEAST BE CIVIL TO EACH OTHER, LARS. ENJOY THE SHOW.
THANKS, MAN.
LARS! DOES DAVE KNOW YOU'RE HERE?
YEAH. I JUST TALKED TO HIM. EVERYTHING'S COOL.
I'M SORRY ABOUT CLIFF. THAT REALLY SUCKS.
YEAH. WE'RE REALLY STILL IN SHOCK. WE'VE DECIDED TO CARRY ON, THOUGH.
6

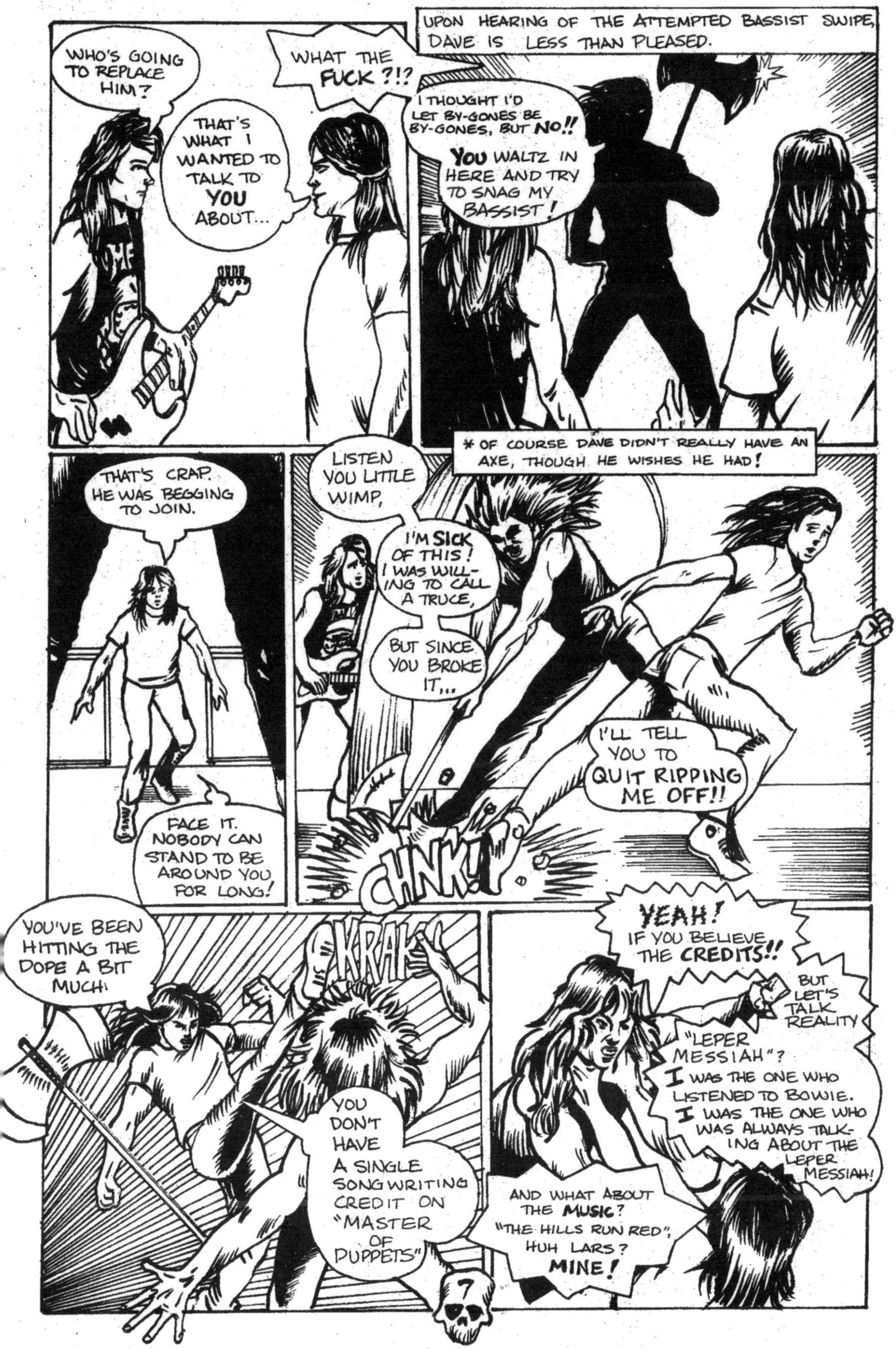
UPON HEARING OF THE ATTEMPTED BASSIST SWIPE, DAVE IS LESS THAN PLEASED.
WHO'S GOING TO REPLACE HIM?
WHAT THE FUCK ?!?
THAT'S WHAT I WANTED TO TALK TO YOU ABOUT...
I THOUGHT I'D LET BY-GONES BE BY-GONES, BUT NO!!
YOU WALTZ IN HERE AND TRY TO SNAG MY BASSIST!
* OF COURSE DAVE DIDN'T REALLY HAVE AN AXE, THOUGH HE WISHES HE HAD!
THAT'S CRAP. HE WAS BEGGING TO JOIN.
LISTEN YOU LITTLE WIMP,
I'M SICK OF THIS! I WAS WILLING TO CALL A TRUCE,
BUT SINCE YOU BROKE IT,..
I'LL TELL YOU TO QUIT RIPPING ME OFF!!
FACE IT. NOBODY CAN STAND TO BE AROUND YOU FOR LONG!
CHNK!
YOU'VE BEEN HITTING THE DOPE A BIT MUCH!
KRAK!
YOU DON'T HAVE A SINGLE SONGWRITING CREDIT ON "MASTER OF PUPPETS"
YEAH! IF YOU BELIEVE THE CREDITS!!
BUT LET'S TALK REALITY
"LEPER MESSIAH"? I WAS THE ONE WHO LISTENED TO BOWIE. I WAS THE ONE WHO WAS ALWAYS TALKING ABOUT THE LEPER MESSIAH!
AND WHAT ABOUT THE MUSIC? "THE HILLS RUN RED", HUH LARS? MINE!

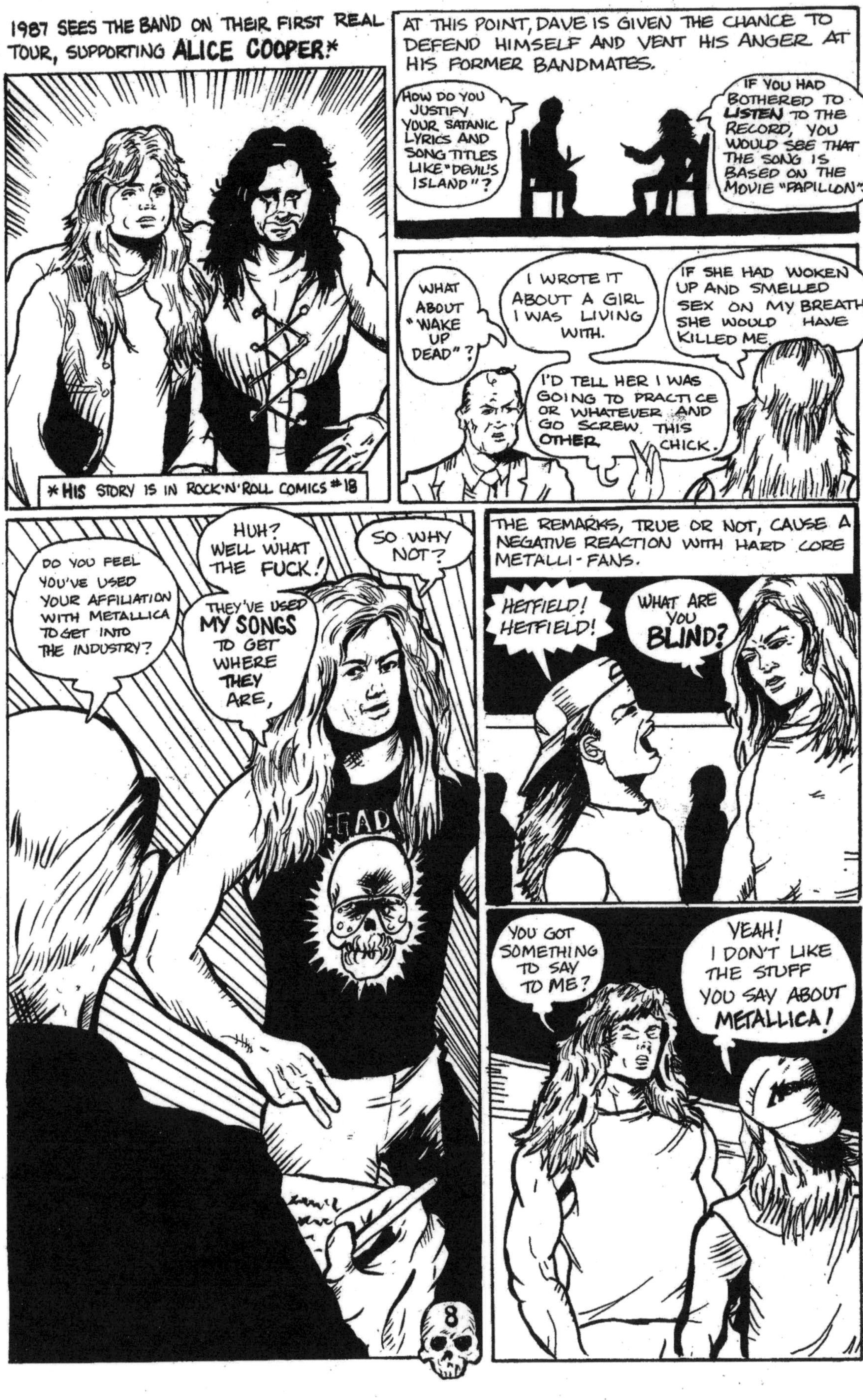

1987 SEES THE BAND ON THEIR FIRST REAL TOUR, SUPPORTING ALICE COOPER.*
* HIS STORY IS IN ROCK'N'ROLL COMICS #18
AT THIS POINT, DAVE IS GIVEN THE CHANCE TO DEFEND HIMSELF AND VENT HIS ANGER AT HIS FORMER BANDMATES.
HOW DO YOU JUSTIFY YOUR SATANIC LYRICS AND SONG TITLES LIKE "DEVIL'S ISLAND"?
IF YOU HAD BOTHERED TO LISTEN TO THE RECORD, YOU WOULD SEE THAT THE SONG IS BASED ON THE MOVIE "PAPILLON".
WHAT ABOUT "WAKE UP DEAD"?
I WROTE IT ABOUT A GIRL I WAS LIVING WITH.
I'D TELL HER I WAS GOING TO PRACTICE OR WHATEVER AND GO SCREW THIS OTHER CHICK.
IF SHE HAD WOKEN UP AND SMELLED SEX ON MY BREATH, SHE WOULD HAVE KILLED ME.
DO YOU FEEL YOU'VE USED YOUR AFFILIATION WITH METALLICA TO GET INTO THE INDUSTRY?
HUH? WELL WHAT THE FUCK!
THEY'VE USED MY SONGS TO GET WHERE THEY ARE,
SO WHY NOT?
THE REMARKS, TRUE OR NOT, CAUSE A NEGATIVE REACTION WITH HARD CORE METALLI-FANS.
HETFIELD! HETFIELD!
WHAT ARE YOU BLIND?
YOU GOT SOMETHING TO SAY TO ME?
YEAH! I DON'T LIKE THE STUFF YOU SAY ABOUT METALLICA!

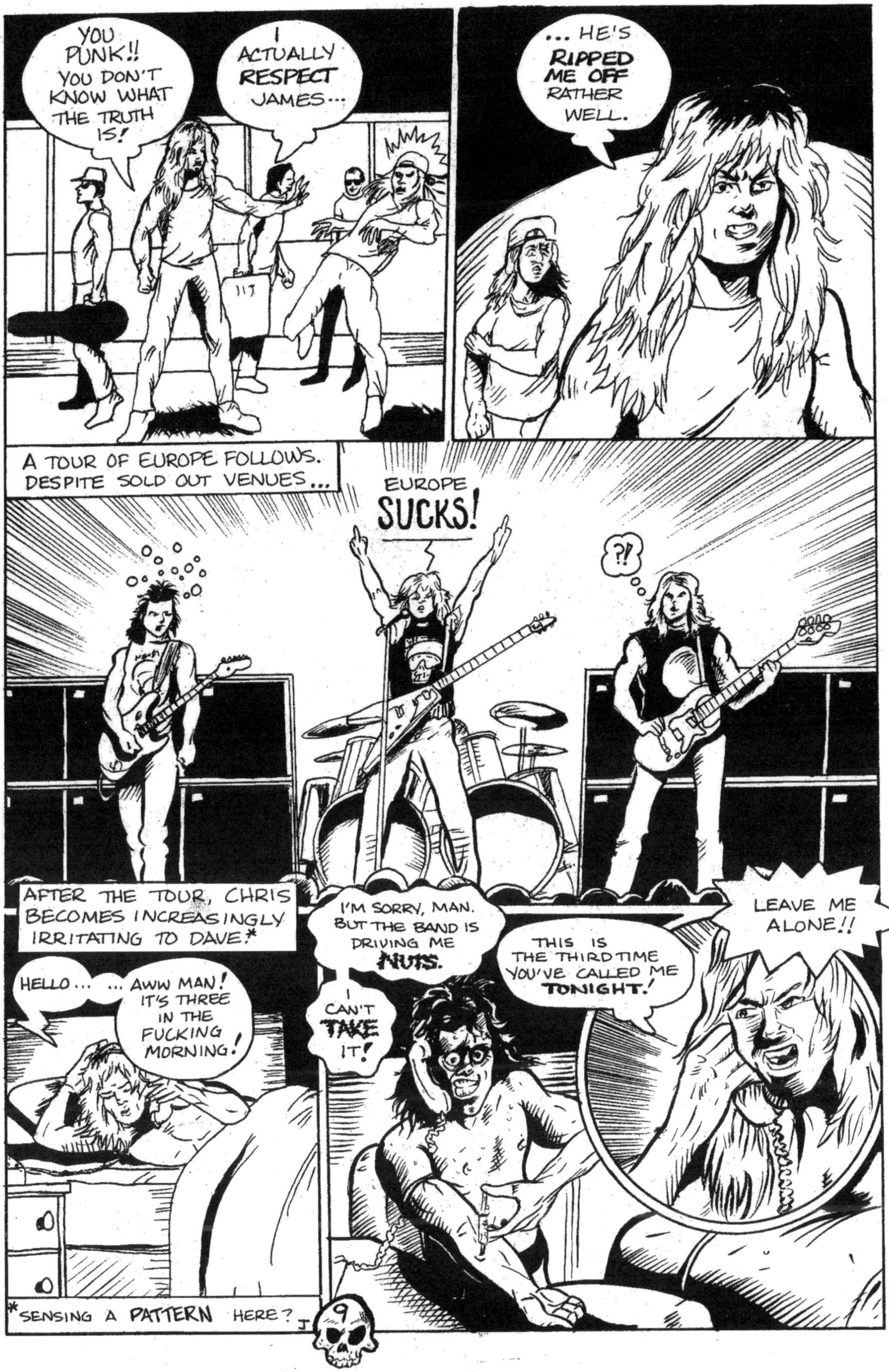

YOU PUNK!! YOU DON'T KNOW WHAT THE TRUTH IS!
I ACTUALLY RESPECT JAMES...
... HE'S RIPPED ME OFF RATHER WELL.
A TOUR OF EUROPE FOLLOWS. DESPITE SOLD OUT VENUES...
EUROPE SUCKS!
?!
AFTER THE TOUR, CHRIS BECOMES INCREASINGLY IRRITATING TO DAVE.*
HELLO....
... AWW MAN! IT'S THREE IN THE FUCKING MORNING!
I'M SORRY, MAN. BUT THE BAND IS DRIVING ME NUTS.
I CAN'T TAKE IT!
THIS IS THE THIRD TIME YOU'VE CALLED ME TONIGHT!
LEAVE ME ALONE!!
*SENSING A PATTERN HERE?

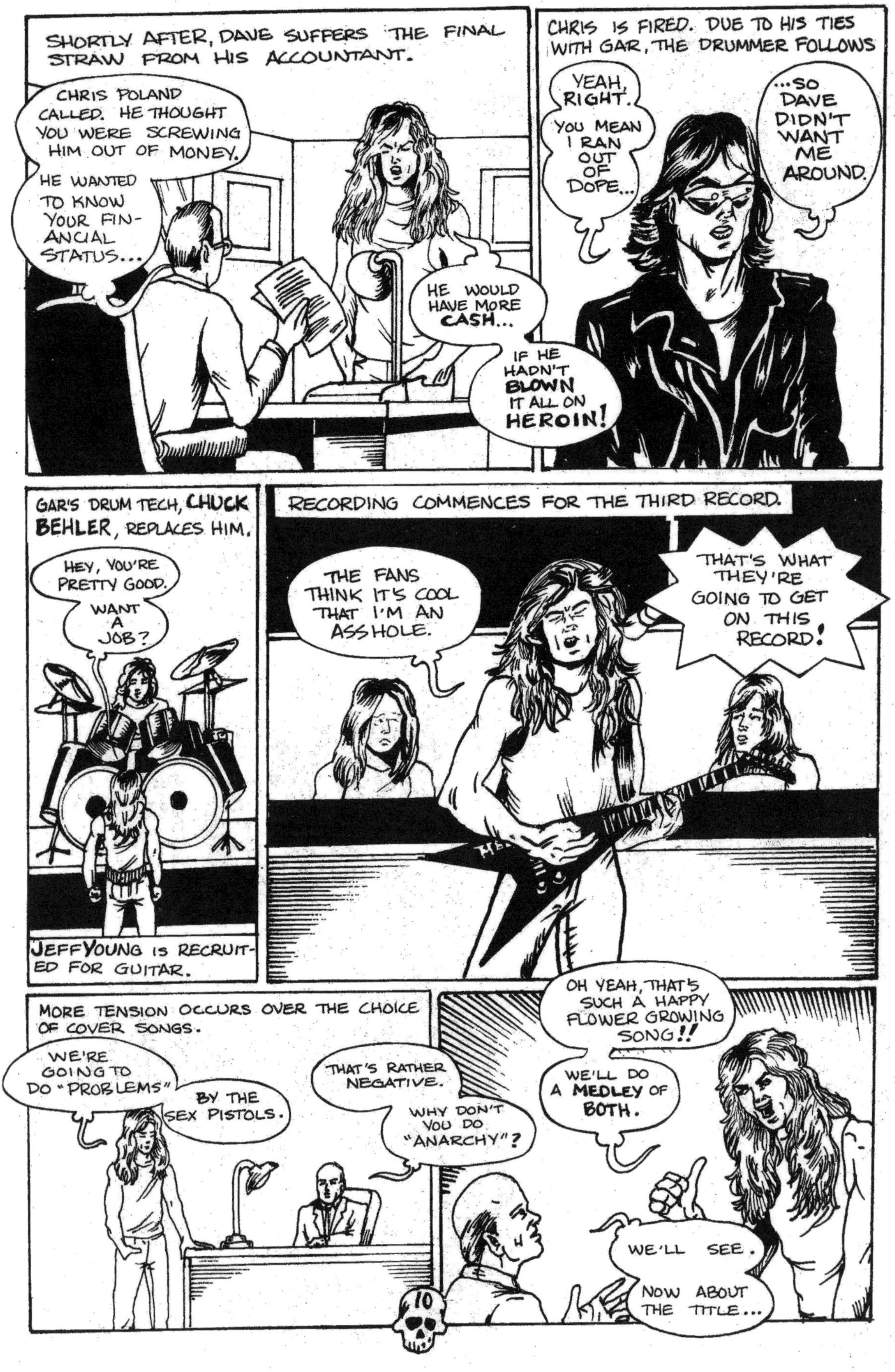

SHORTLY AFTER, DAVE SUFFERS THE FINAL STRAW FROM HIS ACCOUNTANT.
CHRIS POLAND CALLED. HE THOUGHT YOU WERE SCREWING HIM OUT OF MONEY.
HE WANTED TO KNOW YOUR FIN-ANCIAL STATUS...
HE WOULD HAVE MORE CASH...
IF HE HADN'T BLOWN IT ALL ON HEROIN!
CHRIS IS FIRED. DUE TO HIS TIES WITH GAR, THE DRUMMER FOLLOWS
YEAH, RIGHT.
YOU MEAN I RAN OUT OF DOPE...
...SO DAVE DIDN'T WANT ME AROUND.
GAR'S DRUM TECH, CHUCK BEHLER, REPLACES HIM.
HEY, YOU'RE PRETTY GOOD.
WANT A JOB?
JEFF YOUNG IS RECRUIT-ED FOR GUITAR.
RECORDING COMMENCES FOR THE THIRD RECORD.
THE FANS THINK IT'S COOL THAT I'M AN ASSHOLE.
THAT'S WHAT THEY'RE GOING TO GET ON THIS RECORD!
MORE TENSION OCCURS OVER THE CHOICE OF COVER SONGS.
WE'RE GOING TO DO "PROBLEMS"
BY THE SEX PISTOLS.
THAT'S RATHER NEGATIVE.
WHY DON'T YOU DO "ANARCHY"?
OH YEAH, THAT'S SUCH A HAPPY FLOWER GROWING SONG!!
WE'LL DO A MEDLEY OF BOTH.
WE'LL SEE.
NOW ABOUT THE TITLE...

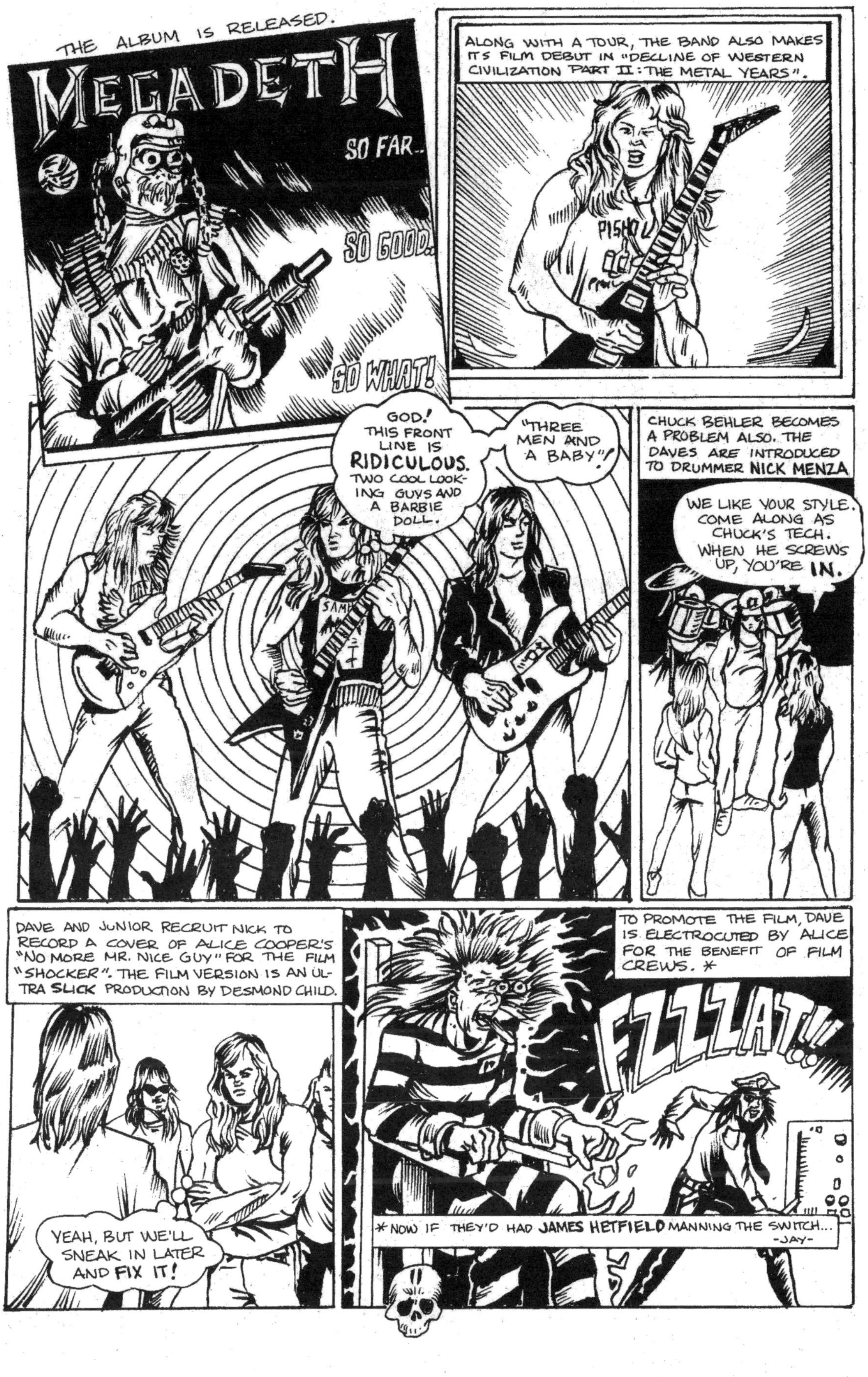
THE ALBUM IS RELEASED.
MEGADETH
SO FAR...
SO GOOD...
SO WHAT!
ALONG WITH A TOUR, THE BAND ALSO MAKES ITS FILM DEBUT IN "DECLINE OF WESTERN CIVILIZATION PART II: THE METAL YEARS".
GOD! THIS FRONT LINE IS RIDICULOUS. TWO COOL LOOKING GUYS AND A BARBIE DOLL.
"THREE MEN AND A BABY"!
CHUCK BEHLER BECOMES A PROBLEM ALSO. THE DAVES ARE INTRODUCED TO DRUMMER NICK MENZA
WE LIKE YOUR STYLE. COME ALONG AS CHUCK'S TECH. WHEN HE SCREWS UP, YOU'RE IN.
DAVE AND JUNIOR RECRUIT NICK TO RECORD A COVER OF ALICE COOPER'S "NO MORE MR. NICE GUY" FOR THE FILM "SHOCKER". THE FILM VERSION IS AN ULTRA SLICK PRODUCTION BY DESMOND CHILD.
YEAH, BUT WE'LL SNEAK IN LATER AND FIX IT!
TO PROMOTE THE FILM, DAVE IS ELECTROCUTED BY ALICE FOR THE BENEFIT OF FILM CREWS. *
FZZZAT!!!
* NOW IF THEY'D HAD JAMES HETFIELD MANNING THE SWITCH...
-JAY-

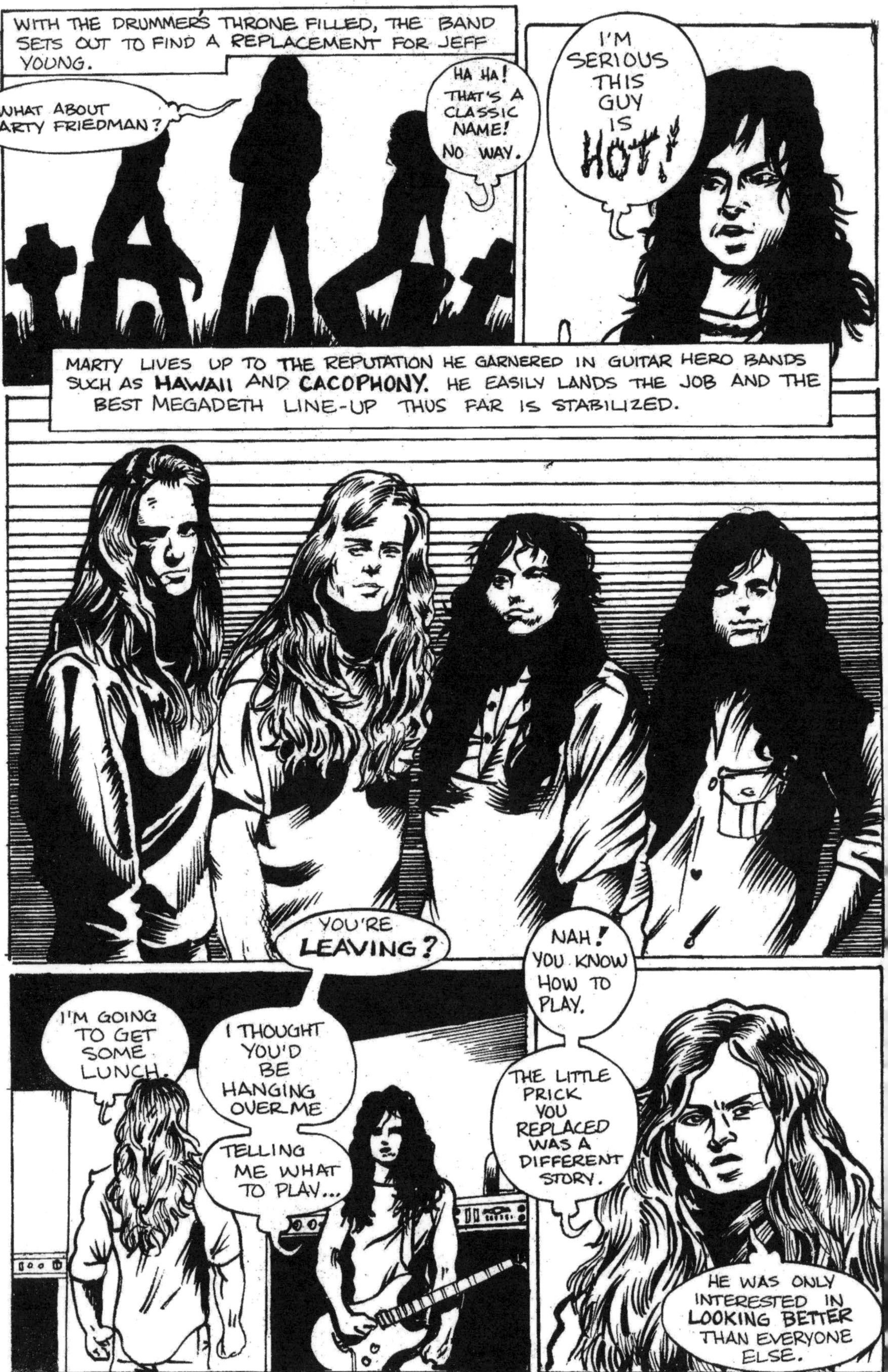
WITH THE DRUMMER'S THRONE FILLED, THE BAND SETS OUT TO FIND A REPLACEMENT FOR JEFF YOUNG.
WHAT ABOUT MARTY FRIEDMAN?
HA HA! THAT'S A CLASSIC NAME! NO WAY.
I'M SERIOUS THIS GUY IS HOT!
MARTY LIVES UP TO THE REPUTATION HE GARNERED IN GUITAR HERO BANDS SUCH AS HAWAII AND CACOPHONY. HE EASILY LANDS THE JOB AND THE BEST MEGADETH LINE-UP THUS FAR IS STABILIZED.
I'M GOING TO GET SOME LUNCH.
YOU'RE LEAVING?
I THOUGHT YOU'D BE HANGING OVER ME
TELLING ME WHAT TO PLAY...
NAH! YOU KNOW HOW TO PLAY.
THE LITTLE PRICK YOU REPLACED WAS A DIFFERENT STORY.
HE WAS ONLY INTERESTED IN LOOKING BETTER THAN EVERYONE ELSE.

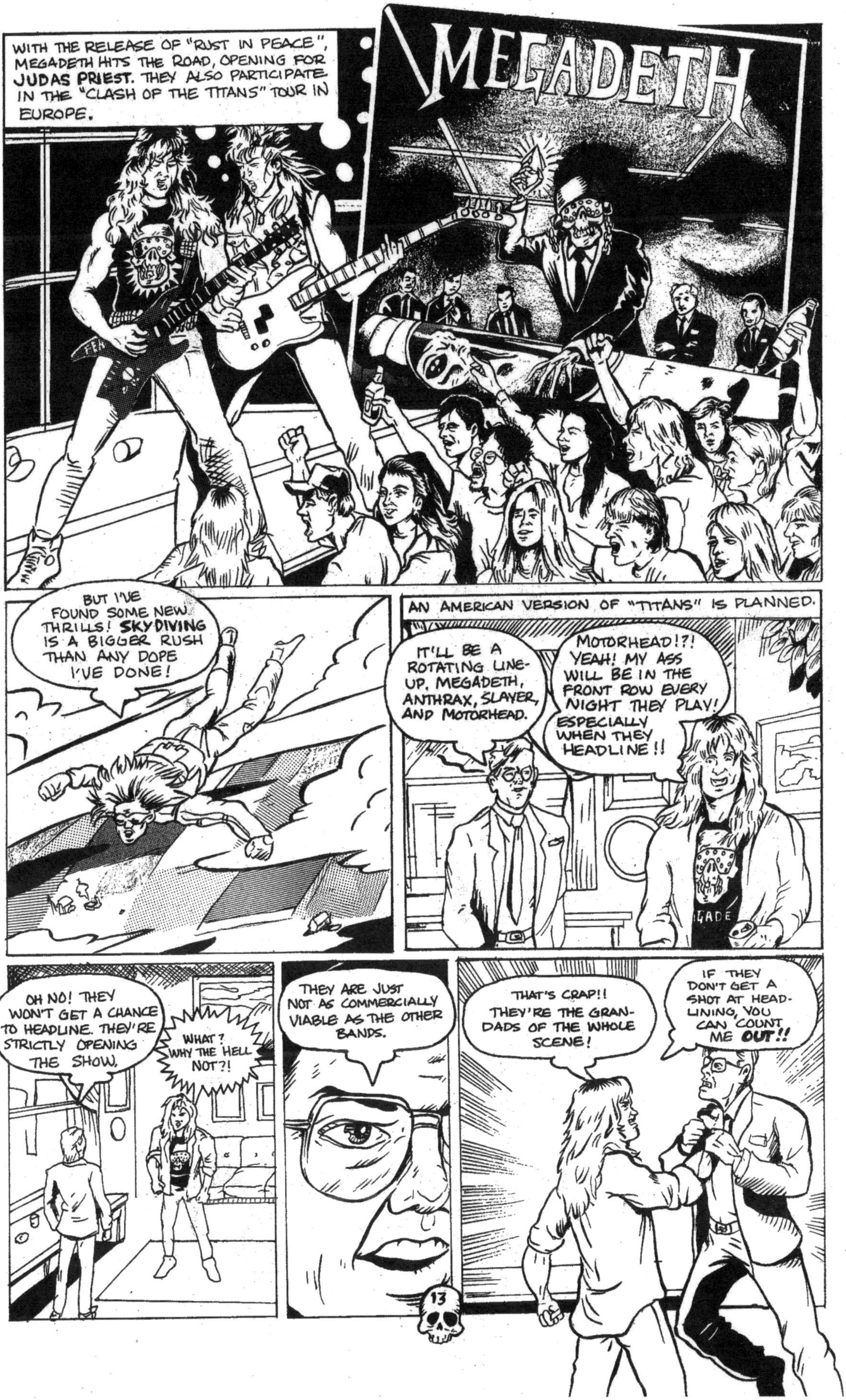

WITH THE RELEASE OF "RUST IN PEACE", MEGADETH HITS THE ROAD, OPENING FOR **JUDAS PRIEST.** THEY ALSO PARTICIPATE IN THE "CLASH OF THE TITANS" TOUR IN EUROPE.
MEGADETH
BUT I'VE FOUND SOME NEW THRILLS! **SKYDIVING** IS A BIGGER RUSH THAN ANY DOPE I'VE DONE!
AN AMERICAN VERSION OF "TITANS" IS PLANNED.
IT'LL BE A ROTATING LINE-UP. MEGADETH, ANTHRAX, SLAYER, AND MOTORHEAD.
MOTORHEAD!?! YEAH! MY ASS WILL BE IN THE FRONT ROW EVERY NIGHT THEY PLAY! ESPECIALLY WHEN THEY HEADLINE!!
OH NO! THEY WON'T GET A CHANCE TO HEADLINE. THEY'RE STRICTLY OPENING THE SHOW.
WHAT? WHY THE HELL NOT?!
THEY ARE JUST NOT AS COMMERCIALLY VIABLE AS THE OTHER BANDS.
THAT'S CRAP!! THEY'RE THE GRAN-DADS OF THE WHOLE SCENE!
IF THEY DON'T GET A SHOT AT HEAD-LINING, YOU CAN COUNT ME **OUT!!**

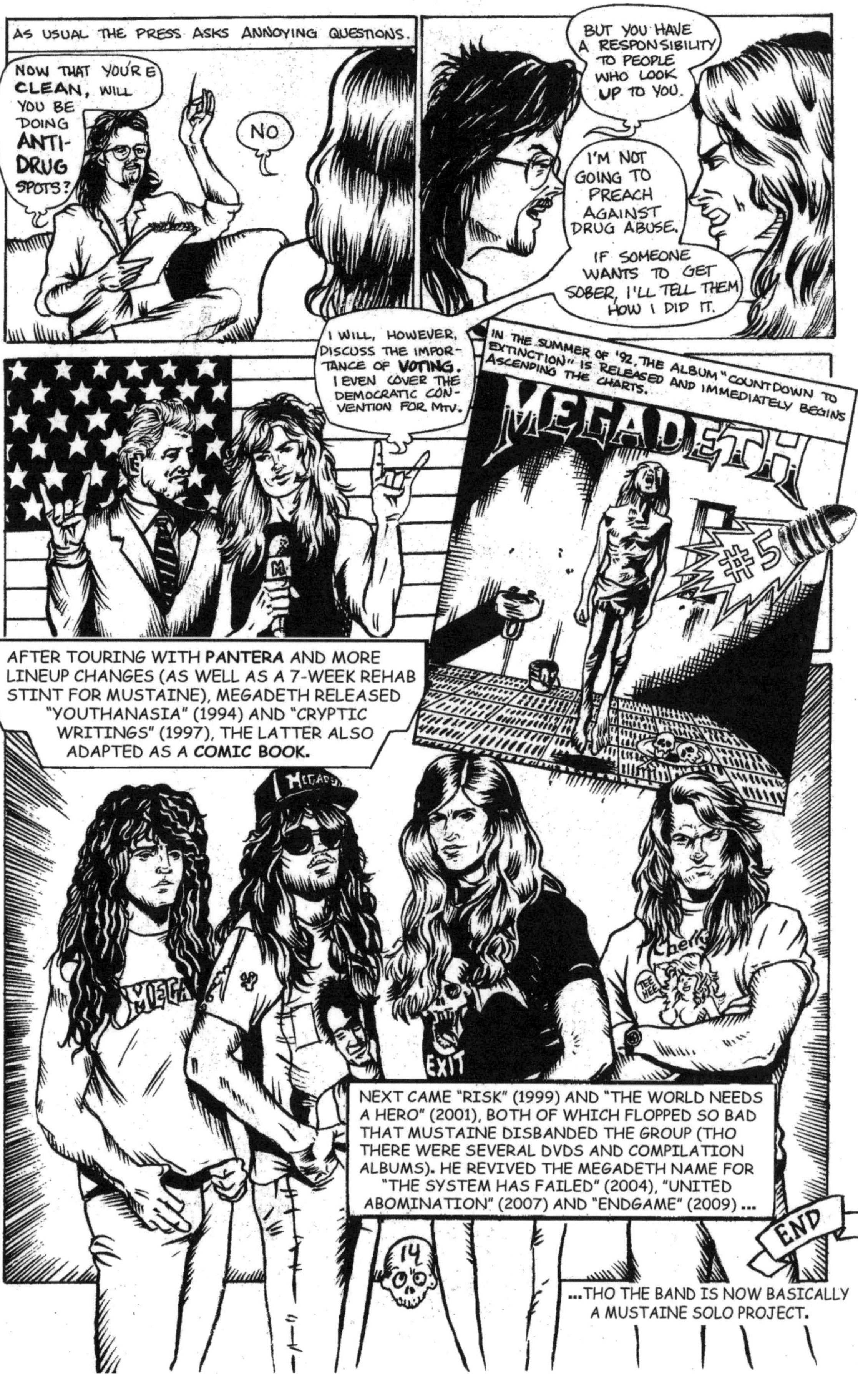
AS USUAL THE PRESS ASKS ANNOYING QUESTIONS.
NOW THAT YOU'RE CLEAN, WILL YOU BE DOING ANTI-DRUG SPOTS?
NO.
BUT YOU HAVE A RESPONSIBILITY TO PEOPLE WHO LOOK UP TO YOU.
I'M NOT GOING TO PREACH AGAINST DRUG ABUSE.
IF SOMEONE WANTS TO GET SOBER, I'LL TELL THEM HOW I DID IT.
I WILL, HOWEVER, DISCUSS THE IMPORTANCE OF VOTING. I EVEN COVER THE DEMOCRATIC CONVENTION FOR MTV.
IN THE SUMMER OF '92, THE ALBUM "COUNTDOWN TO EXTINCTION" IS RELEASED AND IMMEDIATELY BEGINS ASCENDING THE CHARTS.
MEGADETH
#5
AFTER TOURING WITH PANTERA AND MORE LINEUP CHANGES (AS WELL AS A 7-WEEK REHAB STINT FOR MUSTAINE), MEGADETH RELEASED "YOUTHANASIA" (1994) AND "CRYPTIC WRITINGS" (1997), THE LATTER ALSO ADAPTED AS A COMIC BOOK.
EXIT
TEE HEE
NEXT CAME "RISK" (1999) AND "THE WORLD NEEDS A HERO" (2001), BOTH OF WHICH FLOPPED SO BAD THAT MUSTAINE DISBANDED THE GROUP (THO THERE WERE SEVERAL DVDS AND COMPILATION ALBUMS). HE REVIVED THE MEGADETH NAME FOR "THE SYSTEM HAS FAILED" (2004), "UNITED ABOMINATION" (2007) AND "ENDGAME" (2009)...
END
...THO THE BAND IS NOW BASICALLY A MUSTAINE SOLO PROJECT.

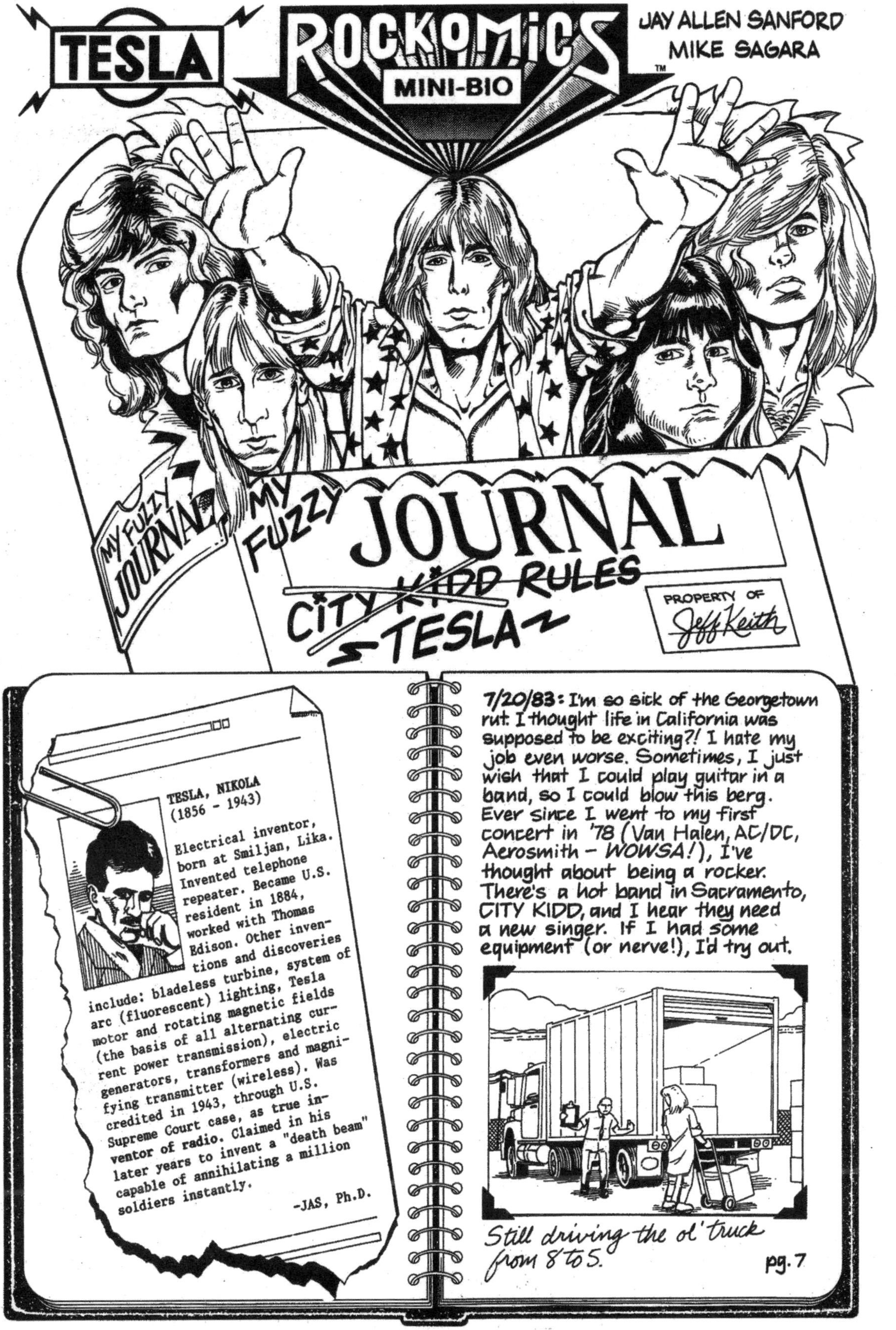
TESLA
ROCKOMICS
MINI-BIO
TM
JAY ALLEN SANFORD
MIKE SAGARA
MY FUZZY JOURNAL
MY FUZZY
JOURNAL
CITY KIDD RULES
TESLA
PROPERTY OF
Jeff Keith
TESLA, NIKOLA
(1856 - 1943)
Electrical inventor, born at Smiljan, Lika. Invented telephone repeater. Became U.S. resident in 1884, worked with Thomas Edison. Other inventions and discoveries include: bladeless turbine, system of arc (fluorescent) lighting, Tesla motor and rotating magnetic fields (the basis of all alternating current power transmission), electric generators, transformers and magnifying transmitter (wireless). Was credited in 1943, through U.S. Supreme Court case, as true inventor of radio. Claimed in his later years to invent a "death beam" capable of annihilating a million soldiers instantly.
-JAS, Ph.D.
7/20/83: I'm so sick of the Georgetown rut. I thought life in California was supposed to be exciting?! I hate my job even worse. Sometimes, I just wish that I could play guitar in a band, so I could blow this berg. Ever since I went to my first concert in '78 (Van Halen, AC/DC, Aerosmith - WOWSA!), I've thought about being a rocker. There's a hot band in Sacramento, CITY KIDD, and I hear they need a new singer. If I had some equipment (or nerve!), I'd try out.
Still driving the ol' truck from 8 to 5.
pg. 7

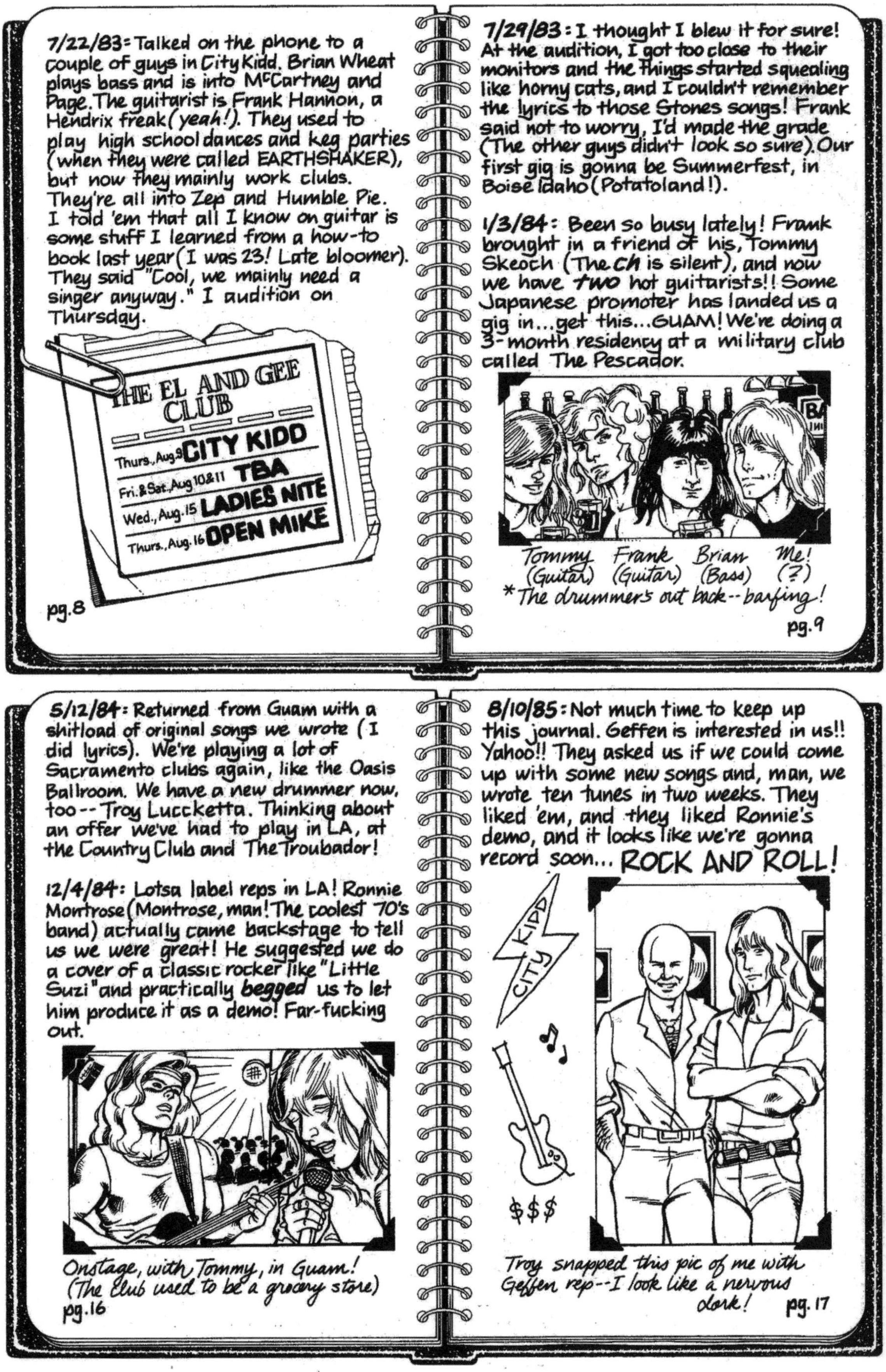
7/22/83: Talked on the phone to a couple of guys in City Kidd. Brian Wheat plays bass and is into McCartney and Page. The guitarist is Frank Hannon, a Hendrix freak (yeah!). They used to play high school dances and keg parties (when they were called EARTHSHAKER), but now they mainly work clubs. They're all into Zep and Humble Pie. I told 'em that all I know on guitar is some stuff I learned from a how-to book last year (I was 23! Late bloomer). They said "Cool, we mainly need a singer anyway." I audition on Thursday.
THE EL AND GEE CLUB
Thurs., Aug. 9 CITY KIDD
Fri. & Sat., Aug 10 & 11 TBA
Wed., Aug. 15 LADIES NITE
Thurs., Aug. 16 OPEN MIKE
pg. 8
7/29/83: I thought I blew it for sure! At the audition, I got too close to their monitors and the things started squealing like horny cats, and I couldn't remember the lyrics to those Stones songs! Frank said not to worry, I'd made the grade (The other guys didn't look so sure). Our first gig is gonna be Summerfest, in Boise Idaho (Potatoland!).
1/3/84: Been so busy lately! Frank brought in a friend of his, Tommy Skeoch (The ch is silent), and now we have two hot guitarists!! Some Japanese promoter has landed us a gig in... get this... GUAM! We're doing a 3-month residency at a military club called The Pescador.
Tommy (Guitar) Frank (Guitar) Brian (Bass) Me! (?)
*The drummer's out back--barfing!
pg. 9
5/12/84: Returned from Guam with a shitload of original songs we wrote (I did lyrics). We're playing a lot of Sacramento clubs again, like the Oasis Ballroom. We have a new drummer now, too -- Troy Luccketta. Thinking about an offer we've had to play in LA, at the Country Club and The Troubador!
12/4/84: Lotsa label reps in LA! Ronnie Montrose (Montrose, man! The coolest 70's band) actually came backstage to tell us we were great! He suggested we do a cover of a classic rocker like "Little Suzi" and practically begged us to let him produce it as a demo! Far-fucking out.
Onstage, with Tommy, in Guam! (The club used to be a grocery store)
pg. 16
8/10/85: Not much time to keep up this journal. Geffen is interested in us!! Yahoo!! They asked us if we could come up with some new songs and, man, we wrote ten tunes in two weeks. They liked 'em, and they liked Ronnie's demo, and it looks like we're gonna record soon... ROCK AND ROLL!
CITY KIDD
$$$
Troy snapped this pic of me with Geffen rep--I look like a nervous dork!
pg. 17

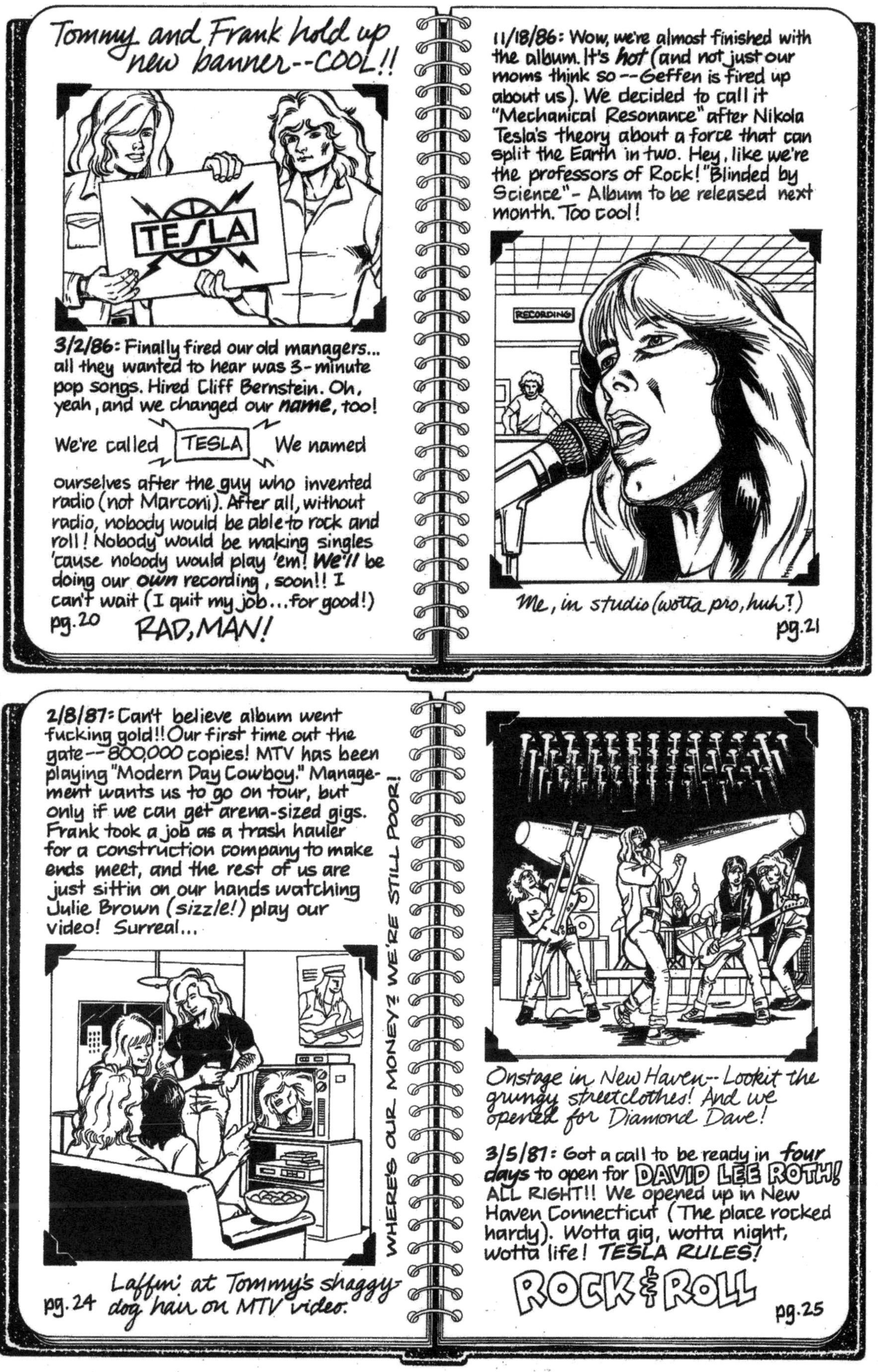
Tommy and Frank hold up new banner--COOL!!
TESLA
3/2/86: Finally fired our old managers... all they wanted to hear was 3-minute pop songs. Hired Cliff Bernstein. Oh, yeah, and we changed our name, too!
We're called TESLA We named ourselves after the guy who invented radio (not Marconi). After all, without radio, nobody would be able to rock and roll! Nobody would be making singles 'cause nobody would play 'em! We'll be doing our own recording, soon!! I can't wait (I quit my job... for good!)
RAD, MAN!
pg. 20
11/18/86: Wow, we're almost finished with the album. It's hot (and not just our moms think so --Geffen is fired up about us). We decided to call it "Mechanical Resonance" after Nikola Tesla's theory about a force that can split the Earth in two. Hey, like we're the professors of Rock! "Blinded by Science" - Album to be released next month. Too cool!
RECORDING
Me, in studio (wotta pro, huh?)
pg. 21
2/8/87: Can't believe album went fucking gold!! Our first time out the gate-- 800,000 copies! MTV has been playing "Modern Day Cowboy." Management wants us to go on tour, but only if we can get arena-sized gigs. Frank took a job as a trash hauler for a construction company to make ends meet, and the rest of us are just sittin on our hands watching Julie Brown (sizzle!) play our video! Surreal...
Laffin' at Tommy's shaggy-dog hair on MTV video.
WHERE'S OUR MONEY? WE'RE STILL POOR!
pg. 24
Onstage in New Haven-- Lookit the grungy streetclothes! And we opened for Diamond Dave!
3/5/87: Got a call to be ready in four days to open for DAVID LEE ROTH! ALL RIGHT!! We opened up in New Haven Connecticut (The place rocked hardy). Wotta gig, wotta night, wotta life! TESLA RULES!
ROCK & ROLL
pg. 25

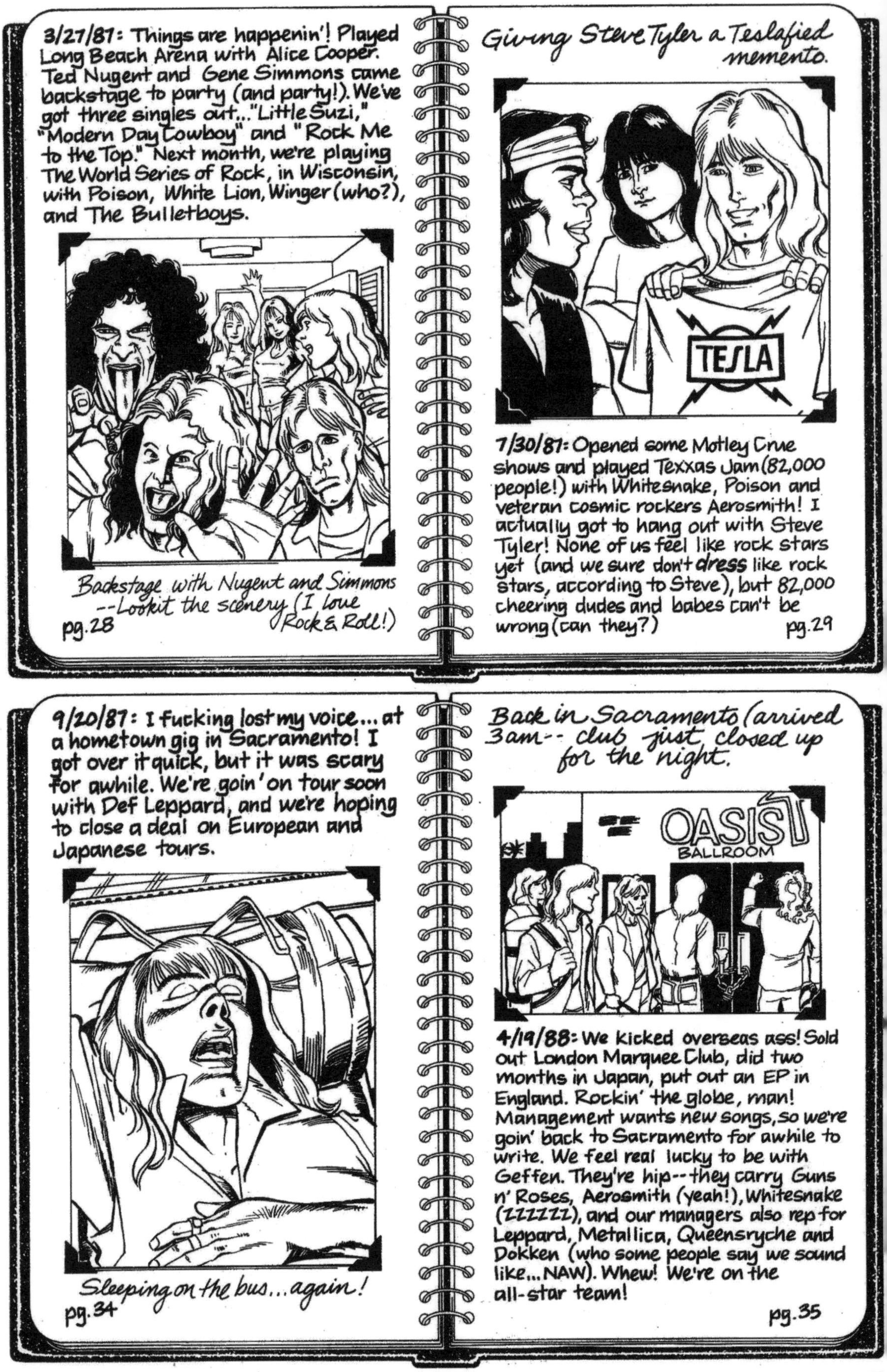
3/27/87: Things are happenin'! Played Long Beach Arena with Alice Cooper. Ted Nugent and Gene Simmons came backstage to party (and party!). We've got three singles out..."Little Suzi," "Modern Day Cowboy" and "Rock Me to the Top." Next month, we're playing The World Series of Rock, in Wisconsin, with Poison, White Lion, Winger (who?), and The Bulletboys.
Backstage with Nugent and Simmons --Lookit the scenery (I love Rock & Roll!)
pg.28
Giving Steve Tyler a Teslafied memento.
TESLA
7/30/87: Opened some Motley Crue shows and played Texxas Jam (82,000 people!) with Whitesnake, Poison and veteran cosmic rockers Aerosmith! I actually got to hang out with Steve Tyler! None of us feel like rock stars yet (and we sure don't dress like rock stars, according to Steve), but 82,000 cheering dudes and babes can't be wrong (can they?)
pg.29
9/20/87: I fucking lost my voice... at a hometown gig in Sacramento! I got over it quick, but it was scary for awhile. We're goin' on tour soon with Def Leppard, and we're hoping to close a deal on European and Japanese tours.
Sleeping on the bus... again!
pg.34
Back in Sacramento (arrived 3am-- club just closed up for the night.
OASIS
BALLROOM
4/19/88: We kicked overseas ass! Sold out London Marquee Club, did two months in Japan, put out an EP in England. Rockin' the globe, man! Management wants new songs, so we're goin' back to Sacramento for awhile to write. We feel real lucky to be with Geffen. They're hip-- they carry Guns n' Roses, Aerosmith (yeah!), Whitesnake (ZZZZZZ), and our managers also rep for Leppard, Metallica, Queensryche and Dokken (who some people say we sound like...NAW). Whew! We're on the all-star team!
pg.35

12/16/88: Spent almost 8 months (Seemed like years...how does Pink Floyd *do* it?) in Bearsville Studio (Woodstock N.Y.) recording. Frank got married while we were up there! We decided to call the new album "The Great Radio Controversy" after Nikola Tesla's landmark court case (The guy croaked right after!). Just call us Nikola's P.R. firm!

Frank's wedding (The poor lovestruck fool!)
pg. 42

1/27/89: Record is out in stores, man, and the buzz is even better than the first time! We rocked harder, put more guitars up front... the first single is "Hang Tough." We're chompin' at the bit for a headline tour, but the timing's not right yet. We're opening for Poison now. Cliff (Bernstein, manager) says sales are lookin' good already on "Radio Controversy."

Jamming with C.C. Deville (Sound check, San Diego)
pg. 43

7/5/89: WE DID IT!!! We're beginning the first-ever official headlining TESLA TOUR!!

"Radio Controversy" is in the American top 20! Look, ma, we're genuine ROCK STARS (maybe I should finally buy some new jeans... NAW).

Bret Michaels (Poison) wishes us good luck on our headlining tour!
pg. 46

Bill Board TOP 20 Tesla

HEAVY METAL HEROES
Hard rocking Tesla style

TESLA So this is success?

CIRCUS TESLA STRAIGHT TO THE TOP

Powerline TESLA

HIT PARADER
Modern Day Cowboys TESLA

24 MOST PROMISING ROCKERS
Jeff Keith: from big rigs to the big time

JEFF KEITH'S FUZZY JOURNAL WAS COMPILED USING PUBLISHED MATERIAL FROM INTERVIEWS WITH KEITH AND THE MEMBERS OF TESLA
Jay

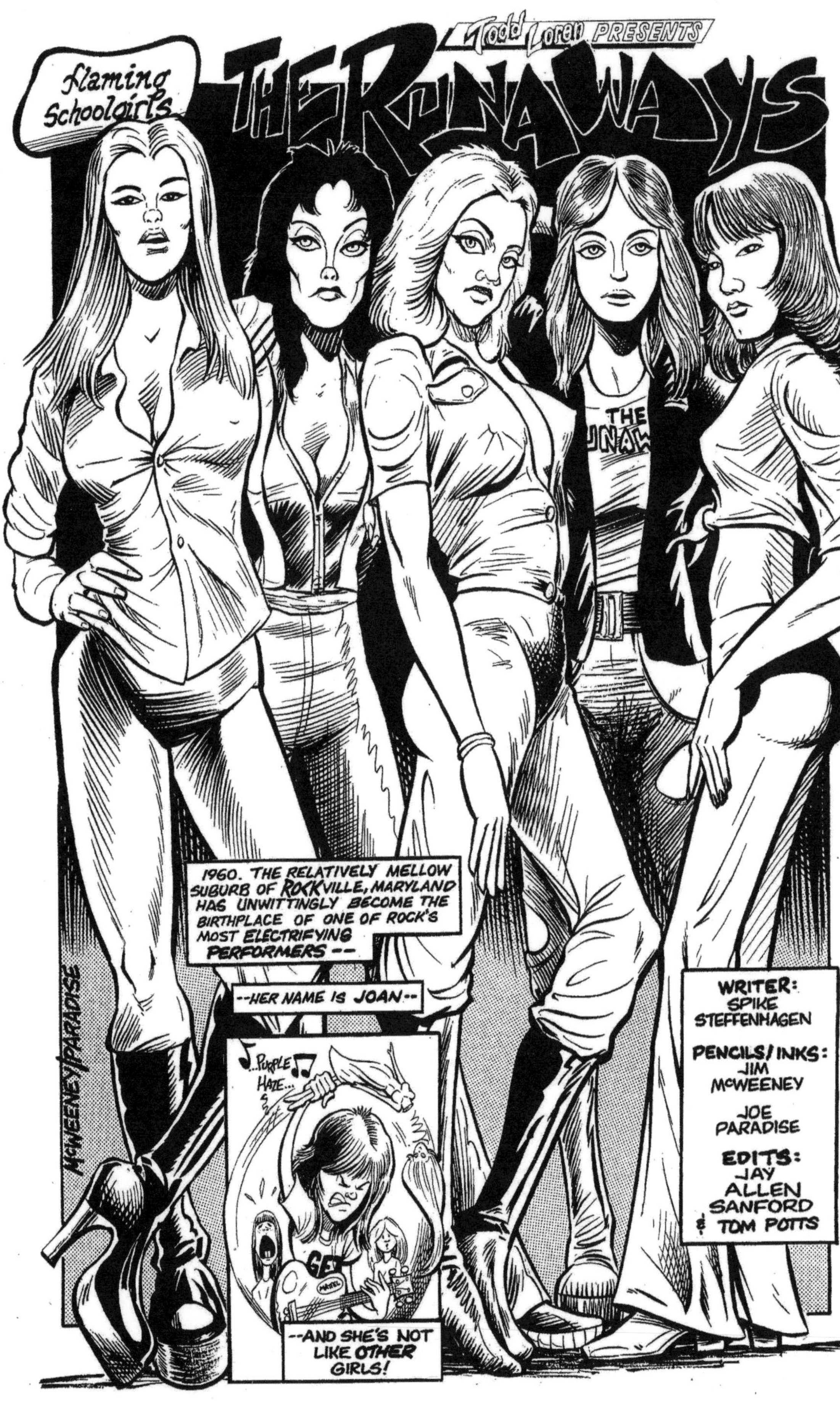
Todd Loren PRESENTS
THE RUNAWAYS
Flaming Schoolgirls
1960. THE RELATIVELY MELLOW SUBURB OF ROCKVILLE, MARYLAND HAS UNWITTINGLY BECOME THE BIRTHPLACE OF ONE OF ROCK'S MOST ELECTRIFYING PERFORMERS --
--HER NAME IS JOAN--
...PURPLE HAZE...
--AND SHE'S NOT LIKE OTHER GIRLS!
WRITER: SPIKE STEFFENHAGEN
PENCILS/INKS: JIM McWEENEY
JOE PARADISE
EDITS: JAY ALLEN SANFORD & TOM POTTS
McWEENEY/PARADISE

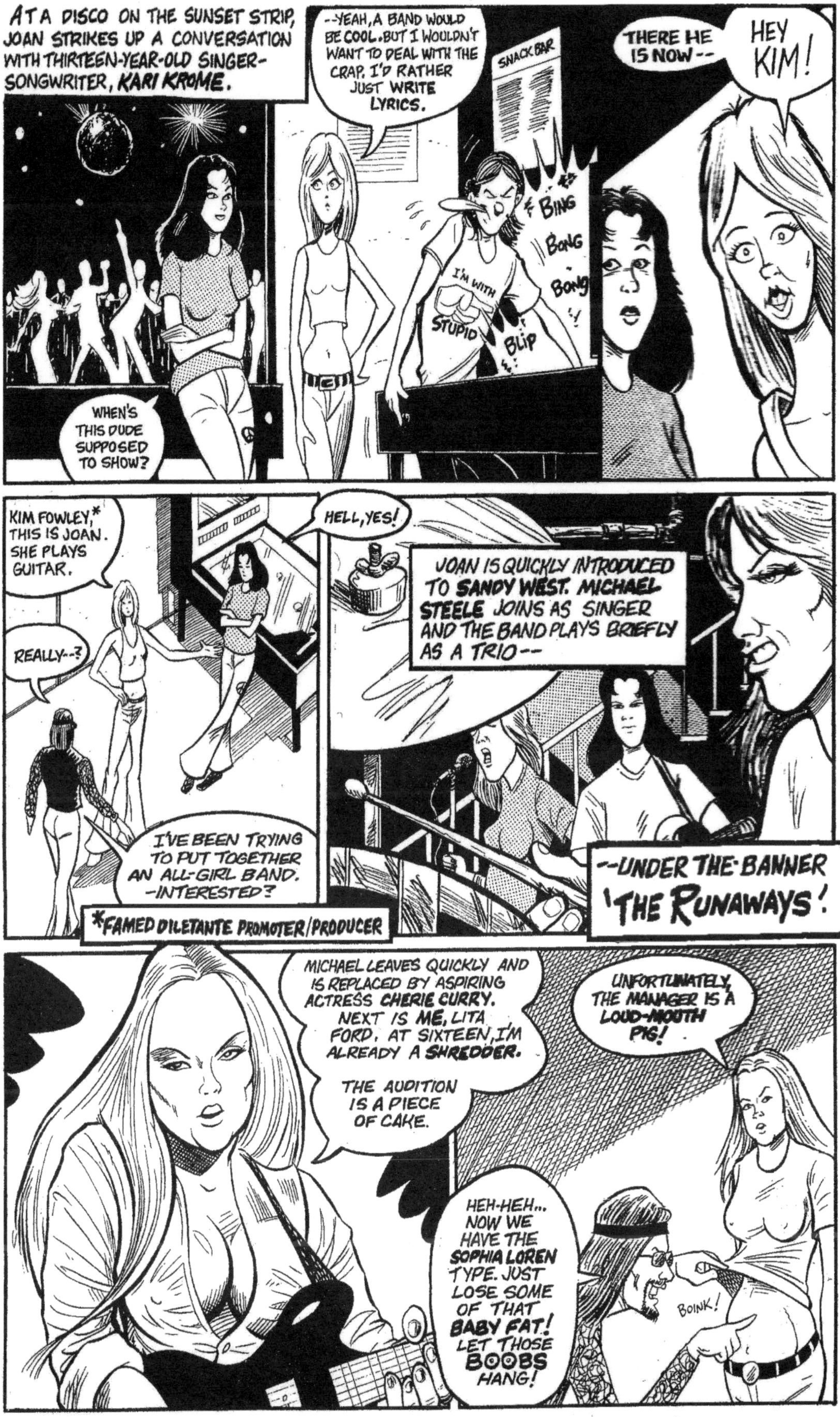

AT A DISCO ON THE SUNSET STRIP, JOAN STRIKES UP A CONVERSATION WITH THIRTEEN-YEAR-OLD SINGER-SONGWRITER, KARI KROME.
WHEN'S THIS DUDE SUPPOSED TO SHOW?
--YEAH, A BAND WOULD BE COOL. BUT I WOULDN'T WANT TO DEAL WITH THE CRAP. I'D RATHER JUST WRITE LYRICS.
SNACK BAR
I'M WITH STUPID
BING
BONG
BONG
BLIP
THERE HE IS NOW--
HEY KIM!
KIM FOWLEY,* THIS IS JOAN. SHE PLAYS GUITAR.
REALLY--?
I'VE BEEN TRYING TO PUT TOGETHER AN ALL-GIRL BAND. -INTERESTED?
HELL, YES!
*FAMED DILETANTE PROMOTER/PRODUCER
JOAN IS QUICKLY INTRODUCED TO SANDY WEST. MICHAEL STEELE JOINS AS SINGER AND THE BAND PLAYS BRIEFLY AS A TRIO--
--UNDER THE BANNER 'THE RUNAWAYS'!
MICHAEL LEAVES QUICKLY AND IS REPLACED BY ASPIRING ACTRESS CHERIE CURRY. NEXT IS ME, LITA FORD. AT SIXTEEN, I'M ALREADY A SHREDDER.
THE AUDITION IS A PIECE OF CAKE.
UNFORTUNATELY, THE MANAGER IS A LOUD-MOUTH PIG!
HEH-HEH... NOW WE HAVE THE SOPHIA LOREN TYPE. JUST LOSE SOME OF THAT BABY FAT! LET THOSE BOOBS HANG!
BOINK!

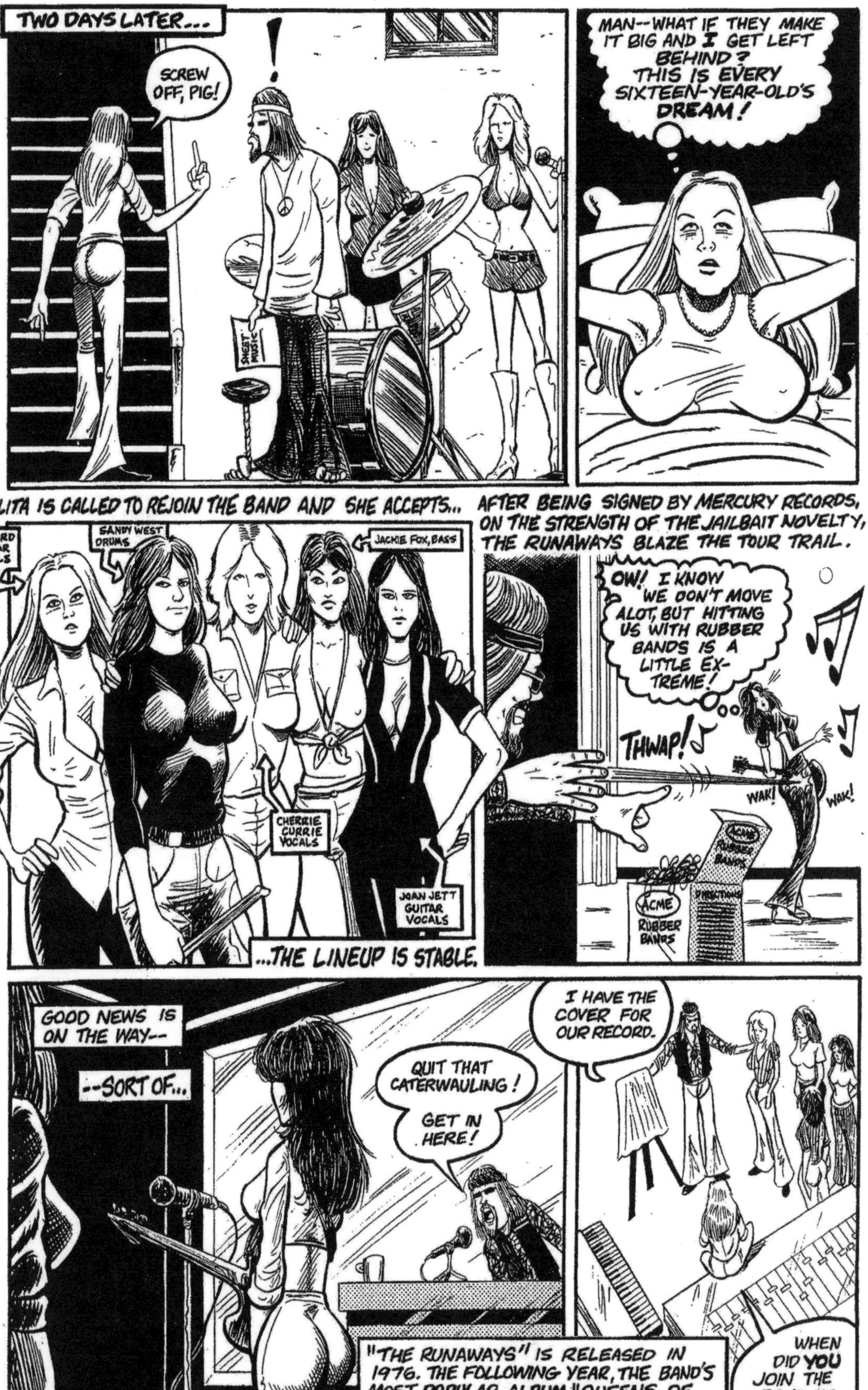
TWO DAYS LATER...
SCREW OFF, PIG!
!
SHEET MUSIC
MAN--WHAT IF THEY MAKE IT BIG AND I GET LEFT BEHIND? THIS IS EVERY SIXTEEN-YEAR-OLD'S DREAM!
LITA IS CALLED TO REJOIN THE BAND AND SHE ACCEPTS...
LITA FORD GUITAR VOCALS
SANDY WEST DRUMS
JACKIE FOX, BASS
CHERRIE CURRIE VOCALS
JOAN JETT GUITAR VOCALS
...THE LINEUP IS STABLE.
AFTER BEING SIGNED BY MERCURY RECORDS, ON THE STRENGTH OF THE JAILBAIT NOVELTY, THE RUNAWAYS BLAZE THE TOUR TRAIL.
OW! I KNOW WE DON'T MOVE ALOT, BUT HITTING US WITH RUBBER BANDS IS A LITTLE EX-TREME!
THWAP!
WAK!
WAK!
ACME RUBBER BANDS
ACME RUBBER BANDS
GOOD NEWS IS ON THE WAY--
--SORT OF...
QUIT THAT CATERWAULING!
GET IN HERE!
I HAVE THE COVER FOR OUR RECORD.
"THE RUNAWAYS" IS RELEASED IN 1976. THE FOLLOWING YEAR, THE BAND'S MOST POPULAR ALBUM "QUEENS OF NOISE" IS RELEASED.
WHEN DID YOU JOIN THE BAND, MR. FOWLEY?

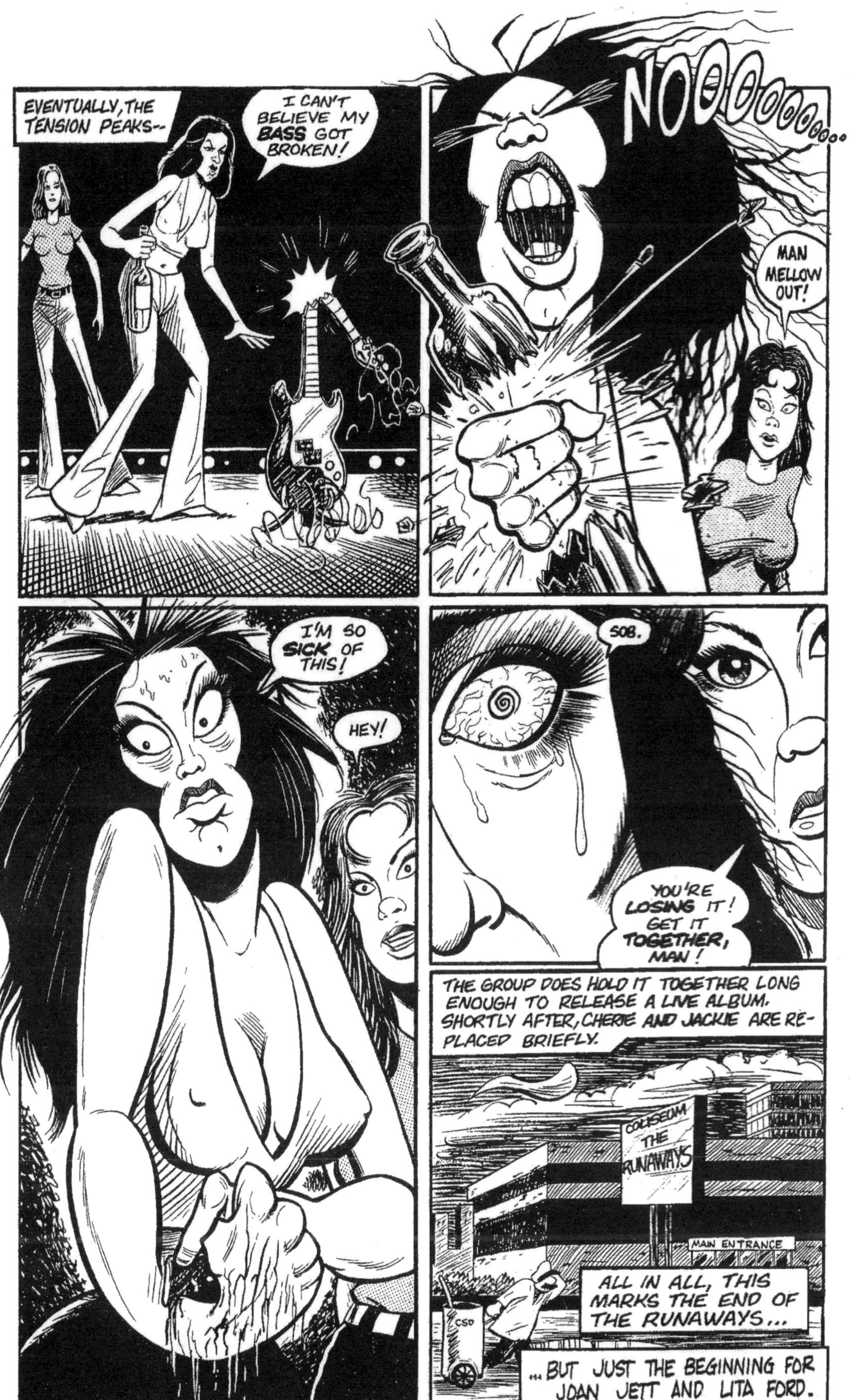
EVENTUALLY, THE TENSION PEAKS--
I CAN'T BELIEVE MY BASS GOT BROKEN!
NOOOOOOOo...
MAN MELLOW OUT!
I'M SO SICK OF THIS!
HEY!
SOB.
YOU'RE LOSING IT! GET IT TOGETHER, MAN!
THE GROUP DOES HOLD IT TOGETHER LONG ENOUGH TO RELEASE A LIVE ALBUM. SHORTLY AFTER, CHERIE AND JACKIE ARE REPLACED BRIEFLY.
COLISEUM THE RUNAWAYS
MAIN ENTRANCE
ALL IN ALL, THIS MARKS THE END OF THE RUNAWAYS...
...BUT JUST THE BEGINNING FOR JOAN JETT AND LITA FORD.

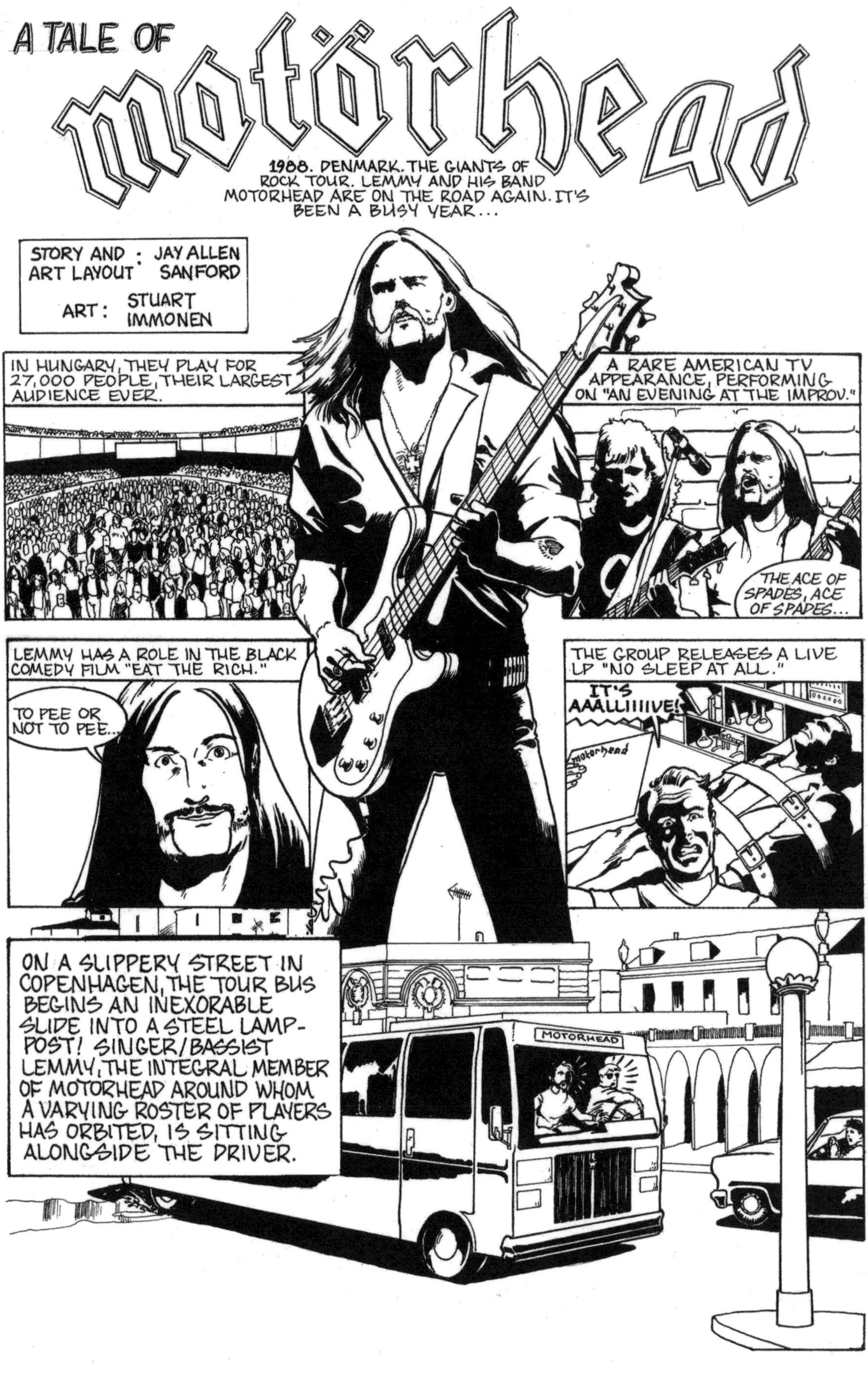
A TALE OF
motörhead
1988. DENMARK. THE GIANTS OF ROCK TOUR. LEMMY AND HIS BAND MOTORHEAD ARE ON THE ROAD AGAIN. IT'S BEEN A BUSY YEAR...
STORY AND ART LAYOUT: JAY ALLEN SANFORD
ART: STUART IMMONEN
IN HUNGARY, THEY PLAY FOR 27,000 PEOPLE, THEIR LARGEST AUDIENCE EVER.
A RARE AMERICAN TV APPEARANCE, PERFORMING ON "AN EVENING AT THE IMPROV."
THE ACE OF SPADES, ACE OF SPADES...
LEMMY HAS A ROLE IN THE BLACK COMEDY FILM "EAT THE RICH."
TO PEE OR NOT TO PEE...
THE GROUP RELEASES A LIVE LP "NO SLEEP AT ALL."
IT'S AAALLIIIIIVE!
motorhead
ON A SLIPPERY STREET IN COPENHAGEN, THE TOUR BUS BEGINS AN INEXORABLE SLIDE INTO A STEEL LAMP-POST! SINGER/BASSIST LEMMY, THE INTEGRAL MEMBER OF MOTORHEAD AROUND WHOM A VARYING ROSTER OF PLAYERS HAS ORBITED, IS SITTING ALONGSIDE THE DRIVER.
MOTORHEAD

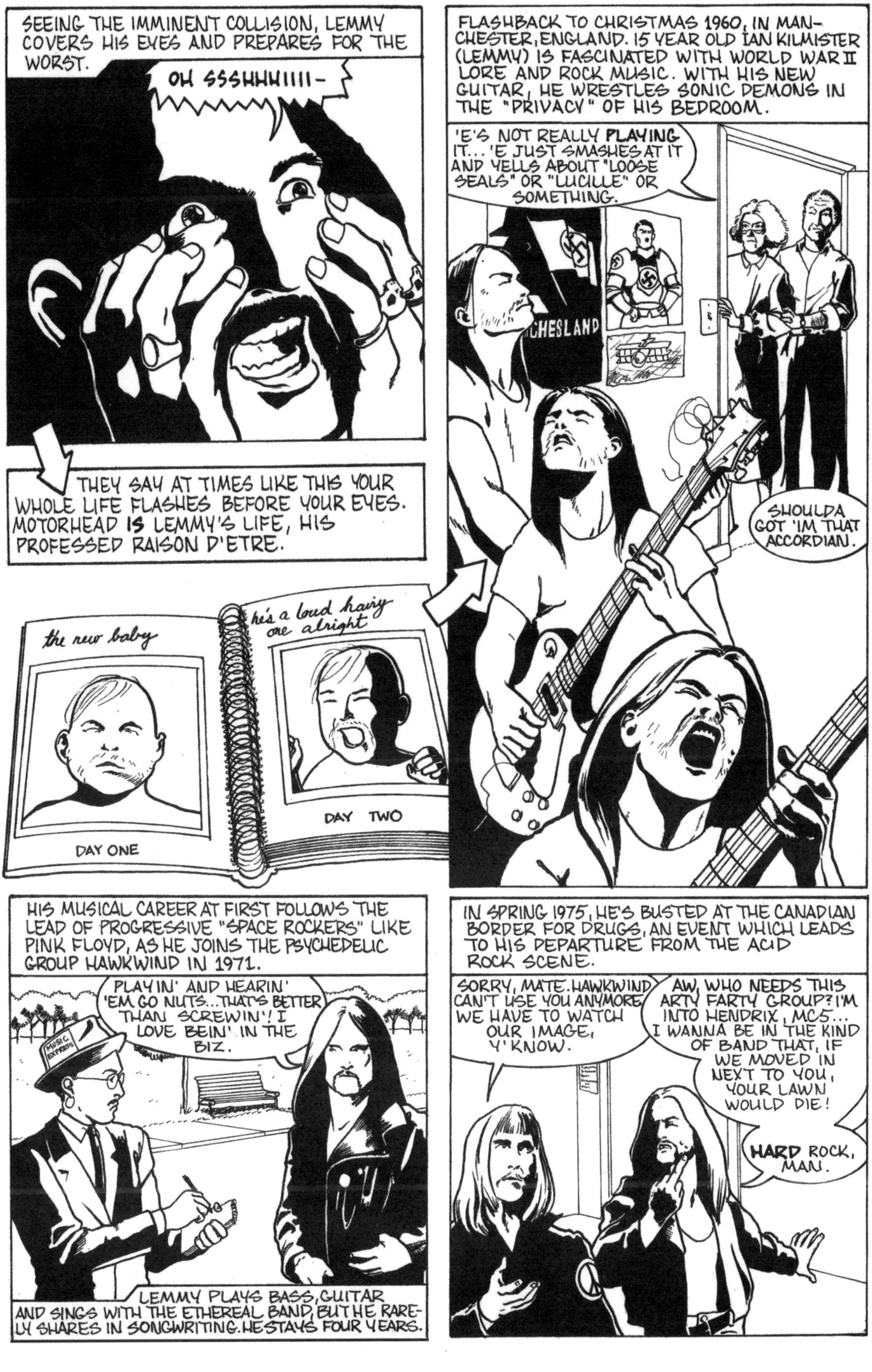
SEEING THE IMMINENT COLLISION, LEMMY COVERS HIS EYES AND PREPARES FOR THE WORST.
OH SSSHHHIIII-
THEY SAY AT TIMES LIKE THIS YOUR WHOLE LIFE FLASHES BEFORE YOUR EYES. MOTORHEAD IS LEMMY'S LIFE, HIS PROFESSED RAISON D'ETRE.
the new baby
DAY ONE
he's a loud hairy one alright
DAY TWO
FLASHBACK TO CHRISTMAS 1960, IN MANCHESTER, ENGLAND. 15 YEAR OLD IAN KILMISTER (LEMMY) IS FASCINATED WITH WORLD WAR II LORE AND ROCK MUSIC. WITH HIS NEW GUITAR, HE WRESTLES SONIC DEMONS IN THE "PRIVACY" OF HIS BEDROOM.
'E'S NOT REALLY PLAYING IT... 'E JUST SMASHES AT IT AND YELLS ABOUT "LOOSE SEALS" OR "LUCILLE" OR SOMETHING.
CHESLAND
SHOULDA GOT 'IM THAT ACCORDIAN.
HIS MUSICAL CAREER AT FIRST FOLLOWS THE LEAD OF PROGRESSIVE "SPACE ROCKERS" LIKE PINK FLOYD, AS HE JOINS THE PSYCHEDELIC GROUP HAWKWIND IN 1971.
PLAYIN' AND HEARIN' 'EM GO NUTS...THAT'S BETTER THAN SCREWIN'! I LOVE BEIN' IN THE BIZ.
MUSIC EXPRESS
LEMMY PLAYS BASS, GUITAR AND SINGS WITH THE ETHEREAL BAND, BUT HE RARELY SHARES IN SONGWRITING. HE STAYS FOUR YEARS.
IN SPRING 1975, HE'S BUSTED AT THE CANADIAN BORDER FOR DRUGS, AN EVENT WHICH LEADS TO HIS DEPARTURE FROM THE ACID ROCK SCENE.
SORRY, MATE. HAWKWIND CAN'T USE YOU ANYMORE. WE HAVE TO WATCH OUR IMAGE, Y'KNOW.
AW, WHO NEEDS THIS ARTY FARTY GROUP? I'M INTO HENDRIX, MC5... I WANNA BE IN THE KIND OF BAND THAT, IF WE MOVED IN NEXT TO YOU, YOUR LAWN WOULD DIE!
HARD ROCK, MAN.

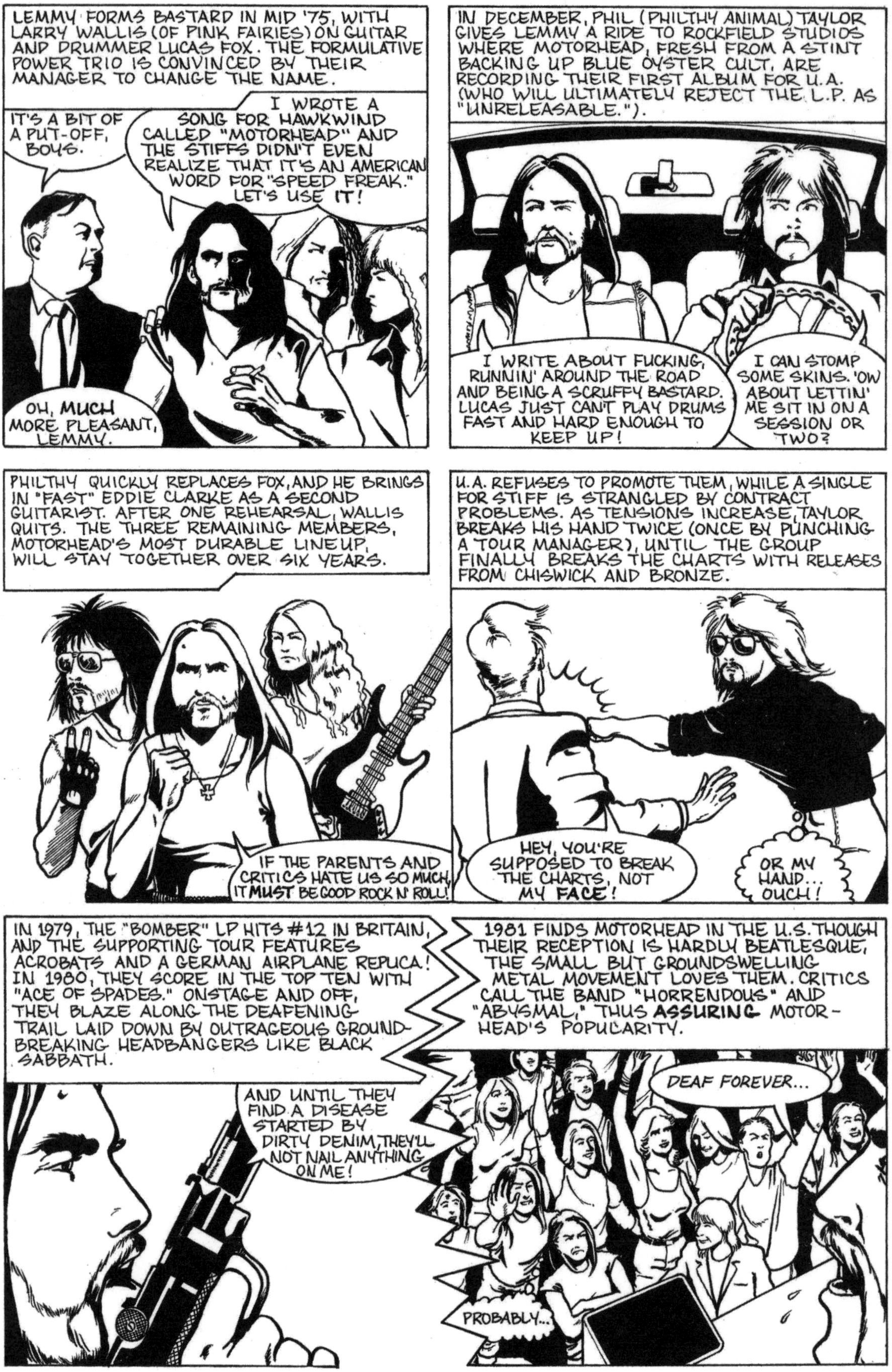
LEMMY FORMS BASTARD IN MID '75, WITH LARRY WALLIS (OF PINK FAIRIES) ON GUITAR AND DRUMMER LUCAS FOX. THE FORMULATIVE POWER TRIO IS CONVINCED BY THEIR MANAGER TO CHANGE THE NAME.
IT'S A BIT OF A PUT-OFF, BOYS.
I WROTE A SONG FOR HAWKWIND CALLED "MOTORHEAD" AND THE STIFFS DIDN'T EVEN REALIZE THAT IT'S AN AMERICAN WORD FOR "SPEED FREAK." LET'S USE IT!
OH, MUCH MORE PLEASANT, LEMMY.
IN DECEMBER, PHIL (PHILTHY ANIMAL) TAYLOR GIVES LEMMY A RIDE TO ROCKFIELD STUDIOS WHERE MOTORHEAD, FRESH FROM A STINT BACKING UP BLUE OYSTER CULT, ARE RECORDING THEIR FIRST ALBUM FOR U.A. (WHO WILL ULTIMATELY REJECT THE L.P. AS "UNRELEASABLE.").
I WRITE ABOUT FUCKING, RUNNIN' AROUND THE ROAD AND BEING A SCRUFFY BASTARD. LUCAS JUST CAN'T PLAY DRUMS FAST AND HARD ENOUGH TO KEEP UP!
I CAN STOMP SOME SKINS. 'OW ABOUT LETTIN' ME SIT IN ON A SESSION OR TWO?
PHILTHY QUICKLY REPLACES FOX, AND HE BRINGS IN "FAST" EDDIE CLARKE AS A SECOND GUITARIST. AFTER ONE REHEARSAL, WALLIS QUITS. THE THREE REMAINING MEMBERS, MOTORHEAD'S MOST DURABLE LINEUP, WILL STAY TOGETHER OVER SIX YEARS.
IF THE PARENTS AND CRITICS HATE US SO MUCH, IT MUST BE GOOD ROCK N' ROLL!
U.A. REFUSES TO PROMOTE THEM, WHILE A SINGLE FOR STIFF IS STRANGLED BY CONTRACT PROBLEMS. AS TENSIONS INCREASE, TAYLOR BREAKS HIS HAND TWICE (ONCE BY PUNCHING A TOUR MANAGER), UNTIL THE GROUP FINALLY BREAKS THE CHARTS WITH RELEASES FROM CHISWICK AND BRONZE.
HEY, YOU'RE SUPPOSED TO BREAK THE CHARTS, NOT MY FACE!
OR MY HAND... OUCH!
IN 1979, THE "BOMBER" LP HITS #12 IN BRITAIN, AND THE SUPPORTING TOUR FEATURES ACROBATS AND A GERMAN AIRPLANE REPLICA! IN 1980, THEY SCORE IN THE TOP TEN WITH "ACE OF SPADES." ONSTAGE AND OFF, THEY BLAZE ALONG THE DEAFENING TRAIL LAID DOWN BY OUTRAGEOUS GROUND-BREAKING HEADBANGERS LIKE BLACK SABBATH.
AND UNTIL THEY FIND A DISEASE STARTED BY DIRTY DENIM, THEY'LL NOT NAIL ANYTHING ON ME!
1981 FINDS MOTORHEAD IN THE U.S. THOUGH THEIR RECEPTION IS HARDLY BEATLESQUE, THE SMALL BUT GROUNDSWELLING METAL MOVEMENT LOVES THEM. CRITICS CALL THE BAND "HORRENDOUS" AND "ABYSMAL," THUS ASSURING MOTOR-HEAD'S POPULARITY.
DEAF FOREVER...
PROBABLY...

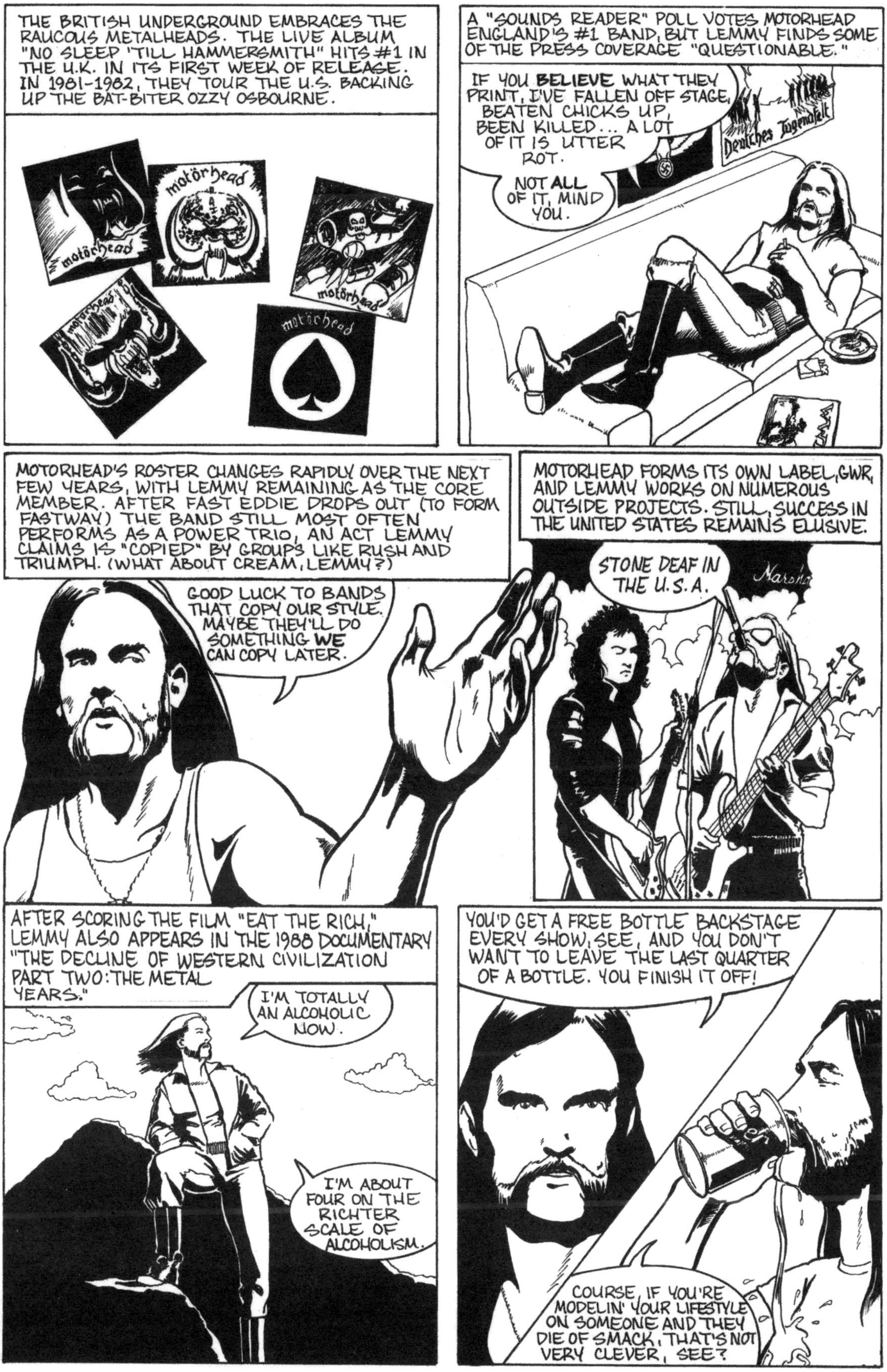

THE BRITISH UNDERGROUND EMBRACES THE RAUCOUS METALHEADS. THE LIVE ALBUM "NO SLEEP 'TILL HAMMERSMITH" HITS #1 IN THE U.K. IN ITS FIRST WEEK OF RELEASE. IN 1981-1982, THEY TOUR THE U.S. BACKING UP THE BAT-BITER OZZY OSBOURNE.
A "SOUNDS READER" POLL VOTES MOTORHEAD ENGLAND'S #1 BAND, BUT LEMMY FINDS SOME OF THE PRESS COVERAGE "QUESTIONABLE."
IF YOU **BELIEVE** WHAT THEY PRINT, I'VE FALLEN OFF STAGE, BEATEN CHICKS UP, BEEN KILLED... A LOT OF IT IS UTTER ROT.
NOT **ALL** OF IT, MIND YOU.
MOTORHEAD'S ROSTER CHANGES RAPIDLY OVER THE NEXT FEW YEARS, WITH LEMMY REMAINING AS THE CORE MEMBER. AFTER FAST EDDIE DROPS OUT (TO FORM FASTWAY) THE BAND STILL MOST OFTEN PERFORMS AS A POWER TRIO, AN ACT LEMMY CLAIMS IS "COPIED" BY GROUPS LIKE RUSH AND TRIUMPH. (WHAT ABOUT CREAM, LEMMY?)
GOOD LUCK TO BANDS THAT COPY OUR STYLE. MAYBE THEY'LL DO SOMETHING **WE** CAN COPY LATER.
MOTORHEAD FORMS ITS OWN LABEL, GWR, AND LEMMY WORKS ON NUMEROUS OUTSIDE PROJECTS. STILL, SUCCESS IN THE UNITED STATES REMAINS ELUSIVE.
STONE DEAF IN THE U.S.A.
AFTER SCORING THE FILM "EAT THE RICH," LEMMY ALSO APPEARS IN THE 1988 DOCUMENTARY "THE DECLINE OF WESTERN CIVILIZATION PART TWO: THE METAL YEARS."
I'M TOTALLY AN ALCOHOLIC NOW.
I'M ABOUT FOUR ON THE RICHTER SCALE OF ALCOHOLISM.
YOU'D GET A FREE BOTTLE BACKSTAGE EVERY SHOW, SEE, AND YOU DON'T WANT TO LEAVE THE LAST QUARTER OF A BOTTLE. YOU FINISH IT OFF!
COURSE, IF YOU'RE MODELIN' YOUR LIFESTYLE ON SOMEONE AND THEY DIE OF SMACK, THAT'S NOT VERY CLEVER, SEE?

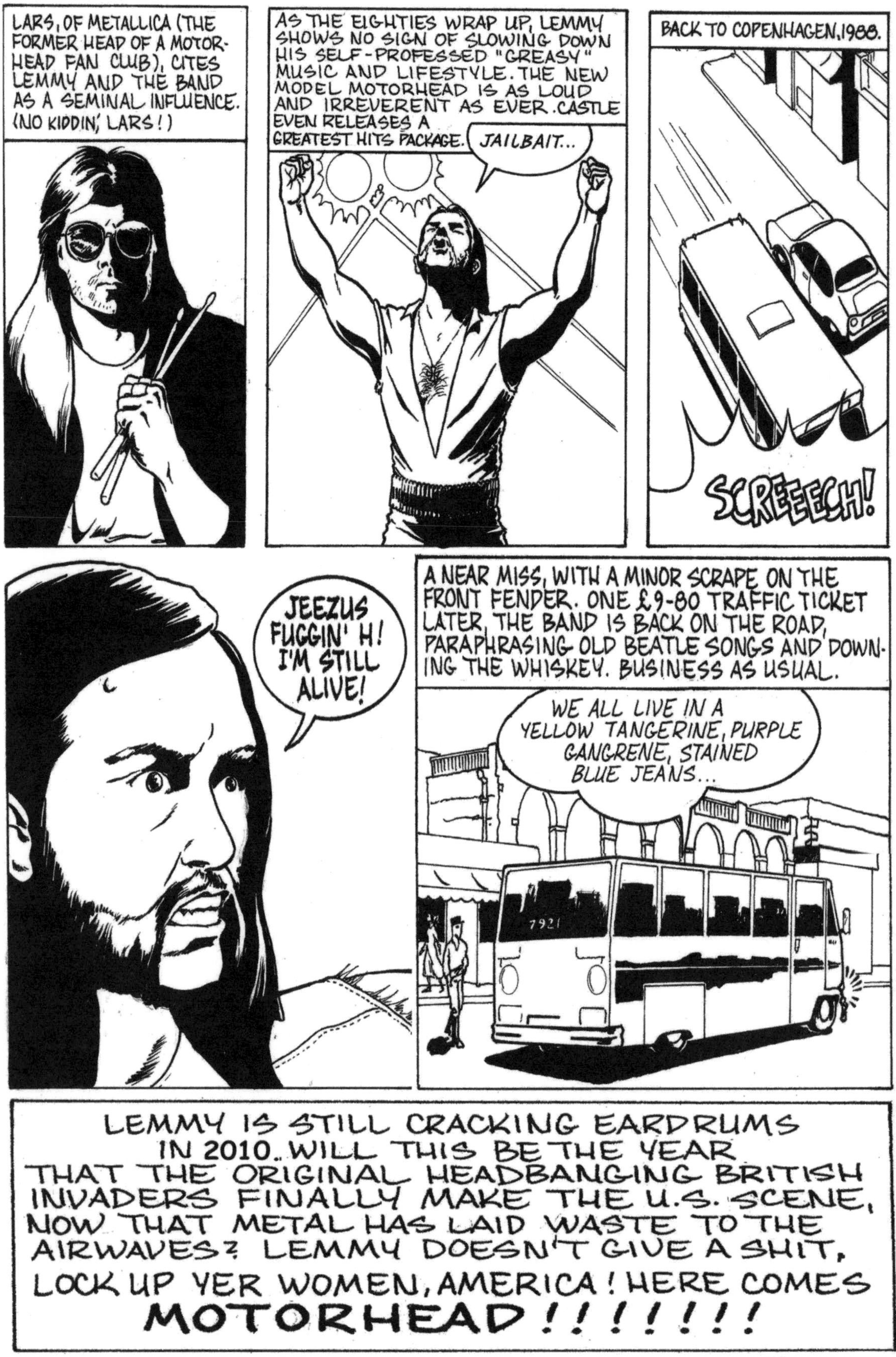
LARS, OF METALLICA (THE FORMER HEAD OF A MOTORHEAD FAN CLUB), CITES LEMMY AND THE BAND AS A SEMINAL INFLUENCE. (NO KIDDIN', LARS!)
AS THE EIGHTIES WRAP UP, LEMMY SHOWS NO SIGN OF SLOWING DOWN HIS SELF-PROFESSED "GREASY" MUSIC AND LIFESTYLE. THE NEW MODEL MOTORHEAD IS AS LOUD AND IRREVERENT AS EVER. CASTLE EVEN RELEASES A GREATEST HITS PACKAGE.
JAILBAIT...
BACK TO COPENHAGEN, 1988.
SCREEECH!
JEEZUS FUGGIN' H! I'M STILL ALIVE!
A NEAR MISS, WITH A MINOR SCRAPE ON THE FRONT FENDER. ONE £9-80 TRAFFIC TICKET LATER, THE BAND IS BACK ON THE ROAD, PARAPHRASING OLD BEATLE SONGS AND DOWNING THE WHISKEY. BUSINESS AS USUAL.
WE ALL LIVE IN A YELLOW TANGERINE, PURPLE GANGRENE, STAINED BLUE JEANS...
7921
LEMMY IS STILL CRACKING EARDRUMS IN 2010. WILL THIS BE THE YEAR THAT THE ORIGINAL HEADBANGING BRITISH INVADERS FINALLY MAKE THE U.S. SCENE, NOW THAT METAL HAS LAID WASTE TO THE AIRWAVES? LEMMY DOESN'T GIVE A SHIT.
LOCK UP YER WOMEN, AMERICA! HERE COMES MOTORHEAD!!!!!!!
END

METALLICA'S GREATEST HITS

OUR STORY BEGINS WITH YOUNG LARS ULRICH (BORN IN DENMARK, 1963). HE'S A ROCK FAN FROM EARLY ON— IN 1975, HE'S PUMPING HIS FIST IN THE SMOKY AIR AT A COPENHAGEN BLACK SABBATH CONCERT.

AFTER THE SHOW, LARS AND A FRIEND PLAN TO WAIT OUTSIDE THE BACKSTAGE DOOR FOR THEIR HERO.

STORY: JAY ALLEN SANFORD, TODD LOREN, TOM POTTS
ART: MARSHALL ROSS, SCOTT PENTZER, LARRY NADOLSKY

YOU LADS REALLY HOLD YER OWN IN A FLICKIN' MOB DON 'TCHA? 'S A GOOD TALENT TO HAVE IF YA EVER GET *FAMOUS* AND FIGHT THROUGH THE LOUTS EVERY TIME YOU JUST WANNA GO TO A PUB!

WOULD YOU...WOULD YOU SIGN MY POSTER FOR ME?

SURE!

THROUGH HIS TEENS, LARS IS AN ACCOMPLISHED TENNIS PLAYER (AS IS HIS FATHER).

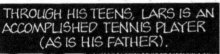

HE EVEN CONSIDERS TAKING UP THE SPORT AS A PROFESSION.

YAWN

SMOKE ON THE WATER AND FIRE IN THE SKY

HEY, LARS, QUITE A "RACKET" YOU'RE MAKING, HEH, HEH!

SO?! I'VE SEEN *YOU* USING A BROOM FOR A MIKESTAND!

YEAH, IT RELIEVES THE *TENSION* SOMETIMES, TO JUST JUMP AROUND AND ROCK OUT!

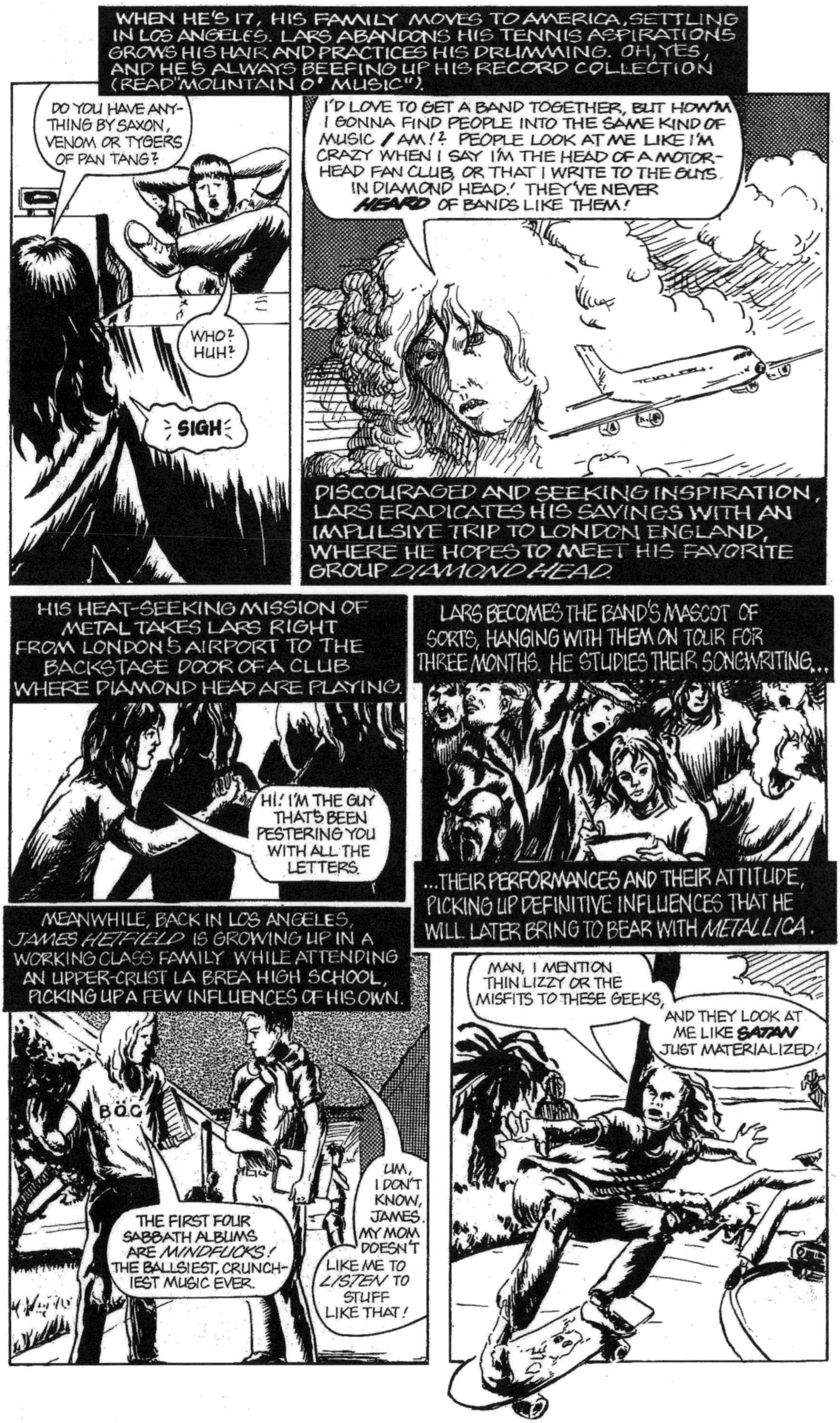
WHEN HE'S 17, HIS FAMILY MOVES TO AMERICA, SETTLING IN LOS ANGELES. LARS ABANDONS HIS TENNIS ASPIRATIONS GROWS HIS HAIR AND PRACTICES HIS DRUMMING. OH, YES, AND HE'S ALWAYS BEEFING UP HIS RECORD COLLECTION (READ "MOUNTAIN O' MUSIC").
DO YOU HAVE ANYTHING BY SAXON, VENOM OR TYGERS OF PAN TANG?
WHO? HUH?
SIGH
I'D LOVE TO GET A BAND TOGETHER, BUT HOW'M I GONNA FIND PEOPLE INTO THE SAME KIND OF MUSIC I AM!? PEOPLE LOOK AT ME LIKE I'M CRAZY WHEN I SAY I'M THE HEAD OF A MOTORHEAD FAN CLUB, OR THAT I WRITE TO THE GUYS IN DIAMOND HEAD! THEY'VE NEVER HEARD OF BANDS LIKE THEM!
DISCOURAGED AND SEEKING INSPIRATION, LARS ERADICATES HIS SAVINGS WITH AN IMPULSIVE TRIP TO LONDON ENGLAND, WHERE HE HOPES TO MEET HIS FAVORITE GROUP DIAMOND HEAD.
HIS HEAT-SEEKING MISSION OF METAL TAKES LARS RIGHT FROM LONDON'S AIRPORT TO THE BACKSTAGE DOOR OF A CLUB WHERE DIAMOND HEAD ARE PLAYING.
HI! I'M THE GUY THAT'S BEEN PESTERING YOU WITH ALL THE LETTERS.
LARS BECOMES THE BAND'S MASCOT OF SORTS, HANGING WITH THEM ON TOUR FOR THREE MONTHS. HE STUDIES THEIR SONGWRITING...
...THEIR PERFORMANCES AND THEIR ATTITUDE, PICKING UP DEFINITIVE INFLUENCES THAT HE WILL LATER BRING TO BEAR WITH METALLICA.
MEANWHILE, BACK IN LOS ANGELES, JAMES HETFIELD IS GROWING UP IN A WORKING CLASS FAMILY WHILE ATTENDING AN UPPER-CRUST LA BREA HIGH SCHOOL, PICKING UP A FEW INFLUENCES OF HIS OWN.
B.O.C
THE FIRST FOUR SABBATH ALBUMS ARE MINDFUCKS! THE BALLSIEST, CRUNCHIEST MUSIC EVER.
UM, I DON'T KNOW, JAMES. MY MOM DOESN'T LIKE ME TO LISTEN TO STUFF LIKE THAT!
MAN, I MENTION THIN LIZZY OR THE MISFITS TO THESE GEEKS,
AND THEY LOOK AT ME LIKE SATAN JUST MATERIALIZED!

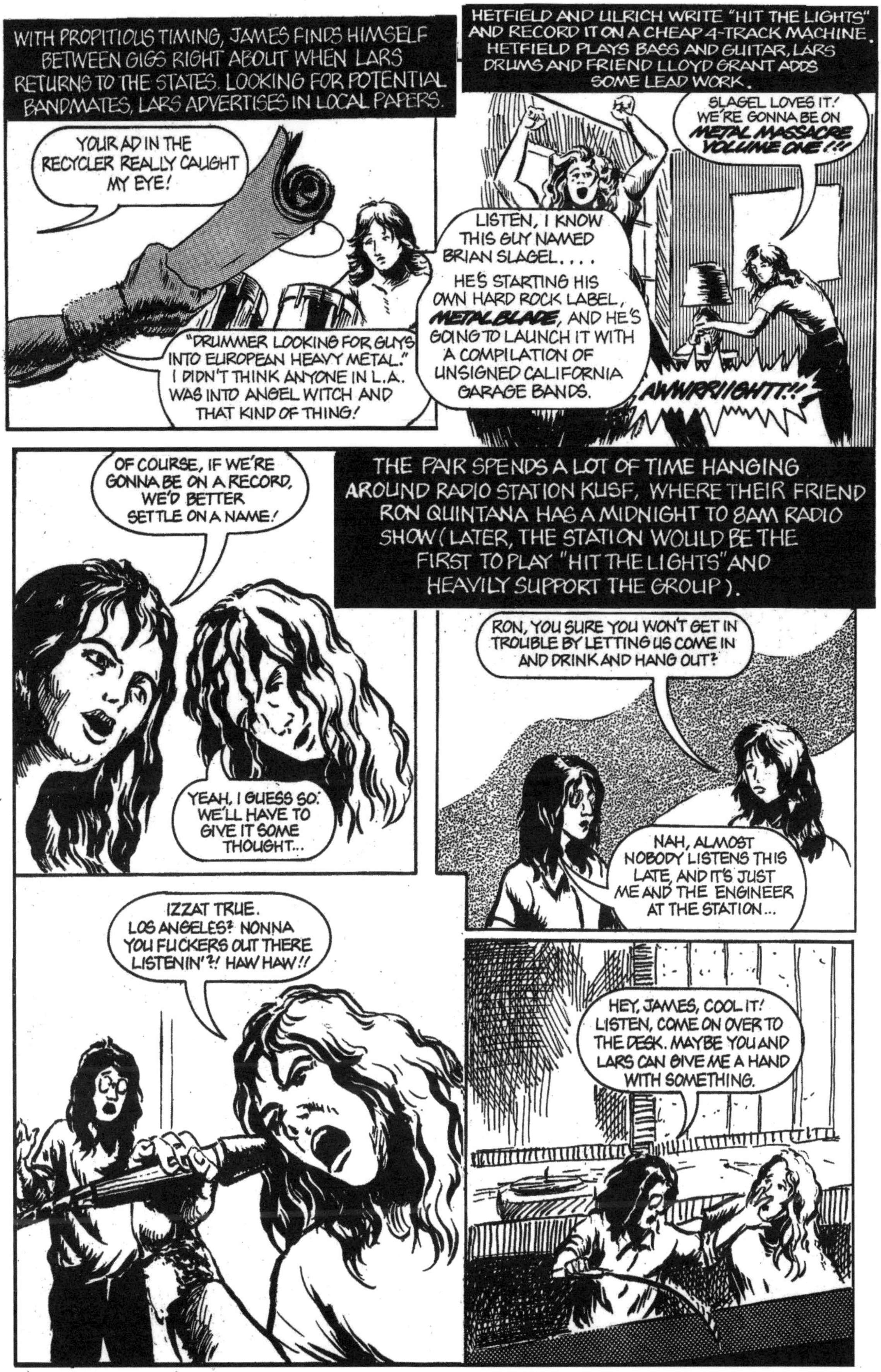

WITH PROPITIOUS TIMING, JAMES FINDS HIMSELF BETWEEN GIGS RIGHT ABOUT WHEN LARS RETURNS TO THE STATES. LOOKING FOR POTENTIAL BANDMATES, LARS ADVERTISES IN LOCAL PAPERS.
YOUR AD IN THE RECYCLER REALLY CAUGHT MY EYE!
"DRUMMER LOOKING FOR GUYS INTO EUROPEAN HEAVY METAL." I DIDN'T THINK ANYONE IN L.A. WAS INTO ANGEL WITCH AND THAT KIND OF THING!
HETFIELD AND ULRICH WRITE "HIT THE LIGHTS" AND RECORD IT ON A CHEAP 4-TRACK MACHINE. HETFIELD PLAYS BASS AND GUITAR, LARS DRUMS AND FRIEND LLOYD GRANT ADDS SOME LEAD WORK.
LISTEN, I KNOW THIS GUY NAMED BRIAN SLAGEL....
HE'S STARTING HIS OWN HARD ROCK LABEL, METAL BLADE, AND HE'S GOING TO LAUNCH IT WITH A COMPILATION OF UNSIGNED CALIFORNIA GARAGE BANDS.
SLAGEL LOVES IT! WE'RE GONNA BE ON METAL MASSACRE VOLUME ONE!!!
AWWRRIIGHTT!!
OF COURSE, IF WE'RE GONNA BE ON A RECORD, WE'D BETTER SETTLE ON A NAME!
YEAH, I GUESS SO. WE'LL HAVE TO GIVE IT SOME THOUGHT...
THE PAIR SPENDS A LOT OF TIME HANGING AROUND RADIO STATION KUSF, WHERE THEIR FRIEND RON QUINTANA HAS A MIDNIGHT TO 8AM RADIO SHOW (LATER, THE STATION WOULD BE THE FIRST TO PLAY "HIT THE LIGHTS" AND HEAVILY SUPPORT THE GROUP).
RON, YOU SURE YOU WON'T GET IN TROUBLE BY LETTING US COME IN AND DRINK AND HANG OUT?
NAH, ALMOST NOBODY LISTENS THIS LATE, AND IT'S JUST ME AND THE ENGINEER AT THE STATION...
IZZAT TRUE. LOS ANGELES? NONNA YOU FUCKERS OUT THERE LISTENIN'?! HAW HAW!!
HEY, JAMES, COOL IT! LISTEN, COME ON OVER TO THE DESK. MAYBE YOU AND LARS CAN GIVE ME A HAND WITH SOMETHING.

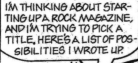

I'M THINKING ABOUT STARTING UP A ROCK MAGAZINE, AND I'M TRYING TO PICK A TITLE. HERE'S A LIST OF POSSIBILITIES I WROTE UP.

LOOK IT OVER AND LET ME KNOW WHAT YOU THINK...

... I GOTTA DO THE NEXT INTRO.

THERE'S SOME GREAT NAMES HERE. *METAFORCE, METAL MANIA, METALLICA...*

METALLICA?! *THAT'S* COOL! SOUNDS LIKE METAL AND VODKA!

HEY RON, CALL YOUR MAGAZINE *METAL MANIA!*

'CAUSE *WE'RE* GONNA USE *METALLICA!*

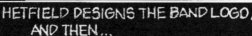

HETFIELD DESIGNS THE BAND LOGO, AND THEN...

CHECK IT OUT! OUR SONG ON THE RADIO! KUSF IS TREATIN' US RIGHT!

I HEAR THAT THE METAL MASSACRE RECORD IS DOING SO GOOD THAT IT'S BEEN LICENSED FOR CANADIAN DISTRIBUTION!

YEAH, WE SHOULD RECORD A CLEANER TAKE FOR THE RE-RELEASE.

I CAN TRY ANOTHER AD IN THE TABLOID PAPERS, SEE IF WE CAN FIND SOME OTHER PLAYERS WHO WANT TO METALLIROCK!

WHICH IS HOW THEY HOOK UP WITH SPEED FRETSTER *DAVE MUSTAINE* AND POWER BASSIST *RON McGOVNEY* (WHOM JAMES HAD ALREADY MET). AT FIRST, HETFIELD IS ONLY THE SINGER, BUT WHEN A SEARCH FOR RHYTHM GUITARIST FAILS (EVERYONE WANTS TO PLAY LEAD), HETFIELD TAKES ON THE VOCALS *AND* THE GUITAR FILLS (ONCE HE LEARNS TO SING AND PLAY SIMULTANEOUSLY).

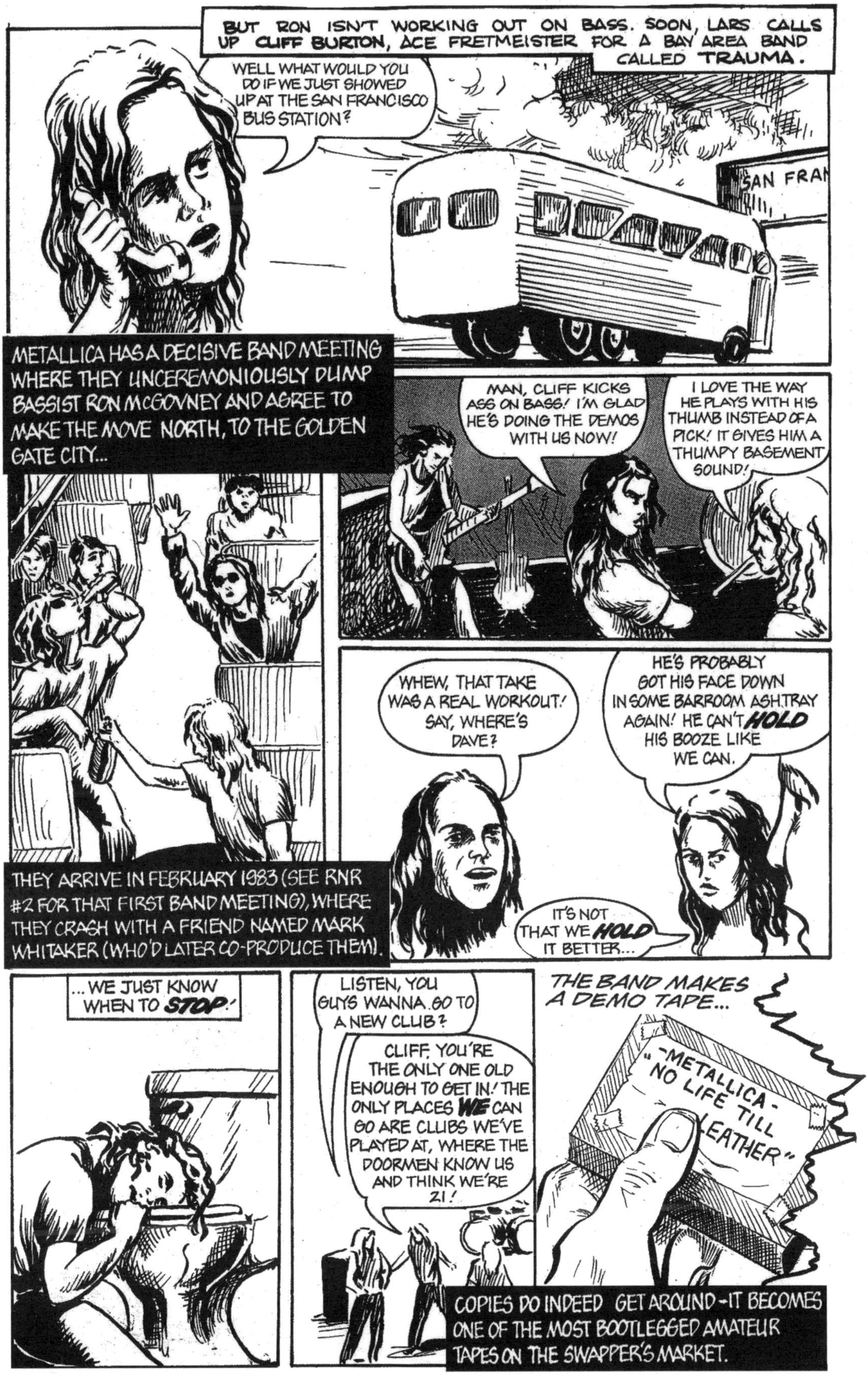
BUT RON ISN'T WORKING OUT ON BASS. SOON, LARS CALLS UP CLIFF BURTON, ACE FRETMEISTER FOR A BAY AREA BAND CALLED TRAUMA.
WELL WHAT WOULD YOU DO IF WE JUST SHOWED UP AT THE SAN FRANCISCO BUS STATION?
SAN FRAN
METALLICA HAS A DECISIVE BAND MEETING WHERE THEY UNCEREMONIOUSLY DUMP BASSIST RON MCGOVNEY AND AGREE TO MAKE THE MOVE NORTH, TO THE GOLDEN GATE CITY...
MAN, CLIFF KICKS ASS ON BASS! I'M GLAD HE'S DOING THE DEMOS WITH US NOW!
I LOVE THE WAY HE PLAYS WITH HIS THUMB INSTEAD OF A PICK! IT GIVES HIM A THUMPY BASEMENT SOUND!
WHEW, THAT TAKE WAS A REAL WORKOUT! SAY, WHERE'S DAVE?
HE'S PROBABLY GOT HIS FACE DOWN IN SOME BARROOM ASHTRAY AGAIN! HE CAN'T HOLD HIS BOOZE LIKE WE CAN.
IT'S NOT THAT WE HOLD IT BETTER...
THEY ARRIVE IN FEBRUARY 1983 (SEE RNR #2 FOR THAT FIRST BAND MEETING), WHERE THEY CRASH WITH A FRIEND NAMED MARK WHITAKER (WHO'D LATER CO-PRODUCE THEM).
...WE JUST KNOW WHEN TO STOP!
LISTEN, YOU GUYS WANNA GO TO A NEW CLUB?
CLIFF, YOU'RE THE ONLY ONE OLD ENOUGH TO GET IN! THE ONLY PLACES WE CAN GO ARE CLUBS WE'VE PLAYED AT, WHERE THE DOORMEN KNOW US AND THINK WE'RE 21!
THE BAND MAKES A DEMO TAPE...
"-METALLICA- NO LIFE TILL LEATHER"
COPIES DO INDEED GET AROUND-IT BECOMES ONE OF THE MOST BOOTLEGGED AMATEUR TAPES ON THE SWAPPER'S MARKET.

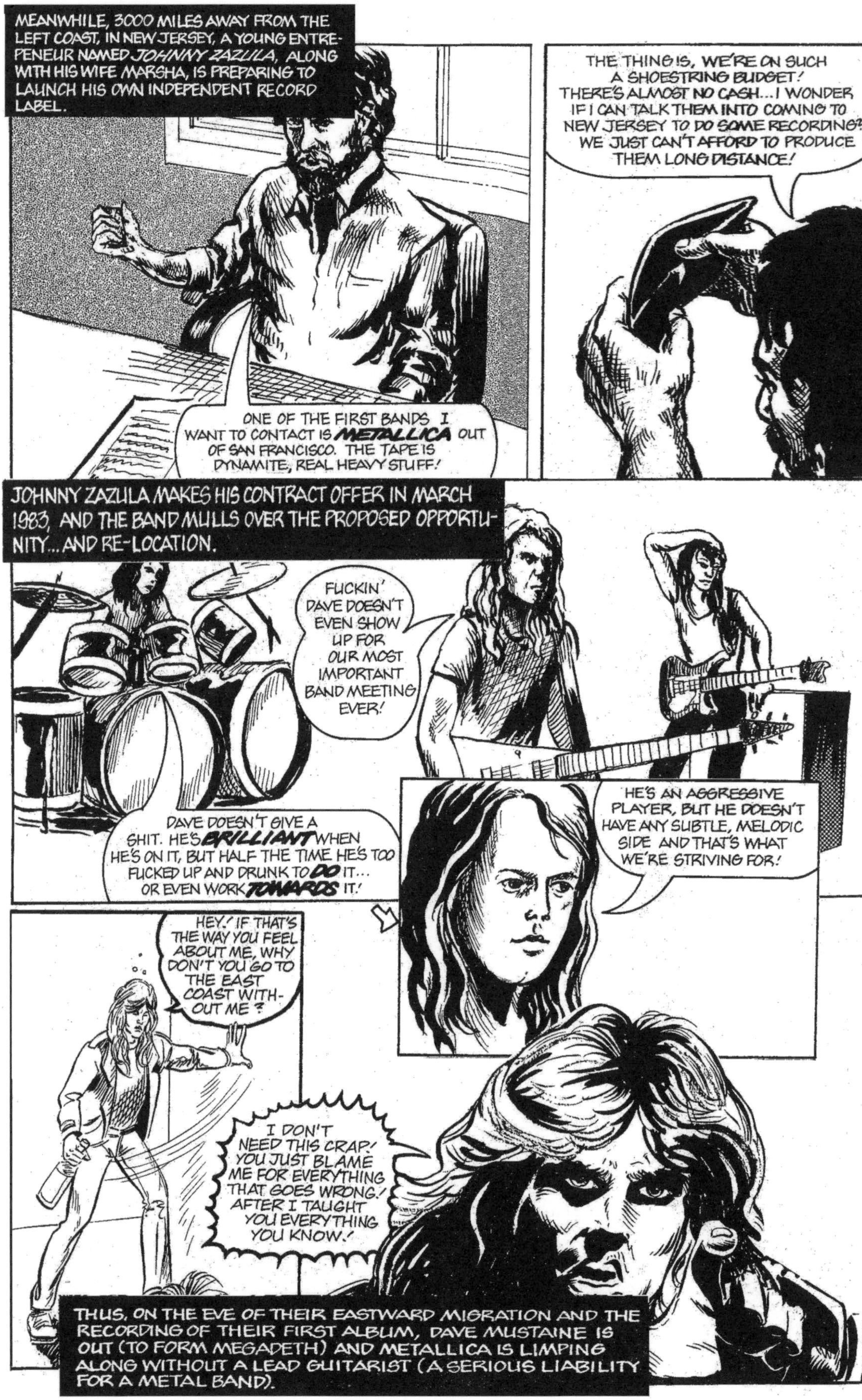
MEANWHILE, 3000 MILES AWAY FROM THE LEFT COAST, IN NEW JERSEY, A YOUNG ENTREPENEUR NAMED JOHNNY ZAZULA, ALONG WITH HIS WIFE MARSHA, IS PREPARING TO LAUNCH HIS OWN INDEPENDENT RECORD LABEL.
ONE OF THE FIRST BANDS I WANT TO CONTACT IS METALLICA OUT OF SAN FRANCISCO. THE TAPE IS DYNAMITE, REAL HEAVY STUFF!
THE THING IS, WE'RE ON SUCH A SHOESTRING BUDGET! THERE'S ALMOST NO CASH... I WONDER IF I CAN TALK THEM INTO COMING TO NEW JERSEY TO DO SOME RECORDING? WE JUST CAN'T AFFORD TO PRODUCE THEM LONG DISTANCE!
JOHNNY ZAZULA MAKES HIS CONTRACT OFFER IN MARCH 1983, AND THE BAND MULLS OVER THE PROPOSED OPPORTUNITY... AND RE-LOCATION.
FUCKIN' DAVE DOESN'T EVEN SHOW UP FOR OUR MOST IMPORTANT BAND MEETING EVER!
DAVE DOESN'T GIVE A SHIT. HE'S BRILLIANT WHEN HE'S ON IT, BUT HALF THE TIME HE'S TOO FUCKED UP AND DRUNK TO DO IT... OR EVEN WORK TOWARDS IT!
HE'S AN AGGRESSIVE PLAYER, BUT HE DOESN'T HAVE ANY SUBTLE, MELODIC SIDE AND THAT'S WHAT WE'RE STRIVING FOR!
HEY! IF THAT'S THE WAY YOU FEEL ABOUT ME, WHY DON'T YOU GO TO THE EAST COAST WITHOUT ME?
I DON'T NEED THIS CRAP! YOU JUST BLAME ME FOR EVERYTHING THAT GOES WRONG! AFTER I TAUGHT YOU EVERYTHING YOU KNOW!
THUS, ON THE EVE OF THEIR EASTWARD MIGRATION AND THE RECORDING OF THEIR FIRST ALBUM, DAVE MUSTAINE IS OUT (TO FORM MEGADETH) AND METALLICA IS LIMPING ALONG WITHOUT A LEAD GUITARIST (A SERIOUS LIABILITY FOR A METAL BAND).

METALLICA'S CANNY DIVINING ROD COULDN'T HAVE SETTLED ON A MORE SUITABLE AXE-SLINGER, A PERFECT METALLURGICAL MATCH. KIRK (BORN IN SF) STUDIED GUITAR WITH ACE WIREWIZARD *JOE SATRIANI* (ALSO STEVE VAI'S INSTRUCTOR).

KIRK IS INDOCTRINATED INTO A DISCIPLINED, ALCHEMIC WORLD OF BLISTERS, GUITAR HARMONIES, MODES, APPREGGIOS, THREE OCTAVE SCALES AND LOTS OF TECHNOLOGY THEORY.

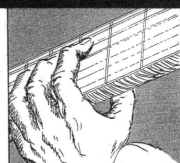

IN MAY 1983 (TWO MONTHS AFTER BEING SIGNED), THE GROUP ENTERS THE STUDIO TO RECORD THEIR FIRST LP, *KILL 'EM ALL*, WITH PAUL CURCIO PRODUCING (METALLICA LATER SUMS UP HIS CONTRIBUTION AS "A GREAT COFFEE GO-FER").

MUSIC AMERICA STUDIOS

THEY RE-RECORD THEIR DEMO SONGS, PLUS SOME NEW COMPOSITIONS AND, OF COURSE, "HIT THE LIGHTS" ONCE AGAIN (THEIR THIRD VERSION IF YOU'RE COUNTING).

I'VE GOT A GREAT IDEA ABOUT WHAT TO CALL OUR FIRST ALBUM... *METAL UP YOUR ASS!*

SOMEHOW, I GET THE FEELING THAT AN INDIE COMPANY LIKE MEGAFORCE WOULD HAVE TROUBLE SELLING A RECORD LIKE THAT.

THE ALBUM IS OUT IN THE SUMMER OF '83 (ON THE NEW *MUSIC FOR NATIONS* LABEL IN ENGLAND, WHERE METALLICA HITS #1 IN *KERRANG* AND *SOUNDS* READER POLLS).

THEN WE'LL GO WITH OUR ORIGINAL TITLE, *KILL 'EM ALL*, AND USE A MORE SUBTLE COVER. MAYBE A MALLET LYING IN A PUDDLE OF BLOOD!

OH, *MUCH* MORE SUBTLE, LARS!

KILL 'EM ALL

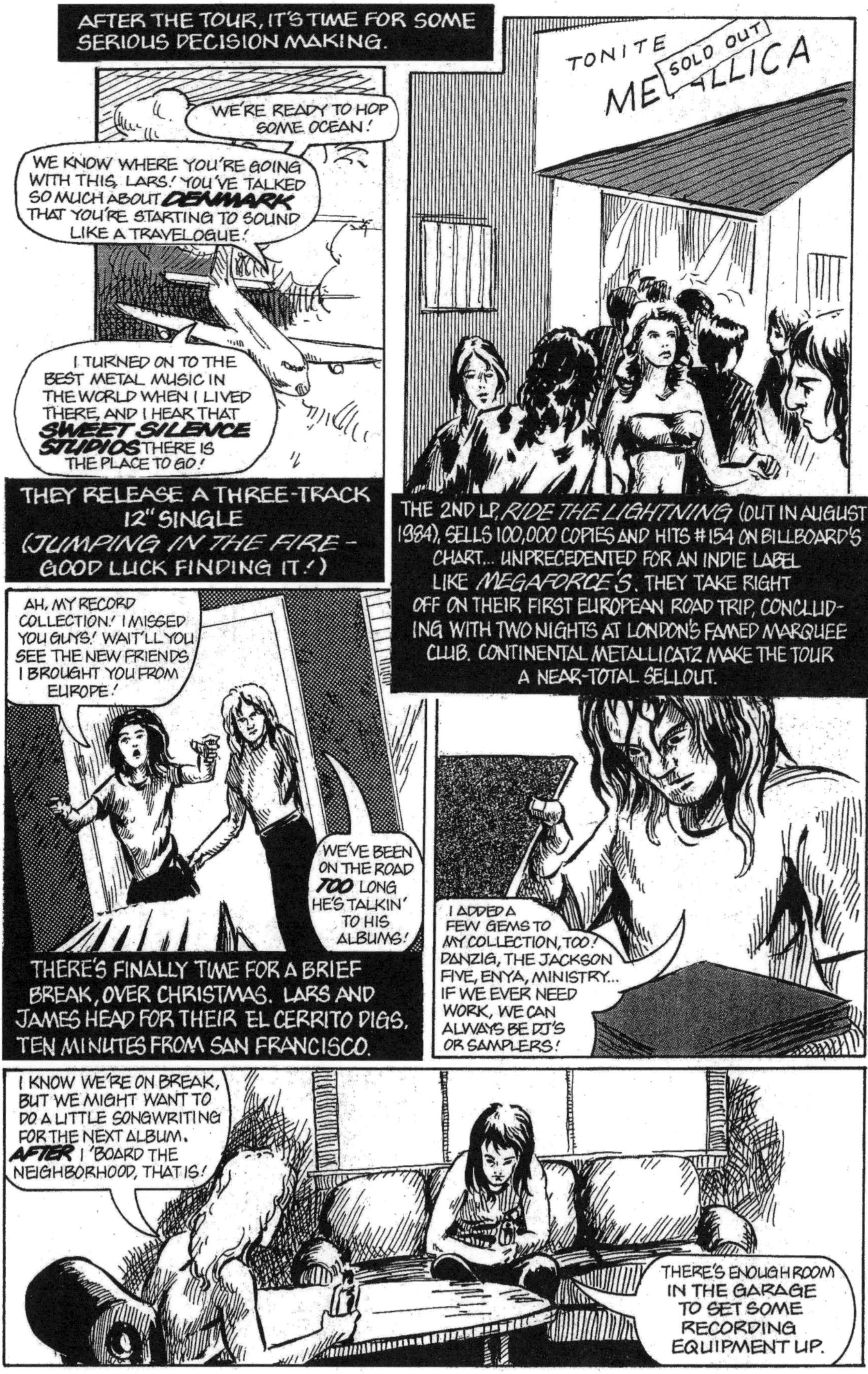
AFTER THE TOUR, IT'S TIME FOR SOME SERIOUS DECISION MAKING.
WE'RE READY TO HOP SOME OCEAN!
WE KNOW WHERE YOU'RE GOING WITH THIS, LARS! YOU'VE TALKED SO MUCH ABOUT DENMARK THAT YOU'RE STARTING TO SOUND LIKE A TRAVELOGUE!
I TURNED ON TO THE BEST METAL MUSIC IN THE WORLD WHEN I LIVED THERE, AND I HEAR THAT SWEET SILENCE STUDIOS THERE IS THE PLACE TO GO!
TONITE
SOLD OUT
METALLICA
THEY RELEASE A THREE-TRACK 12" SINGLE (JUMPING IN THE FIRE - GOOD LUCK FINDING IT!)
THE 2ND LP, RIDE THE LIGHTNING (OUT IN AUGUST 1984), SELLS 100,000 COPIES AND HITS #154 ON BILLBOARD'S CHART... UNPRECEDENTED FOR AN INDIE LABEL LIKE MEGAFORCE'S. THEY TAKE RIGHT OFF ON THEIR FIRST EUROPEAN ROAD TRIP, CONCLUDING WITH TWO NIGHTS AT LONDON'S FAMED MARQUEE CLUB. CONTINENTAL METALLICATZ MAKE THE TOUR A NEAR-TOTAL SELLOUT.
AH, MY RECORD COLLECTION! I MISSED YOU GUYS! WAIT'LL YOU SEE THE NEW FRIENDS I BROUGHT YOU FROM EUROPE!
WE'VE BEEN ON THE ROAD TOO LONG HE'S TALKIN' TO HIS ALBUMS!
THERE'S FINALLY TIME FOR A BRIEF BREAK, OVER CHRISTMAS. LARS AND JAMES HEAD FOR THEIR EL CERRITO DIGS, TEN MINUTES FROM SAN FRANCISCO.
I ADDED A FEW GEMS TO MY COLLECTION, TOO! DANZIG, THE JACKSON FIVE, ENYA, MINISTRY... IF WE EVER NEED WORK, WE CAN ALWAYS BE DJ'S OR SAMPLERS!
I KNOW WE'RE ON BREAK, BUT WE MIGHT WANT TO DO A LITTLE SONGWRITING FOR THE NEXT ALBUM. AFTER I 'BOARD THE NEIGHBORHOOD, THAT IS!
THERE'S ENOUGH ROOM IN THE GARAGE TO SET SOME RECORDING EQUIPMENT UP.

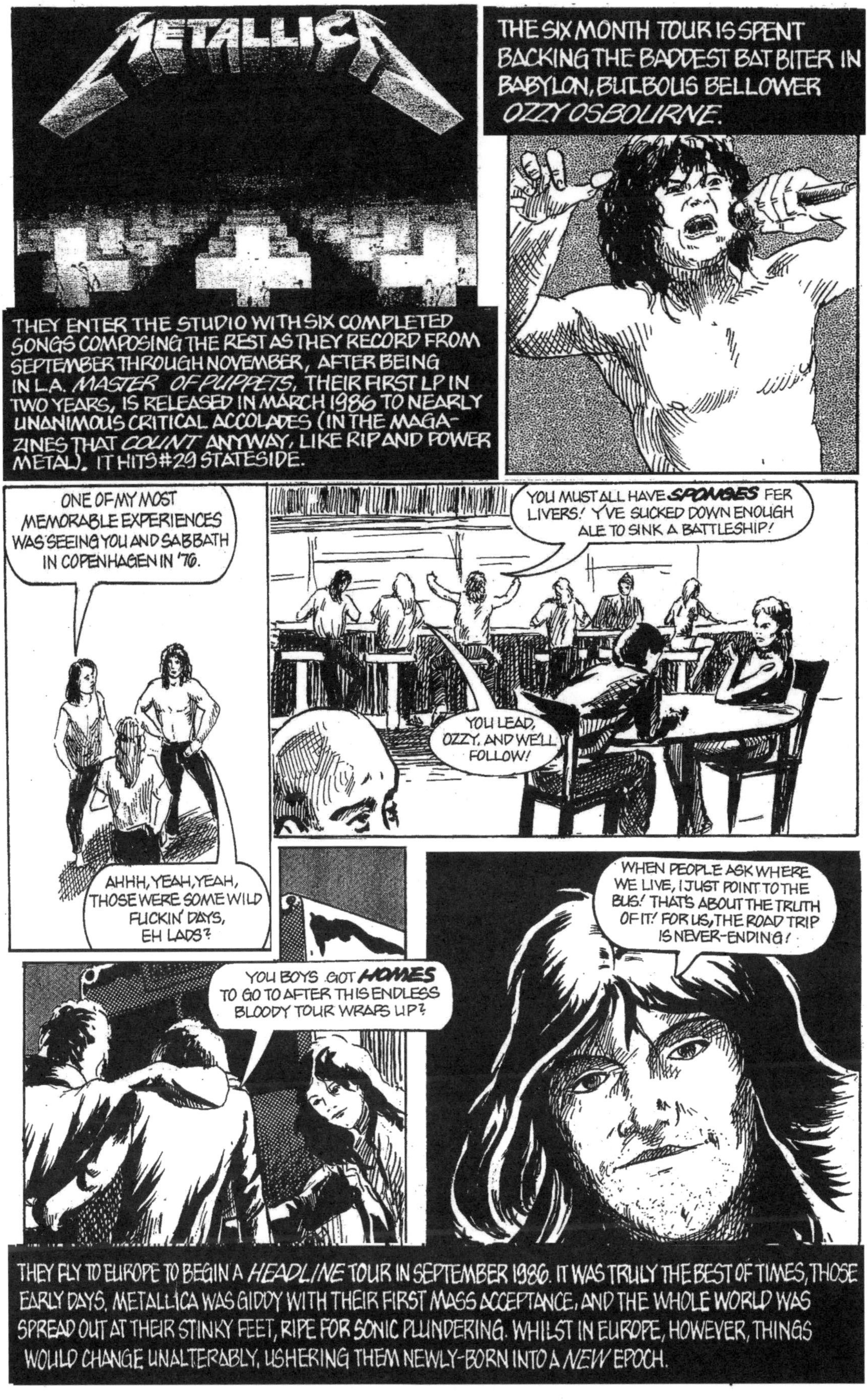
METALLICA
THE SIX MONTH TOUR IS SPENT BACKING THE BADDEST BAT BITER IN BABYLON, BULBOUS BELLOWER *OZZY OSBOURNE*.
THEY ENTER THE STUDIO WITH SIX COMPLETED SONGS COMPOSING THE REST AS THEY RECORD FROM SEPTEMBER THROUGH NOVEMBER, AFTER BEING IN L.A. *MASTER OF PUPPETS*, THEIR FIRST LP IN TWO YEARS, IS RELEASED IN MARCH 1986 TO NEARLY UNANIMOUS CRITICAL ACCOLADES (IN THE MAGAZINES THAT *COUNT* ANYWAY, LIKE RIP AND POWER METAL). IT HITS #29 STATESIDE.
ONE OF MY MOST MEMORABLE EXPERIENCES WAS SEEING YOU AND SABBATH IN COPENHAGEN IN '76.
AHHH, YEAH, YEAH, THOSE WERE SOME WILD FUCKIN' DAYS, EH LADS?
YOU MUST ALL HAVE **SPONGES** FER LIVERS! Y'VE SUCKED DOWN ENOUGH ALE TO SINK A BATTLESHIP!
YOU LEAD, OZZY, AND WE'LL FOLLOW!
YOU BOYS GOT **HOMES** TO GO TO AFTER THIS ENDLESS BLOODY TOUR WRAPS UP?
WHEN PEOPLE ASK WHERE WE LIVE, I JUST POINT TO THE BUS! THAT'S ABOUT THE TRUTH OF IT! FOR US, THE ROAD TRIP IS NEVER-ENDING!
THEY FLY TO EUROPE TO BEGIN A *HEADLINE* TOUR IN SEPTEMBER 1986. IT WAS TRULY THE BEST OF TIMES, THOSE EARLY DAYS. METALLICA WAS GIDDY WITH THEIR FIRST MASS ACCEPTANCE, AND THE WHOLE WORLD WAS SPREAD OUT AT THEIR STINKY FEET, RIPE FOR SONIC PLUNDERING. WHILST IN EUROPE, HOWEVER, THINGS WOULD CHANGE UNALTERABLY, USHERING THEM NEWLY-BORN INTO A *NEW* EPOCH.

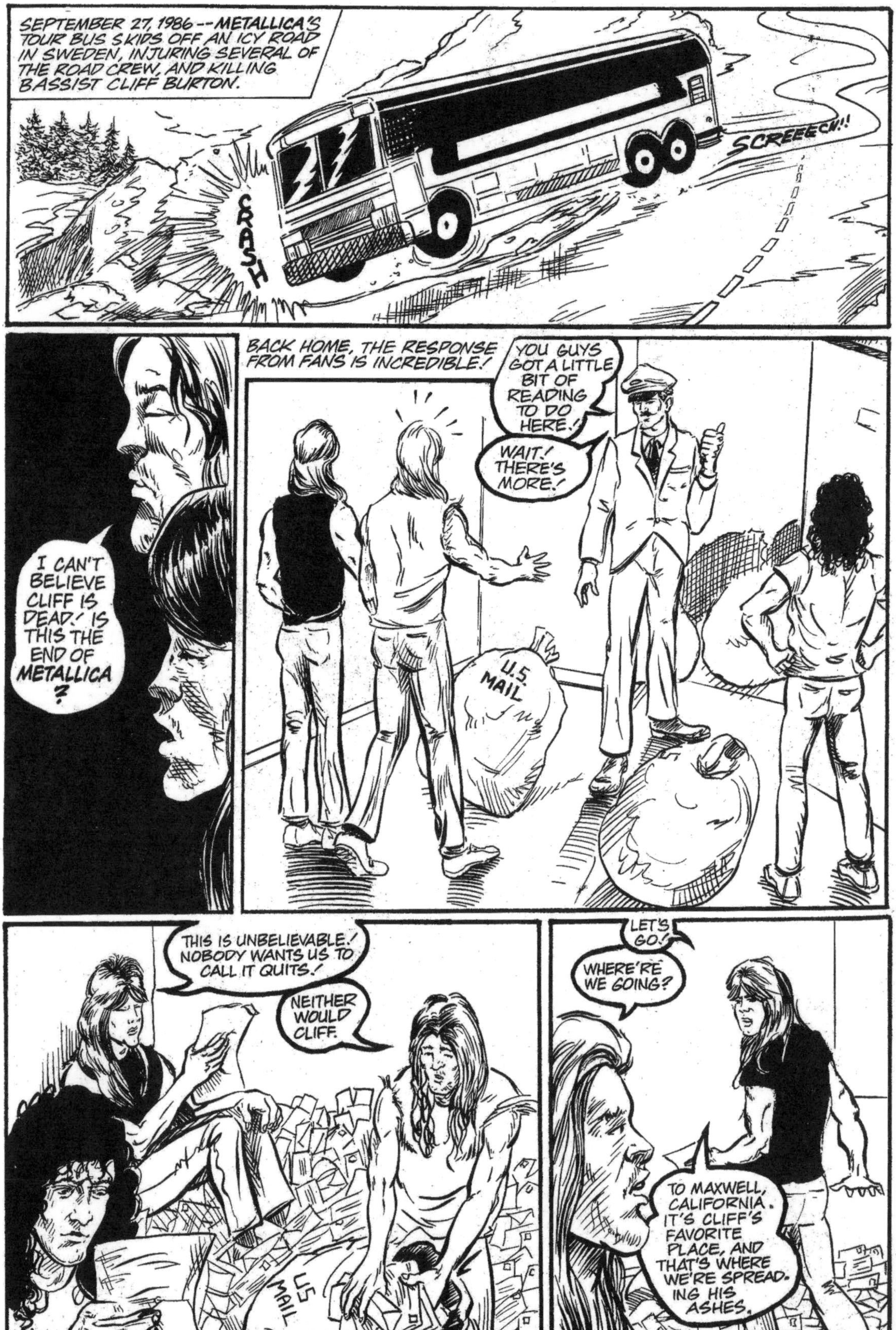
SEPTEMBER 27, 1986 -- METALLICA'S TOUR BUS SKIDS OFF AN ICY ROAD IN SWEDEN, INJURING SEVERAL OF THE ROAD CREW, AND KILLING BASSIST CLIFF BURTON.
CRASH
SCREEEECH!!
I CAN'T BELIEVE CLIFF IS DEAD! IS THIS THE END OF METALLICA?
BACK HOME, THE RESPONSE FROM FANS IS INCREDIBLE!
YOU GUYS GOT A LITTLE BIT OF READING TO DO HERE!
WAIT! THERE'S MORE!
U.S. MAIL
THIS IS UNBELIEVABLE! NOBODY WANTS US TO CALL IT QUITS!
NEITHER WOULD CLIFF.
US MAIL
LET'S GO!
WHERE'RE WE GOING?
TO MAXWELL, CALIFORNIA. IT'S CLIFF'S FAVORITE PLACE, AND THAT'S WHERE WE'RE SPREAD-ING HIS ASHES.

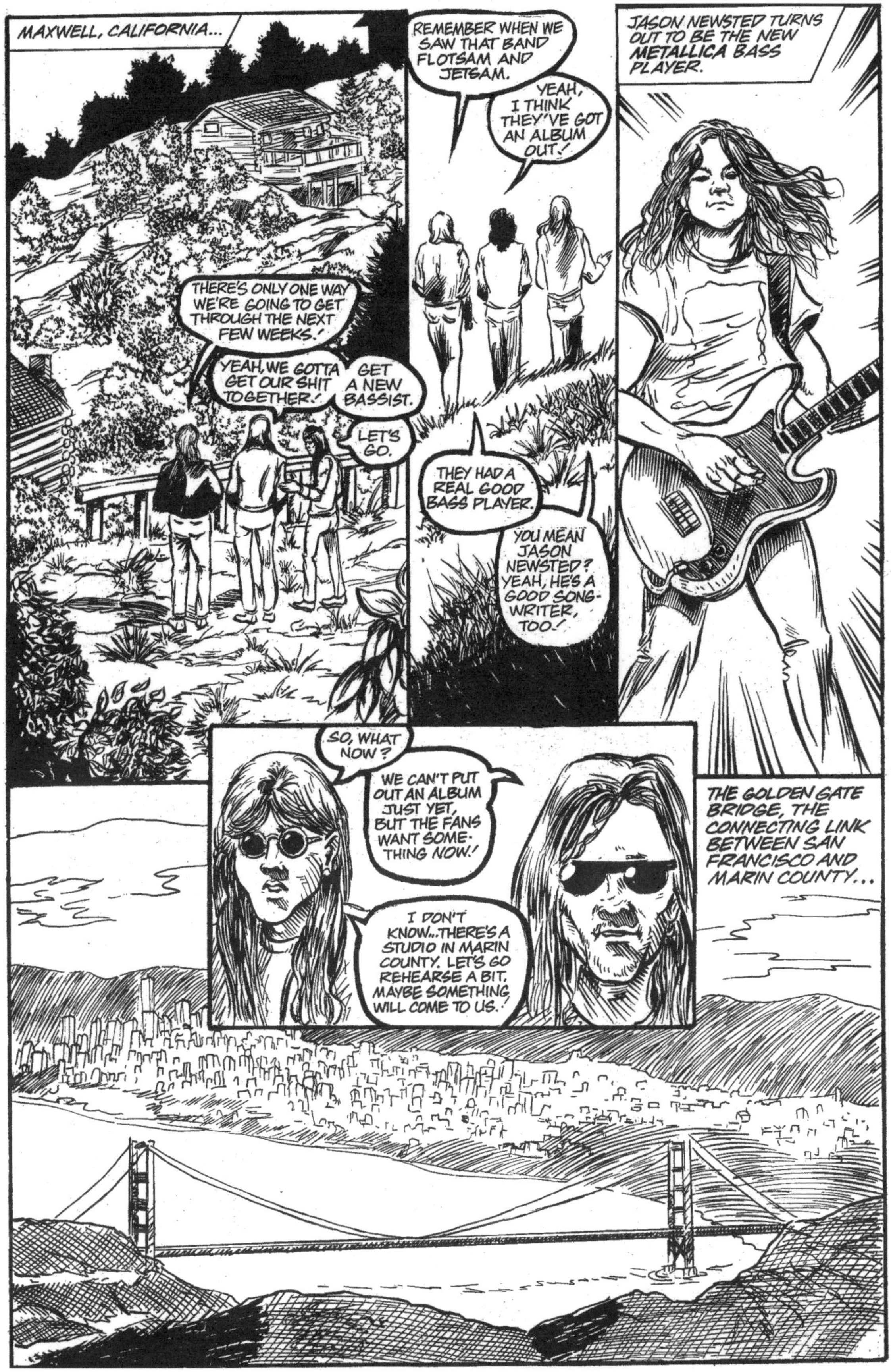
MAXWELL, CALIFORNIA...
THERE'S ONLY ONE WAY WE'RE GOING TO GET THROUGH THE NEXT FEW WEEKS!
YEAH, WE GOTTA GET OUR SHIT TOGETHER!
GET A NEW BASSIST.
LET'S GO.
REMEMBER WHEN WE SAW THAT BAND FLOTSAM AND JETSAM.
YEAH, I THINK THEY'VE GOT AN ALBUM OUT!
THEY HAD A REAL GOOD BASS PLAYER.
YOU MEAN JASON NEWSTED? YEAH, HE'S A GOOD SONG-WRITER, TOO!
JASON NEWSTED TURNS OUT TO BE THE NEW METALLICA BASS PLAYER.
SO, WHAT NOW?
WE CAN'T PUT OUT AN ALBUM JUST YET, BUT THE FANS WANT SOME-THING NOW!
I DON'T KNOW...THERE'S A STUDIO IN MARIN COUNTY. LET'S GO REHEARSE A BIT. MAYBE SOMETHING WILL COME TO US.
THE GOLDEN GATE BRIDGE, THE CONNECTING LINK BETWEEN SAN FRANCISCO AND MARIN COUNTY...

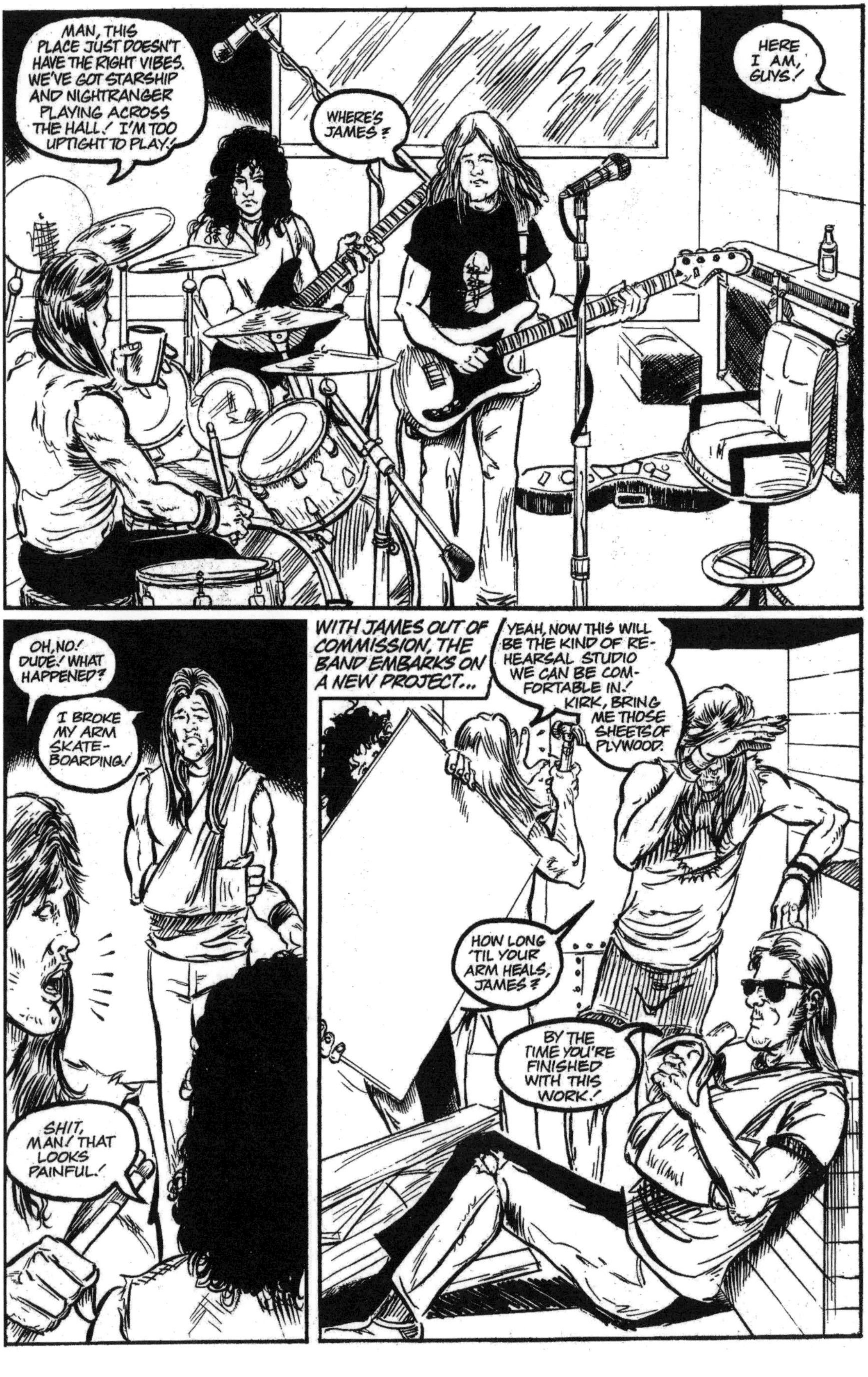

MAN, THIS PLACE JUST DOESN'T HAVE THE RIGHT VIBES. WE'VE GOT STARSHIP AND NIGHTRANGER PLAYING ACROSS THE HALL! I'M TOO UPTIGHT TO PLAY!
WHERE'S JAMES?
HERE I AM, GUYS!
OH, NO! DUDE! WHAT HAPPENED?
I BROKE MY ARM SKATE-BOARDING!
SHIT, MAN! THAT LOOKS PAINFUL!
WITH JAMES OUT OF COMMISSION, THE BAND EMBARKS ON A NEW PROJECT...
YEAH, NOW THIS WILL BE THE KIND OF RE-HEARSAL STUDIO WE CAN BE COM-FORTABLE IN! KIRK, BRING ME THOSE SHEETS OF PLYWOOD.
HOW LONG 'TIL YOUR ARM HEALS, JAMES?
BY THE TIME YOU'RE FINISHED WITH THIS WORK!

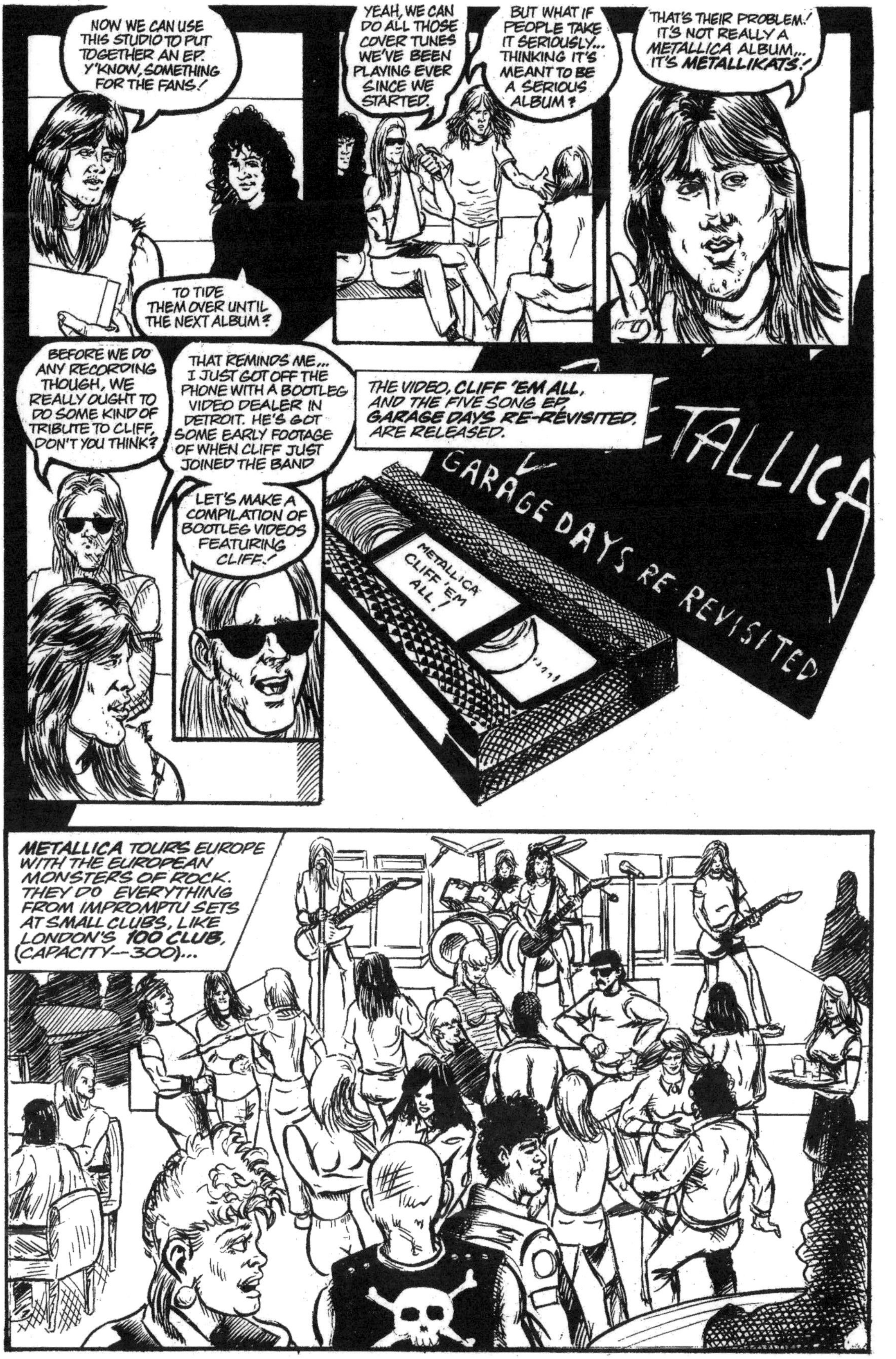
NOW WE CAN USE THIS STUDIO TO PUT TOGETHER AN EP. Y'KNOW, SOMETHING FOR THE FANS!
TO TIDE THEM OVER UNTIL THE NEXT ALBUM?
YEAH, WE CAN DO ALL THOSE COVER TUNES WE'VE BEEN PLAYING EVER SINCE WE STARTED.
BUT WHAT IF PEOPLE TAKE IT SERIOUSLY... THINKING IT'S MEANT TO BE A SERIOUS ALBUM?
THAT'S THEIR PROBLEM! IT'S NOT REALLY A METALLICA ALBUM... IT'S METALLIKATS!
BEFORE WE DO ANY RECORDING THOUGH, WE REALLY OUGHT TO DO SOME KIND OF TRIBUTE TO CLIFF, DON'T YOU THINK?
THAT REMINDS ME... I JUST GOT OFF THE PHONE WITH A BOOTLEG VIDEO DEALER IN DETROIT. HE'S GOT SOME EARLY FOOTAGE OF WHEN CLIFF JUST JOINED THE BAND
LET'S MAKE A COMPILATION OF BOOTLEG VIDEOS FEATURING CLIFF!
THE VIDEO, CLIFF 'EM ALL, AND THE FIVE SONG EP, GARAGE DAYS RE-REVISITED, ARE RELEASED.
METALLICA CLIFF 'EM ALL!
ETALLICA
GARAGE DAYS RE-REVISITED
METALLICA TOURS EUROPE WITH THE EUROPEAN MONSTERS OF ROCK. THEY DO EVERYTHING FROM IMPROMPTU SETS AT SMALL CLUBS, LIKE LONDON'S 100 CLUB, (CAPACITY--300)...

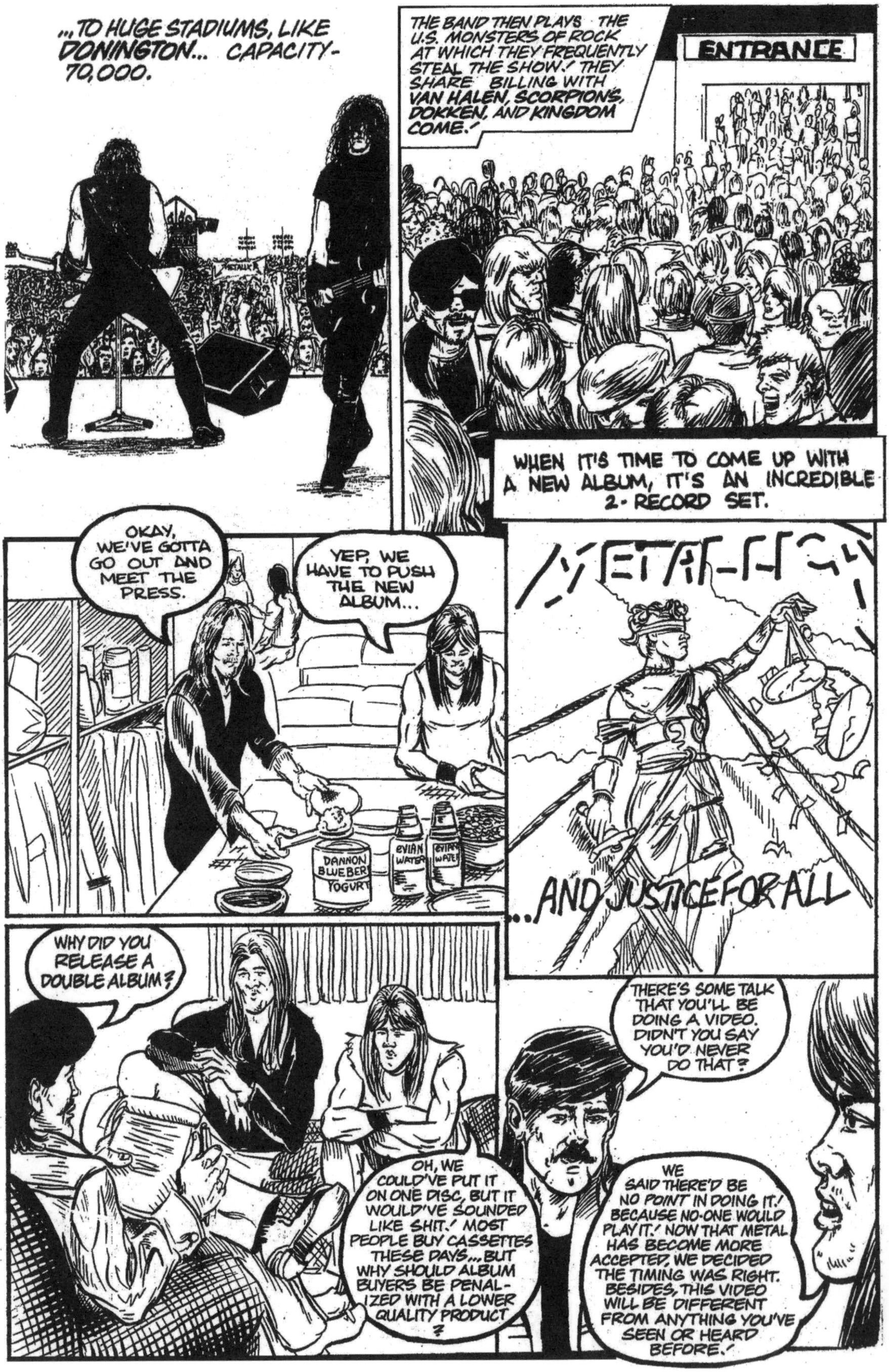
...TO HUGE STADIUMS, LIKE DONINGTON... CAPACITY-70,000.
THE BAND THEN PLAYS THE U.S. MONSTERS OF ROCK AT WHICH THEY FREQUENTLY STEAL THE SHOW! THEY SHARE BILLING WITH VAN HALEN, SCORPIONS, DOKKEN, AND KINGDOM COME!
ENTRANCE
WHEN IT'S TIME TO COME UP WITH A NEW ALBUM, IT'S AN INCREDIBLE 2-RECORD SET.
OKAY, WE'VE GOTTA GO OUT AND MEET THE PRESS.
YEP, WE HAVE TO PUSH THE NEW ALBUM...
DANNON BLUEBERRY YOGURT
EVIAN WATER
EVIAN WATER
...AND JUSTICE FOR ALL
WHY DID YOU RELEASE A DOUBLE ALBUM?
OH, WE COULD'VE PUT IT ON ONE DISC, BUT IT WOULD'VE SOUNDED LIKE SHIT! MOST PEOPLE BUY CASSETTES THESE DAYS... BUT WHY SHOULD ALBUM BUYERS BE PENALIZED WITH A LOWER QUALITY PRODUCT?
THERE'S SOME TALK THAT YOU'LL BE DOING A VIDEO. DIDN'T YOU SAY YOU'D NEVER DO THAT?
WE SAID THERE'D BE NO POINT IN DOING IT! BECAUSE NO-ONE WOULD PLAY IT! NOW THAT METAL HAS BECOME MORE ACCEPTED, WE DECIDED THE TIMING WAS RIGHT. BESIDES, THIS VIDEO WILL BE DIFFERENT FROM ANYTHING YOU'VE SEEN OR HEARD BEFORE!

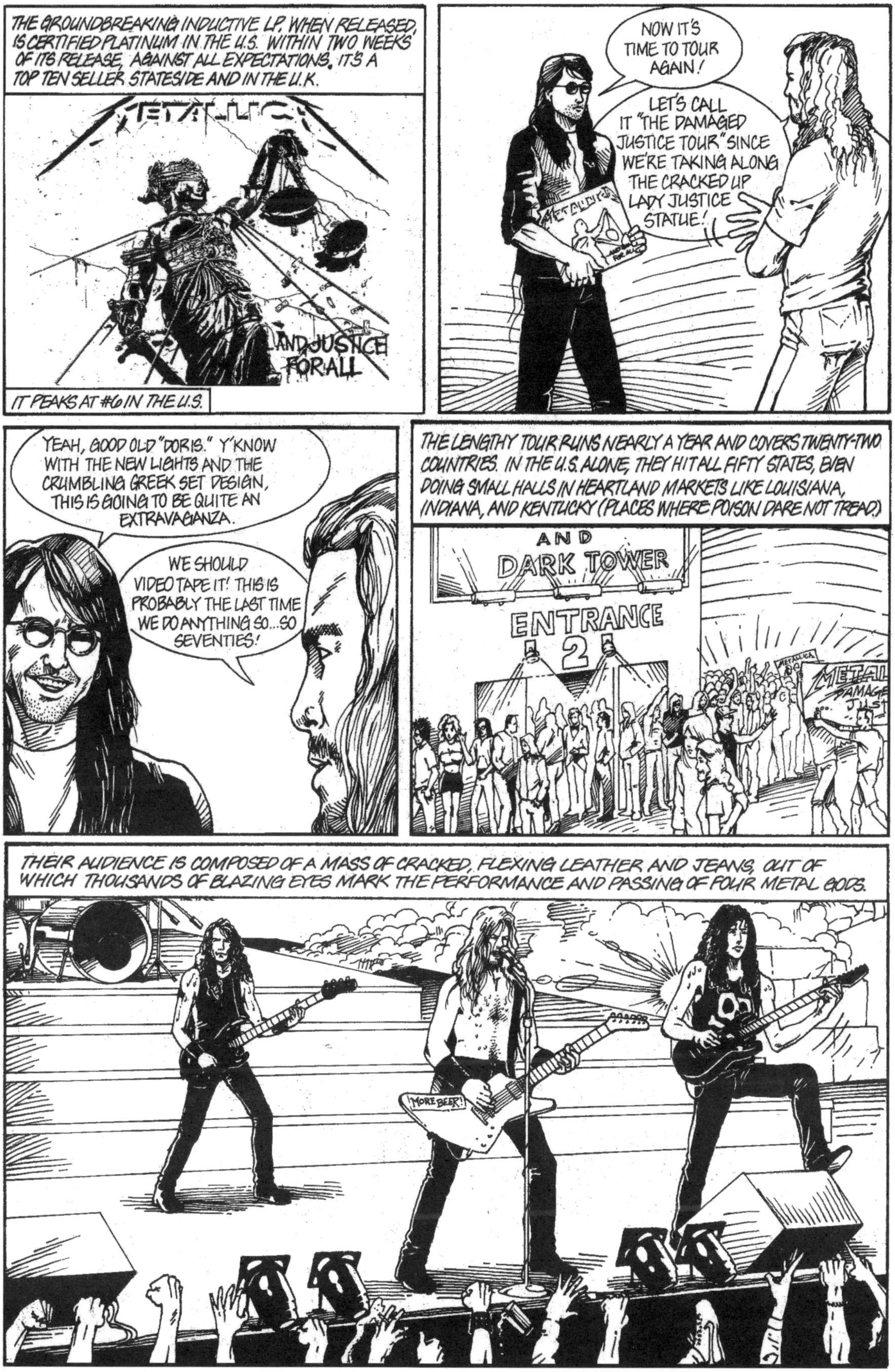
THE GROUNDBREAKING INDUCTIVE LP, WHEN RELEASED, IS CERTIFIED PLATINUM IN THE U.S. WITHIN TWO WEEKS OF ITS RELEASE. AGAINST ALL EXPECTATIONS, IT'S A TOP TEN SELLER STATESIDE AND IN THE U.K.
METALLICA
...AND JUSTICE FOR ALL
IT PEAKS AT #6 IN THE U.S.
NOW IT'S TIME TO TOUR AGAIN!
LET'S CALL IT "THE DAMAGED JUSTICE TOUR" SINCE WE'RE TAKING ALONG THE CRACKED UP LADY JUSTICE STATUE!
YEAH, GOOD OLD "DORIS." Y'KNOW WITH THE NEW LIGHTS AND THE CRUMBLING GREEK SET DESIGN, THIS IS GOING TO BE QUITE AN EXTRAVAGANZA.
WE SHOULD VIDEO TAPE IT! THIS IS PROBABLY THE LAST TIME WE DO ANYTHING SO...SO SEVENTIES!
THE LENGTHY TOUR RUNS NEARLY A YEAR AND COVERS TWENTY-TWO COUNTRIES. IN THE U.S. ALONE, THEY HIT ALL FIFTY STATES, EVEN DOING SMALL HALLS IN HEARTLAND MARKETS LIKE LOUISIANA, INDIANA, AND KENTUCKY (PLACES WHERE POISON DARE NOT TREAD.)
AND
DARK TOWER
ENTRANCE
2
METALLICA
THEIR AUDIENCE IS COMPOSED OF A MASS OF CRACKED, FLEXING LEATHER AND JEANS, OUT OF WHICH THOUSANDS OF BLAZING EYES MARK THE PERFORMANCE AND PASSING OF FOUR METAL GODS.
MORE BEER!

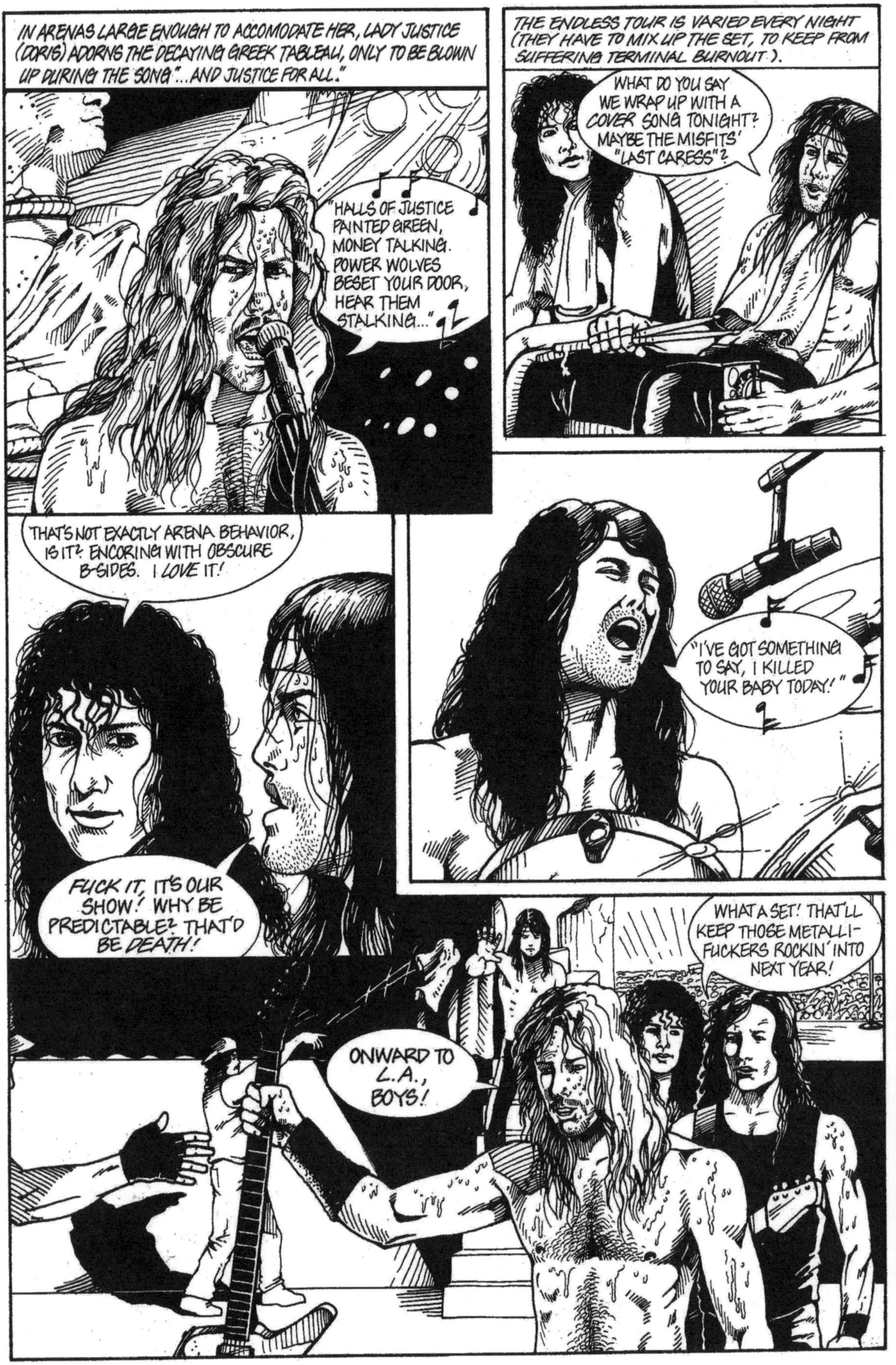
IN ARENAS LARGE ENOUGH TO ACCOMODATE HER, LADY JUSTICE (DORIS) ADORNS THE DECAYING GREEK TABLEAU, ONLY TO BE BLOWN UP DURING THE SONG "...AND JUSTICE FOR ALL."
"HALLS OF JUSTICE PAINTED GREEN, MONEY TALKING. POWER WOLVES BESET YOUR DOOR, HEAR THEM STALKING..."
THE ENDLESS TOUR IS VARIED EVERY NIGHT (THEY HAVE TO MIX UP THE SET, TO KEEP FROM SUFFERING TERMINAL BURNOUT).
WHAT DO YOU SAY WE WRAP UP WITH A COVER SONG TONIGHT? MAYBE THE MISFITS' "LAST CARESS"?
THAT'S NOT EXACTLY ARENA BEHAVIOR, IS IT? ENCORING WITH OBSCURE B-SIDES. I LOVE IT!
FUCK IT, IT'S OUR SHOW! WHY BE PREDICTABLE? THAT'D BE DEATH!
"I'VE GOT SOMETHING TO SAY, I KILLED YOUR BABY TODAY!"
WHAT A SET! THAT'LL KEEP THOSE METALLI-FUCKERS ROCKIN' INTO NEXT YEAR!
ONWARD TO L.A., BOYS!

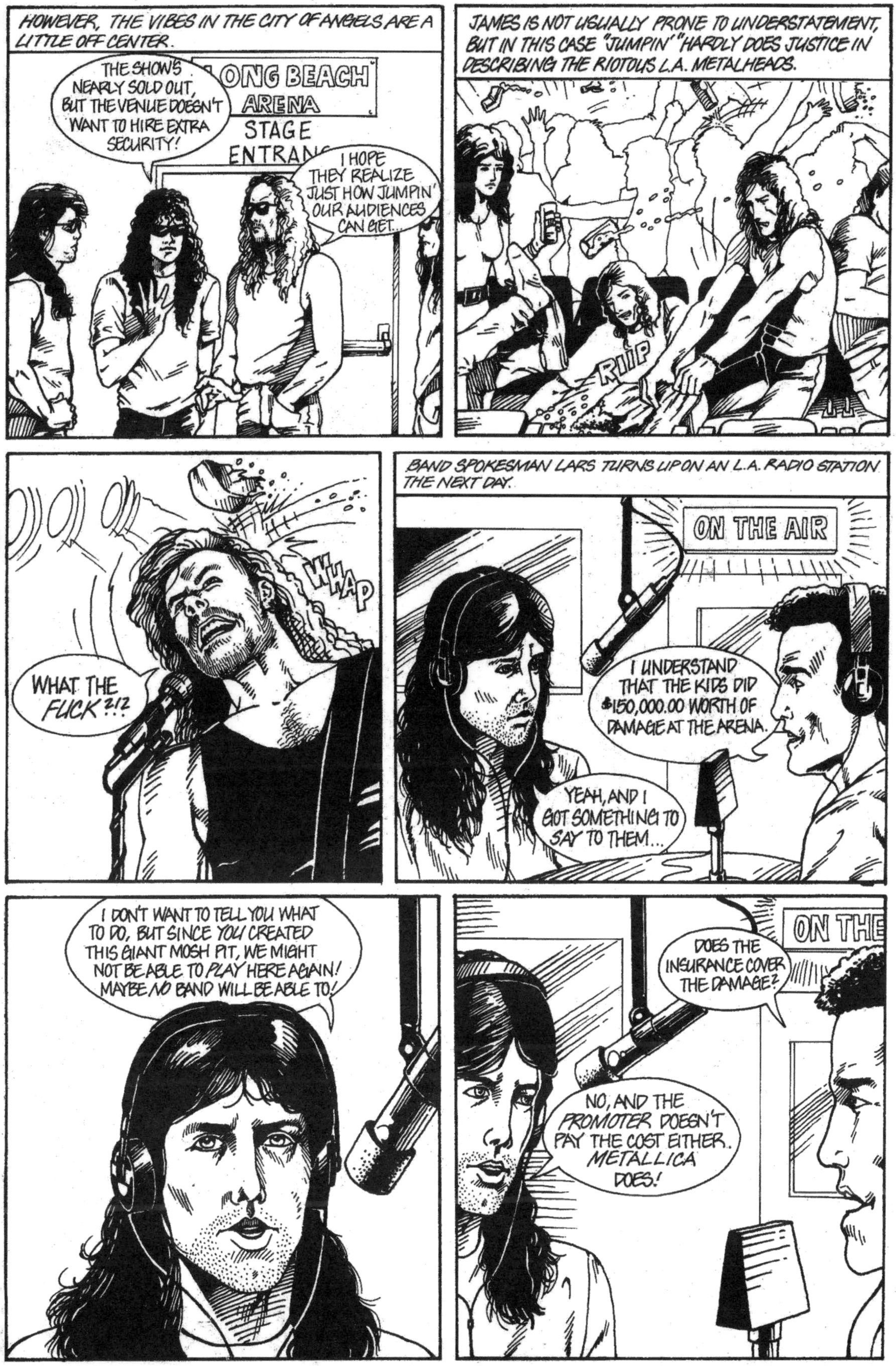
HOWEVER, THE VIBES IN THE CITY OF ANGELS ARE A LITTLE OFF CENTER.
LONG BEACH ARENA
STAGE ENTRAN
THE SHOW'S NEARLY SOLD OUT, BUT THE VENUE DOESN'T WANT TO HIRE EXTRA SECURITY!
I HOPE THEY REALIZE JUST HOW JUMPIN' OUR AUDIENCES CAN GET...
JAMES IS NOT USUALLY PRONE TO UNDERSTATEMENT, BUT IN THIS CASE "JUMPIN'" HARDLY DOES JUSTICE IN DESCRIBING THE RIOTOUS L.A. METALHEADS.
RIP
WHAP
WHAT THE FUCK ?!?
BAND SPOKESMAN LARS TURNS UP ON AN L.A. RADIO STATION THE NEXT DAY.
ON THE AIR
I UNDERSTAND THAT THE KIDS DID $150,000.00 WORTH OF DAMAGE AT THE ARENA.
YEAH, AND I GOT SOMETHING TO SAY TO THEM...
I DON'T WANT TO TELL YOU WHAT TO DO, BUT SINCE YOU CREATED THIS GIANT MOSH PIT, WE MIGHT NOT BE ABLE TO PLAY HERE AGAIN! MAYBE NO BAND WILL BE ABLE TO!
ON THE
DOES THE INSURANCE COVER THE DAMAGE?
NO, AND THE PROMOTER DOESN'T PAY THE COST EITHER. METALLICA DOES!

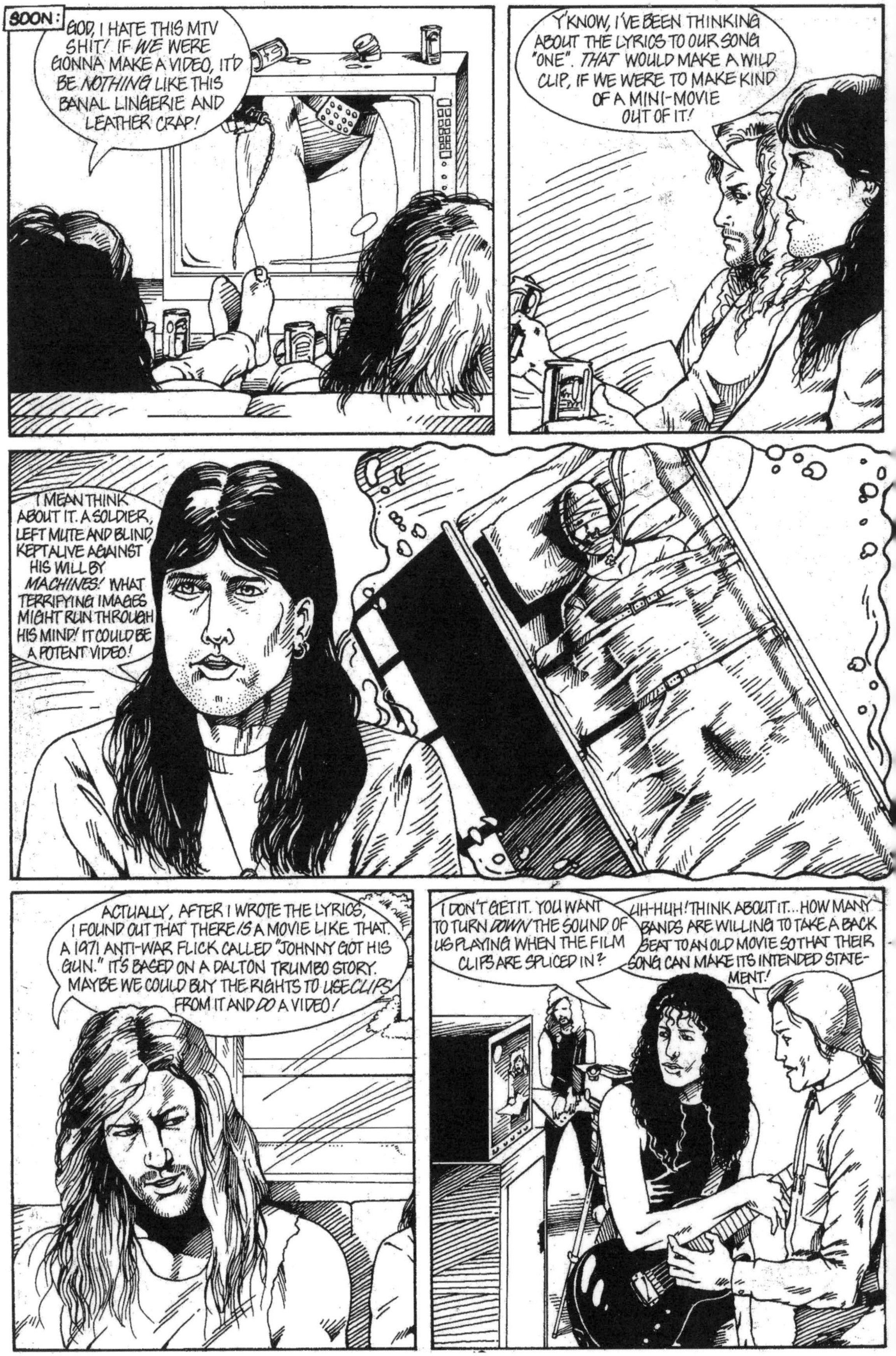
SOON:
GOD, I HATE THIS MTV SHIT! IF WE WERE GONNA MAKE A VIDEO, IT'D BE NOTHING LIKE THIS BANAL LINGERIE AND LEATHER CRAP!
Y'KNOW, I'VE BEEN THINKING ABOUT THE LYRICS TO OUR SONG "ONE". THAT WOULD MAKE A WILD CLIP, IF WE WERE TO MAKE KIND OF A MINI-MOVIE OUT OF IT!
I MEAN THINK ABOUT IT. A SOLDIER, LEFT MUTE AND BLIND, KEPT ALIVE AGAINST HIS WILL BY MACHINES! WHAT TERRIFYING IMAGES MIGHT RUN THROUGH HIS MIND! IT COULD BE A POTENT VIDEO!
ACTUALLY, AFTER I WROTE THE LYRICS, I FOUND OUT THAT THERE IS A MOVIE LIKE THAT. A 1971 ANTI-WAR FLICK CALLED "JOHNNY GOT HIS GUN." IT'S BASED ON A DALTON TRUMBO STORY. MAYBE WE COULD BUY THE RIGHTS TO USE CLIPS FROM IT AND DO A VIDEO!
I DON'T GET IT. YOU WANT TO TURN DOWN THE SOUND OF US PLAYING WHEN THE FILM CLIPS ARE SPLICED IN?
UH-HUH! THINK ABOUT IT... HOW MANY BANDS ARE WILLING TO TAKE A BACK SEAT TO AN OLD MOVIE SO THAT THEIR SONG CAN MAKE ITS INTENDED STATEMENT!

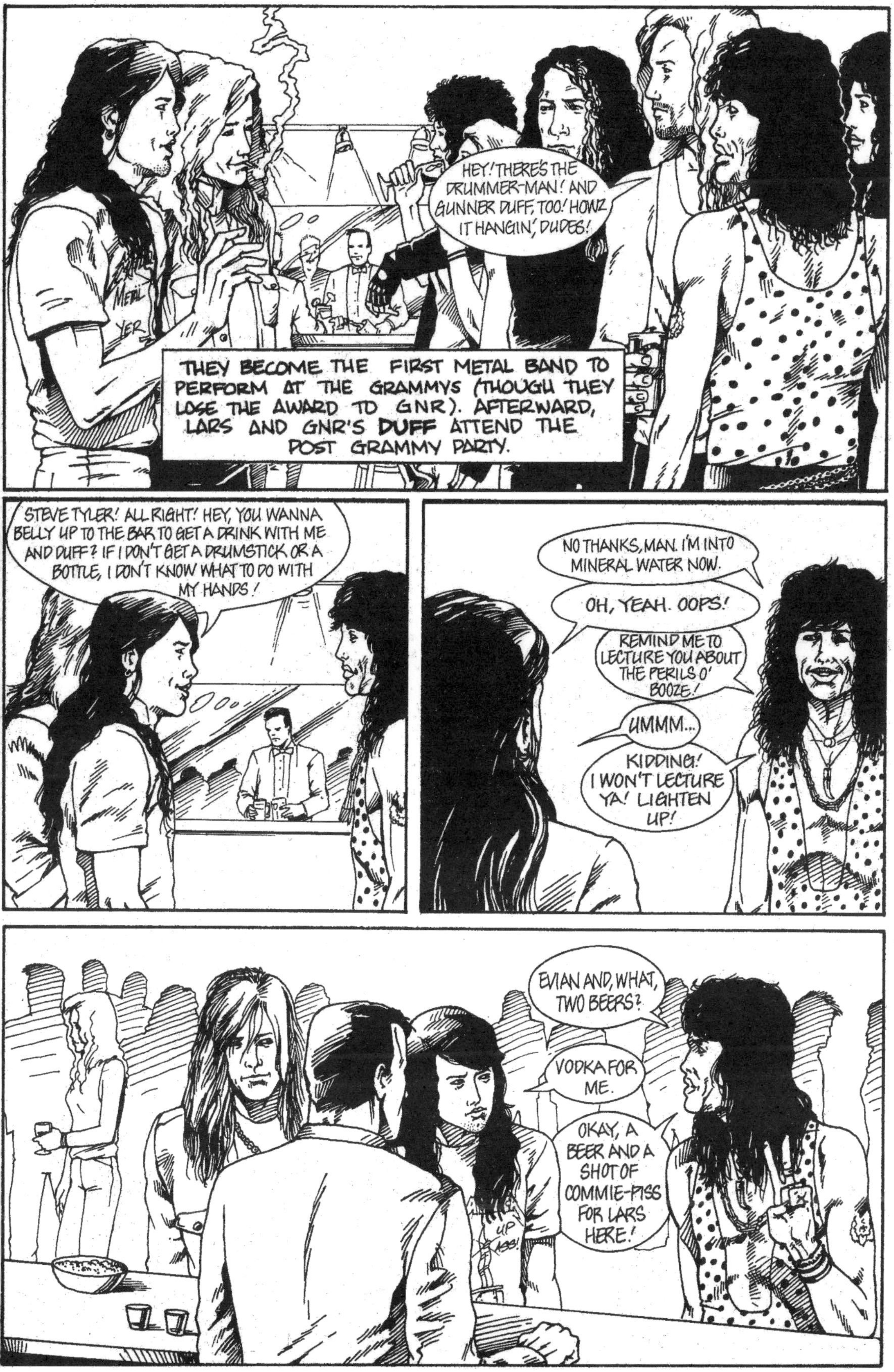

HEY! THERE'S THE DRUMMER-MAN! AND GUNNER DUFF, TOO! HOWZ IT HANGIN', DUDES!
THEY BECOME THE FIRST METAL BAND TO PERFORM AT THE GRAMMYS (THOUGH THEY LOSE THE AWARD TO GNR). AFTERWARD, LARS AND GNR'S DUFF ATTEND THE POST GRAMMY PARTY.
STEVE TYLER! ALL RIGHT! HEY, YOU WANNA BELLY UP TO THE BAR TO GET A DRINK WITH ME AND DUFF? IF I DON'T GET A DRUMSTICK OR A BOTTLE, I DON'T KNOW WHAT TO DO WITH MY HANDS!
NO THANKS, MAN. I'M INTO MINERAL WATER NOW.
OH, YEAH. OOPS!
REMIND ME TO LECTURE YOU ABOUT THE PERILS O' BOOZE!
UMMM...
KIDDING! I WON'T LECTURE YA! LIGHTEN UP!
EVIAN AND, WHAT, TWO BEERS?
VODKA FOR ME.
OKAY, A BEER AND A SHOT OF COMMIE-PISS FOR LARS HERE!

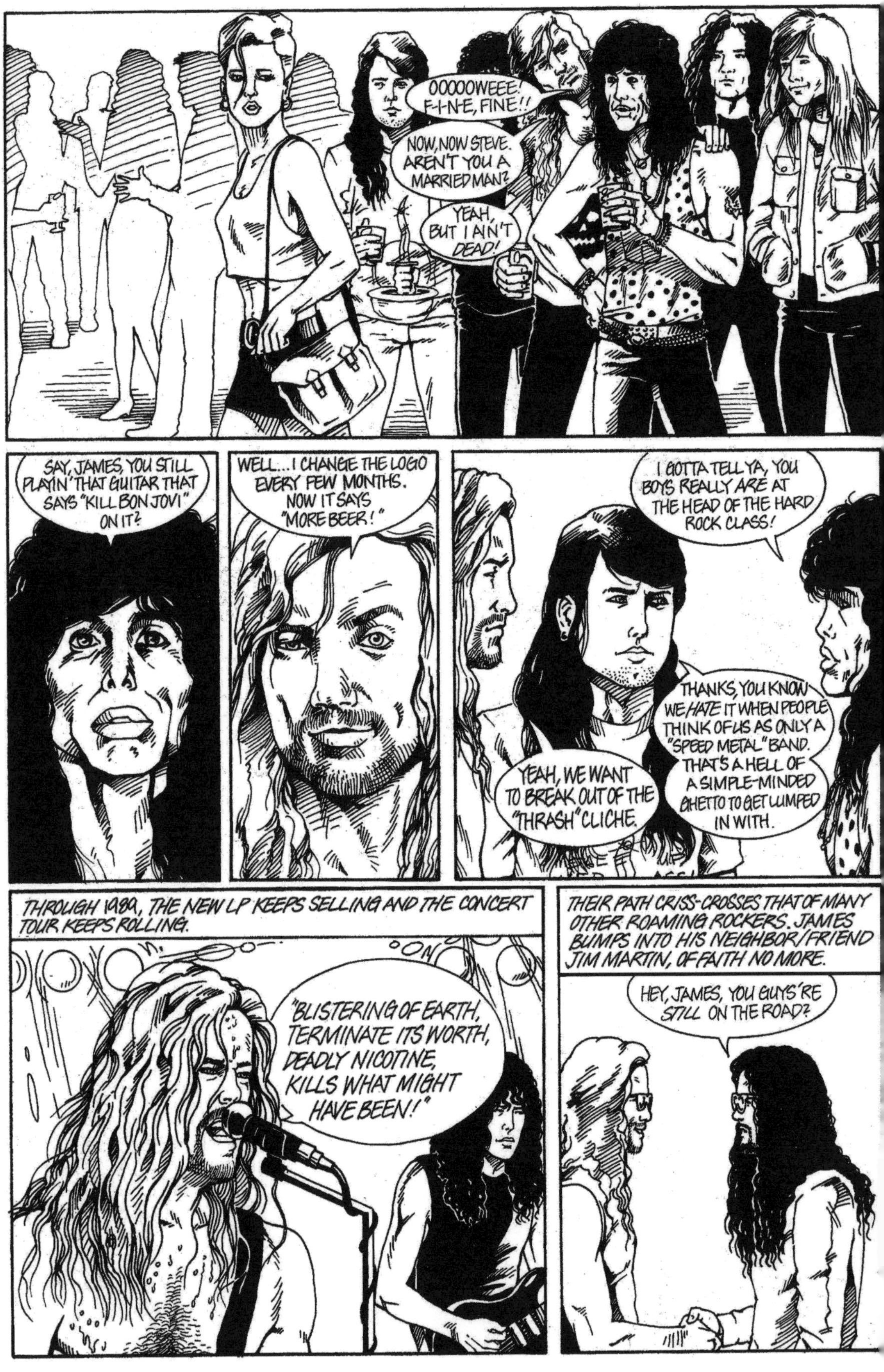
OOOOOWEEE! F-I-N-E, FINE!!
NOW, NOW STEVE. AREN'T YOU A MARRIED MAN?
YEAH, BUT I AIN'T *DEAD!*
SAY, JAMES, YOU STILL PLAYIN' THAT GUITAR THAT SAYS "KILL BON JOVI" ON IT?
WELL... I CHANGE THE LOGO EVERY FEW MONTHS. NOW IT SAYS "MORE BEER!"
I GOTTA TELL YA, YOU BOYS REALLY *ARE* AT THE HEAD OF THE HARD ROCK CLASS!
THANKS, YOU KNOW WE *HATE* IT WHEN PEOPLE THINK OF US AS ONLY A "SPEED METAL" BAND. THAT'S A HELL OF A SIMPLE-MINDED GHETTO TO GET LUMPED IN WITH.
YEAH, WE WANT TO BREAK OUT OF THE "THRASH" CLICHE.
THROUGH 1989, THE NEW LP KEEPS SELLING AND THE CONCERT TOUR KEEPS ROLLING.
"BLISTERING OF EARTH, TERMINATE ITS WORTH, DEADLY NICOTINE, KILLS WHAT MIGHT HAVE BEEN!"
THEIR PATH CRISS-CROSSES THAT OF MANY OTHER ROAMING ROCKERS. JAMES BUMPS INTO HIS NEIGHBOR/FRIEND JIM MARTIN, OF FAITH NO MORE.
HEY, JAMES, YOU GUYS'RE *STILL* ON THE ROAD?

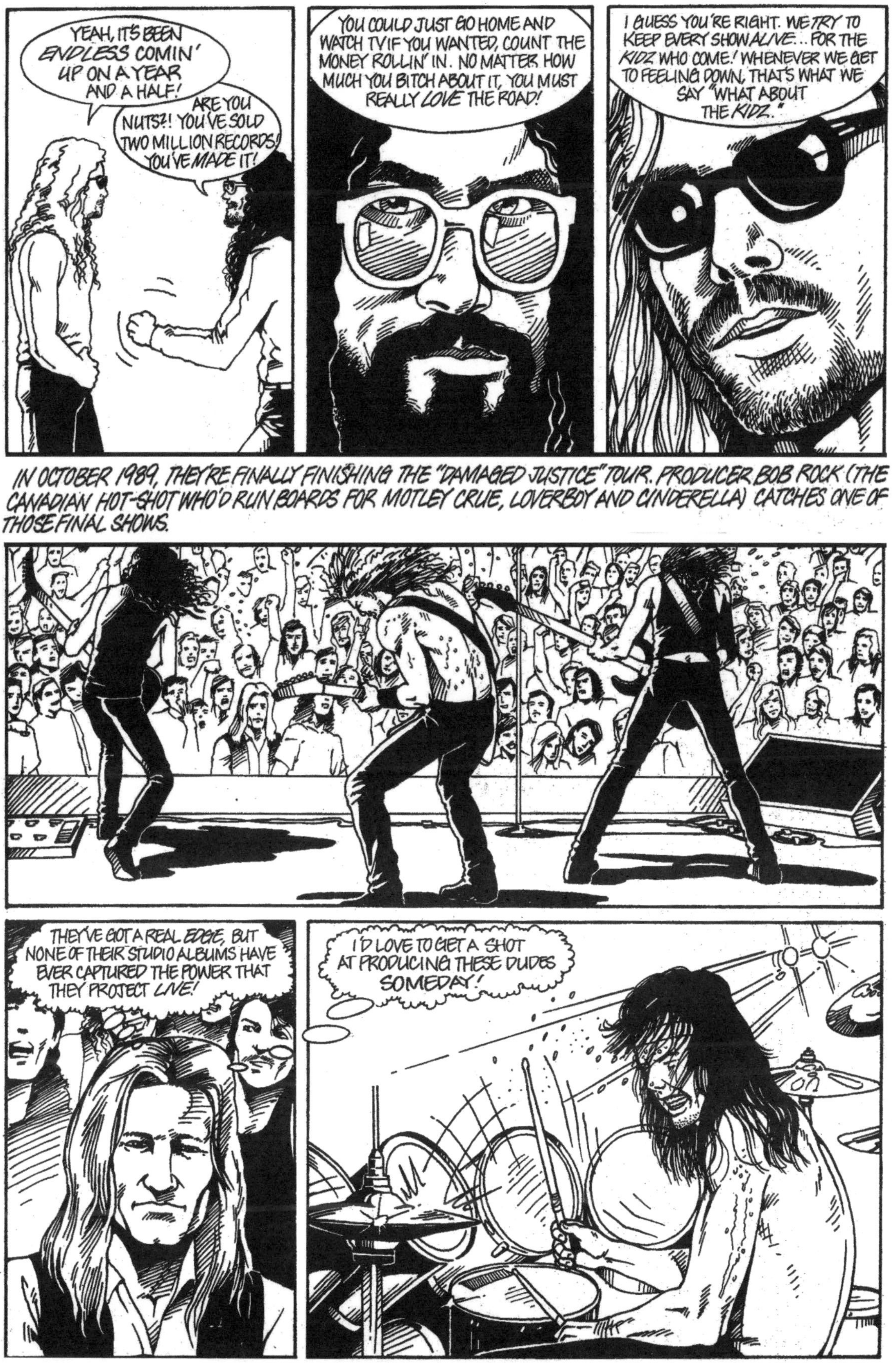
YEAH, IT'S BEEN ENDLESS COMIN' UP ON A YEAR AND A HALF!
ARE YOU NUTS?! YOU'VE SOLD TWO MILLION RECORDS! YOU'VE MADE IT!
YOU COULD JUST GO HOME AND WATCH TV IF YOU WANTED, COUNT THE MONEY ROLLIN' IN. NO MATTER HOW MUCH YOU BITCH ABOUT IT, YOU MUST REALLY LOVE THE ROAD!
I GUESS YOU'RE RIGHT. WE TRY TO KEEP EVERY SHOW ALIVE... FOR THE KIDZ WHO COME! WHENEVER WE GET TO FEELING DOWN, THAT'S WHAT WE SAY "WHAT ABOUT THE KIDZ."
IN OCTOBER 1989, THEY'RE FINALLY FINISHING THE "DAMAGED JUSTICE" TOUR. PRODUCER BOB ROCK (THE CANADIAN HOT-SHOT WHO'D RUN BOARDS FOR MOTLEY CRUE, LOVERBOY AND CINDERELLA) CATCHES ONE OF THOSE FINAL SHOWS.
THEY'VE GOT A REAL EDGE, BUT NONE OF THEIR STUDIO ALBUMS HAVE EVER CAPTURED THE POWER THAT THEY PROJECT LIVE!
I'D LOVE TO GET A SHOT AT PRODUCING THESE DUDES SOMEDAY!

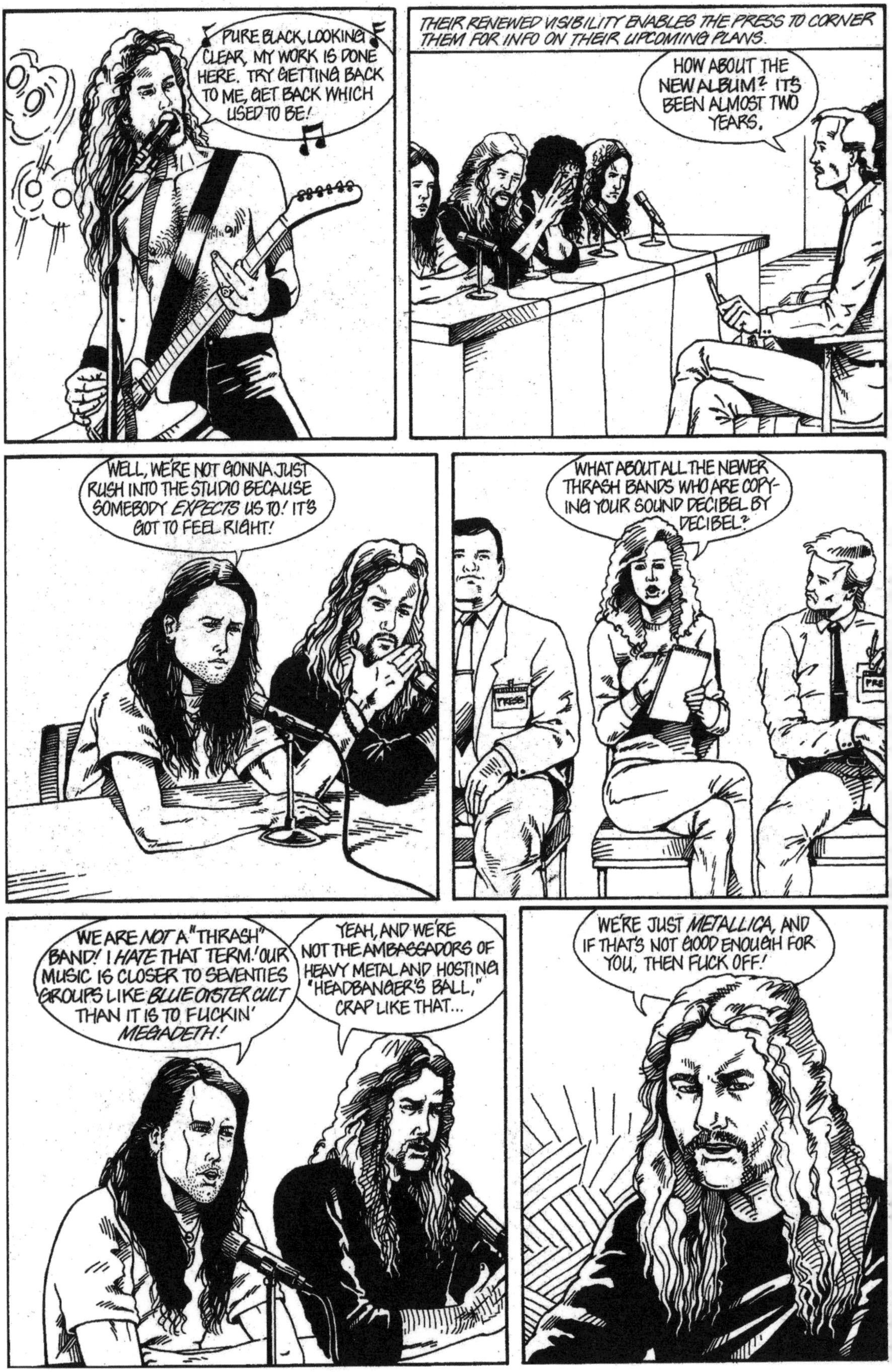
PURE BLACK, LOOKING CLEAR, MY WORK IS DONE HERE. TRY GETTING BACK TO ME, GET BACK WHICH USED TO BE!
THEIR RENEWED VISIBILITY ENABLES THE PRESS TO CORNER THEM FOR INFO ON THEIR UPCOMING PLANS.
HOW ABOUT THE NEW ALBUM? IT'S BEEN ALMOST TWO YEARS.
WELL, WE'RE NOT GONNA JUST RUSH INTO THE STUDIO BECAUSE SOMEBODY EXPECTS US TO! IT'S GOT TO FEEL RIGHT!
WHAT ABOUT ALL THE NEWER THRASH BANDS WHO ARE COPYING YOUR SOUND DECIBEL BY DECIBEL?
PRESS
WE ARE NOT A "THRASH" BAND! I HATE THAT TERM! OUR MUSIC IS CLOSER TO SEVENTIES GROUPS LIKE BLUE OYSTER CULT THAN IT IS TO FUCKIN' MEGADETH!
YEAH, AND WE'RE NOT THE AMBASSADORS OF HEAVY METAL AND HOSTING "HEADBANGER'S BALL," CRAP LIKE THAT...
WE'RE JUST METALLICA, AND IF THAT'S NOT GOOD ENOUGH FOR YOU, THEN FUCK OFF!

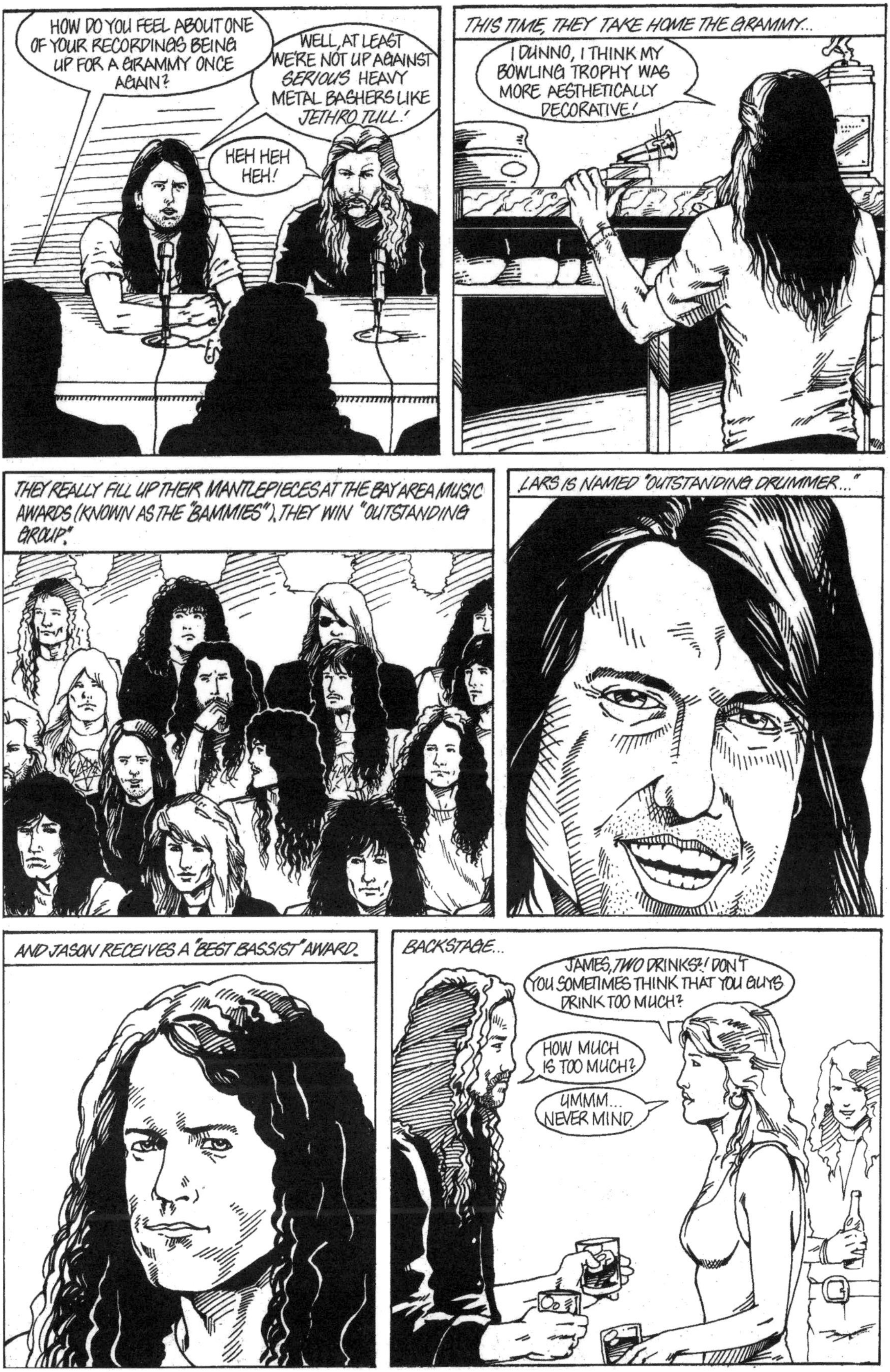
HOW DO YOU FEEL ABOUT ONE OF YOUR RECORDINGS BEING UP FOR A GRAMMY ONCE AGAIN?
WELL, AT LEAST WE'RE NOT UP AGAINST SERIOUS HEAVY METAL BASHERS LIKE JETHRO TULL!
HEH HEH HEH!
THIS TIME, THEY TAKE HOME THE GRAMMY...
I DUNNO, I THINK MY BOWLING TROPHY WAS MORE AESTHETICALLY DECORATIVE!
THEY REALLY FILL UP THEIR MANTLEPIECES AT THE BAY AREA MUSIC AWARDS (KNOWN AS THE "BAMMIES"). THEY WIN "OUTSTANDING GROUP".
LARS IS NAMED "OUTSTANDING DRUMMER..."
AND JASON RECEIVES A "BEST BASSIST" AWARD.
BACKSTAGE...
JAMES, TWO DRINKS?! DON'T YOU SOMETIMES THINK THAT YOU GUYS DRINK TOO MUCH?
HOW MUCH IS TOO MUCH?
UMMM... NEVER MIND.

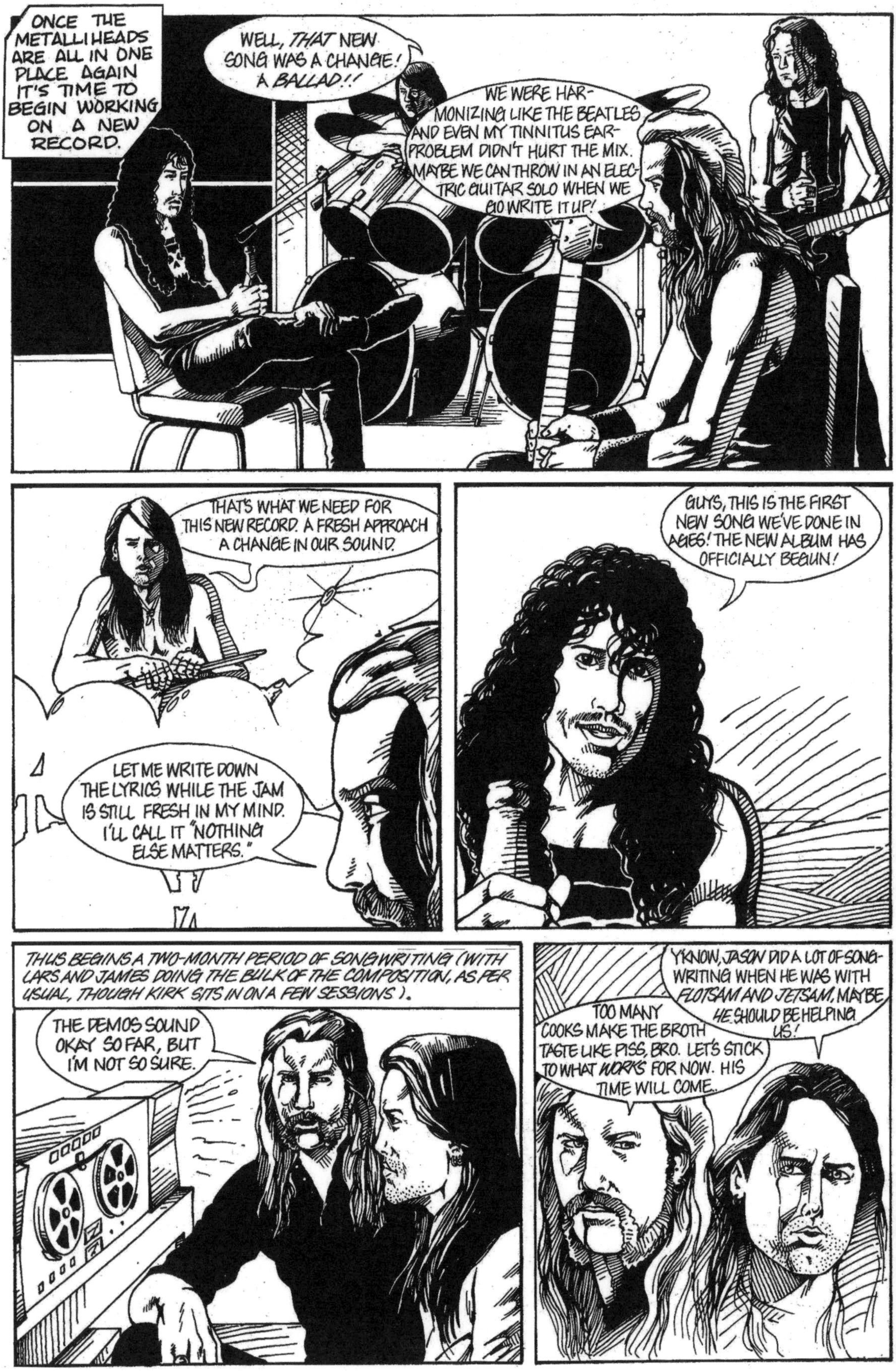
ONCE THE METALLIHEADS ARE ALL IN ONE PLACE AGAIN IT'S TIME TO BEGIN WORKING ON A NEW RECORD.
WELL, *THAT* NEW SONG WAS A CHANGE! A *BALLAD*!!
WE WERE HARMONIZING LIKE THE BEATLES AND EVEN MY TINNITUS EAR-PROBLEM DIDN'T HURT THE MIX. MAYBE WE CAN THROW IN AN ELECTRIC GUITAR SOLO WHEN WE GO WRITE IT UP!
THAT'S WHAT WE NEED FOR THIS NEW RECORD. A FRESH APPROACH A CHANGE IN OUR SOUND.
LET ME WRITE DOWN THE LYRICS WHILE THE JAM IS STILL FRESH IN MY MIND. I'LL CALL IT "NOTHING ELSE MATTERS."
GUYS, THIS IS THE FIRST NEW SONG WE'VE DONE IN AGES! THE NEW ALBUM HAS OFFICIALLY BEGUN!
THUS BEGINS A TWO-MONTH PERIOD OF SONGWRITING (WITH LARS AND JAMES DOING THE BULK OF THE COMPOSITION, AS PER USUAL, THOUGH KIRK SITS IN ON A FEW SESSIONS).
THE DEMOS SOUND OKAY SO FAR, BUT I'M NOT SO SURE.
Y'KNOW, JASON DID A LOT OF SONGWRITING WHEN HE WAS WITH *FLOTSAM AND JETSAM*. MAYBE *HE* SHOULD BE HELPING US!
TOO MANY COOKS MAKE THE BROTH TASTE LIKE PISS, BRO. LET'S STICK TO WHAT *WORKS* FOR NOW. HIS TIME WILL COME.

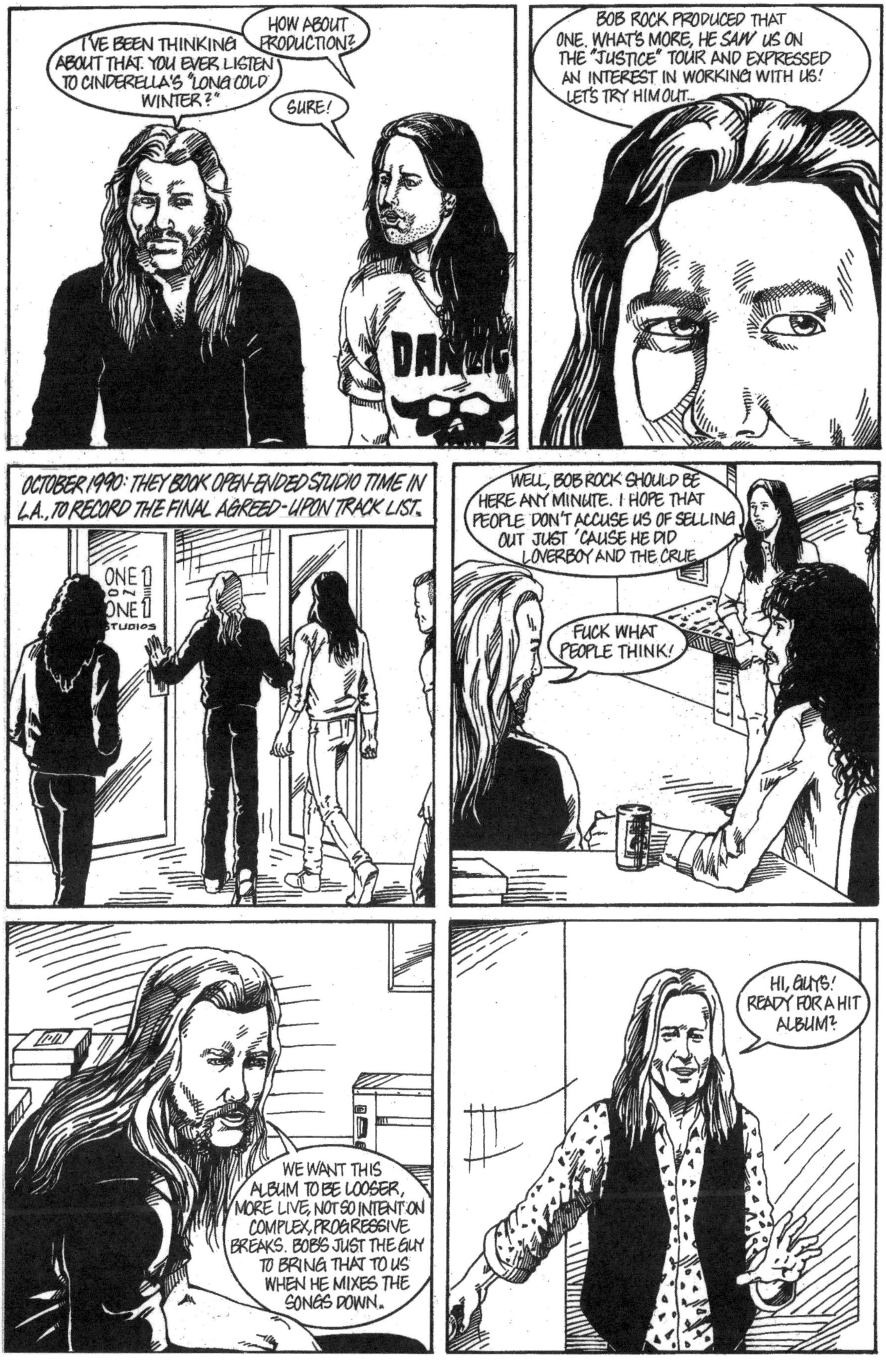
I'VE BEEN THINKING ABOUT THAT. YOU EVER LISTEN TO CINDERELLA'S "LONG COLD WINTER?"
HOW ABOUT PRODUCTION?
SURE!
BOB ROCK PRODUCED THAT ONE. WHAT'S MORE, HE SAW US ON THE "JUSTICE" TOUR AND EXPRESSED AN INTEREST IN WORKING WITH US! LET'S TRY HIM OUT...
DANZIG
OCTOBER 1990: THEY BOOK OPEN-ENDED STUDIO TIME IN L.A., TO RECORD THE FINAL AGREED-UPON TRACK LIST.
ONE ON ONE STUDIOS
WELL, BOB ROCK SHOULD BE HERE ANY MINUTE. I HOPE THAT PEOPLE DON'T ACCUSE US OF SELLING OUT JUST 'CAUSE HE DID LOVERBOY AND THE CRUE.
FUCK WHAT PEOPLE THINK!
WE WANT THIS ALBUM TO BE LOOSER, MORE LIVE, NOT SO INTENT ON COMPLEX, PROGRESSIVE BREAKS. BOB'S JUST THE GUY TO BRING THAT TO US WHEN HE MIXES THE SONGS DOWN.
HI, GUYS! READY FOR A HIT ALBUM?

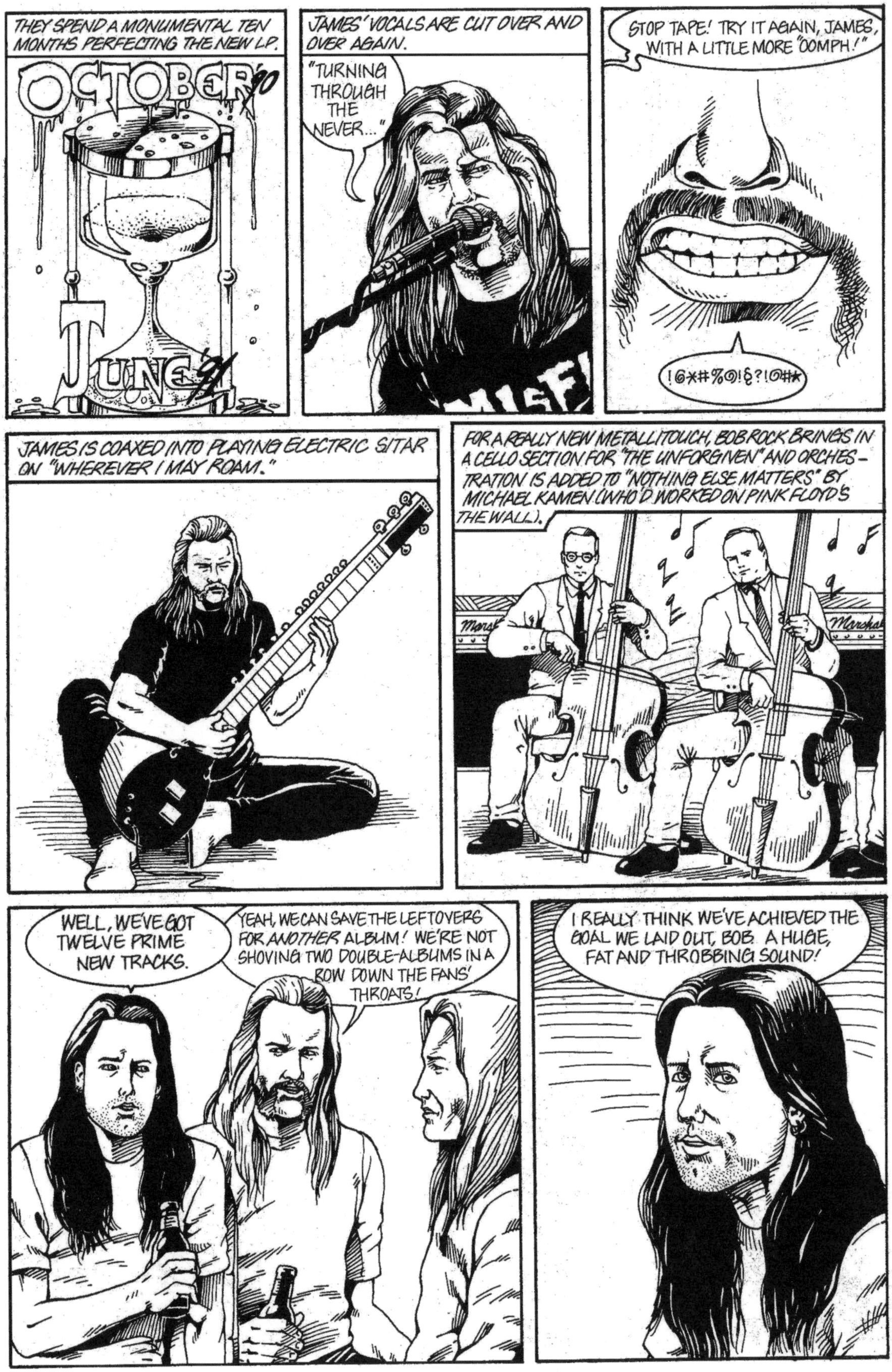
THEY SPEND A MONUMENTAL TEN MONTHS PERFECTING THE NEW LP.
OCTOBER '90
JUNE '91
JAMES' VOCALS ARE CUT OVER AND OVER AGAIN.
"TURNING THROUGH THE NEVER..."
STOP TAPE! TRY IT AGAIN, JAMES, WITH A LITTLE MORE "OOMPH!"
!@*#%@!§?!@#*
JAMES IS COAXED INTO PLAYING ELECTRIC SITAR ON "WHEREVER I MAY ROAM."
FOR A REALLY NEW METALLITOUCH, BOB ROCK BRINGS IN A CELLO SECTION FOR "THE UNFORGIVEN" AND ORCHESTRATION IS ADDED TO "NOTHING ELSE MATTERS" BY MICHAEL KAMEN (WHO'D WORKED ON PINK FLOYD'S THE WALL).
WELL, WE'VE GOT TWELVE PRIME NEW TRACKS.
YEAH, WE CAN SAVE THE LEFTOVERS FOR ANOTHER ALBUM! WE'RE NOT SHOVING TWO DOUBLE-ALBUMS IN A ROW DOWN THE FANS' THROATS!
I REALLY THINK WE'VE ACHIEVED THE GOAL WE LAID OUT, BOB. A HUGE, FAT AND THROBBING SOUND!

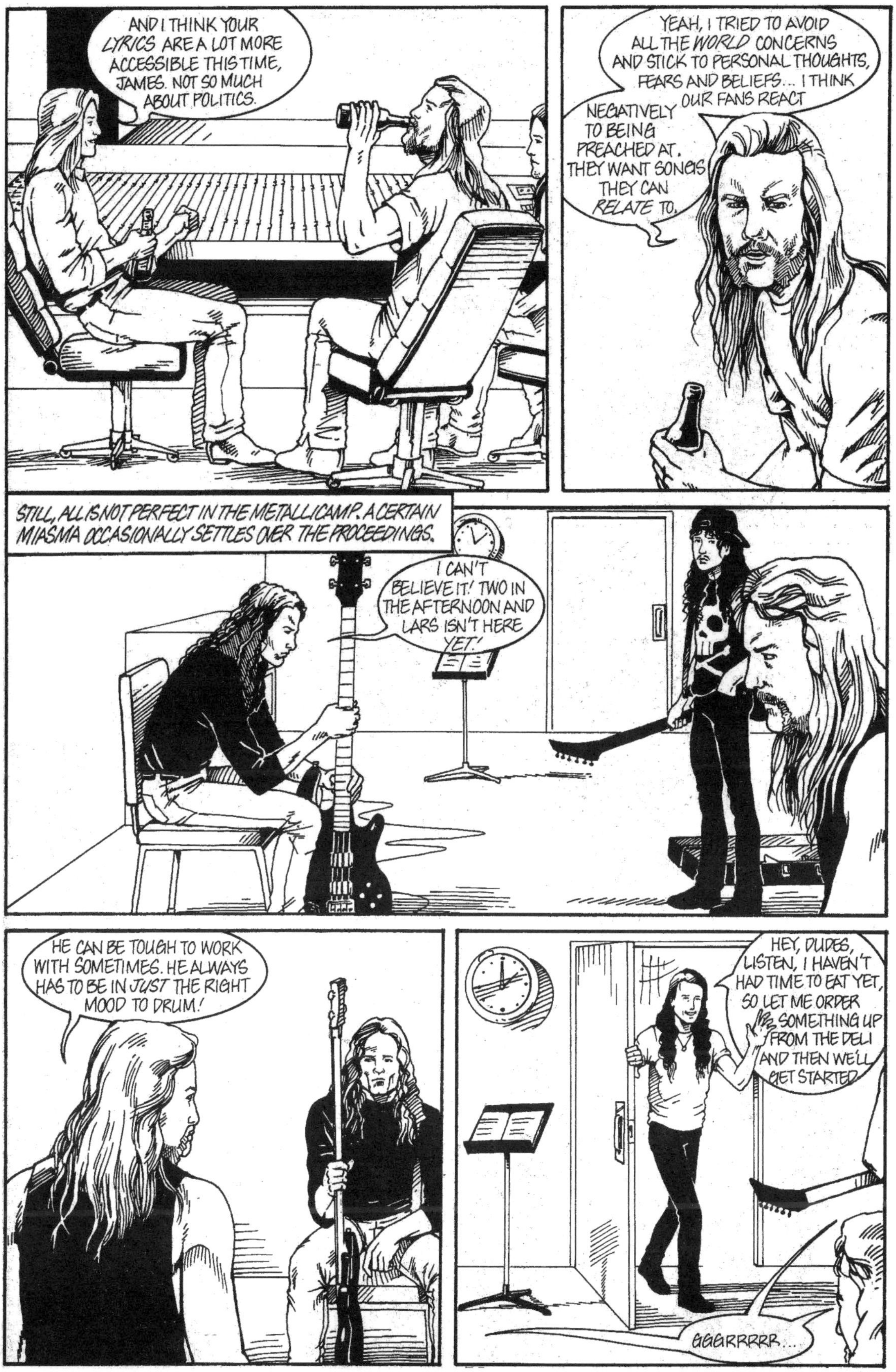
AND I THINK YOUR LYRICS ARE A LOT MORE ACCESSIBLE THIS TIME, JAMES. NOT SO MUCH ABOUT POLITICS.
YEAH, I TRIED TO AVOID ALL THE WORLD CONCERNS AND STICK TO PERSONAL THOUGHTS, FEARS AND BELIEFS... I THINK OUR FANS REACT
NEGATIVELY TO BEING PREACHED AT. THEY WANT SONGS THEY CAN RELATE TO.
STILL, ALL IS NOT PERFECT IN THE METALLICAMP. A CERTAIN MIASMA OCCASIONALLY SETTLES OVER THE PROCEEDINGS.
I CAN'T BELIEVE IT! TWO IN THE AFTERNOON AND LARS ISN'T HERE YET!
HE CAN BE TOUGH TO WORK WITH SOMETIMES. HE ALWAYS HAS TO BE IN JUST THE RIGHT MOOD TO DRUM!
HEY, DUDES, LISTEN, I HAVEN'T HAD TIME TO EAT YET, SO LET ME ORDER SOMETHING UP FROM THE DELI AND THEN WE'LL GET STARTED.
GGGRRRRR...

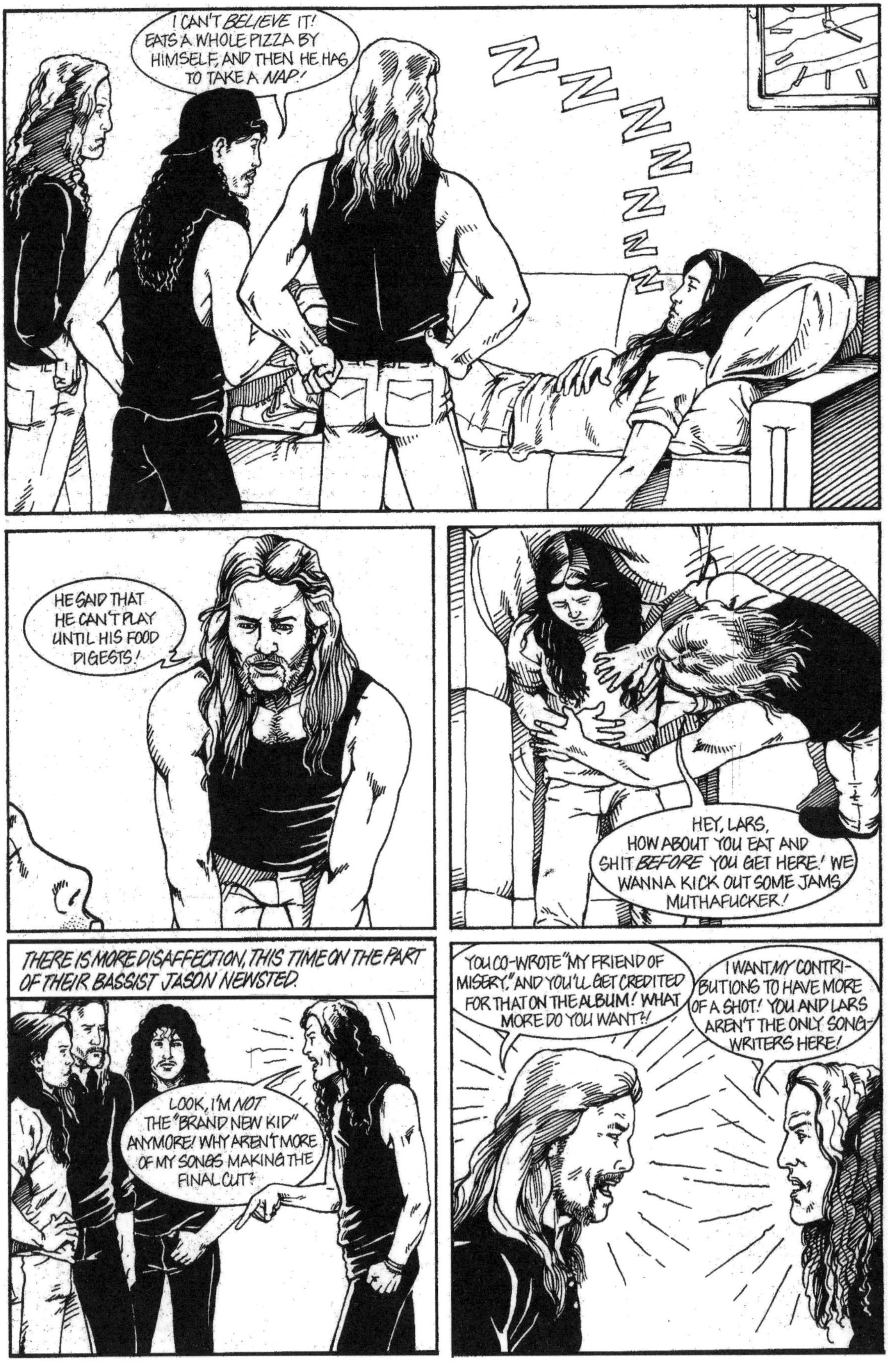

I CAN'T *BELIEVE* IT! EATS A WHOLE PIZZA BY HIMSELF, AND THEN HE HAS TO TAKE A *NAP*!
ZZZZZZZ
HE SAID THAT HE CAN'T PLAY UNTIL HIS FOOD DIGESTS!
HEY, LARS, HOW ABOUT YOU EAT AND SHIT *BEFORE* YOU GET HERE! WE WANNA KICK OUT SOME JAMS MUTHAFUCKER!
THERE IS MORE DISAFFECTION, THIS TIME ON THE PART OF THEIR BASSIST JASON NEWSTED.
LOOK, I'M *NOT* THE "BRAND NEW KID" ANYMORE! WHY AREN'T MORE OF MY SONGS MAKING THE FINAL CUT?
YOU CO-WROTE "MY FRIEND OF MISERY," AND YOU'LL GET CREDITED FOR THAT ON THE ALBUM! WHAT MORE DO YOU WANT?!
I WANT *MY* CONTRIBUTIONS TO HAVE MORE OF A SHOT! YOU AND LARS AREN'T THE ONLY SONGWRITERS HERE!

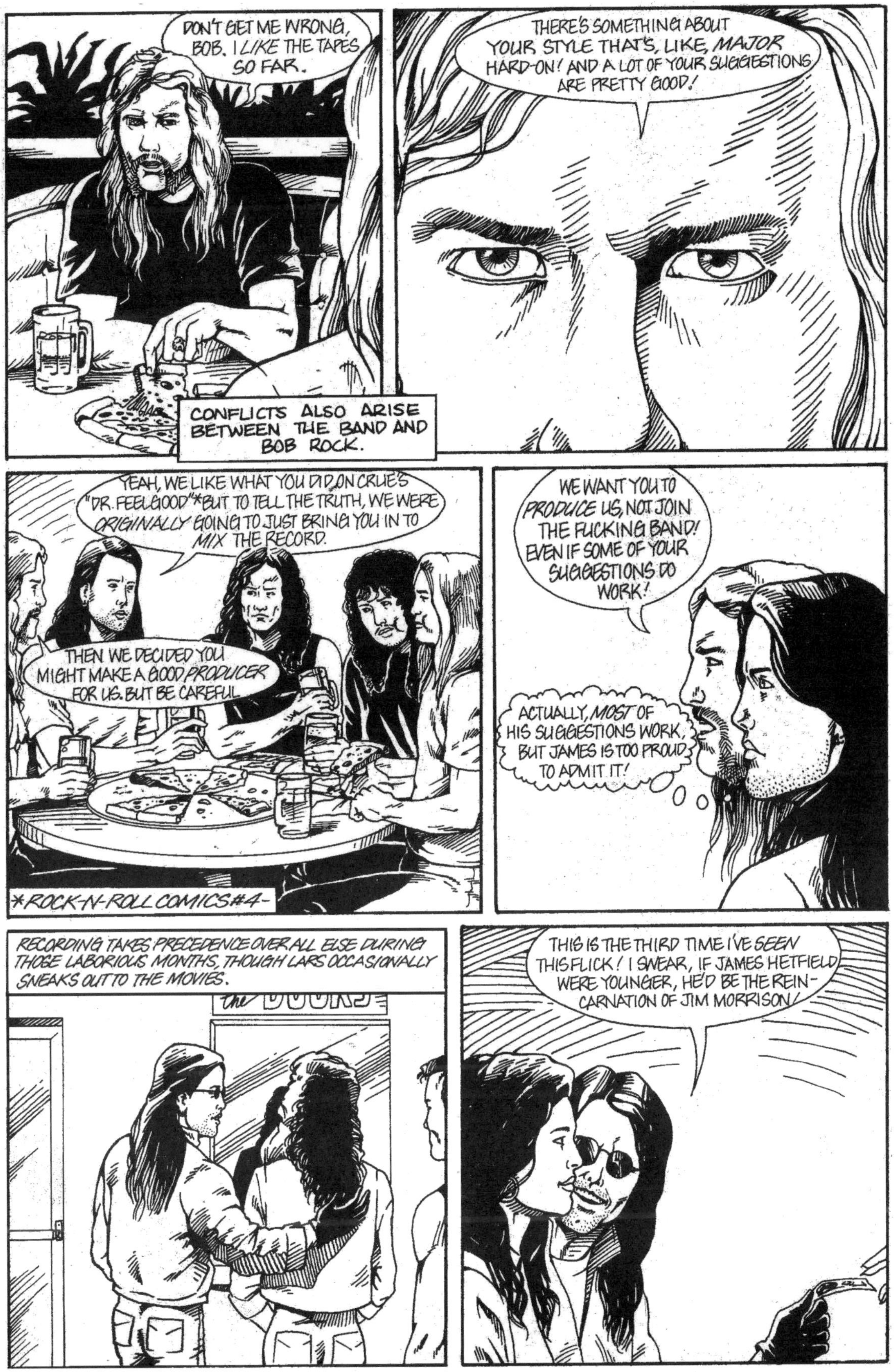
DON'T GET ME WRONG, BOB. I LIKE THE TAPES SO FAR.
CONFLICTS ALSO ARISE BETWEEN THE BAND AND BOB ROCK.
THERE'S SOMETHING ABOUT YOUR STYLE THAT'S, LIKE, MAJOR HARD-ON! AND A LOT OF YOUR SUGGESTIONS ARE PRETTY GOOD!
YEAH, WE LIKE WHAT YOU DID ON CRUE'S "DR. FEELGOOD"* BUT TO TELL THE TRUTH, WE WERE ORIGINALLY GOING TO JUST BRING YOU IN TO MIX THE RECORD.
THEN WE DECIDED YOU MIGHT MAKE A GOOD PRODUCER FOR US. BUT BE CAREFUL.
*ROCK-N-ROLL COMICS #4-
WE WANT YOU TO PRODUCE US, NOT JOIN THE FUCKING BAND! EVEN IF SOME OF YOUR SUGGESTIONS DO WORK!
ACTUALLY, MOST OF HIS SUGGESTIONS WORK, BUT JAMES IS TOO PROUD TO ADMIT IT!
RECORDING TAKES PRECEDENCE OVER ALL ELSE DURING THOSE LABORIOUS MONTHS, THOUGH LARS OCCASIONALLY SNEAKS OUT TO THE MOVIES.
THIS IS THE THIRD TIME I'VE SEEN THIS FLICK! I SWEAR, IF JAMES HETFIELD WERE YOUNGER, HE'D BE THE REIN-CARNATION OF JIM MORRISON!

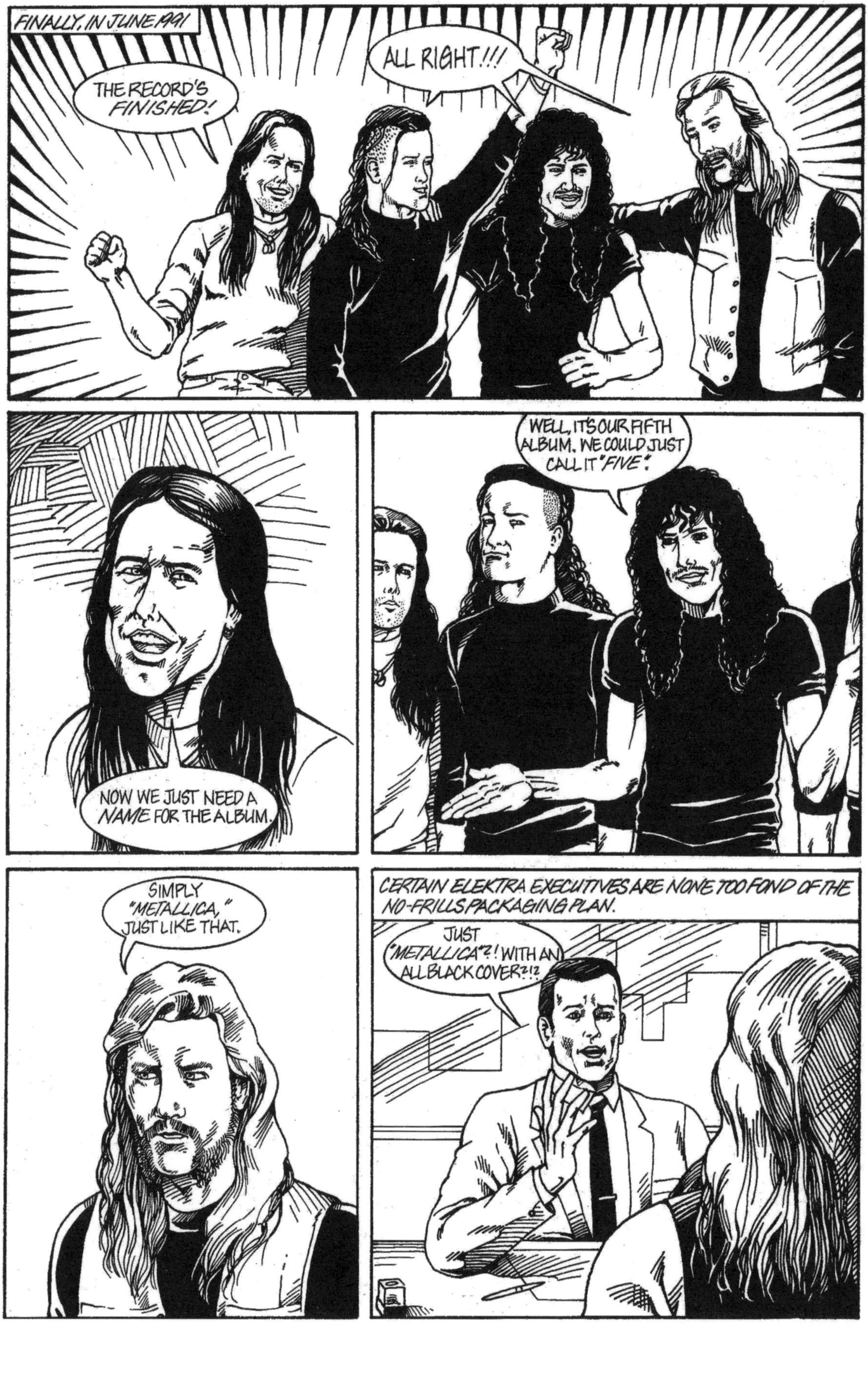
FINALLY, IN JUNE 1991
THE RECORD'S FINISHED!
ALL RIGHT!!!
NOW WE JUST NEED A NAME FOR THE ALBUM.
WELL, IT'S OUR FIFTH ALBUM. WE COULD JUST CALL IT "FIVE"!
SIMPLY "METALLICA," JUST LIKE THAT.
CERTAIN ELEKTRA EXECUTIVES ARE NONE TOO FOND OF THE NO-FRILLS PACKAGING PLAN.
JUST "METALLICA"?! WITH AN ALL BLACK COVER?!?

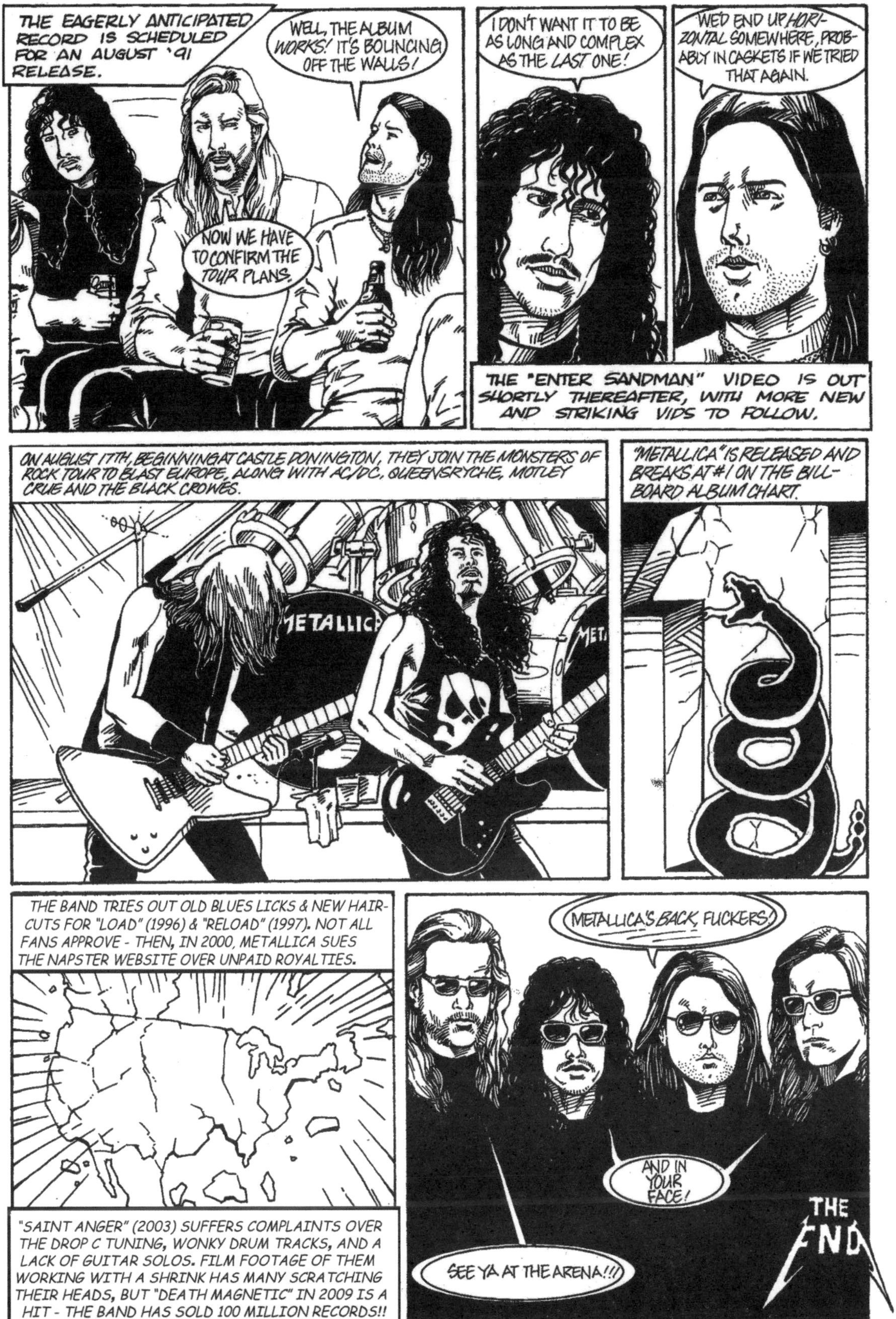
THE EAGERLY ANTICIPATED RECORD IS SCHEDULED FOR AN AUGUST '91 RELEASE.
WELL, THE ALBUM WORKS! IT'S BOUNCING OFF THE WALLS!
NOW WE HAVE TO CONFIRM THE TOUR PLANS.
I DON'T WANT IT TO BE AS LONG AND COMPLEX AS THE LAST ONE!
WE'D END UP HORIZONTAL SOMEWHERE, PROBABLY IN CASKETS IF WE TRIED THAT AGAIN.
THE "ENTER SANDMAN" VIDEO IS OUT SHORTLY THEREAFTER, WITH MORE NEW AND STRIKING VIDS TO FOLLOW.
ON AUGUST 17TH, BEGINNING AT CASTLE DONINGTON, THEY JOIN THE MONSTERS OF ROCK TOUR TO BLAST EUROPE, ALONG WITH AC/DC, QUEENSRYCHE, MOTLEY CRUE AND THE BLACK CROWES.
METALLICA
"METALLICA" IS RELEASED AND BREAKS AT #1 ON THE BILLBOARD ALBUM CHART.
THE BAND TRIES OUT OLD BLUES LICKS & NEW HAIRCUTS FOR "LOAD" (1996) & "RELOAD" (1997). NOT ALL FANS APPROVE - THEN, IN 2000, METALLICA SUES THE NAPSTER WEBSITE OVER UNPAID ROYALTIES.
"SAINT ANGER" (2003) SUFFERS COMPLAINTS OVER THE DROP C TUNING, WONKY DRUM TRACKS, AND A LACK OF GUITAR SOLOS. FILM FOOTAGE OF THEM WORKING WITH A SHRINK HAS MANY SCRATCHING THEIR HEADS, BUT "DEATH MAGNETIC" IN 2009 IS A HIT - THE BAND HAS SOLD 100 MILLION RECORDS!!
METALLICA'S BACK, FUCKERS!
AND IN YOUR FACE!
SEE YA AT THE ARENA!!!
THE END

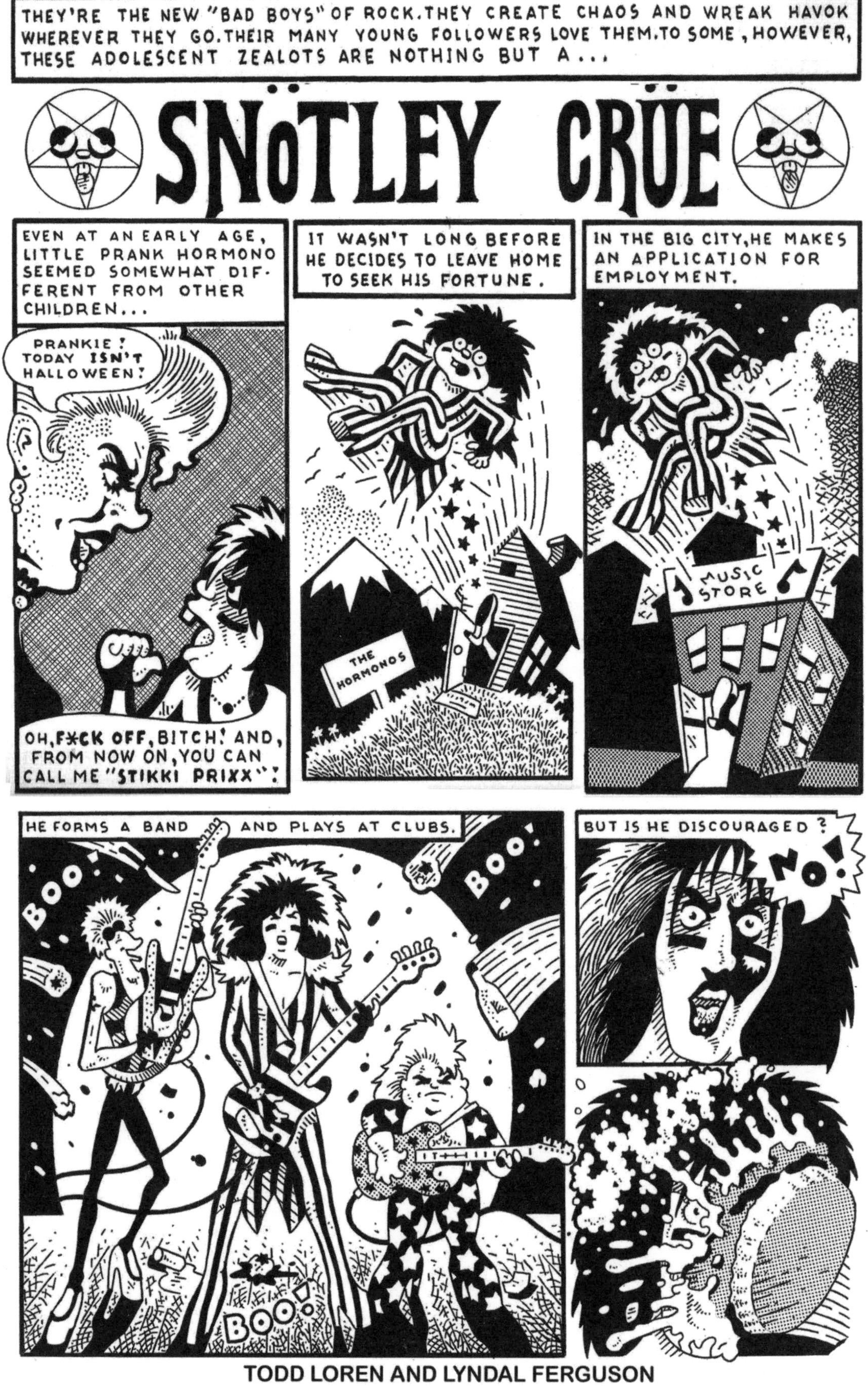
THEY'RE THE NEW "BAD BOYS" OF ROCK. THEY CREATE CHAOS AND WREAK HAVOK WHEREVER THEY GO. THEIR MANY YOUNG FOLLOWERS LOVE THEM. TO SOME, HOWEVER, THESE ADOLESCENT ZEALOTS ARE NOTHING BUT A...
SNöTLEY CRÜE
EVEN AT AN EARLY AGE, LITTLE PRANK HORMONO SEEMED SOMEWHAT DIFFERENT FROM OTHER CHILDREN...
PRANKIE! TODAY ISN'T HALLOWEEN!
OH, F*CK OFF, BITCH! AND, FROM NOW ON, YOU CAN CALL ME "STIKKI PRIXX"!
IT WASN'T LONG BEFORE HE DECIDES TO LEAVE HOME TO SEEK HIS FORTUNE.
THE HORMONOS
IN THE BIG CITY, HE MAKES AN APPLICATION FOR EMPLOYMENT.
MUSIC STORE
HE FORMS A BAND AND PLAYS AT CLUBS.
BOO!
BOO!
BOO!
BUT IS HE DISCOURAGED?
NO!

TODD LOREN AND LYNDAL FERGUSON

HE LEARNS TO SET HIMSELF ON FIRE.

HE SOON FORMS A NEW GROUP : SNÖTLEY CRÜE !

STIKKI PRIXX

BASS, HAIR SPRAY

SCUMMY FLEA

DRUMS, VACANT STARES

VINCE SQUEAL

VOCALS, PEROXIDE

MICK MARSBAR

LEAD GUITAR , MAX FACTOR CONSULTANT

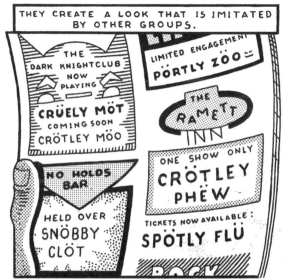

THEY CREATE A LOOK THAT IS IMITATED BY OTHER GROUPS.

THE DARK KNIGHTCLUB NOW PLAYING

CRÜELY MÖT COMING SOON CRÖTLEY MÖO

NO HOLDS BAR

HELD OVER SNÖBBY CLÖT

LIMITED ENGAGEMENT PÖRTLY ZÖO

THE RAMETT INN

ONE SHOW ONLY CRÖTLEY PHËW

TICKETS NOW AVAILABLE : SPÖTLY FLÜ

SOME PEOPLE THINK THEY **ARE** BAD.

THIS "SNÖTLEY CRÜE" IS A GROUP OF SATAN WORSHIPPERS.

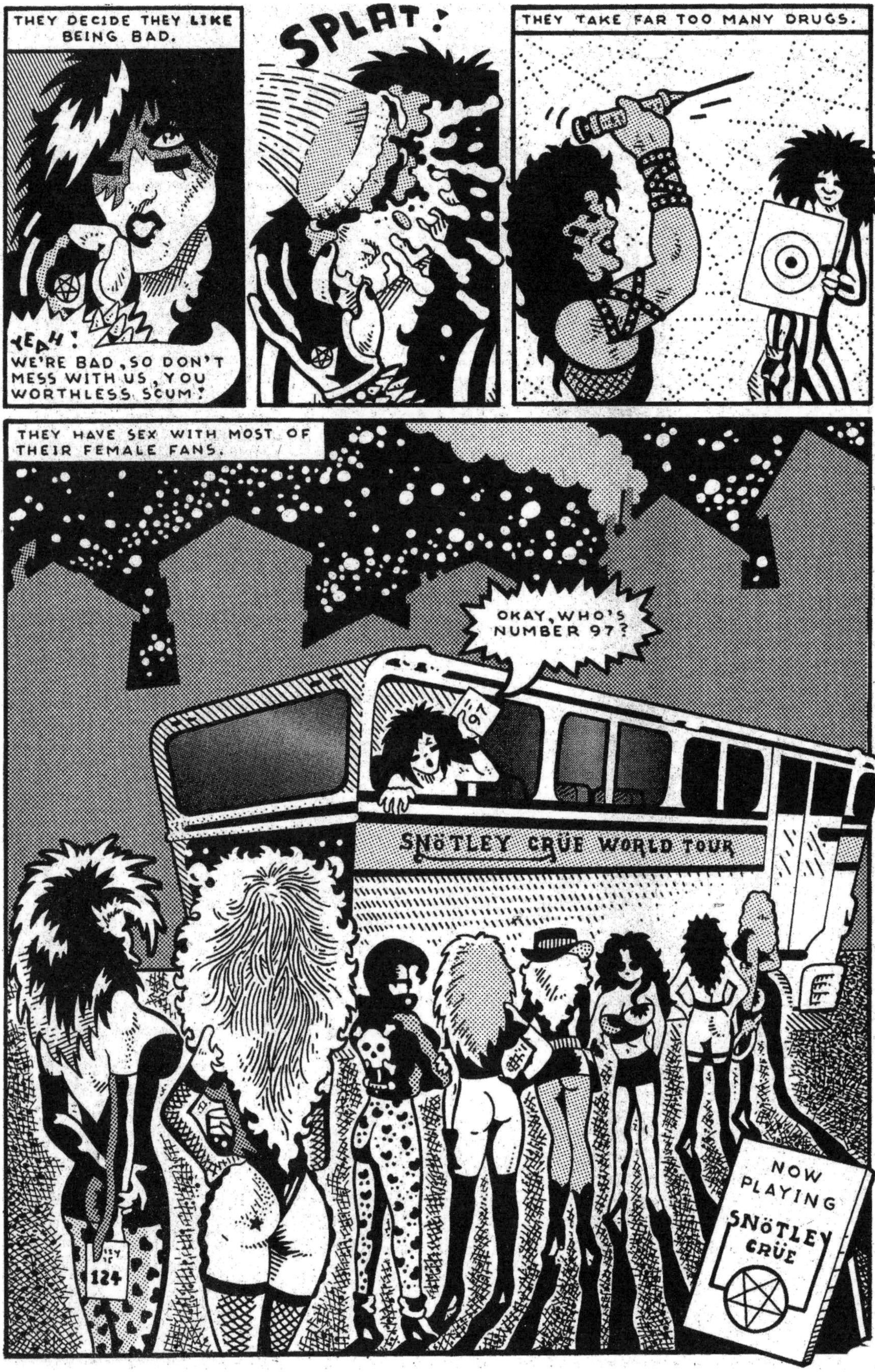
THEY DECIDE THEY LIKE BEING BAD.
YEAH!
WE'RE BAD, SO DON'T MESS WITH US, YOU WORTHLESS SCUM!
SPLAT!
THEY TAKE FAR TOO MANY DRUGS.
THEY HAVE SEX WITH MOST OF THEIR FEMALE FANS.
OKAY, WHO'S NUMBER 97?
97
SNöTLEY CRüE WORLD TOUR
124
NOW PLAYING SNöTLEY CRüE

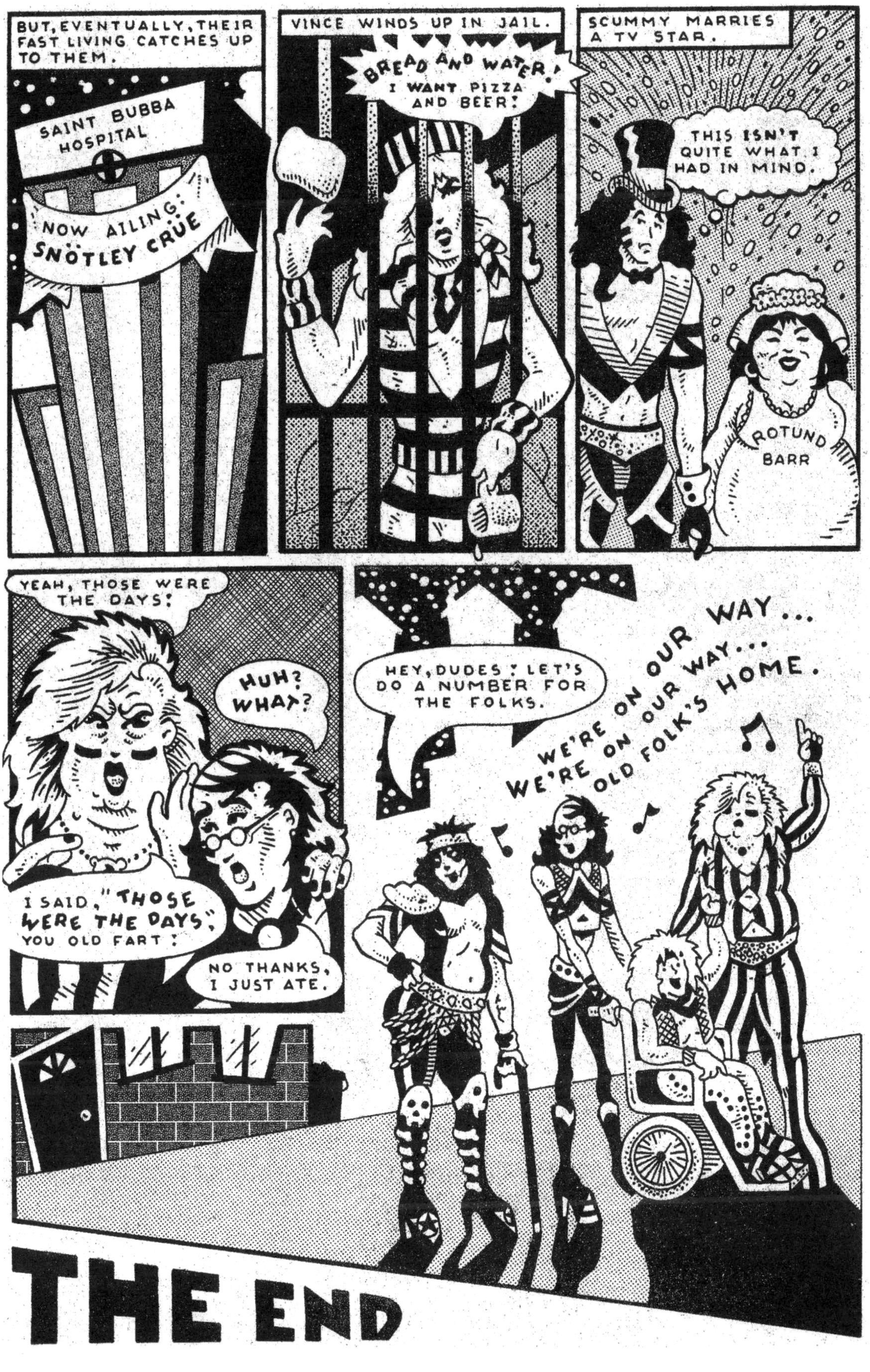
BUT, EVENTUALLY, THEIR FAST LIVING CATCHES UP TO THEM.
SAINT BUBBA HOSPITAL
NOW AILING: SNÖTLEY CRÜE
VINCE WINDS UP IN JAIL.
BREAD AND WATER! I WANT PIZZA AND BEER!
SCUMMY MARRIES A TV STAR.
THIS ISN'T QUITE WHAT I HAD IN MIND.
ROTUND BARR
YEAH, THOSE WERE THE DAYS!
HUH? WHAT?
I SAID, "THOSE WERE THE DAYS", YOU OLD FART!
NO THANKS, I JUST ATE.
HEY, DUDES! LET'S DO A NUMBER FOR THE FOLKS.
WE'RE ON OUR WAY...
WE'RE ON OUR WAY...
OLD FOLK'S HOME.
THE END

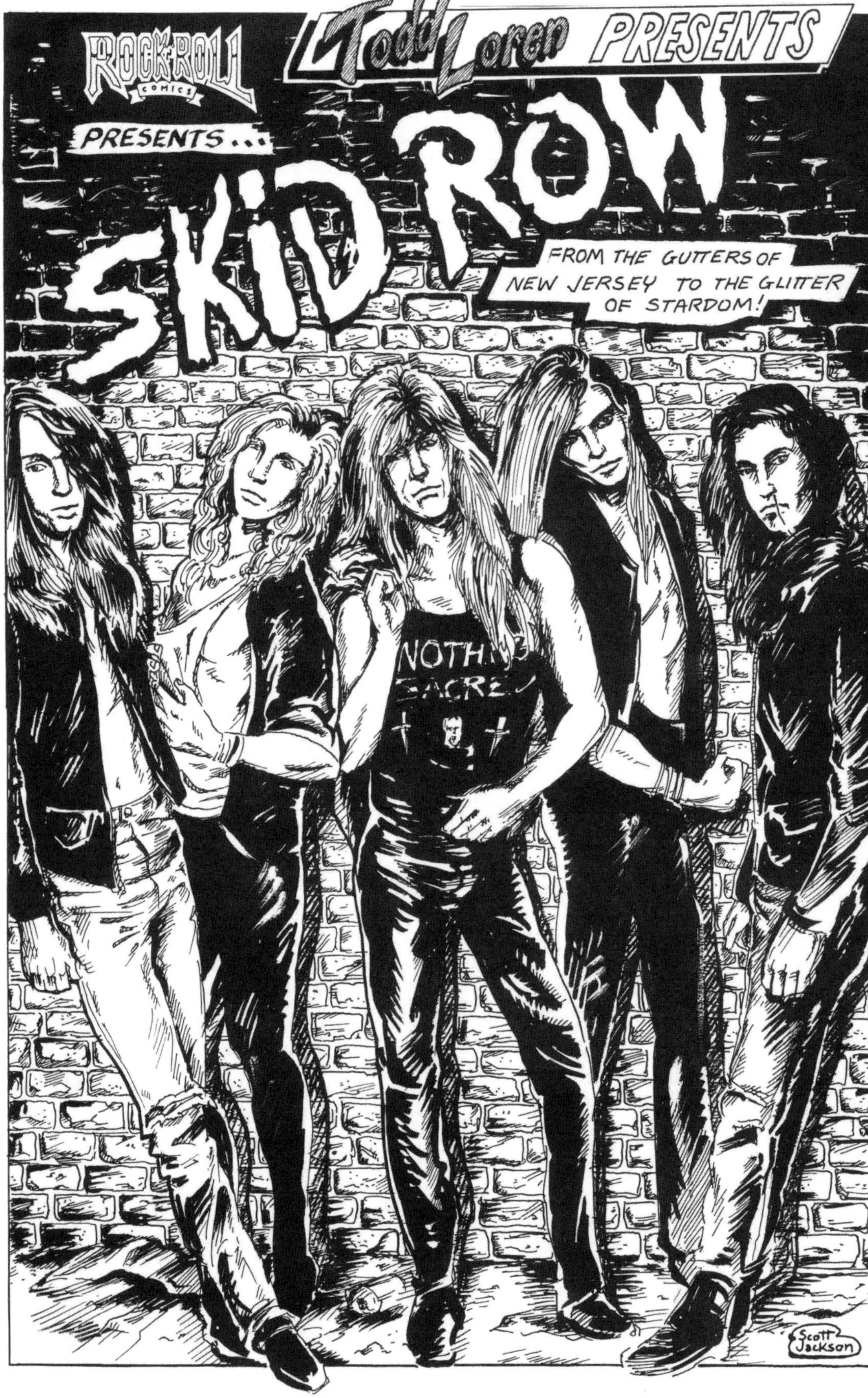
ROCK 'N' ROLL COMICS
Todd Loren PRESENTS
PRESENTS...
SKID ROW
FROM THE GUTTERS OF NEW JERSEY TO THE GLITTER OF STARDOM!
Scott Jackson

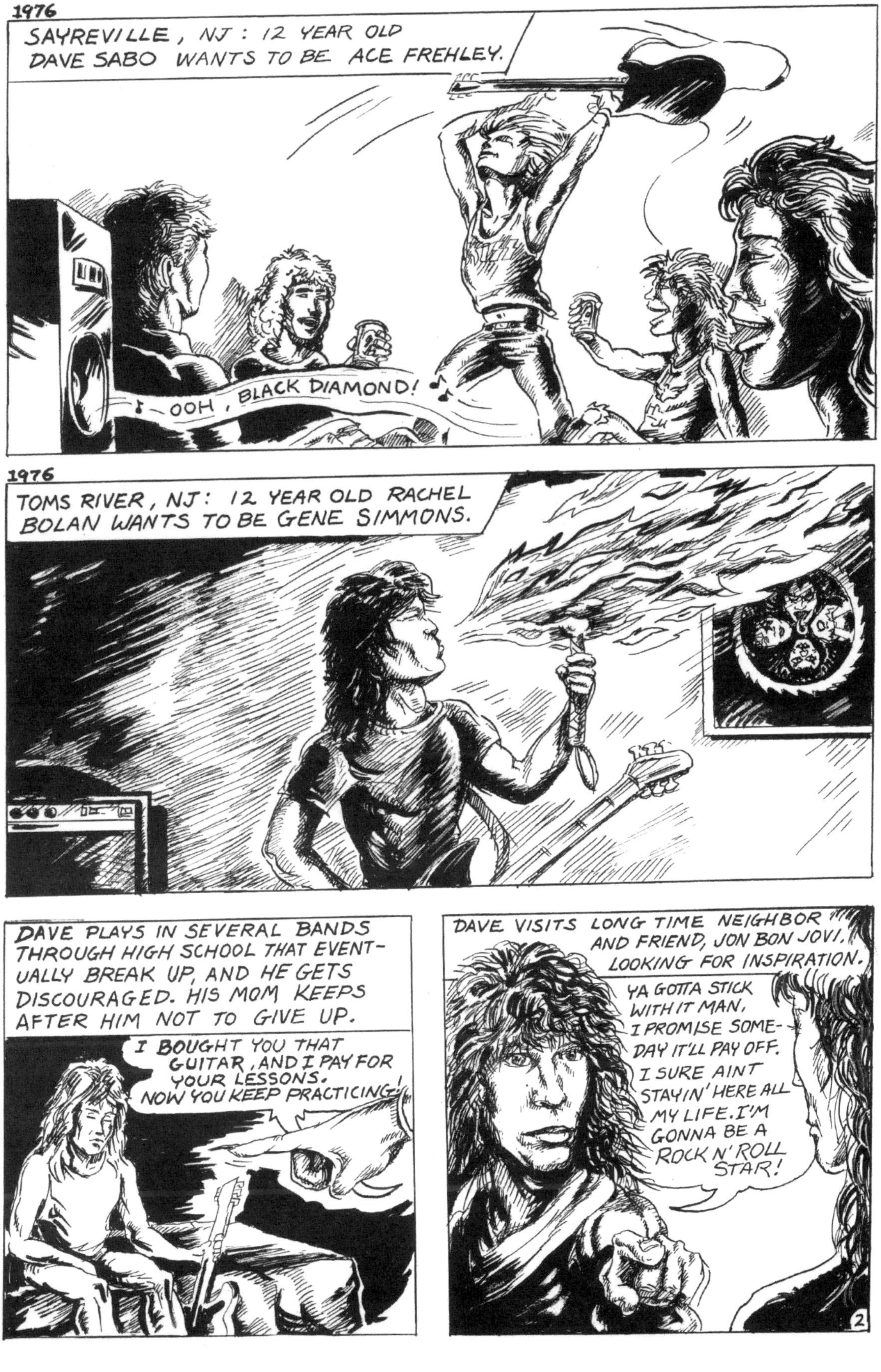
1976
SAYREVILLE, NJ: 12 YEAR OLD DAVE SABO WANTS TO BE ACE FREHLEY.
OOH, BLACK DIAMOND!
1976
TOMS RIVER, NJ: 12 YEAR OLD RACHEL BOLAN WANTS TO BE GENE SIMMONS.
DAVE PLAYS IN SEVERAL BANDS THROUGH HIGH SCHOOL THAT EVENTUALLY BREAK UP, AND HE GETS DISCOURAGED. HIS MOM KEEPS AFTER HIM NOT TO GIVE UP.
I BOUGHT YOU THAT GUITAR, AND I PAY FOR YOUR LESSONS. NOW YOU KEEP PRACTICING!
DAVE VISITS LONG TIME NEIGHBOR AND FRIEND, JON BON JOVI, LOOKING FOR INSPIRATION.
YA GOTTA STICK WITH IT MAN, I PROMISE SOMEDAY IT'LL PAY OFF. I SURE AINT STAYIN' HERE ALL MY LIFE. I'M GONNA BE A ROCK N' ROLL STAR!
2

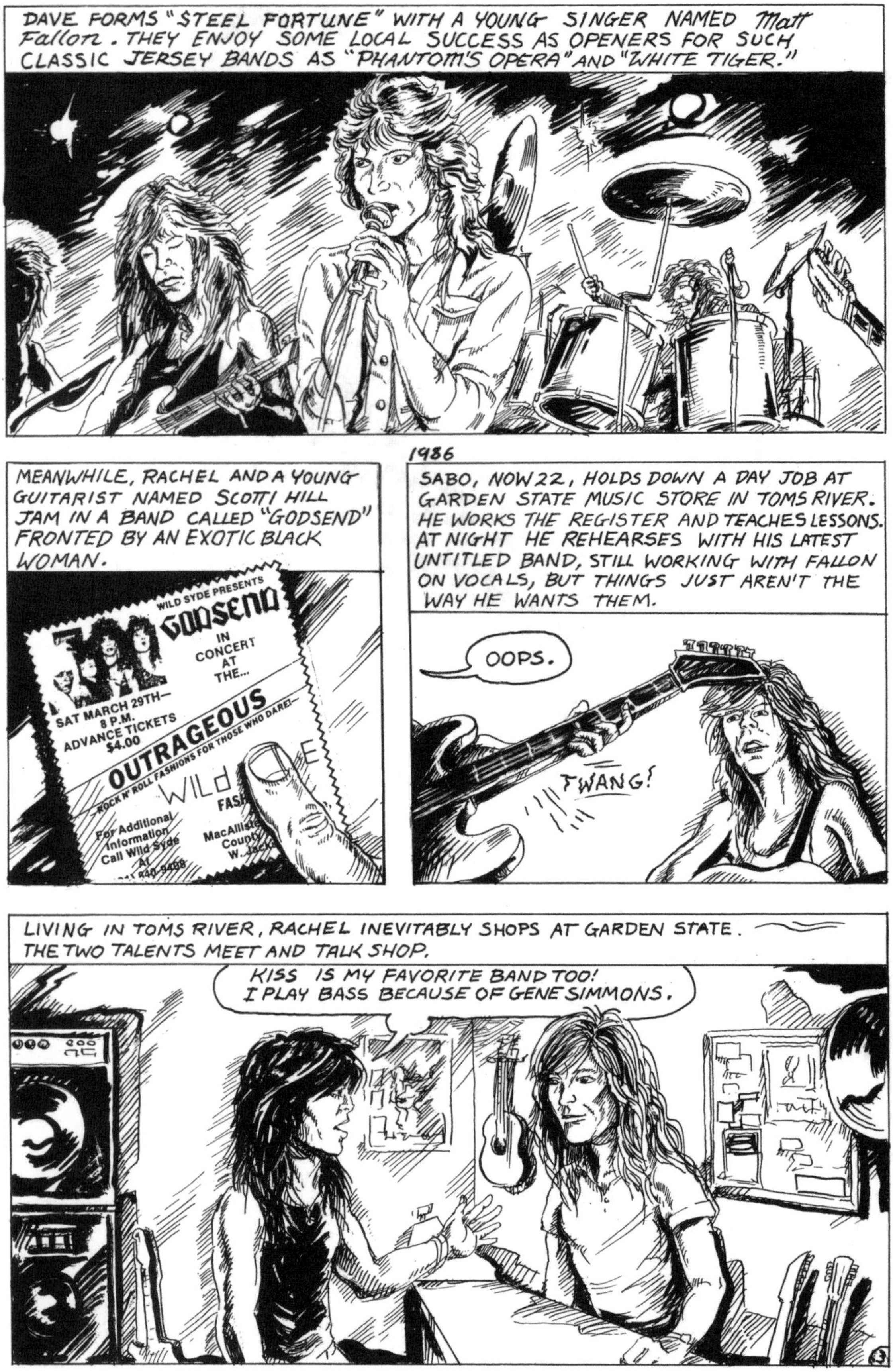
DAVE FORMS "STEEL FORTUNE" WITH A YOUNG SINGER NAMED Matt Fallon. THEY ENJOY SOME LOCAL SUCCESS AS OPENERS FOR SUCH CLASSIC JERSEY BANDS AS "PHANTOM'S OPERA" AND "WHITE TIGER."
1986
MEANWHILE, RACHEL AND A YOUNG GUITARIST NAMED SCOTTI HILL JAM IN A BAND CALLED "GODSEND" FRONTED BY AN EXOTIC BLACK WOMAN.
WILD SYDE PRESENTS
GODSEND
IN CONCERT AT THE...
SAT MARCH 29TH— 8 P.M.
ADVANCE TICKETS $4.00
OUTRAGEOUS
ROCK N' ROLL FASHIONS FOR THOSE WHO DARE!
For Additional Information Call Wild Syde At
SABO, NOW 22, HOLDS DOWN A DAY JOB AT GARDEN STATE MUSIC STORE IN TOMS RIVER. HE WORKS THE REGISTER AND TEACHES LESSONS. AT NIGHT HE REHEARSES WITH HIS LATEST UNTITLED BAND, STILL WORKING WITH FALLON ON VOCALS, BUT THINGS JUST AREN'T THE WAY HE WANTS THEM.
OOPS.
TWANG!
LIVING IN TOMS RIVER, RACHEL INEVITABLY SHOPS AT GARDEN STATE. THE TWO TALENTS MEET AND TALK SHOP.
KISS IS MY FAVORITE BAND TOO! I PLAY BASS BECAUSE OF GENE SIMMONS.
3

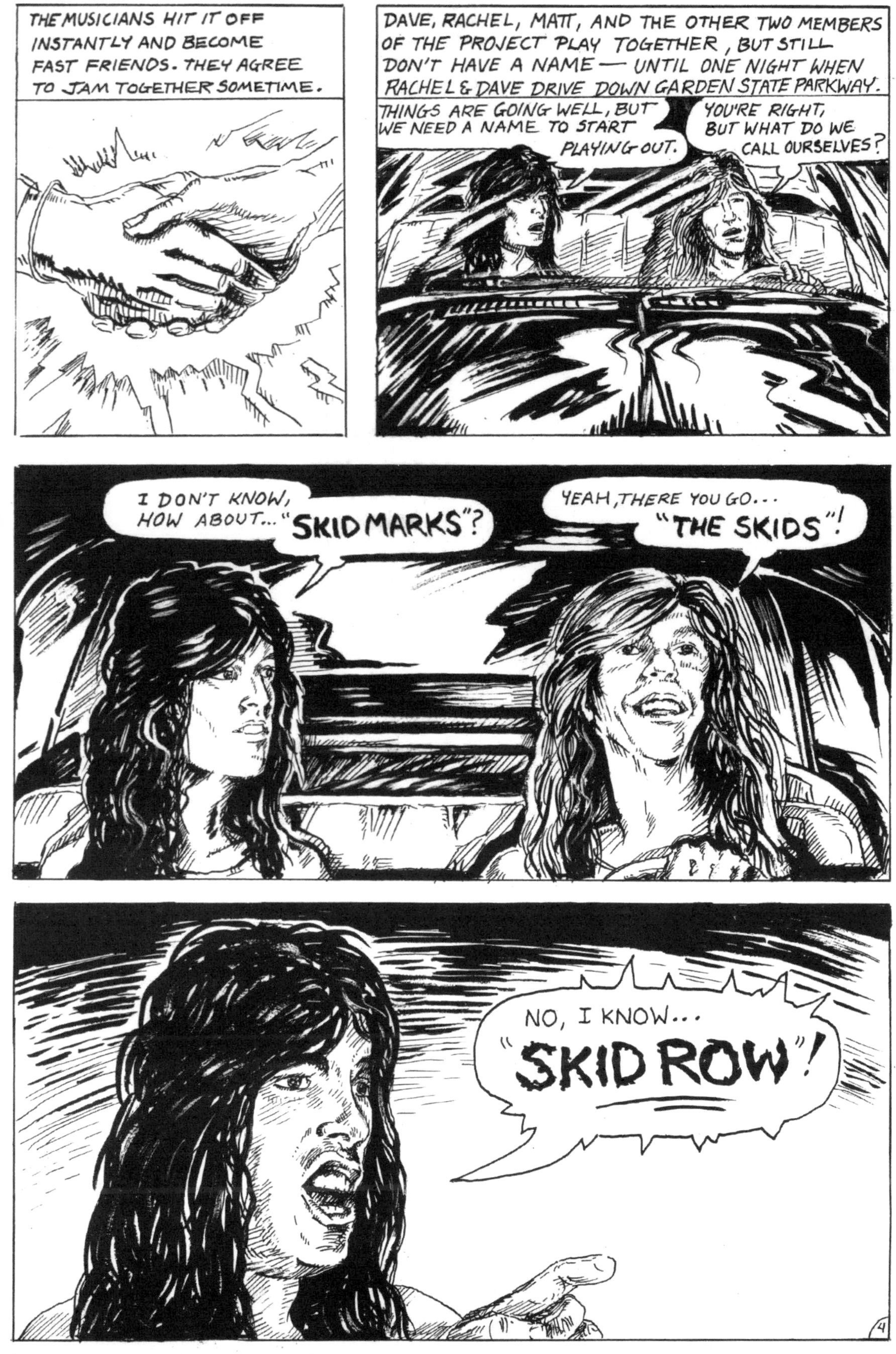
THE MUSICIANS HIT IT OFF INSTANTLY AND BECOME FAST FRIENDS. THEY AGREE TO JAM TOGETHER SOMETIME.
DAVE, RACHEL, MATT, AND THE OTHER TWO MEMBERS OF THE PROJECT PLAY TOGETHER, BUT STILL DON'T HAVE A NAME — UNTIL ONE NIGHT WHEN RACHEL & DAVE DRIVE DOWN GARDEN STATE PARKWAY.
THINGS ARE GOING WELL, BUT WE NEED A NAME TO START PLAYING OUT.
YOU'RE RIGHT, BUT WHAT DO WE CALL OURSELVES?
I DON'T KNOW, HOW ABOUT... "SKID MARKS"?
YEAH, THERE YOU GO... "THE SKIDS"!
NO, I KNOW... "SKID ROW"!

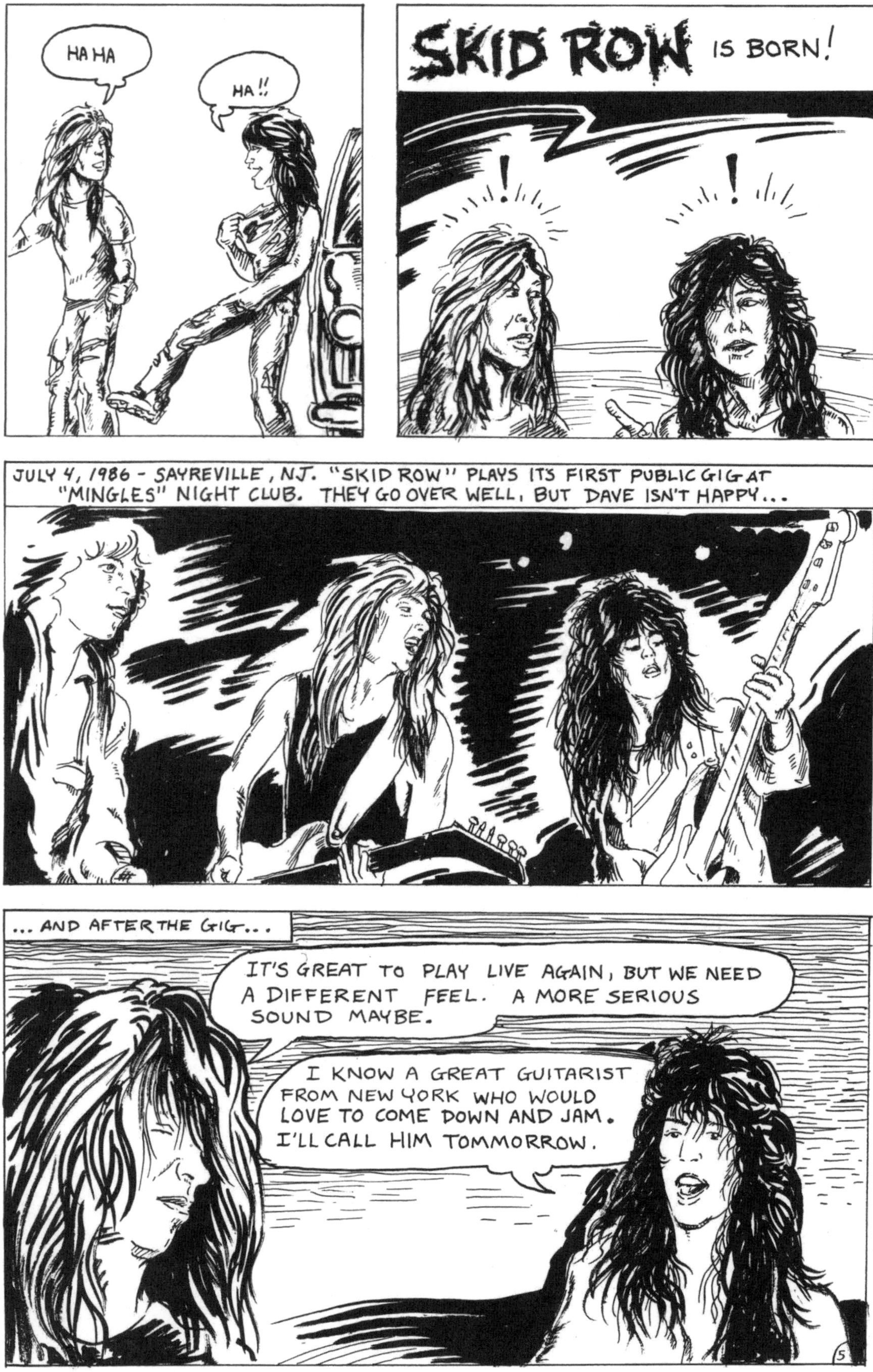
HA HA
HA!!
SKID ROW IS BORN!
!
!
JULY 4, 1986 - SAYREVILLE, N.J. "SKID ROW" PLAYS IT'S FIRST PUBLIC GIG AT "MINGLES" NIGHT CLUB. THEY GO OVER WELL, BUT DAVE ISN'T HAPPY...
... AND AFTER THE GIG...
IT'S GREAT TO PLAY LIVE AGAIN, BUT WE NEED A DIFFERENT FEEL. A MORE SERIOUS SOUND MAYBE.
I KNOW A GREAT GUITARIST FROM NEW YORK WHO WOULD LOVE TO COME DOWN AND JAM. I'LL CALL HIM TOMMORROW.
5

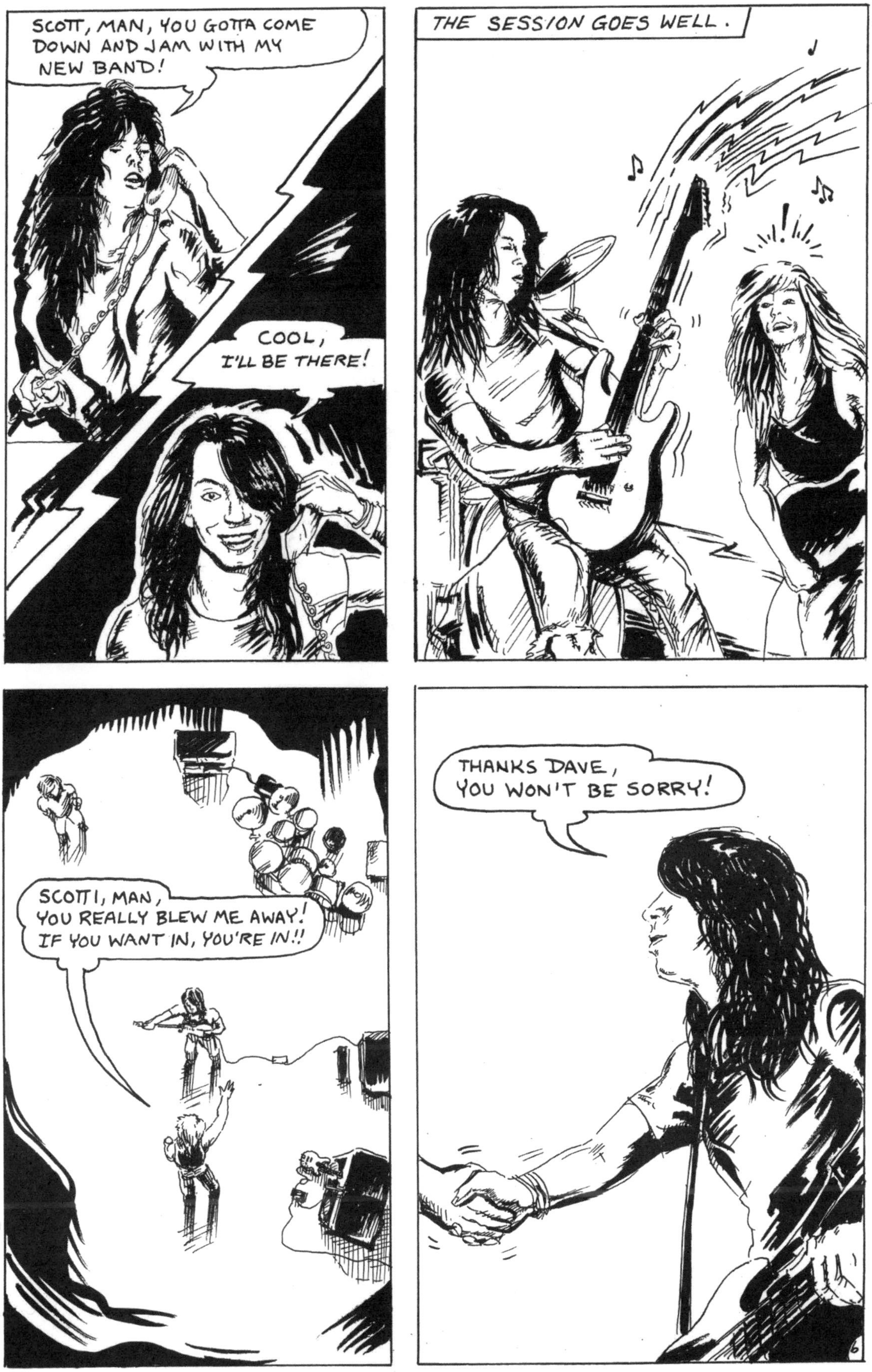
SCOTT, MAN, YOU GOTTA COME DOWN AND JAM WITH MY NEW BAND!
COOL, I'LL BE THERE!
THE SESSION GOES WELL.
SCOTTI, MAN, YOU REALLY BLEW ME AWAY! IF YOU WANT IN, YOU'RE IN!!
THANKS DAVE, YOU WON'T BE SORRY!
6

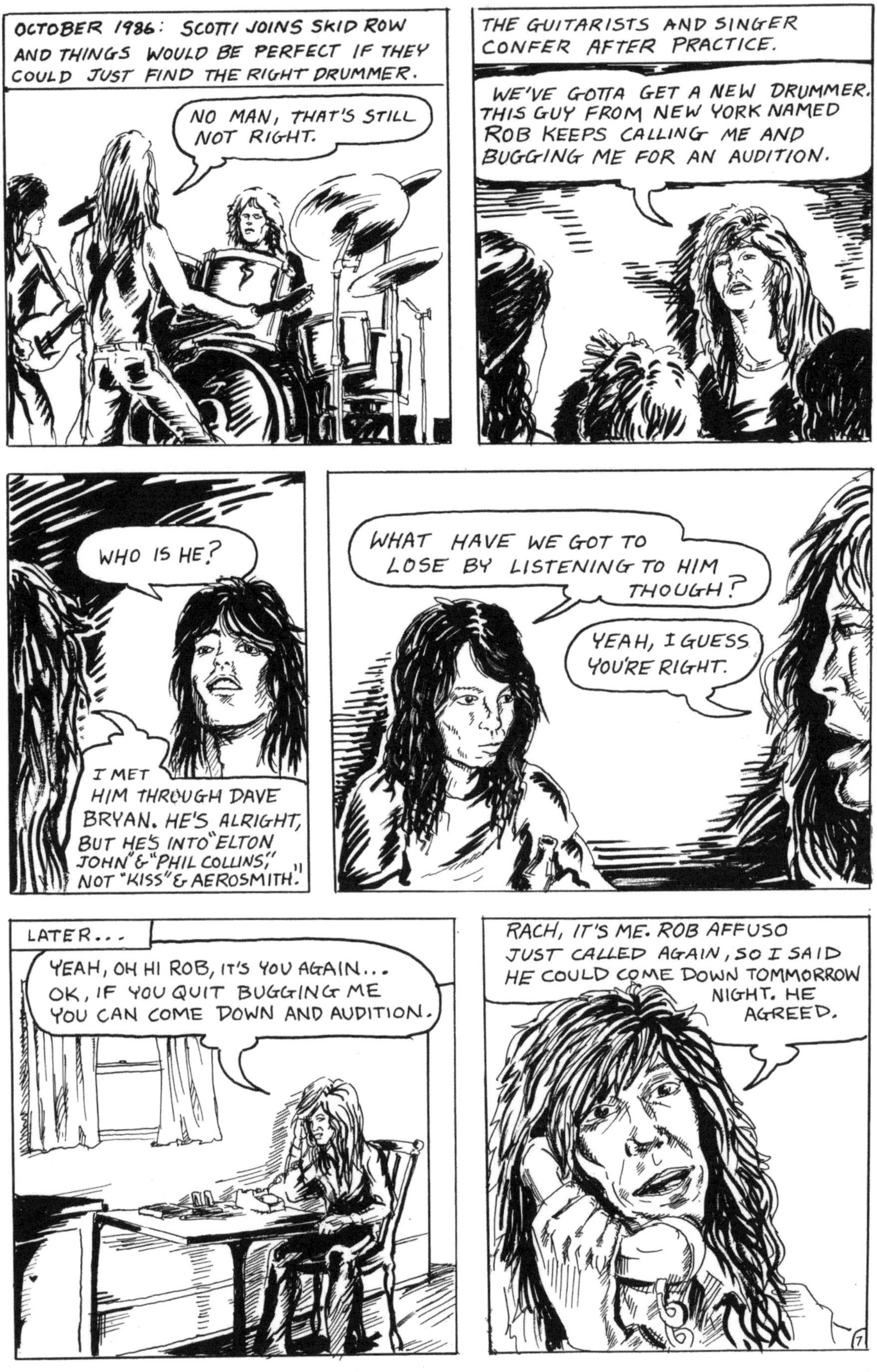
OCTOBER 1986: SCOTTI JOINS SKID ROW AND THINGS WOULD BE PERFECT IF THEY COULD JUST FIND THE RIGHT DRUMMER.
NO MAN, THAT'S STILL NOT RIGHT.
THE GUITARISTS AND SINGER CONFER AFTER PRACTICE.
WE'VE GOTTA GET A NEW DRUMMER. THIS GUY FROM NEW YORK NAMED ROB KEEPS CALLING ME AND BUGGING ME FOR AN AUDITION.
WHO IS HE?
I MET HIM THROUGH DAVE BRYAN. HE'S ALRIGHT, BUT HE'S INTO "ELTON JOHN" & "PHIL COLLINS," NOT "KISS" & AEROSMITH."
WHAT HAVE WE GOT TO LOSE BY LISTENING TO HIM THOUGH?
YEAH, I GUESS YOU'RE RIGHT.
LATER...
YEAH, OH HI ROB, IT'S YOU AGAIN... OK, IF YOU QUIT BUGGING ME YOU CAN COME DOWN AND AUDITION.
RACH, IT'S ME. ROB AFFUSO JUST CALLED AGAIN, SO I SAID HE COULD COME DOWN TOMMORROW NIGHT. HE AGREED.
7

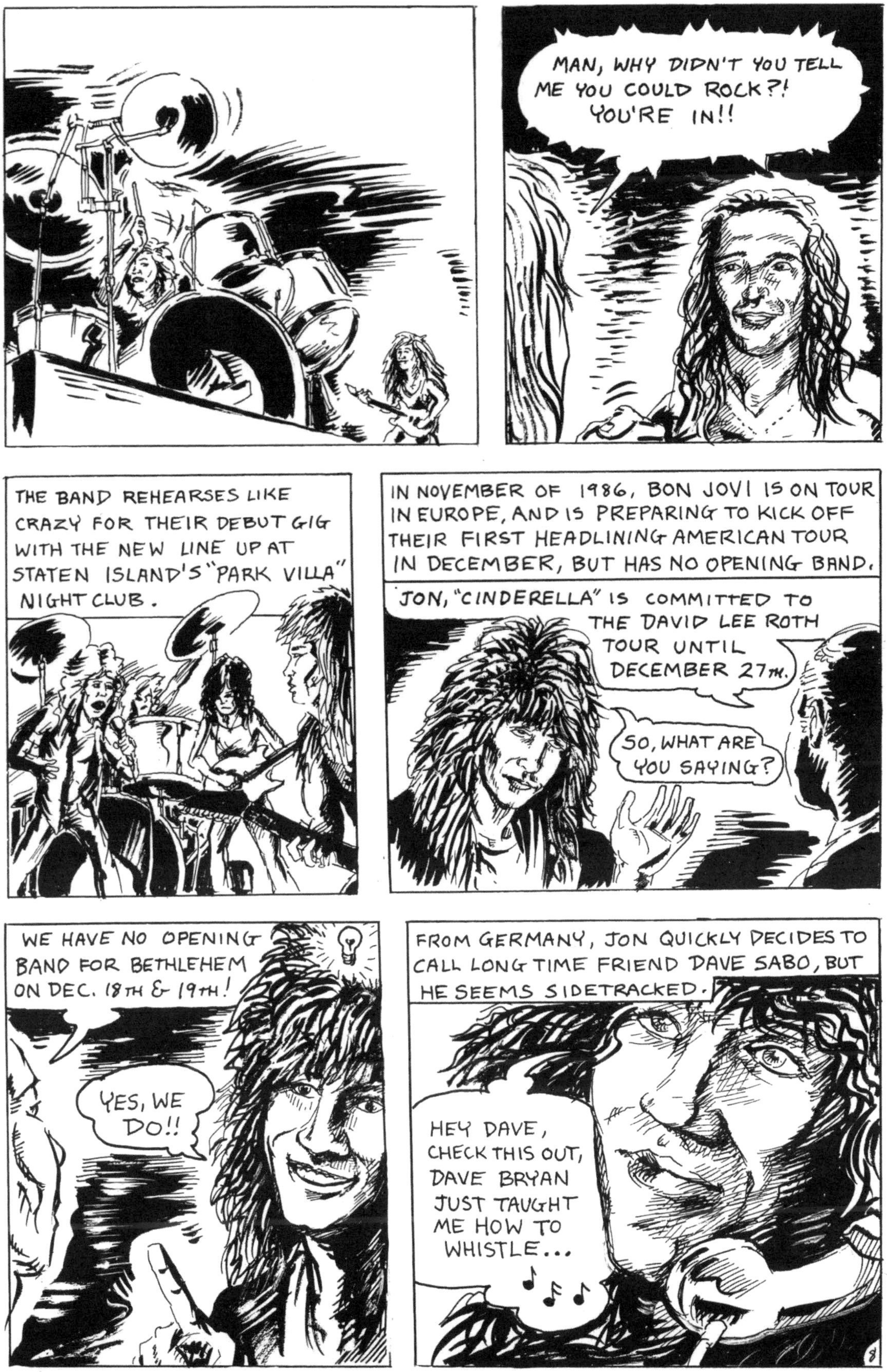
MAN, WHY DIDN'T YOU TELL ME YOU COULD ROCK?! YOU'RE IN!!
THE BAND REHEARSES LIKE CRAZY FOR THEIR DEBUT GIG WITH THE NEW LINE UP AT STATEN ISLAND'S "PARK VILLA" NIGHT CLUB.
IN NOVEMBER OF 1986, BON JOVI IS ON TOUR IN EUROPE, AND IS PREPARING TO KICK OFF THEIR FIRST HEADLINING AMERICAN TOUR IN DECEMBER, BUT HAS NO OPENING BAND.
JON, "CINDERELLA" IS COMMITTED TO THE DAVID LEE ROTH TOUR UNTIL DECEMBER 27TH.
SO, WHAT ARE YOU SAYING?
WE HAVE NO OPENING BAND FOR BETHLEHEM ON DEC. 18TH & 19TH!
YES, WE DO!!
FROM GERMANY, JON QUICKLY DECIDES TO CALL LONG TIME FRIEND DAVE SABO, BUT HE SEEMS SIDETRACKED.
HEY DAVE, CHECK THIS OUT, DAVE BRYAN JUST TAUGHT ME HOW TO WHISTLE...

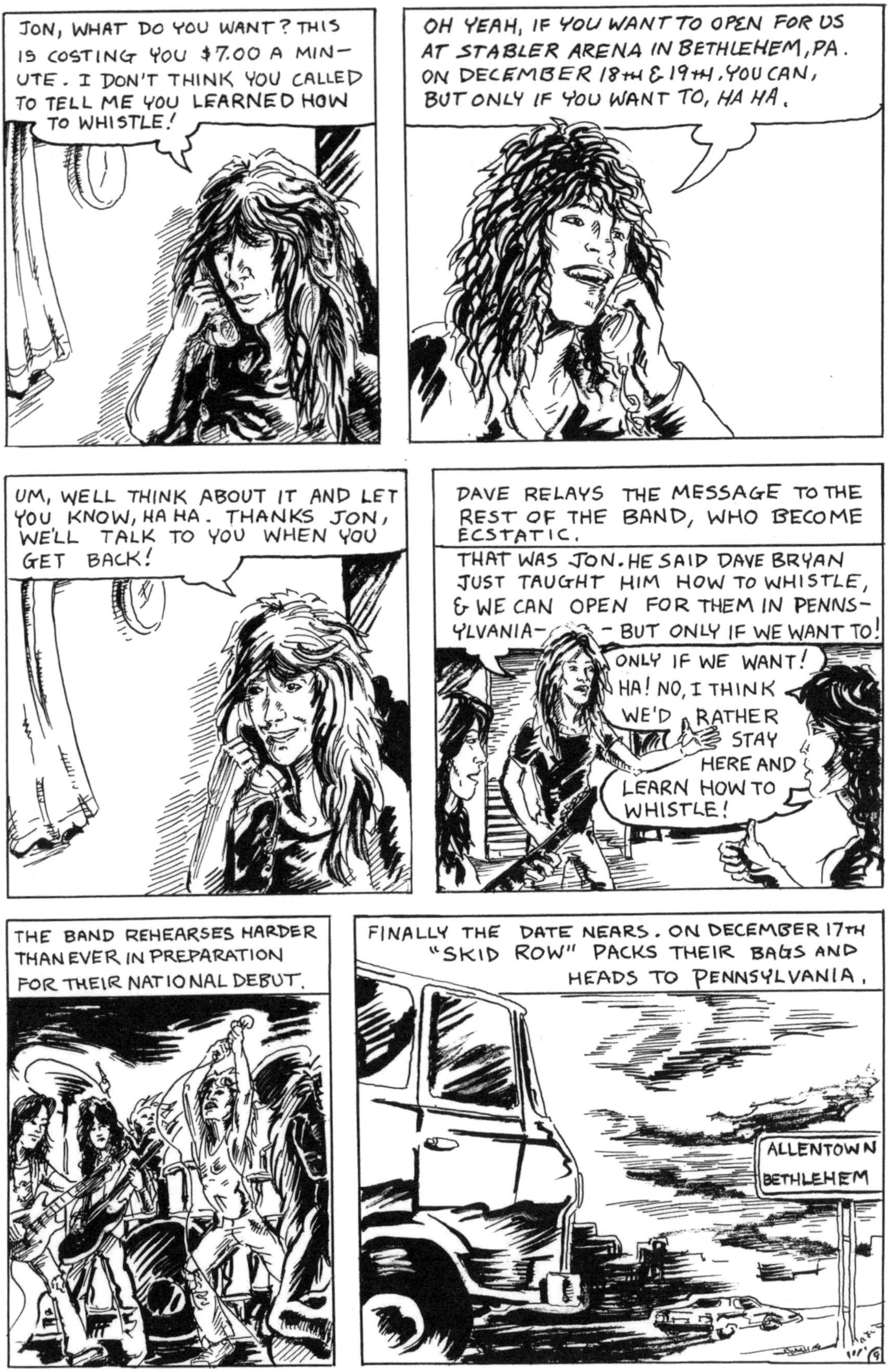
JON, WHAT DO YOU WANT? THIS IS COSTING YOU $7.00 A MIN-UTE. I DON'T THINK YOU CALLED TO TELL ME YOU LEARNED HOW TO WHISTLE!
OH YEAH, IF YOU WANT TO OPEN FOR US AT STABLER ARENA IN BETHLEHEM, PA. ON DECEMBER 18TH & 19TH, YOU CAN, BUT ONLY IF YOU WANT TO, HA HA.
UM, WELL THINK ABOUT IT AND LET YOU KNOW, HA HA. THANKS JON, WE'LL TALK TO YOU WHEN YOU GET BACK!
DAVE RELAYS THE MESSAGE TO THE REST OF THE BAND, WHO BECOME ECSTATIC.
THAT WAS JON. HE SAID DAVE BRYAN JUST TAUGHT HIM HOW TO WHISTLE, & WE CAN OPEN FOR THEM IN PENNSYLVANIA— —BUT ONLY IF WE WANT TO!
ONLY IF WE WANT! HA! NO, I THINK WE'D RATHER STAY HERE AND LEARN HOW TO WHISTLE!
THE BAND REHEARSES HARDER THAN EVER IN PREPARATION FOR THEIR NATIONAL DEBUT.
FINALLY THE DATE NEARS. ON DECEMBER 17TH "SKID ROW" PACKS THEIR BAGS AND HEADS TO PENNSYLVANIA.
ALLENTOWN
BETHLEHEM

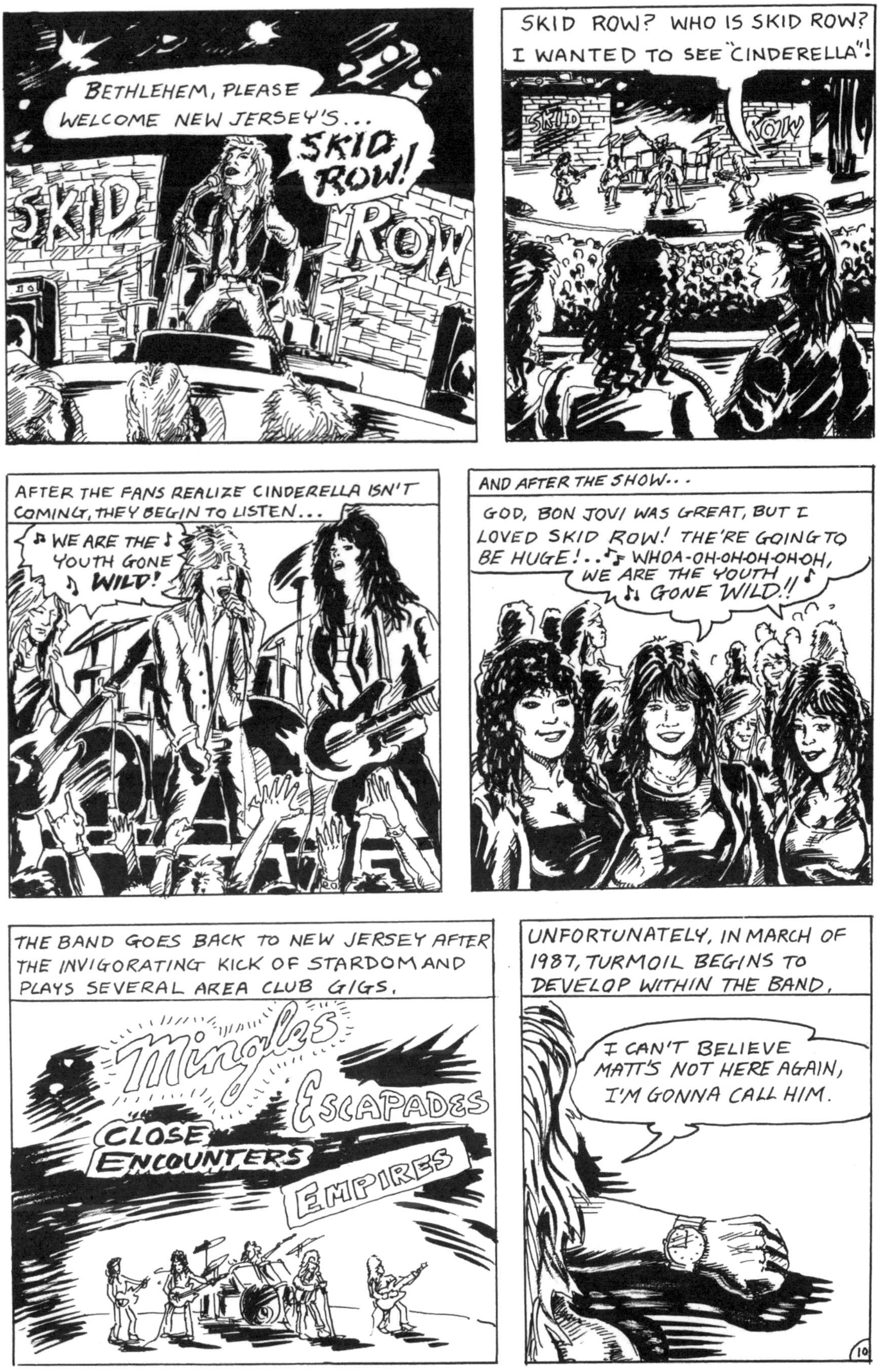
BETHLEHEM, PLEASE WELCOME NEW JERSEY'S...
SKID ROW!
SKID
ROW
SKID ROW? WHO IS SKID ROW? I WANTED TO SEE "CINDERELLA"!
SKID
ROW
AFTER THE FANS REALIZE CINDERELLA ISN'T COMING, THEY BEGIN TO LISTEN...
♫ WE ARE THE ♪ YOUTH GONE ♫ WILD!
AND AFTER THE SHOW...
GOD, BON JOVI WAS GREAT, BUT I LOVED SKID ROW! THE'RE GOING TO BE HUGE!..♫ WHOA-OH-OH-OH-OH-OH, WE ARE THE YOUTH ♪ ♫ GONE WILD!!
THE BAND GOES BACK TO NEW JERSEY AFTER THE INVIGORATING KICK OF STARDOM AND PLAYS SEVERAL AREA CLUB GIGS.
Mingles
Escapades
CLOSE ENCOUNTERS
EMPIRES
UNFORTUNATELY, IN MARCH OF 1987, TURMOIL BEGINS TO DEVELOP WITHIN THE BAND.
I CAN'T BELIEVE MATT'S NOT HERE AGAIN, I'M GONNA CALL HIM.
10

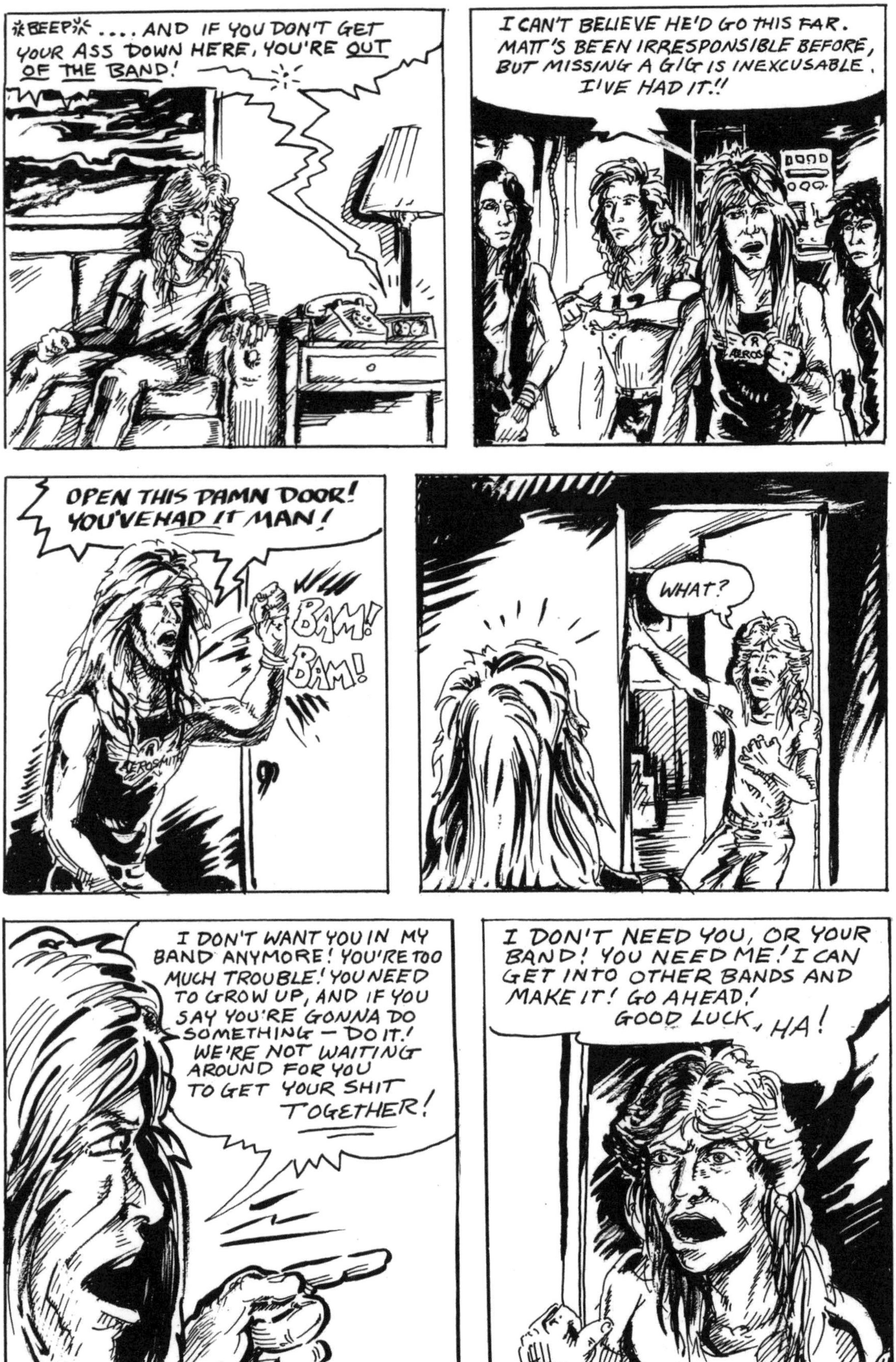
BEEP .... AND IF YOU DON'T GET YOUR ASS DOWN HERE, YOU'RE OUT OF THE BAND!
I CAN'T BELIEVE HE'D GO THIS FAR. MATT'S BEEN IRRESPONSIBLE BEFORE, BUT MISSING A GIG IS INEXCUSABLE. I'VE HAD IT!!
AEROS
OPEN THIS DAMN DOOR! YOU'VE HAD IT MAN!
BAM! BAM!
AEROSMITH
WHAT?
I DON'T WANT YOU IN MY BAND ANYMORE! YOU'RE TOO MUCH TROUBLE! YOU NEED TO GROW UP, AND IF YOU SAY YOU'RE GONNA DO SOMETHING — DO IT! WE'RE NOT WAITING AROUND FOR YOU TO GET YOUR SHIT TOGETHER!
I DON'T NEED YOU, OR YOUR BAND! YOU NEED ME! I CAN GET INTO OTHER BANDS AND MAKE IT! GO AHEAD! GOOD LUCK, HA!

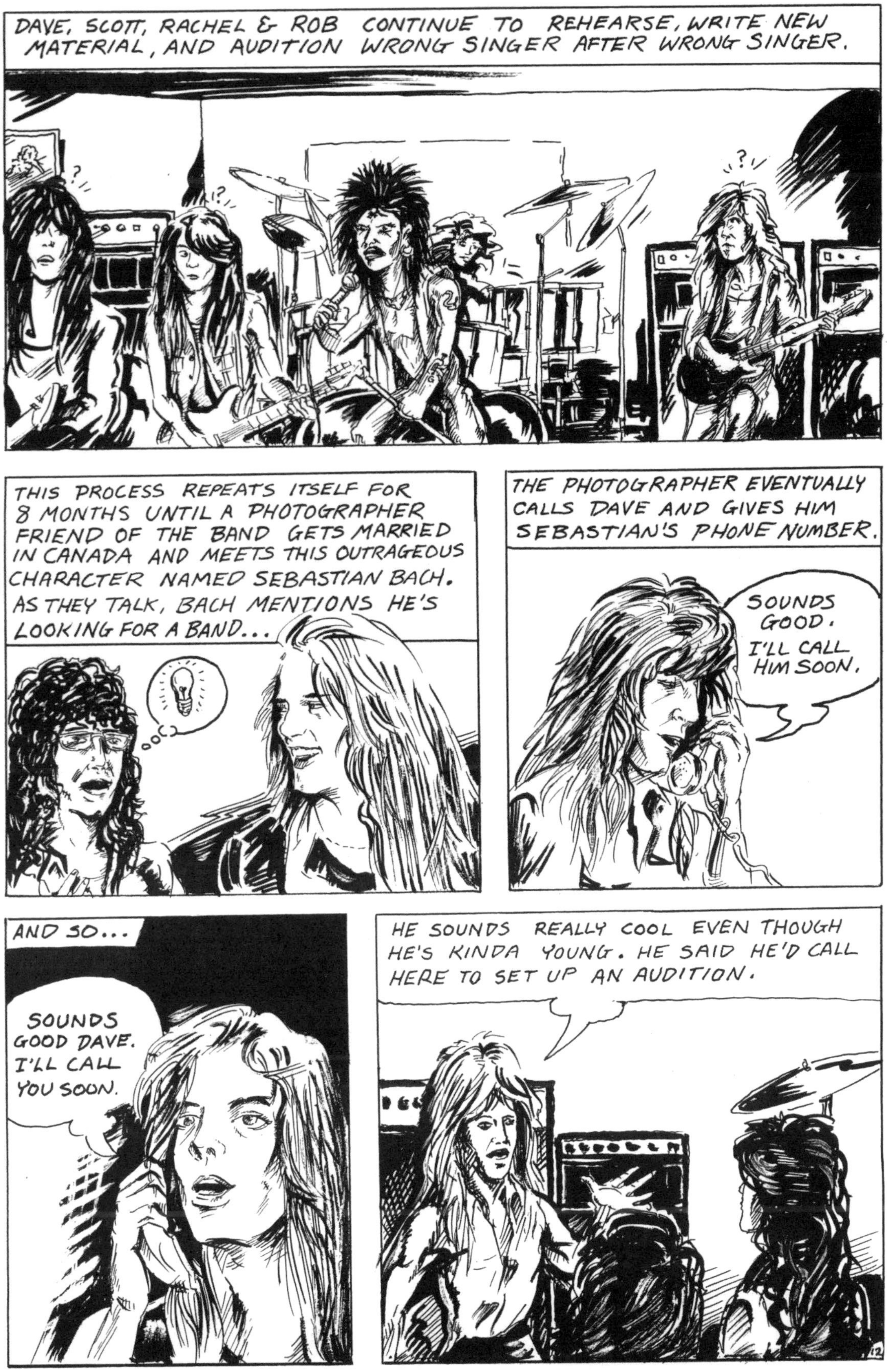
DAVE, SCOTT, RACHEL & ROB CONTINUE TO REHEARSE, WRITE NEW MATERIAL, AND AUDITION WRONG SINGER AFTER WRONG SINGER.
THIS PROCESS REPEATS ITSELF FOR 8 MONTHS UNTIL A PHOTOGRAPHER FRIEND OF THE BAND GETS MARRIED IN CANADA AND MEETS THIS OUTRAGEOUS CHARACTER NAMED SEBASTIAN BACH. AS THEY TALK, BACH MENTIONS HE'S LOOKING FOR A BAND...
THE PHOTOGRAPHER EVENTUALLY CALLS DAVE AND GIVES HIM SEBASTIAN'S PHONE NUMBER.
SOUNDS GOOD. I'LL CALL HIM SOON.
AND SO...
SOUNDS GOOD DAVE. I'LL CALL YOU SOON.
HE SOUNDS REALLY COOL EVEN THOUGH HE'S KINDA YOUNG. HE SAID HE'D CALL HERE TO SET UP AN AUDITION.
12

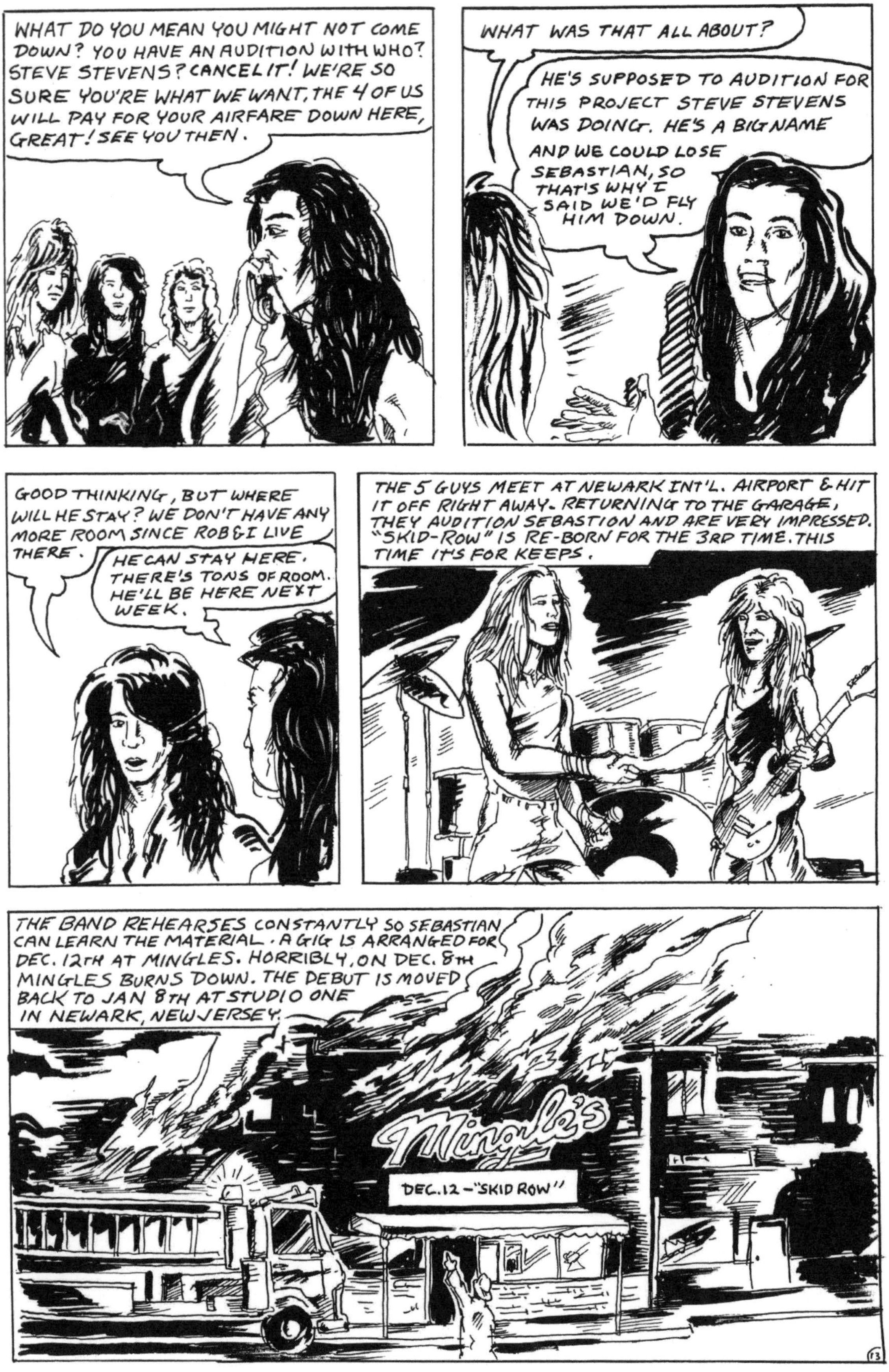
WHAT DO YOU MEAN YOU MIGHT NOT COME DOWN? YOU HAVE AN AUDITION WITH WHO? STEVE STEVENS? CANCEL IT! WE'RE SO SURE YOU'RE WHAT WE WANT, THE 4 OF US WILL PAY FOR YOUR AIRFARE DOWN HERE, GREAT! SEE YOU THEN.
WHAT WAS THAT ALL ABOUT?
HE'S SUPPOSED TO AUDITION FOR THIS PROJECT STEVE STEVENS WAS DOING. HE'S A BIG NAME AND WE COULD LOSE SEBASTIAN, SO THAT'S WHY I SAID WE'D FLY HIM DOWN.
GOOD THINKING, BUT WHERE WILL HE STAY? WE DON'T HAVE ANY MORE ROOM SINCE ROB&I LIVE THERE.
HE CAN STAY HERE. THERE'S TONS OF ROOM. HE'LL BE HERE NEXT WEEK.
THE 5 GUYS MEET AT NEWARK INT'L. AIRPORT & HIT IT OFF RIGHT AWAY. RETURNING TO THE GARAGE, THEY AUDITION SEBASTION AND ARE VERY IMPRESSED. "SKID-ROW" IS RE-BORN FOR THE 3RD TIME. THIS TIME IT'S FOR KEEPS.
THE BAND REHEARSES CONSTANTLY SO SEBASTIAN CAN LEARN THE MATERIAL. A GIG IS ARRANGED FOR DEC. 12TH AT MINGLES. HORRIBLY, ON DEC. 8TH MINGLES BURNS DOWN. THE DEBUT IS MOVED BACK TO JAN 8TH AT STUDIO ONE IN NEWARK, NEW JERSEY.
Mingle's
DEC.12 – "SKID ROW"
13

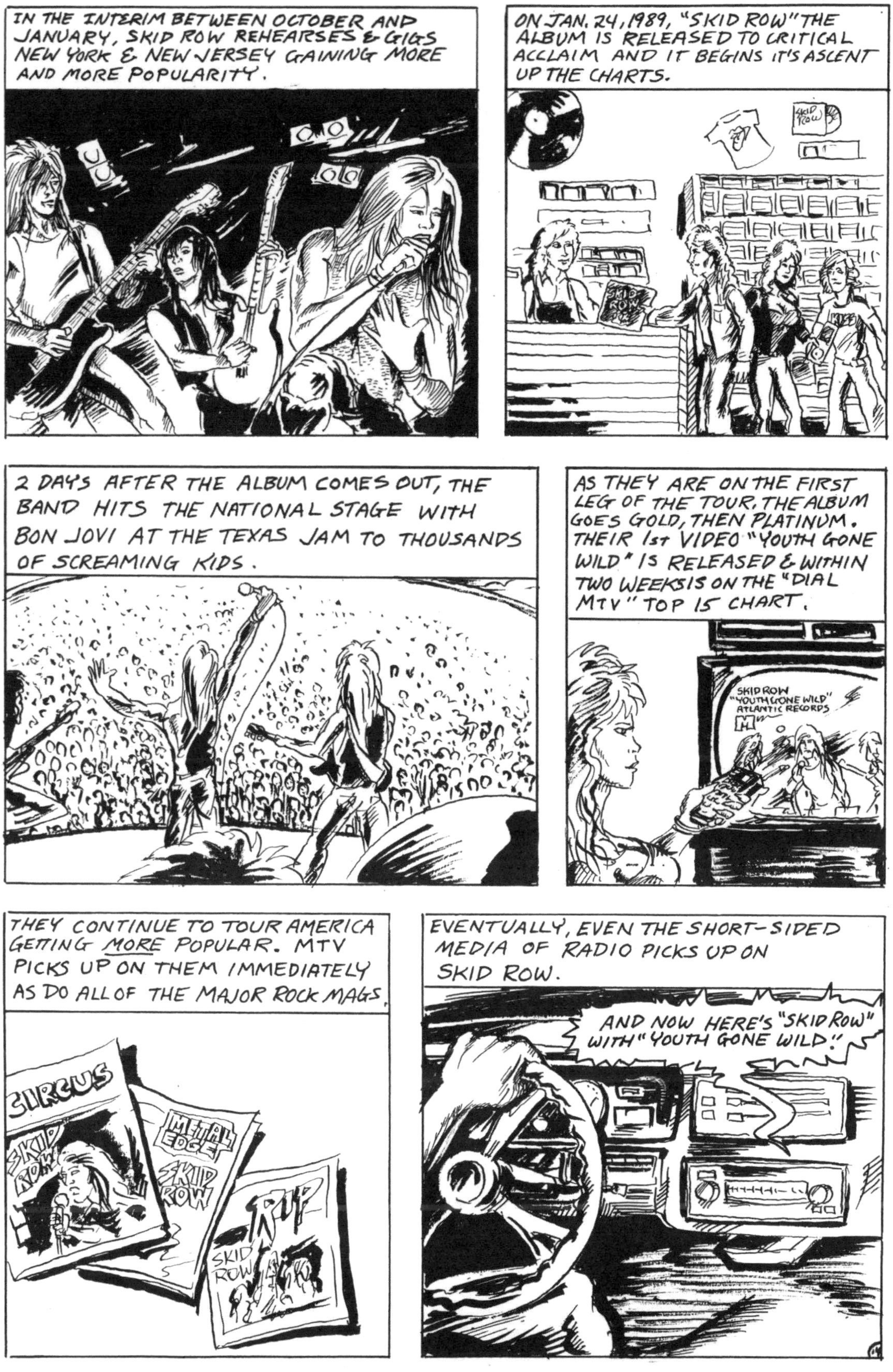
IN THE INTERIM BETWEEN OCTOBER AND JANUARY, SKID ROW REHEARSES & GIGS NEW YORK & NEW JERSEY GAINING MORE AND MORE POPULARITY.
ON JAN. 24, 1989, "SKID ROW" THE ALBUM IS RELEASED TO CRITICAL ACCLAIM AND IT BEGINS IT'S ASCENT UP THE CHARTS.
SKID ROW
2 DAYS AFTER THE ALBUM COMES OUT, THE BAND HITS THE NATIONAL STAGE WITH BON JOVI AT THE TEXAS JAM TO THOUSANDS OF SCREAMING KIDS.
AS THEY ARE ON THE FIRST LEG OF THE TOUR, THE ALBUM GOES GOLD, THEN PLATINUM. THEIR 1st VIDEO "YOUTH GONE WILD" IS RELEASED & WITHIN TWO WEEKS IS ON THE "DIAL MTV" TOP 15 CHART.
SKID ROW "YOUTH GONE WILD" ATLANTIC RECORDS
THEY CONTINUE TO TOUR AMERICA GETTING MORE POPULAR. MTV PICKS UP ON THEM IMMEDIATELY AS DO ALL OF THE MAJOR ROCK MAGS.
CIRCUS
SKID ROW
METAL EDGE
SKID ROW
RIP
SKID ROW
EVENTUALLY, EVEN THE SHORT-SIDED MEDIA OF RADIO PICKS UP ON SKID ROW.
AND NOW HERE'S "SKID ROW" WITH "YOUTH GONE WILD"!

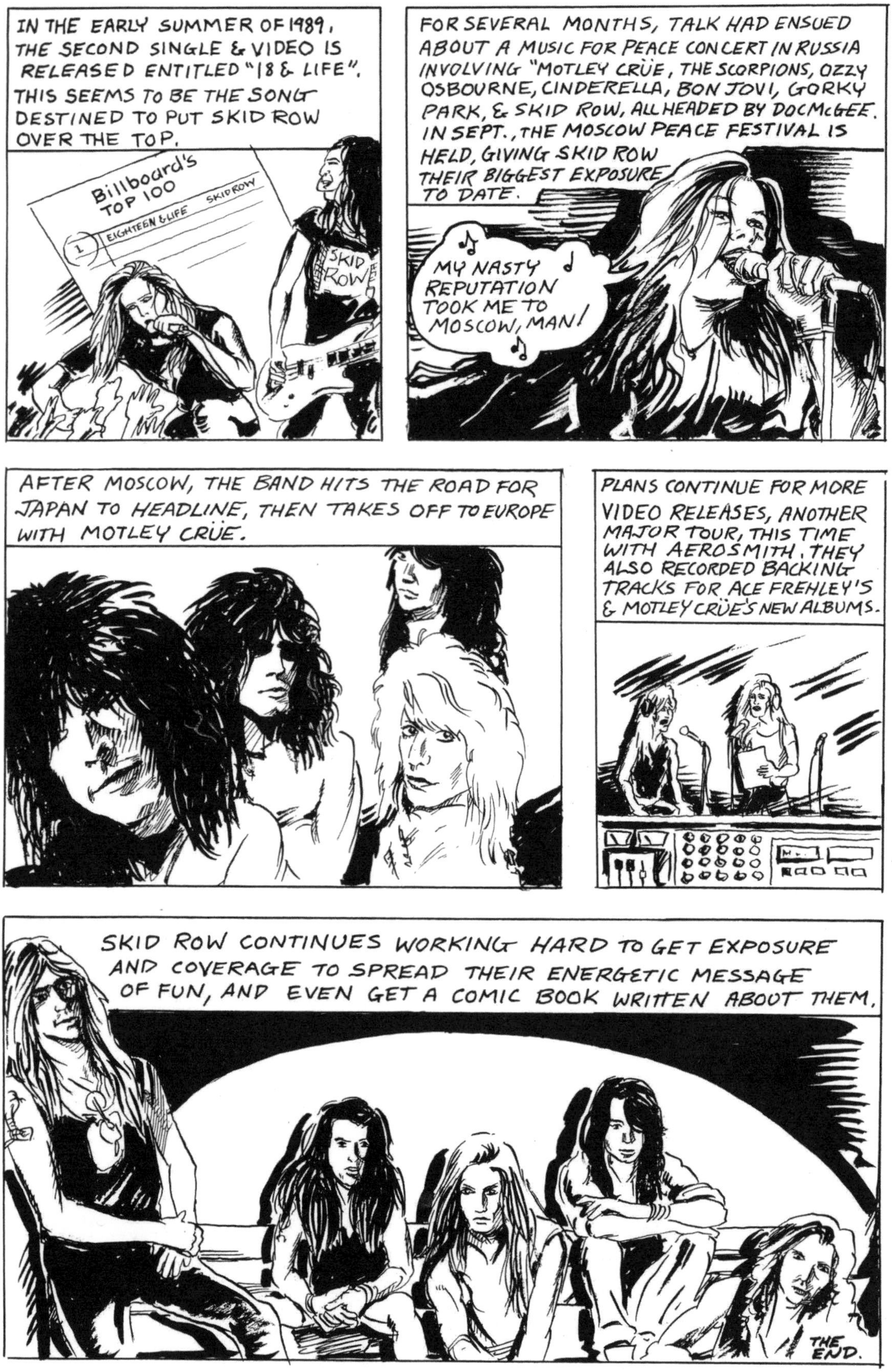
IN THE EARLY SUMMER OF 1989, THE SECOND SINGLE & VIDEO IS RELEASED ENTITLED "18 & LIFE". THIS SEEMS TO BE THE SONG DESTINED TO PUT SKID ROW OVER THE TOP.
Billboard's TOP 100
1 EIGHTEEN & LIFE SKID ROW
SKID ROW
FOR SEVERAL MONTHS, TALK HAD ENSUED ABOUT A MUSIC FOR PEACE CONCERT IN RUSSIA INVOLVING "MOTLEY CRÜE, THE SCORPIONS, OZZY OSBOURNE, CINDERELLA, BON JOVI, GORKY PARK, & SKID ROW, ALL HEADED BY DOC McGEE. IN SEPT., THE MOSCOW PEACE FESTIVAL IS HELD, GIVING SKID ROW THEIR BIGGEST EXPOSURE TO DATE.
MY NASTY REPUTATION TOOK ME TO MOSCOW, MAN!
AFTER MOSCOW, THE BAND HITS THE ROAD FOR JAPAN TO HEADLINE, THEN TAKES OFF TO EUROPE WITH MOTLEY CRÜE.
PLANS CONTINUE FOR MORE VIDEO RELEASES, ANOTHER MAJOR TOUR, THIS TIME WITH AEROSMITH. THEY ALSO RECORDED BACKING TRACKS FOR ACE FREHLEY'S & MOTLEY CRÜE'S NEW ALBUMS.
SKID ROW CONTINUES WORKING HARD TO GET EXPOSURE AND COVERAGE TO SPREAD THEIR ENERGETIC MESSAGE OF FUN, AND EVEN GET A COMIC BOOK WRITTEN ABOUT THEM.
THE END.

THIS IS AN UNAUTHORIZED BIOGRAPHY!

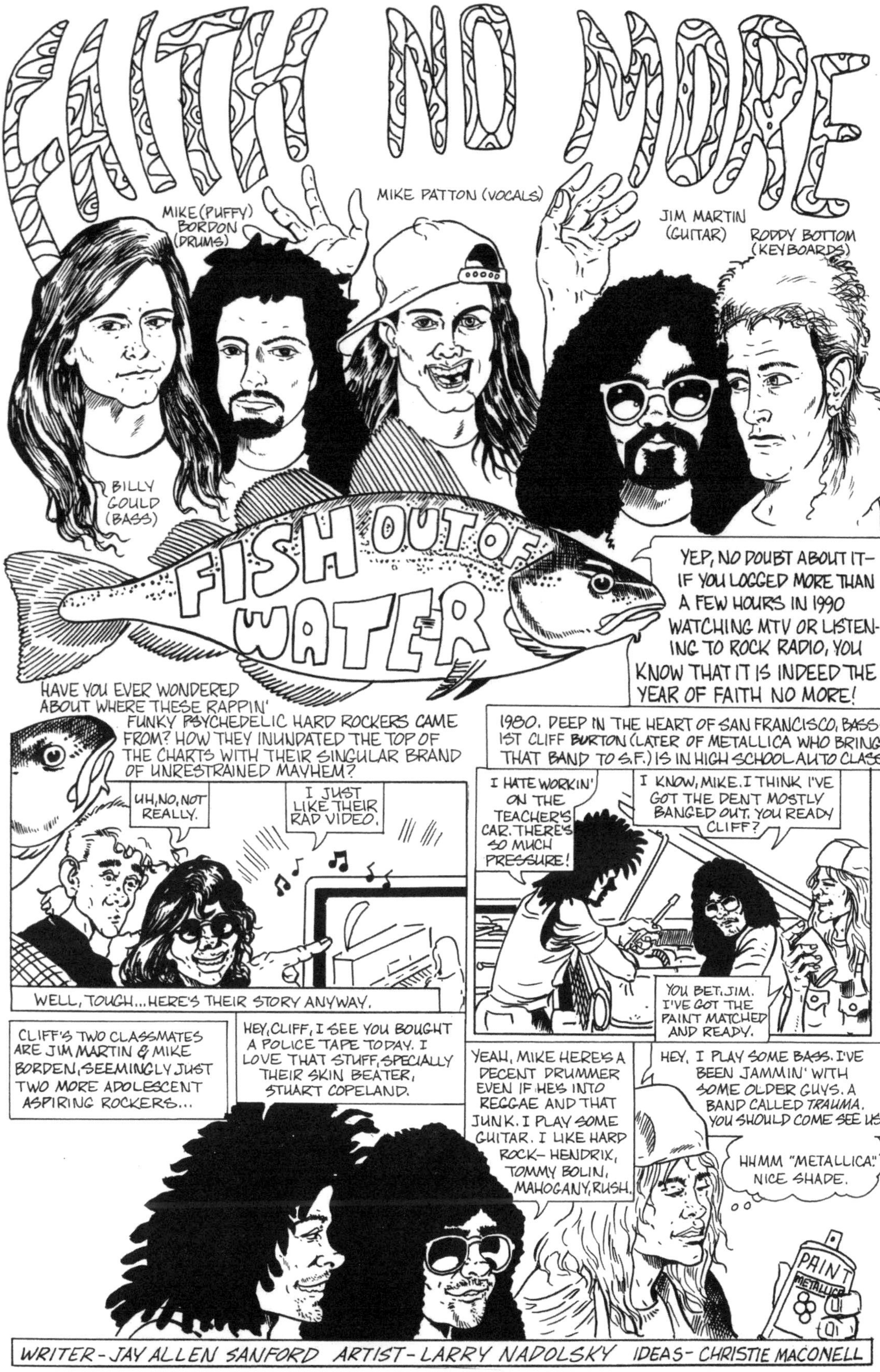
FAITH NO MORE
MIKE (PUFFY) BORDON (DRUMS)
MIKE PATTON (VOCALS)
JIM MARTIN (GUITAR)
RODDY BOTTOM (KEYBOARDS)
BILLY GOULD (BASS)
FISH OUT OF WATER
YEP, NO DOUBT ABOUT IT- IF YOU LOGGED MORE THAN A FEW HOURS IN 1990 WATCHING MTV OR LISTENING TO ROCK RADIO, YOU KNOW THAT IT IS INDEED THE YEAR OF FAITH NO MORE!
HAVE YOU EVER WONDERED ABOUT WHERE THESE RAPPIN' FUNKY PSYCHEDELIC HARD ROCKERS CAME FROM? HOW THEY INUNDATED THE TOP OF THE CHARTS WITH THEIR SINGULAR BRAND OF UNRESTRAINED MAYHEM?
UH, NO, NOT REALLY.
I JUST LIKE THEIR RAD VIDEO.
WELL, TOUGH... HERE'S THEIR STORY ANYWAY.
1980. DEEP IN THE HEART OF SAN FRANCISCO, BASSIST CLIFF BURTON (LATER OF METALLICA WHO BRINGS THAT BAND TO S.F.) IS IN HIGH SCHOOL AUTO CLASS.
I HATE WORKIN' ON THE TEACHER'S CAR. THERE'S SO MUCH PRESSURE!
I KNOW, MIKE. I THINK I'VE GOT THE DENT MOSTLY BANGED OUT. YOU READY CLIFF?
YOU BET, JIM. I'VE GOT THE PAINT MATCHED AND READY.
CLIFF'S TWO CLASSMATES ARE JIM MARTIN & MIKE BORDEN, SEEMINGLY JUST TWO MORE ADOLESCENT ASPIRING ROCKERS...
HEY, CLIFF, I SEE YOU BOUGHT A POLICE TAPE TODAY. I LOVE THAT STUFF, SPECIALLY THEIR SKIN BEATER, STUART COPELAND.
YEAH, MIKE HERE'S A DECENT DRUMMER EVEN IF HE'S INTO REGGAE AND THAT JUNK. I PLAY SOME GUITAR. I LIKE HARD ROCK- HENDRIX, TOMMY BOLIN, MAHOGANY, RUSH.
HEY, I PLAY SOME BASS. I'VE BEEN JAMMIN' WITH SOME OLDER GUYS. A BAND CALLED TRAUMA. YOU SHOULD COME SEE US.
HHMM "METALLICA." NICE SHADE.
PAINT
METALLICA
WRITER - JAY ALLEN SANFORD ARTIST - LARRY NADOLSKY IDEAS - CHRISTIE MACONELL

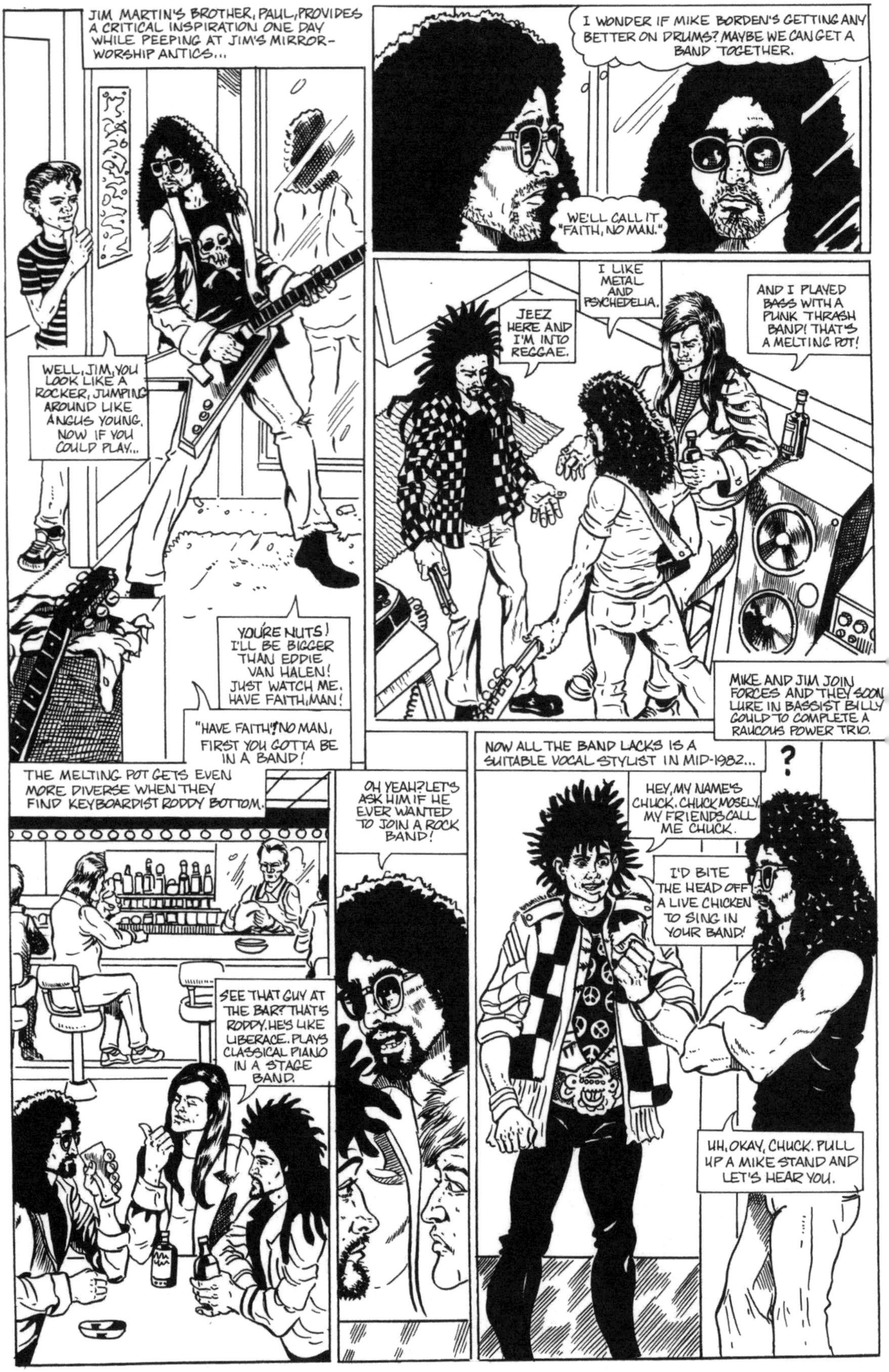

JIM MARTIN'S BROTHER, PAUL, PROVIDES A CRITICAL INSPIRATION ONE DAY WHILE PEEPING AT JIM'S MIRROR-WORSHIP ANTICS...
WELL, JIM, YOU LOOK LIKE A ROCKER, JUMPING AROUND LIKE ANGUS YOUNG. NOW IF YOU COULD PLAY...
YOU'RE NUTS! I'LL BE BIGGER THAN EDDIE VAN HALEN! JUST WATCH ME. HAVE FAITH, MAN!
"HAVE FAITH"? NO MAN, FIRST YOU GOTTA BE IN A BAND!
I WONDER IF MIKE BORDEN'S GETTING ANY BETTER ON DRUMS? MAYBE WE CAN GET A BAND TOGETHER.
WE'LL CALL IT "FAITH, NO MAN."
JEEZ HERE AND I'M INTO REGGAE.
I LIKE METAL AND PSYCHEDELIA.
AND I PLAYED BASS WITH A PUNK THRASH BAND! THAT'S A MELTING POT!
MIKE AND JIM JOIN FORCES AND THEY SOON LURE IN BASSIST BILLY GOULD TO COMPLETE A RAUCOUS POWER TRIO.
THE MELTING POT GETS EVEN MORE DIVERSE WHEN THEY FIND KEYBOARDIST RODDY BOTTOM.
SEE THAT GUY AT THE BAR? THAT'S RODDY. HE'S LIKE LIBERACE. PLAYS CLASSICAL PIANO IN A STAGE BAND.
OH YEAH? LET'S ASK HIM IF HE EVER WANTED TO JOIN A ROCK BAND!
NOW ALL THE BAND LACKS IS A SUITABLE VOCAL STYLIST IN MID-1982...
?
HEY, MY NAME'S CHUCK. CHUCK MOSELY. MY FRIENDS CALL ME CHUCK.
I'D BITE THE HEAD OFF A LIVE CHICKEN TO SING IN YOUR BAND!
UH, OKAY, CHUCK. PULL UP A MIKE STAND AND LET'S HEAR YOU.

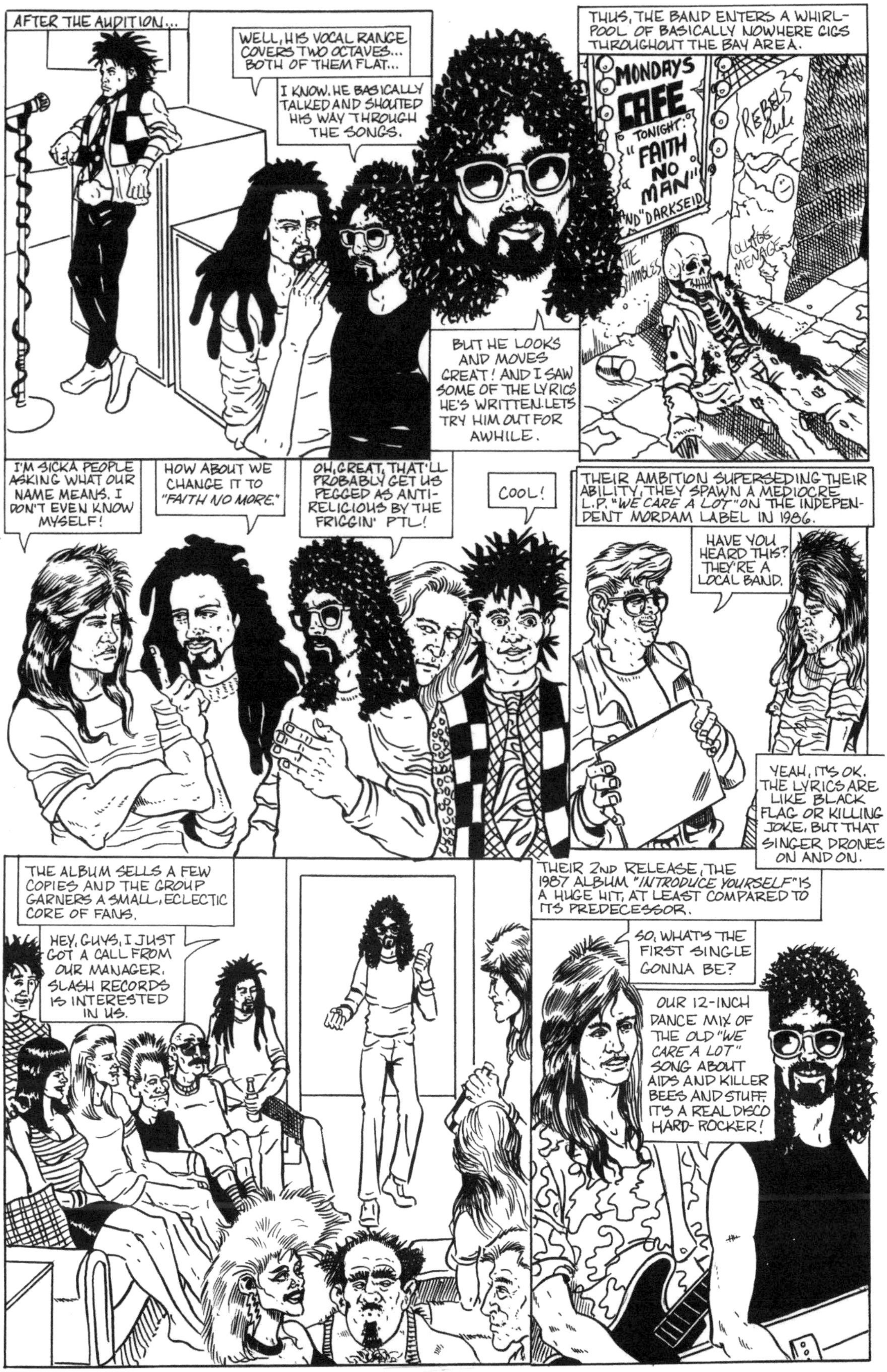
AFTER THE AUDITION...
WELL, HIS VOCAL RANGE COVERS TWO OCTAVES... BOTH OF THEM FLAT...
I KNOW. HE BASICALLY TALKED AND SHOUTED HIS WAY THROUGH THE SONGS.
BUT HE LOOKS AND MOVES GREAT! AND I SAW SOME OF THE LYRICS HE'S WRITTEN. LET'S TRY HIM OUT FOR AWHILE.
THUS, THE BAND ENTERS A WHIRLPOOL OF BASICALLY NOWHERE GIGS THROUGHOUT THE BAY AREA.
MONDAY'S CAFE TONIGHT: "FAITH NO MAN" AND DARKSEID
REBELS RULE
THE SHAMBLES
I'M SICKA PEOPLE ASKING WHAT OUR NAME MEANS. I DON'T EVEN KNOW MYSELF!
HOW ABOUT WE CHANGE IT TO "FAITH NO MORE."
OH, GREAT. THAT'LL PROBABLY GET US PEGGED AS ANTI-RELIGIOUS BY THE FRIGGIN' PTL!
COOL!
THEIR AMBITION SUPERSEDING THEIR ABILITY, THEY SPAWN A MEDIOCRE L.P. "WE CARE A LOT" ON THE INDEPENDENT MORDAM LABEL IN 1986.
HAVE YOU HEARD THIS? THEY'RE A LOCAL BAND.
YEAH, IT'S OK. THE LYRICS ARE LIKE BLACK FLAG OR KILLING JOKE, BUT THAT SINGER DRONES ON AND ON.
THE ALBUM SELLS A FEW COPIES AND THE GROUP GARNERS A SMALL, ECLECTIC CORE OF FANS.
HEY, GUYS, I JUST GOT A CALL FROM OUR MANAGER. SLASH RECORDS IS INTERESTED IN US.
THEIR 2ND RELEASE, THE 1987 ALBUM "INTRODUCE YOURSELF" IS A HUGE HIT, AT LEAST COMPARED TO ITS PREDECESSOR.
SO, WHAT'S THE FIRST SINGLE GONNA BE?
OUR 12-INCH DANCE MIX OF THE OLD "WE CARE A LOT" SONG ABOUT AIDS AND KILLER BEES AND STUFF. IT'S A REAL DISCO HARD-ROCKER!

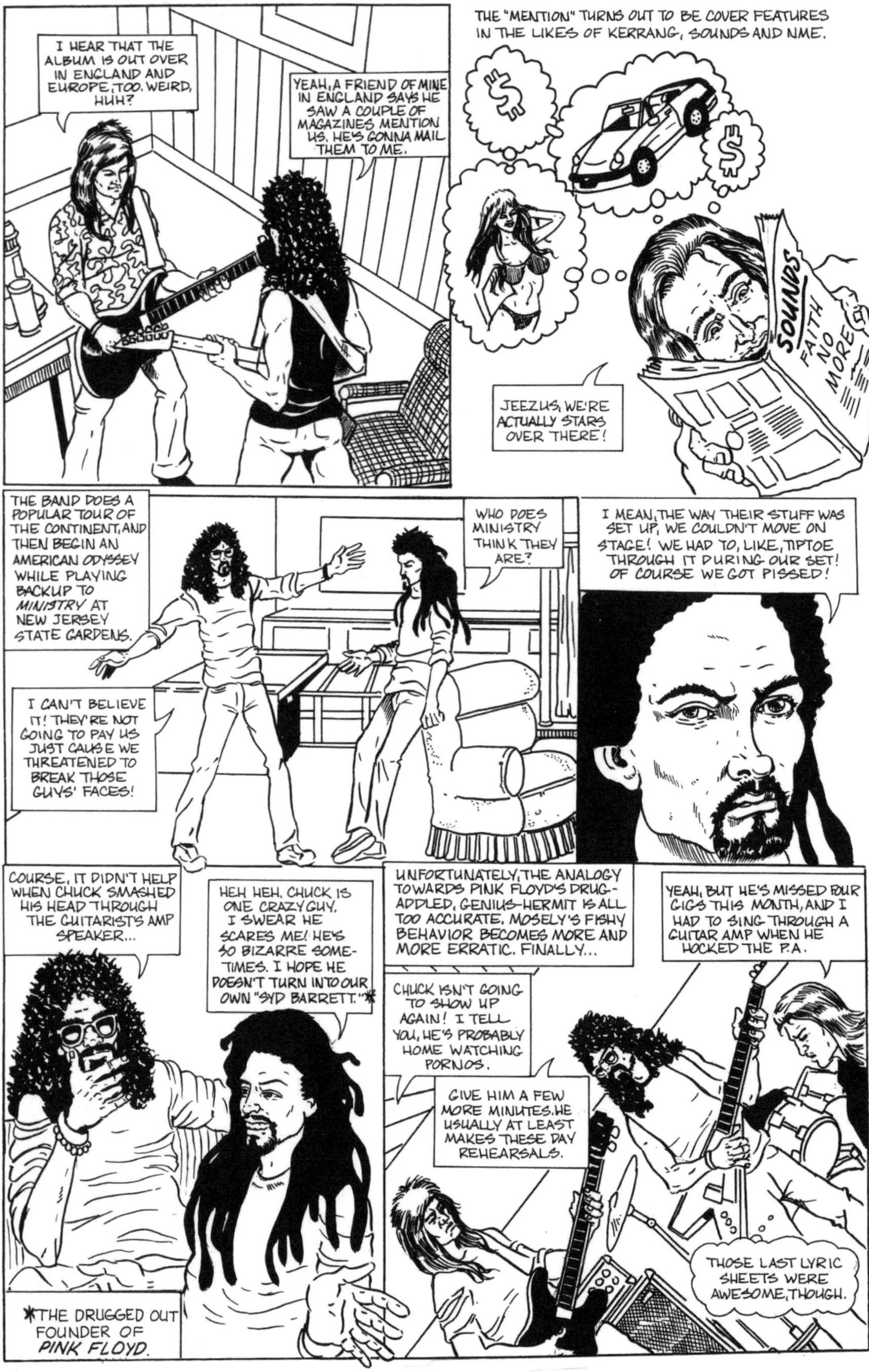

I HEAR THAT THE ALBUM IS OUT OVER IN ENGLAND AND EUROPE, TOO. WEIRD, HUH?
YEAH, A FRIEND OF MINE IN ENGLAND SAYS HE SAW A COUPLE OF MAGAZINES MENTION US. HE'S GONNA MAIL THEM TO ME.
THE "MENTION" TURNS OUT TO BE COVER FEATURES IN THE LIKES OF KERRANG, SOUNDS AND NME.
SOUNDS
FAITH NO MORE
JEEZUS, WE'RE ACTUALLY STARS OVER THERE!
THE BAND DOES A POPULAR TOUR OF THE CONTINENT, AND THEN BEGIN AN AMERICAN ODYSSEY WHILE PLAYING BACKUP TO MINISTRY AT NEW JERSEY STATE GARDENS.
WHO DOES MINISTRY THINK THEY ARE?
I CAN'T BELIEVE IT! THEY'RE NOT GOING TO PAY US JUST CAUSE WE THREATENED TO BREAK THOSE GUYS' FACES!
I MEAN, THE WAY THEIR STUFF WAS SET UP, WE COULDN'T MOVE ON STAGE! WE HAD TO, LIKE, TIPTOE THROUGH IT DURING OUR SET! OF COURSE WE GOT PISSED!
COURSE, IT DIDN'T HELP WHEN CHUCK SMASHED HIS HEAD THROUGH THE GUITARIST'S AMP SPEAKER...
HEH HEH. CHUCK IS ONE CRAZY GUY. I SWEAR HE SCARES ME! HE'S SO BIZARRE SOMETIMES. I HOPE HE DOESN'T TURN INTO OUR OWN "SYD BARRETT."*
*THE DRUGGED OUT FOUNDER OF PINK FLOYD.
UNFORTUNATELY, THE ANALOGY TOWARDS PINK FLOYD'S DRUG-ADDLED, GENIUS-HERMIT IS ALL TOO ACCURATE. MOSELY'S FISHY BEHAVIOR BECOMES MORE AND MORE ERRATIC. FINALLY...
CHUCK ISN'T GOING TO SHOW UP AGAIN! I TELL YOU, HE'S PROBABLY HOME WATCHING PORNOS.
YEAH, BUT HE'S MISSED FOUR GIGS THIS MONTH, AND I HAD TO SING THROUGH A GUITAR AMP WHEN HE HOCKED THE P.A.
GIVE HIM A FEW MORE MINUTES. HE USUALLY AT LEAST MAKES THESE DAY REHEARSALS.
THOSE LAST LYRIC SHEETS WERE AWESOME, THOUGH.

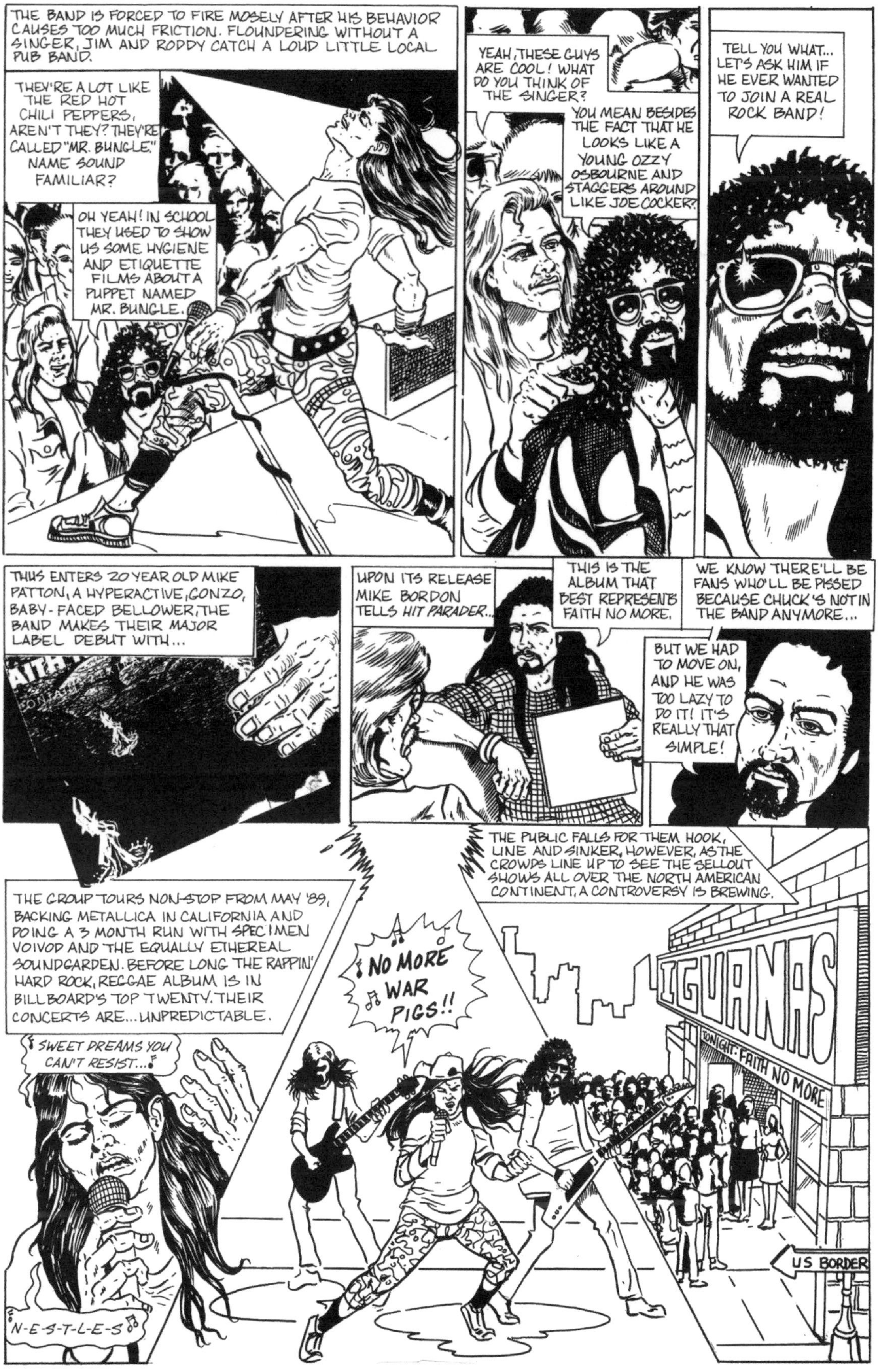
THE BAND IS FORCED TO FIRE MOSELY AFTER HIS BEHAVIOR CAUSES TOO MUCH FRICTION. FLOUNDERING WITHOUT A SINGER, JIM AND RODDY CATCH A LOUD LITTLE LOCAL PUB BAND.
THEY'RE A LOT LIKE THE RED HOT CHILI PEPPERS, AREN'T THEY? THEY'RE CALLED "MR. BUNGLE." NAME SOUND FAMILIAR?
OH YEAH! IN SCHOOL THEY USED TO SHOW US SOME HYGIENE AND ETIQUETTE FILMS ABOUT A PUPPET NAMED MR. BUNGLE.
YEAH, THESE GUYS ARE COOL! WHAT DO YOU THINK OF THE SINGER?
YOU MEAN BESIDES THE FACT THAT HE LOOKS LIKE A YOUNG OZZY OSBOURNE AND STAGGERS AROUND LIKE JOE COCKER?
TELL YOU WHAT... LET'S ASK HIM IF HE EVER WANTED TO JOIN A REAL ROCK BAND!
THUS ENTERS 20 YEAR OLD MIKE PATTON, A HYPERACTIVE, GONZO, BABY-FACED BELLOWER, THE BAND MAKES THEIR MAJOR LABEL DEBUT WITH...
UPON ITS RELEASE MIKE BORDON TELLS *HIT PARADER*...
THIS IS THE ALBUM THAT BEST REPRESENTS FAITH NO MORE.
WE KNOW THERE'LL BE FANS WHO'LL BE PISSED BECAUSE CHUCK'S NOT IN THE BAND ANYMORE...
BUT WE HAD TO MOVE ON, AND HE WAS TOO LAZY TO DO IT! IT'S REALLY THAT SIMPLE!
THE GROUP TOURS NON-STOP FROM MAY '89, BACKING METALLICA IN CALIFORNIA AND DOING A 3 MONTH RUN WITH SPECIMEN VOIVOD AND THE EQUALLY ETHEREAL SOUNDGARDEN. BEFORE LONG THE RAPPIN' HARD ROCK, REGGAE ALBUM IS IN BILLBOARD'S TOP TWENTY. THEIR CONCERTS ARE... UNPREDICTABLE.
SWEET DREAMS YOU CAN'T RESIST...
N-E-S-T-L-E-S
NO MORE WAR PIGS!!
THE PUBLIC FALLS FOR THEM HOOK, LINE AND SINKER, HOWEVER, AS THE CROWDS LINE UP TO SEE THE SELLOUT SHOWS ALL OVER THE NORTH AMERICAN CONTINENT, A CONTROVERSY IS BREWING.
IGUANAS
TONIGHT: FAITH NO MORE
US BORDER

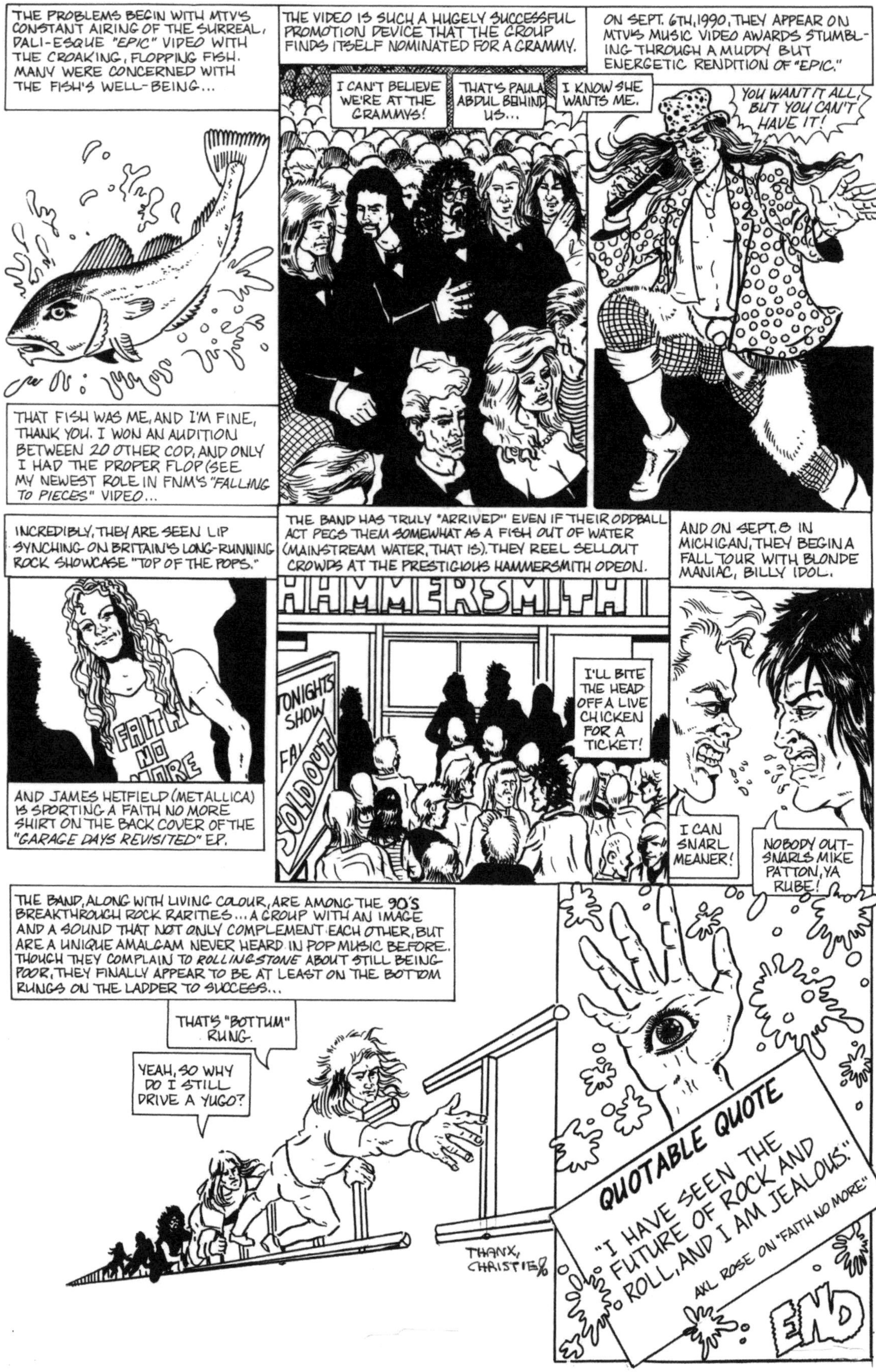
THE PROBLEMS BEGIN WITH MTV'S CONSTANT AIRING OF THE SURREAL, DALI-ESQUE "EPIC" VIDEO WITH THE CROAKING, FLOPPING FISH. MANY WERE CONCERNED WITH THE FISH'S WELL-BEING...
THAT FISH WAS ME, AND I'M FINE, THANK YOU. I WON AN AUDITION BETWEEN 20 OTHER COD, AND ONLY I HAD THE PROPER FLOP (SEE MY NEWEST ROLE IN FNM'S "FALLING TO PIECES" VIDEO...
THE VIDEO IS SUCH A HUGELY SUCCESSFUL PROMOTION DEVICE THAT THE GROUP FINDS ITSELF NOMINATED FOR A GRAMMY.
I CAN'T BELIEVE WE'RE AT THE GRAMMYS!
THAT'S PAULA ABDUL BEHIND US...
I KNOW SHE WANTS ME.
ON SEPT. 6TH, 1990, THEY APPEAR ON MTV'S MUSIC VIDEO AWARDS STUMBLING THROUGH A MUDDY BUT ENERGETIC RENDITION OF "EPIC."
YOU WANT IT ALL, BUT YOU CAN'T HAVE IT!
INCREDIBLY, THEY ARE SEEN LIP SYNCHING ON BRITAIN'S LONG-RUNNING ROCK SHOWCASE "TOP OF THE POPS."
FAITH NO MORE
AND JAMES HETFIELD (METALLICA) IS SPORTING A FAITH NO MORE SHIRT ON THE BACK COVER OF THE "GARAGE DAYS REVISITED" EP.
THE BAND HAS TRULY "ARRIVED" EVEN IF THEIR ODDBALL ACT PEGS THEM SOMEWHAT AS A FISH OUT OF WATER (MAINSTREAM WATER, THAT IS). THEY REEL SELLOUT CROWDS AT THE PRESTIGIOUS HAMMERSMITH ODEON.
HAMMERSMITH
TONIGHTS SHOW
SOLD OUT
I'LL BITE THE HEAD OFF A LIVE CHICKEN FOR A TICKET!
AND ON SEPT. 8 IN MICHIGAN, THEY BEGIN A FALL TOUR WITH BLONDE MANIAC, BILLY IDOL.
I CAN SNARL MEANER!
NOBODY OUT-SNARLS MIKE PATTON, YA RUBE!
THE BAND, ALONG WITH LIVING COLOUR, ARE AMONG THE 90'S BREAKTHROUGH ROCK RARITIES... A GROUP WITH AN IMAGE AND A SOUND THAT NOT ONLY COMPLEMENT EACH OTHER, BUT ARE A UNIQUE AMALGAM NEVER HEARD IN POP MUSIC BEFORE. THOUGH THEY COMPLAIN TO ROLLING STONE ABOUT STILL BEING POOR, THEY FINALLY APPEAR TO BE AT LEAST ON THE BOTTOM RUNGS ON THE LADDER TO SUCCESS...
THAT'S "BOTTUM" RUNG.
YEAH, SO WHY DO I STILL DRIVE A YUGO?
THANX, CHRISTIE
QUOTABLE QUOTE
"I HAVE SEEN THE FUTURE OF ROCK AND ROLL, AND I AM JEALOUS."
AXL ROSE ON "FAITH NO MORE"
END

GUNS 'N' ROSES GREATEST HITS

STORY: Todd Loren, Jay Allen Sanford
ART: Stuart Immonen, Mike Sagara, Jim McWeeney

DUFF McKAGEN

STEVEN ADLER

AXL AND IZZY FROM L.A. GUNS JOIN SLASH, STEVEN, AND DUFF FROM HOLLYWOOD ROSE.

SLASH

AXL ROSE

IZZY STRADLIN

EVEN WITH THE PERMANENT LINE-UP, THE BEGINNING IS TOUGH AS GLAM ROCK DOMINATES THE L.A. SCENE.

EDITOR: Tom Potts
J.A.S.

GUNS N' ROSES SUCKS!

POISON RULES!

SPEAKING OF POISON...

HEY, MAN, YOU'LL BE SORRY IF YOU BOOK GUNS N' ROSES. THEY'LL **DESTROY** YOUR CLUB.

JUST LOOK AT THEM. GUNS N' ROSES ARE NOTHING BUT A BUNCH OF DRUG ADDICTS. IF THEY PLAY HERE THEY'LL RUIN YOUR CLUBS REPUTATION

THIS SUCKS! NO ONE WANTS US! SOMEONE'S FUCKING US UP!

BUT WHO? AND **WHY**?

UM... I THINK I KNOW.

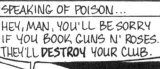

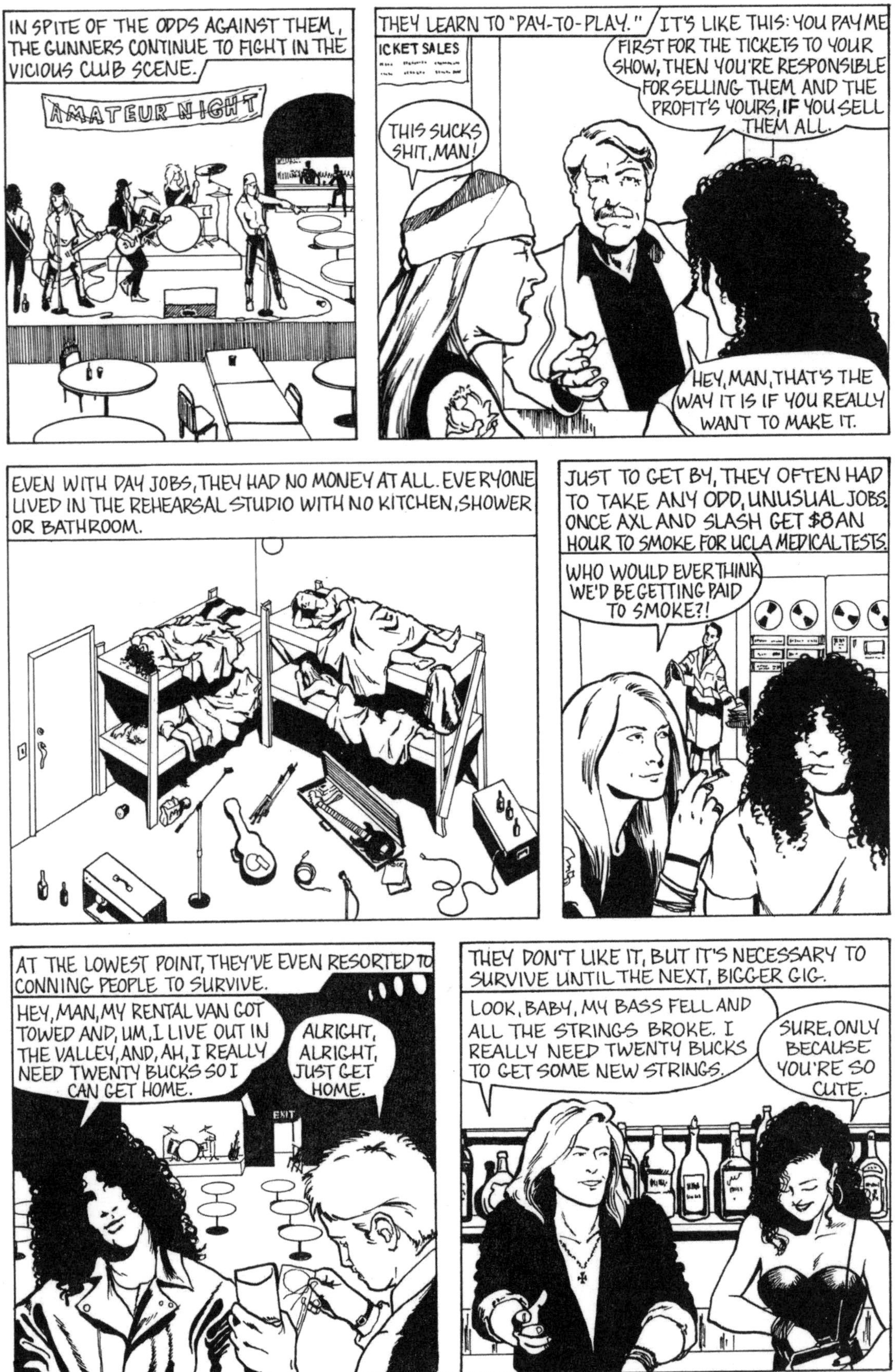
IN SPITE OF THE ODDS AGAINST THEM, THE GUNNERS CONTINUE TO FIGHT IN THE VICIOUS CLUB SCENE.
AMATEUR NIGHT
THEY LEARN TO "PAY-TO-PLAY."
ICKET SALES
IT'S LIKE THIS: YOU PAY ME FIRST FOR THE TICKETS TO YOUR SHOW, THEN YOU'RE RESPONSIBLE FOR SELLING THEM AND THE PROFIT'S YOURS, IF YOU SELL THEM ALL.
THIS SUCKS SHIT, MAN!
HEY, MAN, THAT'S THE WAY IT IS IF YOU REALLY WANT TO MAKE IT.
EVEN WITH DAY JOBS, THEY HAD NO MONEY AT ALL. EVERYONE LIVED IN THE REHEARSAL STUDIO WITH NO KITCHEN, SHOWER OR BATHROOM.
JUST TO GET BY, THEY OFTEN HAD TO TAKE ANY ODD, UNUSUAL JOBS. ONCE AXL AND SLASH GET $8 AN HOUR TO SMOKE FOR UCLA MEDICAL TESTS.
WHO WOULD EVER THINK WE'D BE GETTING PAID TO SMOKE?!
AT THE LOWEST POINT, THEY'VE EVEN RESORTED TO CONNING PEOPLE TO SURVIVE.
HEY, MAN, MY RENTAL VAN GOT TOWED AND, UM, I LIVE OUT IN THE VALLEY, AND, AH, I REALLY NEED TWENTY BUCKS SO I CAN GET HOME.
ALRIGHT, ALRIGHT, JUST GET HOME.
EXIT
THEY DON'T LIKE IT, BUT IT'S NECESSARY TO SURVIVE UNTIL THE NEXT, BIGGER GIG.
LOOK, BABY, MY BASS FELL AND ALL THE STRINGS BROKE. I REALLY NEED TWENTY BUCKS TO GET SOME NEW STRINGS.
SURE, ONLY BECAUSE YOU'RE SO CUTE.

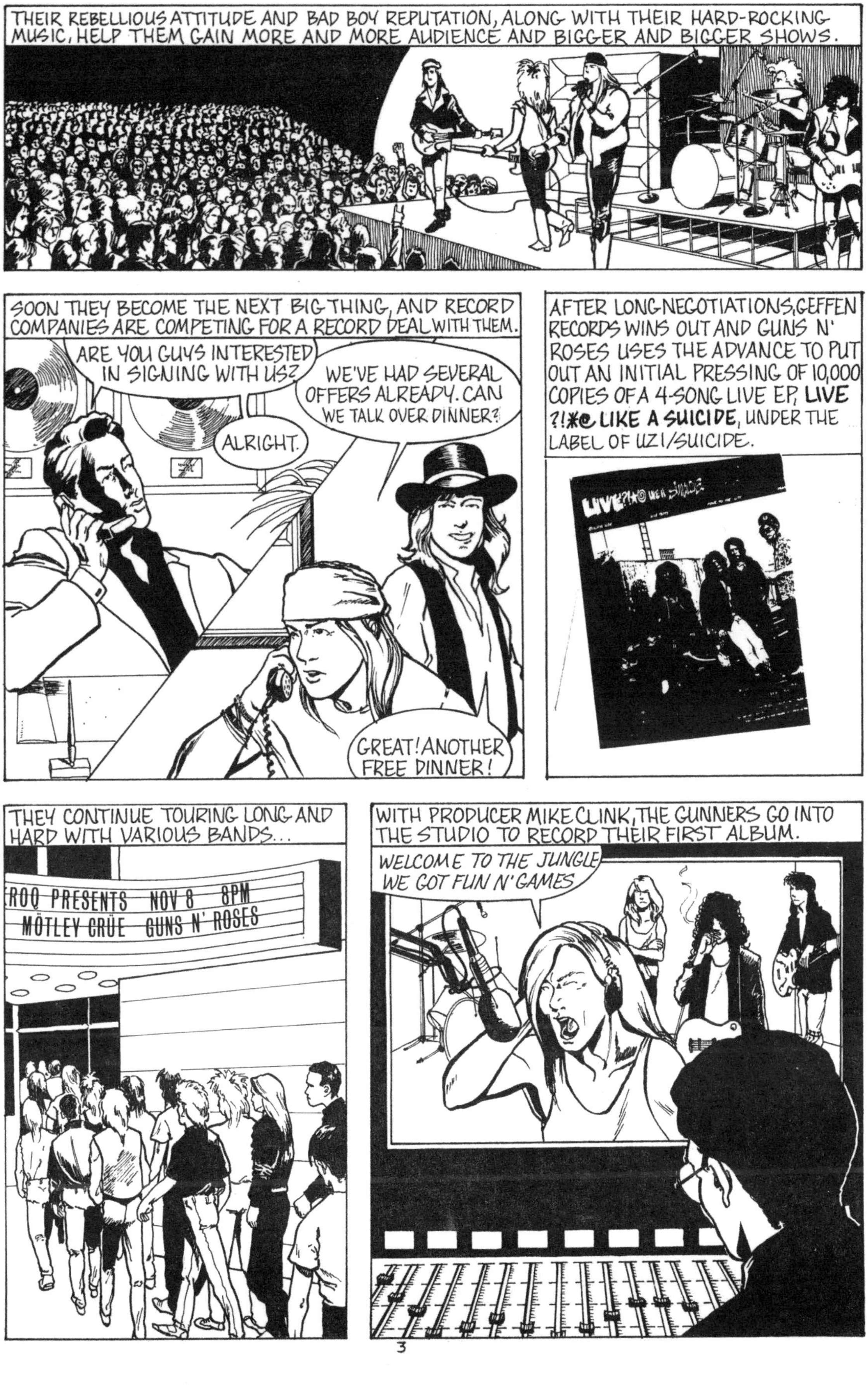
THEIR REBELLIOUS ATTITUDE AND BAD BOY REPUTATION, ALONG WITH THEIR HARD-ROCKING MUSIC, HELP THEM GAIN MORE AND MORE AUDIENCE AND BIGGER AND BIGGER SHOWS.
SOON THEY BECOME THE NEXT BIG THING, AND RECORD COMPANIES ARE COMPETING FOR A RECORD DEAL WITH THEM.
ARE YOU GUYS INTERESTED IN SIGNING WITH US?
WE'VE HAD SEVERAL OFFERS ALREADY. CAN WE TALK OVER DINNER?
ALRIGHT.
GREAT! ANOTHER FREE DINNER!
AFTER LONG NEGOTIATIONS, GEFFEN RECORDS WINS OUT AND GUNS N' ROSES USES THE ADVANCE TO PUT OUT AN INITIAL PRESSING OF 10,000 COPIES OF A 4-SONG LIVE EP, **LIVE ?!*@ LIKE A SUICIDE**, UNDER THE LABEL OF UZI/SUICIDE.
THEY CONTINUE TOURING LONG AND HARD WITH VARIOUS BANDS...
ROQ PRESENTS NOV 8 8PM
MÖTLEY CRÜE GUNS N' ROSES
WITH PRODUCER MIKE CLINK, THE GUNNERS GO INTO THE STUDIO TO RECORD THEIR FIRST ALBUM.
WELCOME TO THE JUNGLE WE GOT FUN N' GAMES

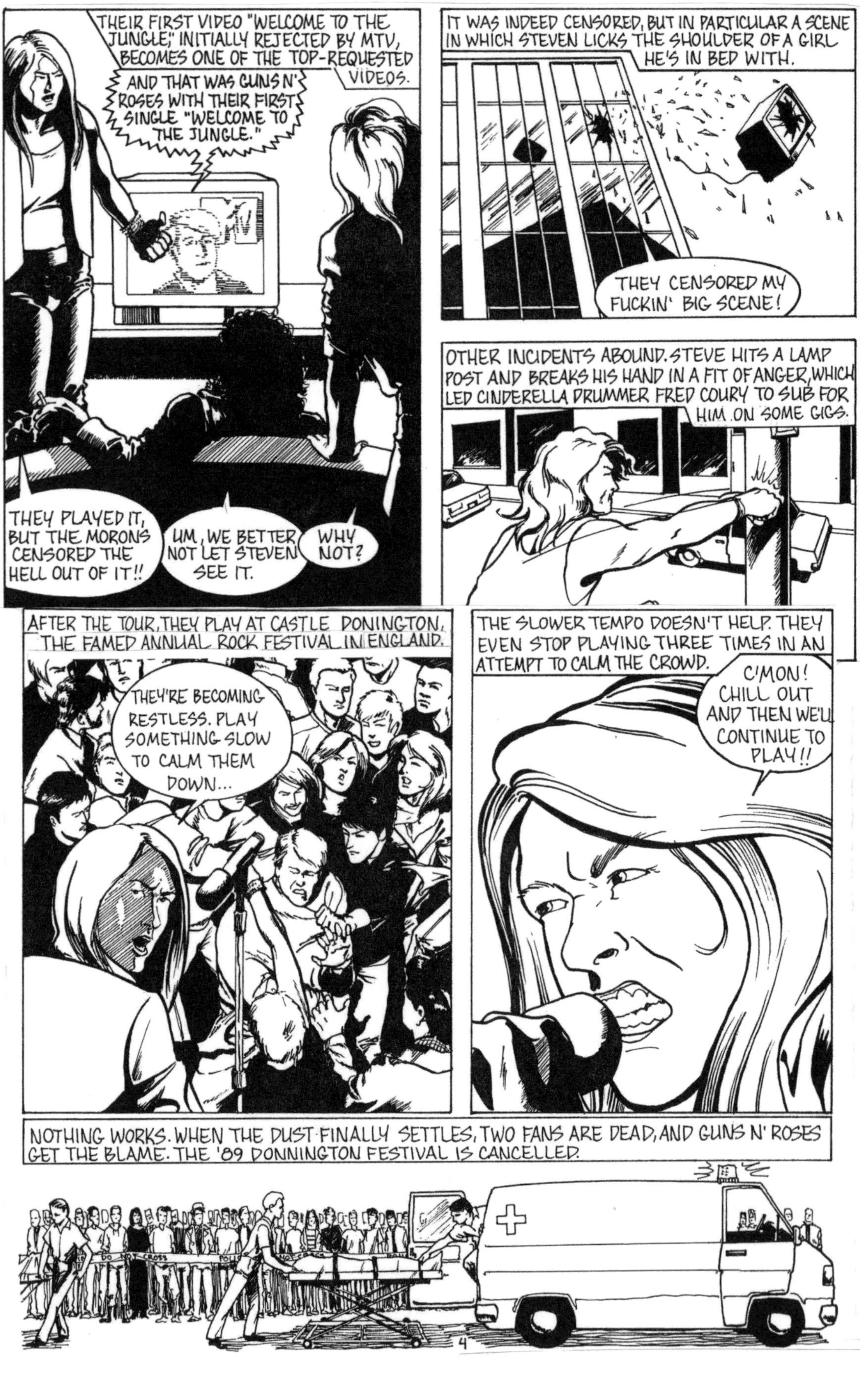
THEIR FIRST VIDEO "WELCOME TO THE JUNGLE," INITIALLY REJECTED BY MTV, BECOMES ONE OF THE TOP-REQUESTED VIDEOS.
AND THAT WAS GUNS N' ROSES WITH THEIR FIRST SINGLE "WELCOME TO THE JUNGLE."
THEY PLAYED IT, BUT THE MORONS CENSORED THE HELL OUT OF IT!!
UM, WE BETTER NOT LET STEVEN SEE IT.
WHY NOT?
IT WAS INDEED CENSORED, BUT IN PARTICULAR A SCENE IN WHICH STEVEN LICKS THE SHOULDER OF A GIRL HE'S IN BED WITH.
THEY CENSORED MY FUCKIN' BIG SCENE!
OTHER INCIDENTS ABOUND. STEVE HITS A LAMP POST AND BREAKS HIS HAND IN A FIT OF ANGER, WHICH LED CINDERELLA DRUMMER FRED COURY TO SUB FOR HIM ON SOME GIGS.
AFTER THE TOUR, THEY PLAY AT CASTLE DONINGTON, THE FAMED ANNUAL ROCK FESTIVAL IN ENGLAND.
THEY'RE BECOMING RESTLESS. PLAY SOMETHING SLOW TO CALM THEM DOWN...
THE SLOWER TEMPO DOESN'T HELP. THEY EVEN STOP PLAYING THREE TIMES IN AN ATTEMPT TO CALM THE CROWD.
C'MON! CHILL OUT AND THEN WE'LL CONTINUE TO PLAY!!
NOTHING WORKS. WHEN THE DUST FINALLY SETTLES, TWO FANS ARE DEAD, AND GUNS N' ROSES GET THE BLAME. THE '89 DONNINGTON FESTIVAL IS CANCELLED.
DO NOT CROSS

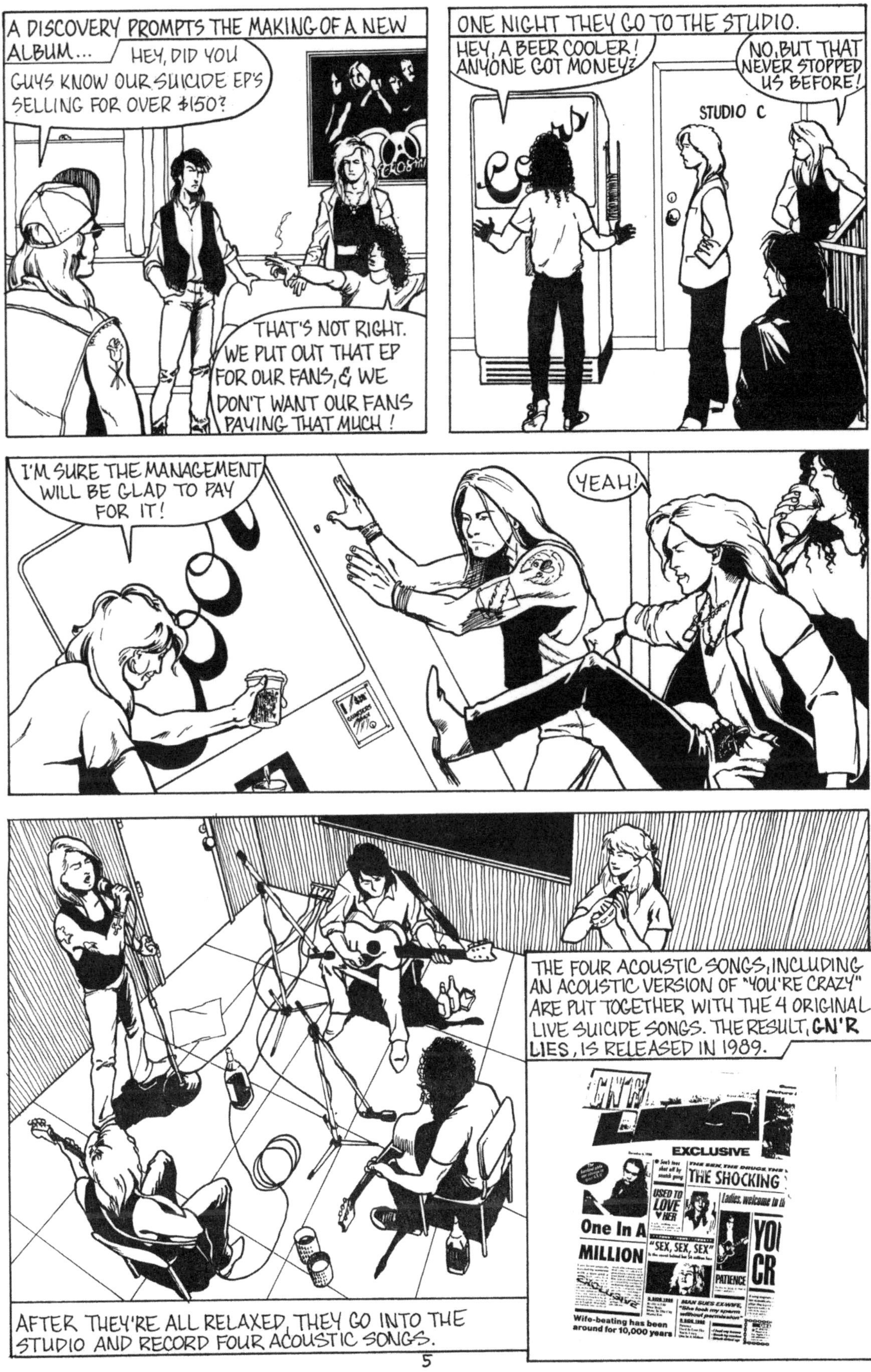
A DISCOVERY PROMPTS THE MAKING OF A NEW ALBUM...
HEY, DID YOU GUYS KNOW OUR SUICIDE EP'S SELLING FOR OVER $150?
THAT'S NOT RIGHT. WE PUT OUT THAT EP FOR OUR FANS, & WE DON'T WANT OUR FANS PAYING THAT MUCH!
ONE NIGHT THEY GO TO THE STUDIO.
HEY, A BEER COOLER! ANYONE GOT MONEY?
NO, BUT THAT NEVER STOPPED US BEFORE!
STUDIO C
I'M SURE THE MANAGEMENT WILL BE GLAD TO PAY FOR IT!
YEAH!
AFTER THEY'RE ALL RELAXED, THEY GO INTO THE STUDIO AND RECORD FOUR ACOUSTIC SONGS.
THE FOUR ACOUSTIC SONGS, INCLUDING AN ACOUSTIC VERSION OF "YOU'RE CRAZY" ARE PUT TOGETHER WITH THE 4 ORIGINAL LIVE SUICIDE SONGS. THE RESULT, GN'R LIES, IS RELEASED IN 1989.
EXCLUSIVE
THE SHOCKING
USED TO LOVE HER
One In A MILLION
"SEX, SEX, SEX"
PATIENCE
Wife-beating has been around for 10,000 years

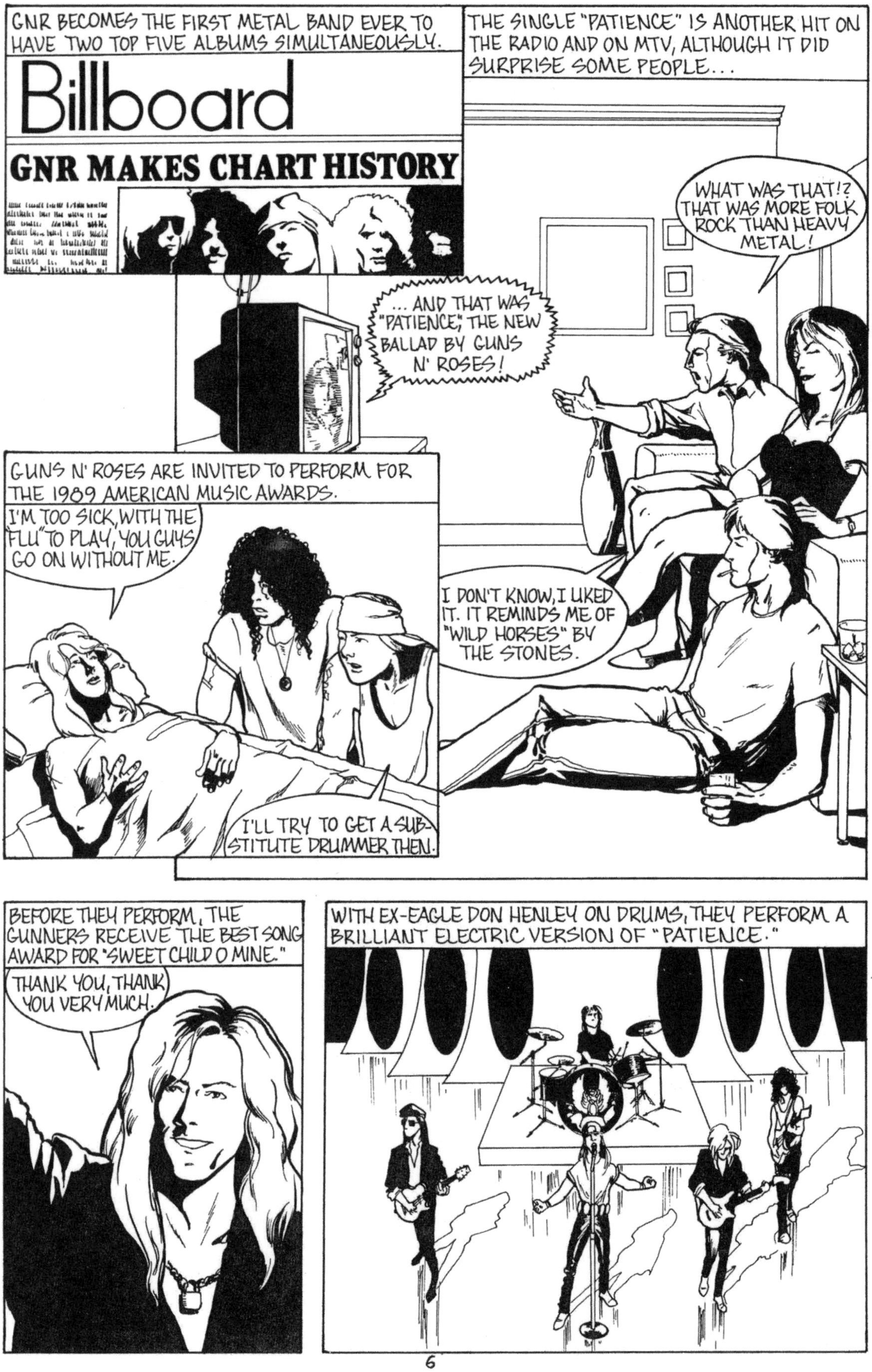
GNR BECOMES THE FIRST METAL BAND EVER TO HAVE TWO TOP FIVE ALBUMS SIMULTANEOUSLY.
Billboard
GNR MAKES CHART HISTORY
THE SINGLE "PATIENCE" IS ANOTHER HIT ON THE RADIO AND ON MTV, ALTHOUGH IT DID SURPRISE SOME PEOPLE...
... AND THAT WAS "PATIENCE," THE NEW BALLAD BY GUNS N' ROSES!
WHAT WAS THAT!? THAT WAS MORE FOLK ROCK THAN HEAVY METAL!
I DON'T KNOW, I LIKED IT. IT REMINDS ME OF "WILD HORSES" BY THE STONES.
GUNS N' ROSES ARE INVITED TO PERFORM FOR THE 1989 AMERICAN MUSIC AWARDS.
I'M TOO SICK, WITH THE "FLU" TO PLAY, YOU GUYS GO ON WITHOUT ME.
I'LL TRY TO GET A SUBSTITUTE DRUMMER THEN.
BEFORE THEY PERFORM, THE GUNNERS RECEIVE THE BEST SONG AWARD FOR "SWEET CHILD O MINE."
THANK YOU, THANK YOU VERY MUCH.
WITH EX-EAGLE DON HENLEY ON DRUMS, THEY PERFORM A BRILLIANT ELECTRIC VERSION OF "PATIENCE."

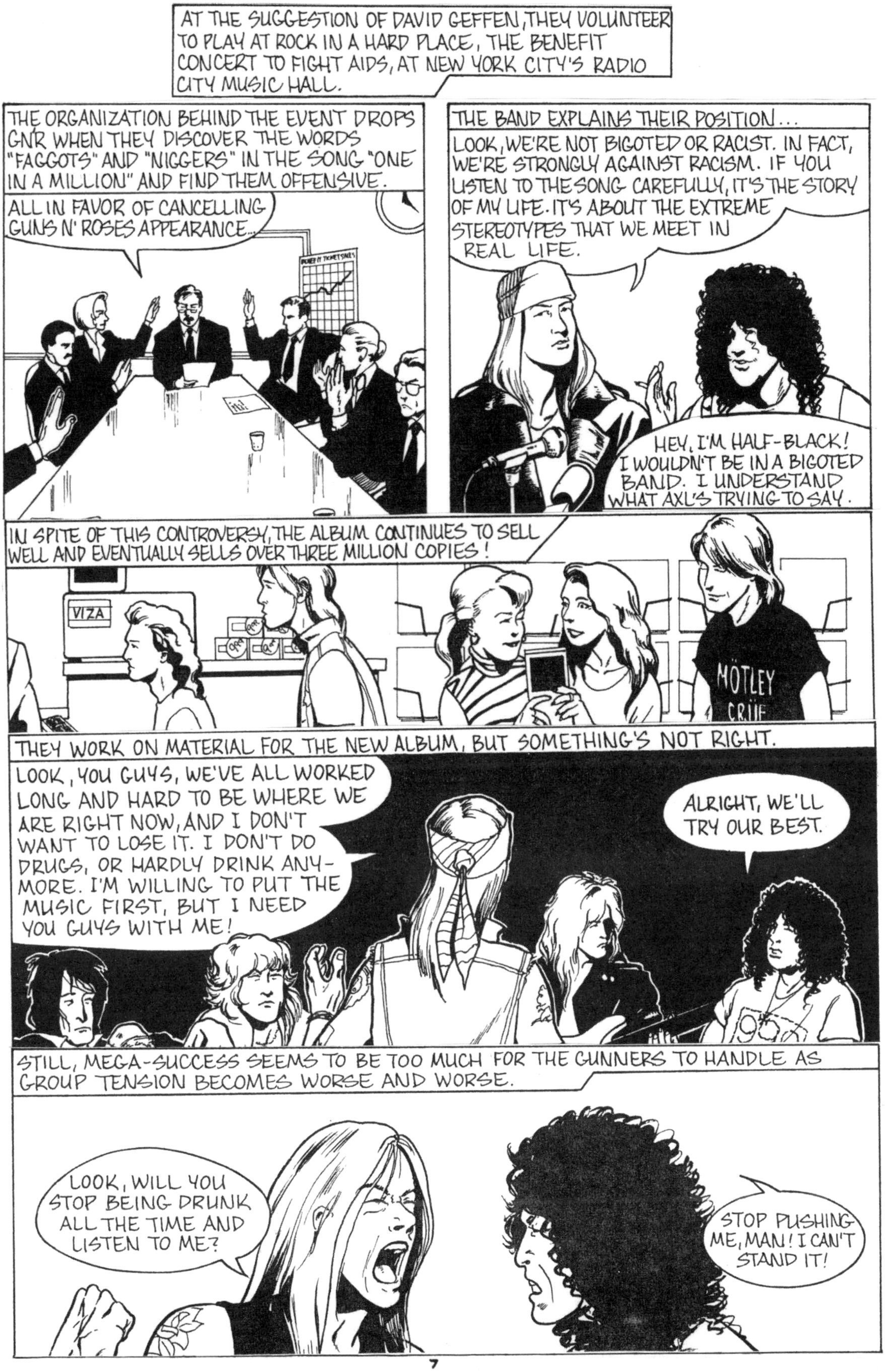
AT THE SUGGESTION OF DAVID GEFFEN, THEY VOLUNTEER TO PLAY AT ROCK IN A HARD PLACE, THE BENEFIT CONCERT TO FIGHT AIDS, AT NEW YORK CITY'S RADIO CITY MUSIC HALL.
THE ORGANIZATION BEHIND THE EVENT DROPS GN'R WHEN THEY DISCOVER THE WORDS "FAGGOTS" AND "NIGGERS" IN THE SONG "ONE IN A MILLION" AND FIND THEM OFFENSIVE.
ALL IN FAVOR OF CANCELLING GUNS N' ROSES APPEARANCE...
THE BAND EXPLAINS THEIR POSITION...
LOOK, WE'RE NOT BIGOTED OR RACIST. IN FACT, WE'RE STRONGLY AGAINST RACISM. IF YOU LISTEN TO THE SONG CAREFULLY, IT'S THE STORY OF MY LIFE. IT'S ABOUT THE EXTREME STEREOTYPES THAT WE MEET IN REAL LIFE.
HEY, I'M HALF-BLACK! I WOULDN'T BE IN A BIGOTED BAND. I UNDERSTAND WHAT AXL'S TRYING TO SAY.
IN SPITE OF THIS CONTROVERSY, THE ALBUM CONTINUES TO SELL WELL AND EVENTUALLY SELLS OVER THREE MILLION COPIES!
VIZA
MÖTLEY CRÜE
THEY WORK ON MATERIAL FOR THE NEW ALBUM, BUT SOMETHING'S NOT RIGHT.
LOOK, YOU GUYS, WE'VE ALL WORKED LONG AND HARD TO BE WHERE WE ARE RIGHT NOW, AND I DON'T WANT TO LOSE IT. I DON'T DO DRUGS, OR HARDLY DRINK ANY-MORE. I'M WILLING TO PUT THE MUSIC FIRST, BUT I NEED YOU GUYS WITH ME!
ALRIGHT, WE'LL TRY OUR BEST.
STILL, MEGA-SUCCESS SEEMS TO BE TOO MUCH FOR THE GUNNERS TO HANDLE AS GROUP TENSION BECOMES WORSE AND WORSE.
LOOK, WILL YOU STOP BEING DRUNK ALL THE TIME AND LISTEN TO ME?
STOP PUSHING ME, MAN! I CAN'T STAND IT!

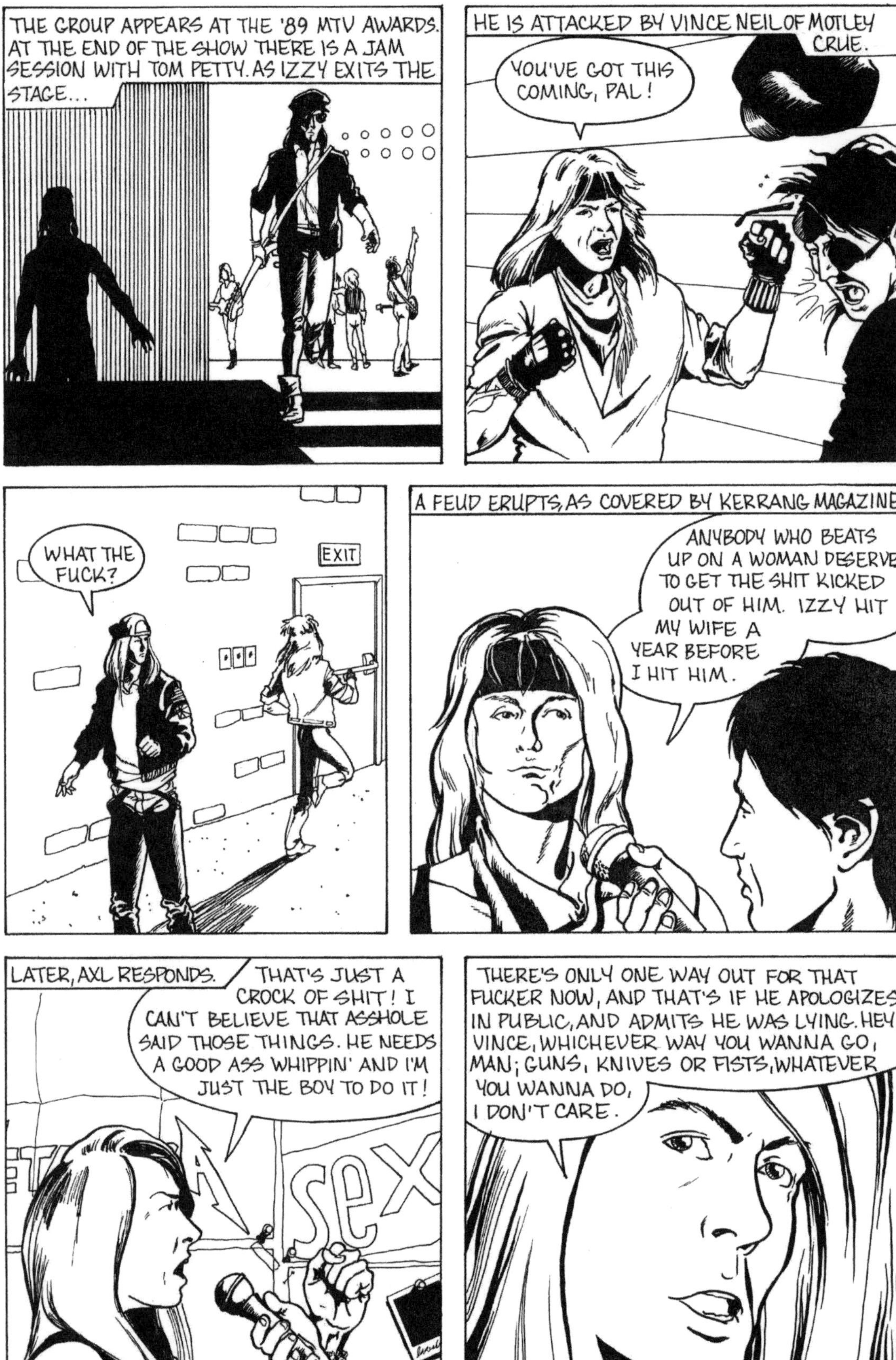
THE GROUP APPEARS AT THE '89 MTV AWARDS. AT THE END OF THE SHOW THERE IS A JAM SESSION WITH TOM PETTY. AS IZZY EXITS THE STAGE...
HE IS ATTACKED BY VINCE NEIL OF MOTLEY CRUE.
YOU'VE GOT THIS COMING, PAL!
WHAT THE FUCK?
EXIT
A FEUD ERUPTS, AS COVERED BY KERRANG MAGAZINE.
ANYBODY WHO BEATS UP ON A WOMAN DESERVES TO GET THE SHIT KICKED OUT OF HIM. IZZY HIT MY WIFE A YEAR BEFORE I HIT HIM.
LATER, AXL RESPONDS.
THAT'S JUST A CROCK OF SHIT! I CAN'T BELIEVE THAT ASSHOLE SAID THOSE THINGS. HE NEEDS A GOOD ASS WHIPPIN' AND I'M JUST THE BOY TO DO IT!
sex
THERE'S ONLY ONE WAY OUT FOR THAT FUCKER NOW, AND THAT'S IF HE APOLOGIZES IN PUBLIC, AND ADMITS HE WAS LYING. HEY, VINCE, WHICHEVER WAY YOU WANNA GO, MAN; GUNS, KNIVES OR FISTS, WHATEVER YOU WANNA DO, I DON'T CARE.

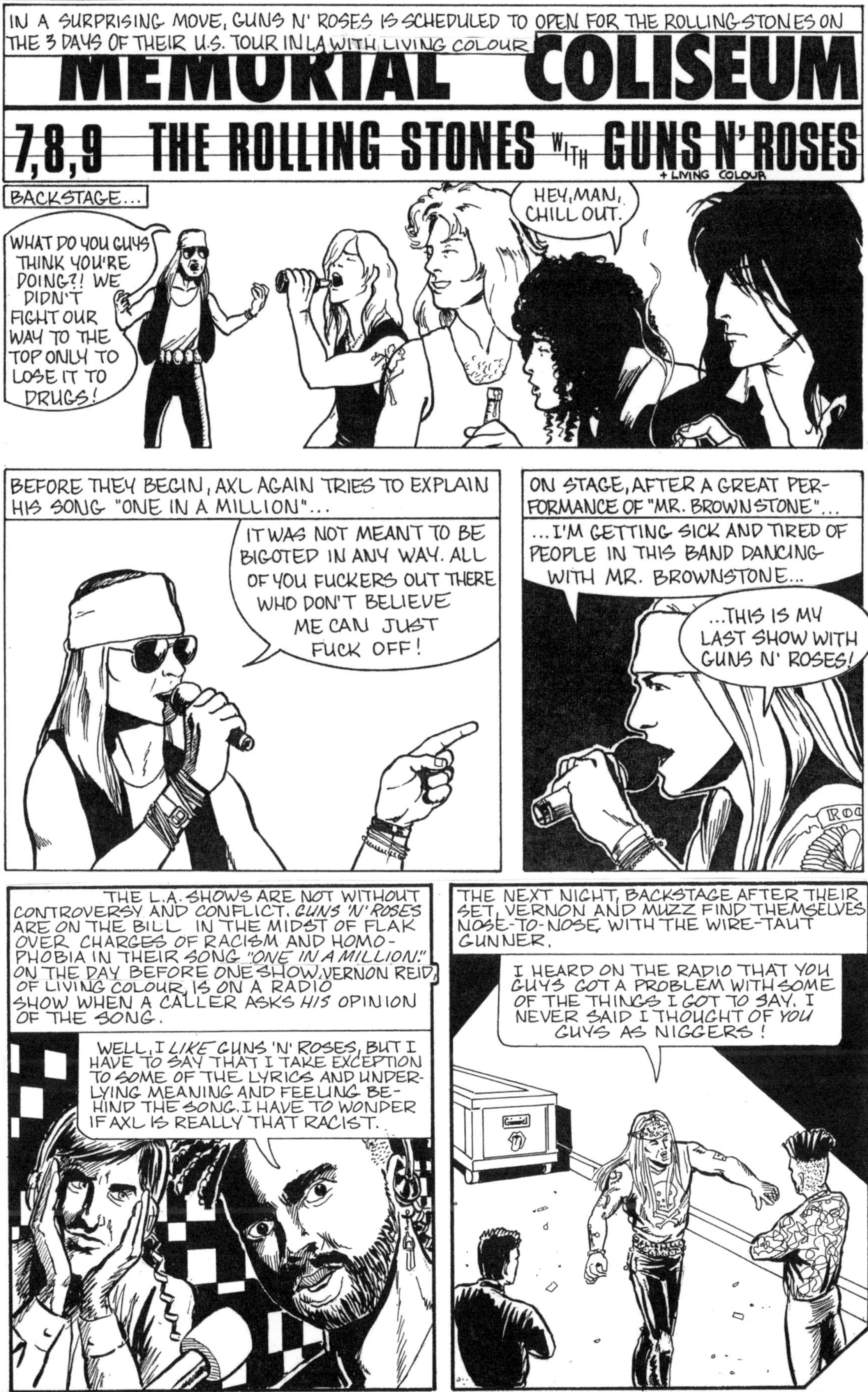
IN A SURPRISING MOVE, GUNS N' ROSES IS SCHEDULED TO OPEN FOR THE ROLLING STONES ON THE 3 DAYS OF THEIR U.S. TOUR IN L.A. WITH LIVING COLOUR
MEMORIAL COLISEUM
7,8,9 THE ROLLING STONES WITH GUNS N' ROSES
+ LIVING COLOUR
BACKSTAGE...
WHAT DO YOU GUYS THINK YOU'RE DOING?! WE DIDN'T FIGHT OUR WAY TO THE TOP ONLY TO LOSE IT TO DRUGS!
HEY, MAN, CHILL OUT.
BEFORE THEY BEGIN, AXL AGAIN TRIES TO EXPLAIN HIS SONG "ONE IN A MILLION"...
IT WAS NOT MEANT TO BE BIGOTED IN ANY WAY. ALL OF YOU FUCKERS OUT THERE WHO DON'T BELIEVE ME CAN JUST FUCK OFF!
ON STAGE, AFTER A GREAT PERFORMANCE OF "MR. BROWNSTONE"...
...I'M GETTING SICK AND TIRED OF PEOPLE IN THIS BAND DANCING WITH MR. BROWNSTONE...
...THIS IS MY LAST SHOW WITH GUNS N' ROSES!
THE L.A. SHOWS ARE NOT WITHOUT CONTROVERSY AND CONFLICT. GUNS 'N' ROSES ARE ON THE BILL IN THE MIDST OF FLAK OVER CHARGES OF RACISM AND HOMOPHOBIA IN THEIR SONG "ONE IN A MILLION." ON THE DAY BEFORE ONE SHOW, VERNON REID, OF LIVING COLOUR, IS ON A RADIO SHOW WHEN A CALLER ASKS HIS OPINION OF THE SONG.
WELL, I LIKE GUNS 'N' ROSES, BUT I HAVE TO SAY THAT I TAKE EXCEPTION TO SOME OF THE LYRICS AND UNDERLYING MEANING AND FEELING BEHIND THE SONG. I HAVE TO WONDER IF AXL IS REALLY THAT RACIST.
THE NEXT NIGHT, BACKSTAGE AFTER THEIR SET, VERNON AND MUZZ FIND THEMSELVES NOSE-TO-NOSE WITH THE WIRE-TAUT GUNNER.
I HEARD ON THE RADIO THAT YOU GUYS GOT A PROBLEM WITH SOME OF THE THINGS I GOT TO SAY. I NEVER SAID I THOUGHT OF YOU GUYS AS NIGGERS!

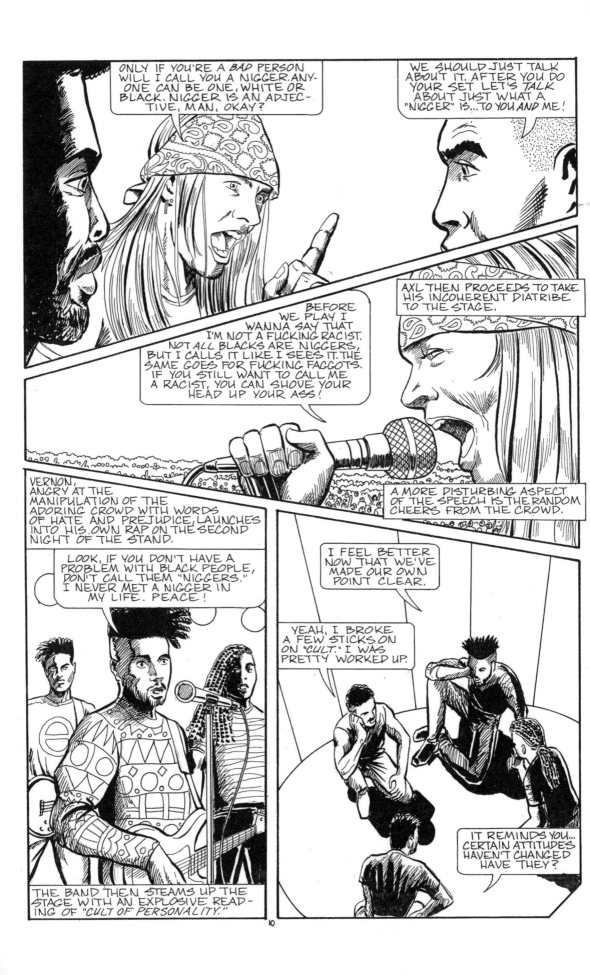

ONLY IF YOU'RE A *BAD* PERSON WILL I CALL YOU A NIGGER. ANY-ONE CAN BE ONE, WHITE OR BLACK. NIGGER IS AN ADJEC-TIVE, MAN, OKAY?

WE SHOULD JUST TALK ABOUT IT. AFTER YOU DO YOUR SET LET'S *TALK* ABOUT JUST WHAT A "NIGGER" IS...TO YOU AND ME!

BEFORE WE PLAY I WANNA SAY THAT I'M NOT A FUCKING RACIST. NOT ALL BLACKS ARE NIGGERS, BUT I CALLS IT LIKE I SEES IT. THE SAME GOES FOR FUCKING FAGGOTS. IF YOU STILL WANT TO CALL ME A RACIST, YOU CAN SHOVE YOUR HEAD UP YOUR ASS!

AXL THEN PROCEEDS TO TAKE HIS INCOHERENT DIATRIBE TO THE STAGE.

A MORE DISTURBING ASPECT OF THE SPEECH IS THE RANDOM CHEERS FROM THE CROWD.

VERNON, ANGRY AT THE MANIPULATION OF THE ADORING CROWD WITH WORDS OF HATE AND PREJUDICE, LAUNCHES INTO HIS OWN RAP ON THE SECOND NIGHT OF THE STAND.

LOOK, IF YOU DON'T HAVE A PROBLEM WITH BLACK PEOPLE, DON'T CALL THEM "NIGGERS." I NEVER MET A NIGGER IN MY LIFE. PEACE!

THE BAND THEN STEAMS UP THE STAGE WITH AN EXPLOSIVE READ-ING OF "*CULT OF PERSONALITY.*"

I FEEL BETTER NOW THAT WE'VE MADE OUR OWN POINT CLEAR.

YEAH, I BROKE A FEW STICKS ON ON "*CULT.*" I WAS PRETTY WORKED UP.

IT REMINDS YOU... CERTAIN ATTITUDES HAVEN'T CHANGED HAVE THEY?

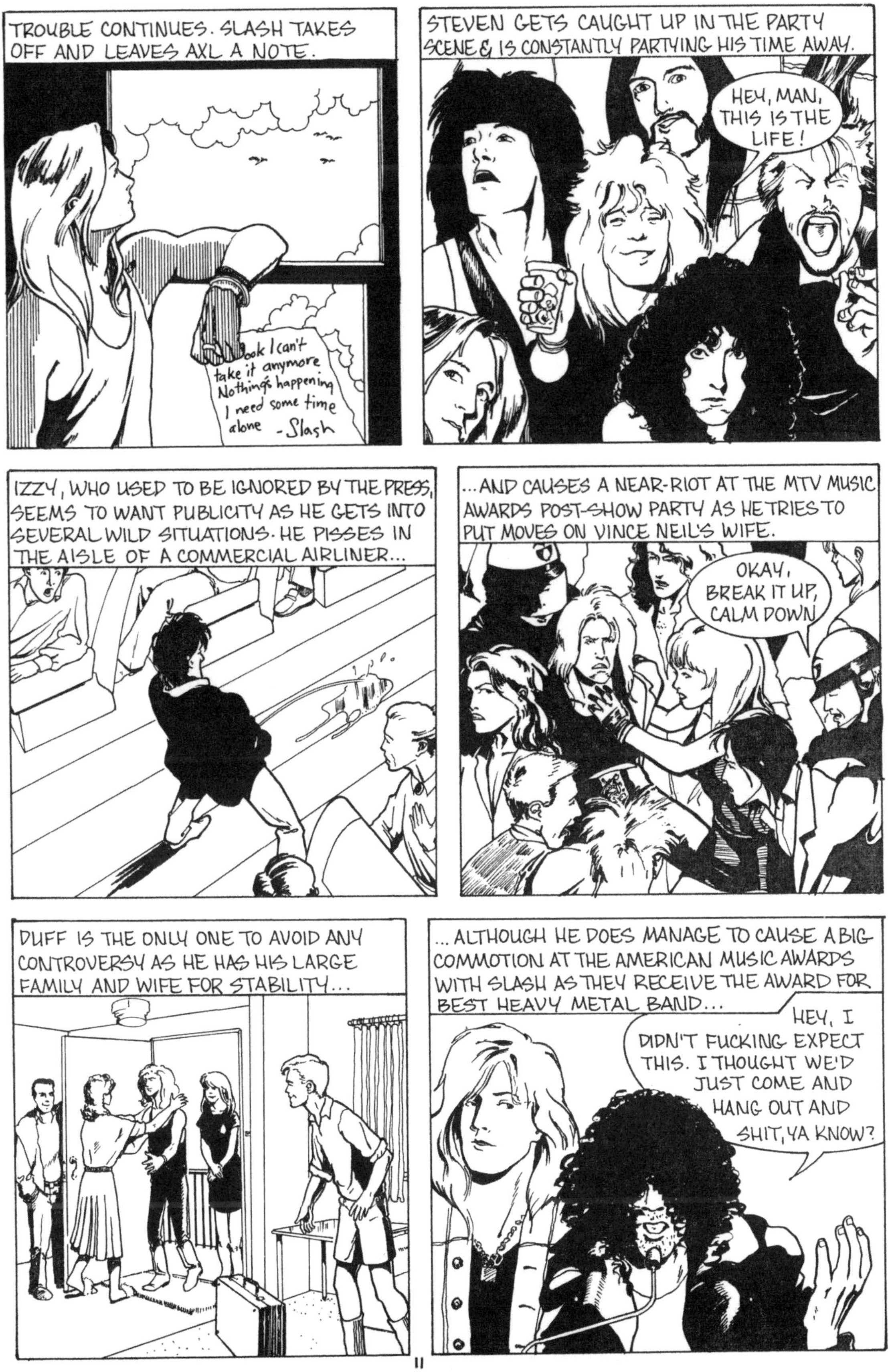
TROUBLE CONTINUES. SLASH TAKES OFF AND LEAVES AXL A NOTE.
ook I can't take it anymore Nothing's happening I need some time alone -Slash
STEVEN GETS CAUGHT UP IN THE PARTY SCENE & IS CONSTANTLY PARTYING HIS TIME AWAY.
HEY, MAN, THIS IS THE LIFE!
IZZY, WHO USED TO BE IGNORED BY THE PRESS, SEEMS TO WANT PUBLICITY AS HE GETS INTO SEVERAL WILD SITUATIONS. HE PISSES IN THE AISLE OF A COMMERCIAL AIRLINER...
...AND CAUSES A NEAR-RIOT AT THE MTV MUSIC AWARDS POST-SHOW PARTY AS HE TRIES TO PUT MOVES ON VINCE NEIL'S WIFE.
OKAY, BREAK IT UP, CALM DOWN
DUFF IS THE ONLY ONE TO AVOID ANY CONTROVERSY AS HE HAS HIS LARGE FAMILY AND WIFE FOR STABILITY...
... ALTHOUGH HE DOES MANAGE TO CAUSE A BIG COMMOTION AT THE AMERICAN MUSIC AWARDS WITH SLASH AS THEY RECEIVE THE AWARD FOR BEST HEAVY METAL BAND...
HEY, I DIDN'T FUCKING EXPECT THIS. I THOUGHT WE'D JUST COME AND HANG OUT AND SHIT, YA KNOW?

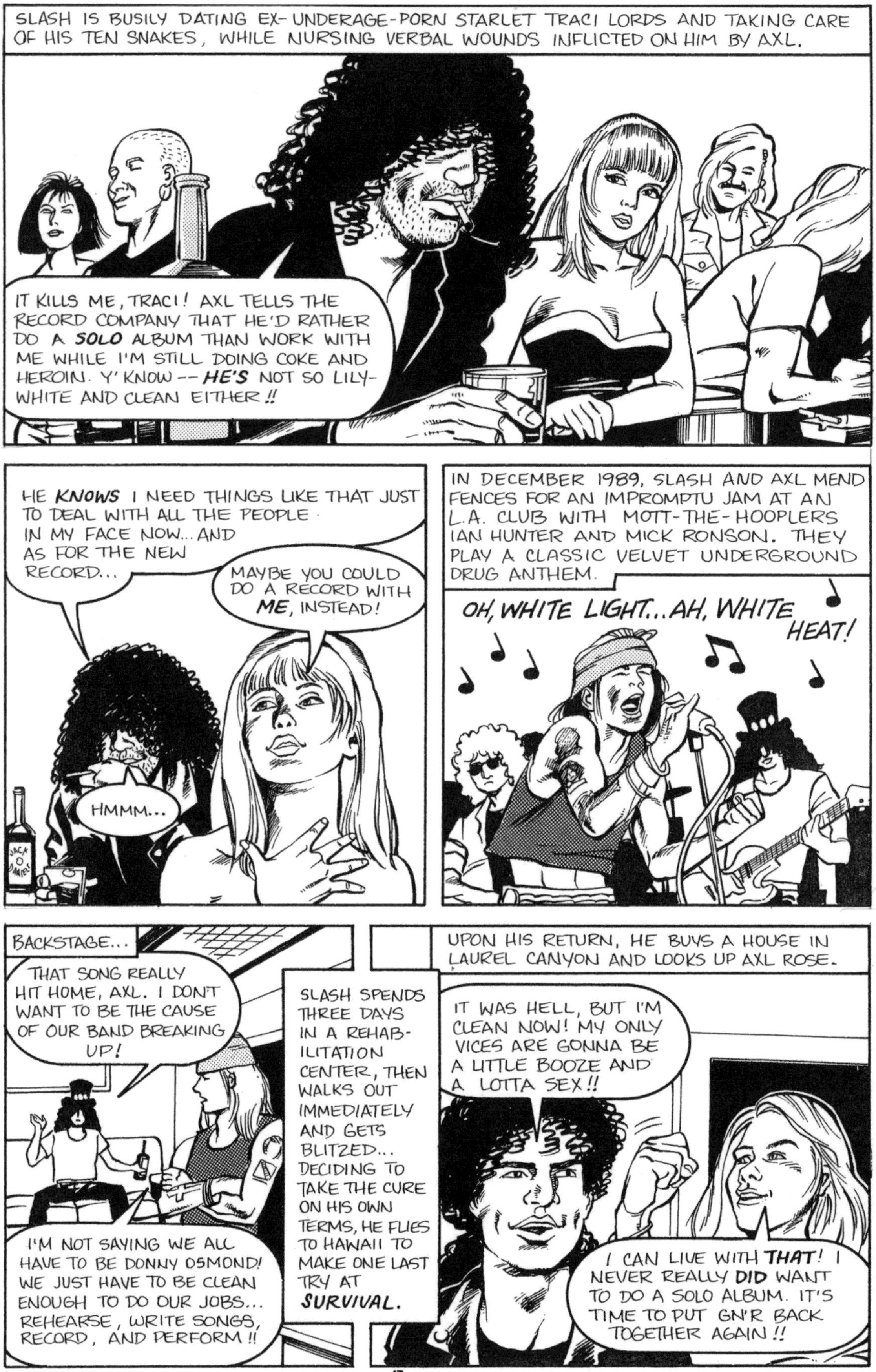

SLASH IS BUSILY DATING EX-UNDERAGE-PORN STARLET TRACI LORDS AND TAKING CARE OF HIS TEN SNAKES, WHILE NURSING VERBAL WOUNDS INFLICTED ON HIM BY AXL.
IT KILLS ME, TRACI! AXL TELLS THE RECORD COMPANY THAT HE'D RATHER DO A **SOLO** ALBUM THAN WORK WITH ME WHILE I'M STILL DOING COKE AND HEROIN. Y' KNOW -- **HE'S** NOT SO LILY-WHITE AND CLEAN EITHER!!
HE **KNOWS** I NEED THINGS LIKE THAT JUST TO DEAL WITH ALL THE PEOPLE IN MY FACE NOW... AND AS FOR THE NEW RECORD...
MAYBE YOU COULD DO A RECORD WITH **ME**, INSTEAD!
HMMM...
IN DECEMBER 1989, SLASH AND AXL MEND FENCES FOR AN IMPROMPTU JAM AT AN L.A. CLUB WITH MOTT-THE-HOOPLERS IAN HUNTER AND MICK RONSON. THEY PLAY A CLASSIC VELVET UNDERGROUND DRUG ANTHEM.
OH, WHITE LIGHT... AH, WHITE HEAT!
BACKSTAGE...
THAT SONG REALLY HIT HOME, AXL. I DON'T WANT TO BE THE CAUSE OF OUR BAND BREAKING UP!
I'M NOT SAYING WE ALL HAVE TO BE DONNY OSMOND! WE JUST HAVE TO BE CLEAN ENOUGH TO DO OUR JOBS... REHEARSE, WRITE SONGS, RECORD, AND PERFORM!!
SLASH SPENDS THREE DAYS IN A REHABILITATION CENTER, THEN WALKS OUT IMMEDIATELY AND GETS BLITZED... DECIDING TO TAKE THE CURE ON HIS OWN TERMS, HE FLIES TO HAWAII TO MAKE ONE LAST TRY AT **SURVIVAL**.
UPON HIS RETURN, HE BUYS A HOUSE IN LAUREL CANYON AND LOOKS UP AXL ROSE.
IT WAS HELL, BUT I'M CLEAN NOW! MY ONLY VICES ARE GONNA BE A LITTLE BOOZE AND A LOTTA SEX!!
I CAN LIVE WITH **THAT**! I NEVER REALLY **DID** WANT TO DO A SOLO ALBUM. IT'S TIME TO PUT GN'R BACK TOGETHER AGAIN!!

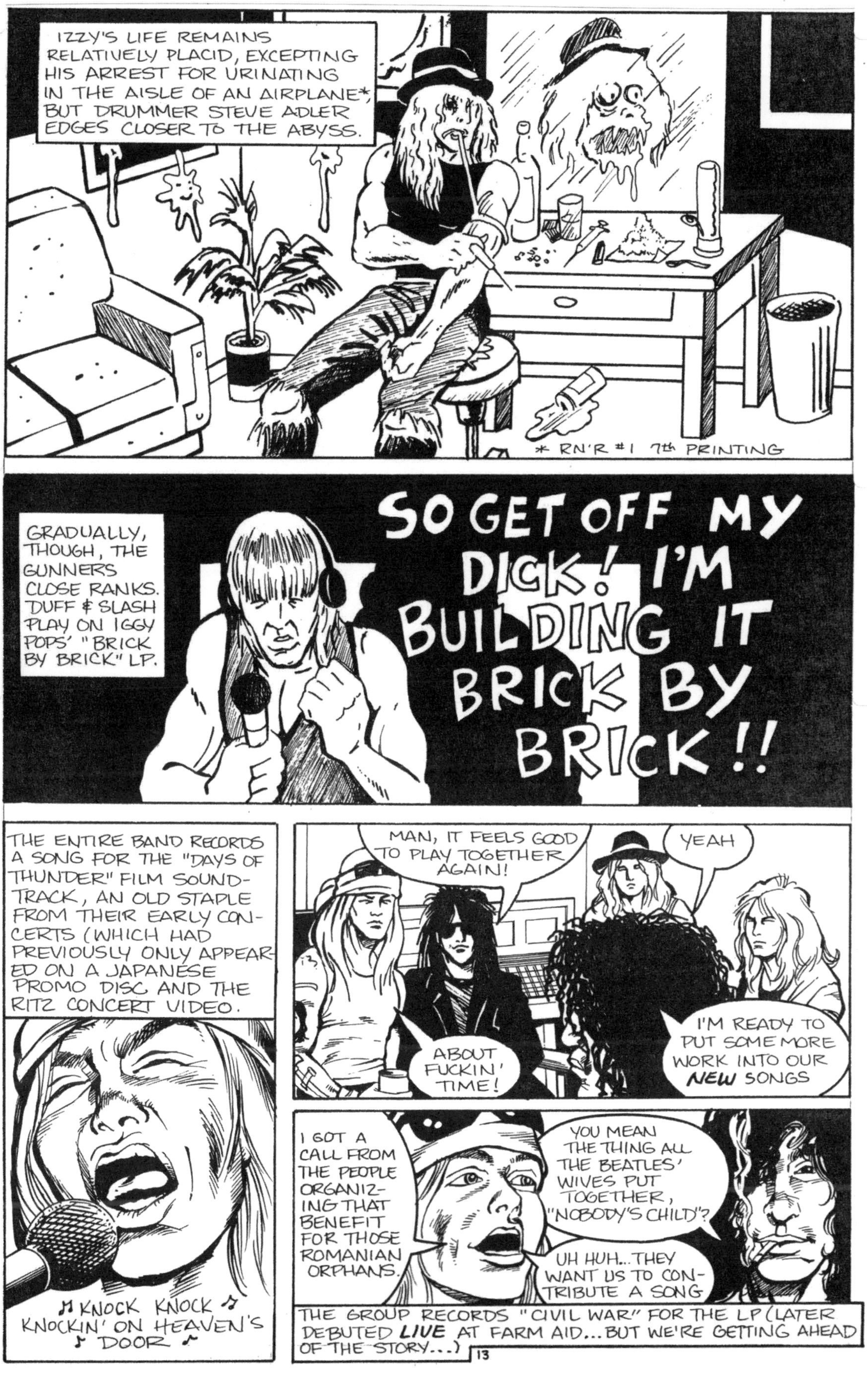
IZZY'S LIFE REMAINS RELATIVELY PLACID, EXCEPTING HIS ARREST FOR URINATING IN THE AISLE OF AN AIRPLANE*, BUT DRUMMER STEVE ADLER EDGES CLOSER TO THE ABYSS.
* RN'R #1 7th PRINTING
GRADUALLY, THOUGH, THE GUNNERS CLOSE RANKS. DUFF & SLASH PLAY ON IGGY POPS' "BRICK BY BRICK" LP.
SO GET OFF MY DICK! I'M BUILDING IT BRICK BY BRICK!!
THE ENTIRE BAND RECORDS A SONG FOR THE "DAYS OF THUNDER" FILM SOUNDTRACK, AN OLD STAPLE FROM THEIR EARLY CONCERTS (WHICH HAD PREVIOUSLY ONLY APPEARED ON A JAPANESE PROMO DISC AND THE RITZ CONCERT VIDEO.
♫ KNOCK KNOCK ♫ KNOCKIN' ON HEAVEN'S ♪ DOOR ♪
MAN, IT FEELS GOOD TO PLAY TOGETHER AGAIN!
YEAH
ABOUT FUCKIN' TIME!
I'M READY TO PUT SOME MORE WORK INTO OUR NEW SONGS
I GOT A CALL FROM THE PEOPLE ORGANIZING THAT BENEFIT FOR THOSE ROMANIAN ORPHANS.
YOU MEAN THE THING ALL THE BEATLES' WIVES PUT TOGETHER, "NOBODY'S CHILD"?
UH HUH... THEY WANT US TO CONTRIBUTE A SONG
THE GROUP RECORDS "CIVIL WAR" FOR THE LP (LATER DEBUTED LIVE AT FARM AID... BUT WE'RE GETTING AHEAD OF THE STORY...)

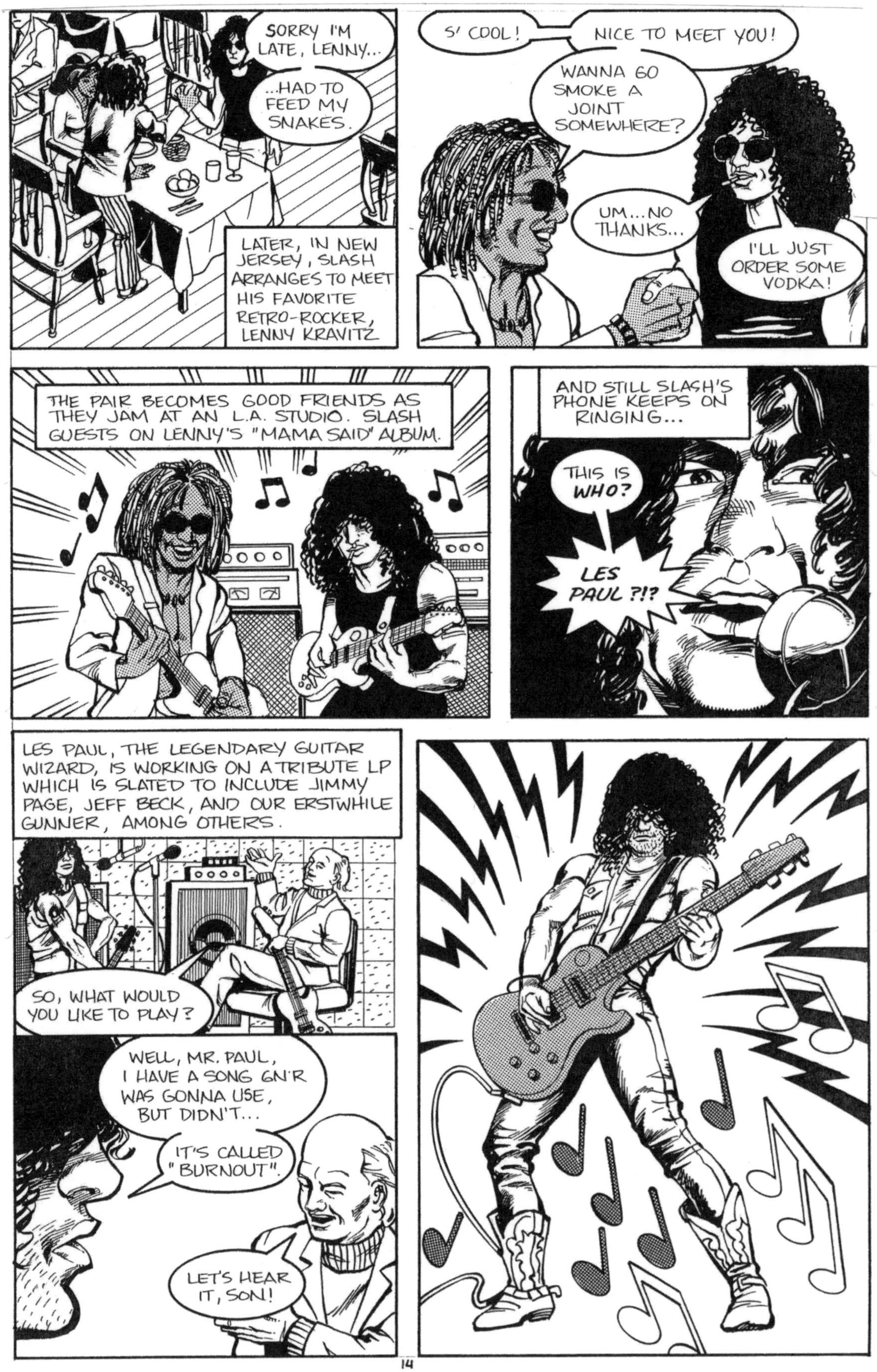
SORRY I'M LATE, LENNY...
...HAD TO FEED MY SNAKES.
LATER, IN NEW JERSEY, SLASH ARRANGES TO MEET HIS FAVORITE RETRO-ROCKER, LENNY KRAVITZ
S' COOL!
NICE TO MEET YOU!
WANNA GO SMOKE A JOINT SOMEWHERE?
UM...NO THANKS...
I'LL JUST ORDER SOME VODKA!
THE PAIR BECOMES GOOD FRIENDS AS THEY JAM AT AN L.A. STUDIO. SLASH GUESTS ON LENNY'S "MAMA SAID" ALBUM.
AND STILL SLASH'S PHONE KEEPS ON RINGING...
THIS IS WHO?
LES PAUL ?!?
LES PAUL, THE LEGENDARY GUITAR WIZARD, IS WORKING ON A TRIBUTE LP WHICH IS SLATED TO INCLUDE JIMMY PAGE, JEFF BECK, AND OUR ERSTWHILE GUNNER, AMONG OTHERS.
SO, WHAT WOULD YOU LIKE TO PLAY?
WELL, MR. PAUL, I HAVE A SONG GN'R WAS GONNA USE, BUT DIDN'T...
IT'S CALLED "BURNOUT".
LET'S HEAR IT, SON!

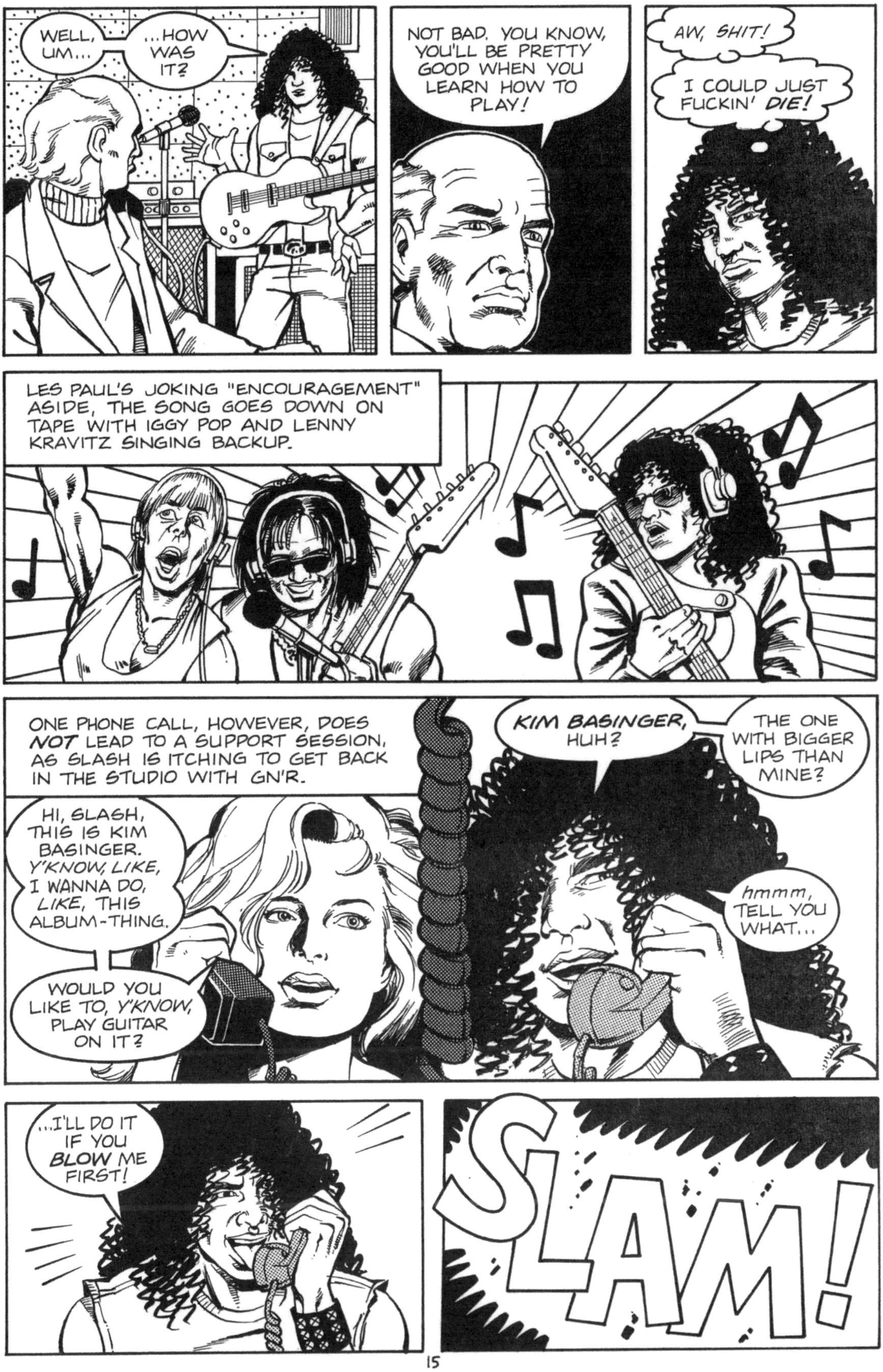
WELL, UM...
...HOW WAS IT?
NOT BAD. YOU KNOW, YOU'LL BE PRETTY GOOD WHEN YOU LEARN HOW TO PLAY!
AW, SHIT!
I COULD JUST FUCKIN' DIE!
LES PAUL'S JOKING "ENCOURAGEMENT" ASIDE, THE SONG GOES DOWN ON TAPE WITH IGGY POP AND LENNY KRAVITZ SINGING BACKUP.
ONE PHONE CALL, HOWEVER, DOES NOT LEAD TO A SUPPORT SESSION, AS SLASH IS ITCHING TO GET BACK IN THE STUDIO WITH GN'R.
HI, SLASH, THIS IS KIM BASINGER. Y'KNOW, LIKE, I WANNA DO, LIKE, THIS ALBUM-THING.
WOULD YOU LIKE TO, Y'KNOW, PLAY GUITAR ON IT?
KIM BASINGER, HUH?
THE ONE WITH BIGGER LIPS THAN MINE?
hmmm, TELL YOU WHAT...
...I'LL DO IT IF YOU BLOW ME FIRST!
SLAM!

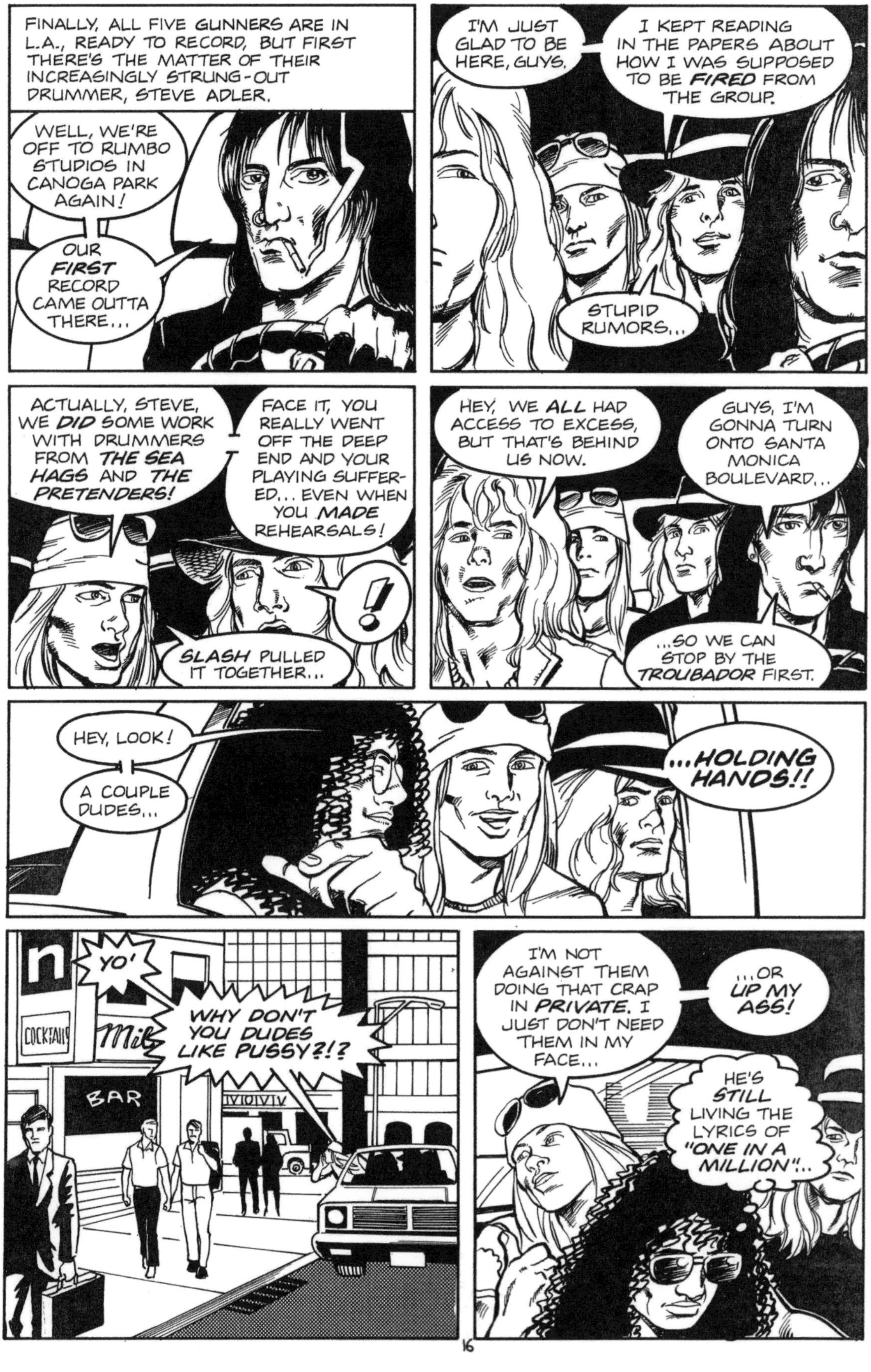
FINALLY, ALL FIVE GUNNERS ARE IN L.A., READY TO RECORD, BUT FIRST THERE'S THE MATTER OF THEIR INCREASINGLY STRUNG-OUT DRUMMER, STEVE ADLER.
WELL, WE'RE OFF TO RUMBO STUDIOS IN CANOGA PARK AGAIN!
OUR FIRST RECORD CAME OUTTA THERE...
I'M JUST GLAD TO BE HERE, GUYS.
I KEPT READING IN THE PAPERS ABOUT HOW I WAS SUPPOSED TO BE FIRED FROM THE GROUP.
STUPID RUMORS...
ACTUALLY, STEVE, WE DID SOME WORK WITH DRUMMERS FROM THE SEA HAGS AND THE PRETENDERS!
FACE IT, YOU REALLY WENT OFF THE DEEP END AND YOUR PLAYING SUFFERED... EVEN WHEN YOU MADE REHEARSALS!
!
SLASH PULLED IT TOGETHER...
HEY, WE ALL HAD ACCESS TO EXCESS, BUT THAT'S BEHIND US NOW.
GUYS, I'M GONNA TURN ONTO SANTA MONICA BOULEVARD...
...SO WE CAN STOP BY THE TROUBADOR FIRST.
HEY, LOOK!
A COUPLE DUDES...
...HOLDING HANDS!!
YO'
WHY DON'T YOU DUDES LIKE PUSSY?!?
COCKTAILS
BAR
I'M NOT AGAINST THEM DOING THAT CRAP IN PRIVATE. I JUST DON'T NEED THEM IN MY FACE...
...OR UP MY ASS!
HE'S STILL LIVING THE LYRICS OF "ONE IN A MILLION"...

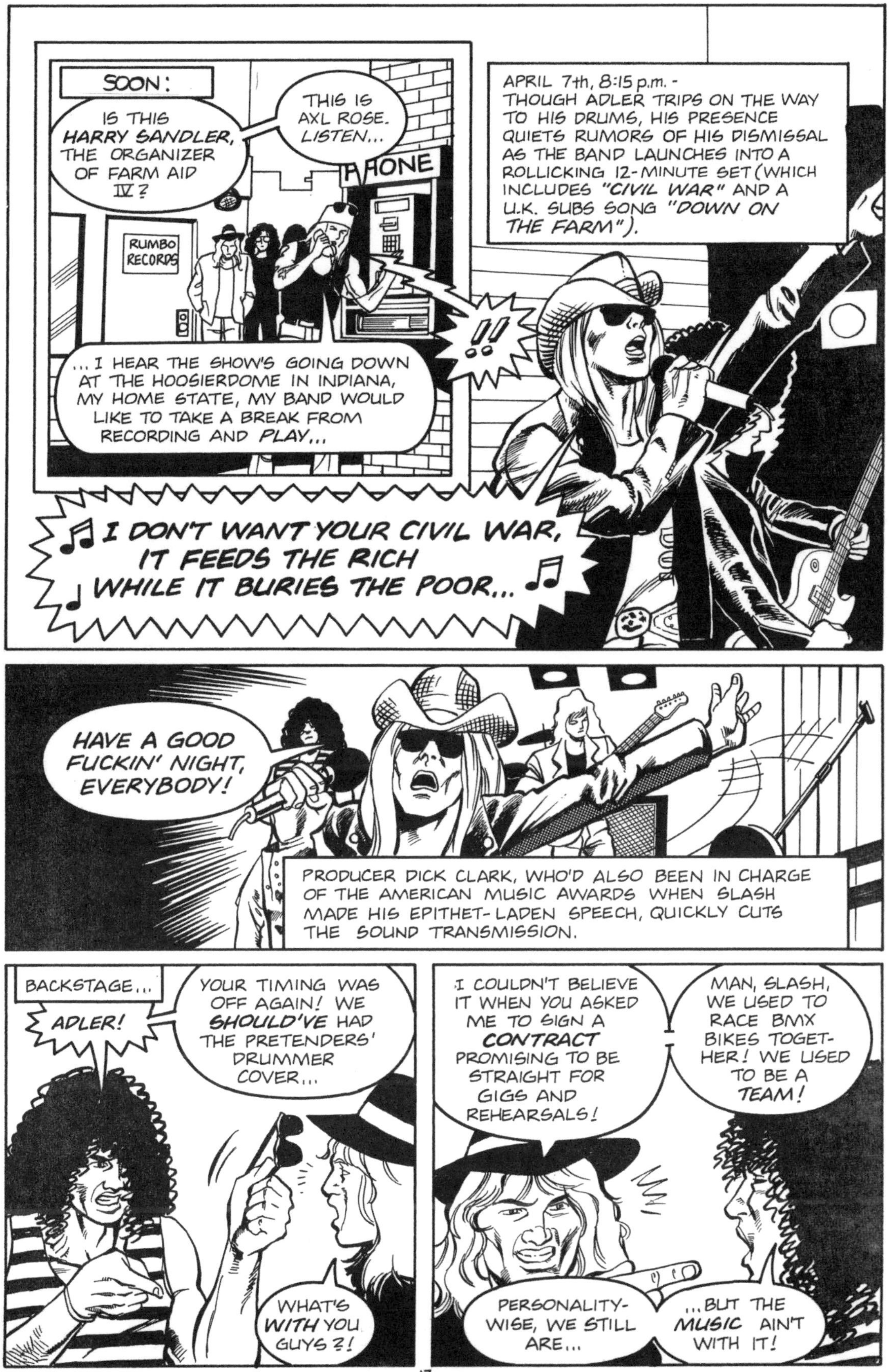
SOON:
IS THIS HARRY SANDLER, THE ORGANIZER OF FARM AID IV?
THIS IS AXL ROSE. LISTEN...
PHONE
RUMBO RECORDS
...I HEAR THE SHOW'S GOING DOWN AT THE HOOSIERDOME IN INDIANA, MY HOME STATE, MY BAND WOULD LIKE TO TAKE A BREAK FROM RECORDING AND PLAY...
!!
APRIL 7th, 8:15 p.m. - THOUGH ADLER TRIPS ON THE WAY TO HIS DRUMS, HIS PRESENCE QUIETS RUMORS OF HIS DISMISSAL AS THE BAND LAUNCHES INTO A ROLLICKING 12-MINUTE SET (WHICH INCLUDES "CIVIL WAR" AND A U.K. SUBS SONG "DOWN ON THE FARM").
I DON'T WANT YOUR CIVIL WAR, IT FEEDS THE RICH WHILE IT BURIES THE POOR...
HAVE A GOOD FUCKIN' NIGHT, EVERYBODY!
PRODUCER DICK CLARK, WHO'D ALSO BEEN IN CHARGE OF THE AMERICAN MUSIC AWARDS WHEN SLASH MADE HIS EPITHET-LADEN SPEECH, QUICKLY CUTS THE SOUND TRANSMISSION.
BACKSTAGE...
ADLER!
YOUR TIMING WAS OFF AGAIN! WE SHOULD'VE HAD THE PRETENDERS' DRUMMER COVER...
WHAT'S WITH YOU GUYS?!
I COULDN'T BELIEVE IT WHEN YOU ASKED ME TO SIGN A CONTRACT PROMISING TO BE STRAIGHT FOR GIGS AND REHEARSALS!
MAN, SLASH, WE USED TO RACE BMX BIKES TOGET-HER! WE USED TO BE A TEAM!
PERSONALITY-WISE, WE STILL ARE...
...BUT THE MUSIC AIN'T WITH IT!

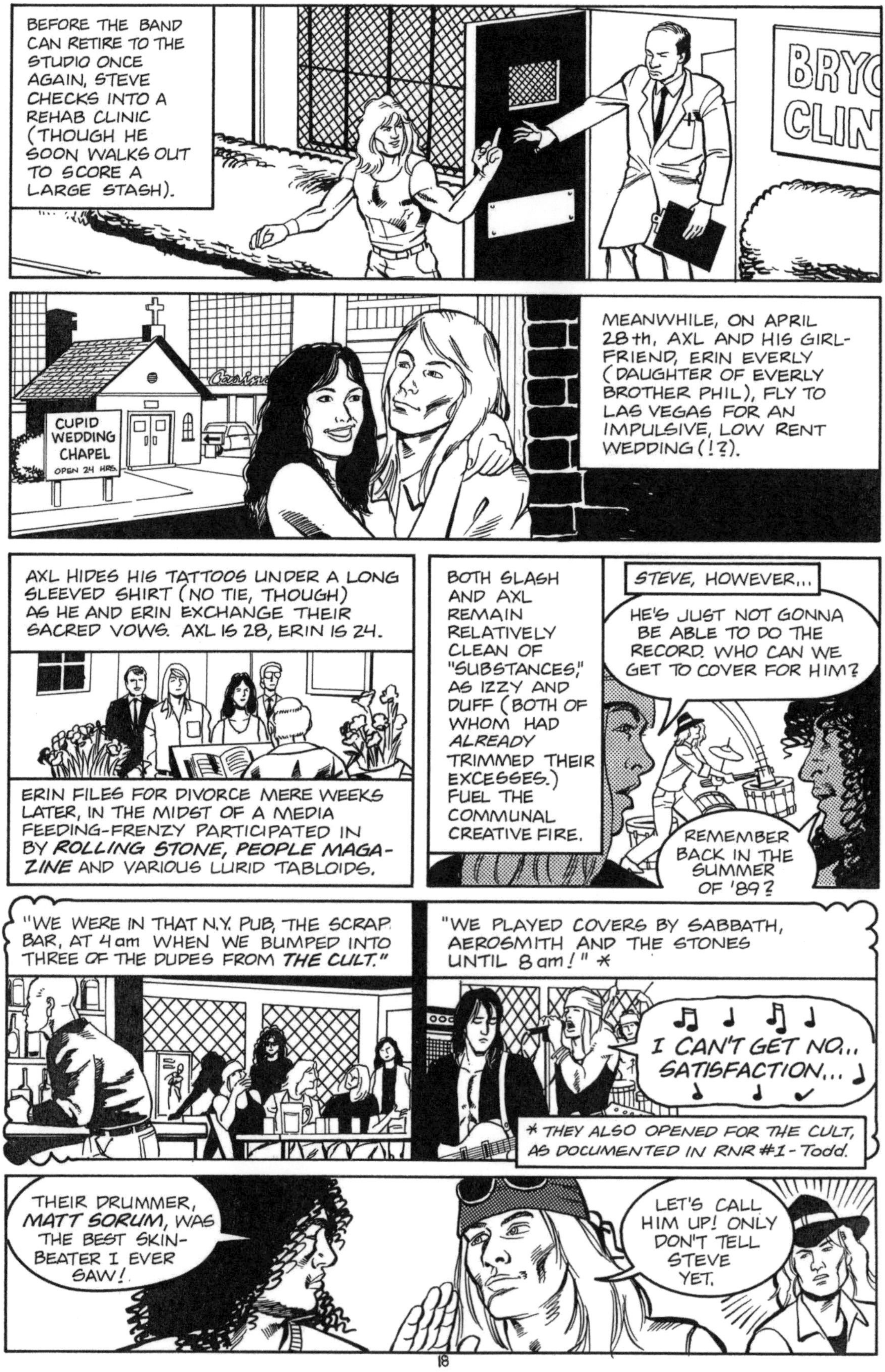
BEFORE THE BAND CAN RETIRE TO THE STUDIO ONCE AGAIN, STEVE CHECKS INTO A REHAB CLINIC (THOUGH HE SOON WALKS OUT TO SCORE A LARGE STASH).
BRYC
CLIN
MEANWHILE, ON APRIL 28th, AXL AND HIS GIRL-FRIEND, ERIN EVERLY (DAUGHTER OF EVERLY BROTHER PHIL), FLY TO LAS VEGAS FOR AN IMPULSIVE, LOW RENT WEDDING (!?).
CUPID WEDDING CHAPEL
OPEN 24 HRS.
AXL HIDES HIS TATTOOS UNDER A LONG SLEEVED SHIRT (NO TIE, THOUGH) AS HE AND ERIN EXCHANGE THEIR SACRED VOWS. AXL IS 28, ERIN IS 24.
ERIN FILES FOR DIVORCE MERE WEEKS LATER, IN THE MIDST OF A MEDIA FEEDING-FRENZY PARTICIPATED IN BY ROLLING STONE, PEOPLE MAGAZINE AND VARIOUS LURID TABLOIDS.
BOTH SLASH AND AXL REMAIN RELATIVELY CLEAN OF "SUBSTANCES," AS IZZY AND DUFF (BOTH OF WHOM HAD ALREADY TRIMMED THEIR EXCESSES.) FUEL THE COMMUNAL CREATIVE FIRE.
STEVE, HOWEVER...
HE'S JUST NOT GONNA BE ABLE TO DO THE RECORD. WHO CAN WE GET TO COVER FOR HIM?
REMEMBER BACK IN THE SUMMER OF '89?
"WE WERE IN THAT N.Y. PUB, THE SCRAP BAR, AT 4am WHEN WE BUMPED INTO THREE OF THE DUDES FROM THE CULT."
"WE PLAYED COVERS BY SABBATH, AEROSMITH AND THE STONES UNTIL 8am!" *
I CAN'T GET NO... SATISFACTION...
* THEY ALSO OPENED FOR THE CULT, AS DOCUMENTED IN RNR #1 - Todd.
THEIR DRUMMER, MATT SORUM, WAS THE BEST SKIN-BEATER I EVER SAW!
LET'S CALL HIM UP! ONLY DON'T TELL STEVE YET.

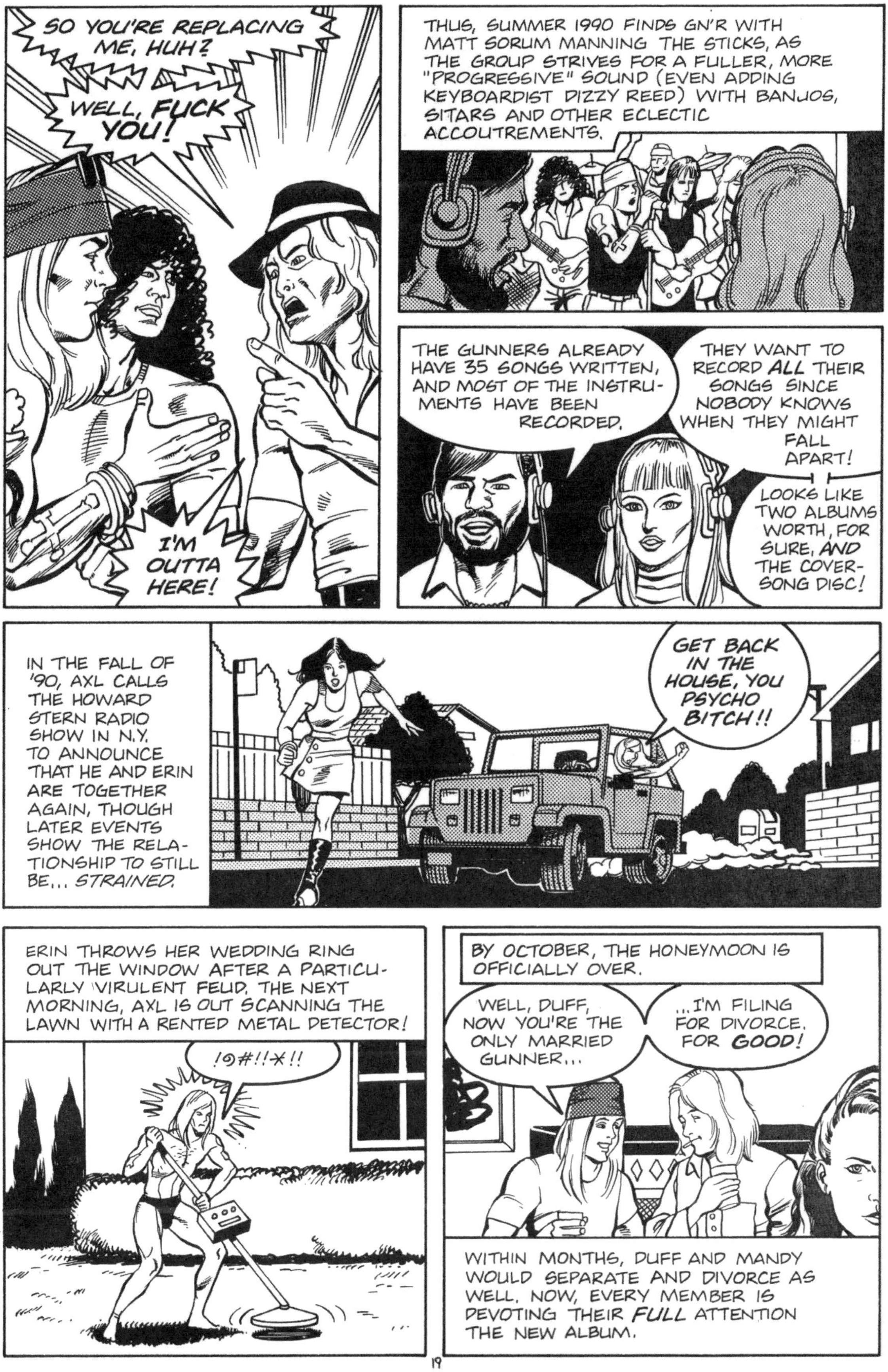

SO YOU'RE REPLACING ME, HUH?
WELL, FUCK YOU!
I'M OUTTA HERE!
THUS, SUMMER 1990 FINDS GN'R WITH MATT SORUM MANNING THE STICKS, AS THE GROUP STRIVES FOR A FULLER, MORE "PROGRESSIVE" SOUND (EVEN ADDING KEYBOARDIST DIZZY REED) WITH BANJOS, SITARS AND OTHER ECLECTIC ACCOUTREMENTS.
THE GUNNERS ALREADY HAVE 35 SONGS WRITTEN, AND MOST OF THE INSTRUMENTS HAVE BEEN RECORDED.
THEY WANT TO RECORD ALL THEIR SONGS SINCE NOBODY KNOWS WHEN THEY MIGHT FALL APART!
LOOKS LIKE TWO ALBUMS WORTH, FOR SURE, AND THE COVER-SONG DISC!
IN THE FALL OF '90, AXL CALLS THE HOWARD STERN RADIO SHOW IN N.Y. TO ANNOUNCE THAT HE AND ERIN ARE TOGETHER AGAIN, THOUGH LATER EVENTS SHOW THE RELATIONSHIP TO STILL BE... STRAINED.
GET BACK IN THE HOUSE, YOU PSYCHO BITCH!!
ERIN THROWS HER WEDDING RING OUT THE WINDOW AFTER A PARTICULARLY VIRULENT FEUD. THE NEXT MORNING, AXL IS OUT SCANNING THE LAWN WITH A RENTED METAL DETECTOR!
!@#!!*!!
BY OCTOBER, THE HONEYMOON IS OFFICIALLY OVER.
WELL, DUFF, NOW YOU'RE THE ONLY MARRIED GUNNER...
...I'M FILING FOR DIVORCE. FOR GOOD!
WITHIN MONTHS, DUFF AND MANDY WOULD SEPARATE AND DIVORCE AS WELL. NOW, EVERY MEMBER IS DEVOTING THEIR FULL ATTENTION THE NEW ALBUM.

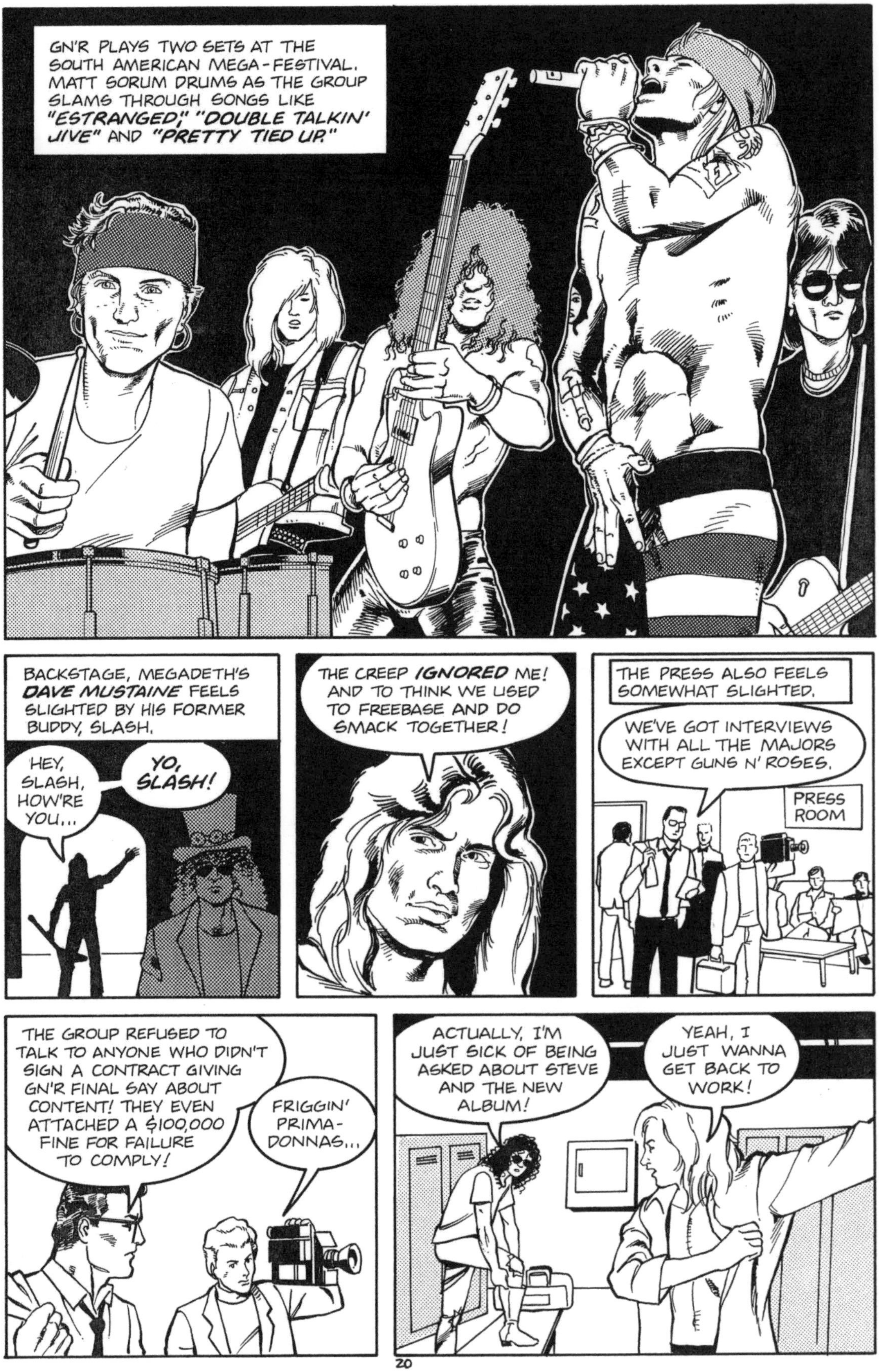

GN'R PLAYS TWO SETS AT THE SOUTH AMERICAN MEGA-FESTIVAL. MATT SORUM DRUMS AS THE GROUP SLAMS THROUGH SONGS LIKE "ESTRANGED," "DOUBLE TALKIN' JIVE" AND "PRETTY TIED UP."
BACKSTAGE, MEGADETH'S DAVE MUSTAINE FEELS SLIGHTED BY HIS FORMER BUDDY, SLASH.
HEY, SLASH, HOW'RE YOU...
YO, SLASH!
THE CREEP IGNORED ME! AND TO THINK WE USED TO FREEBASE AND DO SMACK TOGETHER!
THE PRESS ALSO FEELS SOMEWHAT SLIGHTED.
WE'VE GOT INTERVIEWS WITH ALL THE MAJORS EXCEPT GUNS N' ROSES.
PRESS ROOM
THE GROUP REFUSED TO TALK TO ANYONE WHO DIDN'T SIGN A CONTRACT GIVING GN'R FINAL SAY ABOUT CONTENT! THEY EVEN ATTACHED A $100,000 FINE FOR FAILURE TO COMPLY!
FRIGGIN' PRIMA-DONNAS...
ACTUALLY, I'M JUST SICK OF BEING ASKED ABOUT STEVE AND THE NEW ALBUM!
YEAH, I JUST WANNA GET BACK TO WORK!

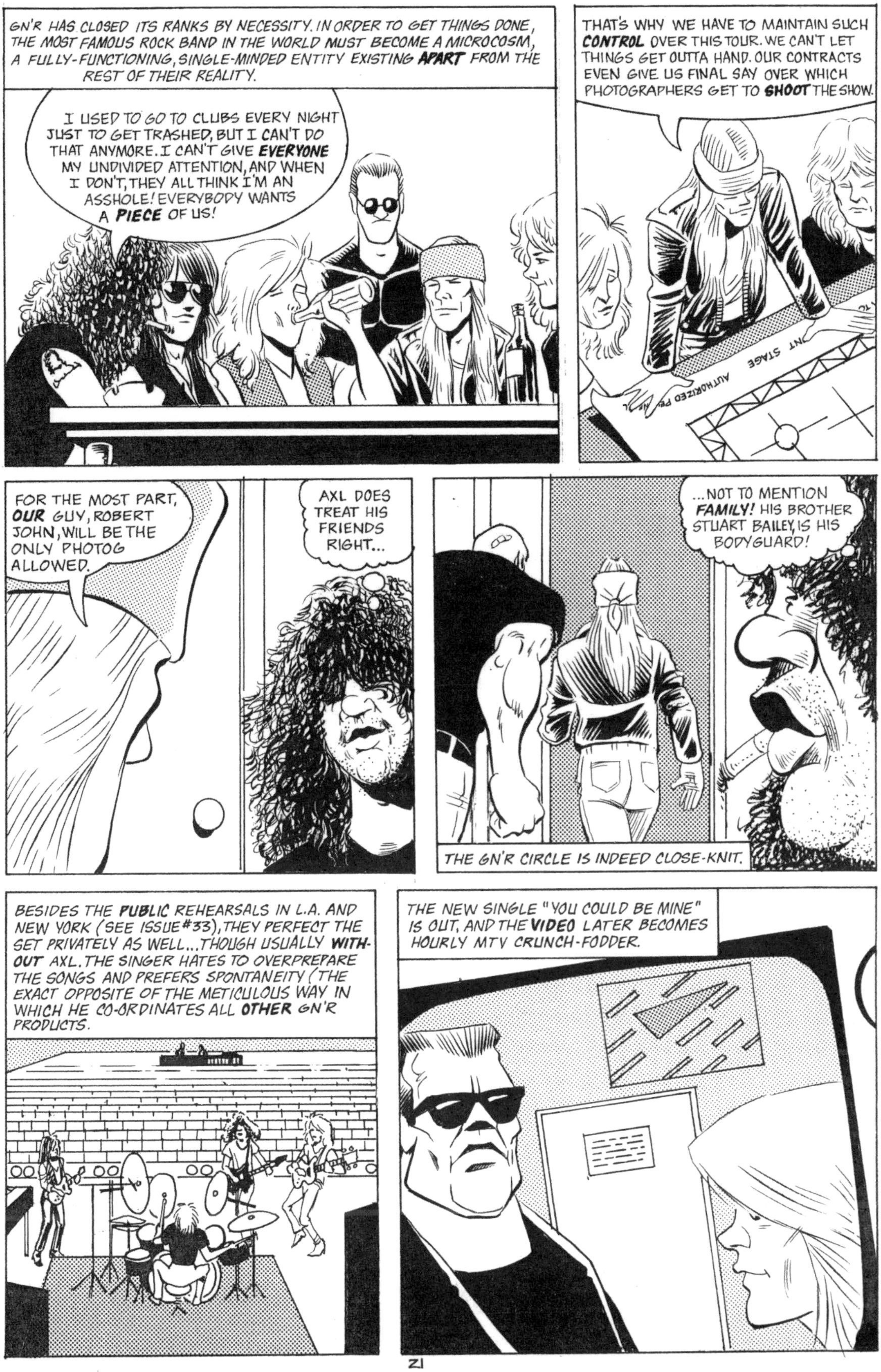
GN'R HAS CLOSED ITS RANKS BY NECESSITY. IN ORDER TO GET THINGS DONE, THE MOST FAMOUS ROCK BAND IN THE WORLD MUST BECOME A MICROCOSM, A FULLY-FUNCTIONING, SINGLE-MINDED ENTITY EXISTING APART FROM THE REST OF THEIR REALITY.
I USED TO GO TO CLUBS EVERY NIGHT JUST TO GET TRASHED, BUT I CAN'T DO THAT ANYMORE. I CAN'T GIVE EVERYONE MY UNDIVIDED ATTENTION, AND WHEN I DON'T, THEY ALL THINK I'M AN ASSHOLE! EVERYBODY WANTS A PIECE OF US!
THAT'S WHY WE HAVE TO MAINTAIN SUCH CONTROL OVER THIS TOUR. WE CAN'T LET THINGS GET OUTTA HAND. OUR CONTRACTS EVEN GIVE US FINAL SAY OVER WHICH PHOTOGRAPHERS GET TO SHOOT THE SHOW.
FOR THE MOST PART, OUR GUY, ROBERT JOHN, WILL BE THE ONLY PHOTOG ALLOWED.
AXL DOES TREAT HIS FRIENDS RIGHT...
...NOT TO MENTION FAMILY! HIS BROTHER STUART BAILEY, IS HIS BODYGUARD!
THE GN'R CIRCLE IS INDEED CLOSE-KNIT.
BESIDES THE PUBLIC REHEARSALS IN L.A. AND NEW YORK (SEE ISSUE #33), THEY PERFECT THE SET PRIVATELY AS WELL...THOUGH USUALLY WITHOUT AXL. THE SINGER HATES TO OVERPREPARE THE SONGS AND PREFERS SPONTANEITY (THE EXACT OPPOSITE OF THE METICULOUS WAY IN WHICH HE CO-ORDINATES ALL OTHER GN'R PRODUCTS.
THE NEW SINGLE "YOU COULD BE MINE" IS OUT, AND THE VIDEO LATER BECOMES HOURLY MTV CRUNCH-FODDER.

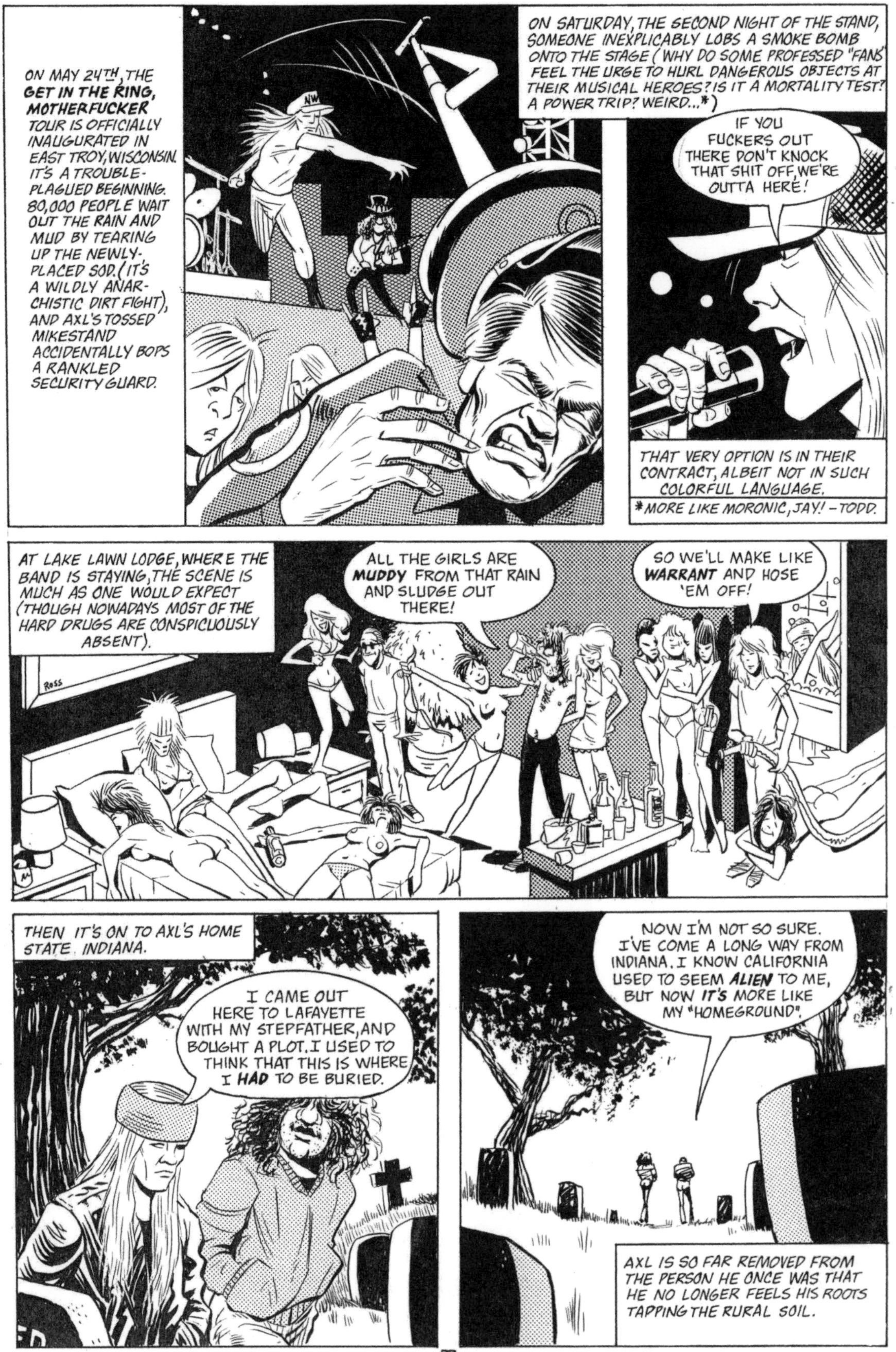

ON MAY 24TH, THE GET IN THE RING, MOTHERFUCKER TOUR IS OFFICIALLY INAUGURATED IN EAST TROY, WISCONSIN. IT'S A TROUBLE-PLAGUED BEGINNING. 80,000 PEOPLE WAIT OUT THE RAIN AND MUD BY TEARING UP THE NEWLY-PLACED SOD. (IT'S A WILDLY ANARCHISTIC DIRT FIGHT), AND AXL'S TOSSED MIKESTAND ACCIDENTALLY BOPS A RANKLED SECURITY GUARD.
NW
ON SATURDAY, THE SECOND NIGHT OF THE STAND, SOMEONE INEXPLICABLY LOBS A SMOKE BOMB ONTO THE STAGE (WHY DO SOME PROFESSED "FANS" FEEL THE URGE TO HURL DANGEROUS OBJECTS AT THEIR MUSICAL HEROES? IS IT A MORTALITY TEST? A POWER TRIP? WEIRD...*)
IF YOU FUCKERS OUT THERE DON'T KNOCK THAT SHIT OFF, WE'RE OUTTA HERE!
THAT VERY OPTION IS IN THEIR CONTRACT, ALBEIT NOT IN SUCH COLORFUL LANGUAGE.
*MORE LIKE MORONIC, JAY! -TODD.
AT LAKE LAWN LODGE, WHERE THE BAND IS STAYING, THE SCENE IS MUCH AS ONE WOULD EXPECT (THOUGH NOWADAYS MOST OF THE HARD DRUGS ARE CONSPICUOUSLY ABSENT).
ALL THE GIRLS ARE MUDDY FROM THAT RAIN AND SLUDGE OUT THERE!
SO WE'LL MAKE LIKE WARRANT AND HOSE 'EM OFF!
ROSS
THEN IT'S ON TO AXL'S HOME STATE, INDIANA.
I CAME OUT HERE TO LAFAYETTE WITH MY STEPFATHER, AND BOUGHT A PLOT. I USED TO THINK THAT THIS IS WHERE I HAD TO BE BURIED.
NOW I'M NOT SO SURE. I'VE COME A LONG WAY FROM INDIANA. I KNOW CALIFORNIA USED TO SEEM ALIEN TO ME, BUT NOW IT'S MORE LIKE MY "HOMEGROUND".
AXL IS SO FAR REMOVED FROM THE PERSON HE ONCE WAS THAT HE NO LONGER FEELS HIS ROOTS TAPPING THE RURAL SOIL.

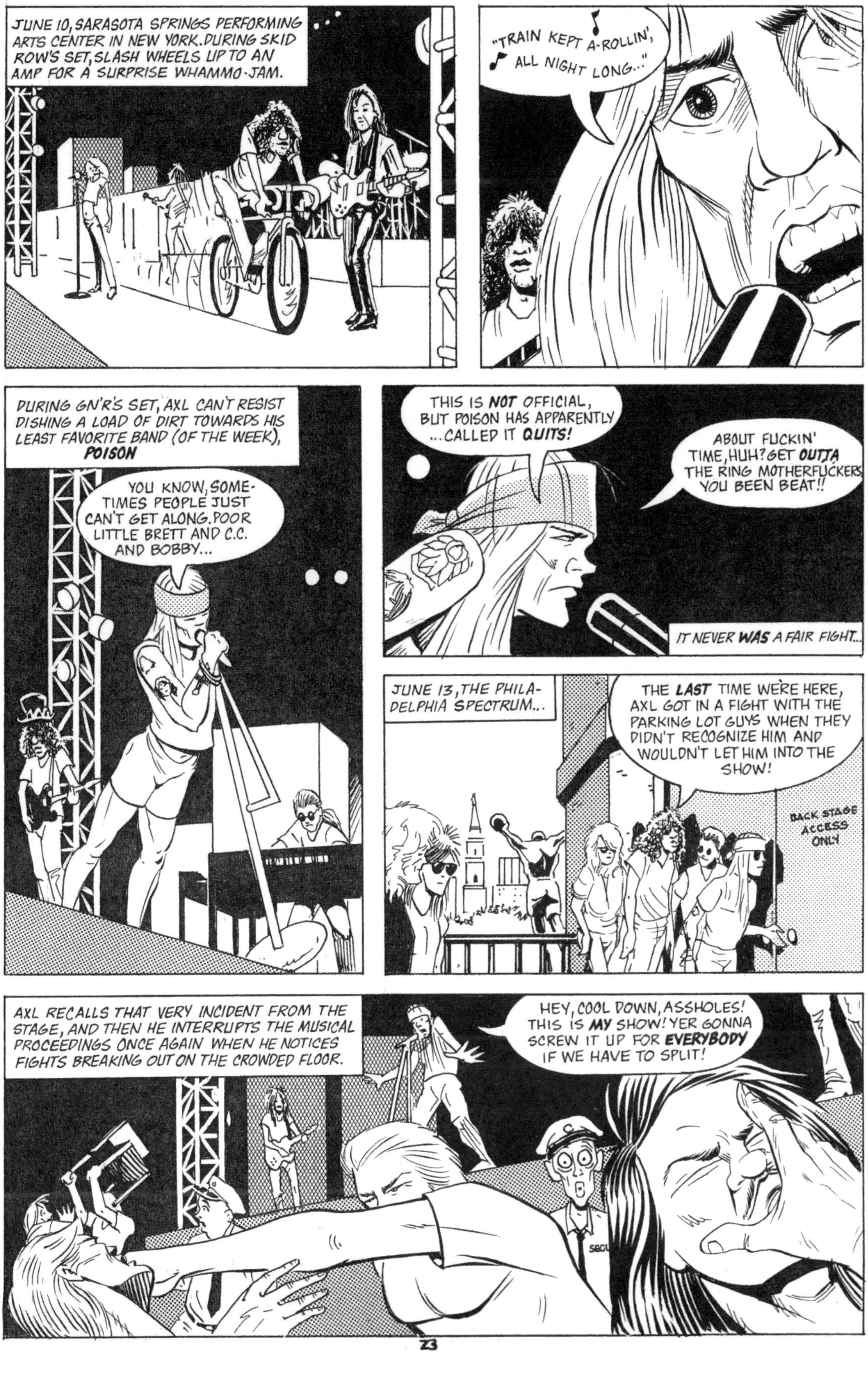
JUNE 10, SARASOTA SPRINGS PERFORMING ARTS CENTER IN NEW YORK. DURING SKID ROW'S SET, SLASH WHEELS UP TO AN AMP FOR A SURPRISE WHAMMO-JAM.
"TRAIN KEPT A-ROLLIN', ALL NIGHT LONG..."
DURING GN'R'S SET, AXL CAN'T RESIST DISHING A LOAD OF DIRT TOWARDS HIS LEAST FAVORITE BAND (OF THE WEEK), POISON
YOU KNOW, SOMETIMES PEOPLE JUST CAN'T GET ALONG. POOR LITTLE BRETT AND C.C. AND BOBBY...
THIS IS NOT OFFICIAL, BUT POISON HAS APPARENTLY ...CALLED IT QUITS!
ABOUT FUCKIN' TIME, HUH? GET OUTTA THE RING MOTHERFUCKERS YOU BEEN BEAT!!
IT NEVER WAS A FAIR FIGHT...
JUNE 13, THE PHILADELPHIA SPECTRUM...
THE LAST TIME WE'RE HERE, AXL GOT IN A FIGHT WITH THE PARKING LOT GUYS WHEN THEY DIDN'T RECOGNIZE HIM AND WOULDN'T LET HIM INTO THE SHOW!
BACK STAGE ACCESS ONLY
AXL RECALLS THAT VERY INCIDENT FROM THE STAGE, AND THEN HE INTERRUPTS THE MUSICAL PROCEEDINGS ONCE AGAIN WHEN HE NOTICES FIGHTS BREAKING OUT ON THE CROWDED FLOOR.
HEY, COOL DOWN, ASSHOLES! THIS IS MY SHOW! YER GONNA SCREW IT UP FOR EVERYBODY IF WE HAVE TO SPLIT!

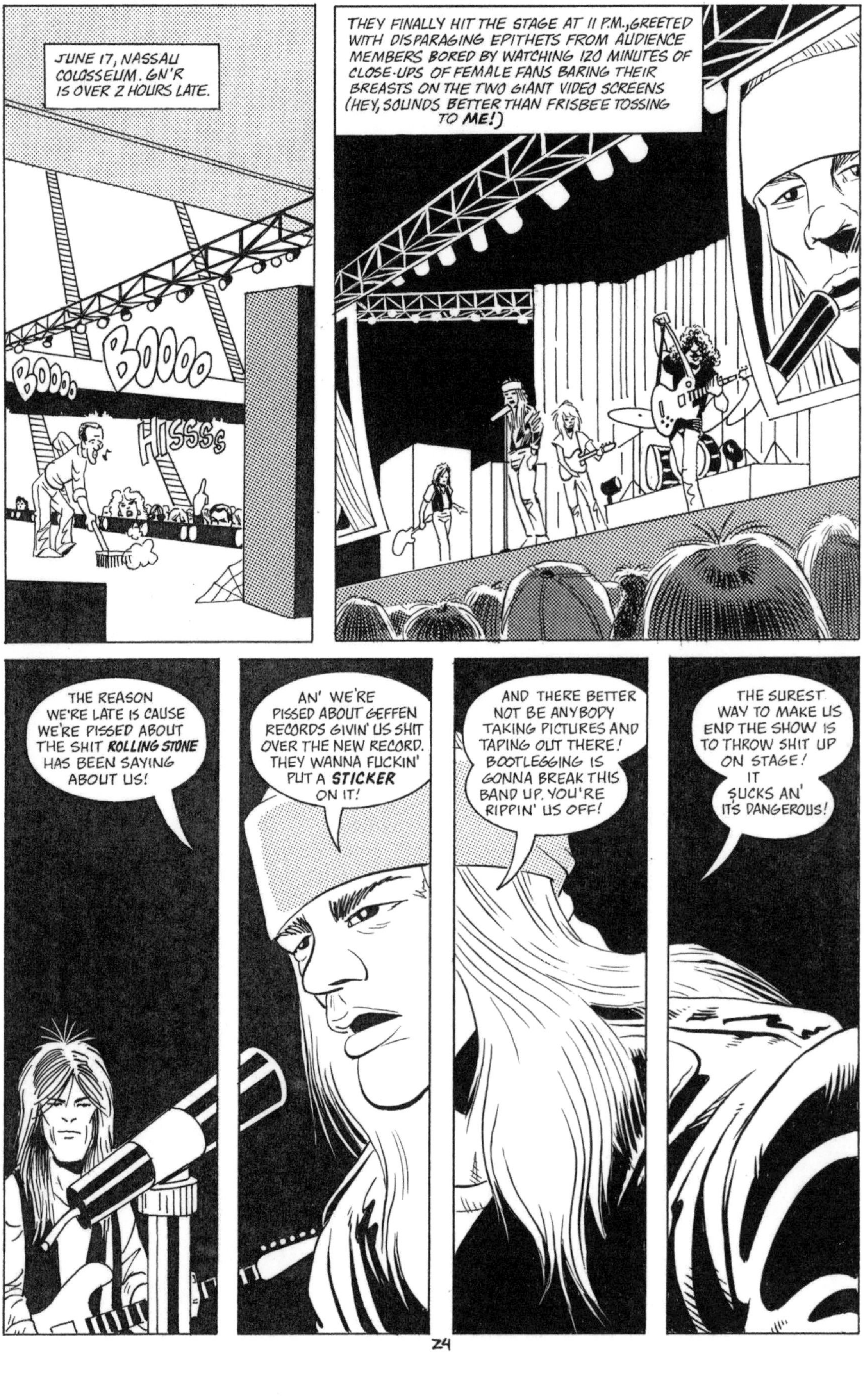
JUNE 17, NASSAU COLOSSEUM. GN'R IS OVER 2 HOURS LATE.
BOOOO
BOOOO
HISSSS
THEY FINALLY HIT THE STAGE AT 11 P.M., GREETED WITH DISPARAGING EPITHETS FROM AUDIENCE MEMBERS BORED BY WATCHING 120 MINUTES OF CLOSE-UPS OF FEMALE FANS BARING THEIR BREASTS ON THE TWO GIANT VIDEO SCREENS (HEY, SOUNDS BETTER THAN FRISBEE TOSSING TO ME!)
THE REASON WE'RE LATE IS CAUSE WE'RE PISSED ABOUT THE SHIT ROLLING STONE HAS BEEN SAYING ABOUT US!
AN' WE'RE PISSED ABOUT GEFFEN RECORDS GIVIN' US SHIT OVER THE NEW RECORD. THEY WANNA FUCKIN' PUT A STICKER ON IT!
AND THERE BETTER NOT BE ANYBODY TAKING PICTURES AND TAPING OUT THERE! BOOTLEGGING IS GONNA BREAK THIS BAND UP. YOU'RE RIPPIN' US OFF!
THE SUREST WAY TO MAKE US END THE SHOW IS TO THROW SHIT UP ON STAGE! IT SUCKS AN' IT'S DANGEROUS!

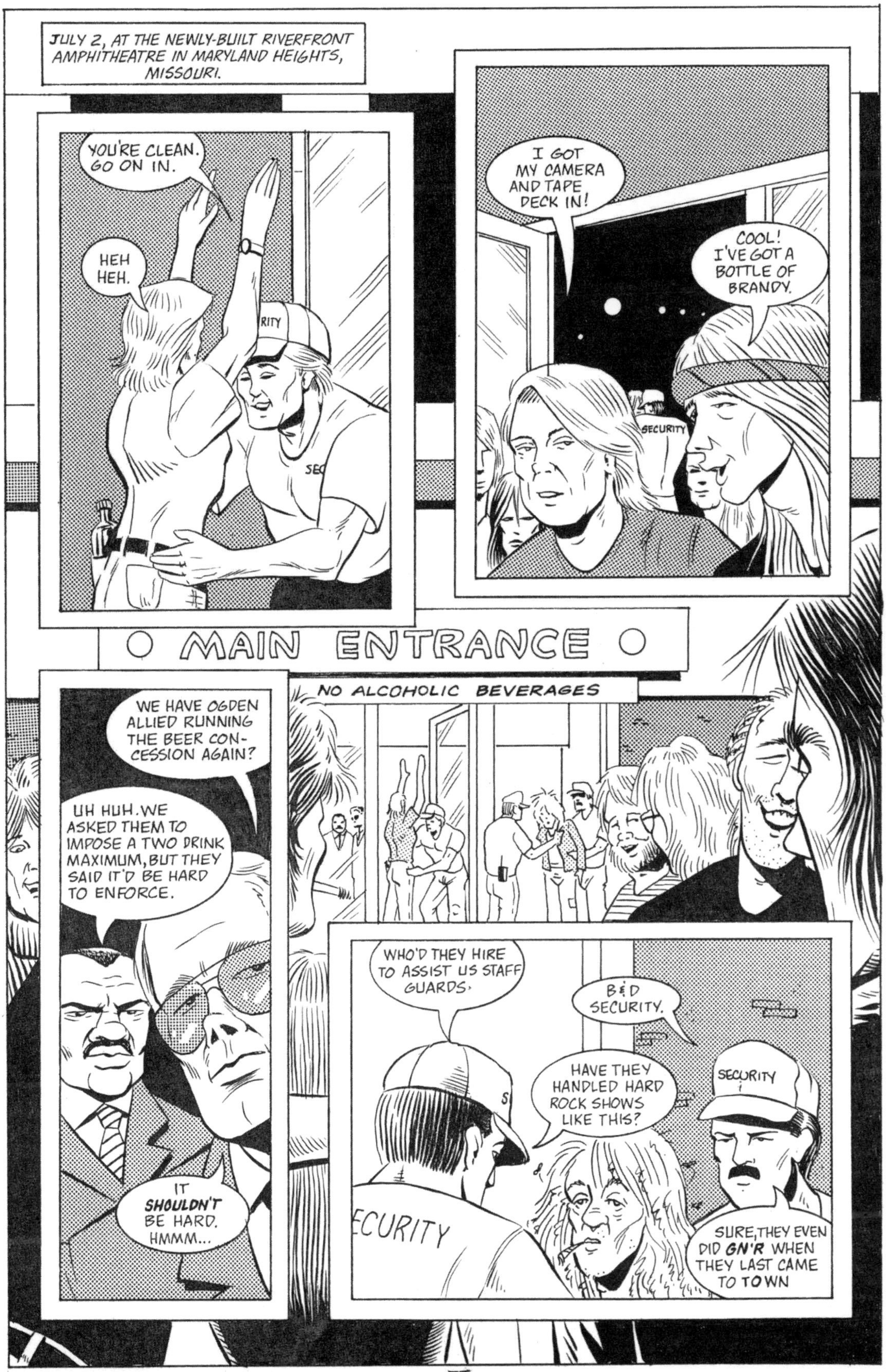

JULY 2, AT THE NEWLY-BUILT RIVERFRONT AMPHITHEATRE IN MARYLAND HEIGHTS, MISSOURI.
YOU'RE CLEAN. GO ON IN.
HEH HEH.
I GOT MY CAMERA AND TAPE DECK IN!
COOL! I'VE GOT A BOTTLE OF BRANDY.
MAIN ENTRANCE
NO ALCOHOLIC BEVERAGES
WE HAVE OGDEN ALLIED RUNNING THE BEER CONCESSION AGAIN?
UH HUH. WE ASKED THEM TO IMPOSE A TWO DRINK MAXIMUM, BUT THEY SAID IT'D BE HARD TO ENFORCE.
IT SHOULDN'T BE HARD. HMMM...
WHO'D THEY HIRE TO ASSIST US STAFF GUARDS.
B&D SECURITY.
HAVE THEY HANDLED HARD ROCK SHOWS LIKE THIS?
SURE, THEY EVEN DID GN'R WHEN THEY LAST CAME TO TOWN

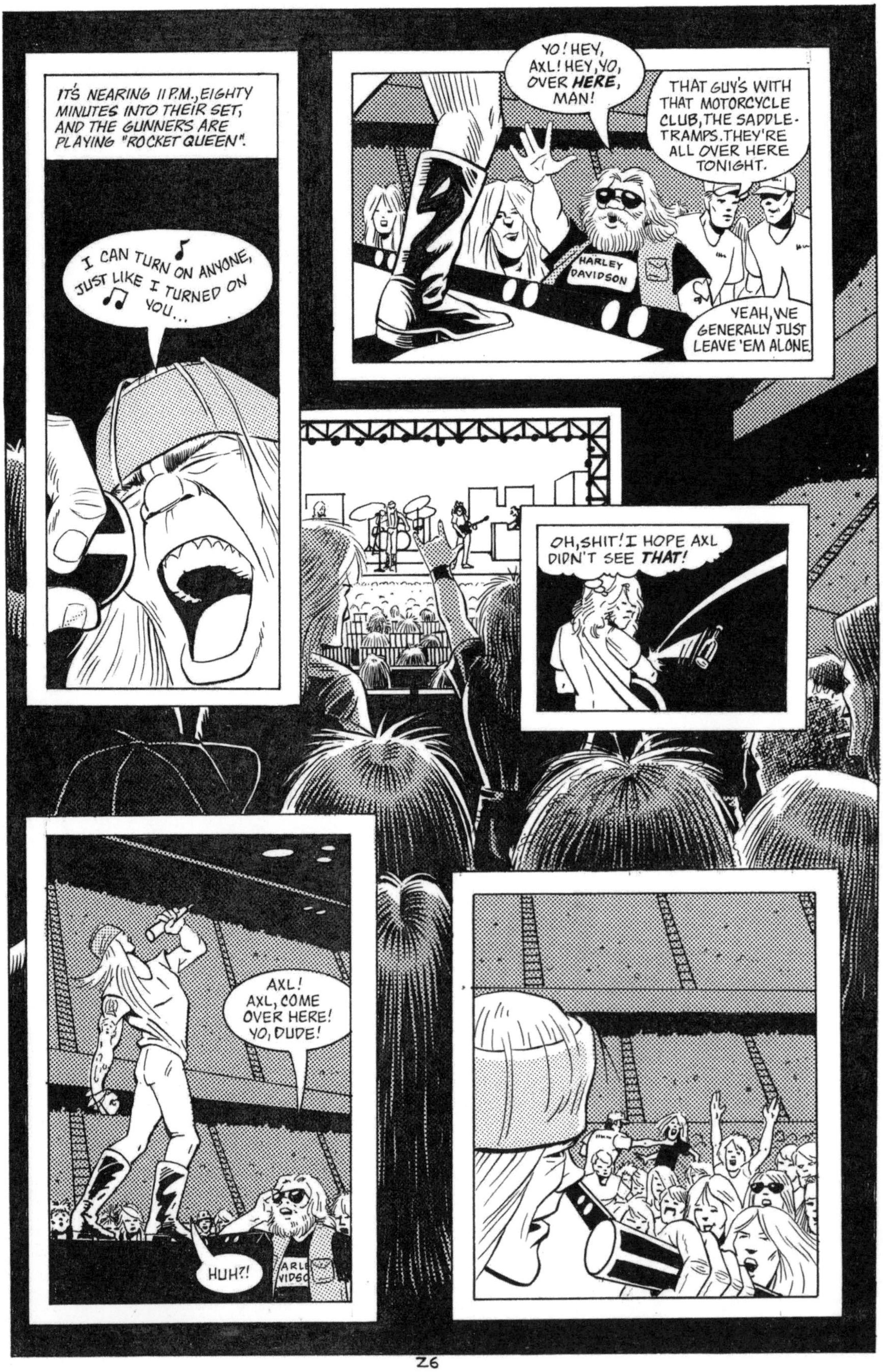
IT'S NEARING 11 P.M., EIGHTY MINUTES INTO THEIR SET, AND THE GUNNERS ARE PLAYING "ROCKET QUEEN".
I CAN TURN ON ANYONE, JUST LIKE I TURNED ON YOU...
YO! HEY, AXL! HEY, YO, OVER HERE, MAN!
HARLEY DAVIDSON
THAT GUY'S WITH THAT MOTORCYCLE CLUB, THE SADDLE-TRAMPS. THEY'RE ALL OVER HERE TONIGHT.
YEAH, WE GENERALLY JUST LEAVE 'EM ALONE.
OH, SHIT! I HOPE AXL DIDN'T SEE THAT!
AXL! AXL, COME OVER HERE! YO, DUDE!
HUH?!

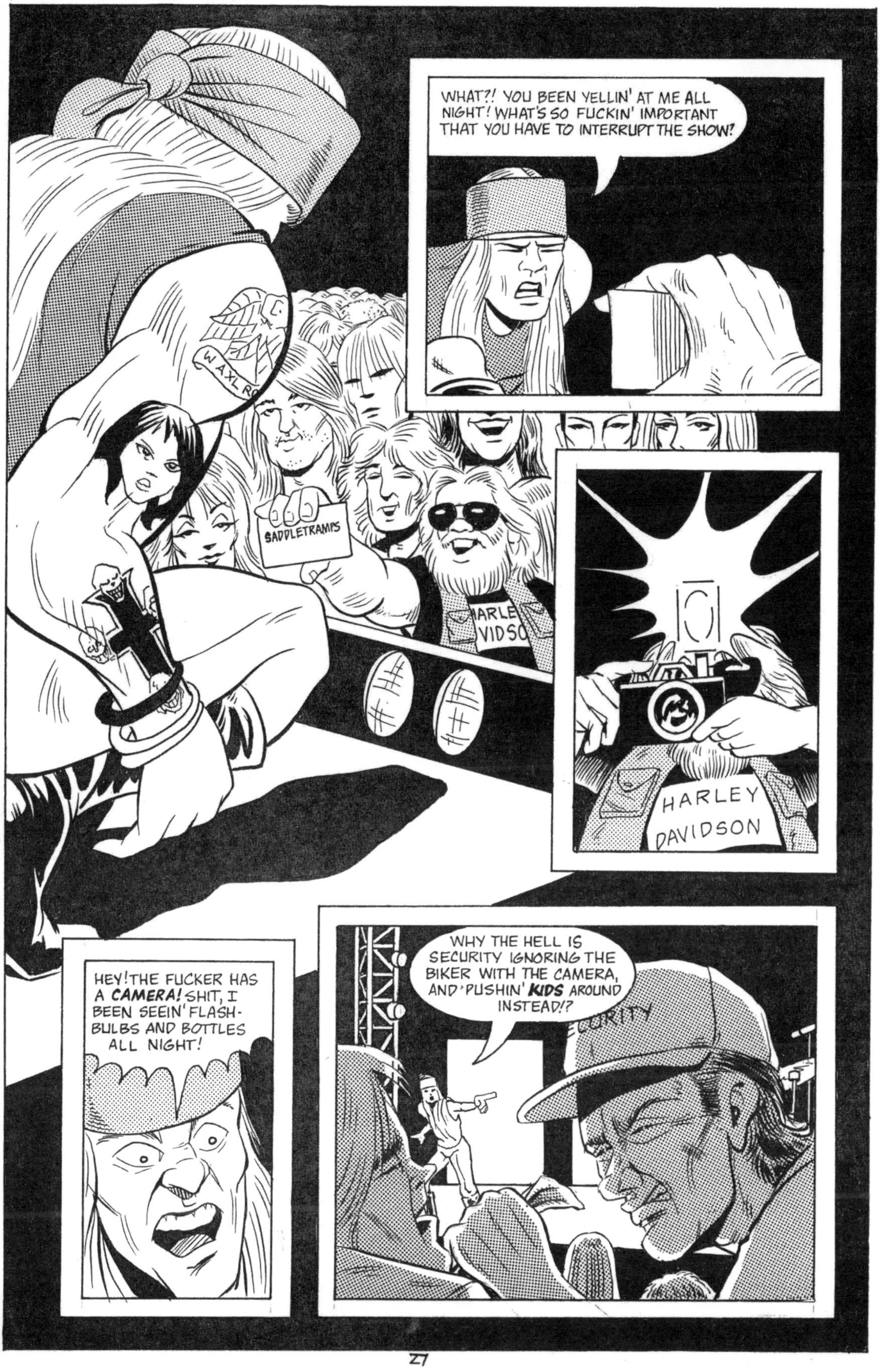
WHAT?! YOU BEEN YELLIN' AT ME ALL NIGHT! WHAT'S SO FUCKIN' IMPORTANT THAT YOU HAVE TO INTERRUPT THE SHOW?
W AXL RO
SADDLETRAMPS
HARLE VIDSO
HARLEY DAVIDSON
HEY! THE FUCKER HAS A CAMERA! SHIT, I BEEN SEEIN' FLASH-BULBS AND BOTTLES ALL NIGHT!
WHY THE HELL IS SECURITY IGNORING THE BIKER WITH THE CAMERA, AND PUSHIN' KIDS AROUND INSTEAD!?
CURITY

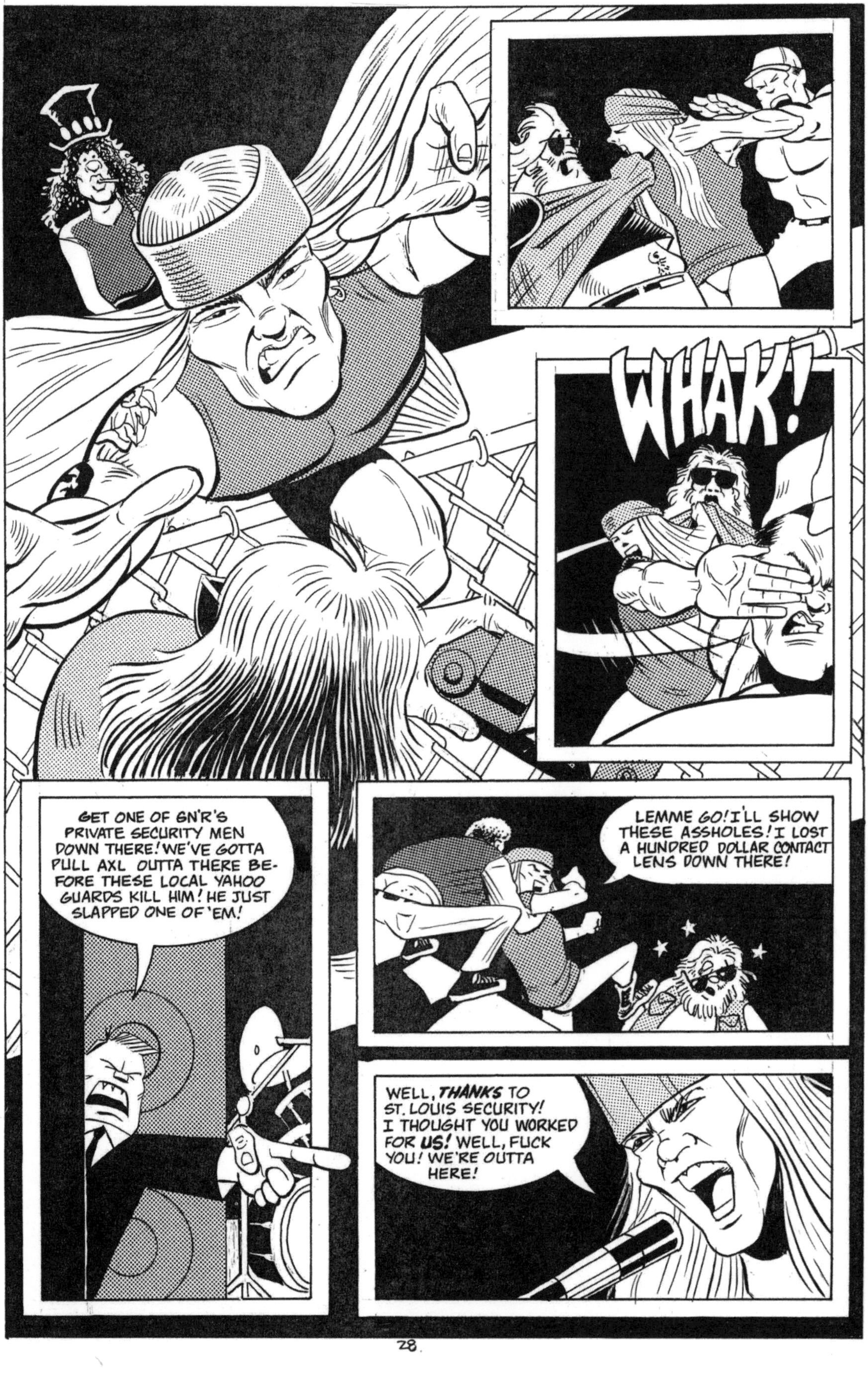
WHAK!
GET ONE OF GN'R'S PRIVATE SECURITY MEN DOWN THERE! WE'VE GOTTA PULL AXL OUTTA THERE BEFORE THESE LOCAL YAHOO GUARDS KILL HIM! HE JUST SLAPPED ONE OF 'EM!
LEMME GO! I'LL SHOW THESE ASSHOLES! I LOST A HUNDRED DOLLAR CONTACT LENS DOWN THERE!
WELL, THANKS TO ST. LOUIS SECURITY! I THOUGHT YOU WORKED FOR US! WELL, FUCK YOU! WE'RE OUTTA HERE!

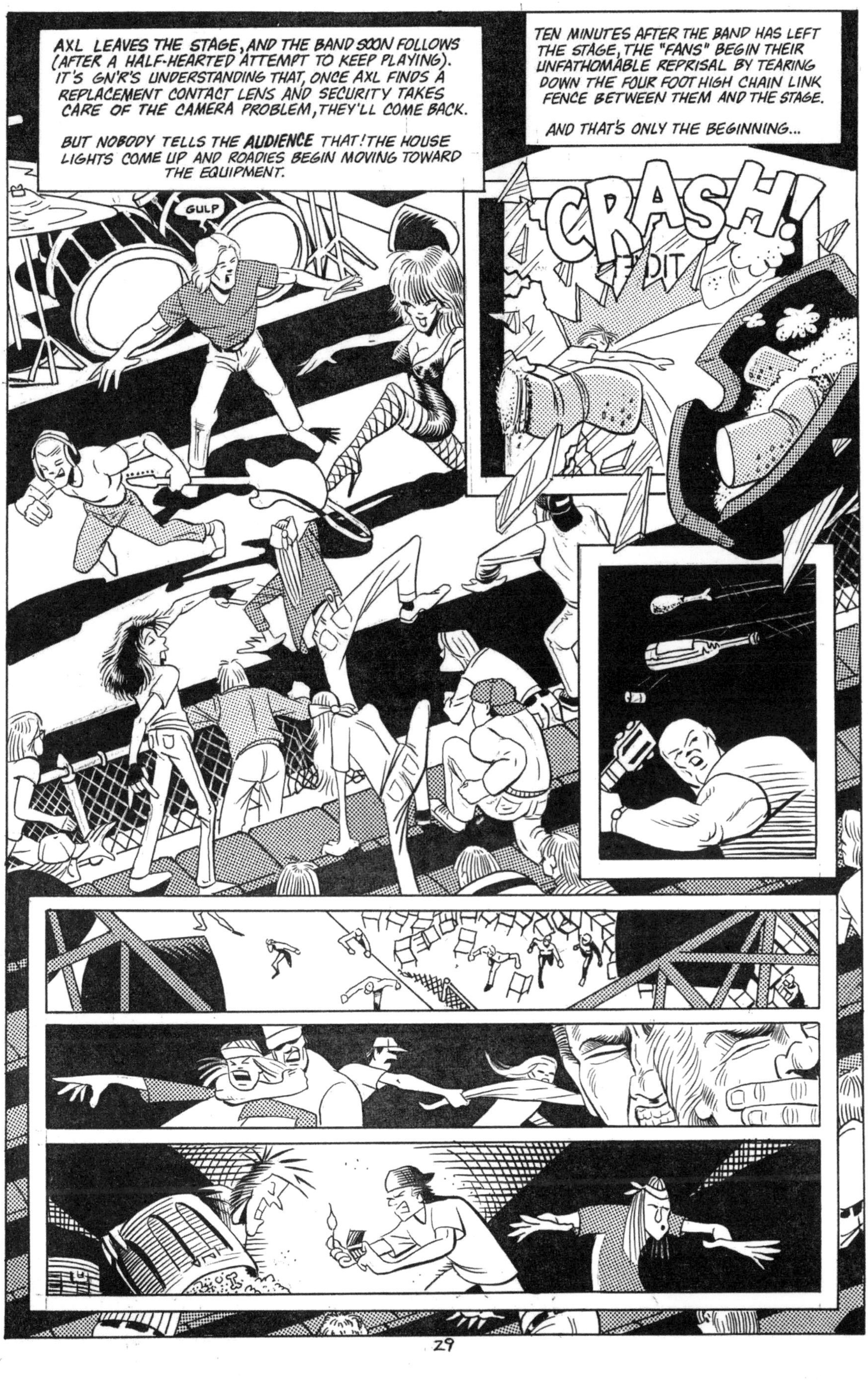
AXL LEAVES THE STAGE, AND THE BAND SOON FOLLOWS (AFTER A HALF-HEARTED ATTEMPT TO KEEP PLAYING). IT'S GN'R'S UNDERSTANDING THAT, ONCE AXL FINDS A REPLACEMENT CONTACT LENS AND SECURITY TAKES CARE OF THE CAMERA PROBLEM, THEY'LL COME BACK.
BUT NOBODY TELLS THE AUDIENCE THAT! THE HOUSE LIGHTS COME UP AND ROADIES BEGIN MOVING TOWARD THE EQUIPMENT.
GULP
TEN MINUTES AFTER THE BAND HAS LEFT THE STAGE, THE "FANS" BEGIN THEIR UNFATHOMABLE REPRISAL BY TEARING DOWN THE FOUR FOOT HIGH CHAIN LINK FENCE BETWEEN THEM AND THE STAGE.
AND THAT'S ONLY THE BEGINNING...
CRASH!

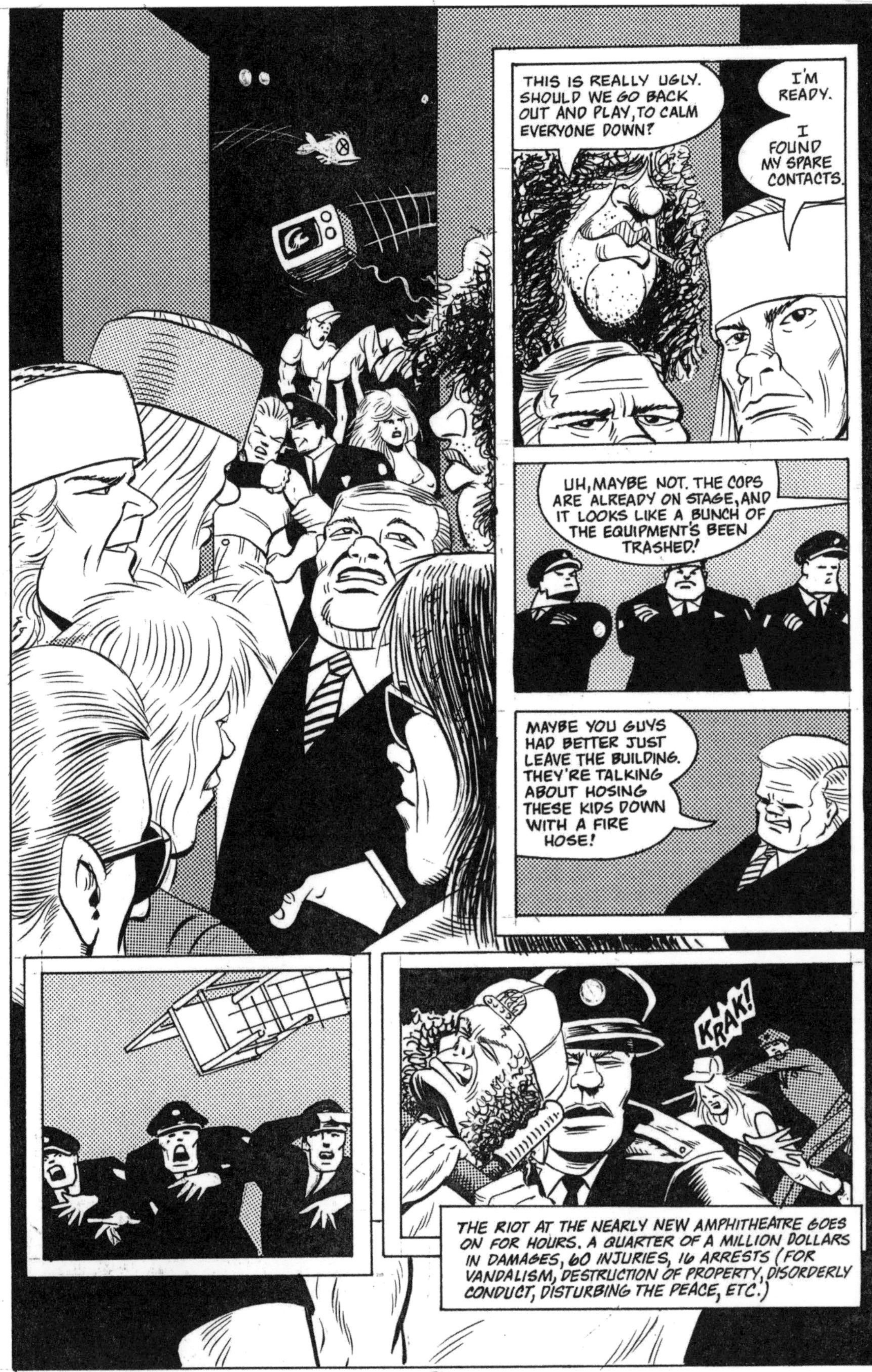
THIS IS REALLY UGLY. SHOULD WE GO BACK OUT AND PLAY, TO CALM EVERYONE DOWN?
I'M READY.
I FOUND MY SPARE CONTACTS.
UH, MAYBE NOT. THE COPS ARE ALREADY ON STAGE, AND IT LOOKS LIKE A BUNCH OF THE EQUIPMENT'S BEEN TRASHED!
MAYBE YOU GUYS HAD BETTER JUST LEAVE THE BUILDING. THEY'RE TALKING ABOUT HOSING THESE KIDS DOWN WITH A FIRE HOSE!
KRAK!
THE RIOT AT THE NEARLY NEW AMPHITHEATRE GOES ON FOR HOURS. A QUARTER OF A MILLION DOLLARS IN DAMAGES, 60 INJURIES, 16 ARRESTS (FOR VANDALISM, DESTRUCTION OF PROPERTY, DISORDERLY CONDUCT, DISTURBING THE PEACE, ETC.)

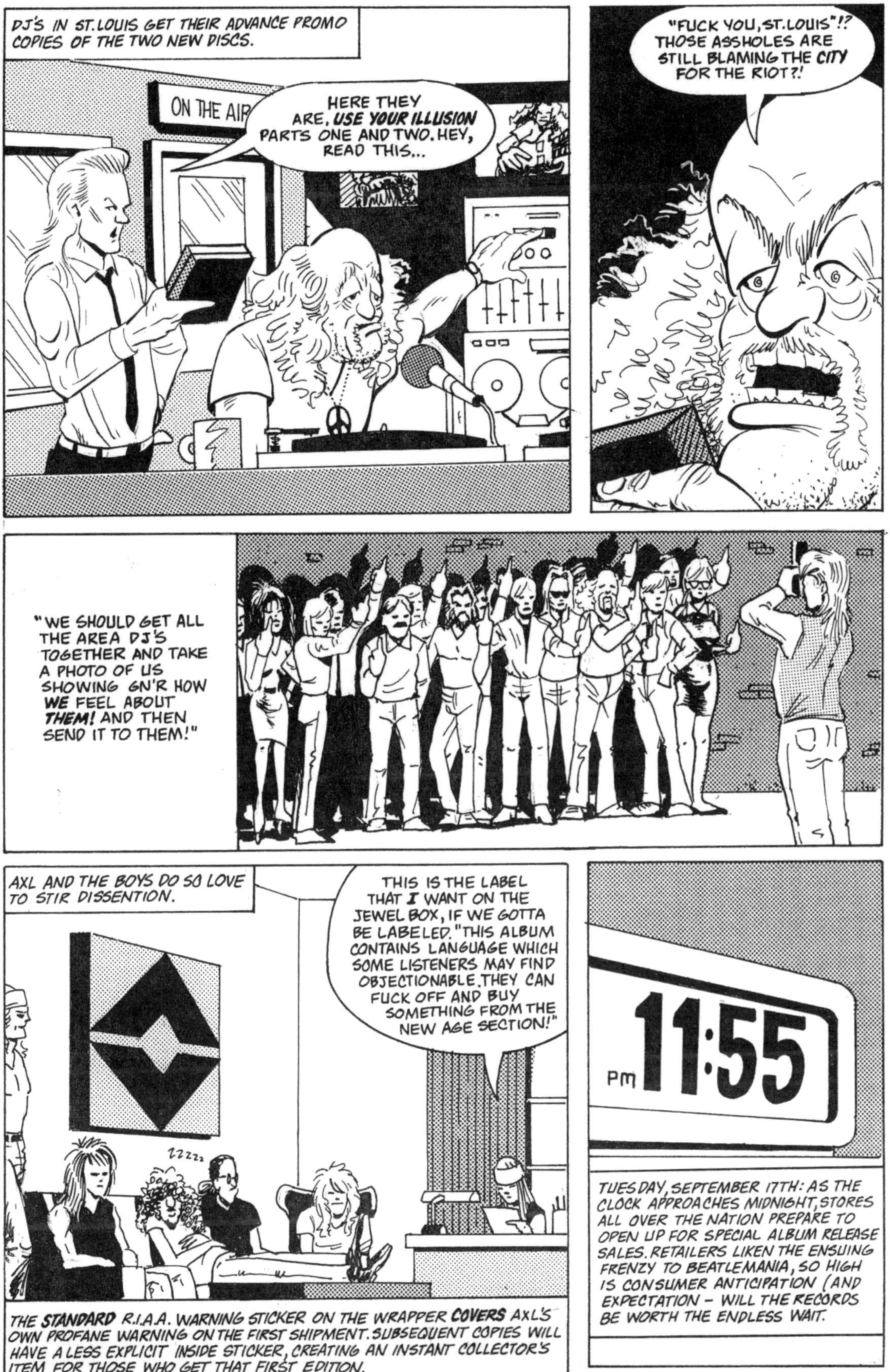
DJ'S IN ST. LOUIS GET THEIR ADVANCE PROMO COPIES OF THE TWO NEW DISCS.
ON THE AIR
HERE THEY ARE, USE YOUR ILLUSION PARTS ONE AND TWO. HEY, READ THIS...
"FUCK YOU, ST. LOUIS"!? THOSE ASSHOLES ARE STILL BLAMING THE CITY FOR THE RIOT?!
"WE SHOULD GET ALL THE AREA DJ'S TOGETHER AND TAKE A PHOTO OF US SHOWING GN'R HOW WE FEEL ABOUT THEM! AND THEN SEND IT TO THEM!"
AXL AND THE BOYS DO SO LOVE TO STIR DISSENTION.
THIS IS THE LABEL THAT I WANT ON THE JEWEL BOX, IF WE GOTTA BE LABELED. "THIS ALBUM CONTAINS LANGUAGE WHICH SOME LISTENERS MAY FIND OBJECTIONABLE. THEY CAN FUCK OFF AND BUY SOMETHING FROM THE NEW AGE SECTION!"
ZZZZZ
THE STANDARD R.I.A.A. WARNING STICKER ON THE WRAPPER COVERS AXL'S OWN PROFANE WARNING ON THE FIRST SHIPMENT. SUBSEQUENT COPIES WILL HAVE A LESS EXPLICIT INSIDE STICKER, CREATING AN INSTANT COLLECTOR'S ITEM FOR THOSE WHO GET THAT FIRST EDITION.
PM 11:55
TUESDAY, SEPTEMBER 17TH: AS THE CLOCK APPROACHES MIDNIGHT, STORES ALL OVER THE NATION PREPARE TO OPEN UP FOR SPECIAL ALBUM RELEASE SALES. RETAILERS LIKEN THE ENSUING FRENZY TO BEATLEMANIA, SO HIGH IS CONSUMER ANTICIPATION (AND EXPECTATION – WILL THE RECORDS BE WORTH THE ENDLESS WAIT.

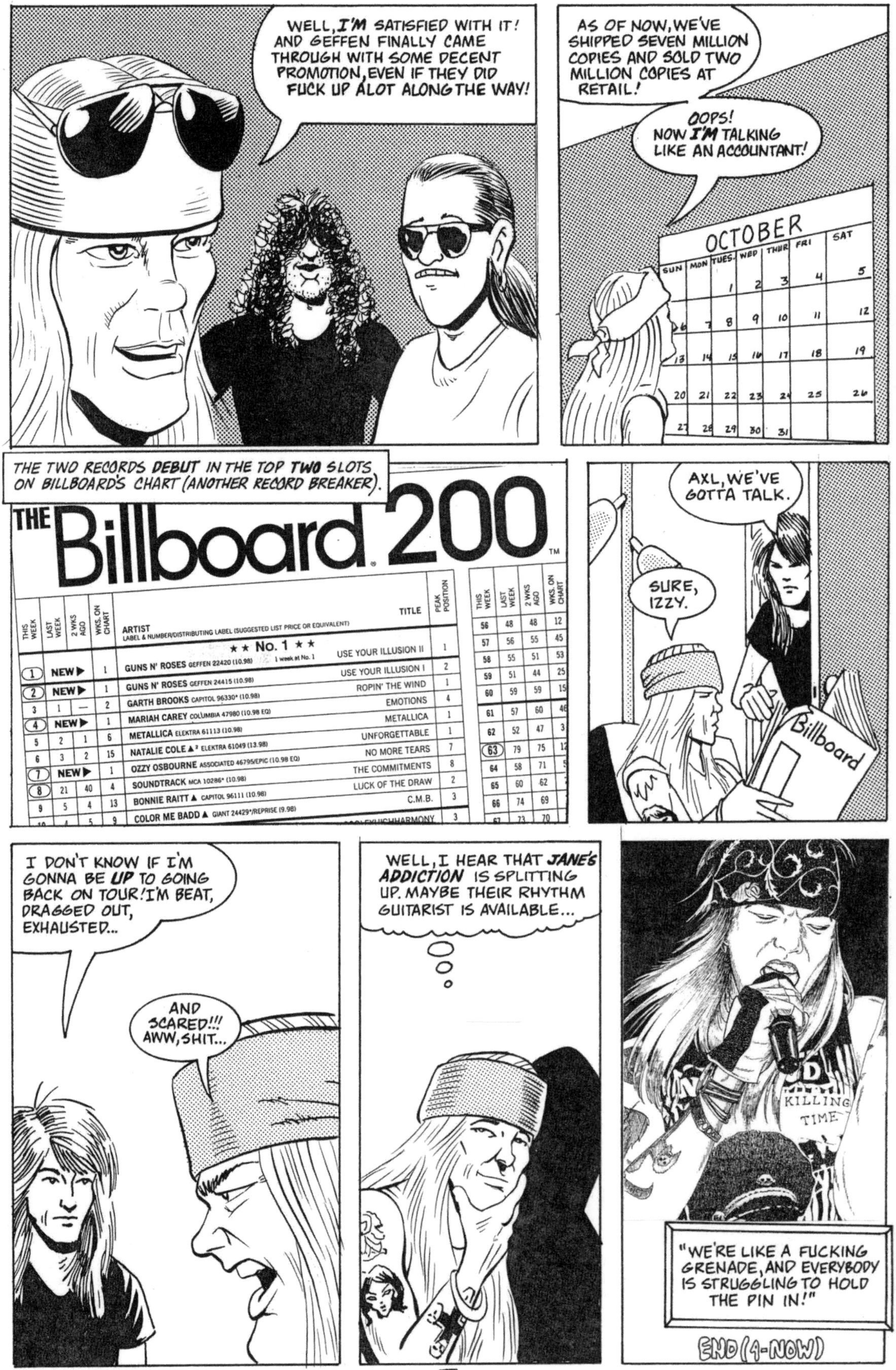
WELL, I'M SATISFIED WITH IT! AND GEFFEN FINALLY CAME THROUGH WITH SOME DECENT PROMOTION, EVEN IF THEY DID FUCK UP ALOT ALONG THE WAY!
AS OF NOW, WE'VE SHIPPED SEVEN MILLION COPIES AND SOLD TWO MILLION COPIES AT RETAIL!
OOPS! NOW I'M TALKING LIKE AN ACCOUNTANT!
OCTOBER
SUN MON TUES. WED THUR FRI SAT
THE TWO RECORDS DEBUT IN THE TOP TWO SLOTS ON BILLBOARD'S CHART (ANOTHER RECORD BREAKER).
THE Billboard 200
THIS WEEK | LAST WEEK | 2 WKS AGO | WKS. ON CHART | ARTIST LABEL & NUMBER/DISTRIBUTING LABEL (SUGGESTED LIST PRICE OR EQUIVALENT) | TITLE | PEAK POSITION
★★ No. 1 ★★
1 NEW ▶ 1 GUNS N' ROSES GEFFEN 24420 (10.98) 1 week at No. 1 USE YOUR ILLUSION II 1
2 NEW ▶ 1 GUNS N' ROSES GEFFEN 24415 (10.98) USE YOUR ILLUSION I 2
3 1 — 2 GARTH BROOKS CAPITOL 96330* (10.98) ROPIN' THE WIND 1
4 NEW ▶ 1 MARIAH CAREY COLUMBIA 47980 (10.98 EQ) EMOTIONS 4
5 2 1 6 METALLICA ELEKTRA 61113 (10.98) METALLICA 1
6 3 2 15 NATALIE COLE ELEKTRA 61049 (13.98) UNFORGETTABLE 1
7 NEW ▶ 1 OZZY OSBOURNE ASSOCIATED 46795/EPIC (10.98 EQ) NO MORE TEARS 7
8 21 40 4 SOUNDTRACK MCA 10286* (10.98) THE COMMITMENTS 8
9 5 4 13 BONNIE RAITT CAPITOL 96111 (10.98) LUCK OF THE DRAW 2
10 4 5 9 COLOR ME BADD GIANT 24429*/REPRISE (9.98) C.M.B. 3
AXL, WE'VE GOTTA TALK.
SURE, IZZY.
Billboard
I DON'T KNOW IF I'M GONNA BE UP TO GOING BACK ON TOUR! I'M BEAT, DRAGGED OUT, EXHAUSTED...
AND SCARED!!! AWW, SHIT...
WELL, I HEAR THAT JANE'S ADDICTION IS SPLITTING UP. MAYBE THEIR RHYTHM GUITARIST IS AVAILABLE...
KILLING TIME
"WE'RE LIKE A FUCKING GRENADE, AND EVERYBODY IS STRUGGLING TO HOLD THE PIN IN!"
END (4-NOW)

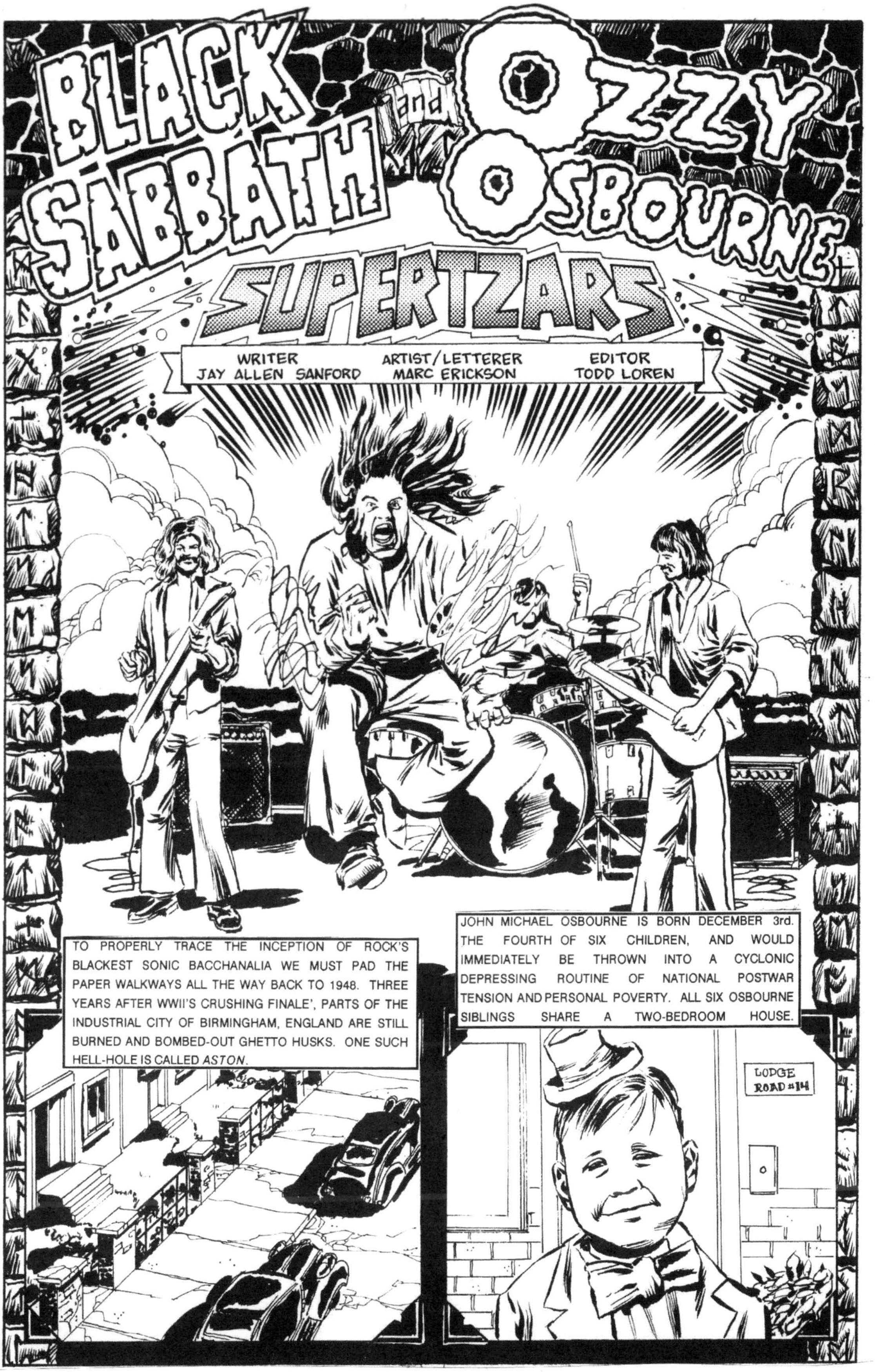
BLACK SABBATH and OZZY OSBOURNE
SUPERTZARS
WRITER JAY ALLEN SANFORD
ARTIST/LETTERER MARC ERICKSON
EDITOR TODD LOREN
TO PROPERLY TRACE THE INCEPTION OF ROCK'S BLACKEST SONIC BACCHANALIA WE MUST PAD THE PAPER WALKWAYS ALL THE WAY BACK TO 1948. THREE YEARS AFTER WWII'S CRUSHING FINALE', PARTS OF THE INDUSTRIAL CITY OF BIRMINGHAM, ENGLAND ARE STILL BURNED AND BOMBED-OUT GHETTO HUSKS. ONE SUCH HELL-HOLE IS CALLED ASTON.
JOHN MICHAEL OSBOURNE IS BORN DECEMBER 3rd. THE FOURTH OF SIX CHILDREN, AND WOULD IMMEDIATELY BE THROWN INTO A CYCLONIC DEPRESSING ROUTINE OF NATIONAL POSTWAR TENSION AND PERSONAL POVERTY. ALL SIX OSBOURNE SIBLINGS SHARE A TWO-BEDROOM HOUSE.
LODGE ROAD #14

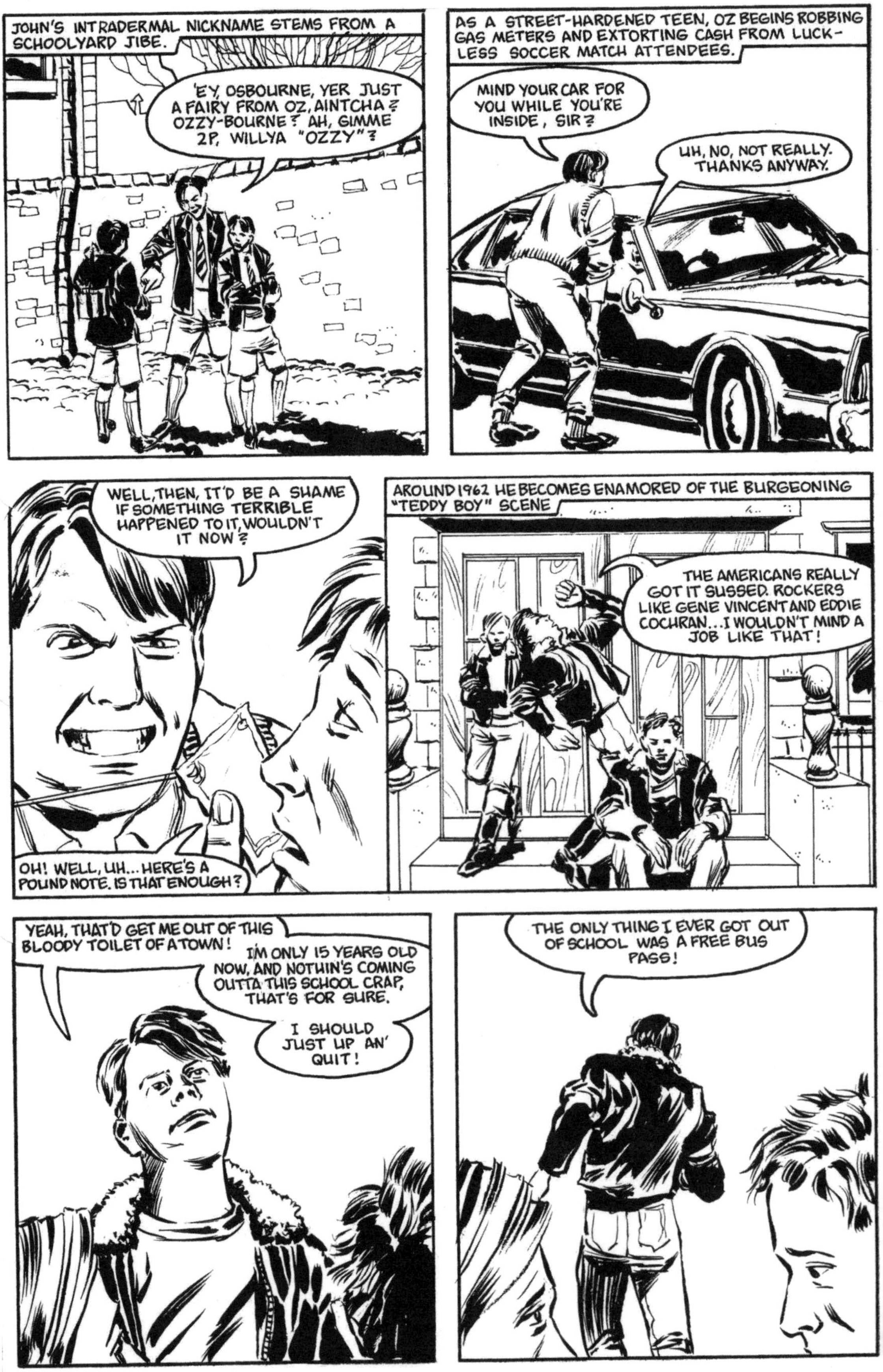
JOHN'S INTRADERMAL NICKNAME STEMS FROM A SCHOOLYARD JIBE.
'EY, OSBOURNE, YER JUST A FAIRY FROM OZ, AINTCHA? OZZY-BOURNE? AH, GIMME 2P, WILLYA "OZZY"?
AS A STREET-HARDENED TEEN, OZ BEGINS ROBBING GAS METERS AND EXTORTING CASH FROM LUCK-LESS SOCCER MATCH ATTENDEES.
MIND YOUR CAR FOR YOU WHILE YOU'RE INSIDE, SIR?
UH, NO, NOT REALLY. THANKS ANYWAY.
WELL, THEN, IT'D BE A SHAME IF SOMETHING TERRIBLE HAPPENED TO IT, WOULDN'T IT NOW?
OH! WELL, UH... HERE'S A POUND NOTE. IS THAT ENOUGH?
AROUND 1962 HE BECOMES ENAMORED OF THE BURGEONING "TEDDY BOY" SCENE
THE AMERICANS REALLY GOT IT SUSSED. ROCKERS LIKE GENE VINCENT AND EDDIE COCHRAN... I WOULDN'T MIND A JOB LIKE THAT!
YEAH, THAT'D GET ME OUT OF THIS BLOODY TOILET OF A TOWN!
I'M ONLY 15 YEARS OLD NOW, AND NOTHIN'S COMING OUTTA THIS SCHOOL CRAP, THAT'S FOR SURE.
I SHOULD JUST UP AN' QUIT!
THE ONLY THING I EVER GOT OUT OF SCHOOL WAS A FREE BUS PASS!

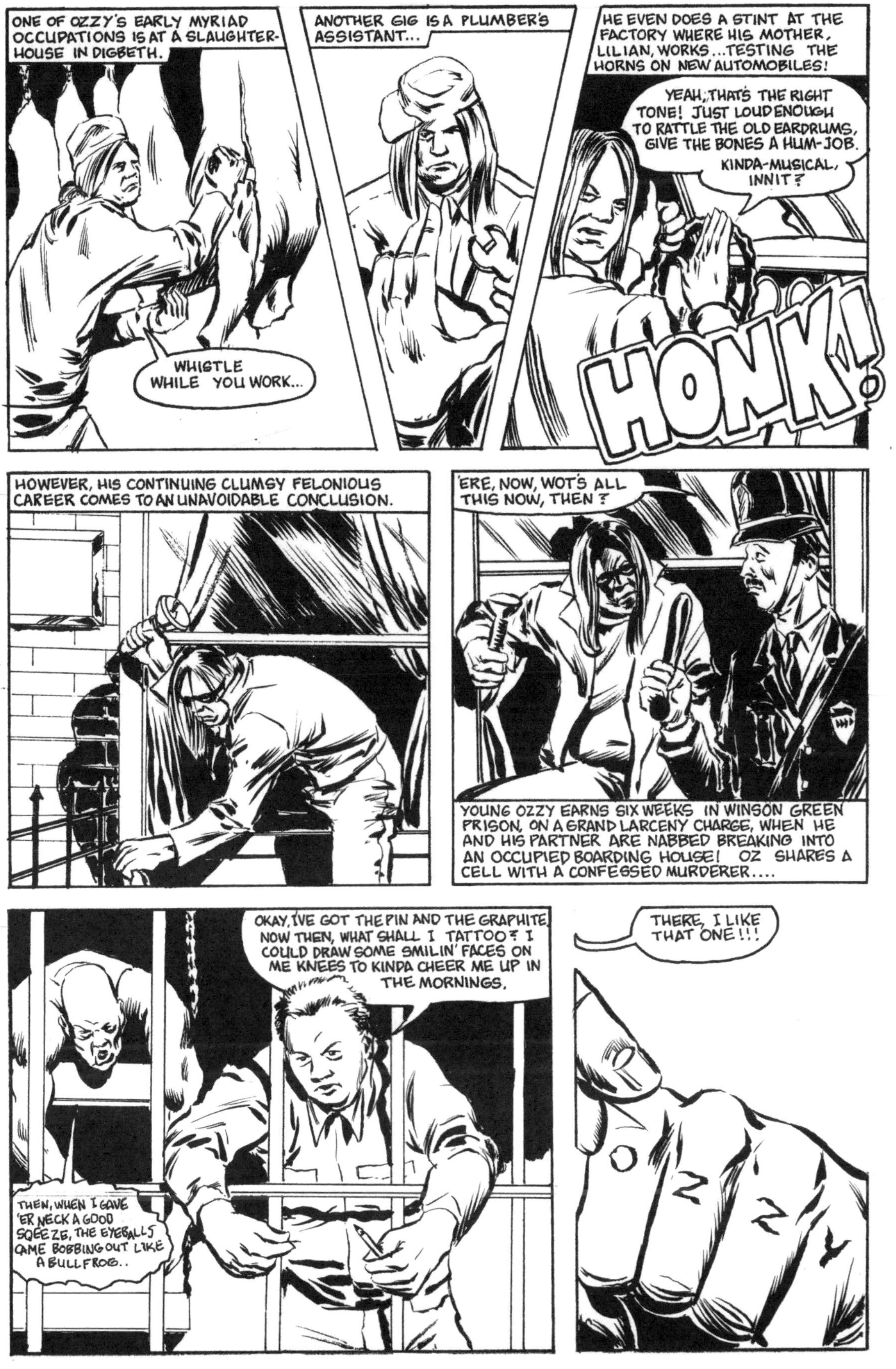
ONE OF OZZY'S EARLY MYRIAD OCCUPATIONS IS AT A SLAUGHTER-HOUSE IN DIGBETH.
WHISTLE WHILE YOU WORK...
ANOTHER GIG IS A PLUMBER'S ASSISTANT...
HE EVEN DOES A STINT AT THE FACTORY WHERE HIS MOTHER, LILIAN, WORKS...TESTING THE HORNS ON NEW AUTOMOBILES!
YEAH, THAT'S THE RIGHT TONE! JUST LOUD ENOUGH TO RATTLE THE OLD EARDRUMS, GIVE THE BONES A HUM-JOB.
KINDA-MUSICAL, INNIT?
HONK!
HOWEVER, HIS CONTINUING CLUMSY FELONIOUS CAREER COMES TO AN UNAVOIDABLE CONCLUSION.
'ERE, NOW, WOT'S ALL THIS NOW, THEN?
YOUNG OZZY EARNS SIX WEEKS IN WINSON GREEN PRISON, ON A GRAND LARCENY CHARGE, WHEN HE AND HIS PARTNER ARE NABBED BREAKING INTO AN OCCUPIED BOARDING HOUSE! OZ SHARES A CELL WITH A CONFESSED MURDERER....
OKAY, I'VE GOT THE PIN AND THE GRAPHITE. NOW THEN, WHAT SHALL I TATTOO? I COULD DRAW SOME SMILIN' FACES ON ME KNEES TO KINDA CHEER ME UP IN THE MORNINGS.
THEN, WHEN I GAVE 'ER NECK A GOOD SQEEZE, THE EYEBALLS CAME BOBBING OUT LIKE A BULLFROG..
THERE, I LIKE THAT ONE!!!
O Z Z Y

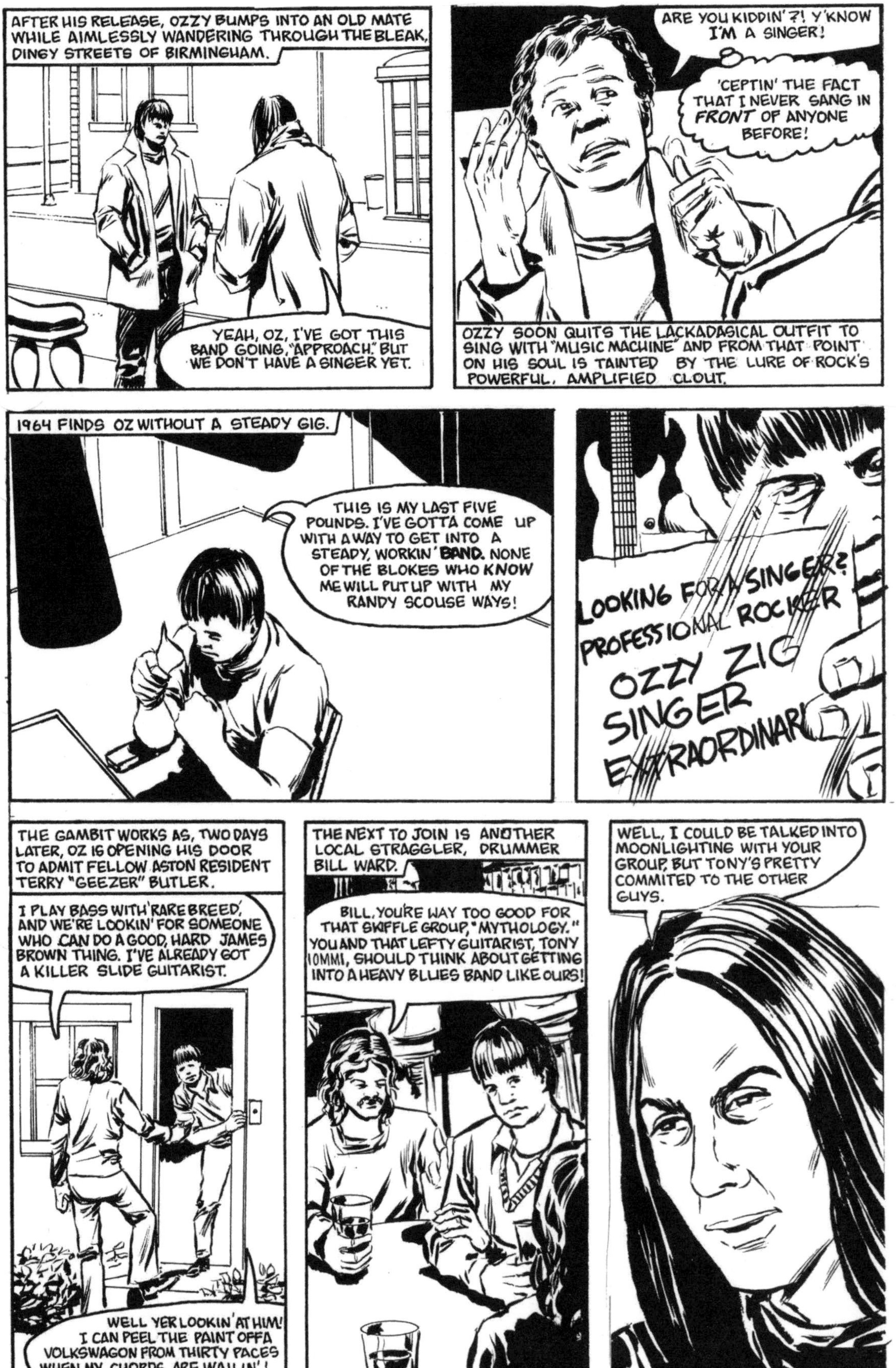
AFTER HIS RELEASE, OZZY BUMPS INTO AN OLD MATE WHILE AIMLESSLY WANDERING THROUGH THE BLEAK, DINGY STREETS OF BIRMINGHAM.
YEAH, OZ, I'VE GOT THIS BAND GOING, "APPROACH." BUT WE DON'T HAVE A SINGER YET.
ARE YOU KIDDIN'?! Y'KNOW I'M A SINGER!
'CEPTIN' THE FACT THAT I NEVER SANG IN FRONT OF ANYONE BEFORE!
OZZY SOON QUITS THE LACKADASICAL OUTFIT TO SING WITH "MUSIC MACHINE" AND FROM THAT POINT ON HIS SOUL IS TAINTED BY THE LURE OF ROCK'S POWERFUL, AMPLIFIED CLOUT.
1964 FINDS OZ WITHOUT A STEADY GIG.
THIS IS MY LAST FIVE POUNDS. I'VE GOTTA COME UP WITH A WAY TO GET INTO A STEADY, WORKIN' BAND. NONE OF THE BLOKES WHO KNOW ME WILL PUT UP WITH MY RANDY SCOUSE WAYS!
LOOKING FOR A SINGER?
PROFESSIONAL ROCKER
OZZY ZIG
SINGER
EXTRAORDINAR
THE GAMBIT WORKS AS, TWO DAYS LATER, OZ IS OPENING HIS DOOR TO ADMIT FELLOW ASTON RESIDENT TERRY "GEEZER" BUTLER.
I PLAY BASS WITH 'RARE BREED', AND WE'RE LOOKIN' FOR SOMEONE WHO CAN DO A GOOD, HARD JAMES BROWN THING. I'VE ALREADY GOT A KILLER SLIDE GUITARIST.
WELL YER LOOKIN' AT HIM! I CAN PEEL THE PAINT OFFA VOLKSWAGON FROM THIRTY PACES WHEN MY CHORDS ARE WAILIN'!
THE NEXT TO JOIN IS ANOTHER LOCAL STRAGGLER, DRUMMER BILL WARD.
BILL, YOU'RE WAY TOO GOOD FOR THAT SKIFFLE GROUP, "MYTHOLOGY." YOU AND THAT LEFTY GUITARIST, TONY IOMMI, SHOULD THINK ABOUT GETTING INTO A HEAVY BLUES BAND LIKE OURS!
WELL, I COULD BE TALKED INTO MOONLIGHTING WITH YOUR GROUP, BUT TONY'S PRETTY COMMITED TO THE OTHER GUYS.

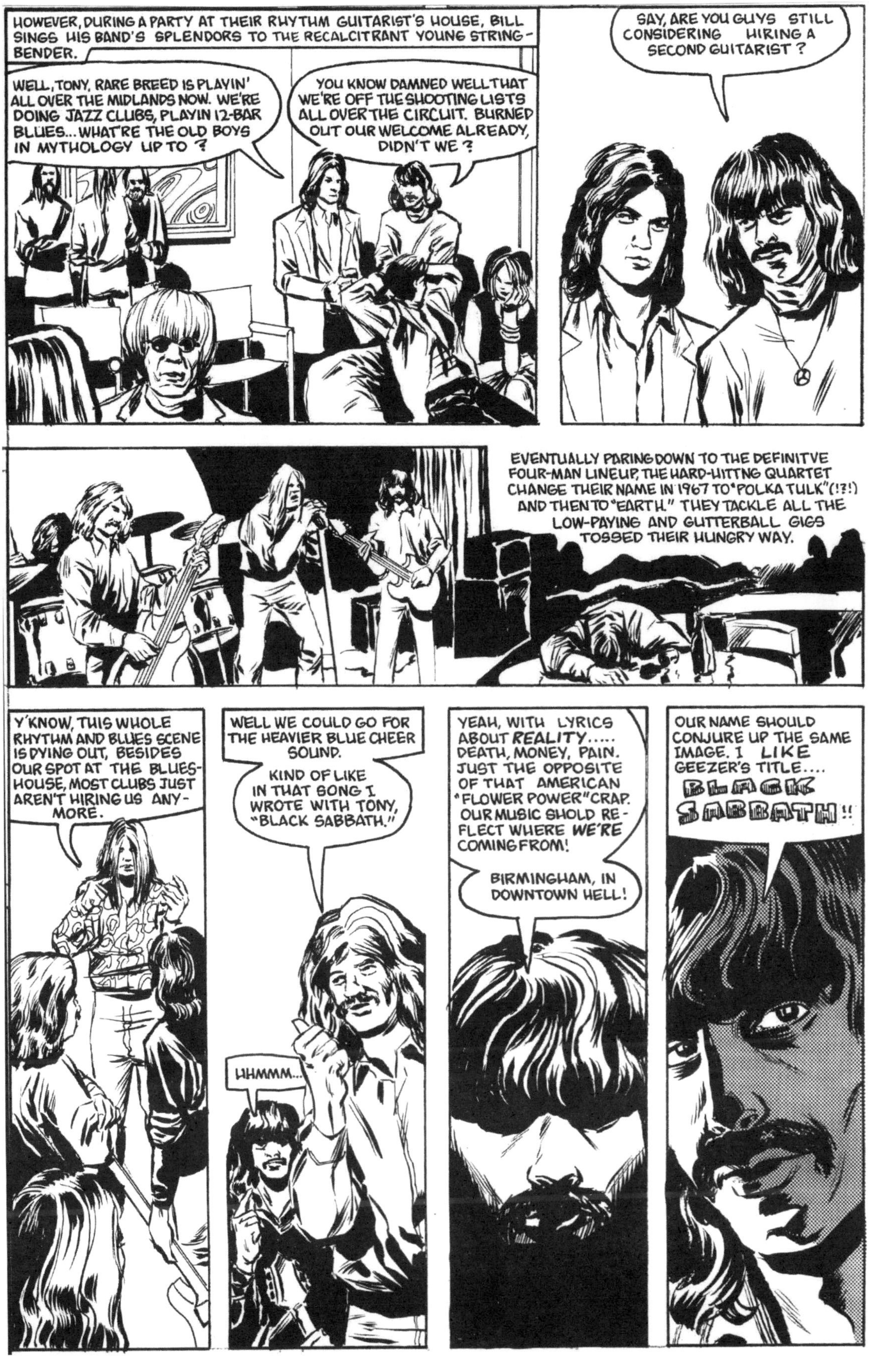
HOWEVER, DURING A PARTY AT THEIR RHYTHM GUITARIST'S HOUSE, BILL SINGS HIS BAND'S SPLENDORS TO THE RECALCITRANT YOUNG STRING-BENDER.
WELL, TONY, RARE BREED IS PLAYIN' ALL OVER THE MIDLANDS NOW. WE'RE DOING JAZZ CLUBS, PLAYIN 12-BAR BLUES... WHAT'RE THE OLD BOYS IN MYTHOLOGY UP TO ?
YOU KNOW DAMNED WELL THAT WE'RE OFF THE SHOOTING LISTS ALL OVER THE CIRCUIT. BURNED OUT OUR WELCOME ALREADY, DIDN'T WE ?
SAY, ARE YOU GUYS STILL CONSIDERING HIRING A SECOND GUITARIST ?
EVENTUALLY PARING DOWN TO THE DEFINITVE FOUR-MAN LINEUP, THE HARD-HITTING QUARTET CHANGE THEIR NAME IN 1967 TO "POLKA TULK" (!?!) AND THEN TO "EARTH." THEY TACKLE ALL THE LOW-PAYING AND GUTTERBALL GIGS TOSSED THEIR HUNGRY WAY.
Y'KNOW, THIS WHOLE RHYTHM AND BLUES SCENE IS DYING OUT, BESIDES OUR SPOT AT THE BLUES-HOUSE, MOST CLUBS JUST AREN'T HIRING US ANY-MORE.
WELL WE COULD GO FOR THE HEAVIER BLUE CHEER SOUND.
KIND OF LIKE IN THAT SONG I WROTE WITH TONY, "BLACK SABBATH."
UHMMM...
YEAH, WITH LYRICS ABOUT REALITY..... DEATH, MONEY, PAIN. JUST THE OPPOSITE OF THAT AMERICAN "FLOWER POWER" CRAP. OUR MUSIC SHOLD RE-FLECT WHERE WE'RE COMING FROM!
BIRMINGHAM, IN DOWNTOWN HELL!
OUR NAME SHOULD CONJURE UP THE SAME IMAGE. I LIKE GEEZER'S TITLE....
BLACK SABBATH!!

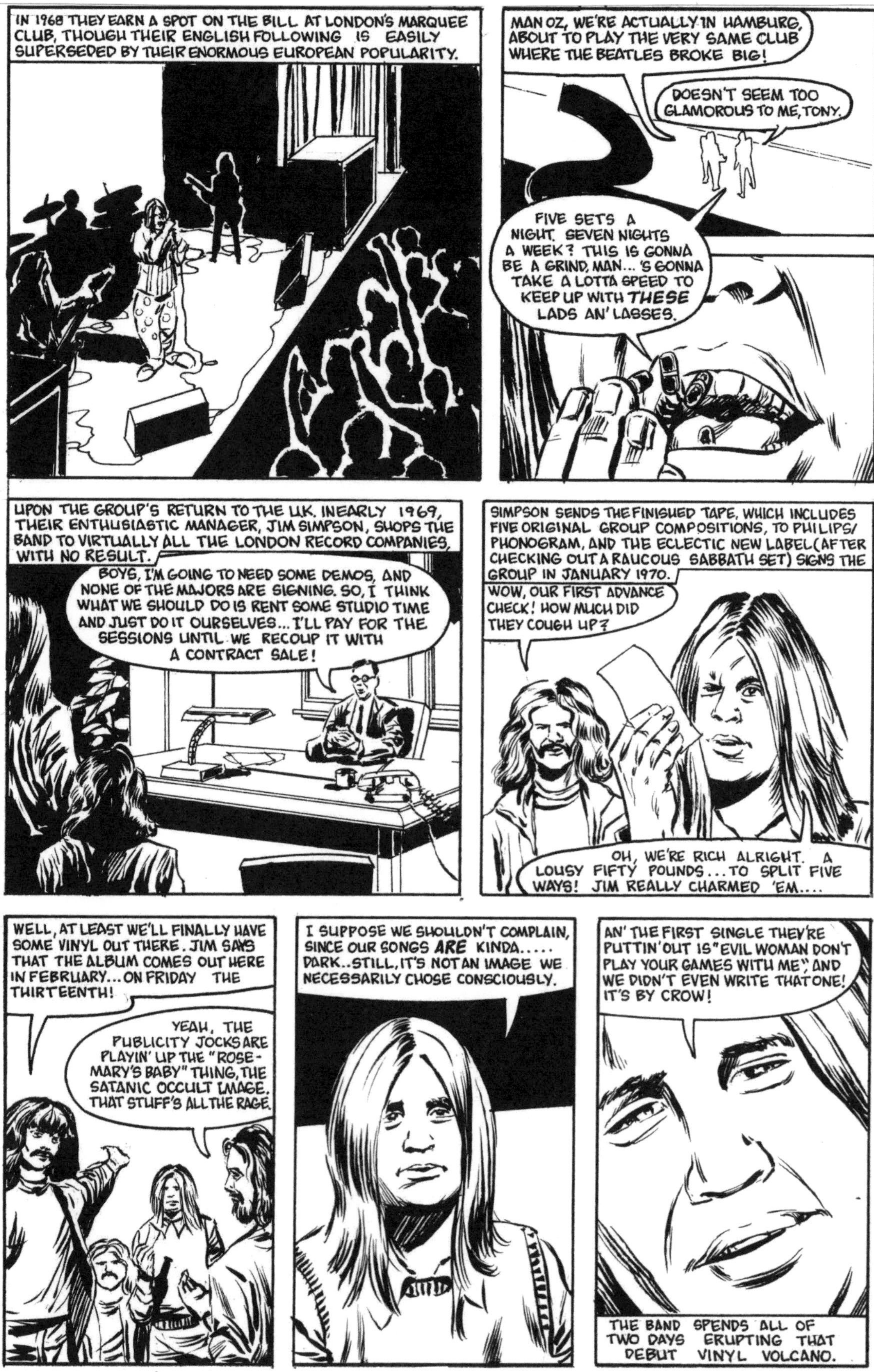

IN 1968 THEY EARN A SPOT ON THE BILL AT LONDON'S MARQUEE CLUB, THOUGH THEIR ENGLISH FOLLOWING IS EASILY SUPERSEDED BY THEIR ENORMOUS EUROPEAN POPULARITY.
MAN OZ, WE'RE ACTUALLY IN HAMBURG, ABOUT TO PLAY THE VERY SAME CLUB WHERE THE BEATLES BROKE BIG!
DOESN'T SEEM TOO GLAMOROUS TO ME, TONY.
FIVE SETS A NIGHT, SEVEN NIGHTS A WEEK? THIS IS GONNA BE A GRIND, MAN... 'S GONNA TAKE A LOTTA SPEED TO KEEP UP WITH THESE LADS AN' LASSES.
UPON THE GROUP'S RETURN TO THE U.K. IN EARLY 1969, THEIR ENTHUSIASTIC MANAGER, JIM SIMPSON, SHOPS THE BAND TO VIRTUALLY ALL THE LONDON RECORD COMPANIES, WITH NO RESULT.
BOYS, I'M GOING TO NEED SOME DEMOS, AND NONE OF THE MAJORS ARE SIGNING. SO, I THINK WHAT WE SHOULD DO IS RENT SOME STUDIO TIME AND JUST DO IT OURSELVES... I'LL PAY FOR THE SESSIONS UNTIL WE RECOUP IT WITH A CONTRACT SALE!
SIMPSON SENDS THE FINISHED TAPE, WHICH INCLUDES FIVE ORIGINAL GROUP COMPOSITIONS, TO PHILIPS/PHONOGRAM, AND THE ECLECTIC NEW LABEL (AFTER CHECKING OUT A RAUCOUS SABBATH SET) SIGNS THE GROUP IN JANUARY 1970.
WOW, OUR FIRST ADVANCE CHECK! HOW MUCH DID THEY COUGH UP?
OH, WE'RE RICH ALRIGHT. A LOUSY FIFTY POUNDS... TO SPLIT FIVE WAYS! JIM REALLY CHARMED 'EM....
WELL, AT LEAST WE'LL FINALLY HAVE SOME VINYL OUT THERE. JIM SAYS THAT THE ALBUM COMES OUT HERE IN FEBRUARY... ON FRIDAY THE THIRTEENTH!
YEAH, THE PUBLICITY JOCKS ARE PLAYIN' UP THE "ROSE-MARY'S BABY" THING, THE SATANIC OCCULT IMAGE. THAT STUFF'S ALL THE RAGE.
I SUPPOSE WE SHOULDN'T COMPLAIN, SINCE OUR SONGS ARE KINDA..... DARK.. STILL, IT'S NOT AN IMAGE WE NECESSARILY CHOSE CONSCIOUSLY.
AN' THE FIRST SINGLE THEY'RE PUTTIN' OUT IS "EVIL WOMAN DON'T PLAY YOUR GAMES WITH ME", AND WE DIDN'T EVEN WRITE THAT ONE! IT'S BY CROW!
THE BAND SPENDS ALL OF TWO DAYS ERUPTING THAT DEBUT VINYL VOLCANO.

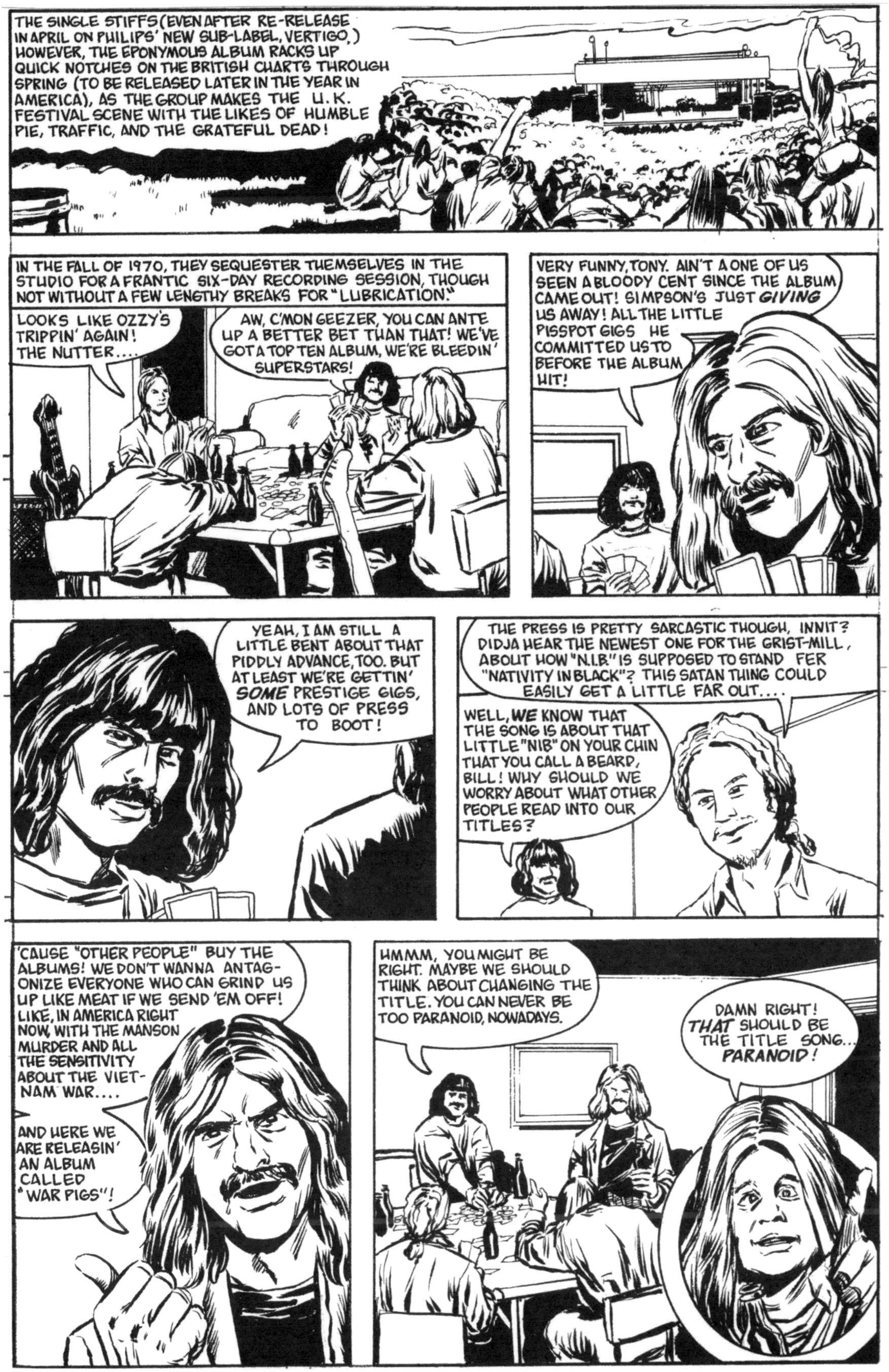

THE SINGLE STIFFS (EVEN AFTER RE-RELEASE IN APRIL ON PHILIPS' NEW SUB-LABEL, VERTIGO,) HOWEVER, THE EPONYMOUS ALBUM RACKS UP QUICK NOTCHES ON THE BRITISH CHARTS THROUGH SPRING (TO BE RELEASED LATER IN THE YEAR IN AMERICA), AS THE GROUP MAKES THE U.K. FESTIVAL SCENE WITH THE LIKES OF HUMBLE PIE, TRAFFIC, AND THE GRATEFUL DEAD!
IN THE FALL OF 1970, THEY SEQUESTER THEMSELVES IN THE STUDIO FOR A FRANTIC SIX-DAY RECORDING SESSION, THOUGH NOT WITHOUT A FEW LENGTHY BREAKS FOR "LUBRICATION."
LOOKS LIKE OZZY'S TRIPPIN' AGAIN! THE NUTTER....
AW, C'MON GEEZER, YOU CAN ANTE UP A BETTER BET THAN THAT! WE'VE GOT A TOP TEN ALBUM, WE'RE BLEEDIN' SUPERSTARS!
VERY FUNNY, TONY. AIN'T A ONE OF US SEEN A BLOODY CENT SINCE THE ALBUM CAME OUT! SIMPSON'S JUST GIVING US AWAY! ALL THE LITTLE PISSPOT GIGS HE COMMITTED US TO BEFORE THE ALBUM HIT!
YEAH, I AM STILL A LITTLE BENT ABOUT THAT PIDDLY ADVANCE, TOO. BUT AT LEAST WE'RE GETTIN' SOME PRESTIGE GIGS, AND LOTS OF PRESS TO BOOT!
THE PRESS IS PRETTY SARCASTIC THOUGH, INNIT? DIDJA HEAR THE NEWEST ONE FOR THE GRIST-MILL, ABOUT HOW "N.I.B." IS SUPPOSED TO STAND FER "NATIVITY IN BLACK"? THIS SATAN THING COULD EASILY GET A LITTLE FAR OUT....
WELL, WE KNOW THAT THE SONG IS ABOUT THAT LITTLE "NIB" ON YOUR CHIN THAT YOU CALL A BEARD, BILL! WHY SHOULD WE WORRY ABOUT WHAT OTHER PEOPLE READ INTO OUR TITLES?
'CAUSE "OTHER PEOPLE" BUY THE ALBUMS! WE DON'T WANNA ANTAGONIZE EVERYONE WHO CAN GRIND US UP LIKE MEAT IF WE SEND 'EM OFF! LIKE, IN AMERICA RIGHT NOW, WITH THE MANSON MURDER AND ALL THE SENSITIVITY ABOUT THE VIET-NAM WAR....
AND HERE WE ARE RELEASIN' AN ALBUM CALLED "WAR PIGS"!
HMMM, YOU MIGHT BE RIGHT. MAYBE WE SHOULD THINK ABOUT CHANGING THE TITLE. YOU CAN NEVER BE TOO PARANOID, NOWADAYS.
DAMN RIGHT! THAT SHOULD BE THE TITLE SONG... PARANOID!

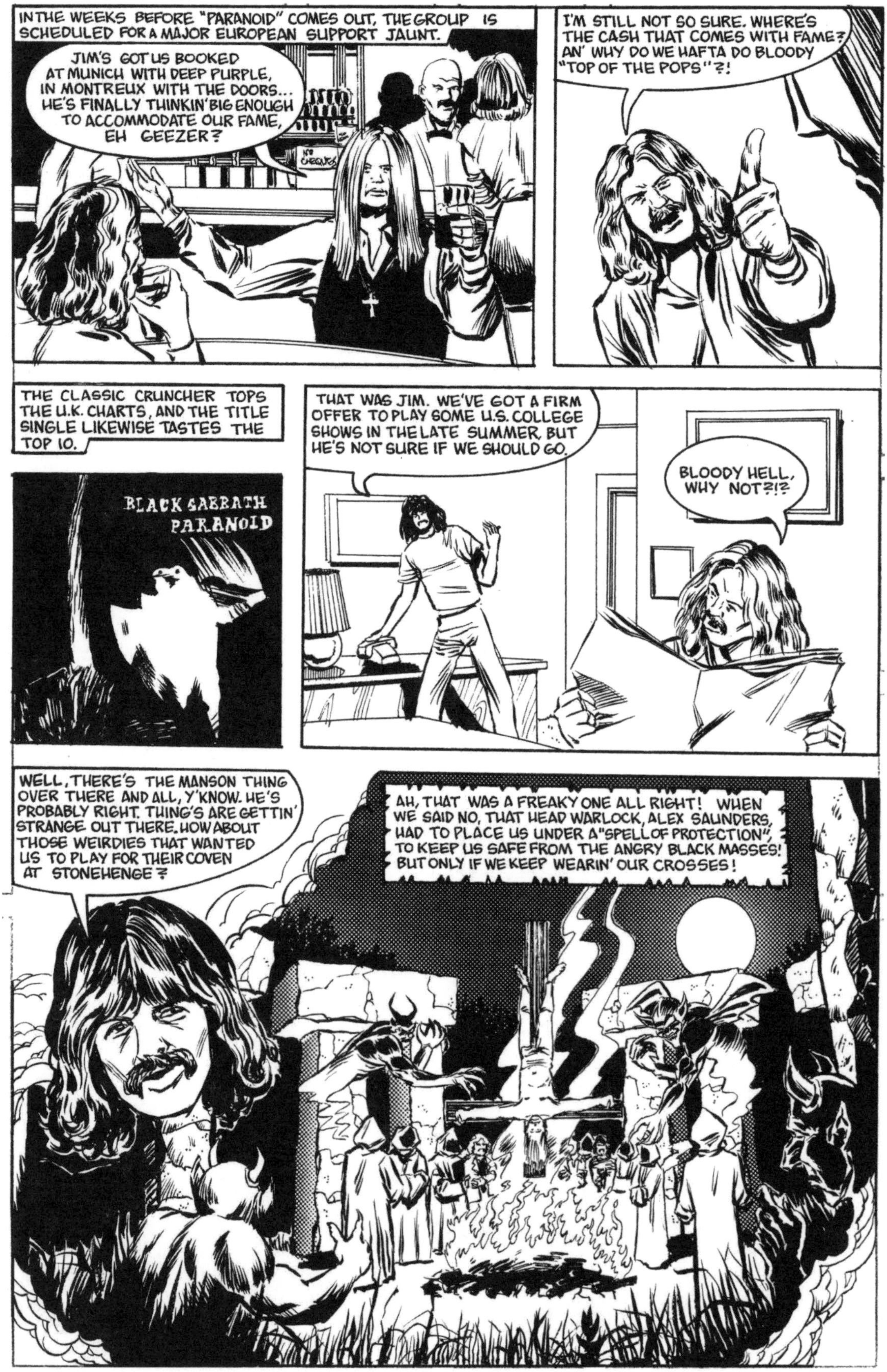

IN THE WEEKS BEFORE "PARANOID" COMES OUT, THE GROUP IS SCHEDULED FOR A MAJOR EUROPEAN SUPPORT JAUNT.
JIM'S GOT US BOOKED AT MUNICH WITH DEEP PURPLE, IN MONTREUX WITH THE DOORS... HE'S FINALLY THINKIN' BIG ENOUGH TO ACCOMMODATE OUR FAME, EH GEEZER?
NO CHEQUES
I'M STILL NOT SO SURE. WHERE'S THE CASH THAT COMES WITH FAME? AN' WHY DO WE HAFTA DO BLOODY "TOP OF THE POPS"?!
THE CLASSIC CRUNCHER TOPS THE U.K. CHARTS, AND THE TITLE SINGLE LIKEWISE TASTES THE TOP 10.
BLACK SABBATH
PARANOID
THAT WAS JIM. WE'VE GOT A FIRM OFFER TO PLAY SOME U.S. COLLEGE SHOWS IN THE LATE SUMMER, BUT HE'S NOT SURE IF WE SHOULD GO.
BLOODY HELL, WHY NOT?!?
WELL, THERE'S THE MANSON THING OVER THERE AND ALL, Y'KNOW. HE'S PROBABLY RIGHT. THING'S ARE GETTIN' STRANGE OUT THERE. HOW ABOUT THOSE WEIRDIES THAT WANTED US TO PLAY FOR THEIR COVEN AT STONEHENGE?
AH, THAT WAS A FREAKY ONE ALL RIGHT! WHEN WE SAID NO, THAT HEAD WARLOCK, ALEX SAUNDERS, HAD TO PLACE US UNDER A "SPELL OF PROTECTION", TO KEEP US SAFE FROM THE ANGRY BLACK MASSES! BUT ONLY IF WE KEEP WEARIN' OUR CROSSES!

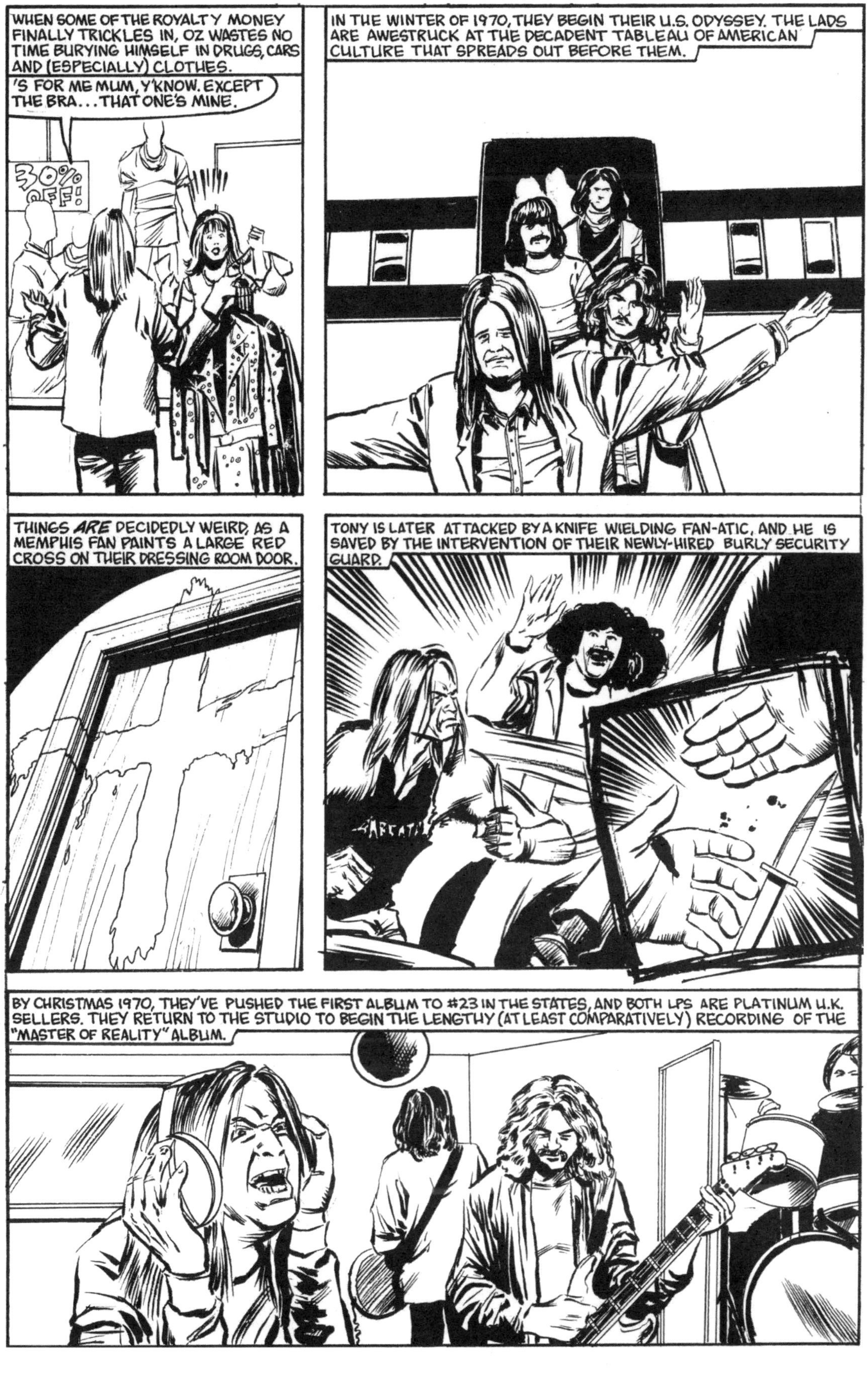
WHEN SOME OF THE ROYALTY MONEY FINALLY TRICKLES IN, OZ WASTES NO TIME BURYING HIMSELF IN DRUGS, CARS AND (ESPECIALLY) CLOTHES.
'S FOR ME MUM, Y'KNOW. EXCEPT THE BRA... THAT ONE'S MINE.
30% OFF!
IN THE WINTER OF 1970, THEY BEGIN THEIR U.S. ODYSSEY. THE LADS ARE AWESTRUCK AT THE DECADENT TABLEAU OF AMERICAN CULTURE THAT SPREADS OUT BEFORE THEM.
THINGS *ARE* DECIDEDLY WEIRD, AS A MEMPHIS FAN PAINTS A LARGE RED CROSS ON THEIR DRESSING ROOM DOOR.
TONY IS LATER ATTACKED BY A KNIFE WIELDING FAN-ATIC, AND HE IS SAVED BY THE INTERVENTION OF THEIR NEWLY-HIRED BURLY SECURITY GUARD.
BY CHRISTMAS 1970, THEY'VE PUSHED THE FIRST ALBUM TO #23 IN THE STATES, AND BOTH LPS ARE PLATINUM U.K. SELLERS. THEY RETURN TO THE STUDIO TO BEGIN THE LENGTHY (AT LEAST COMPARATIVELY) RECORDING OF THE "MASTER OF REALITY" ALBUM.

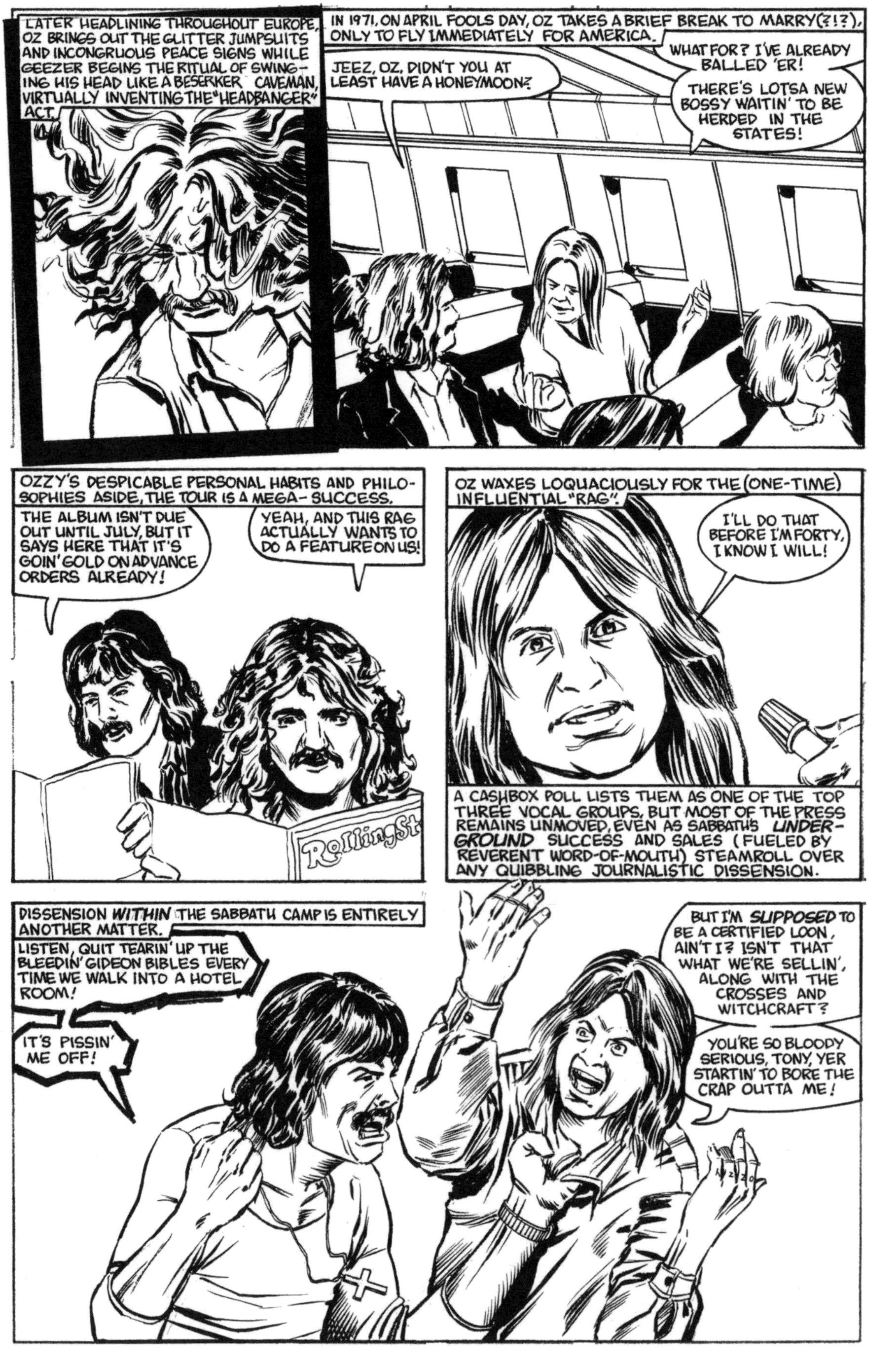
LATER HEADLINING THROUGHOUT EUROPE, OZ BRINGS OUT THE GLITTER JUMPSUITS AND INCONGRUOUS PEACE SIGNS WHILE GEEZER BEGINS THE RITUAL OF SWINGING HIS HEAD LIKE A BESERKER CAVEMAN, VIRTUALLY INVENTING THE "HEADBANGER" ACT.
IN 1971, ON APRIL FOOLS DAY, OZ TAKES A BRIEF BREAK TO MARRY(?!?), ONLY TO FLY IMMEDIATELY FOR AMERICA.
JEEZ, OZ, DIDN'T YOU AT LEAST HAVE A HONEYMOON?
WHAT FOR? I'VE ALREADY BALLED 'ER!
THERE'S LOTSA NEW BOSSY WAITIN' TO BE HERDED IN THE STATES!
OZZY'S DESPICABLE PERSONAL HABITS AND PHILOSOPHIES ASIDE, THE TOUR IS A MEGA-SUCCESS.
THE ALBUM ISN'T DUE OUT UNTIL JULY, BUT IT SAYS HERE THAT IT'S GOIN' GOLD ON ADVANCE ORDERS ALREADY!
YEAH, AND THIS RAG ACTUALLY WANTS TO DO A FEATURE ON US!
RollingSt
OZ WAXES LOQUACIOUSLY FOR THE (ONE-TIME) INFLUENTIAL "RAG".
I'LL DO THAT BEFORE I'M FORTY, I KNOW I WILL!
A CASHBOX POLL LISTS THEM AS ONE OF THE TOP THREE VOCAL GROUPS, BUT MOST OF THE PRESS REMAINS UNMOVED, EVEN AS SABBATH'S UNDERGROUND SUCCESS AND SALES (FUELED BY REVERENT WORD-OF-MOUTH) STEAMROLL OVER ANY QUIBBLING JOURNALISTIC DISSENSION.
DISSENSION WITHIN THE SABBATH CAMP IS ENTIRELY ANOTHER MATTER.
LISTEN, QUIT TEARIN' UP THE BLEEDIN' GIDEON BIBLES EVERY TIME WE WALK INTO A HOTEL ROOM!
IT'S PISSIN' ME OFF!
BUT I'M SUPPOSED TO BE A CERTIFIED LOON, AIN'T I? ISN'T THAT WHAT WE'RE SELLIN', ALONG WITH THE CROSSES AND WITCHCRAFT?
YOU'RE SO BLOODY SERIOUS, TONY, YER STARTIN' TO BORE THE CRAP OUTTA ME!

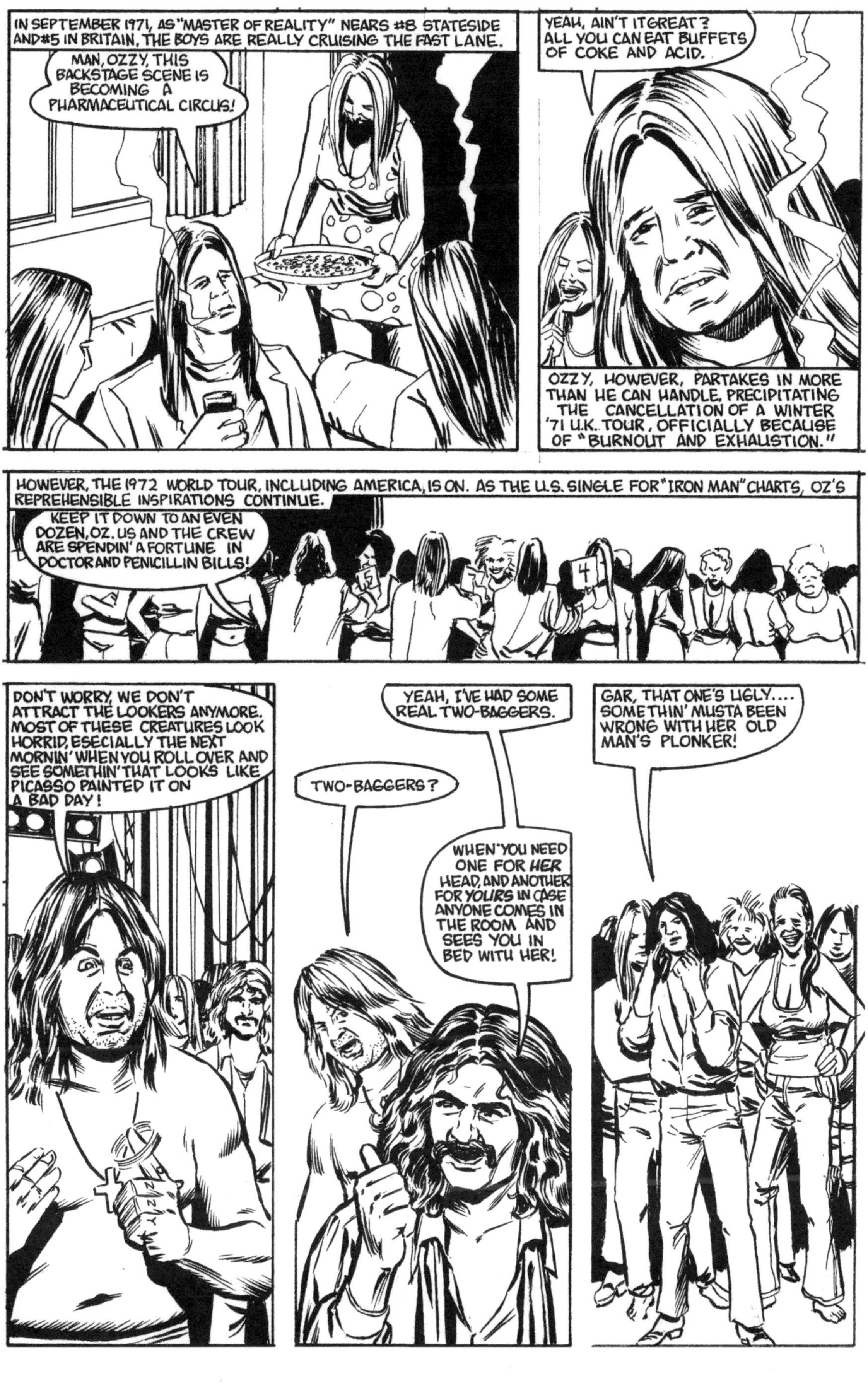
IN SEPTEMBER 1971, AS "MASTER OF REALITY" NEARS #8 STATESIDE AND #5 IN BRITAIN, THE BOYS ARE REALLY CRUISING THE FAST LANE.
MAN, OZZY, THIS BACKSTAGE SCENE IS BECOMING A PHARMACEUTICAL CIRCUS!
YEAH, AIN'T IT GREAT? ALL YOU CAN EAT BUFFETS OF COKE AND ACID.
OZZY, HOWEVER, PARTAKES IN MORE THAN HE CAN HANDLE, PRECIPITATING THE CANCELLATION OF A WINTER '71 U.K. TOUR, OFFICIALLY BECAUSE OF "BURNOUT AND EXHAUSTION."
HOWEVER, THE 1972 WORLD TOUR, INCLUDING AMERICA, IS ON. AS THE U.S. SINGLE FOR "IRON MAN" CHARTS, OZ'S REPREHENSIBLE INSPIRATIONS CONTINUE.
KEEP IT DOWN TO AN EVEN DOZEN, OZ. US AND THE CREW ARE SPENDIN' A FORTUNE IN DOCTOR AND PENICILLIN BILLS!
DON'T WORRY, WE DON'T ATTRACT THE LOOKERS ANYMORE. MOST OF THESE CREATURES LOOK HORRID, ESECIALLY THE NEXT MORNIN' WHEN YOU ROLL OVER AND SEE SOMETHIN' THAT LOOKS LIKE PICASSO PAINTED IT ON A BAD DAY!
YEAH, I'VE HAD SOME REAL TWO-BAGGERS.
TWO-BAGGERS?
WHEN YOU NEED ONE FOR HER HEAD, AND ANOTHER FOR YOURS IN CASE ANYONE COMES IN THE ROOM AND SEES YOU IN BED WITH HER!
GAR, THAT ONE'S UGLY.... SOMETHIN' MUSTA BEEN WRONG WITH HER OLD MAN'S PLONKER!

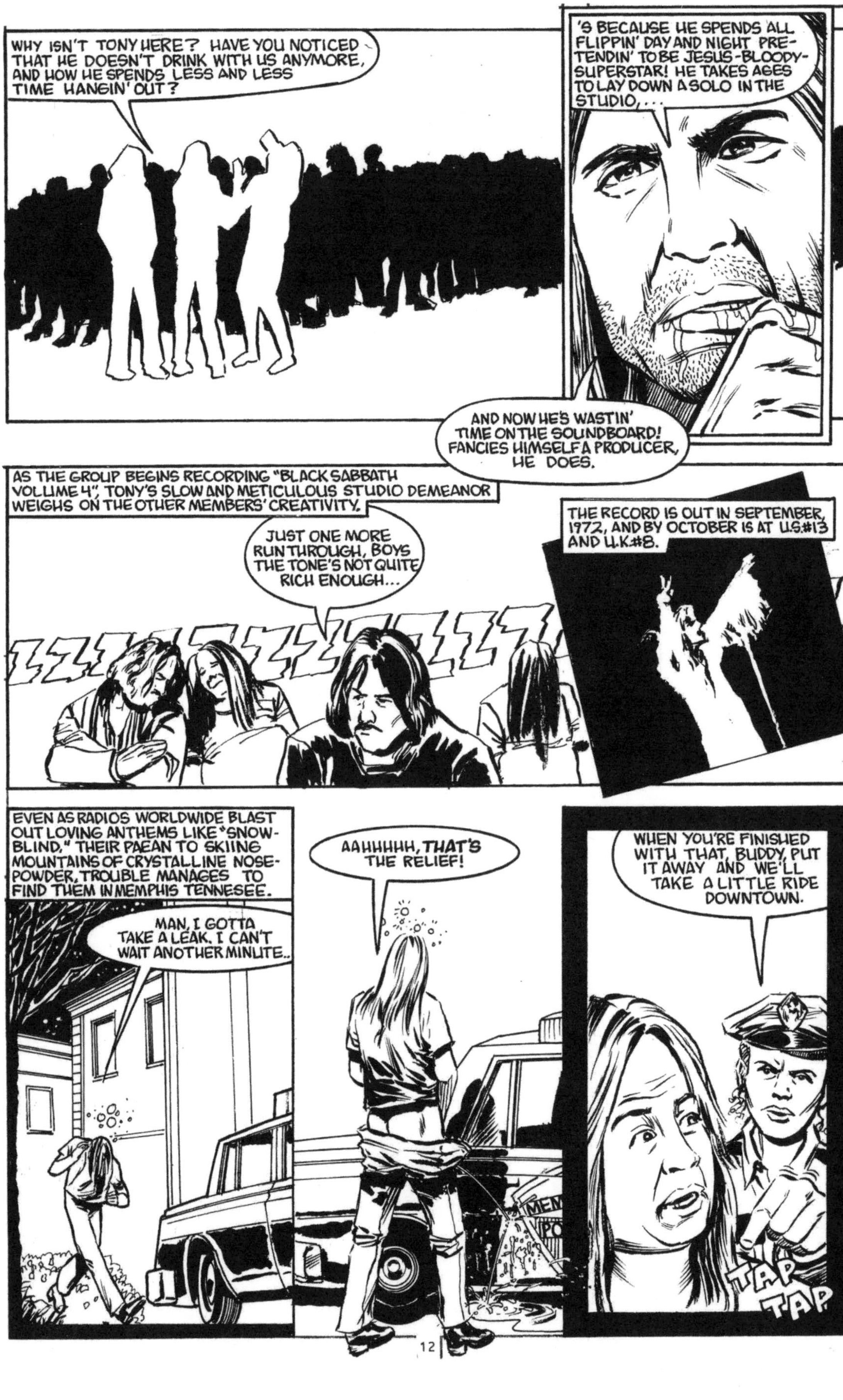
WHY ISN'T TONY HERE? HAVE YOU NOTICED THAT HE DOESN'T DRINK WITH US ANYMORE, AND HOW HE SPENDS LESS AND LESS TIME HANGIN' OUT?
'S BECAUSE HE SPENDS ALL FLIPPIN' DAY AND NIGHT PRETENDIN' TO BE JESUS-BLOODY-SUPERSTAR! HE TAKES AGES TO LAY DOWN A SOLO IN THE STUDIO, . . .
AND NOW HE'S WASTIN' TIME ON THE SOUNDBOARD! FANCIES HIMSELF A PRODUCER, HE DOES.
AS THE GROUP BEGINS RECORDING "BLACK SABBATH VOLUME 4", TONY'S SLOW AND METICULOUS STUDIO DEMEANOR WEIGHS ON THE OTHER MEMBERS' CREATIVITY.
JUST ONE MORE RUN THROUGH, BOYS THE TONE'S NOT QUITE RICH ENOUGH...
ZZZZZZZZZZZZZ
THE RECORD IS OUT IN SEPTEMBER, 1972, AND BY OCTOBER IS AT U.S.#13 AND U.K.#8.
EVEN AS RADIOS WORLDWIDE BLAST OUT LOVING ANTHEMS LIKE "SNOW-BLIND," THEIR PAEAN TO SKIING MOUNTAINS OF CRYSTALLINE NOSE-POWDER, TROUBLE MANAGES TO FIND THEM IN MEMPHIS TENNESEE.
MAN, I GOTTA TAKE A LEAK. I CAN'T WAIT ANOTHER MINUTE..
AAHHHHH, THAT'S THE RELIEF!
WHEN YOU'RE FINISHED WITH THAT, BUDDY, PUT IT AWAY AND WE'LL TAKE A LITTLE RIDE DOWNTOWN.
TAP TAP

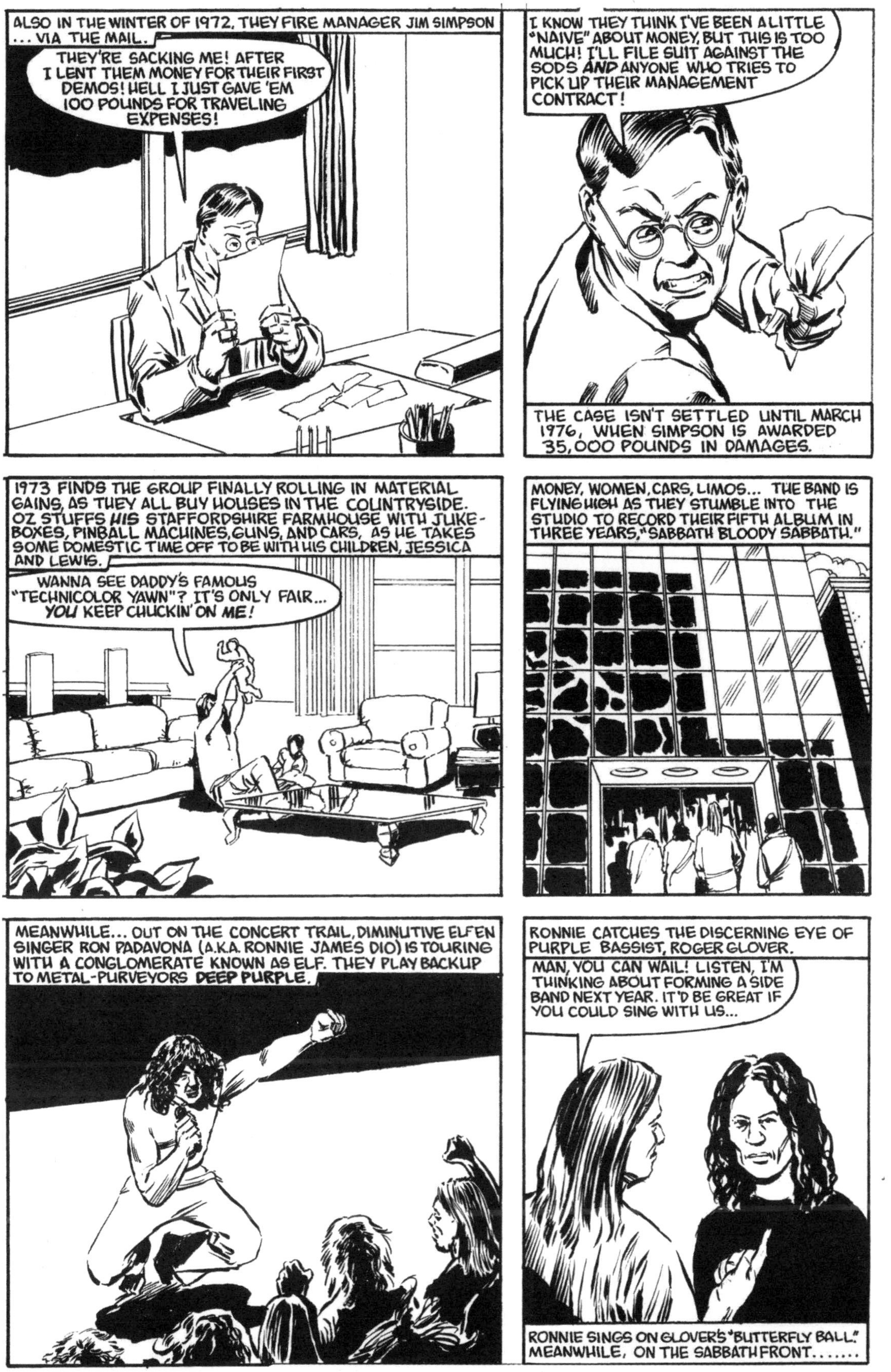
ALSO IN THE WINTER OF 1972, THEY FIRE MANAGER JIM SIMPSON ... VIA THE MAIL.
THEY'RE SACKING ME! AFTER I LENT THEM MONEY FOR THEIR FIRST DEMOS! HELL I JUST GAVE 'EM 100 POUNDS FOR TRAVELING EXPENSES!
I KNOW THEY THINK I'VE BEEN A LITTLE "NAIVE" ABOUT MONEY, BUT THIS IS TOO MUCH! I'LL FILE SUIT AGAINST THE SODS AND ANYONE WHO TRIES TO PICK UP THEIR MANAGEMENT CONTRACT!
THE CASE ISN'T SETTLED UNTIL MARCH 1976, WHEN SIMPSON IS AWARDED 35,000 POUNDS IN DAMAGES.
1973 FINDS THE GROUP FINALLY ROLLING IN MATERIAL GAINS, AS THEY ALL BUY HOUSES IN THE COUNTRYSIDE. OZ STUFFS HIS STAFFORDSHIRE FARMHOUSE WITH JUKE-BOXES, PINBALL MACHINES, GUNS, AND CARS, AS HE TAKES SOME DOMESTIC TIME OFF TO BE WITH HIS CHILDREN, JESSICA AND LEWIS.
WANNA SEE DADDY'S FAMOUS "TECHNICOLOR YAWN"? IT'S ONLY FAIR... YOU KEEP CHUCKIN' ON ME!
MONEY, WOMEN, CARS, LIMOS... THE BAND IS FLYING HIGH AS THEY STUMBLE INTO THE STUDIO TO RECORD THEIR FIFTH ALBUM IN THREE YEARS, "SABBATH BLOODY SABBATH."
MEANWHILE... OUT ON THE CONCERT TRAIL, DIMINUTIVE ELFEN SINGER RON PADAVONA (A.K.A. RONNIE JAMES DIO) IS TOURING WITH A CONGLOMERATE KNOWN AS ELF. THEY PLAY BACKUP TO METAL-PURVEYORS DEEP PURPLE.
RONNIE CATCHES THE DISCERNING EYE OF PURPLE BASSIST, ROGER GLOVER.
MAN, YOU CAN WAIL! LISTEN, I'M THINKING ABOUT FORMING A SIDE BAND NEXT YEAR. IT'D BE GREAT IF YOU COULD SING WITH US...
RONNIE SINGS ON GLOVER'S "BUTTERFLY BALL." MEANWHILE, ON THE SABBATH FRONT.......

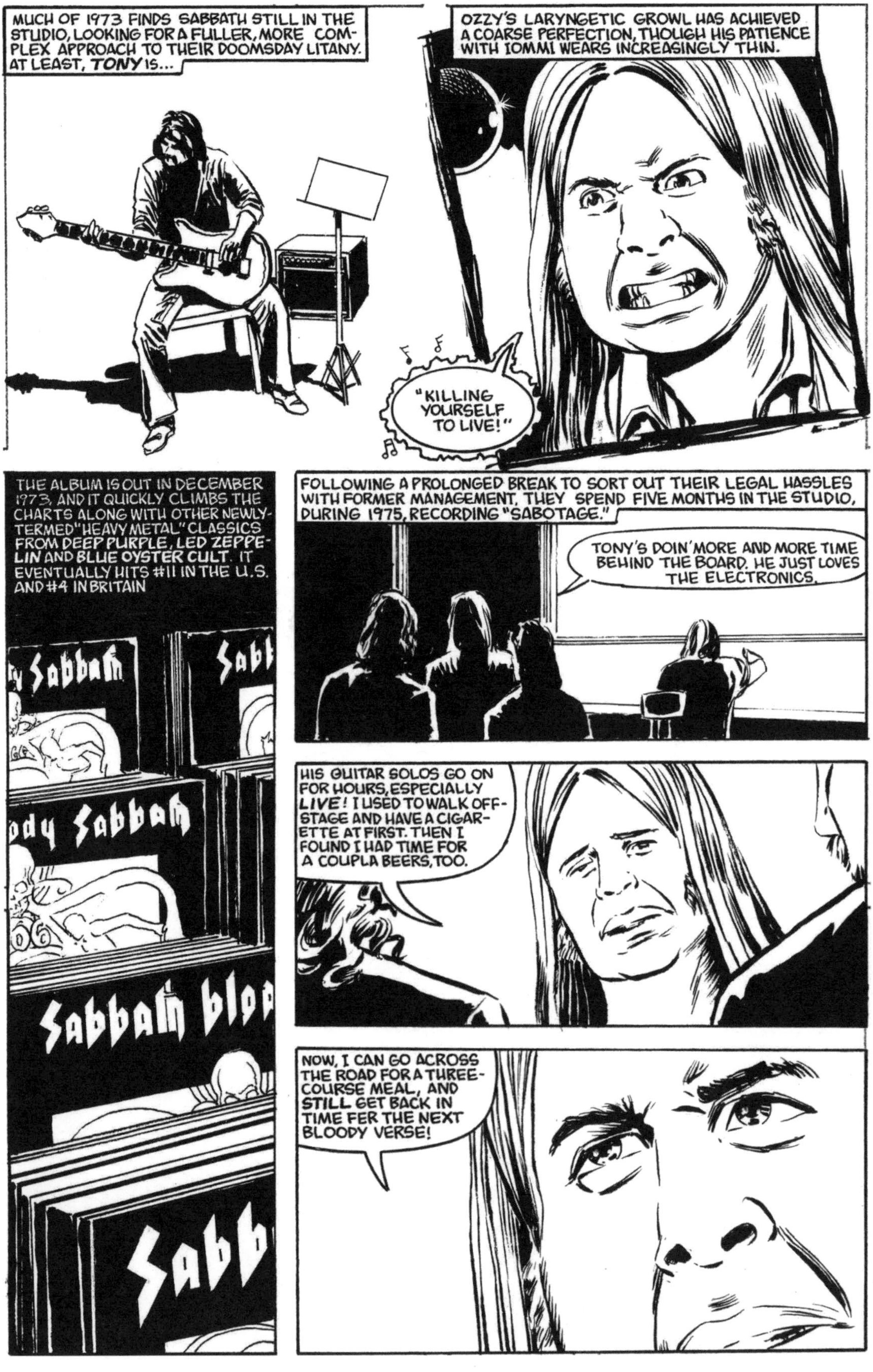
MUCH OF 1973 FINDS SABBATH STILL IN THE STUDIO, LOOKING FOR A FULLER, MORE COMPLEX APPROACH TO THEIR DOOMSDAY LITANY. AT LEAST, TONY IS...
OZZY'S LARYNGETIC GROWL HAS ACHIEVED A COARSE PERFECTION, THOUGH HIS PATIENCE WITH IOMMI WEARS INCREASINGLY THIN.
"KILLING YOURSELF TO LIVE!"
THE ALBUM IS OUT IN DECEMBER 1973, AND IT QUICKLY CLIMBS THE CHARTS ALONG WITH OTHER NEWLY-TERMED "HEAVY METAL" CLASSICS FROM DEEP PURPLE, LED ZEPPELIN AND BLUE OYSTER CULT. IT EVENTUALLY HITS #11 IN THE U.S. AND #4 IN BRITAIN
FOLLOWING A PROLONGED BREAK TO SORT OUT THEIR LEGAL HASSLES WITH FORMER MANAGEMENT, THEY SPEND FIVE MONTHS IN THE STUDIO, DURING 1975, RECORDING "SABOTAGE."
TONY'S DOIN' MORE AND MORE TIME BEHIND THE BOARD. HE JUST LOVES THE ELECTRONICS.
HIS GUITAR SOLOS GO ON FOR HOURS, ESPECIALLY LIVE! I USED TO WALK OFF-STAGE AND HAVE A CIGARETTE AT FIRST. THEN I FOUND I HAD TIME FOR A COUPLA BEERS, TOO.
NOW, I CAN GO ACROSS THE ROAD FOR A THREE-COURSE MEAL, AND STILL GET BACK IN TIME FER THE NEXT BLOODY VERSE!

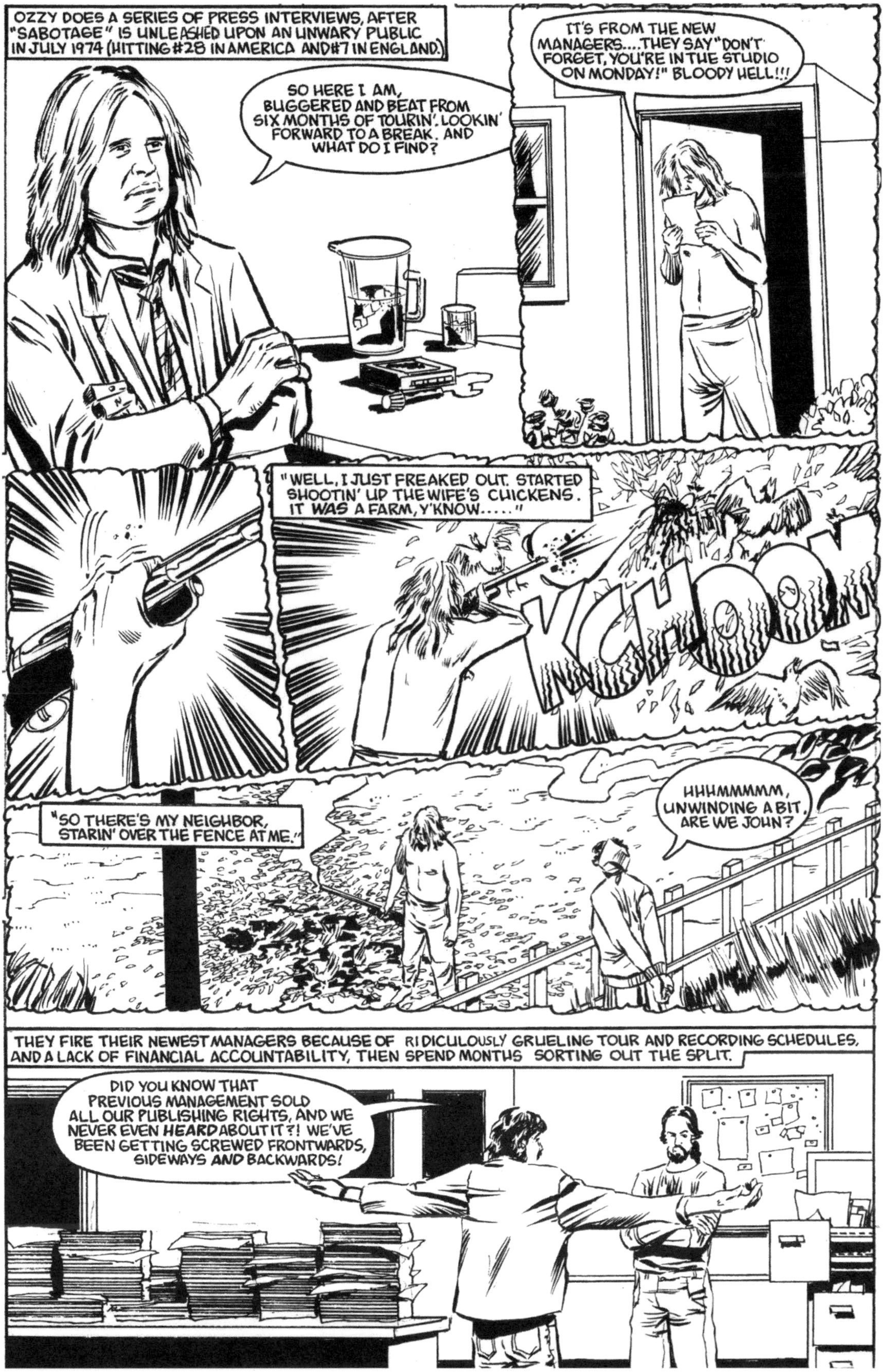

OZZY DOES A SERIES OF PRESS INTERVIEWS, AFTER "SABOTAGE" IS UNLEASHED UPON AN UNWARY PUBLIC IN JULY 1974 (HITTING #28 IN AMERICA AND #7 IN ENGLAND).
SO HERE I AM, BUGGERED AND BEAT FROM SIX MONTHS OF TOURIN'. LOOKIN' FORWARD TO A BREAK. AND WHAT DO I FIND?
IT'S FROM THE NEW MANAGERS....THEY SAY "DON'T FORGET, YOU'RE IN THE STUDIO ON MONDAY!" BLOODY HELL!!!
"WELL, I JUST FREAKED OUT. STARTED SHOOTIN' UP THE WIFE'S CHICKENS. IT WAS A FARM, Y'KNOW....."
KCHOOM
"SO THERE'S MY NEIGHBOR, STARIN' OVER THE FENCE AT ME."
HHHMMMMM, UNWINDING A BIT, ARE WE JOHN?
THEY FIRE THEIR NEWEST MANAGERS BECAUSE OF RIDICULOUSLY GRUELING TOUR AND RECORDING SCHEDULES, AND A LACK OF FINANCIAL ACCOUNTABILITY, THEN SPEND MONTHS SORTING OUT THE SPLIT.
DID YOU KNOW THAT PREVIOUS MANAGEMENT SOLD ALL OUR PUBLISHING RIGHTS, AND WE NEVER EVEN HEARD ABOUT IT?! WE'VE BEEN GETTING SCREWED FRONTWARDS, SIDEWAYS AND BACKWARDS!

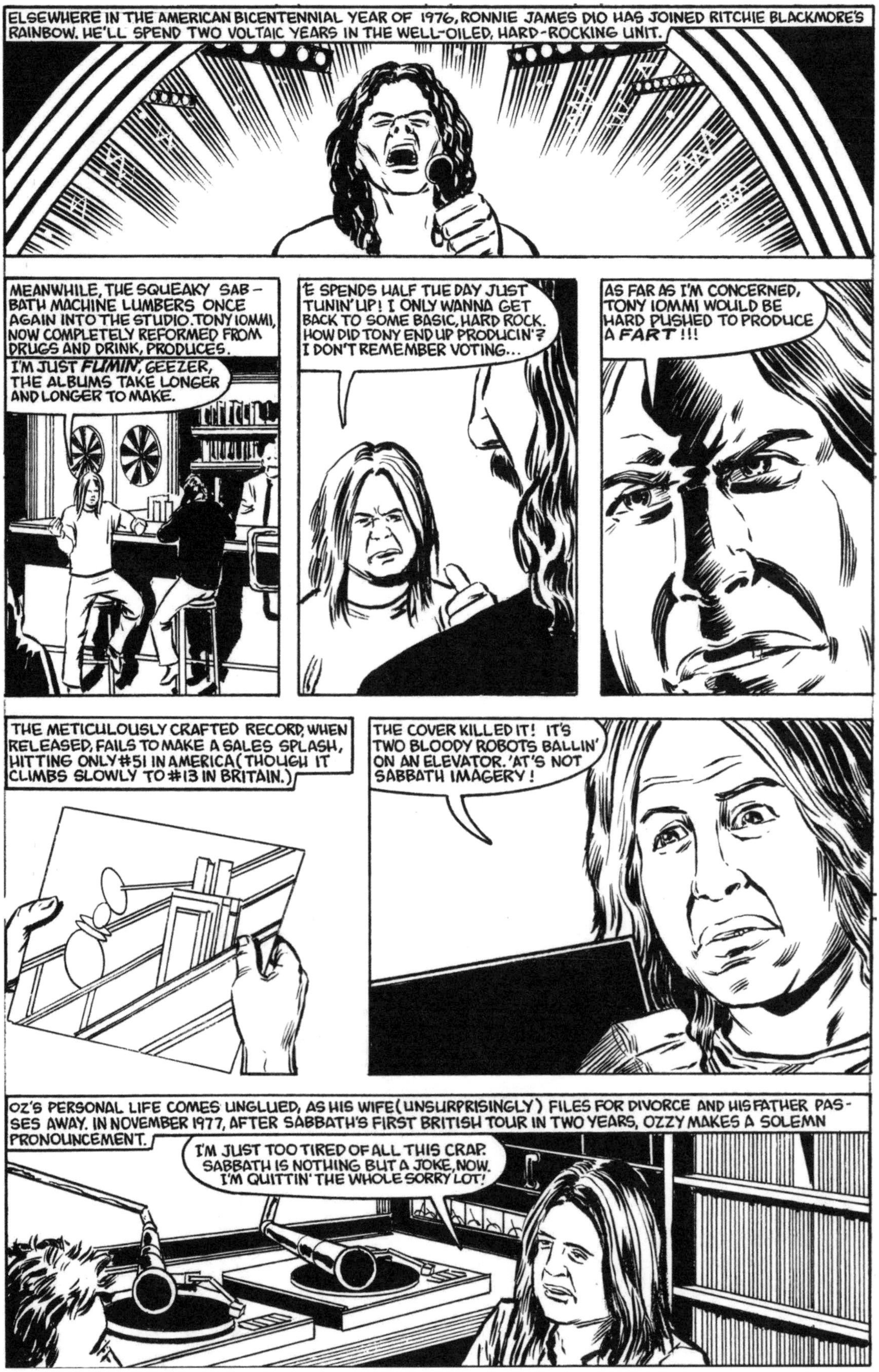
ELSEWHERE IN THE AMERICAN BICENTENNIAL YEAR OF 1976, RONNIE JAMES DIO HAS JOINED RITCHIE BLACKMORE'S RAINBOW. HE'LL SPEND TWO VOLTAIC YEARS IN THE WELL-OILED, HARD-ROCKING UNIT.
MEANWHILE, THE SQUEAKY SAB-BATH MACHINE LUMBERS ONCE AGAIN INTO THE STUDIO. TONY IOMMI, NOW COMPLETELY REFORMED FROM DRUGS AND DRINK, PRODUCES.
I'M JUST FUMIN', GEEZER, THE ALBUMS TAKE LONGER AND LONGER TO MAKE.
'E SPENDS HALF THE DAY JUST TUNIN' UP! I ONLY WANNA GET BACK TO SOME BASIC, HARD ROCK. HOW DID TONY END UP PRODUCIN'? I DON'T REMEMBER VOTING...
AS FAR AS I'M CONCERNED, TONY IOMMI WOULD BE HARD PUSHED TO PRODUCE A FART!!!
THE METICULOUSLY CRAFTED RECORD, WHEN RELEASED, FAILS TO MAKE A SALES SPLASH, HITTING ONLY #51 IN AMERICA (THOUGH IT CLIMBS SLOWLY TO #13 IN BRITAIN.)
THE COVER KILLED IT! IT'S TWO BLOODY ROBOTS BALLIN' ON AN ELEVATOR. 'AT'S NOT SABBATH IMAGERY!
OZ'S PERSONAL LIFE COMES UNGLUED, AS HIS WIFE (UNSURPRISINGLY) FILES FOR DIVORCE AND HIS FATHER PASSES AWAY. IN NOVEMBER 1977, AFTER SABBATH'S FIRST BRITISH TOUR IN TWO YEARS, OZZY MAKES A SOLEMN PRONOUNCEMENT.
I'M JUST TOO TIRED OF ALL THIS CRAP. SABBATH IS NOTHING BUT A JOKE, NOW. I'M QUITTIN' THE WHOLE SORRY LOT!

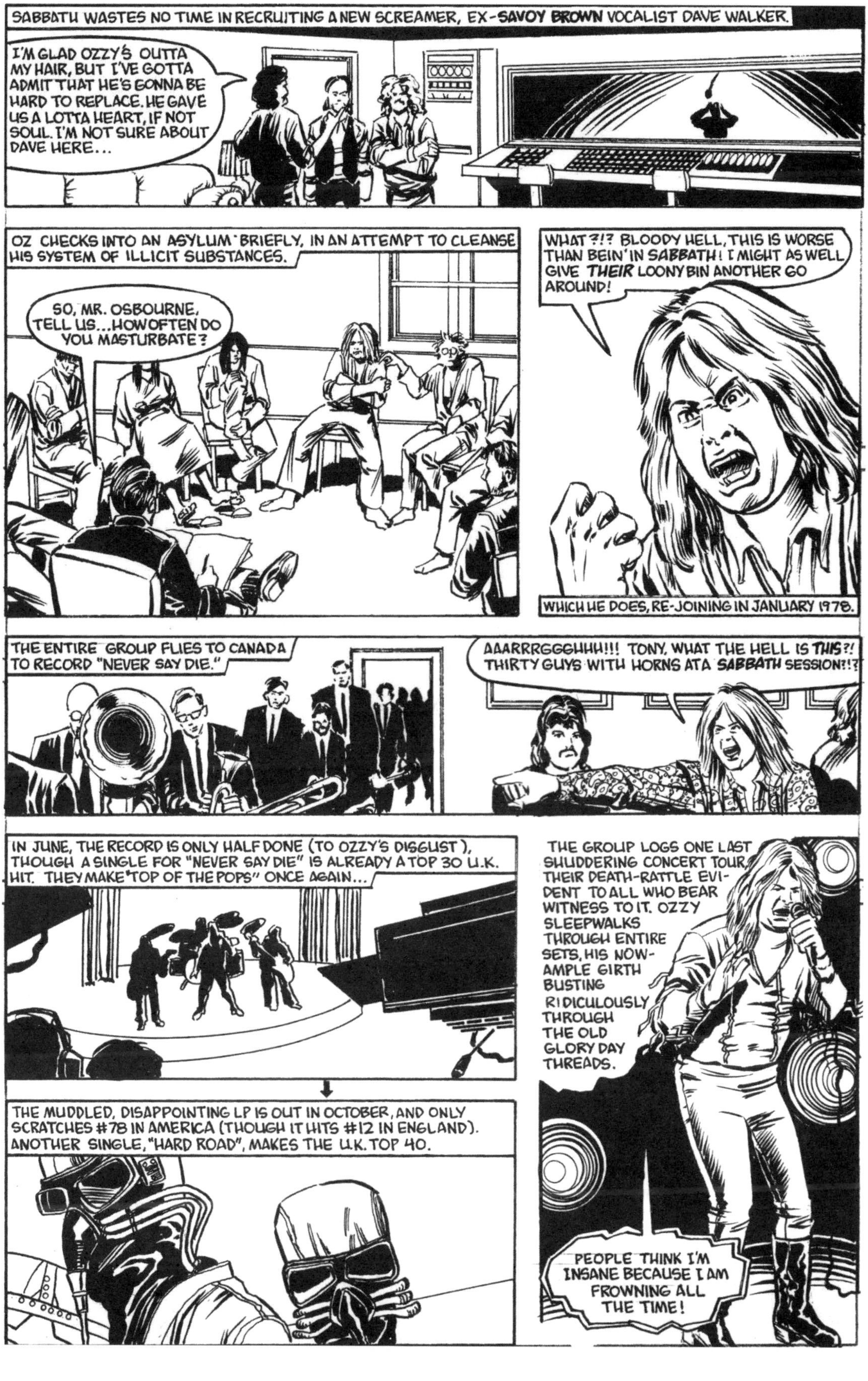
SABBATH WASTES NO TIME IN RECRUITING A NEW SCREAMER, EX-SAVOY BROWN VOCALIST DAVE WALKER.
I'M GLAD OZZY'S OUTTA MY HAIR, BUT I'VE GOTTA ADMIT THAT HE'S GONNA BE HARD TO REPLACE. HE GAVE US A LOTTA HEART, IF NOT SOUL. I'M NOT SURE ABOUT DAVE HERE...
OZ CHECKS INTO AN ASYLUM BRIEFLY, IN AN ATTEMPT TO CLEANSE HIS SYSTEM OF ILLICIT SUBSTANCES.
SO, MR. OSBOURNE, TELL US... HOW OFTEN DO YOU MASTURBATE?
WHAT?!? BLOODY HELL, THIS IS WORSE THAN BEIN' IN SABBATH! I MIGHT AS WELL GIVE THEIR LOONY BIN ANOTHER GO AROUND!
WHICH HE DOES, RE-JOINING IN JANUARY 1978.
THE ENTIRE GROUP FLIES TO CANADA TO RECORD "NEVER SAY DIE."
AAARRRGGGHHH!!! TONY, WHAT THE HELL IS THIS?! THIRTY GUYS WITH HORNS AT A SABBATH SESSION?!?
IN JUNE, THE RECORD IS ONLY HALF DONE (TO OZZY'S DISGUST), THOUGH A SINGLE FOR "NEVER SAY DIE" IS ALREADY A TOP 30 U.K. HIT. THEY MAKE "TOP OF THE POPS" ONCE AGAIN...
THE MUDDLED, DISAPPOINTING LP IS OUT IN OCTOBER, AND ONLY SCRATCHES #78 IN AMERICA (THOUGH IT HITS #12 IN ENGLAND). ANOTHER SINGLE, "HARD ROAD", MAKES THE U.K. TOP 40.
THE GROUP LOGS ONE LAST SHUDDERING CONCERT TOUR, THEIR DEATH-RATTLE EVIDENT TO ALL WHO BEAR WITNESS TO IT. OZZY SLEEPWALKS THROUGH ENTIRE SETS, HIS NOW-AMPLE GIRTH BUSTING RIDICULOUSLY THROUGH THE OLD GLORY DAY THREADS.
PEOPLE THINK I'M INSANE BECAUSE I AM FROWNING ALL THE TIME!

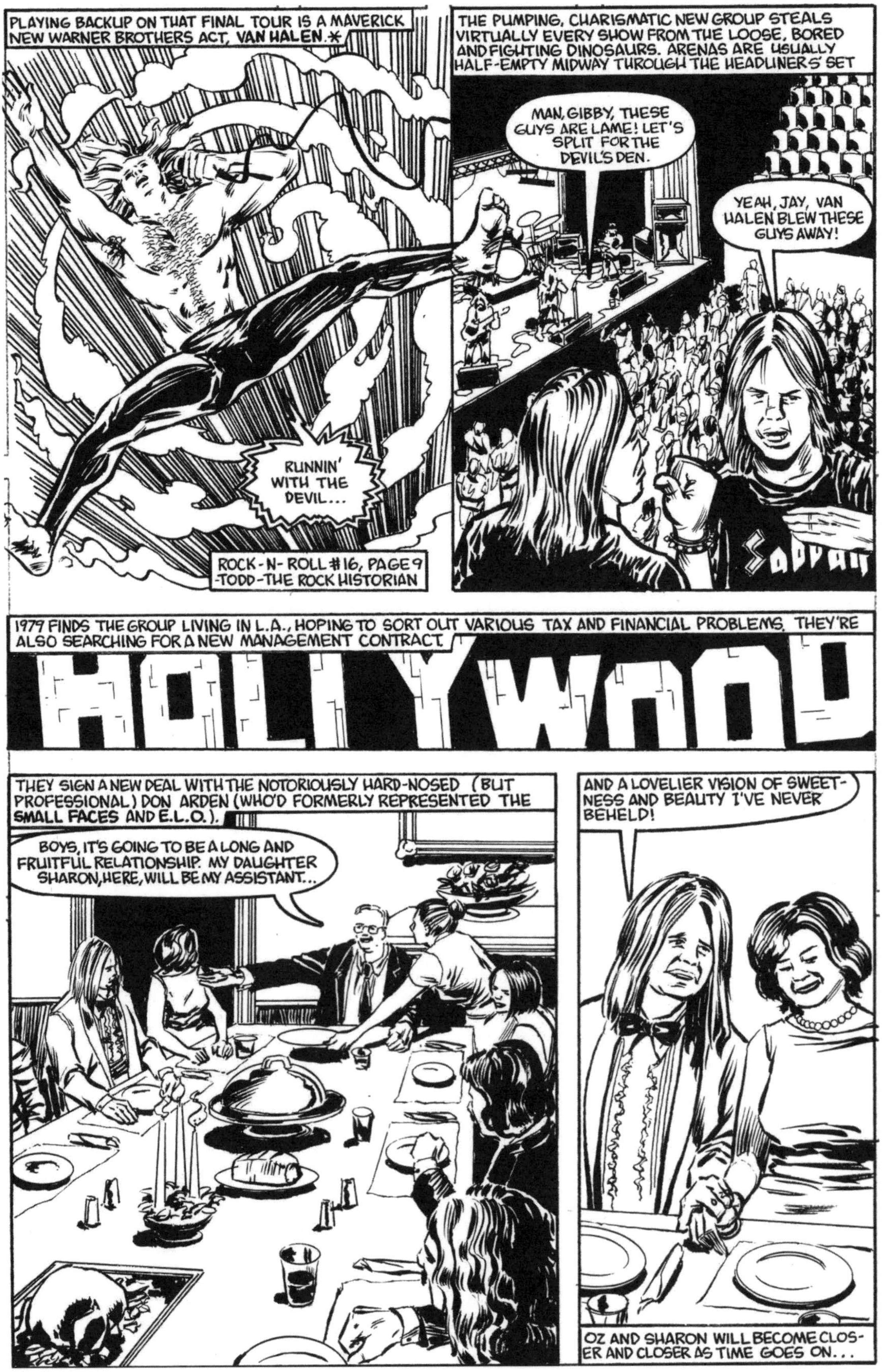
PLAYING BACKUP ON THAT FINAL TOUR IS A MAVERICK NEW WARNER BROTHERS ACT, VAN HALEN.*
RUNNIN' WITH THE DEVIL...
ROCK-N-ROLL #16, PAGE 9 -TODD-THE ROCK HISTORIAN
THE PUMPING, CHARISMATIC NEW GROUP STEALS VIRTUALLY EVERY SHOW FROM THE LOOSE, BORED AND FIGHTING DINOSAURS. ARENAS ARE USUALLY HALF-EMPTY MIDWAY THROUGH THE HEADLINERS' SET
MAN, GIBBY, THESE GUYS ARE LAME! LET'S SPLIT FOR THE DEVIL'S DEN.
YEAH, JAY, VAN HALEN BLEW THESE GUYS AWAY!
1979 FINDS THE GROUP LIVING IN L.A., HOPING TO SORT OUT VARIOUS TAX AND FINANCIAL PROBLEMS. THEY'RE ALSO SEARCHING FOR A NEW MANAGEMENT CONTRACT.
HOLLYWOOD
THEY SIGN A NEW DEAL WITH THE NOTORIOUSLY HARD-NOSED (BUT PROFESSIONAL) DON ARDEN (WHO'D FORMERLY REPRESENTED THE SMALL FACES AND E.L.O.).
BOYS, IT'S GOING TO BE A LONG AND FRUITFUL RELATIONSHIP. MY DAUGHTER SHARON, HERE, WILL BE MY ASSISTANT...
AND A LOVELIER VISION OF SWEETNESS AND BEAUTY I'VE NEVER BEHELD!
OZ AND SHARON WILL BECOME CLOSER AND CLOSER AS TIME GOES ON...

THEY CHOOSE A STUDIO IN L.A., THOUGH TONY EXPRESSES DOUBT AS TO WHETHER OZZY IS PREPARED FOR THE ORDEAL.

IT'S NOT GONNA BE ANOTHER SIX-MONTH LONG SWEAT FOUNDRY, IS IT TONY?

OZ, IF YOU'RE NOT READY TO RECORD, MAYBE YOU SHOULD JUST GO BACK TO ENGLAND AND REST UP. WE'LL LAY DOWN SOME TRACKS AND CALL YOU IN LATER.

AS OZ RETURNS TO THE FARM, TONY EYES A POSSIBLE NEW DI-RECTION.

THIS LITTLE GUY FROM RAINBOW, RONNIE JAMES DIO...HIS TIMBRE AND CONTROL ARE INCREDIBLE!

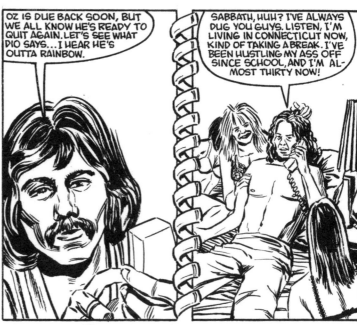

OZ IS DUE BACK SOON, BUT WE ALL KNOW HE'S READY TO QUIT AGAIN. LET'S SEE WHAT DIO SAYS...I HEAR HE'S OUTTA RAINBOW.

SABBATH, HUH? I'VE ALWAYS DUG YOU GUYS. LISTEN, I'M LIVING IN CONNECTICUT NOW, KIND OF TAKING A BREAK. I'VE BEEN HUSTLING MY ASS OFF SINCE SCHOOL, AND I'M AL-MOST THIRTY NOW!

I STUDIED CLASSICAL TRUMPET, AN' THEN PLAYED BASS. IN '72, ROGER GLOVER PRODUCED ELF AND LET US OPEN FOR PURPLE. THEN I JOINED HIS BAND.

WHEN RITCHIE QUIT TO FORM RAINBOW,＊ I WENT ALONG FOR THE RIDE, DID FIVE ALBUMS. I'M NOT SURE IF I'M READY TO COMMIT TO ANOTHER BAND ALREADY! I'LL THINK ABOUT IT..

＊ROCK-N-ROLL #10, —TODD

WELL, GET BACK TO US SOON. I'VE GOT TO KNOW WHAT TO TELL THE RECORD COMPANY BEFORE OZ ARRIVES!

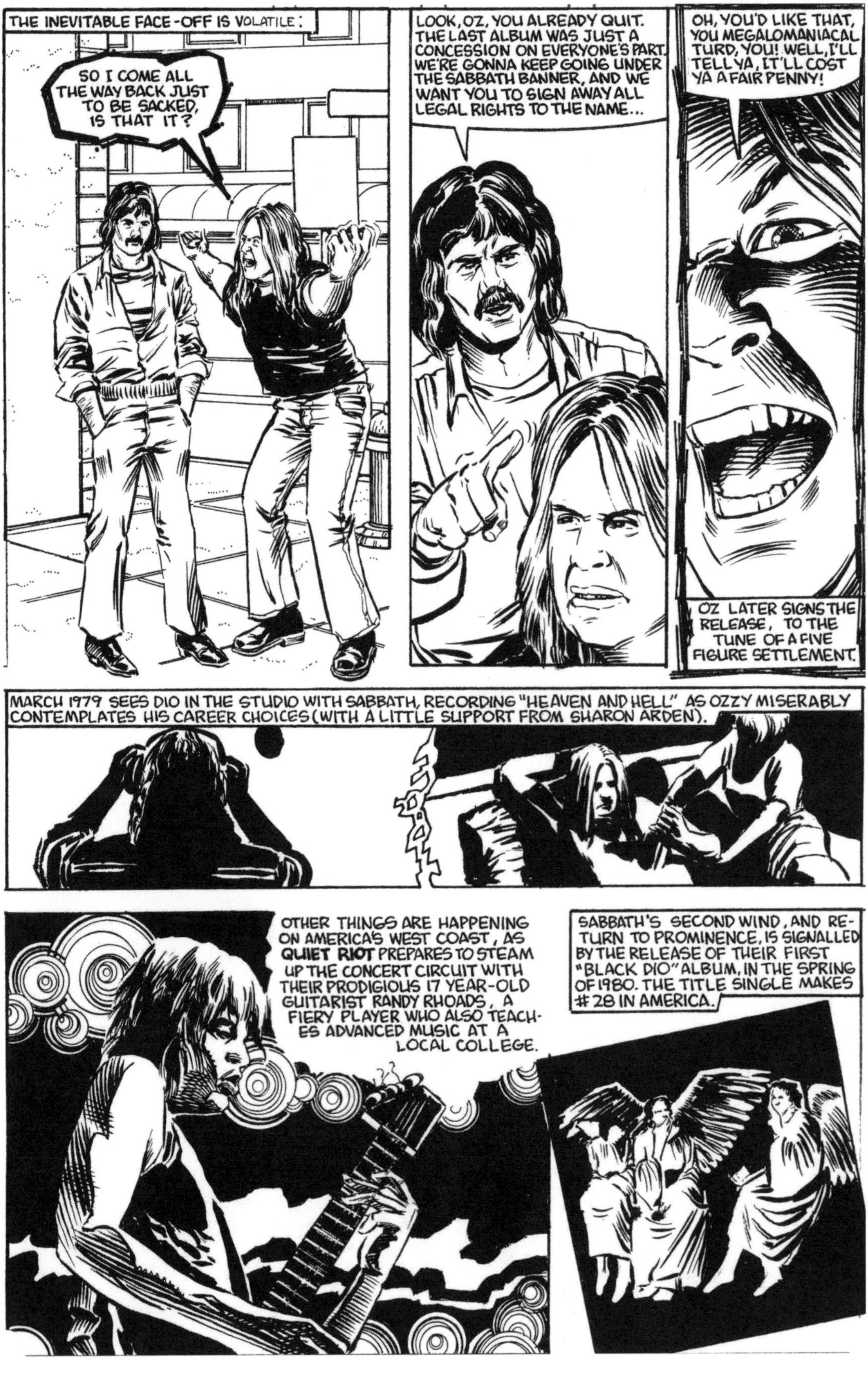

THE INEVITABLE FACE-OFF IS VOLATILE:
SO I COME ALL THE WAY BACK JUST TO BE SACKED, IS THAT IT?
LOOK, OZ, YOU ALREADY QUIT. THE LAST ALBUM WAS JUST A CONCESSION ON EVERYONE'S PART. WE'RE GONNA KEEP GOING UNDER THE SABBATH BANNER, AND WE WANT YOU TO SIGN AWAY ALL LEGAL RIGHTS TO THE NAME...
OH, YOU'D LIKE THAT, YOU MEGALOMANIACAL TURD, YOU! WELL, I'LL TELL YA, IT'LL COST YA A FAIR PENNY!
OZ LATER SIGNS THE RELEASE, TO THE TUNE OF A FIVE FIGURE SETTLEMENT.
MARCH 1979 SEES DIO IN THE STUDIO WITH SABBATH, RECORDING "HEAVEN AND HELL" AS OZZY MISERABLY CONTEMPLATES HIS CAREER CHOICES (WITH A LITTLE SUPPORT FROM SHARON ARDEN).
OTHER THINGS ARE HAPPENING ON AMERICA'S WEST COAST, AS QUIET RIOT PREPARES TO STEAM UP THE CONCERT CIRCUIT WITH THEIR PRODIGIOUS 17 YEAR-OLD GUITARIST RANDY RHOADS, A FIERY PLAYER WHO ALSO TEACHES ADVANCED MUSIC AT A LOCAL COLLEGE.
SABBATH'S SECOND WIND, AND RETURN TO PROMINENCE, IS SIGNALLED BY THE RELEASE OF THEIR FIRST "BLACK DIO" ALBUM, IN THE SPRING OF 1980. THE TITLE SINGLE MAKES #28 IN AMERICA.

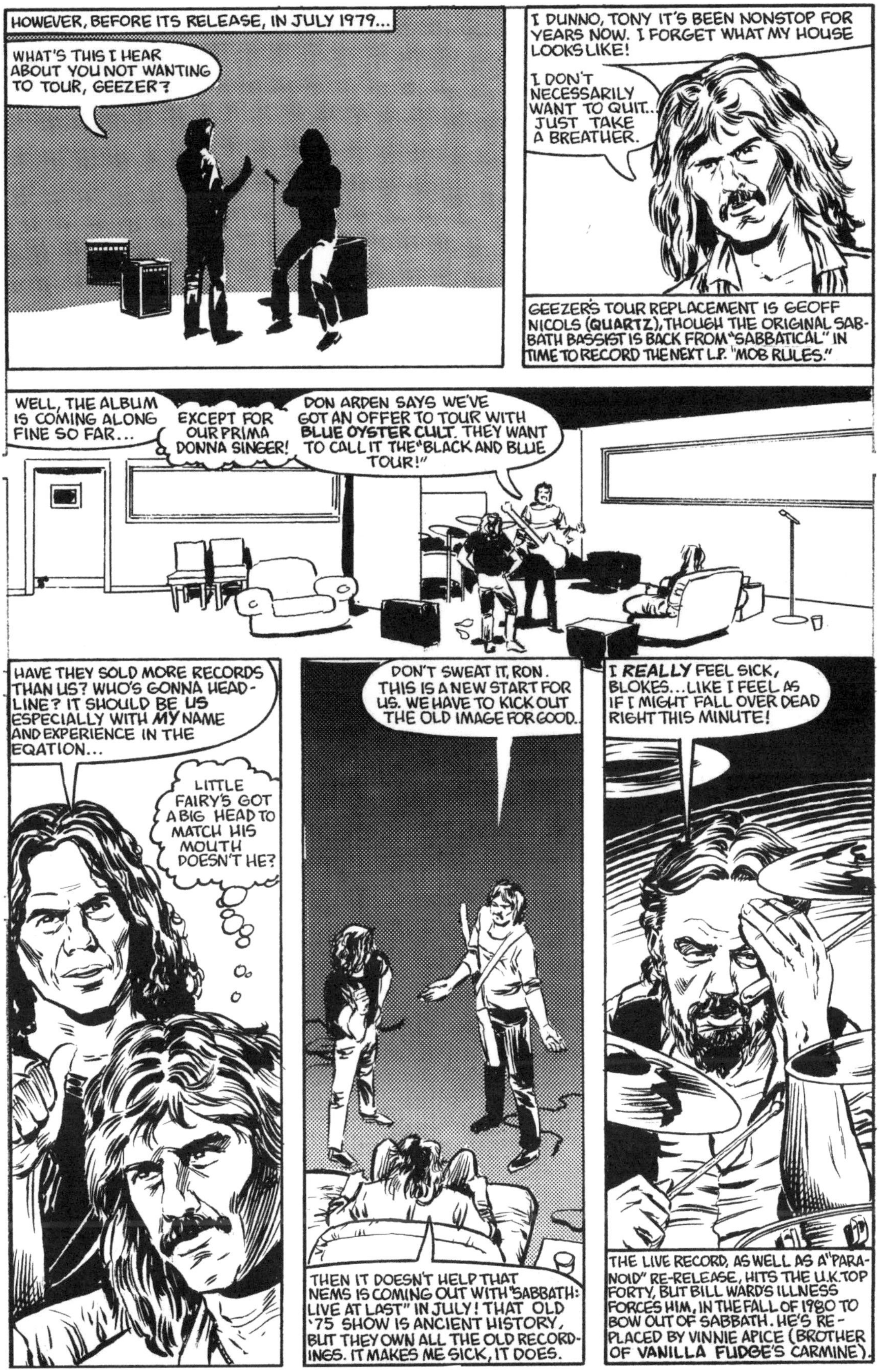

HOWEVER, BEFORE ITS RELEASE, IN JULY 1979...
WHAT'S THIS I HEAR ABOUT YOU NOT WANTING TO TOUR, GEEZER?
I DUNNO, TONY IT'S BEEN NONSTOP FOR YEARS NOW. I FORGET WHAT MY HOUSE LOOKS LIKE!
I DON'T NECESSARILY WANT TO QUIT... JUST TAKE A BREATHER.
GEEZER'S TOUR REPLACEMENT IS GEOFF NICOLS (QUARTZ), THOUGH THE ORIGINAL SABBATH BASSIST IS BACK FROM "SABBATICAL" IN TIME TO RECORD THE NEXT L.P. "MOB RULES."
WELL, THE ALBUM IS COMING ALONG FINE SO FAR...
EXCEPT FOR OUR PRIMA DONNA SINGER!
DON ARDEN SAYS WE'VE GOT AN OFFER TO TOUR WITH BLUE OYSTER CULT. THEY WANT TO CALL IT THE "BLACK AND BLUE TOUR!"
HAVE THEY SOLD MORE RECORDS THAN US? WHO'S GONNA HEADLINE? IT SHOULD BE US ESPECIALLY WITH MY NAME AND EXPERIENCE IN THE EQATION...
LITTLE FAIRY'S GOT A BIG HEAD TO MATCH HIS MOUTH DOESN'T HE?
DON'T SWEAT IT, RON. THIS IS A NEW START FOR US. WE HAVE TO KICK OUT THE OLD IMAGE FOR GOOD.
THEN IT DOESN'T HELP THAT NEMS IS COMING OUT WITH "SABBATH: LIVE AT LAST" IN JULY! THAT OLD '75 SHOW IS ANCIENT HISTORY, BUT THEY OWN ALL THE OLD RECORDINGS. IT MAKES ME SICK, IT DOES.
I REALLY FEEL SICK, BLOKES... LIKE I FEEL AS IF I MIGHT FALL OVER DEAD RIGHT THIS MINUTE!
THE LIVE RECORD, AS WELL AS A "PARANOID" RE-RELEASE, HITS THE U.K. TOP FORTY, BUT BILL WARD'S ILLNESS FORCES HIM, IN THE FALL OF 1980 TO BOW OUT OF SABBATH. HE'S REPLACED BY VINNIE APICE (BROTHER OF VANILLA FUDGE'S CARMINE).

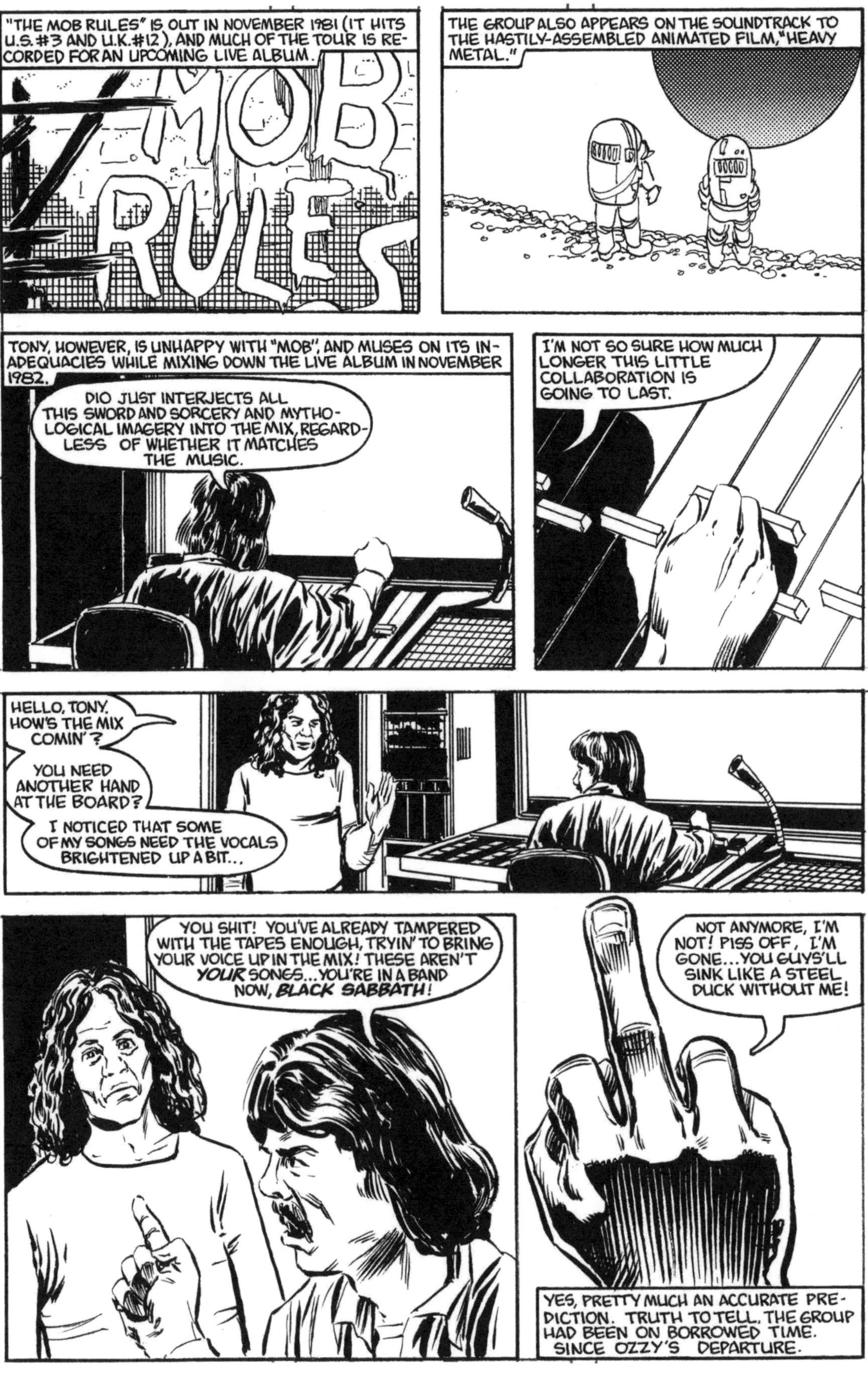
"THE MOB RULES" IS OUT IN NOVEMBER 1981 (IT HITS U.S. #3 AND U.K. #12), AND MUCH OF THE TOUR IS RECORDED FOR AN UPCOMING LIVE ALBUM.
MOB RULES
THE GROUP ALSO APPEARS ON THE SOUNDTRACK TO THE HASTILY-ASSEMBLED ANIMATED FILM, "HEAVY METAL."
TONY, HOWEVER, IS UNHAPPY WITH "MOB", AND MUSES ON ITS INADEQUACIES WHILE MIXING DOWN THE LIVE ALBUM IN NOVEMBER 1982.
DIO JUST INTERJECTS ALL THIS SWORD AND SORCERY AND MYTHOLOGICAL IMAGERY INTO THE MIX, REGARDLESS OF WHETHER IT MATCHES THE MUSIC.
I'M NOT SO SURE HOW MUCH LONGER THIS LITTLE COLLABORATION IS GOING TO LAST.
HELLO, TONY. HOW'S THE MIX COMIN'?
YOU NEED ANOTHER HAND AT THE BOARD?
I NOTICED THAT SOME OF MY SONGS NEED THE VOCALS BRIGHTENED UP A BIT...
YOU SHIT! YOU'VE ALREADY TAMPERED WITH THE TAPES ENOUGH, TRYIN' TO BRING YOUR VOICE UP IN THE MIX! THESE AREN'T *YOUR* SONGS... YOU'RE IN A BAND NOW, *BLACK SABBATH*!
NOT ANYMORE, I'M NOT! PISS OFF, I'M GONE... YOU GUYS'LL SINK LIKE A STEEL DUCK WITHOUT ME!
YES, PRETTY MUCH AN ACCURATE PREDICTION. TRUTH TO TELL, THE GROUP HAD BEEN ON BORROWED TIME SINCE OZZY'S DEPARTURE.

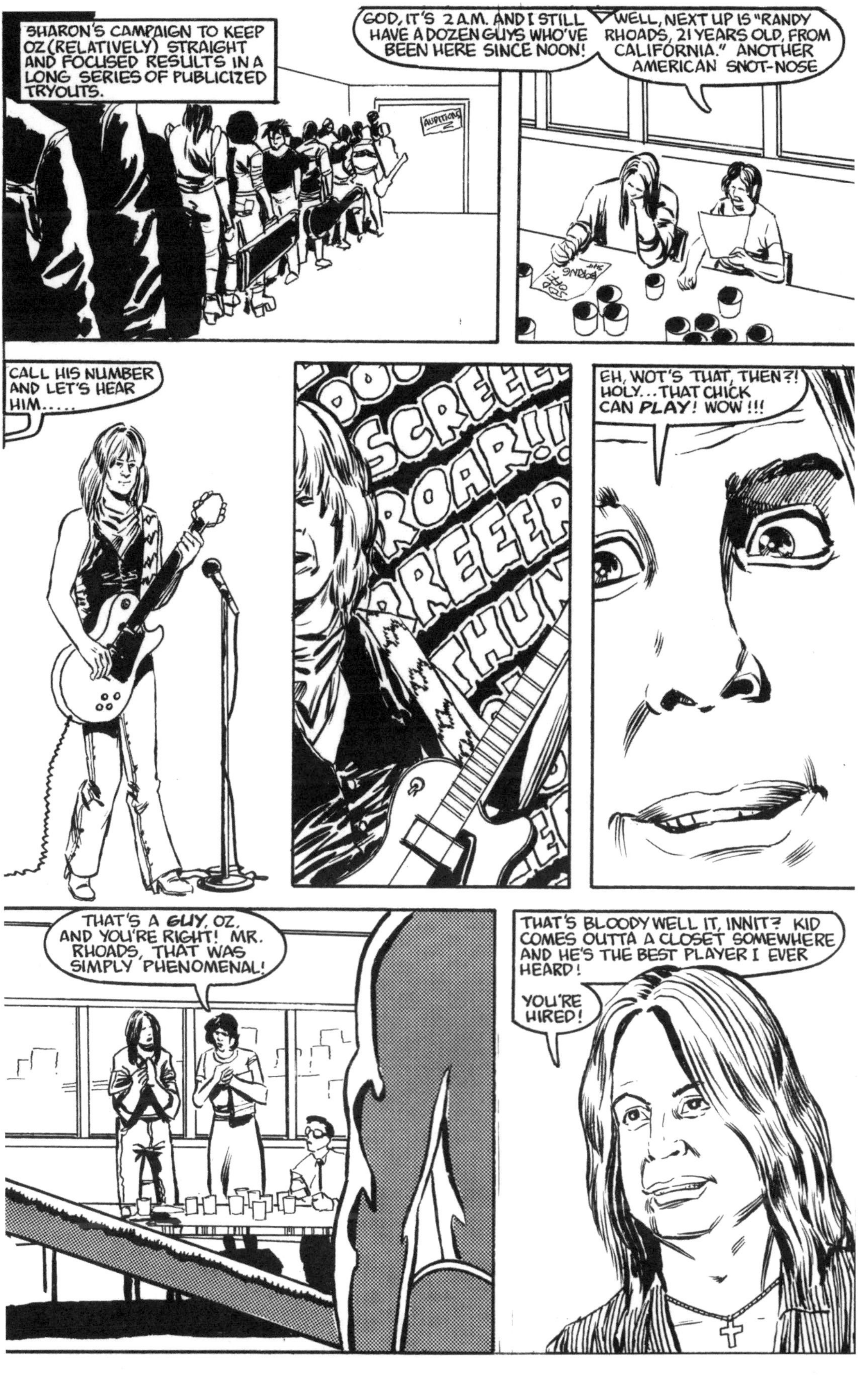
SHARON'S CAMPAIGN TO KEEP OZ (RELATIVELY) STRAIGHT AND FOCUSED RESULTS IN A LONG SERIES OF PUBLICIZED TRYOUTS.
AUDITIONS
GOD, IT'S 2 A.M. AND I STILL HAVE A DOZEN GUYS WHO'VE BEEN HERE SINCE NOON!
WELL, NEXT UP IS "RANDY RHOADS, 21 YEARS OLD, FROM CALIFORNIA." ANOTHER AMERICAN SNOT-NOSE
CALL HIS NUMBER AND LET'S HEAR HIM.....
SCREEE
ROAR!!
REEER
THUN
EH, WOT'S THAT, THEN?! HOLY...THAT CHICK CAN PLAY! WOW!!!
THAT'S A GUY, OZ, AND YOU'RE RIGHT! MR. RHOADS, THAT WAS SIMPLY PHENOMENAL!
THAT'S BLOODY WELL IT, INNIT? KID COMES OUTTA A CLOSET SOMEWHERE AND HE'S THE BEST PLAYER I EVER HEARD!
YOU'RE HIRED!

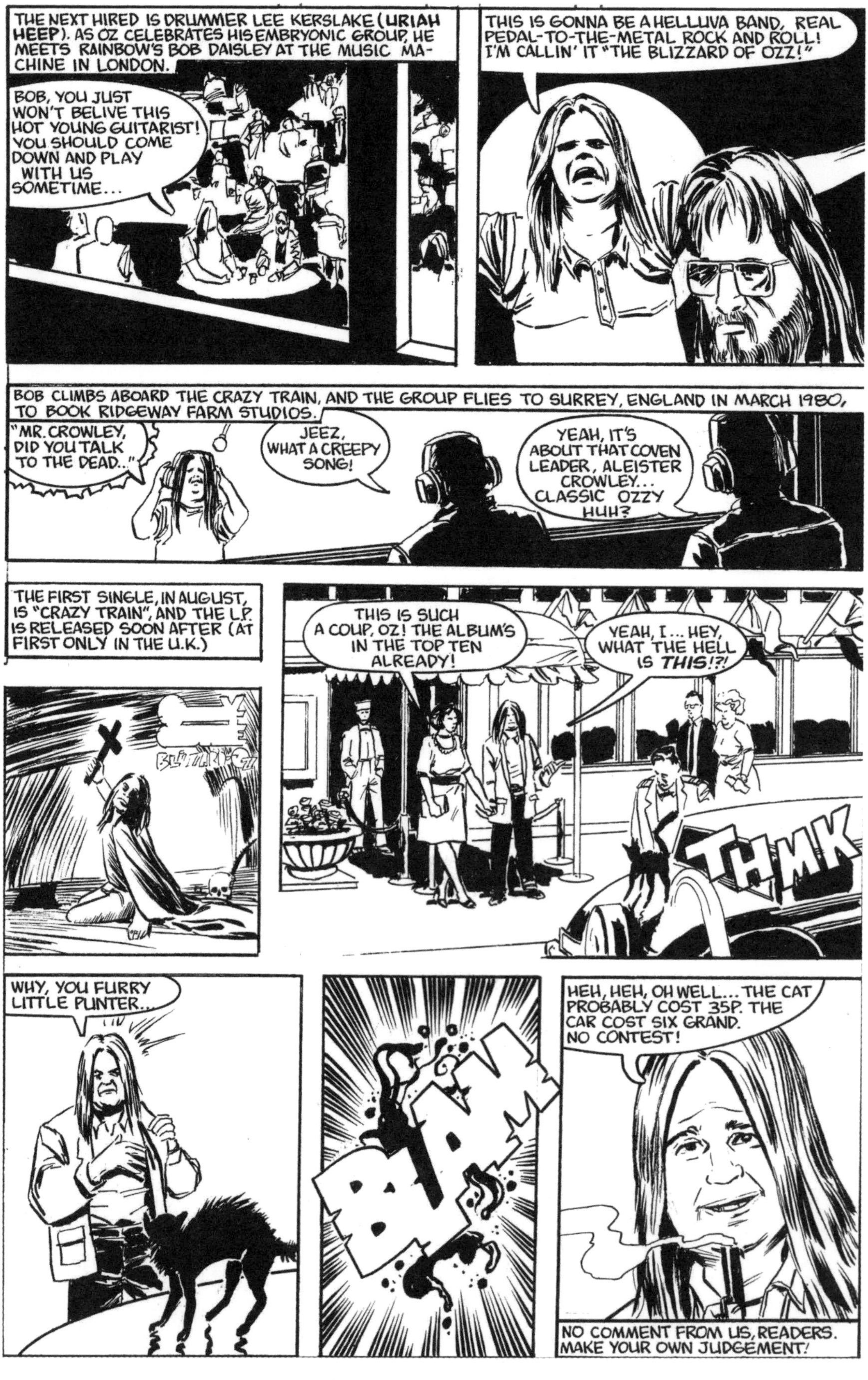
THE NEXT HIRED IS DRUMMER LEE KERSLAKE (URIAH HEEP). AS OZ CELEBRATES HIS EMBRYONIC GROUP, HE MEETS RAINBOW'S BOB DAISLEY AT THE MUSIC MACHINE IN LONDON.
BOB, YOU JUST WON'T BELIVE THIS HOT YOUNG GUITARIST! YOU SHOULD COME DOWN AND PLAY WITH US SOMETIME...
THIS IS GONNA BE A HELLUVA BAND, REAL PEDAL-TO-THE-METAL ROCK AND ROLL! I'M CALLIN' IT "THE BLIZZARD OF OZZ!"
BOB CLIMBS ABOARD THE CRAZY TRAIN, AND THE GROUP FLIES TO SURREY, ENGLAND IN MARCH 1980, TO BOOK RIDGEWAY FARM STUDIOS.
"MR. CROWLEY, DID YOU TALK TO THE DEAD..."
JEEZ, WHAT A CREEPY SONG!
YEAH, IT'S ABOUT THAT COVEN LEADER, ALEISTER CROWLEY... CLASSIC OZZY HUH?
THE FIRST SINGLE, IN AUGUST, IS "CRAZY TRAIN", AND THE L.P. IS RELEASED SOON AFTER (AT FIRST ONLY IN THE U.K.)
THIS IS SUCH A COUP, OZ! THE ALBUM'S IN THE TOP TEN ALREADY!
YEAH, I... HEY, WHAT THE HELL IS *THIS*!?!
THMK
WHY, YOU FURRY LITTLE PUNTER...
BLAM
HEH, HEH, OH WELL... THE CAT PROBABLY COST 35P. THE CAR COST SIX GRAND. NO CONTEST!
NO COMMENT FROM US, READERS. MAKE YOUR OWN JUDGEMENT!

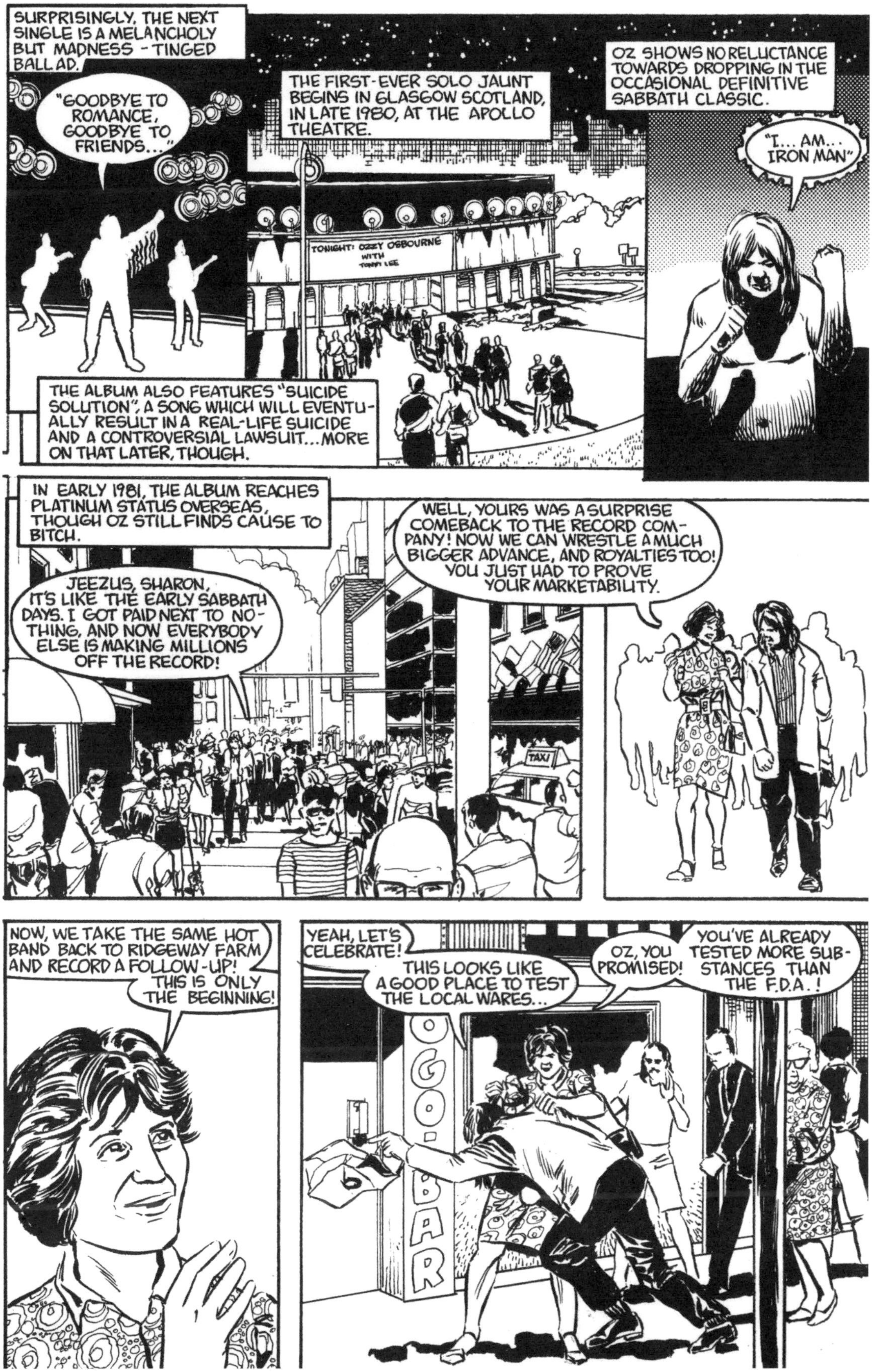

SURPRISINGLY, THE NEXT SINGLE IS A MELANCHOLY BUT MADNESS - TINGED BALLAD.
"GOODBYE TO ROMANCE, GOODBYE TO FRIENDS..."
THE FIRST-EVER SOLO JAUNT BEGINS IN GLASGOW SCOTLAND, IN LATE 1980, AT THE APOLLO THEATRE.
TONIGHT: OZZY OSBOURNE WITH TOMMY LEE
THE ALBUM ALSO FEATURES "SUICIDE SOLUTION", A SONG WHICH WILL EVENTUALLY RESULT IN A REAL-LIFE SUICIDE AND A CONTROVERSIAL LAWSUIT... MORE ON THAT LATER, THOUGH.
OZ SHOWS NO RELUCTANCE TOWARDS DROPPING IN THE OCCASIONAL DEFINITIVE SABBATH CLASSIC.
"I... AM... IRON MAN"
IN EARLY 1981, THE ALBUM REACHES PLATINUM STATUS OVERSEAS, THOUGH OZ STILL FINDS CAUSE TO BITCH.
JEEZUS, SHARON, IT'S LIKE THE EARLY SABBATH DAYS. I GOT PAID NEXT TO NOTHING, AND NOW EVERYBODY ELSE IS MAKING MILLIONS OFF THE RECORD!
WELL, YOURS WAS A SURPRISE COMEBACK TO THE RECORD COMPANY! NOW WE CAN WRESTLE A MUCH BIGGER ADVANCE, AND ROYALTIES TOO! YOU JUST HAD TO PROVE YOUR MARKETABILITY.
TAXI
NOW, WE TAKE THE SAME HOT BAND BACK TO RIDGEWAY FARM AND RECORD A FOLLOW-UP!
THIS IS ONLY THE BEGINNING!
YEAH, LET'S CELEBRATE!
THIS LOOKS LIKE A GOOD PLACE TO TEST THE LOCAL WARES...
OZ, YOU PROMISED!
YOU'VE ALREADY TESTED MORE SUBSTANCES THAN THE F.D.A.!
GO-GO BAR

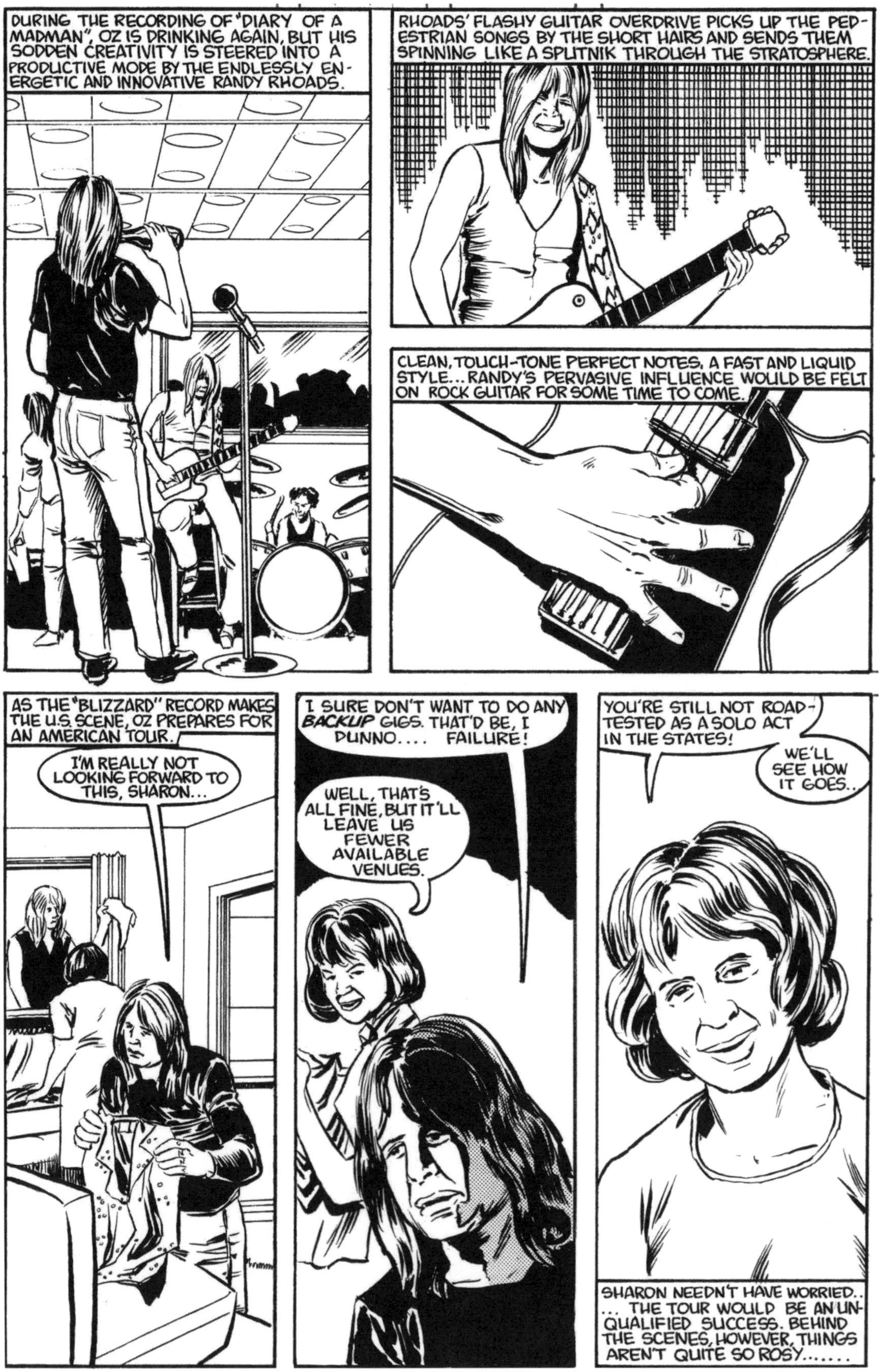
DURING THE RECORDING OF "DIARY OF A MADMAN", OZ IS DRINKING AGAIN, BUT HIS SODDEN CREATIVITY IS STEERED INTO A PRODUCTIVE MODE BY THE ENDLESSLY ENERGETIC AND INNOVATIVE RANDY RHOADS.
RHOADS' FLASHY GUITAR OVERDRIVE PICKS UP THE PEDESTRIAN SONGS BY THE SHORT HAIRS AND SENDS THEM SPINNING LIKE A SPUTNIK THROUGH THE STRATOSPHERE.
CLEAN, TOUCH-TONE PERFECT NOTES, A FAST AND LIQUID STYLE... RANDY'S PERVASIVE INFLUENCE WOULD BE FELT ON ROCK GUITAR FOR SOME TIME TO COME.
AS THE "BLIZZARD" RECORD MAKES THE U.S. SCENE, OZ PREPARES FOR AN AMERICAN TOUR.
I'M REALLY NOT LOOKING FORWARD TO THIS, SHARON...
I SURE DON'T WANT TO DO ANY BACKUP GIGS. THAT'D BE, I DUNNO.... FAILURE!
WELL, THAT'S ALL FINE, BUT IT'LL LEAVE US FEWER AVAILABLE VENUES.
YOU'RE STILL NOT ROAD-TESTED AS A SOLO ACT IN THE STATES!
WE'LL SEE HOW IT GOES..
SHARON NEEDN'T HAVE WORRIED.. ... THE TOUR WOULD BE AN UNQUALIFIED SUCCESS. BEHIND THE SCENES, HOWEVER, THINGS AREN'T QUITE SO ROSY.......

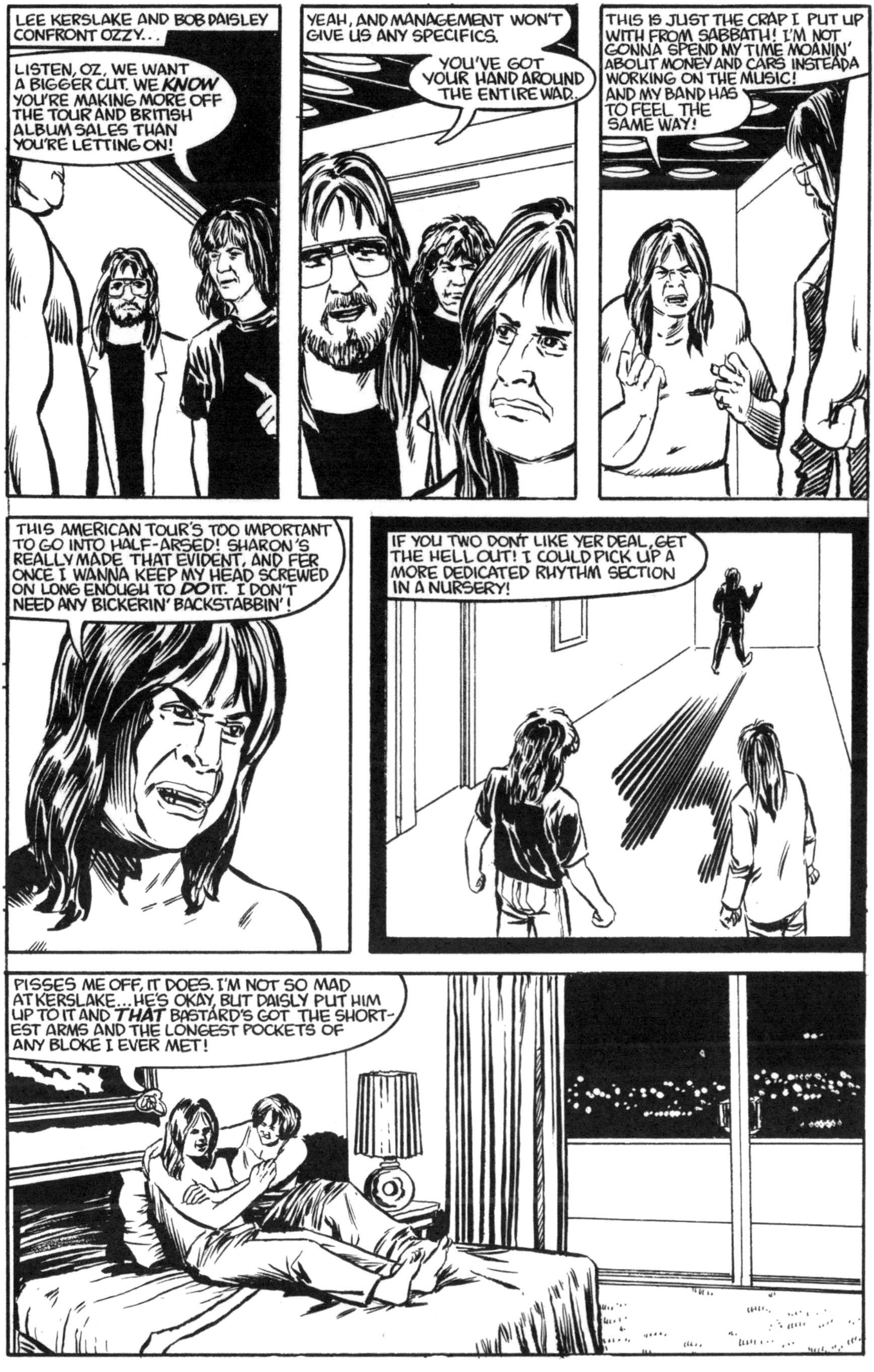
LEE KERSLAKE AND BOB DAISLEY CONFRONT OZZY...
LISTEN, OZ, WE WANT A BIGGER CUT. WE KNOW YOU'RE MAKING MORE OFF THE TOUR AND BRITISH ALBUM SALES THAN YOU'RE LETTING ON!
YEAH, AND MANAGEMENT WON'T GIVE US ANY SPECIFICS.
YOU'VE GOT YOUR HAND AROUND THE ENTIRE WAD.
THIS IS JUST THE CRAP I PUT UP WITH FROM SABBATH! I'M NOT GONNA SPEND MY TIME MOANIN' ABOUT MONEY AND CARS INSTEADA WORKING ON THE MUSIC! AND MY BAND HAS TO FEEL THE SAME WAY!
THIS AMERICAN TOUR'S TOO IMPORTANT TO GO INTO HALF-ARSED! SHARON'S REALLY MADE THAT EVIDENT, AND FER ONCE I WANNA KEEP MY HEAD SCREWED ON LONG ENOUGH TO DO IT. I DON'T NEED ANY BICKERIN' BACKSTABBIN'!
IF YOU TWO DON'T LIKE YER DEAL, GET THE HELL OUT! I COULD PICK UP A MORE DEDICATED RHYTHM SECTION IN A NURSERY!
PISSES ME OFF, IT DOES. I'M NOT SO MAD AT KERSLAKE... HE'S OKAY, BUT DAISLY PUT HIM UP TO IT AND THAT BASTARD'S GOT THE SHORTEST ARMS AND THE LONGEST POCKETS OF ANY BLOKE I EVER MET!

BEFORE THE U.S. TOUR STARTS, AN ELEVENTH HOUR ALTERATION, IN MAY 1981, FINDS DRUMMER TOMMY ALDRIDGE (BLACK OAK ARKANSSAS), A HALF-INDIAN FROM FLORIDA, ALONG FOR THE RIDE. RANDY ALSO BRINGS IN HIS OLD QUIET RIOT BASSIST, FLORIDIAN RUDY SARZO.

THE NEW UNIT REHEARSES IN L.A., AND THE SOUND IS SUITABLY TIGHT.

WE'RE AS READY AS WE'RE GONNA GET, BUT I'M STILL WORRIED ABOUT THE POSSIBILITY OF PLAYING HALF-EMPTY HOUSES.

WELL, WE'VE GOT A LOT OF ADVANCE PUBLICITY OUT, AND TICKET SALES ARE GREAT SO FAR. PLUS, I DON'T KNOW IF OZ TOLD YOU, BUT I THREW OUT ALL HIS TIRED OLD "SABBATH" CLOTHES AND DESIGNED HIM A FLASHY, NEW WARDROBE!

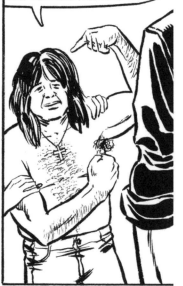

YEAH, I'M LIKE THE SIX MILLION DOLLAR MAN NOW. SHE REBUILT ME... SHE'S EVEN TALKIN' ME INTO DYING MY HAIR LIGHTER AND GETTING A SHAG CUT!

HOWEVER, OMINOUS EVENTS LOOM ON THE HORIZON. OZ GETS INVITED TO A CBS RECORDS CONVENTION, TO HOB-NOB WITH THE EXECUTIVES, AGENTS AND PROMOTERS WHO ARE SUPPOSED TO BE FORCEFEEDING HIM TO THE AMERICAN PUBLIC.

SHARON, I'VE GOT A GREAT IDEA!

A STUNT THAT'LL GET THESE BOOKIE JOCKSTRAPS TO REMEMBER MY NAME FER A CHANGE!

FIRST I NEED TO BUY SOME DOVES...

IT WOULD BE A PARTY THAT NOBODY WOULD EVER FORGET, TO BE SURE!

TO BE CONTINUED NEXT PART TWO:

OZZY OSBOURNE AND BLACK SABBATH II ALL ABOARD THE CRAZY TRAIN!

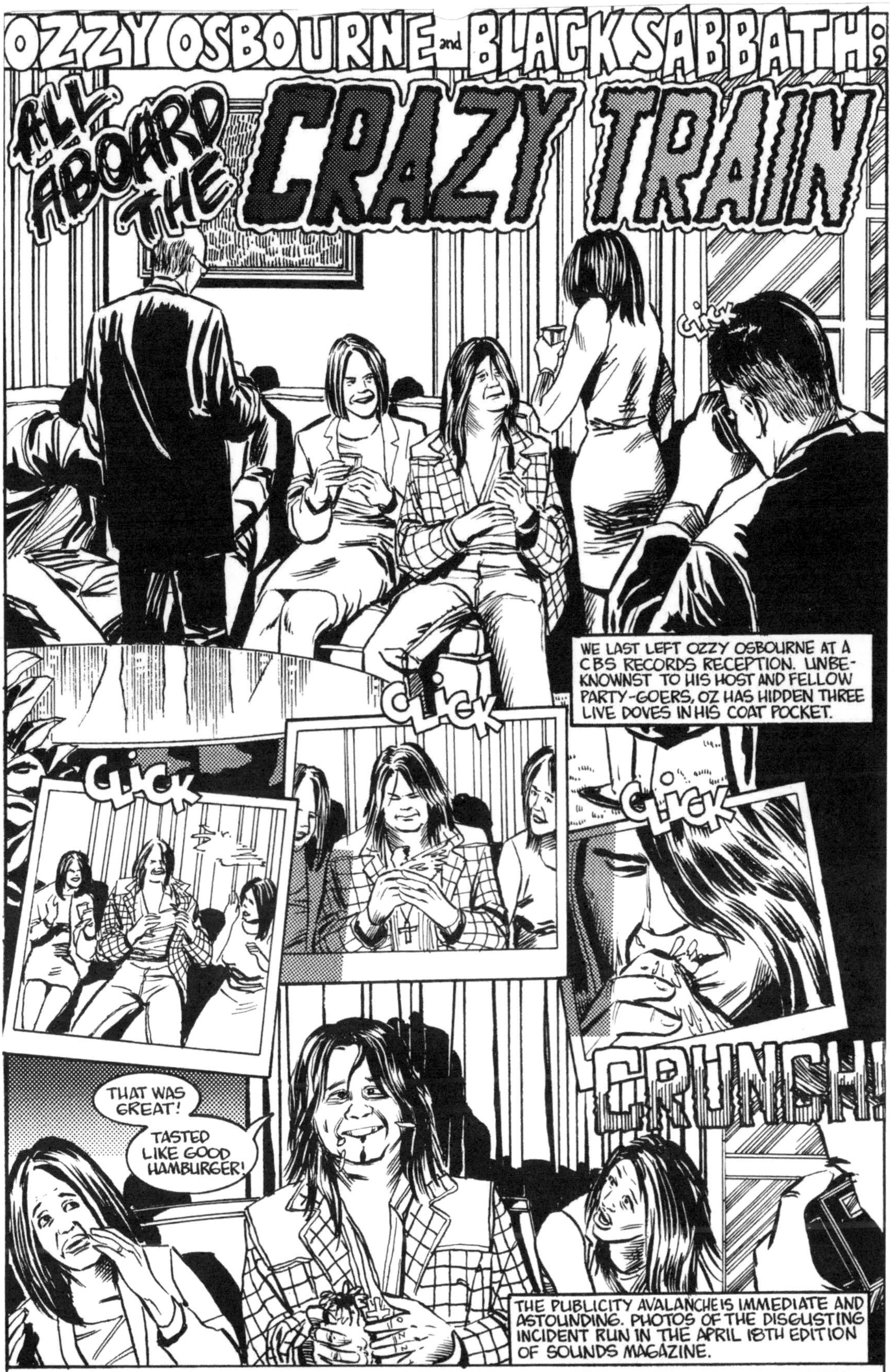
OZZY OSBOURNE and BLACK SABBATH:
ALL ABOARD THE CRAZY TRAIN
CLICK
WE LAST LEFT OZZY OSBOURNE AT A CBS RECORDS RECEPTION. UNBEKNOWNST TO HIS HOST AND FELLOW PARTY-GOERS, OZ HAS HIDDEN THREE LIVE DOVES IN HIS COAT POCKET.
CLICK
CLICK
CLICK
CRUNCH!
THAT WAS GREAT!
TASTED LIKE GOOD HAMBURGER!
THE PUBLICITY AVALANCHE IS IMMEDIATE AND ASTOUNDING. PHOTOS OF THE DISGUSTING INCIDENT RUN IN THE APRIL 18TH EDITION OF SOUNDS MAGAZINE.
WRITER: JAY ALLEN SANFORD ARTIST/LETTERER: MARC ERICKSON EDITED BY TODD LOREN

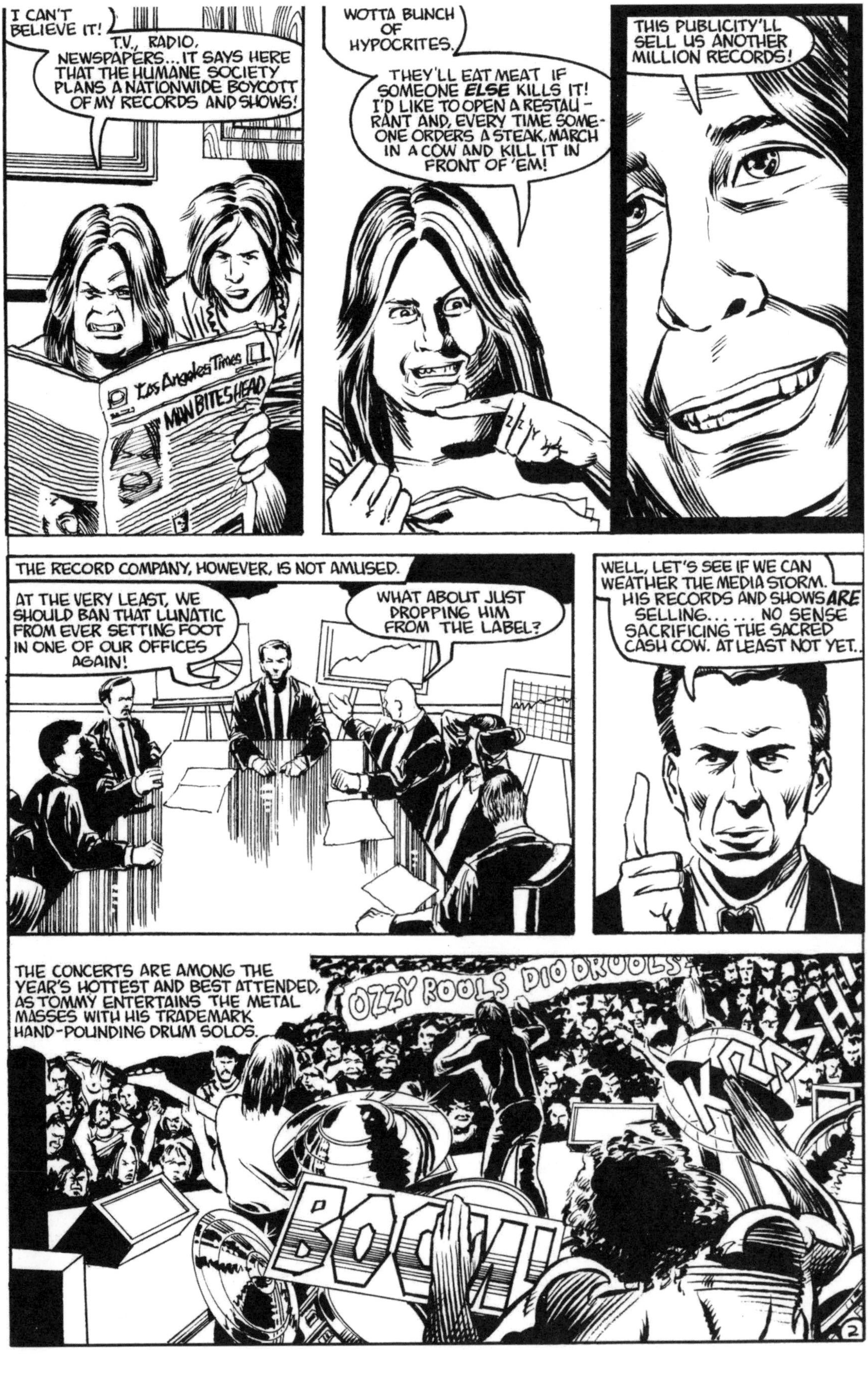
I CAN'T BELIEVE IT!
T.V., RADIO, NEWSPAPERS... IT SAYS HERE THAT THE HUMANE SOCIETY PLANS A NATIONWIDE BOYCOTT OF MY RECORDS AND SHOWS!
Los Angeles Times
MAN BITES HEAD
WOTTA BUNCH OF HYPOCRITES.
THEY'LL EAT MEAT IF SOMEONE *ELSE* KILLS IT! I'D LIKE TO OPEN A RESTAU-RANT AND, EVERY TIME SOME-ONE ORDERS A STEAK, MARCH IN A COW AND KILL IT IN FRONT OF 'EM!
THIS PUBLICITY'LL SELL US ANOTHER MILLION RECORDS!
THE RECORD COMPANY, HOWEVER, IS NOT AMUSED.
AT THE VERY LEAST, WE SHOULD BAN THAT LUNATIC FROM EVER SETTING FOOT IN ONE OF OUR OFFICES AGAIN!
WHAT ABOUT JUST DROPPING HIM FROM THE LABEL?
WELL, LET'S SEE IF WE CAN WEATHER THE MEDIA STORM. HIS RECORDS AND SHOWS *ARE* SELLING...... NO SENSE SACRIFICING THE SACRED CASH COW. AT LEAST NOT YET..
THE CONCERTS ARE AMONG THE YEAR'S HOTTEST AND BEST ATTENDED, AS TOMMY ENTERTAINS THE METAL MASSES WITH HIS TRADEMARK HAND-POUNDING DRUM SOLOS.
OZZY ROOLS
DIO DROOLS
BOOM!

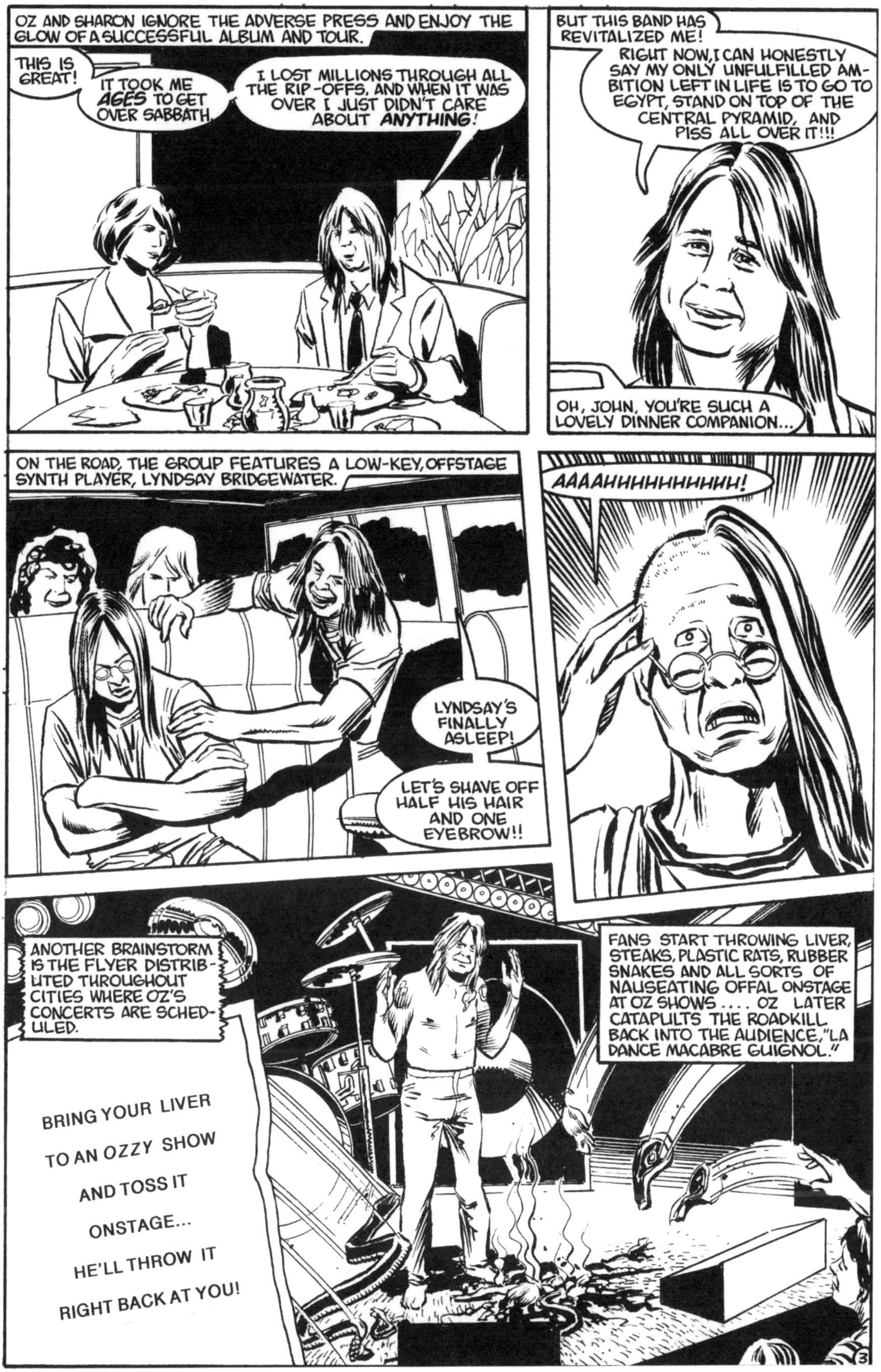

OZ AND SHARON IGNORE THE ADVERSE PRESS AND ENJOY THE GLOW OF A SUCCESSFUL ALBUM AND TOUR.
THIS IS GREAT!
IT TOOK ME AGES TO GET OVER SABBATH.
I LOST MILLIONS THROUGH ALL THE RIP-OFFS, AND WHEN IT WAS OVER I JUST DIDN'T CARE ABOUT ANYTHING!
BUT THIS BAND HAS REVITALIZED ME!
RIGHT NOW, I CAN HONESTLY SAY MY ONLY UNFULFILLED AMBITION LEFT IN LIFE IS TO GO TO EGYPT, STAND ON TOP OF THE CENTRAL PYRAMID, AND PISS ALL OVER IT!!!
OH, JOHN, YOU'RE SUCH A LOVELY DINNER COMPANION...
ON THE ROAD, THE GROUP FEATURES A LOW-KEY, OFFSTAGE SYNTH PLAYER, LYNDSAY BRIDGEWATER.
LYNDSAY'S FINALLY ASLEEP!
LET'S SHAVE OFF HALF HIS HAIR AND ONE EYEBROW!!
AAAAHHHHHHHHH!
ANOTHER BRAINSTORM IS THE FLYER DISTRIBUTED THROUGHOUT CITIES WHERE OZ'S CONCERTS ARE SCHEDULED.
BRING YOUR LIVER TO AN OZZY SHOW AND TOSS IT ONSTAGE... HE'LL THROW IT RIGHT BACK AT YOU!
FANS START THROWING LIVER, STEAKS, PLASTIC RATS, RUBBER SNAKES AND ALL SORTS OF NAUSEATING OFFAL ONSTAGE AT OZ SHOWS.... OZ LATER CATAPULTS THE ROADKILL BACK INTO THE AUDIENCE, "LA DANCE MACABRE GUIGNOL."

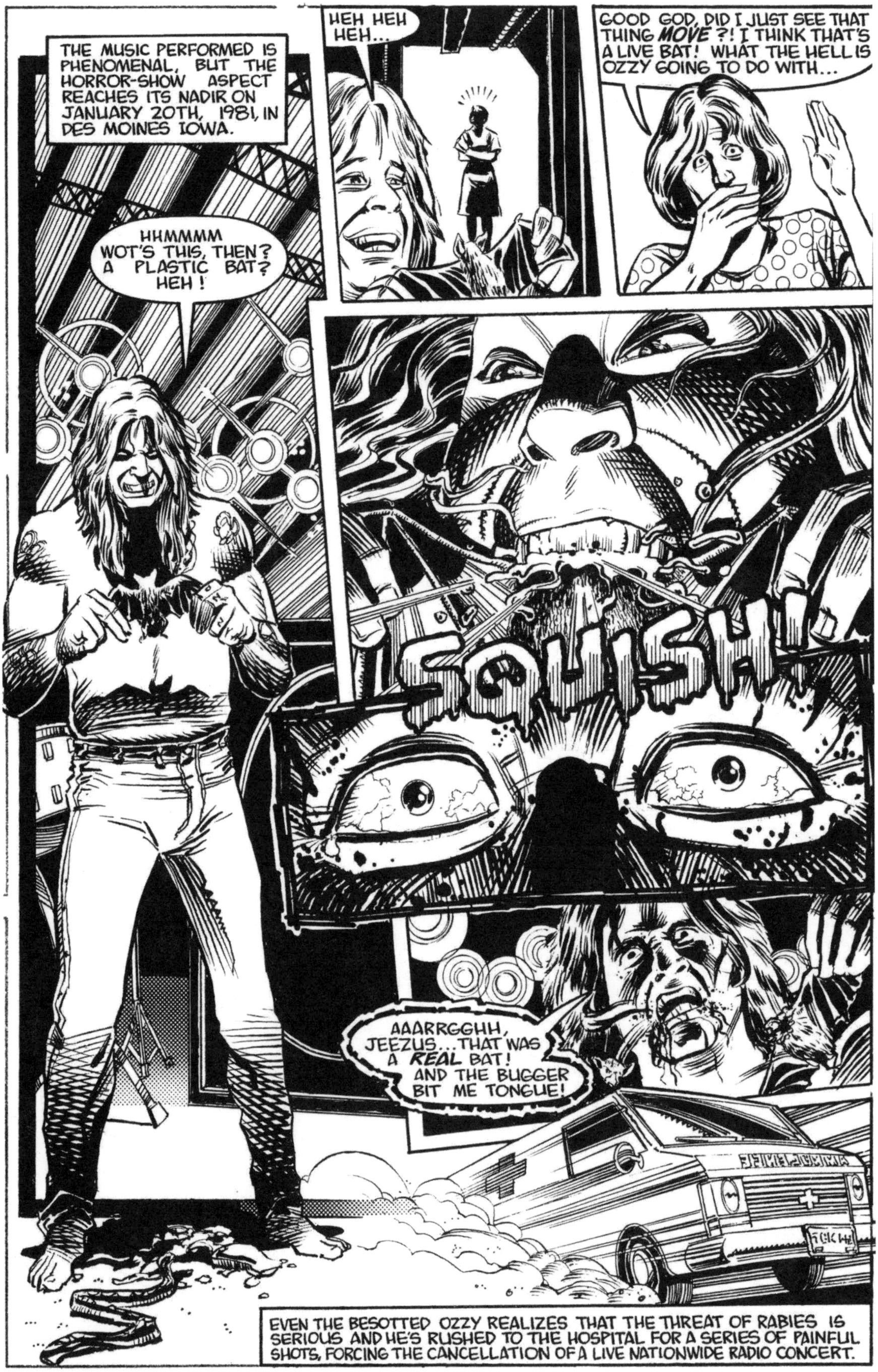
THE MUSIC PERFORMED IS PHENOMENAL, BUT THE HORROR-SHOW ASPECT REACHES ITS NADIR ON JANUARY 20TH, 1981, IN DES MOINES IOWA.
HEH HEH HEH...
GOOD GOD, DID I JUST SEE THAT THING MOVE ?! I THINK THAT'S A LIVE BAT! WHAT THE HELL IS OZZY GOING TO DO WITH...
HHMMMM WOT'S THIS, THEN? A PLASTIC BAT? HEH!
SQUISH!
AAARRGGHH, JEEZUS...THAT WAS A REAL BAT! AND THE BUGGER BIT ME TONGUE!
EVEN THE BESOTTED OZZY REALIZES THAT THE THREAT OF RABIES IS SERIOUS AND HE'S RUSHED TO THE HOSPITAL FOR A SERIES OF PAINFUL SHOTS, FORCING THE CANCELLATION OF A LIVE NATIONWIDE RADIO CONCERT.

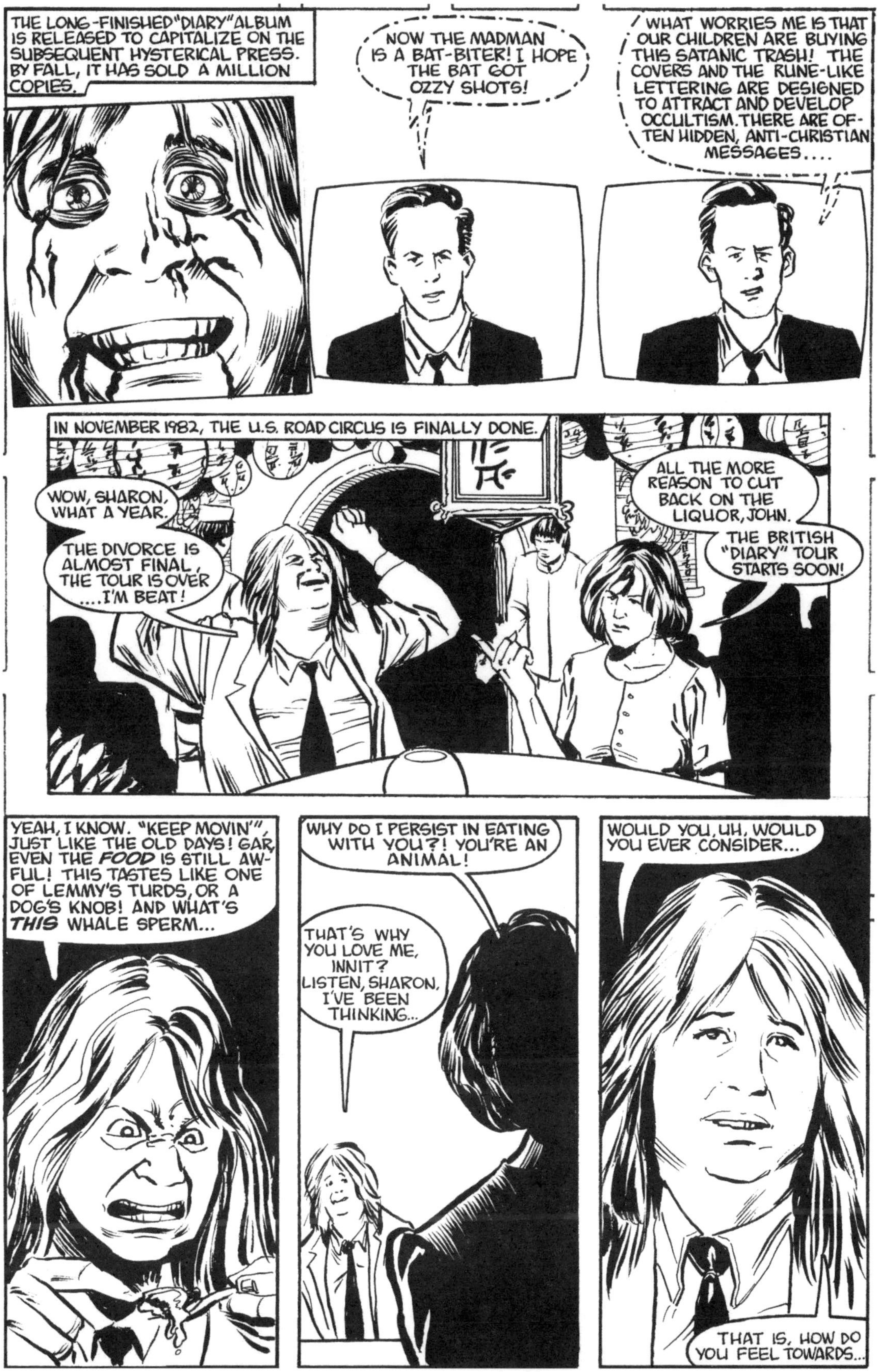
THE LONG-FINISHED "DIARY" ALBUM IS RELEASED TO CAPITALIZE ON THE SUBSEQUENT HYSTERICAL PRESS. BY FALL, IT HAS SOLD A MILLION COPIES.
NOW THE MADMAN IS A BAT-BITER! I HOPE THE BAT GOT OZZY SHOTS!
WHAT WORRIES ME IS THAT OUR CHILDREN ARE BUYING THIS SATANIC TRASH! THE COVERS AND THE RUNE-LIKE LETTERING ARE DESIGNED TO ATTRACT AND DEVELOP OCCULTISM. THERE ARE OFTEN HIDDEN, ANTI-CHRISTIAN MESSAGES....
IN NOVEMBER 1982, THE U.S. ROAD CIRCUS IS FINALLY DONE.
WOW, SHARON, WHAT A YEAR.
THE DIVORCE IS ALMOST FINAL, THE TOUR IS OVER ....I'M BEAT!
ALL THE MORE REASON TO CUT BACK ON THE LIQUOR, JOHN.
THE BRITISH "DIARY" TOUR STARTS SOON!
YEAH, I KNOW. "KEEP MOVIN'", JUST LIKE THE OLD DAYS! GAR, EVEN THE FOOD IS STILL AWFUL! THIS TASTES LIKE ONE OF LEMMY'S TURDS, OR A DOG'S KNOB! AND WHAT'S THIS WHALE SPERM...
WHY DO I PERSIST IN EATING WITH YOU?! YOU'RE AN ANIMAL!
THAT'S WHY YOU LOVE ME, INNIT? LISTEN, SHARON, I'VE BEEN THINKING...
WOULD YOU, UH, WOULD YOU EVER CONSIDER...
THAT IS, HOW DO YOU FEEL TOWARDS...

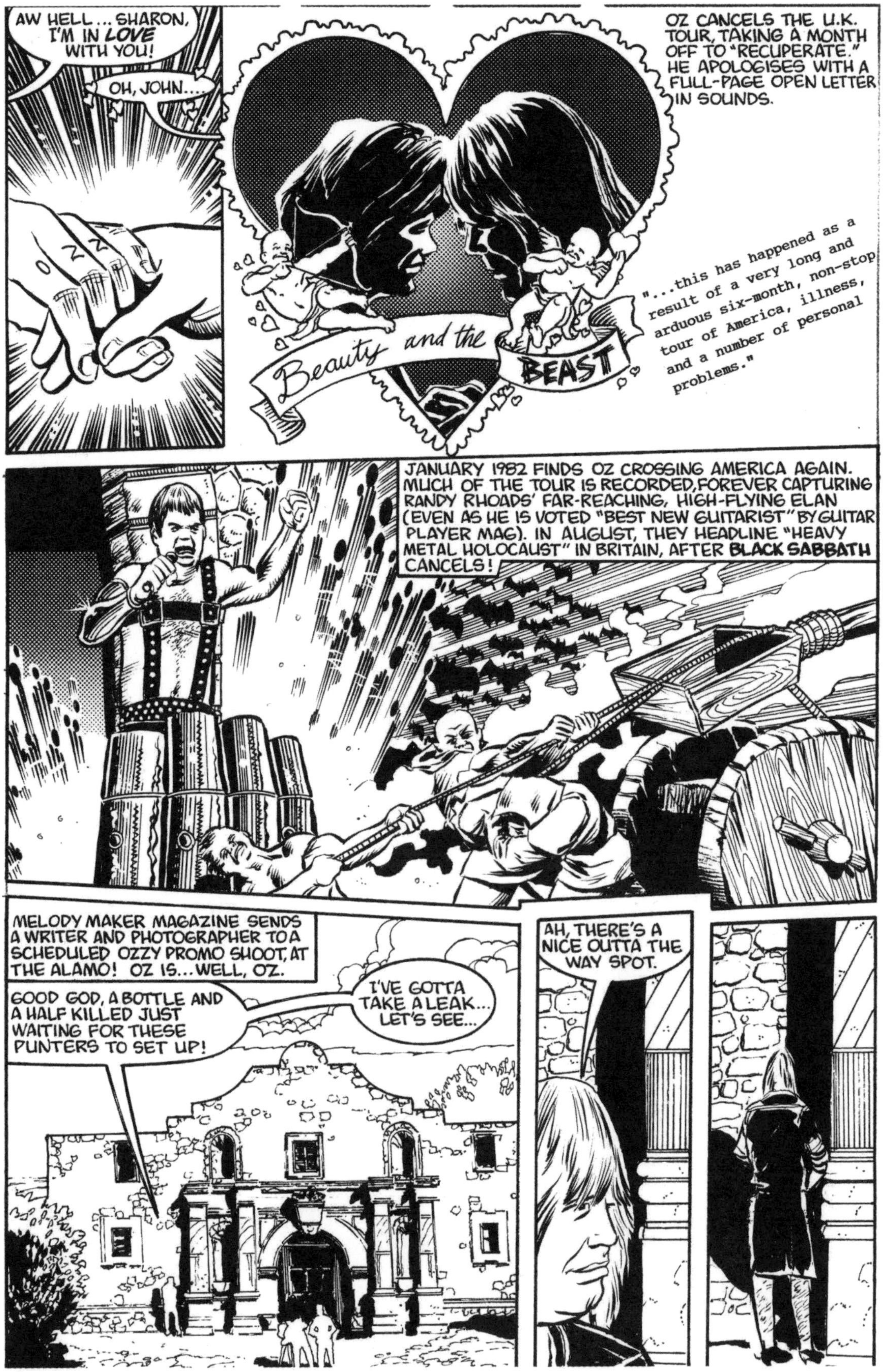
AW HELL... SHARON, I'M IN LOVE WITH YOU!
OH, JOHN....
OZZY
OZ CANCELS THE U.K. TOUR, TAKING A MONTH OFF TO "RECUPERATE." HE APOLOGISES WITH A FULL-PAGE OPEN LETTER IN SOUNDS.
Beauty and the BEAST
"...this has happened as a result of a very long and arduous six-month, non-stop tour of America, illness, and a number of personal problems."
JANUARY 1982 FINDS OZ CROSSING AMERICA AGAIN. MUCH OF THE TOUR IS RECORDED, FOREVER CAPTURING RANDY RHOADS' FAR-REACHING, HIGH-FLYING ELAN (EVEN AS HE IS VOTED "BEST NEW GUITARIST" BY GUITAR PLAYER MAG). IN AUGUST, THEY HEADLINE "HEAVY METAL HOLOCAUST" IN BRITAIN, AFTER BLACK SABBATH CANCELS!
MELODY MAKER MAGAZINE SENDS A WRITER AND PHOTOGRAPHER TO A SCHEDULED OZZY PROMO SHOOT, AT THE ALAMO! OZ IS...WELL, OZ.
GOOD GOD, A BOTTLE AND A HALF KILLED JUST WAITING FOR THESE PUNTERS TO SET UP!
I'VE GOTTA TAKE A LEAK... LET'S SEE...
AH, THERE'S A NICE OUTTA THE WAY SPOT.

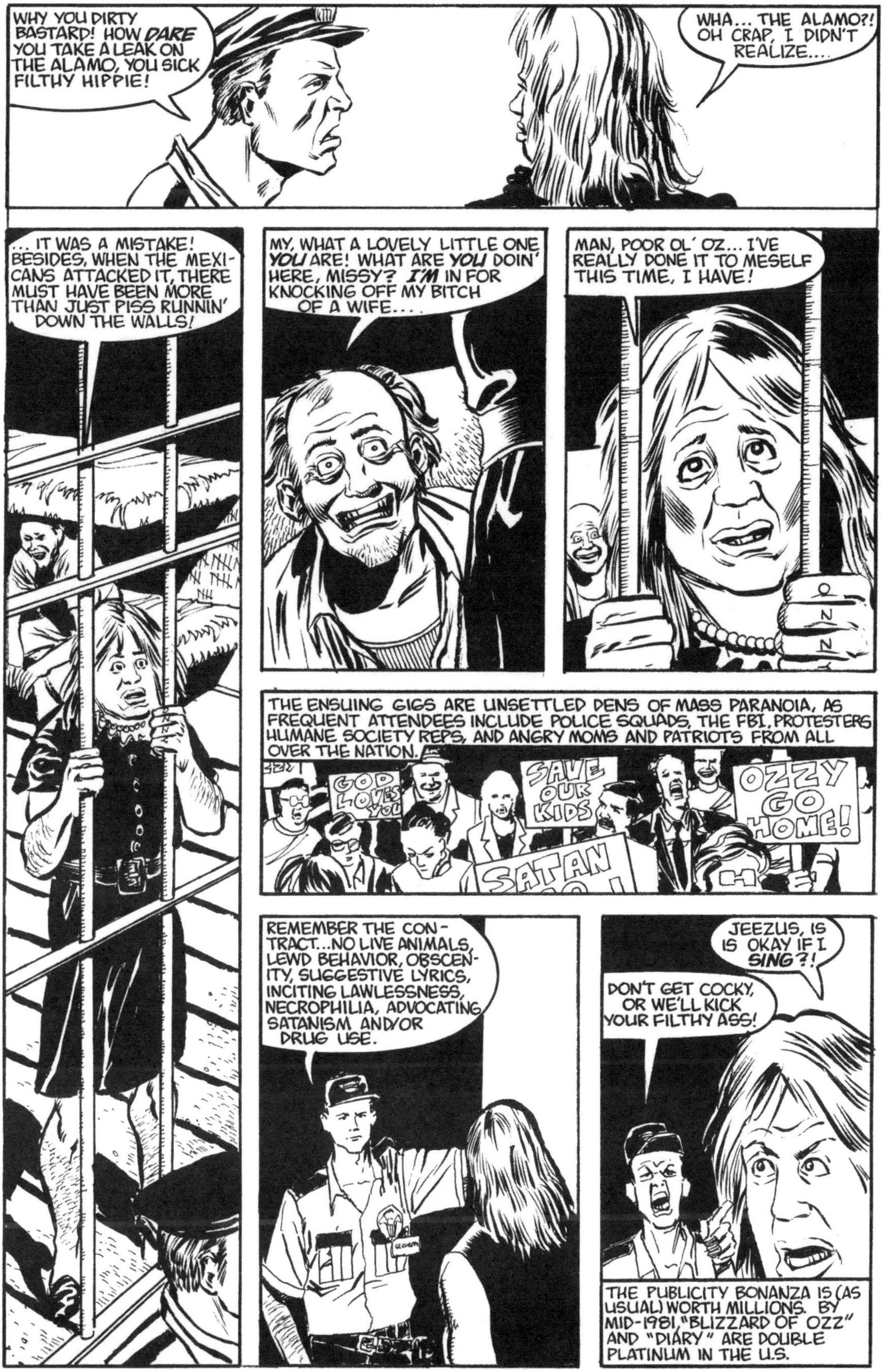
WHY YOU DIRTY BASTARD! HOW *DARE* YOU TAKE A LEAK ON THE ALAMO, YOU SICK FILTHY HIPPIE!
WHA... THE ALAMO?! OH CRAP, I DIDN'T REALIZE....
... IT WAS A MISTAKE! BESIDES, WHEN THE MEXICANS ATTACKED IT, THERE MUST HAVE BEEN MORE THAN JUST PISS RUNNIN' DOWN THE WALLS!
MY, WHAT A LOVELY LITTLE ONE *YOU* ARE! WHAT ARE *YOU* DOIN' HERE, MISSY? *I'M* IN FOR KNOCKING OFF MY BITCH OF A WIFE...
MAN, POOR OL' OZ... I'VE REALLY DONE IT TO MESELF THIS TIME, I HAVE!
THE ENSUING GIGS ARE UNSETTLED DENS OF MASS PARANOIA, AS FREQUENT ATTENDEES INCLUDE POLICE SQUADS, THE FBI, PROTESTERS HUMANE SOCIETY REPS, AND ANGRY MOMS AND PATRIOTS FROM ALL OVER THE NATION.
GOD LOVES YOU
SAVE OUR KIDS
OZZY GO HOME!
SATAN
REMEMBER THE CONTRACT...NO LIVE ANIMALS, LEWD BEHAVIOR, OBSCENITY, SUGGESTIVE LYRICS, INCITING LAWLESSNESS, NECROPHILIA, ADVOCATING SATANISM AND/OR DRUG USE.
JEEZUS, IS IS OKAY IF I *SING*?!
DON'T GET COCKY, OR WE'LL KICK YOUR FILTHY ASS!
THE PUBLICITY BONANZA IS (AS USUAL) WORTH MILLIONS. BY MID-1981, "BLIZZARD OF OZZ" AND "DIARY" ARE DOUBLE PLATINUM IN THE U.S.

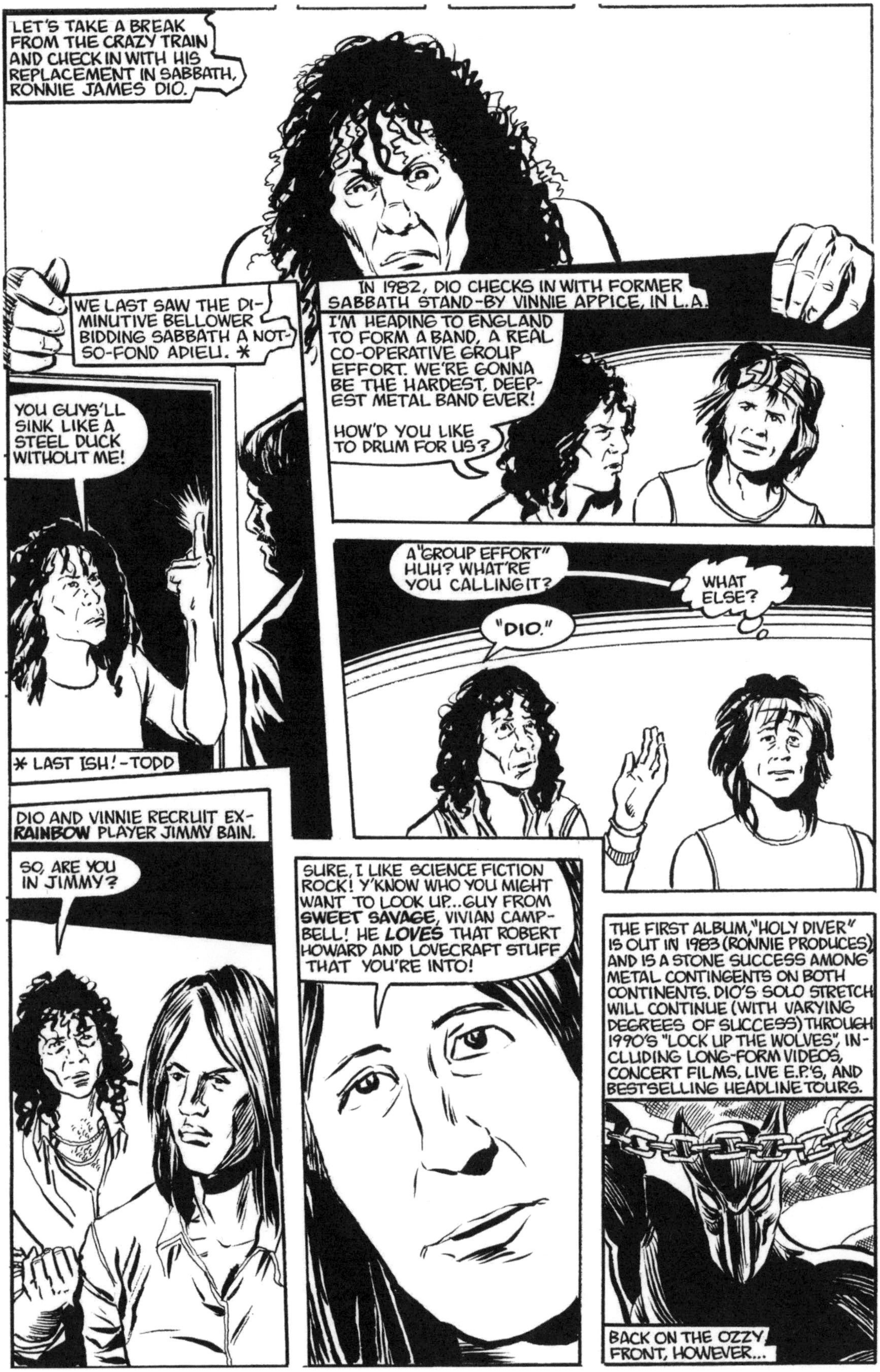
LET'S TAKE A BREAK FROM THE CRAZY TRAIN AND CHECK IN WITH HIS REPLACEMENT IN SABBATH, RONNIE JAMES DIO.
WE LAST SAW THE DIMINUTIVE BELLOWER BIDDING SABBATH A NOT-SO-FOND ADIEU. *
YOU GUYS'LL SINK LIKE A STEEL DUCK WITHOUT ME!
* LAST ISH! -TODD
IN 1982, DIO CHECKS IN WITH FORMER SABBATH STAND-BY VINNIE APPICE, IN L.A.
I'M HEADING TO ENGLAND TO FORM A BAND, A REAL CO-OPERATIVE GROUP EFFORT. WE'RE GONNA BE THE HARDEST, DEEPEST METAL BAND EVER!
HOW'D YOU LIKE TO DRUM FOR US?
A "GROUP EFFORT" HUH? WHAT'RE YOU CALLING IT?
WHAT ELSE?
"DIO."
DIO AND VINNIE RECRUIT EX-RAINBOW PLAYER JIMMY BAIN.
SO, ARE YOU IN JIMMY?
SURE, I LIKE SCIENCE FICTION ROCK! Y'KNOW WHO YOU MIGHT WANT TO LOOK UP...GUY FROM SWEET SAVAGE, VIVIAN CAMPBELL! HE LOVES THAT ROBERT HOWARD AND LOVECRAFT STUFF THAT YOU'RE INTO!
THE FIRST ALBUM, "HOLY DIVER" IS OUT IN 1983 (RONNIE PRODUCES) AND IS A STONE SUCCESS AMONG METAL CONTINGENTS ON BOTH CONTINENTS. DIO'S SOLO STRETCH WILL CONTINUE (WITH VARYING DEGREES OF SUCCESS) THROUGH 1990'S "LOCK UP THE WOLVES", INCLUDING LONG-FORM VIDEOS, CONCERT FILMS, LIVE E.P.'S, AND BESTSELLING HEADLINE TOURS.
BACK ON THE OZZY FRONT, HOWEVER...

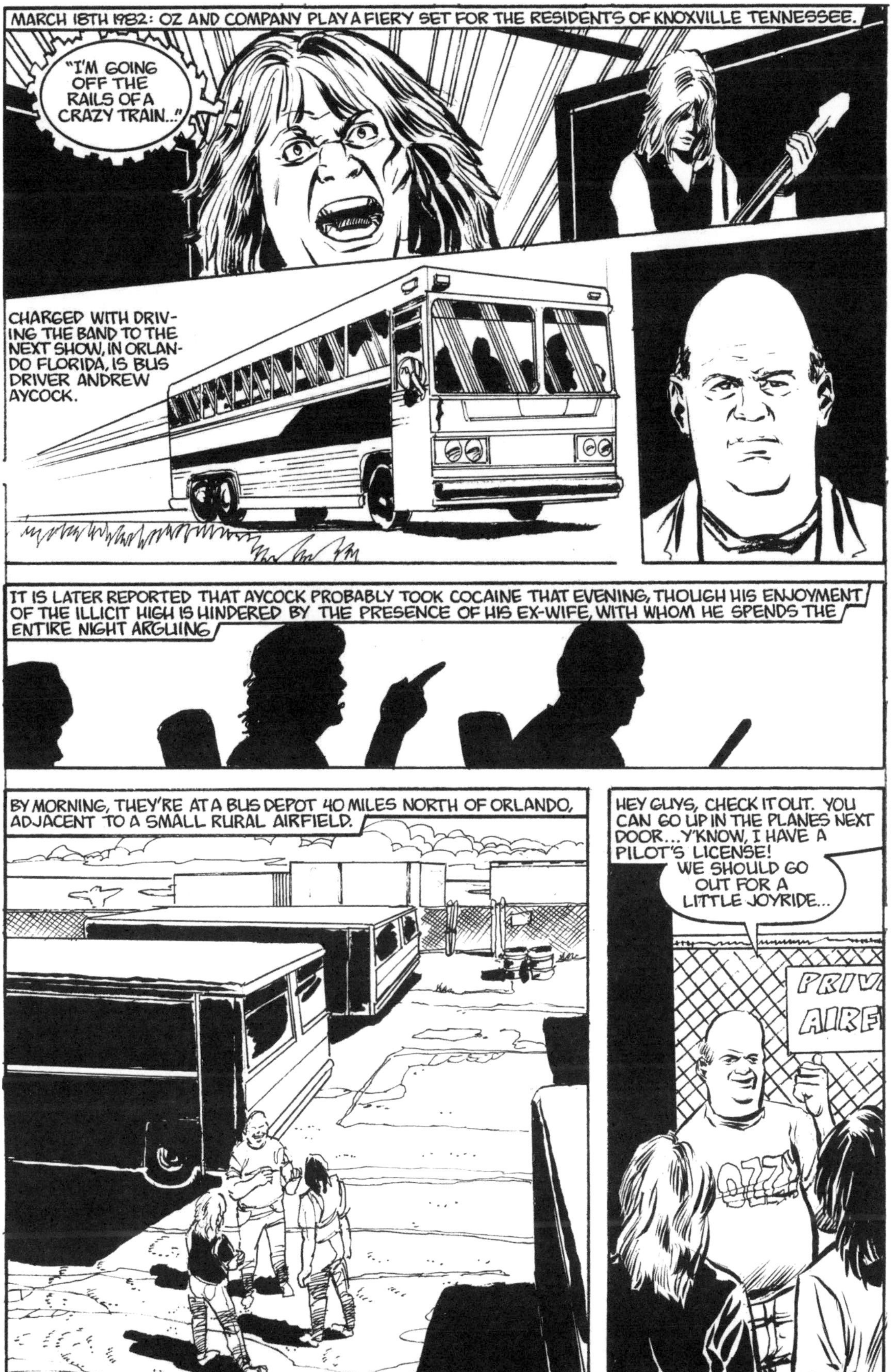
MARCH 18TH 1982: OZ AND COMPANY PLAY A FIERY SET FOR THE RESIDENTS OF KNOXVILLE TENNESSEE.
"I'M GOING OFF THE RAILS OF A CRAZY TRAIN..."
CHARGED WITH DRIVING THE BAND TO THE NEXT SHOW, IN ORLANDO FLORIDA, IS BUS DRIVER ANDREW AYCOCK.
IT IS LATER REPORTED THAT AYCOCK PROBABLY TOOK COCAINE THAT EVENING, THOUGH HIS ENJOYMENT OF THE ILLICIT HIGH IS HINDERED BY THE PRESENCE OF HIS EX-WIFE, WITH WHOM HE SPENDS THE ENTIRE NIGHT ARGUING
BY MORNING, THEY'RE AT A BUS DEPOT 40 MILES NORTH OF ORLANDO, ADJACENT TO A SMALL RURAL AIRFIELD.
HEY GUYS, CHECK IT OUT. YOU CAN GO UP IN THE PLANES NEXT DOOR...Y'KNOW, I HAVE A PILOT'S LICENSE!
WE SHOULD GO OUT FOR A LITTLE JOYRIDE...
PRIV
AIRF
OZZY

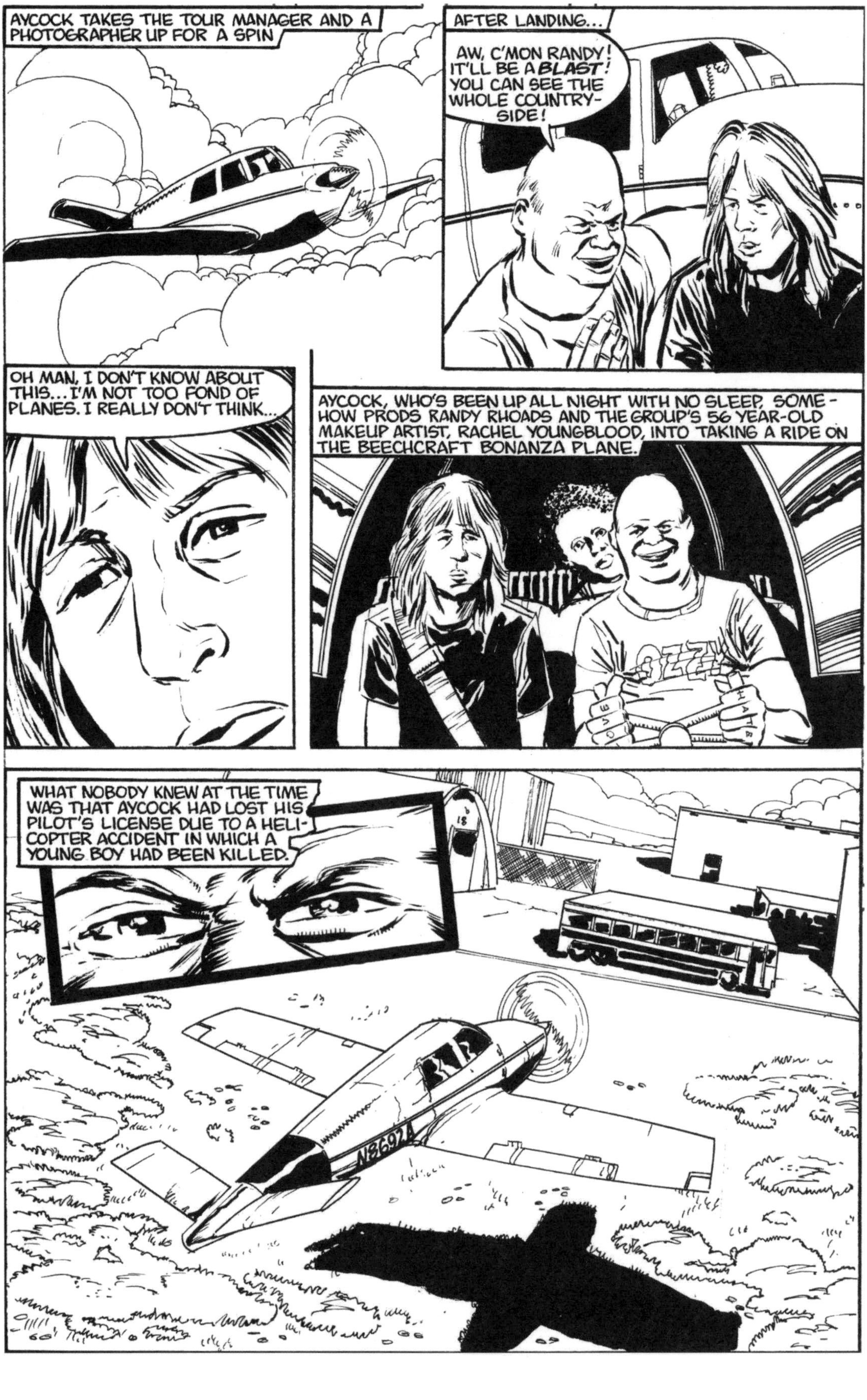
AYCOCK TAKES THE TOUR MANAGER AND A PHOTOGRAPHER UP FOR A SPIN
AFTER LANDING...
AW, C'MON RANDY! IT'LL BE A BLAST! YOU CAN SEE THE WHOLE COUNTRY-SIDE!
OH MAN, I DON'T KNOW ABOUT THIS... I'M NOT TOO FOND OF PLANES. I REALLY DON'T THINK...
AYCOCK, WHO'S BEEN UP ALL NIGHT WITH NO SLEEP, SOME-HOW PRODS RANDY RHOADS AND THE GROUP'S 56 YEAR-OLD MAKEUP ARTIST, RACHEL YOUNGBLOOD, INTO TAKING A RIDE ON THE BEECHCRAFT BONANZA PLANE.
WHAT NOBODY KNEW AT THE TIME WAS THAT AYCOCK HAD LOST HIS PILOT'S LICENSE DUE TO A HELI-COPTER ACCIDENT IN WHICH A YOUNG BOY HAD BEEN KILLED.
N8692A

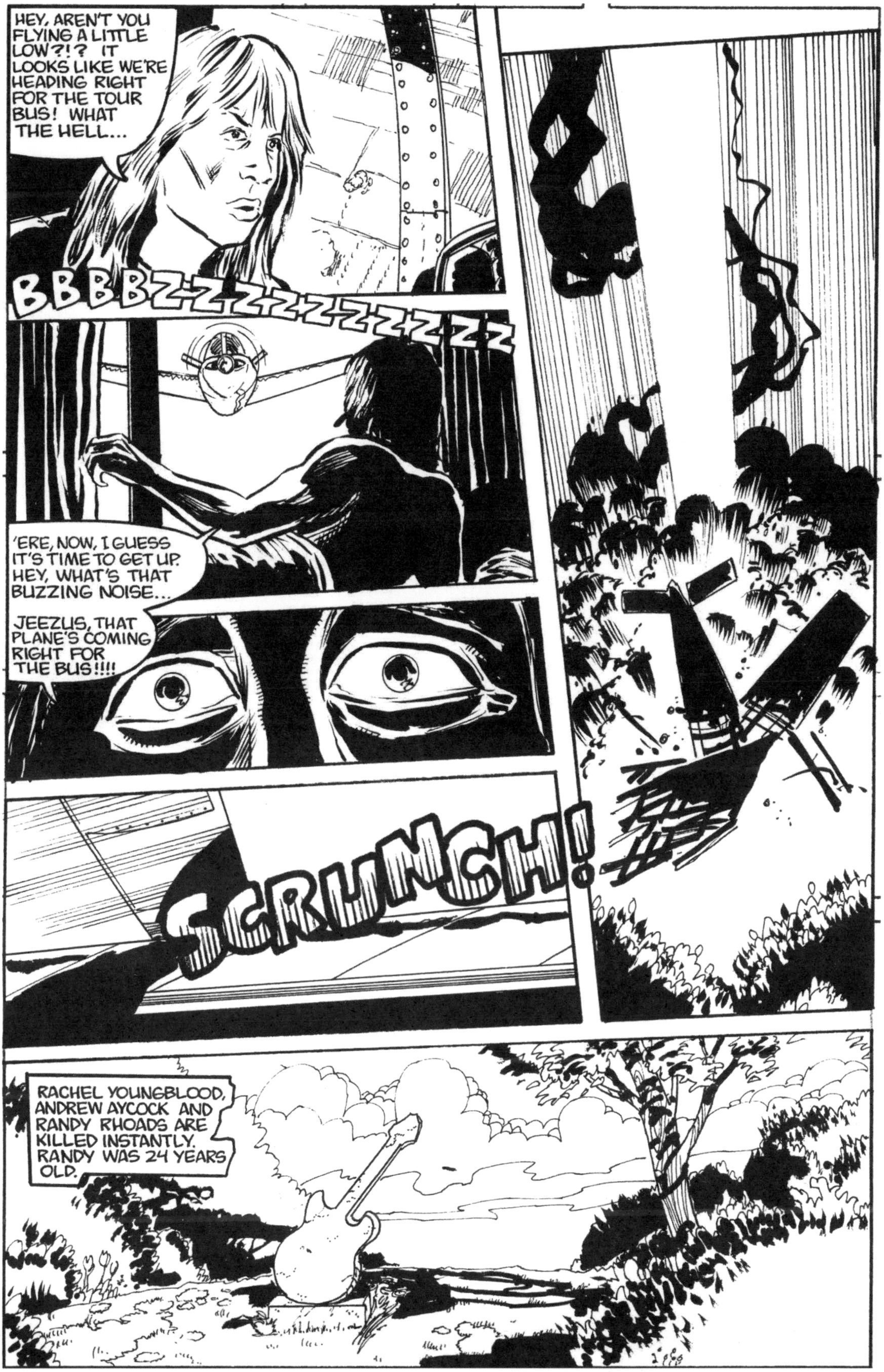
HEY, AREN'T YOU FLYING A LITTLE LOW?!? IT LOOKS LIKE WE'RE HEADING RIGHT FOR THE TOUR BUS! WHAT THE HELL...
BBBBZZZZZZZZZZZZ
'ERE, NOW, I GUESS IT'S TIME TO GET UP. HEY, WHAT'S THAT BUZZING NOISE...
JEEZUS, THAT PLANE'S COMING RIGHT FOR THE BUS!!!!
SCRUNCH!
RACHEL YOUNGBLOOD, ANDREW AYCOCK AND RANDY RHOADS ARE KILLED INSTANTLY. RANDY WAS 24 YEARS OLD.

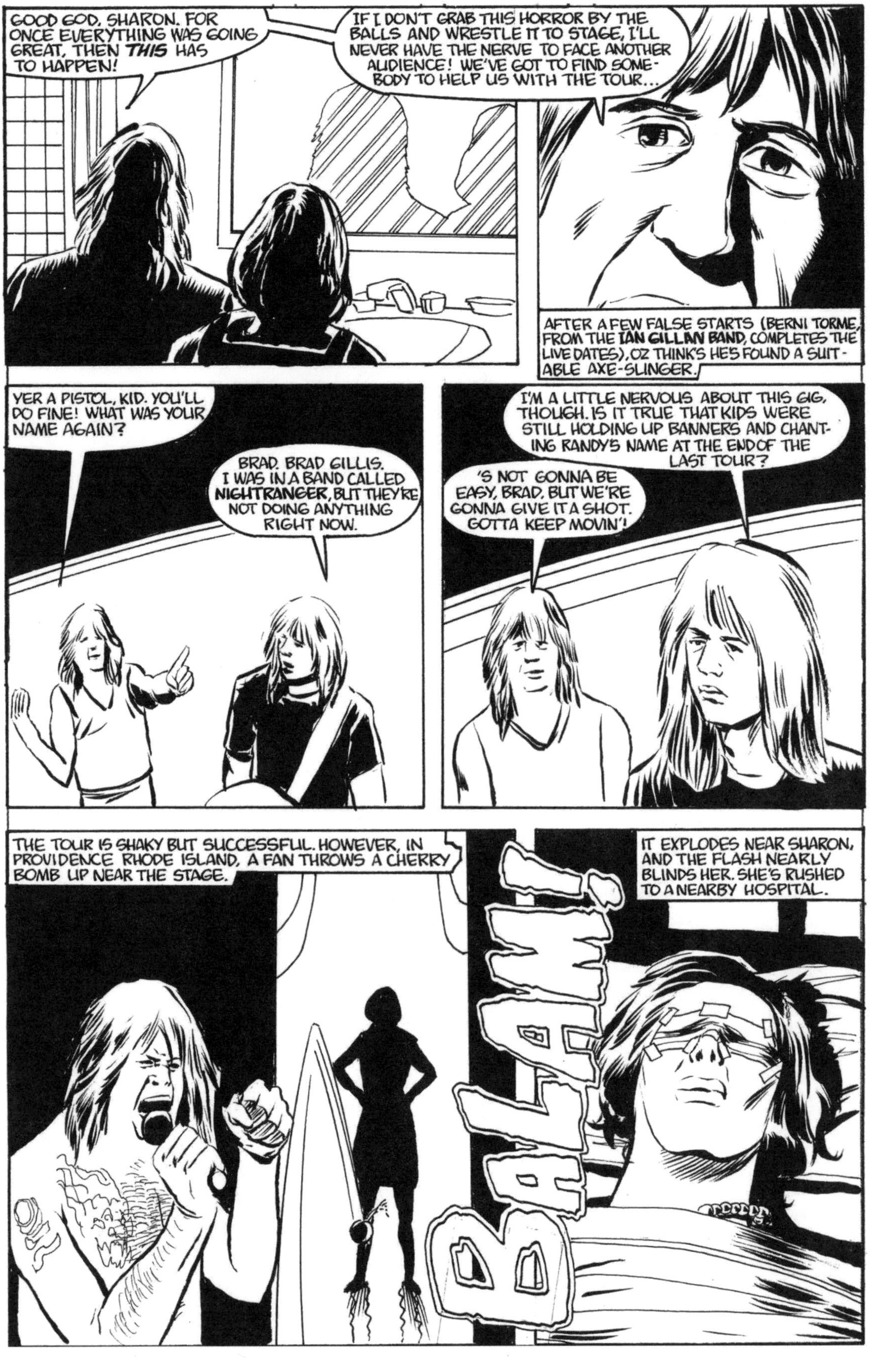
GOOD GOD, SHARON. FOR ONCE EVERYTHING WAS GOING GREAT, THEN THIS HAS TO HAPPEN!
IF I DON'T GRAB THIS HORROR BY THE BALLS AND WRESTLE IT TO STAGE, I'LL NEVER HAVE THE NERVE TO FACE ANOTHER AUDIENCE! WE'VE GOT TO FIND SOMEBODY TO HELP US WITH THE TOUR...
AFTER A FEW FALSE STARTS (BERNI TORME, FROM THE IAN GILLAN BAND, COMPLETES THE LIVE DATES), OZ THINK'S HE'S FOUND A SUITABLE AXE-SLINGER.
YER A PISTOL, KID. YOU'LL DO FINE! WHAT WAS YOUR NAME AGAIN?
BRAD. BRAD GILLIS. I WAS IN A BAND CALLED NIGHTRANGER, BUT THEY'RE NOT DOING ANYTHING RIGHT NOW.
I'M A LITTLE NERVOUS ABOUT THIS GIG, THOUGH. IS IT TRUE THAT KIDS WERE STILL HOLDING UP BANNERS AND CHANTING RANDY'S NAME AT THE END OF THE LAST TOUR?
'S NOT GONNA BE EASY, BRAD, BUT WE'RE GONNA GIVE IT A SHOT. GOTTA KEEP MOVIN'!
THE TOUR IS SHAKY BUT SUCCESSFUL. HOWEVER, IN PROVIDENCE RHODE ISLAND, A FAN THROWS A CHERRY BOMB UP NEAR THE STAGE.
BLAM!!
IT EXPLODES NEAR SHARON, AND THE FLASH NEARLY BLINDS HER. SHE'S RUSHED TO A NEARBY HOSPITAL.

LUCKILY, SHARON ONLY SUFFERS FROM MINOR INJURIES AND IS SOON READY TO BE RELEASED. OZ IS RELIEVED, THOUGH HE'S SOON STAGGERED ONCE AGAIN BY THE ARRIVAL OF SOME *OTHER* CONCERT ATTENDEES

ANOTHER ONE FROM THE ROCK SHOW. HER FRIEND SAYS SHE DID ACID. GOD, IT LOOKS LIKE SHE SLICED OFF HER OWN LEFT INDEX FINGER!

I...I NEVER SEE WHAT HAPPENS BEYOND THE LIGHTS THAT SHINE ON THE FRONT TWO ROWS...IS IT ALWAYS SUCH...MADNESS OUT THERE?

IT IS A SOBER OZZY OSBOURNE WHO ATTEMPTS TO SINK A PSYCHIC ANCHOR WITH A BID FOR DOMESTIC BLISS.

SHARON, THE DIVORCE IS FINAL, AS OF TODAY. WHEN THE TOUR FINISHES UP IN HAWAII, I'D LIKE TO START A *NEW* PROJECT...

LET'S GET MARRIED AND START A FAMILY... RIGHT AWAY!

SOUNDS LIKE A GREAT IDEA!

THE WEDDING TAKES PLACE ON JULY 4TH 1982. TOMMY ALDRIDGE IS BEST MAN, AND THE GROUP COMMANDERS THE WEDDING GROUP'S INSTRU- MENTS TO JAM ON *BEATLE* SONGS ALL NIGHT LONG! MANAGEMENT BEGINS TALKS WITH OZ REGARDING HIS NEXT ALBUM, THOUGH HE BREAKS LONG ENOUGH FOR A LATE NIGHT LARK ON THE LETTERMAN SHOW.

REALLY, DAVID, BATS MAKE GREAT PETS. BET- TER THAN A DOG. AND, BOY, ARE THEY CRUNCHY!

BACK AT THE OFFICE...

THE CONTRACT SPECI- FIES AT LEAST ONE MORE ALBUM BEFORE RE-NEGO- TIATING. WHY THE HELL HAVEN'T YOU GOTTEN BACK INTO THE STUDIO YET?

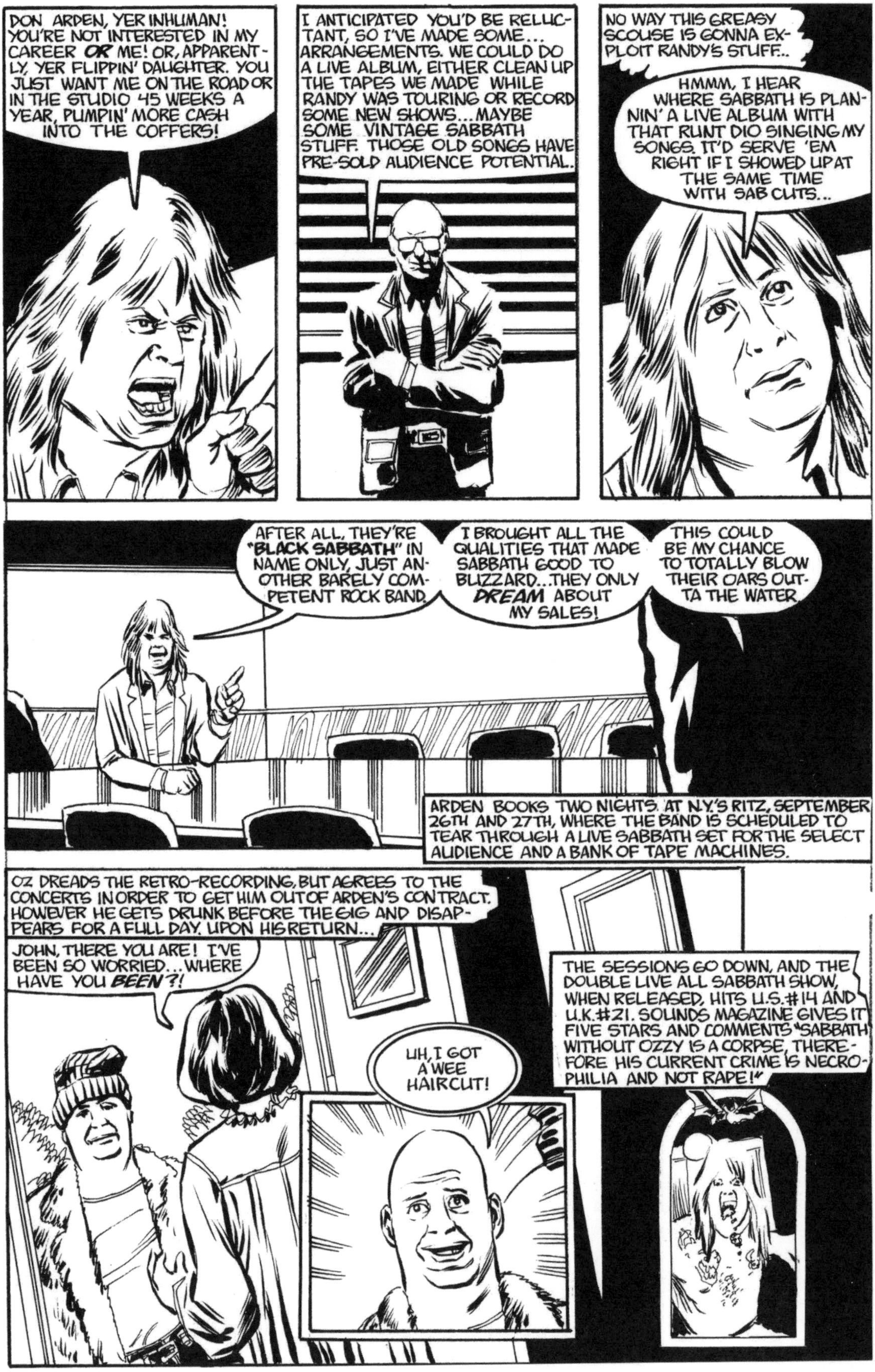
DON ARDEN, YER INHUMAN! YOU'RE NOT INTERESTED IN MY CAREER OR ME! OR, APPARENTLY, YER FLIPPIN' DAUGHTER. YOU JUST WANT ME ON THE ROAD OR IN THE STUDIO 45 WEEKS A YEAR, PUMPIN' MORE CASH INTO THE COFFERS!
I ANTICIPATED YOU'D BE RELUCTANT, SO I'VE MADE SOME... ARRANGEMENTS. WE COULD DO A LIVE ALBUM, EITHER CLEAN UP THE TAPES WE MADE WHILE RANDY WAS TOURING OR RECORD SOME NEW SHOWS... MAYBE SOME VINTAGE SABBATH STUFF. THOSE OLD SONGS HAVE PRE-SOLD AUDIENCE POTENTIAL.
NO WAY THIS GREASY SCOUSE IS GONNA EXPLOIT RANDY'S STUFF..
HMMM, I HEAR WHERE SABBATH IS PLANNIN' A LIVE ALBUM WITH THAT RUNT DIO SINGING MY SONGS. IT'D SERVE 'EM RIGHT IF I SHOWED UP AT THE SAME TIME WITH SAB CUTS...
AFTER ALL, THEY'RE "BLACK SABBATH" IN NAME ONLY, JUST ANOTHER BARELY COMPETENT ROCK BAND.
I BROUGHT ALL THE QUALITIES THAT MADE SABBATH GOOD TO BLIZZARD...THEY ONLY DREAM ABOUT MY SALES!
THIS COULD BE MY CHANCE TO TOTALLY BLOW THEIR OARS OUTTA THE WATER
ARDEN BOOKS TWO NIGHTS AT N.Y.'S RITZ, SEPTEMBER 26TH AND 27TH, WHERE THE BAND IS SCHEDULED TO TEAR THROUGH A LIVE SABBATH SET FOR THE SELECT AUDIENCE AND A BANK OF TAPE MACHINES.
OZ DREADS THE RETRO-RECORDING, BUT AGREES TO THE CONCERTS IN ORDER TO GET HIM OUT OF ARDEN'S CONTRACT. HOWEVER HE GETS DRUNK BEFORE THE GIG AND DISAPPEARS FOR A FULL DAY. UPON HIS RETURN...
JOHN, THERE YOU ARE! I'VE BEEN SO WORRIED... WHERE HAVE YOU BEEN?!
UH, I GOT A WEE HAIRCUT!
THE SESSIONS GO DOWN, AND THE DOUBLE LIVE ALL SABBATH SHOW, WHEN RELEASED, HITS U.S. #14 AND U.K. #21. SOUNDS MAGAZINE GIVES IT FIVE STARS AND COMMENTS "SABBATH WITHOUT OZZY IS A CORPSE, THEREFORE HIS CURRENT CRIME IS NECROPHILIA AND NOT RAPE!"

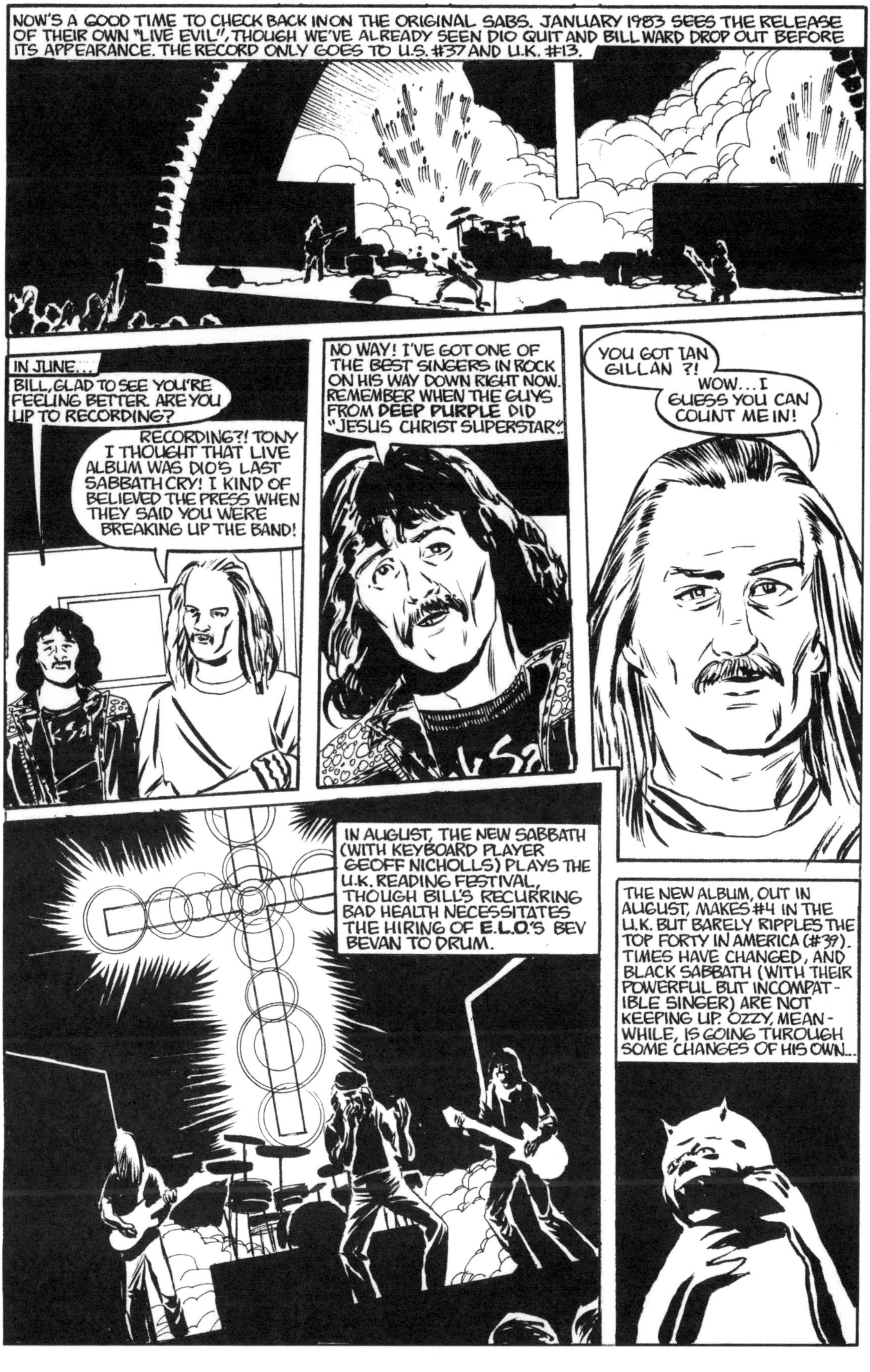

NOW'S A GOOD TIME TO CHECK BACK IN ON THE ORIGINAL SABS. JANUARY 1983 SEES THE RELEASE OF THEIR OWN "LIVE EVIL", THOUGH WE'VE ALREADY SEEN DIO QUIT AND BILL WARD DROP OUT BEFORE ITS APPEARANCE. THE RECORD ONLY GOES TO U.S. #37 AND U.K. #13.
IN JUNE...
BILL, GLAD TO SEE YOU'RE FEELING BETTER. ARE YOU UP TO RECORDING?
RECORDING?! TONY I THOUGHT THAT LIVE ALBUM WAS DIO'S LAST SABBATH CRY! I KIND OF BELIEVED THE PRESS WHEN THEY SAID YOU WERE BREAKING UP THE BAND!
NO WAY! I'VE GOT ONE OF THE BEST SINGERS IN ROCK ON HIS WAY DOWN RIGHT NOW. REMEMBER WHEN THE GUYS FROM DEEP PURPLE DID "JESUS CHRIST SUPERSTAR"?
YOU GOT IAN GILLAN ?!
WOW... I GUESS YOU CAN COUNT ME IN!
IN AUGUST, THE NEW SABBATH (WITH KEYBOARD PLAYER GEOFF NICHOLLS) PLAYS THE U.K. READING FESTIVAL, THOUGH BILL'S RECURRING BAD HEALTH NECESSITATES THE HIRING OF E.L.O.'S BEV BEVAN TO DRUM.
THE NEW ALBUM, OUT IN AUGUST, MAKES #4 IN THE U.K. BUT BARELY RIPPLES THE TOP FORTY IN AMERICA (#39). TIMES HAVE CHANGED, AND BLACK SABBATH (WITH THEIR POWERFUL BUT INCOMPATIBLE SINGER) ARE NOT KEEPING UP. OZZY, MEANWHILE, IS GOING THROUGH SOME CHANGES OF HIS OWN...

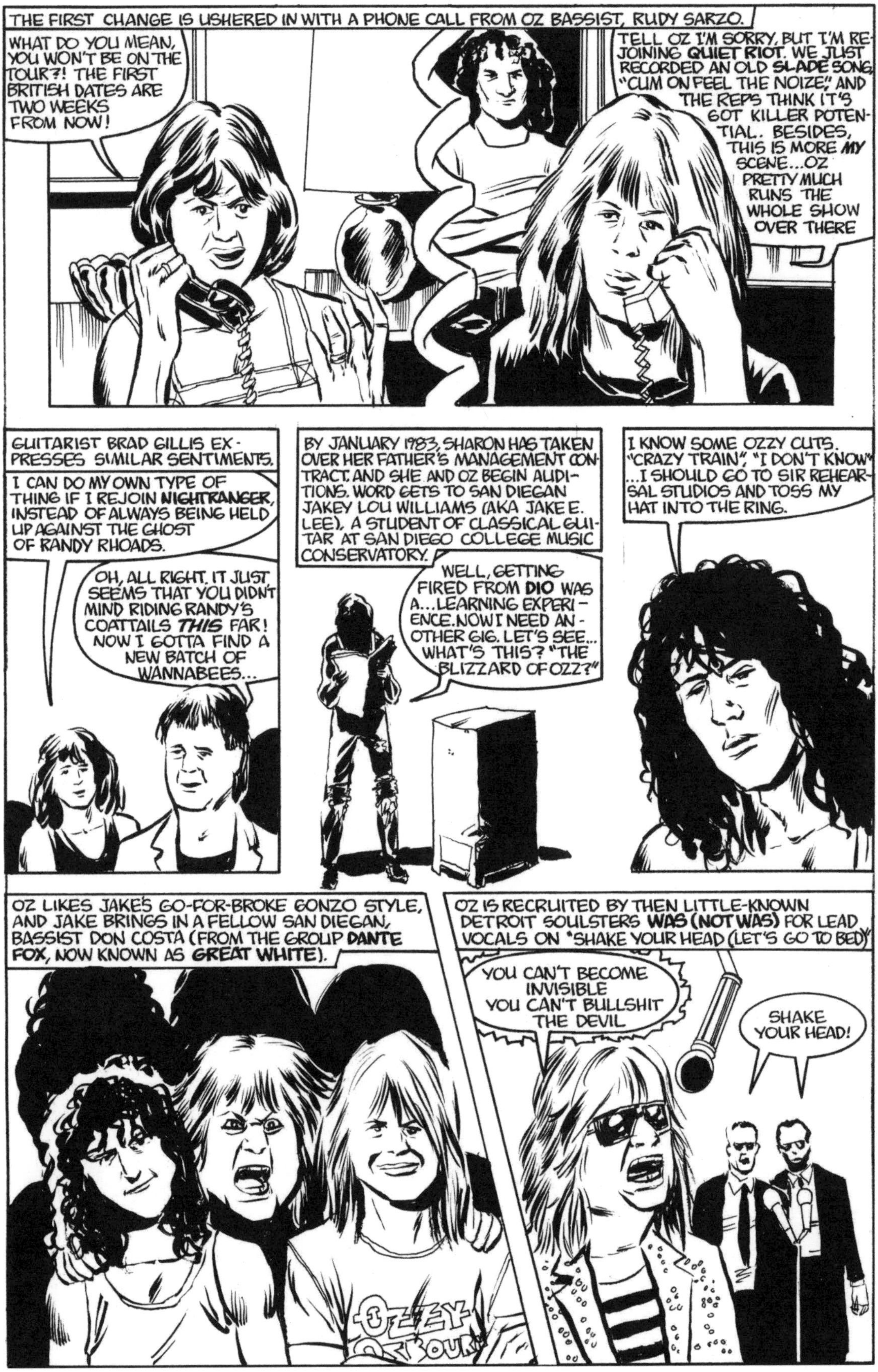

THE FIRST CHANGE IS USHERED IN WITH A PHONE CALL FROM OZ BASSIST, RUDY SARZO.
WHAT DO YOU MEAN, YOU WON'T BE ON THE TOUR?! THE FIRST BRITISH DATES ARE TWO WEEKS FROM NOW!
TELL OZ I'M SORRY, BUT I'M RE-JOINING QUIET RIOT. WE JUST RECORDED AN OLD SLADE SONG, "CUM ON FEEL THE NOIZE," AND THE REPS THINK IT'S GOT KILLER POTEN-TIAL. BESIDES, THIS IS MORE MY SCENE...OZ PRETTY MUCH RUNS THE WHOLE SHOW OVER THERE
GUITARIST BRAD GILLIS EX-PRESSES SIMILAR SENTIMENTS.
I CAN DO MY OWN TYPE OF THING IF I REJOIN NIGHTRANGER, INSTEAD OF ALWAYS BEING HELD UP AGAINST THE GHOST OF RANDY RHOADS.
OH, ALL RIGHT. IT JUST SEEMS THAT YOU DIDN'T MIND RIDING RANDY'S COATTAILS THIS FAR! NOW I GOTTA FIND A NEW BATCH OF WANNABEES...
BY JANUARY 1983, SHARON HAS TAKEN OVER HER FATHER'S MANAGEMENT CON-TRACT. AND SHE AND OZ BEGIN AUDI-TIONS. WORD GETS TO SAN DIEGAN JAKEY LOU WILLIAMS (AKA JAKE E. LEE), A STUDENT OF CLASSICAL GUI-TAR AT SAN DIEGO COLLEGE MUSIC CONSERVATORY.
WELL, GETTING FIRED FROM DIO WAS A...LEARNING EXPERI-ENCE. NOW I NEED AN-OTHER GIG. LET'S SEE... WHAT'S THIS? "THE BLIZZARD OF OZZ?"
I KNOW SOME OZZY CUTS. "CRAZY TRAIN," "I DON'T KNOW" ...I SHOULD GO TO SIR REHEAR-SAL STUDIOS AND TOSS MY HAT INTO THE RING.
OZ LIKES JAKE'S GO-FOR-BROKE GONZO STYLE, AND JAKE BRINGS IN A FELLOW SAN DIEGAN, BASSIST DON COSTA (FROM THE GROUP DANTE FOX, NOW KNOWN AS GREAT WHITE).
OZZY OSBOURNE
OZ IS RECRUITED BY THEN LITTLE-KNOWN DETROIT SOULSTERS WAS (NOT WAS) FOR LEAD VOCALS ON "SHAKE YOUR HEAD (LET'S GO TO BED)"
YOU CAN'T BECOME INVISIBLE YOU CAN'T BULLSHIT THE DEVIL
SHAKE YOUR HEAD!

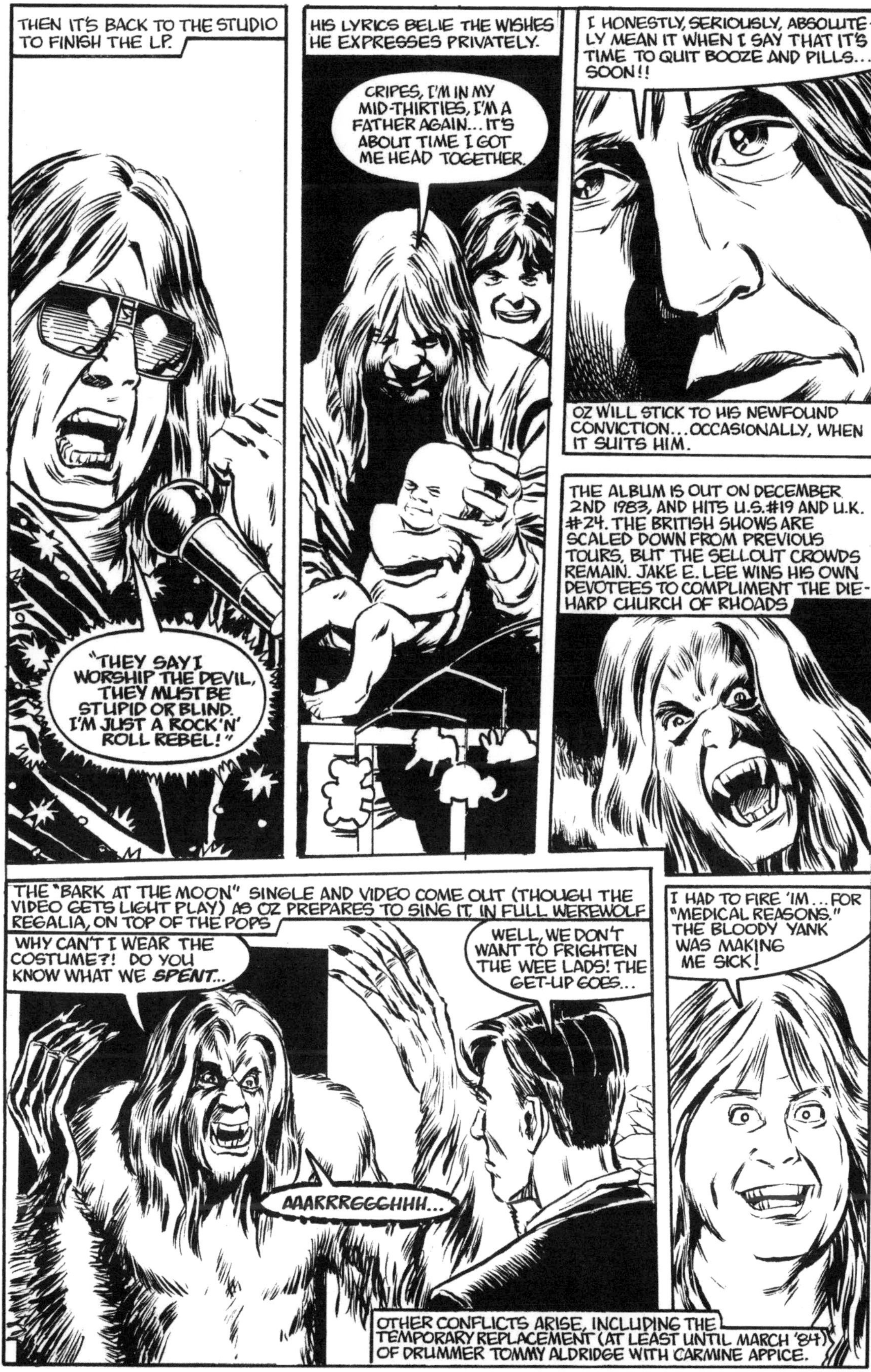

THEN IT'S BACK TO THE STUDIO TO FINISH THE LP.
"THEY SAY I WORSHIP THE DEVIL, THEY MUST BE STUPID OR BLIND. I'M JUST A ROCK 'N' ROLL REBEL!"
HIS LYRICS BELIE THE WISHES HE EXPRESSES PRIVATELY.
CRIPES, I'M IN MY MID-THIRTIES, I'M A FATHER AGAIN... IT'S ABOUT TIME I GOT ME HEAD TOGETHER.
I HONESTLY, SERIOUSLY, ABSOLUTELY MEAN IT WHEN I SAY THAT IT'S TIME TO QUIT BOOZE AND PILLS... SOON!!
OZ WILL STICK TO HIS NEWFOUND CONVICTION... OCCASIONALLY, WHEN IT SUITS HIM.
THE ALBUM IS OUT ON DECEMBER 2ND 1983, AND HITS U.S. #19 AND U.K. #24. THE BRITISH SHOWS ARE SCALED DOWN FROM PREVIOUS TOURS, BUT THE SELLOUT CROWDS REMAIN. JAKE E. LEE WINS HIS OWN DEVOTEES TO COMPLIMENT THE DIE-HARD CHURCH OF RHOADS
THE "BARK AT THE MOON" SINGLE AND VIDEO COME OUT (THOUGH THE VIDEO GETS LIGHT PLAY) AS OZ PREPARES TO SING IT, IN FULL WEREWOLF REGALIA, ON TOP OF THE POPS
WHY CAN'T I WEAR THE COSTUME?! DO YOU KNOW WHAT WE *SPENT*...
WELL, WE DON'T WANT TO FRIGHTEN THE WEE LADS! THE GET-UP GOES...
AAARRRGGGHHH...
I HAD TO FIRE 'IM... FOR "MEDICAL REASONS." THE BLOODY YANK WAS MAKING ME SICK!
OTHER CONFLICTS ARISE, INCLUDING THE TEMPORARY REPLACEMENT (AT LEAST UNTIL MARCH '84) OF DRUMMER TOMMY ALDRIDGE WITH CARMINE APPICE.

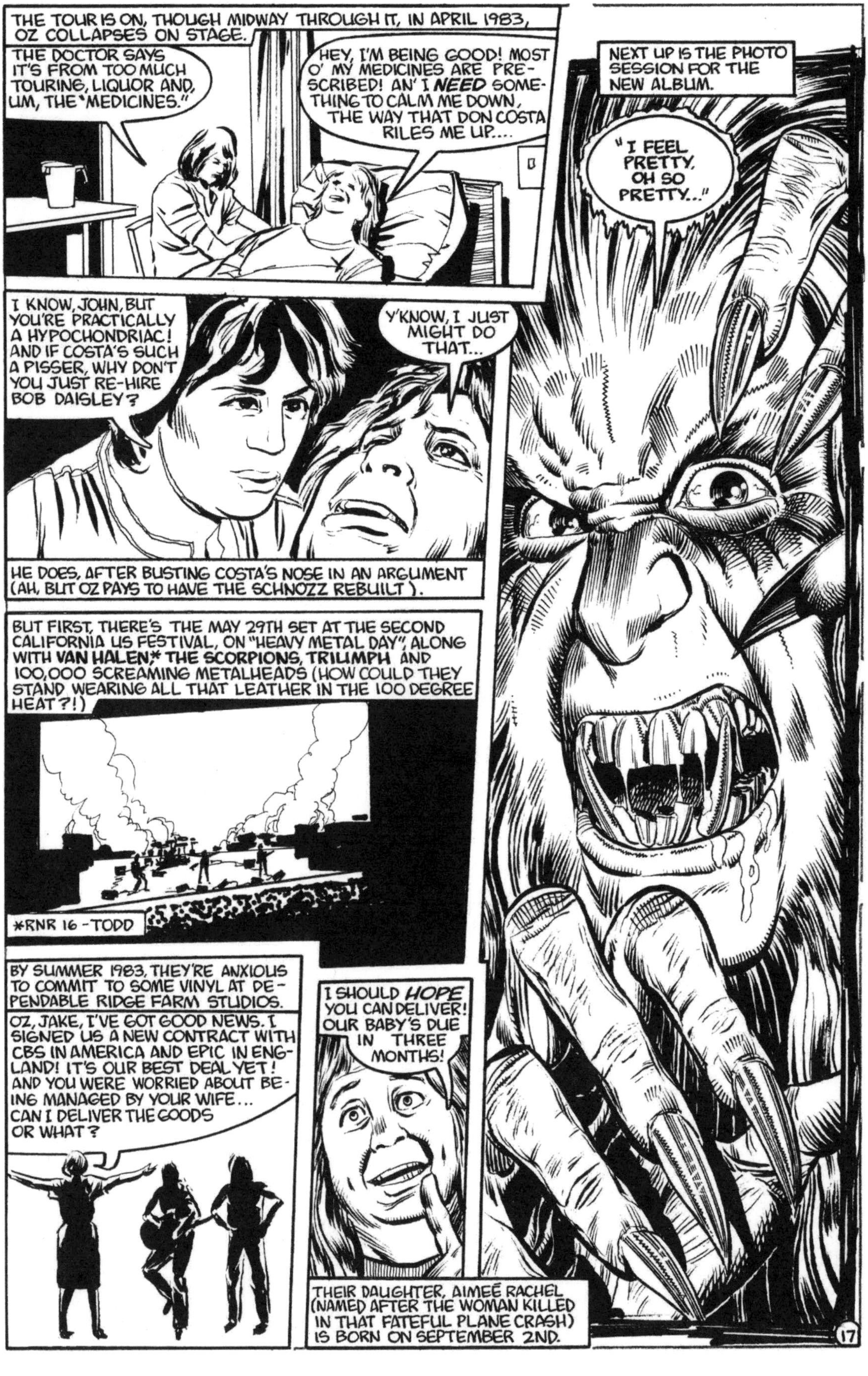
THE TOUR IS ON, THOUGH MIDWAY THROUGH IT, IN APRIL 1983, OZ COLLAPSES ON STAGE.
THE DOCTOR SAYS IT'S FROM TOO MUCH TOURING, LIQUOR AND, UM, THE "MEDICINES."
HEY, I'M BEING GOOD! MOST O' MY MEDICINES ARE PRE-SCRIBED! AN' I NEED SOME-THING TO CALM ME DOWN, THE WAY THAT DON COSTA RILES ME UP....
I KNOW, JOHN, BUT YOU'RE PRACTICALLY A HYPOCHONDRIAC! AND IF COSTA'S SUCH A PISSER, WHY DON'T YOU JUST RE-HIRE BOB DAISLEY?
Y'KNOW, I JUST MIGHT DO THAT...
HE DOES, AFTER BUSTING COSTA'S NOSE IN AN ARGUMENT (AH, BUT OZ PAYS TO HAVE THE SCHNOZZ REBUILT).
BUT FIRST, THERE'S THE MAY 29TH SET AT THE SECOND CALIFORNIA US FESTIVAL, ON "HEAVY METAL DAY", ALONG WITH VAN HALEN,* THE SCORPIONS, TRIUMPH AND 100,000 SCREAMING METALHEADS (HOW COULD THEY STAND WEARING ALL THAT LEATHER IN THE 100 DEGREE HEAT?!)
*RNR 16 - TODD
BY SUMMER 1983, THEY'RE ANXIOUS TO COMMIT TO SOME VINYL AT DE-PENDABLE RIDGE FARM STUDIOS.
OZ, JAKE, I'VE GOT GOOD NEWS. I SIGNED US A NEW CONTRACT WITH CBS IN AMERICA AND EPIC IN ENG-LAND! IT'S OUR BEST DEAL YET! AND YOU WERE WORRIED ABOUT BE-ING MANAGED BY YOUR WIFE... CAN I DELIVER THE GOODS OR WHAT?
I SHOULD HOPE YOU CAN DELIVER! OUR BABY'S DUE IN THREE MONTHS!
THEIR DAUGHTER, AIMEÉ RACHEL (NAMED AFTER THE WOMAN KILLED IN THAT FATEFUL PLANE CRASH) IS BORN ON SEPTEMBER 2ND.
NEXT UP IS THE PHOTO SESSION FOR THE NEW ALBUM.
"I FEEL PRETTY, OH SO PRETTY..."

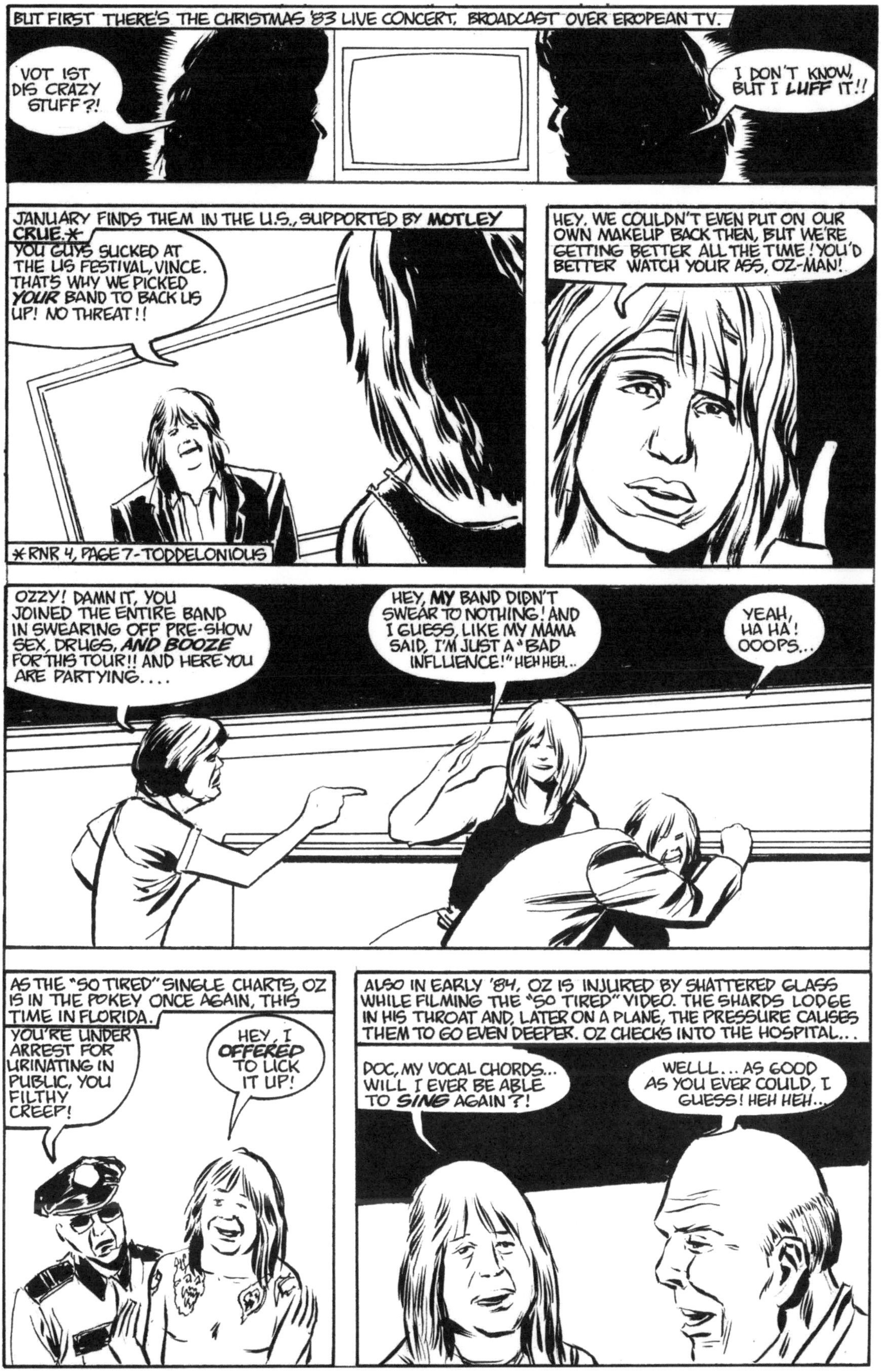
BUT FIRST THERE'S THE CHRISTMAS '83 LIVE CONCERT, BROADCAST OVER EROPEAN TV.
VOT IST DIS CRAZY STUFF?!
I DON'T KNOW, BUT I LUFF IT!!
JANUARY FINDS THEM IN THE U.S., SUPPORTED BY MOTLEY CRUE.*
YOU GUYS SUCKED AT THE US FESTIVAL, VINCE. THAT'S WHY WE PICKED YOUR BAND TO BACK US UP! NO THREAT!!
*RNR 4, PAGE 7-TODDELONIOUS
HEY, WE COULDN'T EVEN PUT ON OUR OWN MAKEUP BACK THEN, BUT WE'RE GETTING BETTER ALL THE TIME! YOU'D BETTER WATCH YOUR ASS, OZ-MAN!
OZZY! DAMN IT, YOU JOINED THE ENTIRE BAND IN SWEARING OFF PRE-SHOW SEX, DRUGS, AND BOOZE FOR THIS TOUR!! AND HERE YOU ARE PARTYING....
HEY, MY BAND DIDN'T SWEAR TO NOTHING! AND I GUESS, LIKE MY MAMA SAID, I'M JUST A "BAD INFLUENCE!" HEH HEH...
YEAH, HA HA! OOOPS...
AS THE "SO TIRED" SINGLE CHARTS, OZ IS IN THE POKEY ONCE AGAIN, THIS TIME IN FLORIDA.
YOU'RE UNDER ARREST FOR URINATING IN PUBLIC, YOU FILTHY CREEP!
HEY, I OFFERED TO LICK IT UP!
ALSO IN EARLY '84, OZ IS INJURED BY SHATTERED GLASS WHILE FILMING THE "SO TIRED" VIDEO. THE SHARDS LODGE IN HIS THROAT AND, LATER ON A PLANE, THE PRESSURE CAUSES THEM TO GO EVEN DEEPER. OZ CHECKS INTO THE HOSPITAL...
DOC, MY VOCAL CHORDS... WILL I EVER BE ABLE TO SING AGAIN?!
WELLL... AS GOOD AS YOU EVER COULD, I GUESS! HEH HEH...

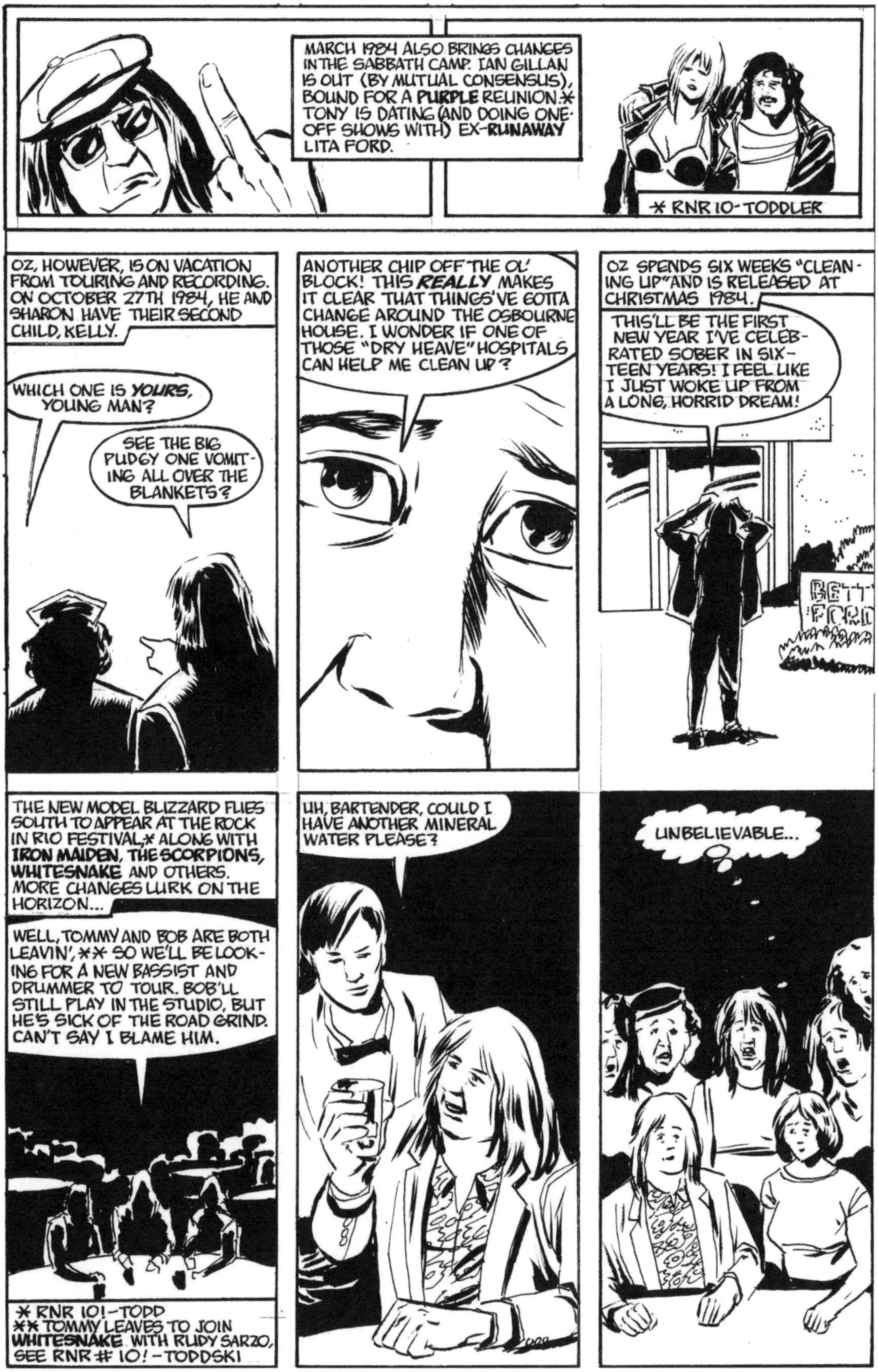
MARCH 1984 ALSO BRINGS CHANGES IN THE SABBATH CAMP. IAN GILLAN IS OUT (BY MUTUAL CONSENSUS), BOUND FOR A PURPLE REUNION.* TONY IS DATING (AND DOING ONE-OFF SHOWS WITH) EX-RUNAWAY LITA FORD.
* RNR 10-TODDLER
OZ, HOWEVER, IS ON VACATION FROM TOURING AND RECORDING. ON OCTOBER 27TH 1984, HE AND SHARON HAVE THEIR SECOND CHILD, KELLY.
WHICH ONE IS YOURS, YOUNG MAN?
SEE THE BIG PUDGY ONE VOMITING ALL OVER THE BLANKETS?
ANOTHER CHIP OFF THE OL' BLOCK! THIS REALLY MAKES IT CLEAR THAT THINGS'VE GOTTA CHANGE AROUND THE OSBOURNE HOUSE. I WONDER IF ONE OF THOSE "DRY HEAVE" HOSPITALS CAN HELP ME CLEAN UP?
OZ SPENDS SIX WEEKS "CLEANING UP" AND IS RELEASED AT CHRISTMAS 1984.
THIS'LL BE THE FIRST NEW YEAR I'VE CELEBRATED SOBER IN SIXTEEN YEARS! I FEEL LIKE I JUST WOKE UP FROM A LONG, HORRID DREAM!
THE NEW MODEL BLIZZARD FLIES SOUTH TO APPEAR AT THE ROCK IN RIO FESTIVAL,* ALONG WITH IRON MAIDEN, THE SCORPIONS, WHITESNAKE AND OTHERS. MORE CHANGES LURK ON THE HORIZON...
WELL, TOMMY AND BOB ARE BOTH LEAVIN',** SO WE'LL BE LOOKING FOR A NEW BASSIST AND DRUMMER TO TOUR. BOB'LL STILL PLAY IN THE STUDIO, BUT HE'S SICK OF THE ROAD GRIND. CAN'T SAY I BLAME HIM.
* RNR 10!-TODD
** TOMMY LEAVES TO JOIN WHITESNAKE WITH RUDY SARZO, SEE RNR # 10!-TODDSKI
UH, BARTENDER, COULD I HAVE ANOTHER MINERAL WATER PLEASE?
UNBELIEVABLE...

OZ, WE'VE GOT TO GET ON WITH HIRING SOME NEW GUNS.

YEAH, I KNOW, JAKE. I'VE BEEN PUTTING IT OFF. I'M NOT LOOKIN' FORWARD TO ANOTHER PARADE OF LEECHES.

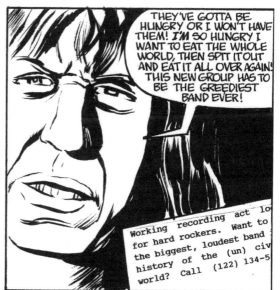

THEY'VE GOTTA BE HUNGRY OR I WON'T HAVE THEM! *I'M* SO HUNGRY I WANT TO EAT THE WHOLE WORLD, THEN SPIT IT OUT AND EAT IT ALL OVER AGAIN! THIS NEW GROUP HAS TO BE THE GREEDIEST BAND EVER!

Working recording act lo for hard rockers. Want to the biggest, loudest band history of the (un) civ world? Call (122) 134-5

THE NEW BOYS ARE DRUMMER RANDY CASTILLO (**LITA FORD BAND**) AND SESSION BASSIST PHILIP SOUSSAN.

THE GROUP BEGINS RECORDING "THE ULTIMATE SIN" IN SPRING. OZ HAS A LITTLE TROUBLE STAYING... FOCUSED.

MAN, OZ, YOU *SWORE*! WE WROTE SOME GREAT, HARD-ROCKING SONGS TOGETHER. LET'S PLAY THEM TOGETHER!! DON'T FALL OFF THE WAGON AND WIG OUT ON US...

I KNOW, I KNOW. YOU DIDN'T KNOW ME TEN YEARS AGO. I'M MR. ROGERS COMPARED TO THEN!

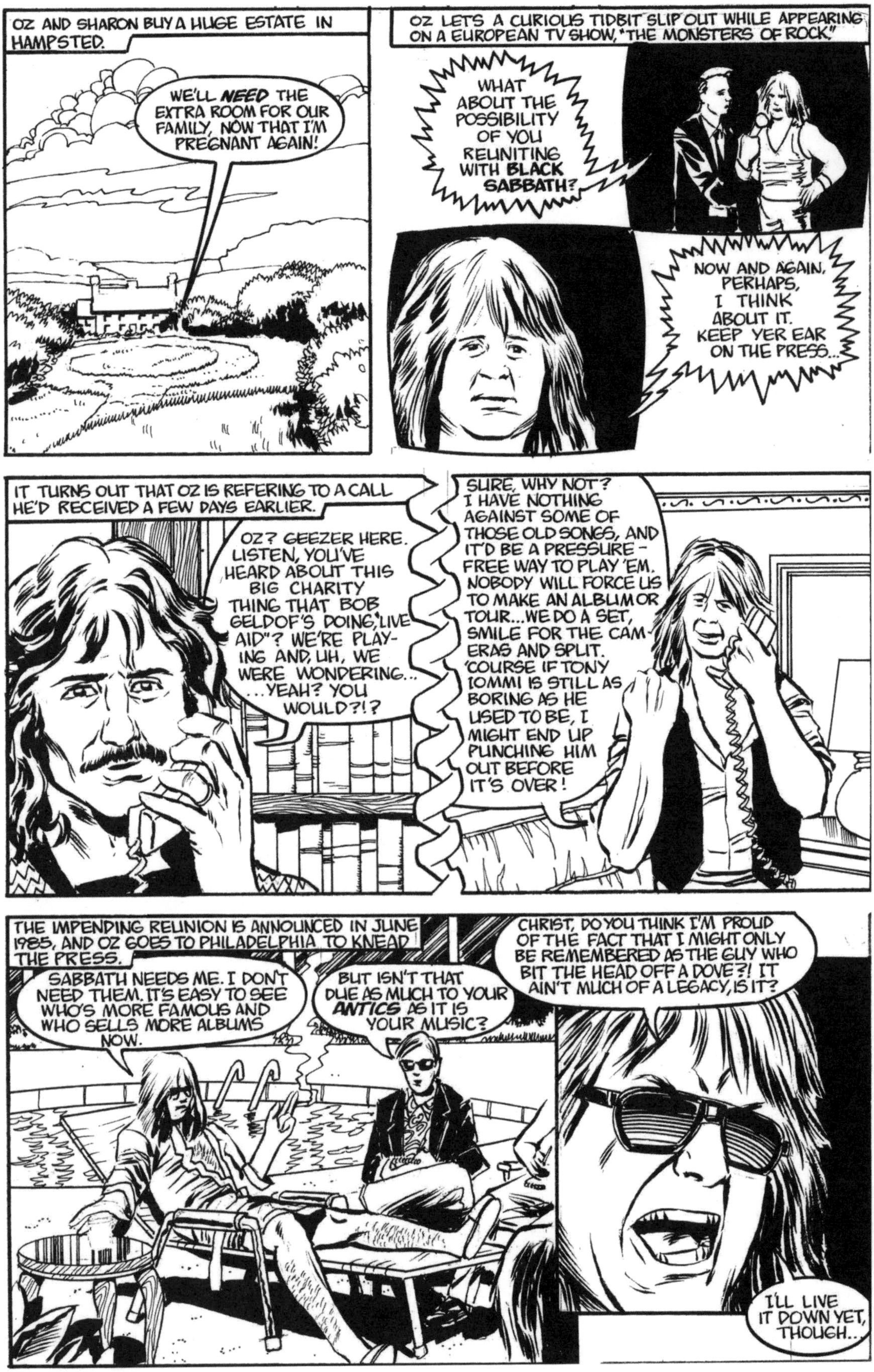
OZ AND SHARON BUY A HUGE ESTATE IN HAMPSTED.
WE'LL NEED THE EXTRA ROOM FOR OUR FAMILY, NOW THAT I'M PREGNANT AGAIN!
OZ LETS A CURIOUS TIDBIT SLIP OUT WHILE APPEARING ON A EUROPEAN TV SHOW, "THE MONSTERS OF ROCK."
WHAT ABOUT THE POSSIBILITY OF YOU REUNITING WITH BLACK SABBATH?
NOW AND AGAIN, PERHAPS, I THINK ABOUT IT. KEEP YER EAR ON THE PRESS...
IT TURNS OUT THAT OZ IS REFERING TO A CALL HE'D RECEIVED A FEW DAYS EARLIER.
OZ? GEEZER HERE. LISTEN, YOU'VE HEARD ABOUT THIS BIG CHARITY THING THAT BOB GELDOF'S DOING, "LIVE AID"? WE'RE PLAYING AND, UH, WE WERE WONDERING... ...YEAH? YOU WOULD?!?
SURE, WHY NOT? I HAVE NOTHING AGAINST SOME OF THOSE OLD SONGS, AND IT'D BE A PRESSURE-FREE WAY TO PLAY 'EM. NOBODY WILL FORCE US TO MAKE AN ALBUM OR TOUR...WE DO A SET, SMILE FOR THE CAMERAS AND SPLIT. 'COURSE IF TONY IOMMI IS STILL AS BORING AS HE USED TO BE, I MIGHT END UP PUNCHING HIM OUT BEFORE IT'S OVER!
THE IMPENDING REUNION IS ANNOUNCED IN JUNE 1985, AND OZ GOES TO PHILADELPHIA TO KNEAD THE PRESS.
SABBATH NEEDS ME. I DON'T NEED THEM. IT'S EASY TO SEE WHO'S MORE FAMOUS AND WHO SELLS MORE ALBUMS NOW.
BUT ISN'T THAT DUE AS MUCH TO YOUR ANTICS AS IT IS YOUR MUSIC?
CHRIST, DO YOU THINK I'M PROUD OF THE FACT THAT I MIGHT ONLY BE REMEMBERED AS THE GUY WHO BIT THE HEAD OFF A DOVE?! IT AIN'T MUCH OF A LEGACY, IS IT?
I'LL LIVE IT DOWN YET, THOUGH...

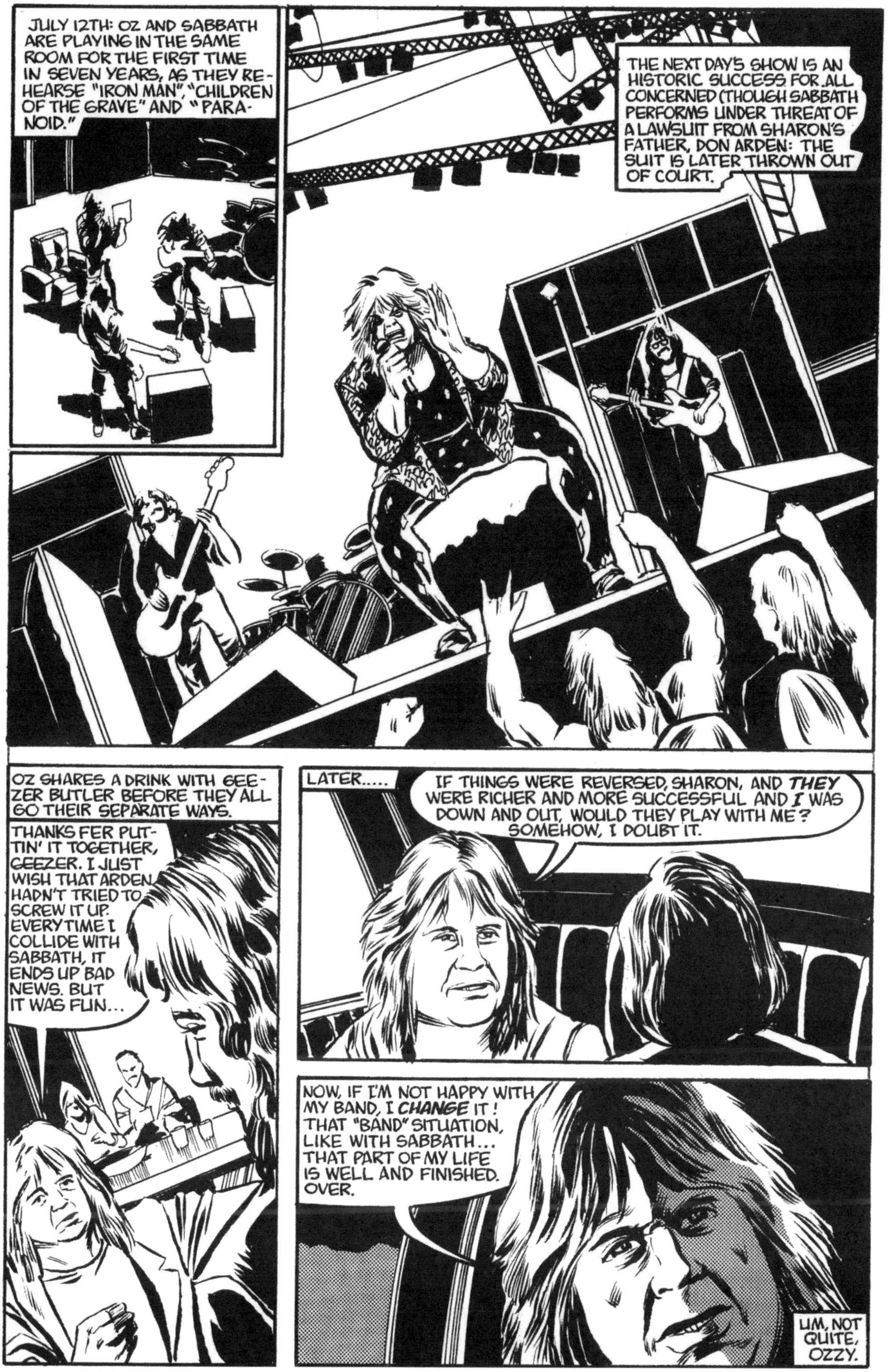
JULY 12TH: OZ AND SABBATH ARE PLAYING IN THE SAME ROOM FOR THE FIRST TIME IN SEVEN YEARS, AS THEY RE-HEARSE "IRON MAN", "CHILDREN OF THE GRAVE" AND "PARA-NOID."
THE NEXT DAY'S SHOW IS AN HISTORIC SUCCESS FOR ALL CONCERNED (THOUGH SABBATH PERFORMS UNDER THREAT OF A LAWSUIT FROM SHARON'S FATHER, DON ARDEN: THE SUIT IS LATER THROWN OUT OF COURT.
OZ SHARES A DRINK WITH GEE-ZER BUTLER BEFORE THEY ALL GO THEIR SEPARATE WAYS.
THANKS FER PUT-TIN' IT TOGETHER, GEEZER. I JUST WISH THAT ARDEN HADN'T TRIED TO SCREW IT UP. EVERY TIME I COLLIDE WITH SABBATH, IT ENDS UP BAD NEWS. BUT IT WAS FUN...
LATER.....
IF THINGS WERE REVERSED, SHARON, AND THEY WERE RICHER AND MORE SUCCESSFUL AND I WAS DOWN AND OUT, WOULD THEY PLAY WITH ME? SOMEHOW, I DOUBT IT.
NOW, IF I'M NOT HAPPY WITH MY BAND, I CHANGE IT! THAT "BAND" SITUATION, LIKE WITH SABBATH... THAT PART OF MY LIFE IS WELL AND FINISHED. OVER.
UM, NOT QUITE, OZZY.

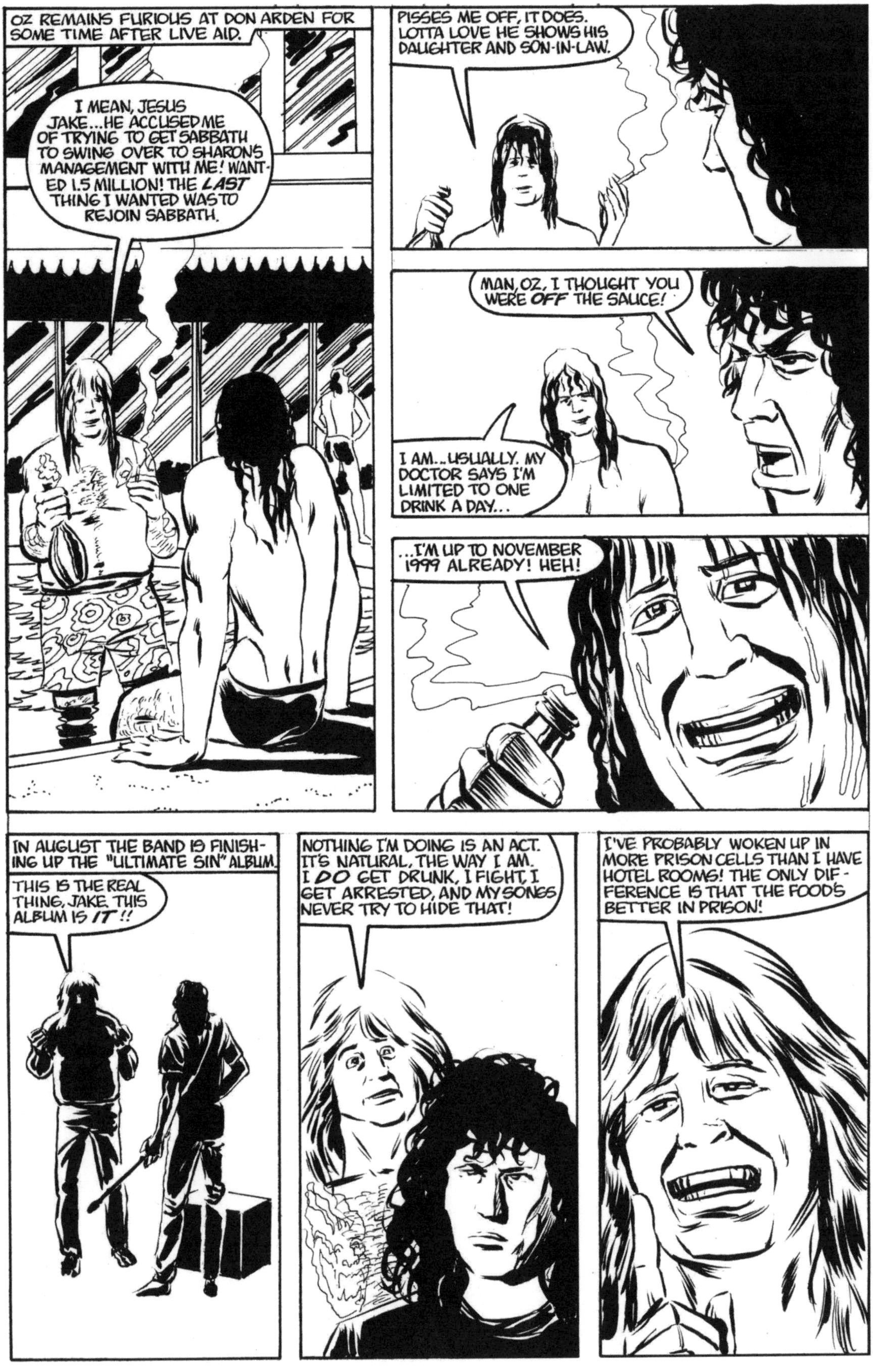
OZ REMAINS FURIOUS AT DON ARDEN FOR SOME TIME AFTER LIVE AID.
I MEAN, JESUS JAKE...HE ACCUSED ME OF TRYING TO GET SABBATH TO SWING OVER TO SHARON'S MANAGEMENT WITH ME! WANTED 1.5 MILLION! THE LAST THING I WANTED WAS TO REJOIN SABBATH.
PISSES ME OFF, IT DOES. LOTTA LOVE HE SHOWS HIS DAUGHTER AND SON-IN-LAW.
MAN, OZ, I THOUGHT YOU WERE OFF THE SAUCE!
I AM...USUALLY. MY DOCTOR SAYS I'M LIMITED TO ONE DRINK A DAY...
...I'M UP TO NOVEMBER 1999 ALREADY! HEH!
IN AUGUST THE BAND IS FINISHING UP THE "ULTIMATE SIN" ALBUM.
THIS IS THE REAL THING, JAKE. THIS ALBUM IS IT!!
NOTHING I'M DOING IS AN ACT. IT'S NATURAL, THE WAY I AM. I DO GET DRUNK, I FIGHT, I GET ARRESTED, AND MY SONGS NEVER TRY TO HIDE THAT!
I'VE PROBABLY WOKEN UP IN MORE PRISON CELLS THAN I HAVE HOTEL ROOMS! THE ONLY DIFFERENCE IS THAT THE FOOD'S BETTER IN PRISON!

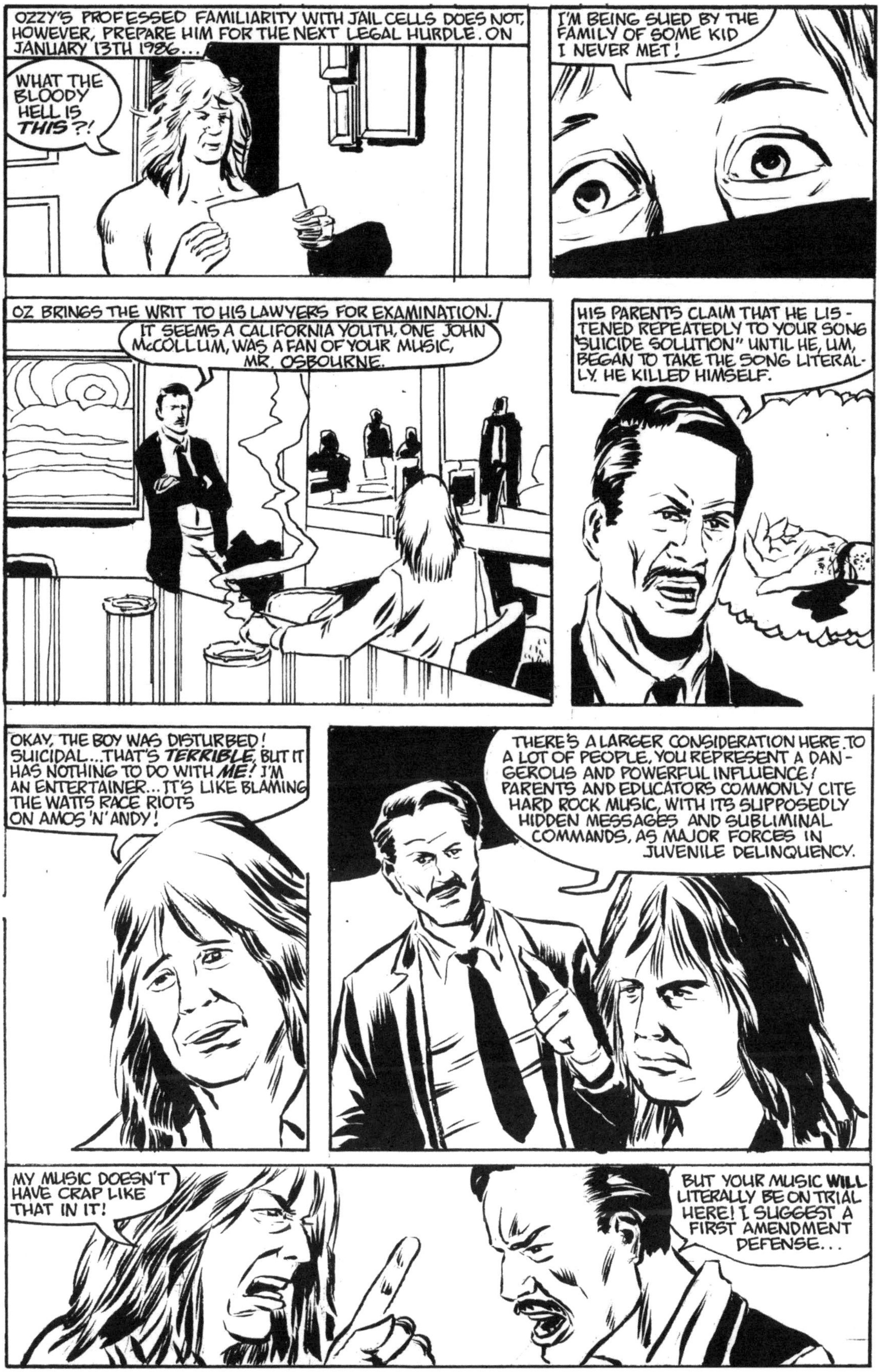
OZZY'S PROFESSED FAMILIARITY WITH JAIL CELLS DOES NOT, HOWEVER, PREPARE HIM FOR THE NEXT LEGAL HURDLE. ON JANUARY 13TH 1986...
WHAT THE BLOODY HELL IS THIS?!
I'M BEING SUED BY THE FAMILY OF SOME KID I NEVER MET!
OZ BRINGS THE WRIT TO HIS LAWYERS FOR EXAMINATION.
IT SEEMS A CALIFORNIA YOUTH, ONE JOHN McCOLLUM, WAS A FAN OF YOUR MUSIC, MR. OSBOURNE.
HIS PARENTS CLAIM THAT HE LIS-TENED REPEATEDLY TO YOUR SONG "SUICIDE SOLUTION" UNTIL HE, UM, BEGAN TO TAKE THE SONG LITERAL-LY. HE KILLED HIMSELF.
OKAY, THE BOY WAS DISTURBED! SUICIDAL...THAT'S TERRIBLE, BUT IT HAS NOTHING TO DO WITH ME! I'M AN ENTERTAINER...IT'S LIKE BLAMING THE WATTS RACE RIOTS ON AMOS 'N' ANDY!
THERE'S A LARGER CONSIDERATION HERE. TO A LOT OF PEOPLE, YOU REPRESENT A DAN-GEROUS AND POWERFUL INFLUENCE! PARENTS AND EDUCATORS COMMONLY CITE HARD ROCK MUSIC, WITH ITS SUPPOSEDLY HIDDEN MESSAGES AND SUBLIMINAL COMMANDS, AS MAJOR FORCES IN JUVENILE DELINQUENCY.
MY MUSIC DOESN'T HAVE CRAP LIKE THAT IN IT!
BUT YOUR MUSIC WILL LITERALLY BE ON TRIAL HERE! I SUGGEST A FIRST AMENDMENT DEFENSE...

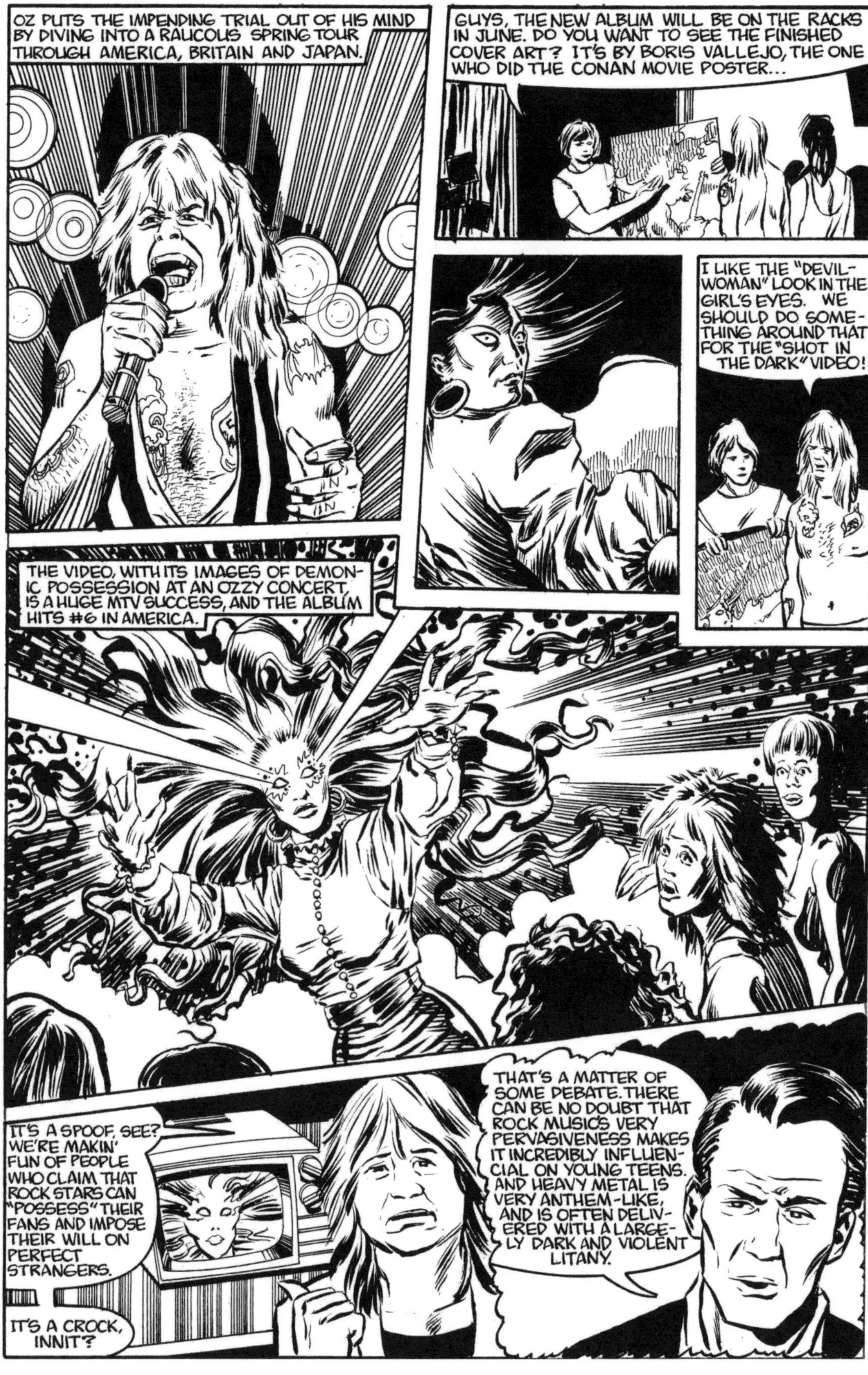
OZ PUTS THE IMPENDING TRIAL OUT OF HIS MIND BY DIVING INTO A RAUCOUS SPRING TOUR THROUGH AMERICA, BRITAIN AND JAPAN.
GUYS, THE NEW ALBUM WILL BE ON THE RACKS IN JUNE. DO YOU WANT TO SEE THE FINISHED COVER ART? IT'S BY BORIS VALLEJO, THE ONE WHO DID THE CONAN MOVIE POSTER...
I LIKE THE "DEVIL-WOMAN" LOOK IN THE GIRL'S EYES. WE SHOULD DO SOMETHING AROUND THAT FOR THE "SHOT IN THE DARK" VIDEO!
THE VIDEO, WITH ITS IMAGES OF DEMONIC POSSESSION AT AN OZZY CONCERT, IS A HUGE MTV SUCCESS, AND THE ALBUM HITS #6 IN AMERICA.
IT'S A SPOOF, SEE? WE'RE MAKIN' FUN OF PEOPLE WHO CLAIM THAT ROCK STARS CAN "POSSESS" THEIR FANS AND IMPOSE THEIR WILL ON PERFECT STRANGERS.
IT'S A CROCK, INNIT?
THAT'S A MATTER OF SOME DEBATE. THERE CAN BE NO DOUBT THAT ROCK MUSIC'S VERY PERVASIVENESS MAKES IT INCREDIBLY INFLUENCIAL ON YOUNG TEENS. AND HEAVY METAL IS VERY ANTHEM-LIKE, AND IS OFTEN DELIVERED WITH A LARGELY DARK AND VIOLENT LITANY.

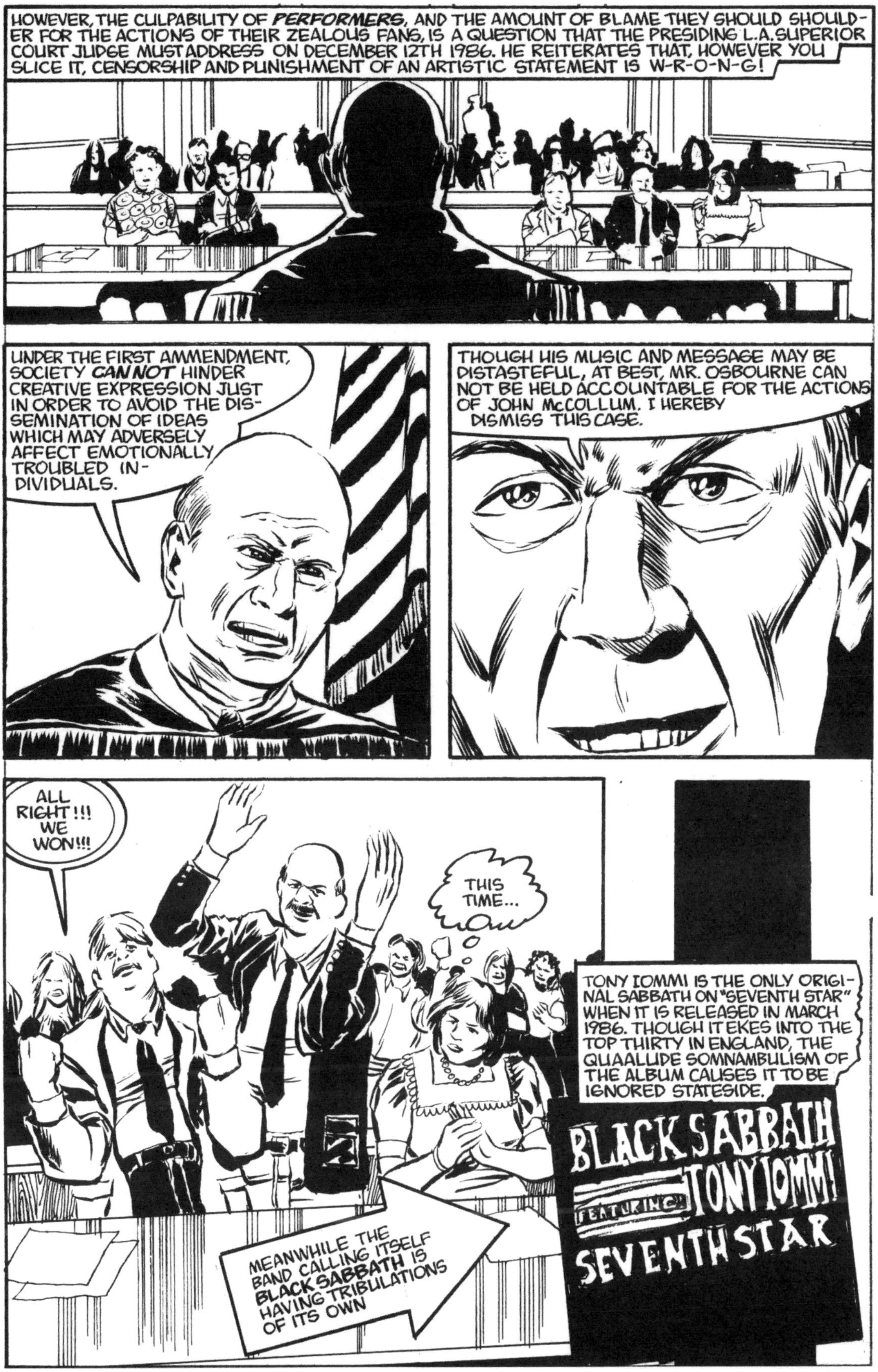
HOWEVER, THE CULPABILITY OF PERFORMERS, AND THE AMOUNT OF BLAME THEY SHOULD SHOULDER FOR THE ACTIONS OF THEIR ZEALOUS FANS, IS A QUESTION THAT THE PRESIDING L.A. SUPERIOR COURT JUDGE MUST ADDRESS ON DECEMBER 12TH 1986. HE REITERATES THAT, HOWEVER YOU SLICE IT, CENSORSHIP AND PUNISHMENT OF AN ARTISTIC STATEMENT IS W-R-O-N-G!
UNDER THE FIRST AMMENDMENT, SOCIETY CAN NOT HINDER CREATIVE EXPRESSION JUST IN ORDER TO AVOID THE DISSEMINATION OF IDEAS WHICH MAY ADVERSELY AFFECT EMOTIONALLY TROUBLED INDIVIDUALS.
THOUGH HIS MUSIC AND MESSAGE MAY BE DISTASTEFUL, AT BEST, MR. OSBOURNE CAN NOT BE HELD ACCOUNTABLE FOR THE ACTIONS OF JOHN McCOLLUM. I HEREBY DISMISS THIS CASE.
ALL RIGHT!!! WE WON!!!
THIS TIME...
TONY IOMMI IS THE ONLY ORIGINAL SABBATH ON "SEVENTH STAR" WHEN IT IS RELEASED IN MARCH 1986. THOUGH IT EKES INTO THE TOP THIRTY IN ENGLAND, THE QUAALUDE SOMNAMBULISM OF THE ALBUM CAUSES IT TO BE IGNORED STATESIDE.
BLACK SABBATH
FEATURING TONY IOMMI
SEVENTH STAR
MEANWHILE THE BAND CALLING ITSELF BLACK SABBATH IS HAVING TRIBULATIONS OF ITS OWN

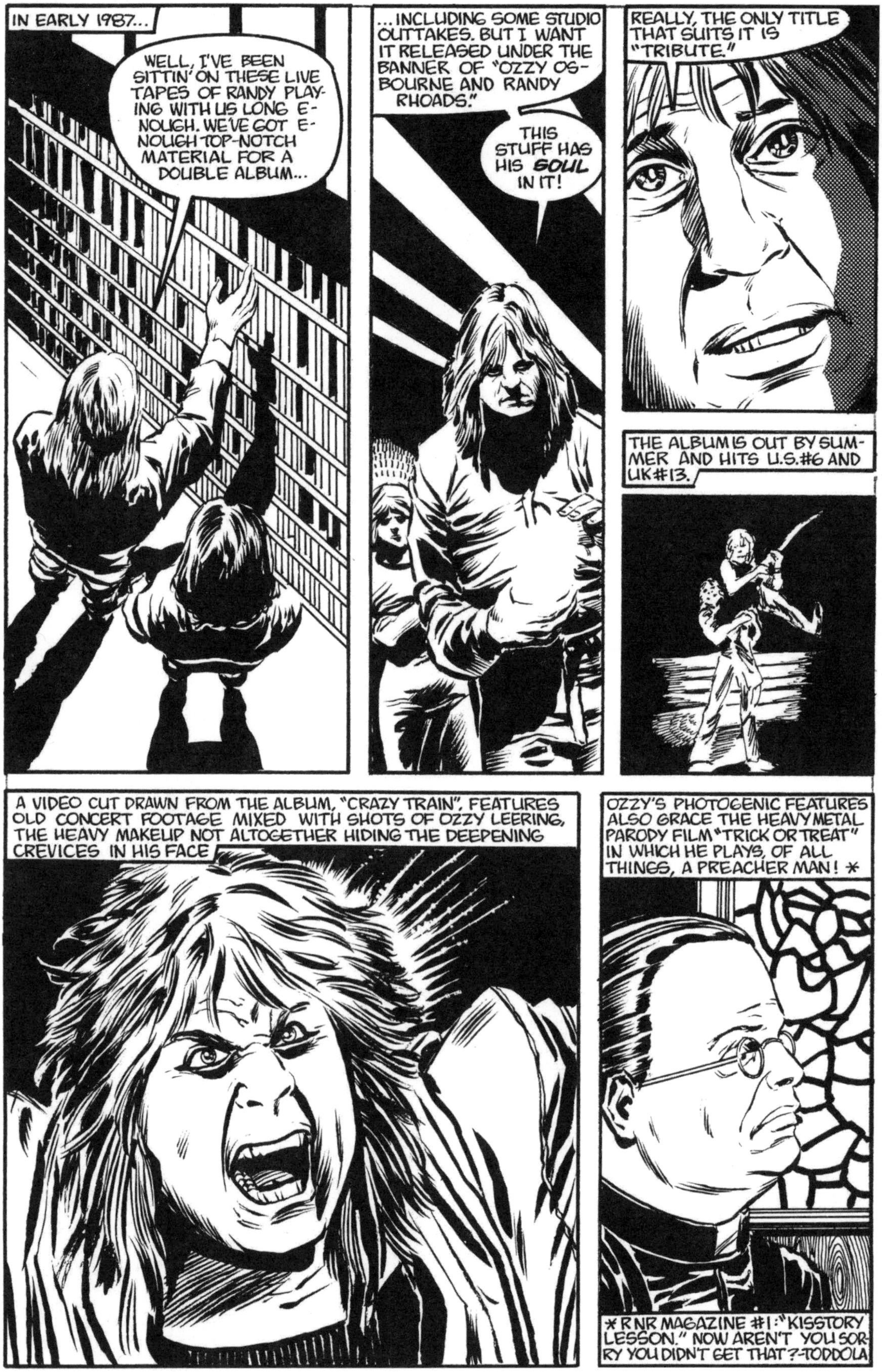
IN EARLY 1987...
WELL, I'VE BEEN SITTIN' ON THESE LIVE TAPES OF RANDY PLAYING WITH US LONG ENOUGH. WE'VE GOT ENOUGH TOP-NOTCH MATERIAL FOR A DOUBLE ALBUM...
...INCLUDING SOME STUDIO OUTTAKES. BUT I WANT IT RELEASED UNDER THE BANNER OF "OZZY OSBOURNE AND RANDY RHOADS."
THIS STUFF HAS HIS SOUL IN IT!
REALLY, THE ONLY TITLE THAT SUITS IT IS "TRIBUTE."
THE ALBUM IS OUT BY SUMMER AND HITS U.S.#6 AND UK#13.
A VIDEO CUT DRAWN FROM THE ALBUM, "CRAZY TRAIN", FEATURES OLD CONCERT FOOTAGE MIXED WITH SHOTS OF OZZY LEERING, THE HEAVY MAKEUP NOT ALTOGETHER HIDING THE DEEPENING CREVICES IN HIS FACE.
OZZY'S PHOTOGENIC FEATURES ALSO GRACE THE HEAVY METAL PARODY FILM "TRICK OR TREAT" IN WHICH HE PLAYS, OF ALL THINGS, A PREACHER MAN! *
* RNR MAGAZINE #1: "KISSTORY LESSON." NOW AREN'T YOU SORRY YOU DIDN'T GET THAT? -TODDOLA

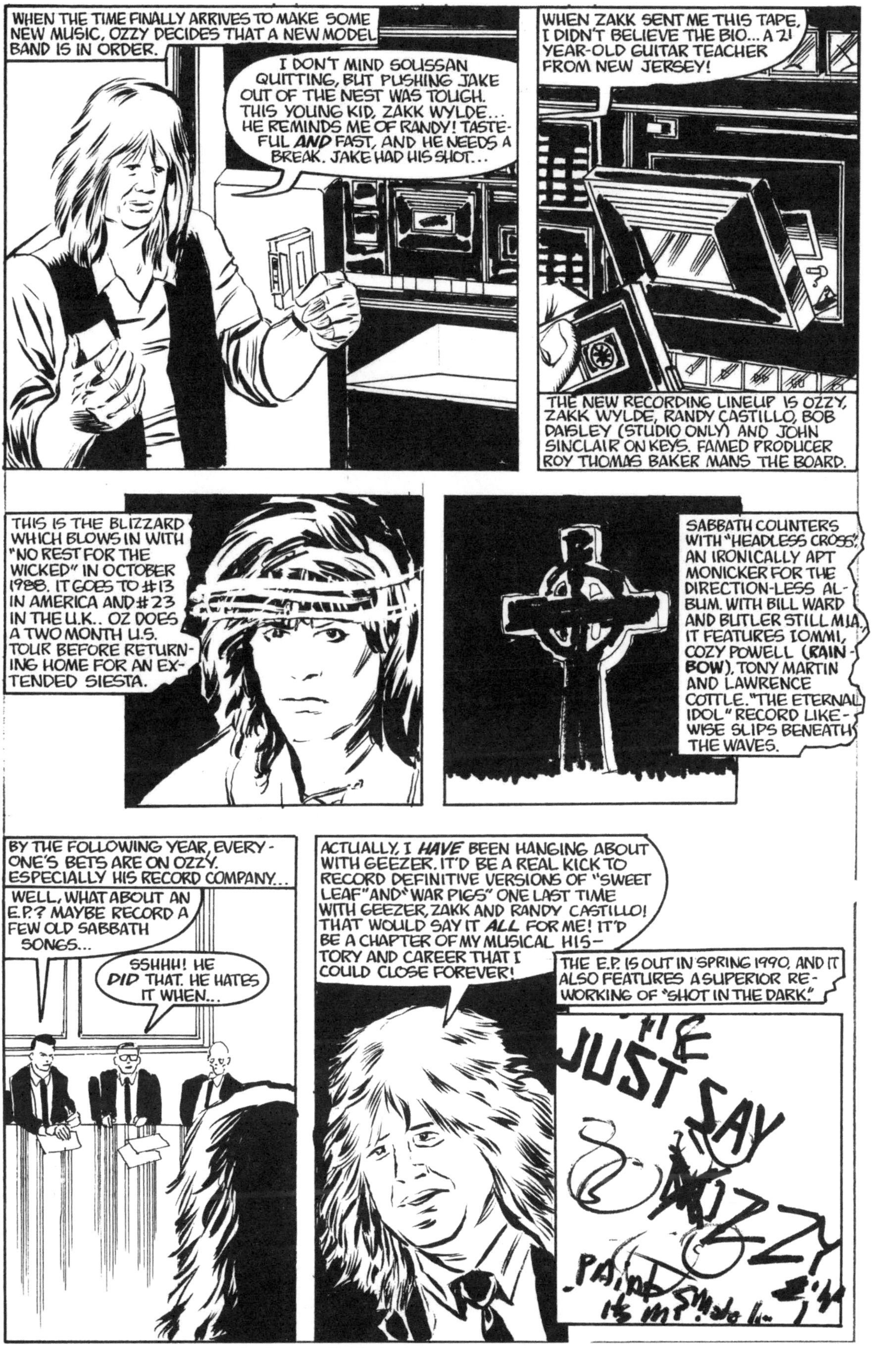
WHEN THE TIME FINALLY ARRIVES TO MAKE SOME NEW MUSIC, OZZY DECIDES THAT A NEW MODEL BAND IS IN ORDER.
I DON'T MIND SOUSSAN QUITTING, BUT PUSHING JAKE OUT OF THE NEST WAS TOUGH. THIS YOUNG KID, ZAKK WYLDE... HE REMINDS ME OF RANDY! TASTEFUL **AND** FAST, AND HE NEEDS A BREAK. JAKE HAD HIS SHOT...
WHEN ZAKK SENT ME THIS TAPE, I DIDN'T BELIEVE THE BIO... A 21 YEAR-OLD GUITAR TEACHER FROM NEW JERSEY!
THE NEW RECORDING LINEUP IS OZZY, ZAKK WYLDE, RANDY CASTILLO, BOB DAISLEY (STUDIO ONLY) AND JOHN SINCLAIR ON KEYS. FAMED PRODUCER ROY THOMAS BAKER MANS THE BOARD.
THIS IS THE BLIZZARD WHICH BLOWS IN WITH "NO REST FOR THE WICKED" IN OCTOBER 1988. IT GOES TO #13 IN AMERICA AND #23 IN THE U.K.. OZ DOES A TWO MONTH U.S. TOUR BEFORE RETURNING HOME FOR AN EXTENDED SIESTA.
SABBATH COUNTERS WITH "HEADLESS CROSS", AN IRONICALLY APT MONICKER FOR THE DIRECTION-LESS ALBUM. WITH BILL WARD AND BUTLER STILL MIA, IT FEATURES IOMMI, COZY POWELL (**RAINBOW**), TONY MARTIN AND LAWRENCE COTTLE. "THE ETERNAL IDOL" RECORD LIKEWISE SLIPS BENEATH THE WAVES.
BY THE FOLLOWING YEAR, EVERYONE'S BETS ARE ON OZZY. ESPECIALLY HIS RECORD COMPANY...
WELL, WHAT ABOUT AN E.P.? MAYBE RECORD A FEW OLD SABBATH SONGS...
SSHHH! HE **DID** THAT. HE HATES IT WHEN...
ACTUALLY, I **HAVE** BEEN HANGING ABOUT WITH GEEZER. IT'D BE A REAL KICK TO RECORD DEFINITIVE VERSIONS OF "SWEET LEAF" AND "WAR PIGS" ONE LAST TIME WITH GEEZER, ZAKK AND RANDY CASTILLO! THAT WOULD SAY IT **ALL** FOR ME! IT'D BE A CHAPTER OF MY MUSICAL HISTORY AND CAREER THAT I COULD CLOSE FOREVER!
THE E.P. IS OUT IN SPRING 1990, AND IT ALSO FEATURES A SUPERIOR REWORKING OF "SHOT IN THE DARK."
JUST SAY OZZY

BACK HOME ON THE FARM...

HOW'S THE E.P. SELLING?

FAIR, I GUESS, FOR A SHORTY. OUR HEAD'S ABOVE WATER.

I READ WHERE SABBATH HAS A NEW ONE COMING OUT AT THE END OF THE YEAR. I'LL BET OUR E.P. OUTSELLS THEIR ALBUM FIVE TO ONE!

A REMARKABLY ACCURATE PREDICTION

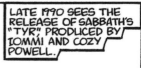

LATE 1990 SEES THE RELEASE OF SABBATH'S "TYR" PRODUCED BY IOMMI AND COZY POWELL.

IRONICALLY, THE NEW SABBATH SONGS AND LYRICS HARKEN BACK TO THE DARK MYTHOLOGY THAT DIO INTRODUCED TO THE BAND (SOMETHING TONY ONCE PROFESSED TO HATING) STAND-OUTS LIKE "SABBATH STONES" SHOW AT LEAST SOME OF THE OLD FIRE.

AND THAT'S THE WAY THINGS STAND AS 1991 GETS WELL UNDERWAY. PERHAPS THINGS WILL EVENT-UALLY TURN OUT LIKE THE ROGER WATERS/PINK FLOYD SPLIT; TWO TALENTED CONTINGENTS PROVID-ING TWICE THE AMOUNT OF GOOD MUSIC THAT THEY HAD WHILE HANDCUFFED TOGETHER. OR PERHAPS BOTH SABBATH AND OZZY ARE TOO FAR PAST THEIR CREATIVE PRIMES TO COME BACK FROM THEIR RESPECTIVE GRAVES. WHATEVER THE FUTURE BRINGS, NOBODY CAN EVER DENY THE BRASS AUDACITY, SOMBER FLAVOR AND IRON INFLUENCE THAT THESE SINGULAR TALENTS HAVE BROUGHT TO ROCK AND ROLL! OZZY OSBOURNE and BLACK SABBATH!

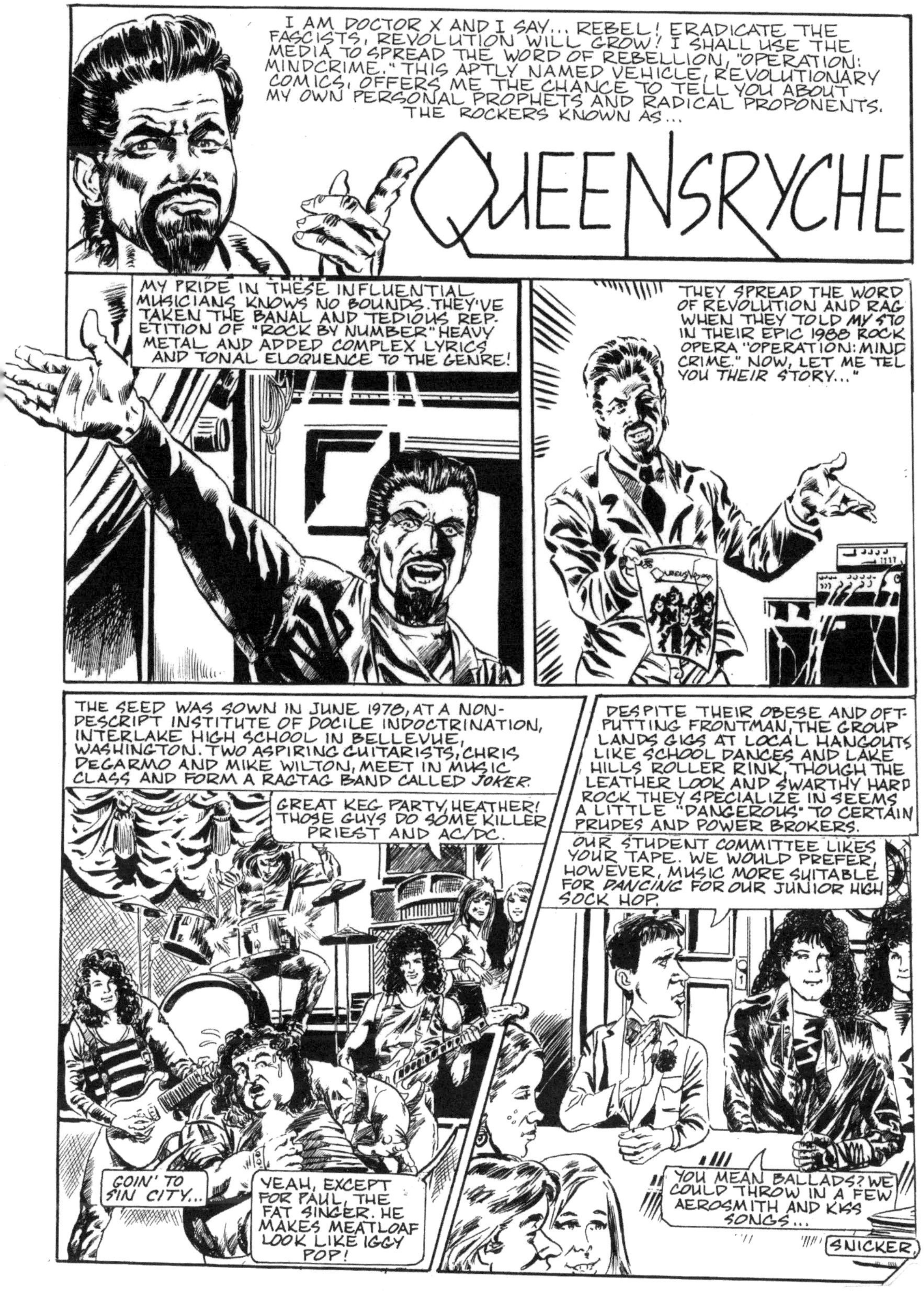
I AM DOCTOR X AND I SAY... REBEL! ERADICATE THE FASCISTS, REVOLUTION WILL GROW! I SHALL USE THE MEDIA TO SPREAD THE WORD OF REBELLION, "OPERATION: MINDCRIME." THIS APTLY NAMED VEHICLE, REVOLUTIONARY COMICS, OFFERS ME THE CHANCE TO TELL YOU ABOUT MY OWN PERSONAL PROPHETS AND RADICAL PROPONENTS. THE ROCKERS KNOWN AS...
QUEENSRYCHE
MY PRIDE IN THESE INFLUENTIAL MUSICIANS KNOWS NO BOUNDS. THEY'VE TAKEN THE BANAL AND TEDIOUS REPETITION OF "ROCK BY NUMBER" HEAVY METAL AND ADDED COMPLEX LYRICS AND TONAL ELOQUENCE TO THE GENRE!
THEY SPREAD THE WORD OF REVOLUTION AND RAG WHEN THEY TOLD MY STO IN THEIR EPIC 1988 ROCK OPERA "OPERATION: MIND CRIME." NOW, LET ME TEL YOU THEIR STORY..."
THE SEED WAS SOWN IN JUNE 1978, AT A NON-DESCRIPT INSTITUTE OF DOCILE INDOCTRINATION, INTERLAKE HIGH SCHOOL IN BELLEVUE, WASHINGTON. TWO ASPIRING GUITARISTS, CHRIS DEGARMO AND MIKE WILTON, MEET IN MUSIC CLASS AND FORM A RAGTAG BAND CALLED JOKER.
GREAT KEG PARTY, HEATHER! THOSE GUYS DO SOME KILLER PRIEST AND AC/DC.
GOIN' TO SIN CITY...
YEAH, EXCEPT FOR PAUL, THE FAT SINGER. HE MAKES MEATLOAF LOOK LIKE IGGY POP!
DESPITE THEIR OBESE AND OFT-PUTTING FRONTMAN, THE GROUP LANDS GIGS AT LOCAL HANGOUTS LIKE SCHOOL DANCES AND LAKE HILLS ROLLER RINK, THOUGH THE LEATHER LOOK AND SWARTHY HARD ROCK THEY SPECIALIZE IN SEEMS A LITTLE "DANGEROUS" TO CERTAIN PRUDES AND POWER BROKERS.
OUR STUDENT COMMITTEE LIKES YOUR TAPE. WE WOULD PREFER, HOWEVER, MUSIC MORE SUITABLE FOR DANCING FOR OUR JUNIOR HIGH SOCK HOP.
YOU MEAN BALLADS? WE COULD THROW IN A FEW AEROSMITH AND KISS SONGS...
SNICKER

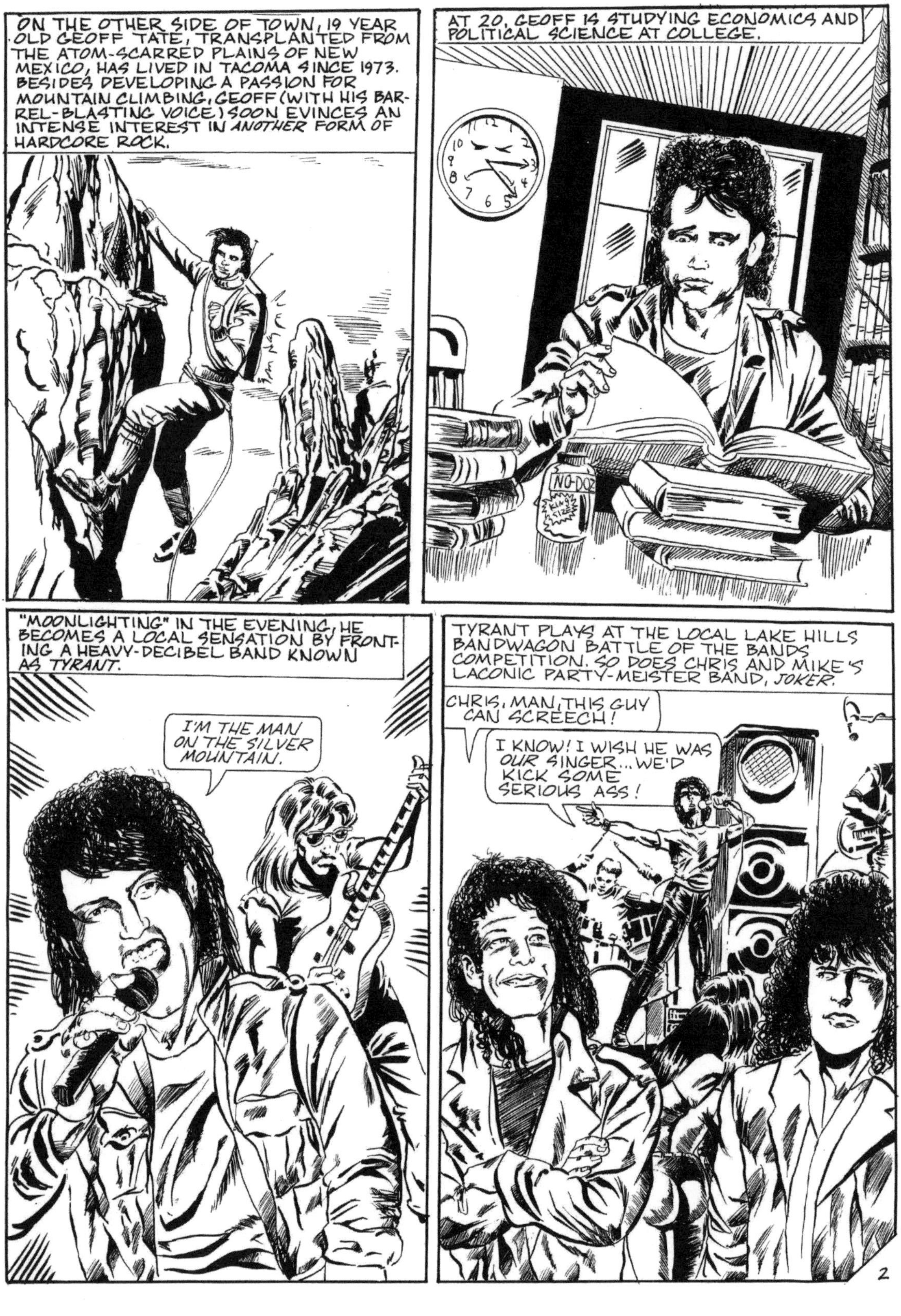
ON THE OTHER SIDE OF TOWN, 19 YEAR OLD GEOFF TATE, TRANSPLANTED FROM THE ATOM-SCARRED PLAINS OF NEW MEXICO, HAS LIVED IN TACOMA SINCE 1973. BESIDES DEVELOPING A PASSION FOR MOUNTAIN CLIMBING, GEOFF (WITH HIS BARREL-BLASTING VOICE) SOON EVINCES AN INTENSE INTEREST IN *ANOTHER* FORM OF HARDCORE ROCK.
AT 20, GEOFF IS STUDYING ECONOMICS AND POLITICAL SCIENCE AT COLLEGE.
NO-DOZ
KING SIZE
"MOONLIGHTING" IN THE EVENING, HE BECOMES A LOCAL SENSATION BY FRONTING A HEAVY-DECIBEL BAND KNOWN AS *TYRANT*.
I'M THE MAN ON THE SILVER MOUNTAIN.
TYRANT PLAYS AT THE LOCAL LAKE HILLS BANDWAGON BATTLE OF THE BANDS COMPETITION. SO DOES CHRIS AND MIKE'S LACONIC PARTY-MEISTER BAND, *JOKER*.
CHRIS, MAN, THIS GUY CAN SCREECH!
I KNOW! I WISH HE WAS *OUR* SINGER... WE'D KICK SOME SERIOUS ASS!

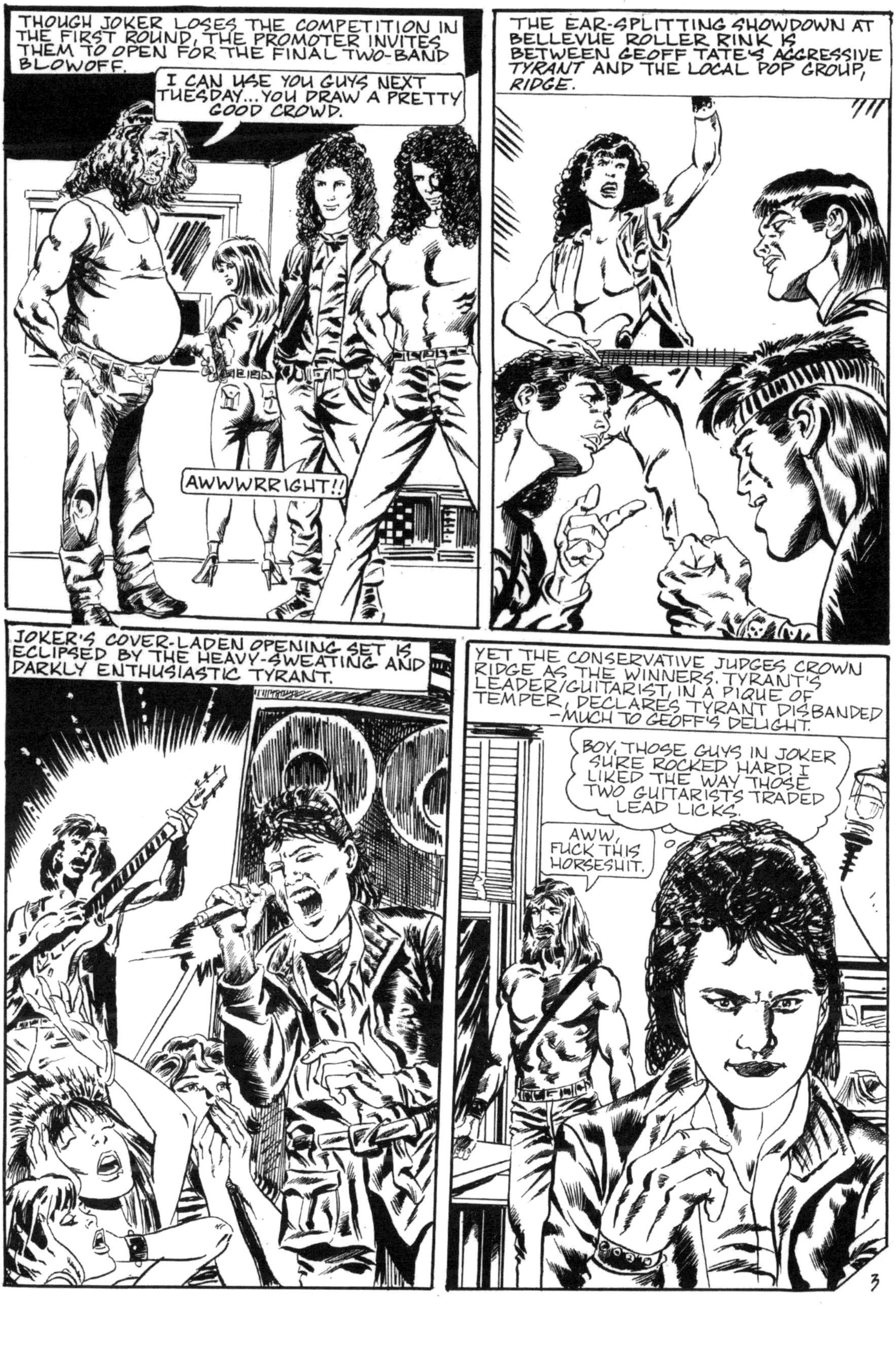
THOUGH JOKER LOSES THE COMPETITION IN THE FIRST ROUND, THE PROMOTER INVITES THEM TO OPEN FOR THE FINAL TWO-BAND BLOWOFF.
I CAN USE YOU GUYS NEXT TUESDAY...YOU DRAW A PRETTY GOOD CROWD.
AWWWRRIGHT!!
THE EAR-SPLITTING SHOWDOWN AT BELLEVUE ROLLER RINK IS BETWEEN GEOFF TATE'S AGGRESSIVE TYRANT AND THE LOCAL POP GROUP, RIDGE.
JOKER'S COVER-LADEN OPENING SET IS ECLIPSED BY THE HEAVY-SWEATING AND DARKLY ENTHUSIASTIC TYRANT.
YET THE CONSERVATIVE JUDGES CROWN RIDGE AS THE WINNERS. TYRANT'S LEADER/GUITARIST, IN A PIQUE OF TEMPER, DECLARES TYRANT DISBANDED -MUCH TO GEOFF'S DELIGHT.
BOY, THOSE GUYS IN JOKER SURE ROCKED HARD. I LIKED THE WAY THOSE TWO GUITARISTS TRADED LEAD LICKS.
AWW, FUCK THIS HORSESHIT.

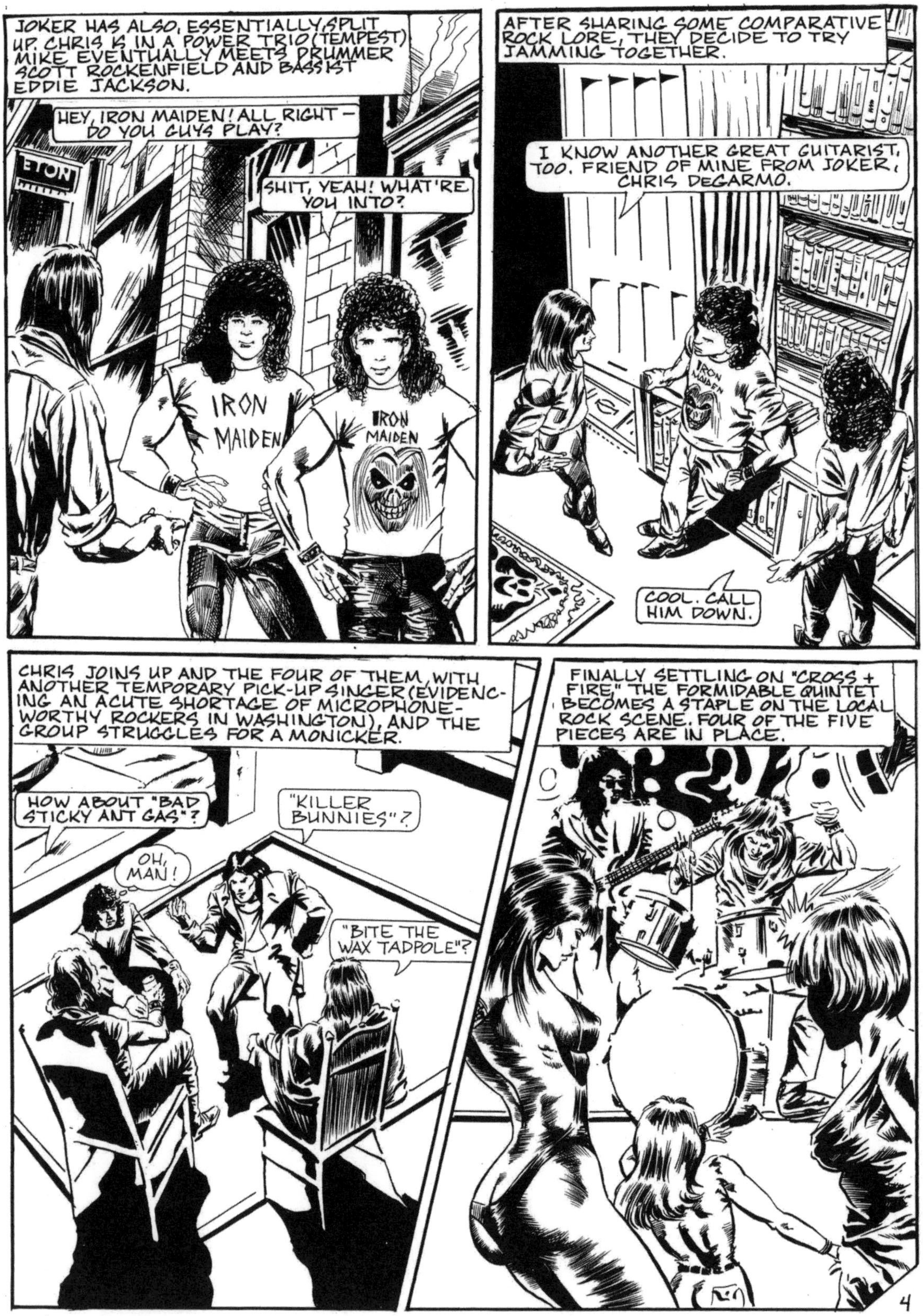
JOKER HAS ALSO, ESSENTIALLY, SPLIT UP. CHRIS IS IN A POWER TRIO (TEMPEST). MIKE EVENTUALLY MEETS DRUMMER SCOTT ROCKENFIELD AND BASSIST EDDIE JACKSON.
HEY, IRON MAIDEN! ALL RIGHT — DO YOU GUYS PLAY?
SHIT, YEAH! WHAT'RE YOU INTO?
IRON MAIDEN
IRON MAIDEN
AFTER SHARING SOME COMPARATIVE ROCK LORE, THEY DECIDE TO TRY JAMMING TOGETHER.
I KNOW ANOTHER GREAT GUITARIST, TOO. FRIEND OF MINE FROM JOKER, CHRIS DeGARMO.
IRON MAIDEN
COOL. CALL HIM DOWN.
CHRIS JOINS UP AND THE FOUR OF THEM, WITH ANOTHER TEMPORARY PICK-UP SINGER (EVIDENCING AN ACUTE SHORTAGE OF MICROPHONE-WORTHY ROCKERS IN WASHINGTON), AND THE GROUP STRUGGLES FOR A MONICKER.
HOW ABOUT "BAD STICKY ANT GAS"?
"KILLER BUNNIES"?
OH, MAN!
"BITE THE WAX TADPOLE"?
FINALLY SETTLING ON "CROSS + FIRE," THE FORMIDABLE QUINTET BECOMES A STAPLE ON THE LOCAL ROCK SCENE. FOUR OF THE FIVE PIECES ARE IN PLACE.

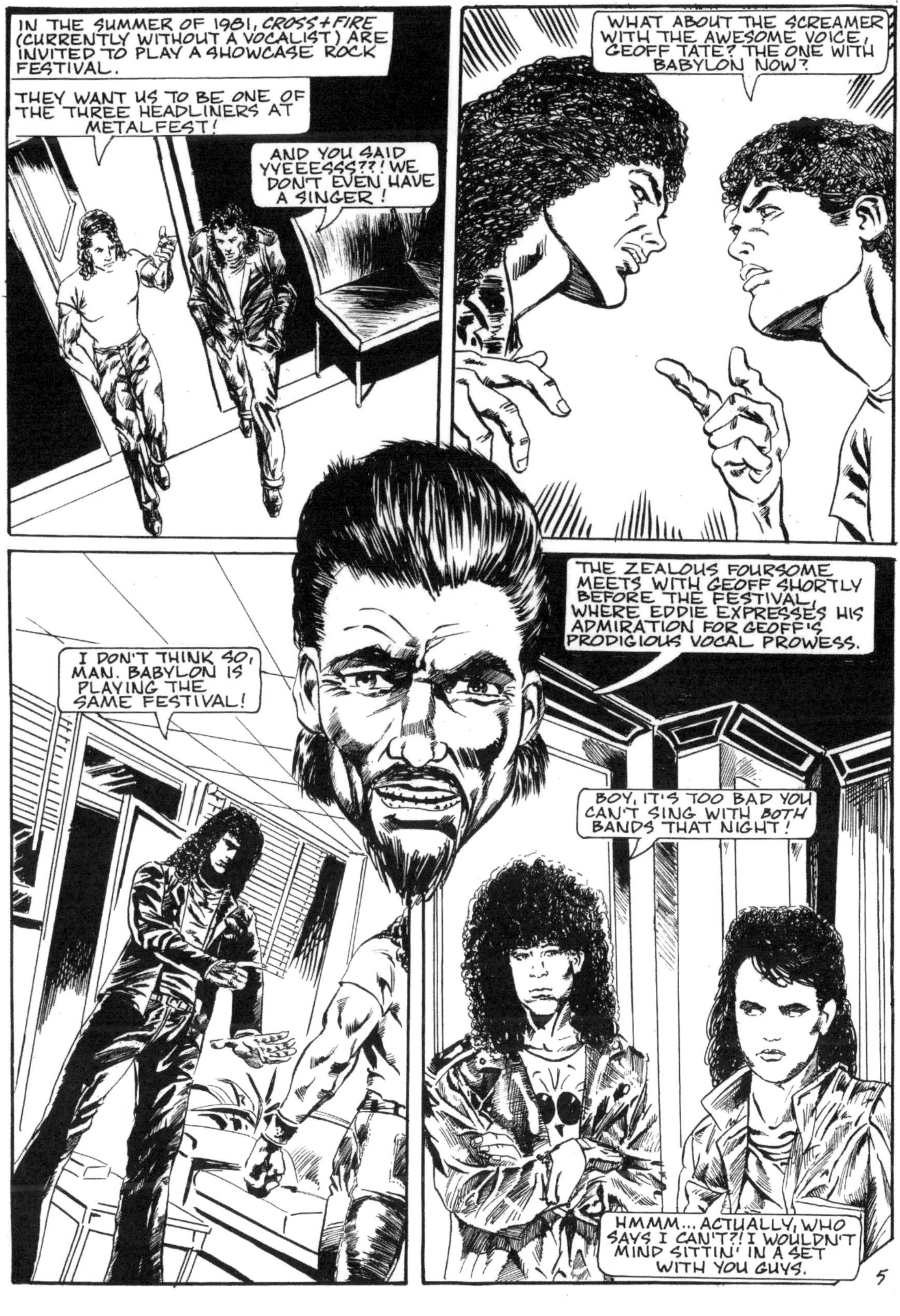

IN THE SUMMER OF 1981, CROSS+FIRE (CURRENTLY WITHOUT A VOCALIST) ARE INVITED TO PLAY A SHOWCASE ROCK FESTIVAL.
THEY WANT US TO BE ONE OF THE THREE HEADLINERS AT METALFEST!
AND YOU SAID YYEEESSS??! WE DON'T EVEN HAVE A SINGER!
WHAT ABOUT THE SCREAMER WITH THE AWESOME VOICE, GEOFF TATE? THE ONE WITH BABYLON NOW?
I DON'T THINK SO, MAN. BABYLON IS PLAYING THE SAME FESTIVAL!
THE ZEALOUS FOURSOME MEETS WITH GEOFF SHORTLY BEFORE THE FESTIVAL, WHERE EDDIE EXPRESSES HIS ADMIRATION FOR GEOFF'S PRODIGIOUS VOCAL PROWESS.
BOY, IT'S TOO BAD YOU CAN'T SING WITH BOTH BANDS THAT NIGHT!
HMMM... ACTUALLY, WHO SAYS I CAN'T?! I WOULDN'T MIND SITTIN' IN A SET WITH YOU GUYS.

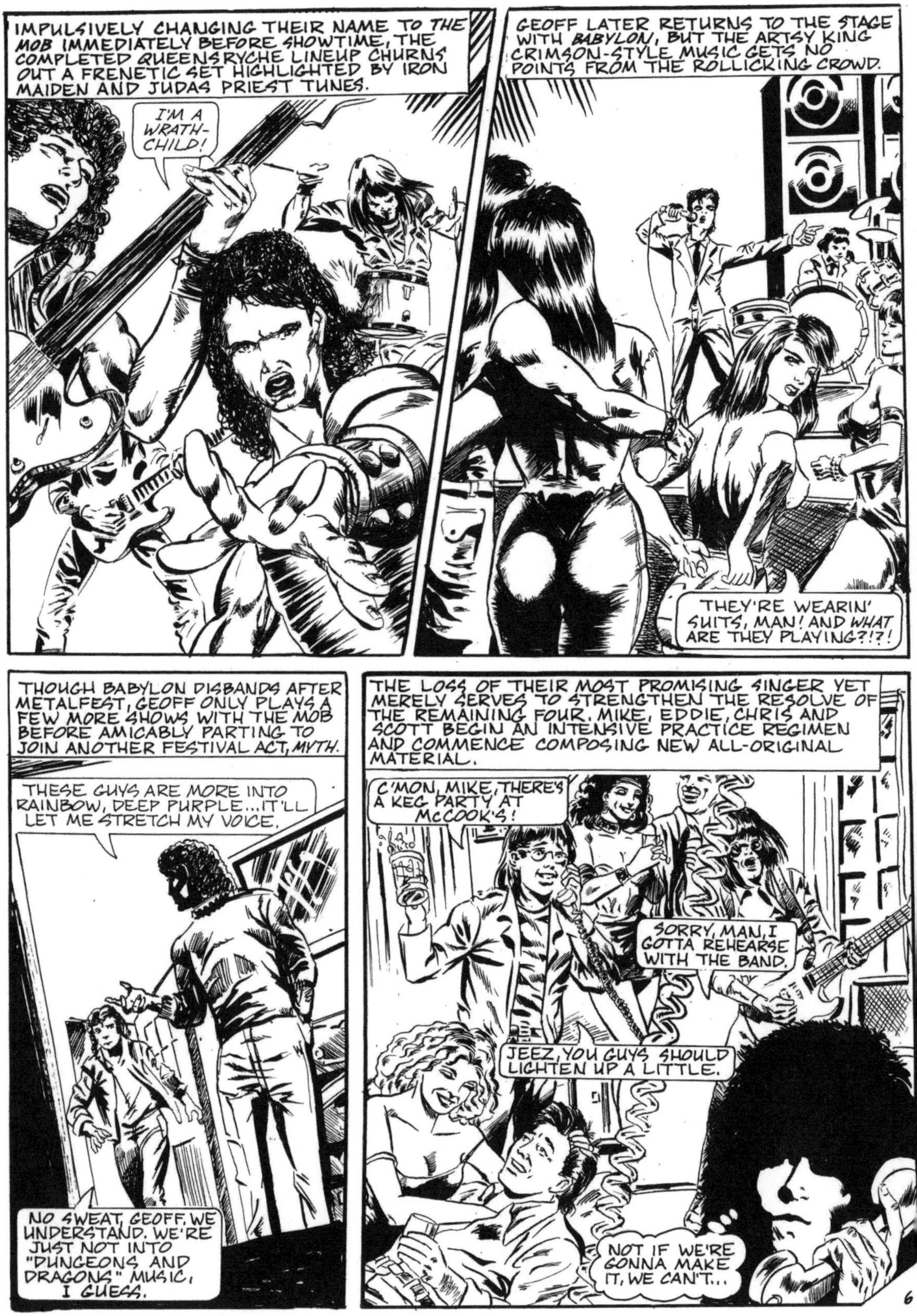
IMPULSIVELY CHANGING THEIR NAME TO THE MOB IMMEDIATELY BEFORE SHOWTIME, THE COMPLETED QUEENSRYCHE LINEUP CHURNS OUT A FRENETIC SET HIGHLIGHTED BY IRON MAIDEN AND JUDAS PRIEST TUNES.
I'M A WRATH-CHILD!
GEOFF LATER RETURNS TO THE STAGE WITH BABYLON, BUT THE ARTSY KING CRIMSON-STYLE MUSIC GETS NO POINTS FROM THE ROLLICKING CROWD.
THEY'RE WEARIN' SUITS, MAN! AND WHAT ARE THEY PLAYING?!?!
THOUGH BABYLON DISBANDS AFTER METALFEST, GEOFF ONLY PLAYS A FEW MORE SHOWS WITH THE MOB BEFORE AMICABLY PARTING TO JOIN ANOTHER FESTIVAL ACT, MYTH.
THESE GUYS ARE MORE INTO RAINBOW, DEEP PURPLE... IT'LL LET ME STRETCH MY VOICE.
NO SWEAT, GEOFF, WE UNDERSTAND. WE'RE JUST NOT INTO "DUNGEONS AND DRAGONS" MUSIC, I GUESS.
THE LOSS OF THEIR MOST PROMISING SINGER YET MERELY SERVES TO STRENGTHEN THE RESOLVE OF THE REMAINING FOUR. MIKE, EDDIE, CHRIS AND SCOTT BEGIN AN INTENSIVE PRACTICE REGIMEN AND COMMENCE COMPOSING NEW ALL-ORIGINAL MATERIAL.
C'MON, MIKE, THERE'S A KEG PARTY AT McCOOK'S!
SORRY, MAN, I GOTTA REHEARSE WITH THE BAND.
JEEZ, YOU GUYS SHOULD LIGHTEN UP A LITTLE.
NOT IF WE'RE GONNA MAKE IT, WE CAN'T...

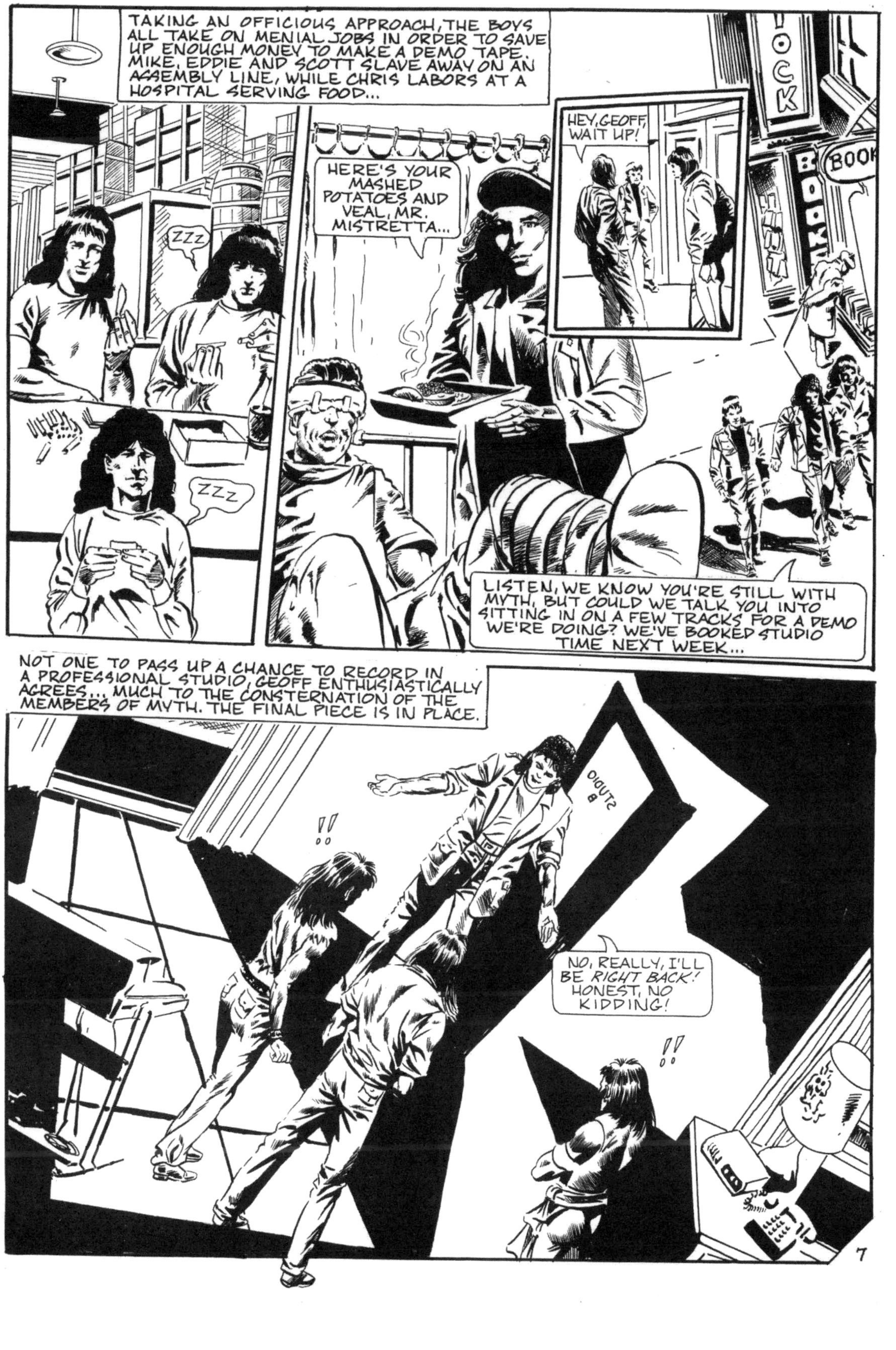
TAKING AN OFFICIOUS APPROACH, THE BOYS ALL TAKE ON MENIAL JOBS IN ORDER TO SAVE UP ENOUGH MONEY TO MAKE A DEMO TAPE. MIKE, EDDIE AND SCOTT SLAVE AWAY ON AN ASSEMBLY LINE, WHILE CHRIS LABORS AT A HOSPITAL SERVING FOOD...
ZZZ
ZZZ
HERE'S YOUR MASHED POTATOES AND VEAL, MR. MISTRETTA...
HEY, GEOFF, WAIT UP!
BOOK
LISTEN, WE KNOW YOU'RE STILL WITH MYTH, BUT COULD WE TALK YOU INTO SITTING IN ON A FEW TRACKS FOR A DEMO WE'RE DOING? WE'VE BOOKED STUDIO TIME NEXT WEEK...
NOT ONE TO PASS UP A CHANCE TO RECORD IN A PROFESSIONAL STUDIO, GEOFF ENTHUSIASTICALLY AGREES... MUCH TO THE CONSTERNATION OF THE MEMBERS OF MYTH. THE FINAL PIECE IS IN PLACE.
STUDIO B
!!
NO, REALLY, I'LL BE *RIGHT BACK!* HONEST, NO KIDDING!
!!

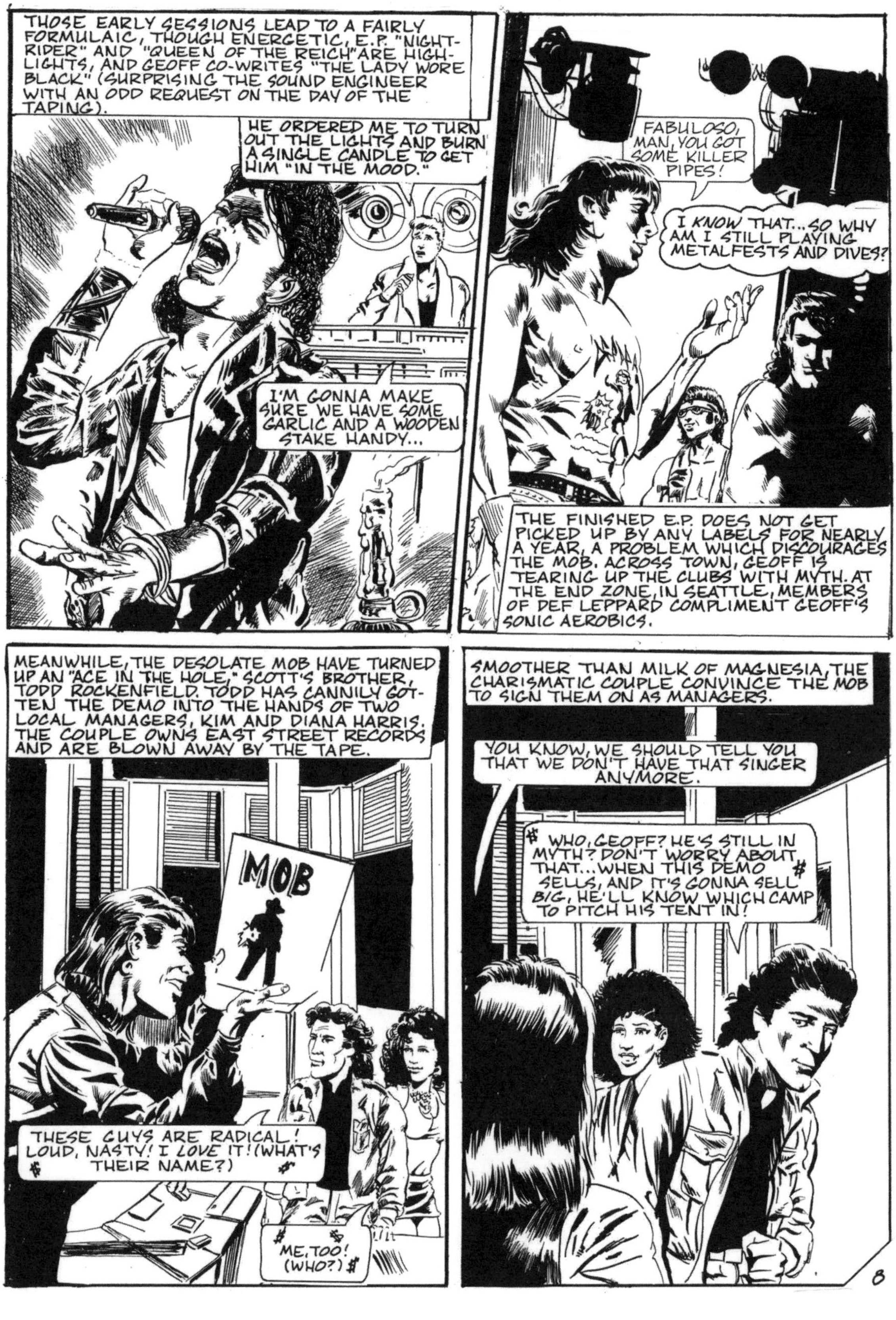
THOSE EARLY SESSIONS LEAD TO A FAIRLY FORMULAIC, THOUGH ENERGETIC, E.P. "NIGHT-RIDER" AND "QUEEN OF THE REICH" ARE HIGH-LIGHTS, AND GEOFF CO-WRITES "THE LADY WORE BLACK" (SURPRISING THE SOUND ENGINEER WITH AN ODD REQUEST ON THE DAY OF THE TAPING).
HE ORDERED ME TO TURN OUT THE LIGHTS AND BURN A SINGLE CANDLE TO GET HIM "IN THE MOOD."
I'M GONNA MAKE SURE WE HAVE SOME GARLIC AND A WOODEN STAKE HANDY...
FABULOSO, MAN, YOU GOT SOME KILLER PIPES!
I KNOW THAT...SO WHY AM I STILL PLAYING METALFESTS AND DIVES?
THE FINISHED E.P. DOES NOT GET PICKED UP BY ANY LABELS FOR NEARLY A YEAR, A PROBLEM WHICH DISCOURAGES THE MOB. ACROSS TOWN, GEOFF IS TEARING UP THE CLUBS WITH MYTH. AT THE END ZONE, IN SEATTLE, MEMBERS OF DEF LEPPARD COMPLIMENT GEOFF'S SONIC AEROBICS.
MEANWHILE, THE DESOLATE MOB HAVE TURNED UP AN "ACE IN THE HOLE," SCOTT'S BROTHER, TODD ROCKENFIELD. TODD HAS CANNILY GOTTEN THE DEMO INTO THE HANDS OF TWO LOCAL MANAGERS, KIM AND DIANA HARRIS. THE COUPLE OWNS EAST STREET RECORDS AND ARE BLOWN AWAY BY THE TAPE.
MOB
THESE GUYS ARE RADICAL! LOUD, NASTY! I LOVE IT! (WHAT'S THEIR NAME?)
ME, TOO! (WHO?)
SMOOTHER THAN MILK OF MAGNESIA, THE CHARISMATIC COUPLE CONVINCE THE MOB TO SIGN THEM ON AS MANAGERS.
YOU KNOW, WE SHOULD TELL YOU THAT WE DON'T HAVE THAT SINGER ANYMORE.
WHO, GEOFF? HE'S STILL IN MYTH? DON'T WORRY ABOUT THAT...WHEN THIS DEMO SELLS, AND IT'S GONNA SELL BIG, HE'LL KNOW WHICH CAMP TO PITCH HIS TENT IN!

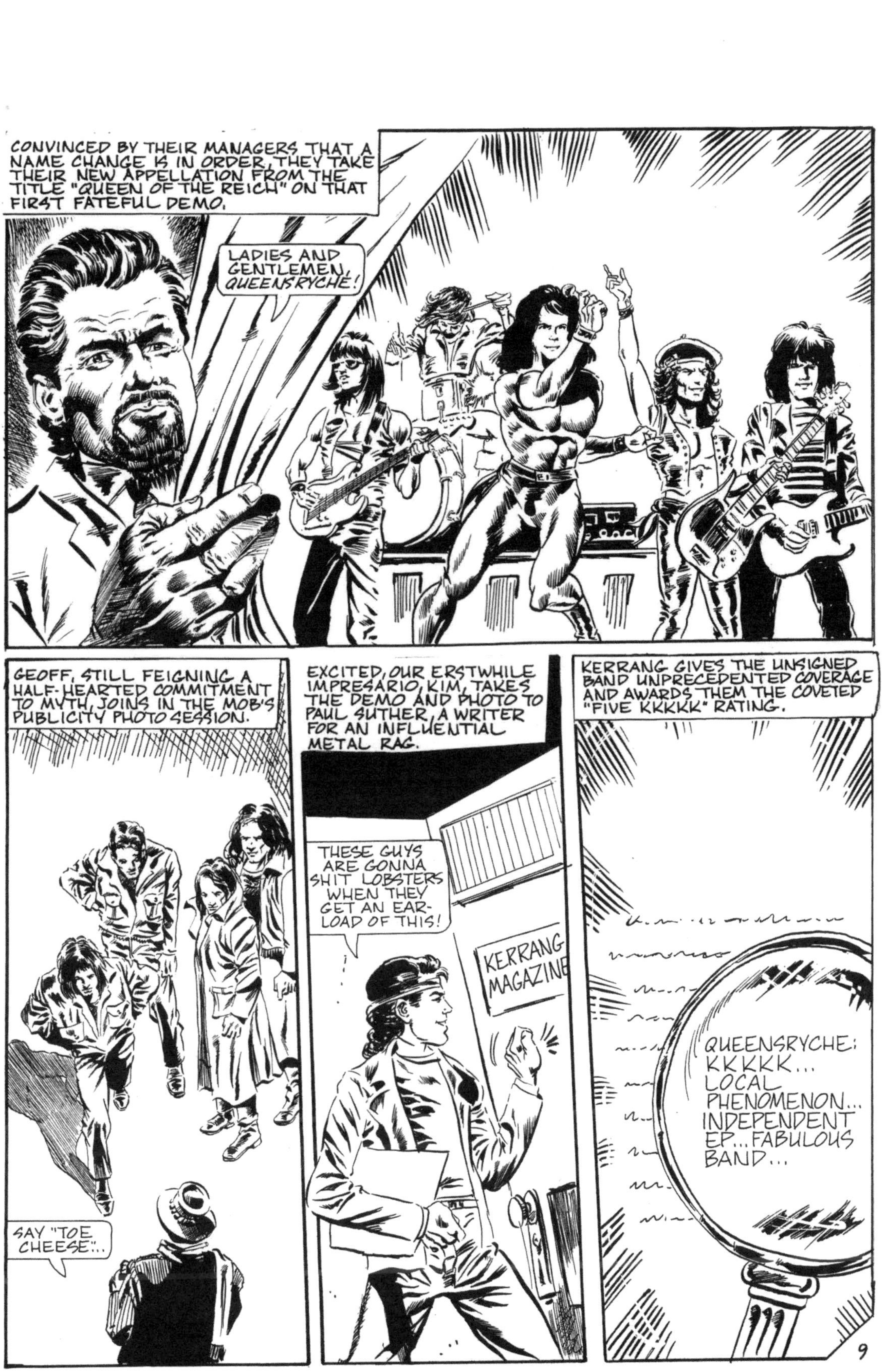

CONVINCED BY THEIR MANAGERS THAT A NAME CHANGE IS IN ORDER, THEY TAKE THEIR NEW APPELLATION FROM THE TITLE "QUEEN OF THE REICH" ON THAT FIRST FATEFUL DEMO.
LADIES AND GENTLEMEN, QUEENSRYCHE!
GEOFF, STILL FEIGNING A HALF-HEARTED COMMITMENT TO MYTH, JOINS IN THE MOB'S PUBLICITY PHOTO SESSION.
SAY "TOE CHEESE"...
EXCITED, OUR ERSTWHILE IMPRESARIO, KIM, TAKES THE DEMO AND PHOTO TO PAUL SUTHER, A WRITER FOR AN INFLUENTIAL METAL RAG.
THESE GUYS ARE GONNA SHIT LOBSTERS WHEN THEY GET AN EAR-LOAD OF THIS!
KERRANG MAGAZINE
KERRANG GIVES THE UNSIGNED BAND UNPRECEDENTED COVERAGE AND AWARDS THEM THE COVETED "FIVE KKKKK" RATING.
QUEENSRYCHE: KKKKK... LOCAL PHENOMENON... INDEPENDENT EP... FABULOUS BAND...

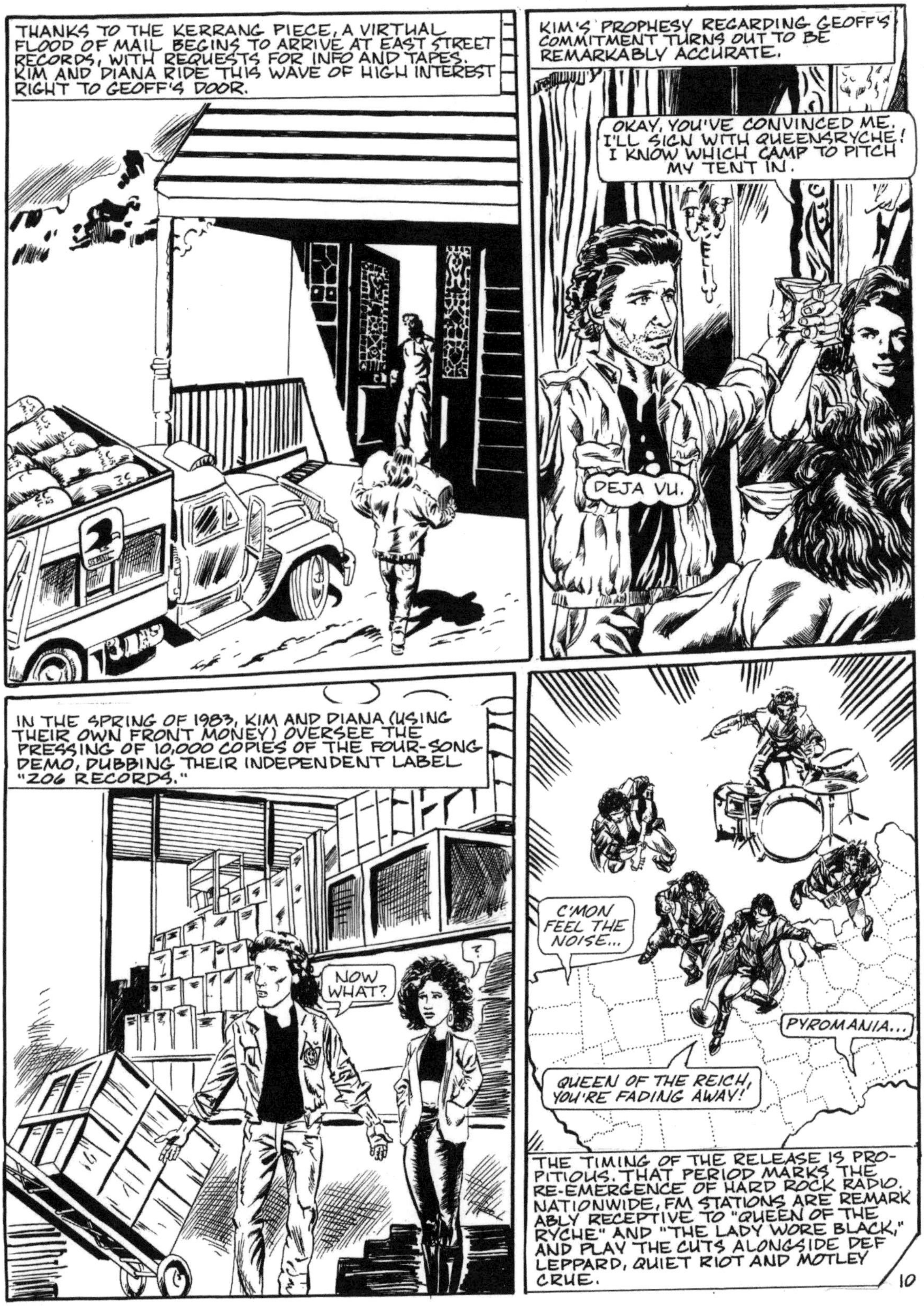
THANKS TO THE KERRANG PIECE, A VIRTUAL FLOOD OF MAIL BEGINS TO ARRIVE AT EAST STREET RECORDS, WITH REQUESTS FOR INFO AND TAPES. KIM AND DIANA RIDE THIS WAVE OF HIGH INTEREST RIGHT TO GEOFF'S DOOR.
KIM'S PROPHESY REGARDING GEOFF'S COMMITMENT TURNS OUT TO BE REMARKABLY ACCURATE.
OKAY, YOU'VE CONVINCED ME. I'LL SIGN WITH QUEENSRYCHE! I KNOW WHICH CAMP TO PITCH MY TENT IN.
DEJA VU.
IN THE SPRING OF 1983, KIM AND DIANA (USING THEIR OWN FRONT MONEY) OVERSEE THE PRESSING OF 10,000 COPIES OF THE FOUR-SONG DEMO, DUBBING THEIR INDEPENDENT LABEL "206 RECORDS."
NOW WHAT?
?
C'MON FEEL THE NOISE...
PYROMANIA...
QUEEN OF THE REICH, YOU'RE FADING AWAY!
THE TIMING OF THE RELEASE IS PROPITIOUS. THAT PERIOD MARKS THE RE-EMERGENCE OF HARD ROCK RADIO. NATIONWIDE, FM STATIONS ARE REMARKABLY RECEPTIVE TO "QUEEN OF THE RYCHE" AND "THE LADY WORE BLACK," AND PLAY THE CUTS ALONGSIDE DEF LEPPARD, QUIET RIOT AND MOTLEY CRUE.

THE RESPONSE TO THE E.P. IS, TO PUT IT MILDLY, POSITIVE.

THE RECORD IS ABSOLUTELY, COMPLETELY SOLD OUT!

AND WE NEVER EVEN PLAYED A QUEENSRYCHE GIG!

SOON...

HEY, YOU GUYS WANNA OPEN A COUPLE OF GIGS FOR ZEBRA?

YEEE-HAAWW!

THOUGH TICKET SALES IN PORTLAND AND SEATTLE HAD BEEN LAGGING, THE ADDITION OF QUEENSRYCHE TO THE BILL CAUSES THE SHOWS TO SELL OUT. THEIR IMPRESSIVE SET BLOWS THE THREE-PIECE ZEBRA OFF THE STAGE.

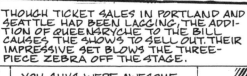

YOU GUYS WERE AWESOME, INCREDIBLE, INCANDESCENT! I HEAR THAT THERE WERE SOME HIGH CALIBER RECORD EXECS OUT THERE TONIGHT.

WOW, REALLY?!

AWW, WISE UP, EDDIE. A BAND DOESN'T GET SIGNED ON THEIR VERY FIRST GIG.

WRONG AGAIN, GEOFF.

EMI-AMERICA CONTRACT

THE INDIE E.P. IS RE-RELEASED ON THE MAJOR LABEL, TO EVEN MORE PERSONAL AND CRITICAL ACCLAIM.

QUEENSRYCHE

HOT SHIT

11

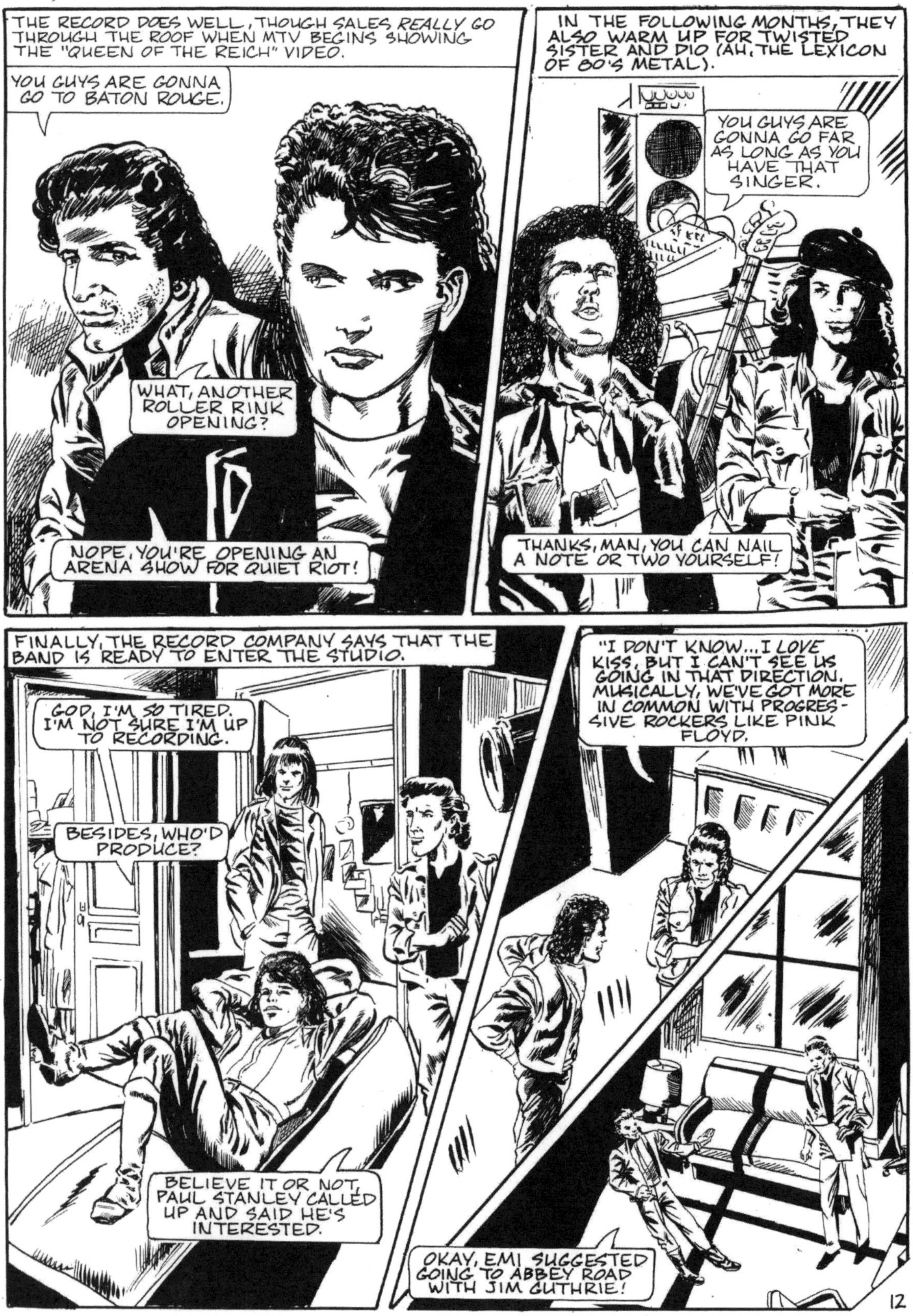
THE RECORD DOES WELL, THOUGH SALES REALLY GO THROUGH THE ROOF WHEN MTV BEGINS SHOWING THE "QUEEN OF THE REICH" VIDEO.
YOU GUYS ARE GONNA GO TO BATON ROUGE.
WHAT, ANOTHER ROLLER RINK OPENING?
NOPE, YOU'RE OPENING AN ARENA SHOW FOR QUIET RIOT!
IN THE FOLLOWING MONTHS, THEY ALSO WARM UP FOR TWISTED SISTER AND DIO (AH, THE LEXICON OF 80'S METAL).
YOU GUYS ARE GONNA GO FAR AS LONG AS YOU HAVE THAT SINGER.
THANKS, MAN, YOU CAN NAIL A NOTE OR TWO YOURSELF!
FINALLY, THE RECORD COMPANY SAYS THAT THE BAND IS READY TO ENTER THE STUDIO.
GOD, I'M SO TIRED. I'M NOT SURE I'M UP TO RECORDING.
BESIDES, WHO'D PRODUCE?
BELIEVE IT OR NOT, PAUL STANLEY CALLED UP AND SAID HE'S INTERESTED.
"I DON'T KNOW... I LOVE KISS, BUT I CAN'T SEE US GOING IN THAT DIRECTION. MUSICALLY, WE'VE GOT MORE IN COMMON WITH PROGRES-SIVE ROCKERS LIKE PINK FLOYD.
OKAY, EMI SUGGESTED GOING TO ABBEY ROAD WITH JIM GUTHRIE!

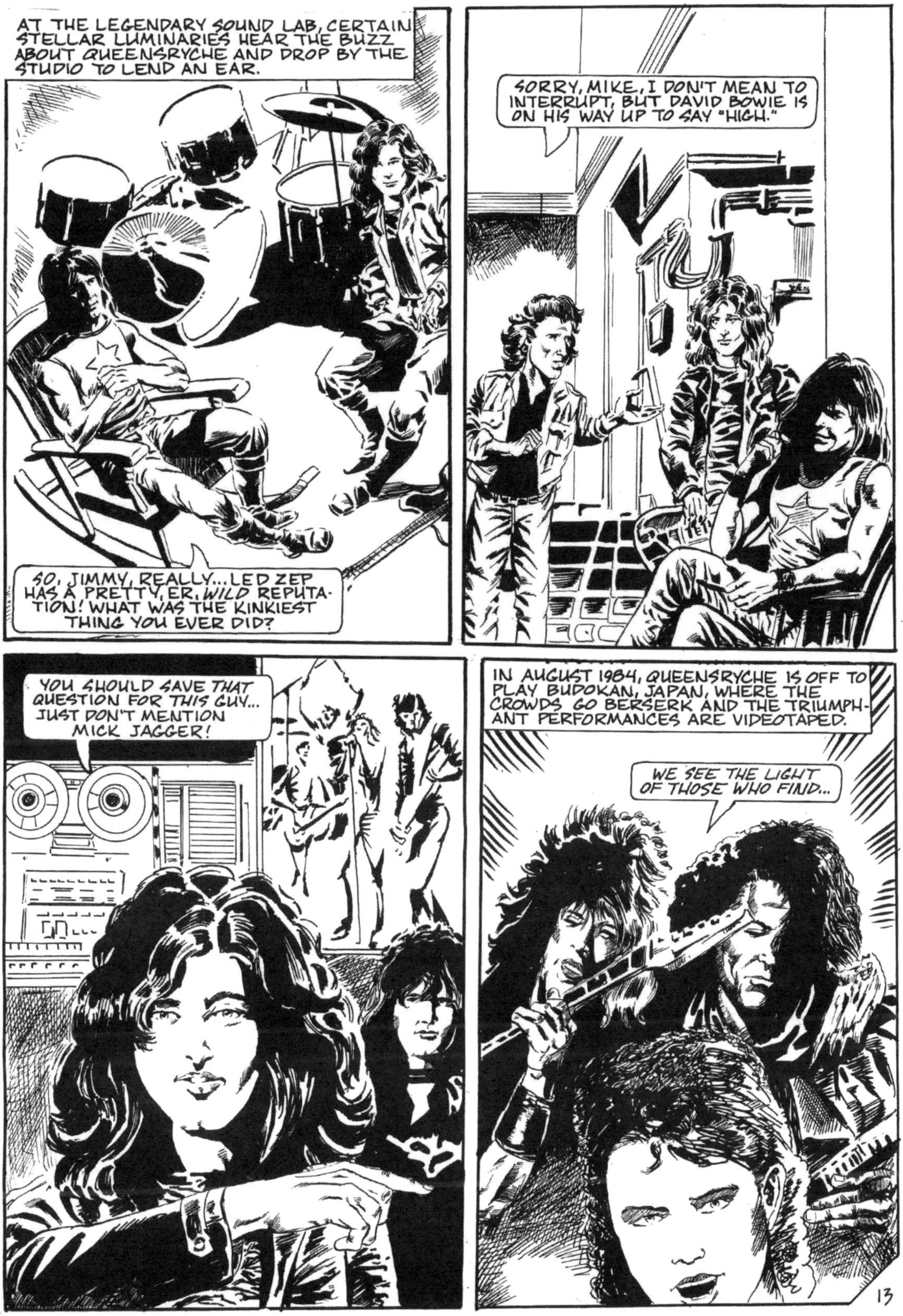

AT THE LEGENDARY SOUND LAB, CERTAIN STELLAR LUMINARIES HEAR THE BUZZ ABOUT QUEENSRYCHE AND DROP BY THE STUDIO TO LEND AN EAR.
SO, JIMMY, REALLY... LED ZEP HAS A PRETTY, ER, *WILD* REPUTATION! WHAT WAS THE KINKIEST THING YOU EVER DID?
SORRY, MIKE, I DON'T MEAN TO INTERRUPT, BUT DAVID BOWIE IS ON HIS WAY UP TO SAY "HIGH."
YOU SHOULD SAVE *THAT* QUESTION FOR *THIS* GUY... JUST DON'T MENTION MICK JAGGER!
IN AUGUST 1984, QUEENSRYCHE IS OFF TO PLAY BUDOKAN, JAPAN, WHERE THE CROWDS GO BERSERK AND THE TRIUMPHANT PERFORMANCES ARE VIDEOTAPED.
WE SEE THE LIGHT OF THOSE WHO FIND...

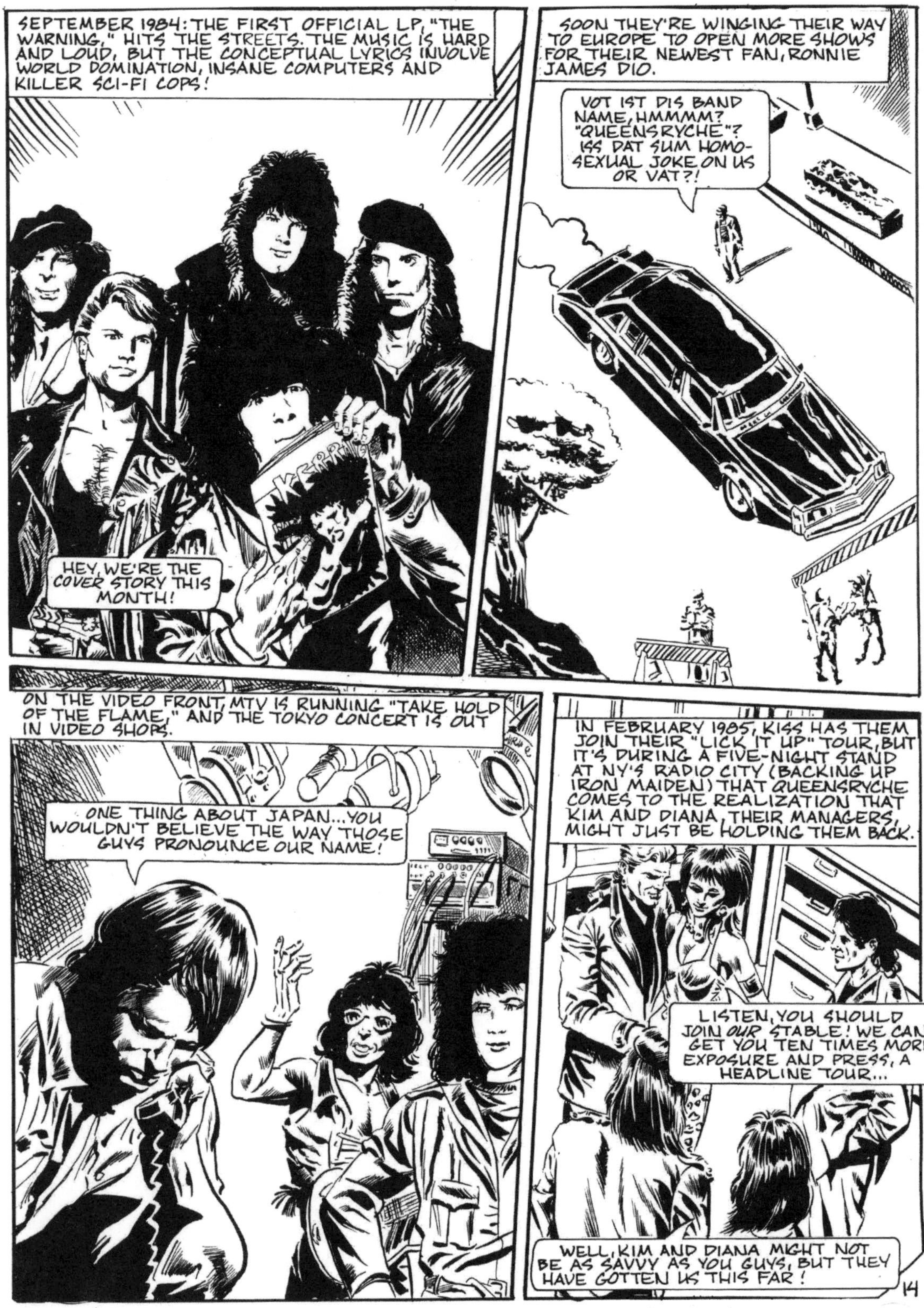
SEPTEMBER 1984: THE FIRST OFFICIAL LP, "THE WARNING," HITS THE STREETS. THE MUSIC IS HARD AND LOUD, BUT THE CONCEPTUAL LYRICS INVOLVE WORLD DOMINATION, INSANE COMPUTERS AND KILLER SCI-FI COPS!
HEY, WE'RE THE COVER STORY THIS MONTH!
SOON THEY'RE WINGING THEIR WAY TO EUROPE TO OPEN MORE SHOWS FOR THEIR NEWEST FAN, RONNIE JAMES DIO.
VOT IST DIS BAND NAME, HMMMM? "QUEENSRYCHE"? ISS DAT SUM HOMO-SEXUAL JOKE ON US OR VAT?!
ON THE VIDEO FRONT, MTV IS RUNNING "TAKE HOLD OF THE FLAME," AND THE TOKYO CONCERT IS OUT IN VIDEO SHOPS.
ONE THING ABOUT JAPAN...YOU WOULDN'T BELIEVE THE WAY THOSE GUYS PRONOUNCE OUR NAME!
IN FEBRUARY 1985, KISS HAS THEM JOIN THEIR "LICK IT UP" TOUR, BUT IT'S DURING A FIVE-NIGHT STAND AT NY'S RADIO CITY (BACKING UP IRON MAIDEN) THAT QUEENSRYCHE COMES TO THE REALIZATION THAT KIM AND DIANA, THEIR MANAGERS, MIGHT JUST BE HOLDING THEM BACK.
LISTEN, YOU SHOULD JOIN OUR STABLE! WE CAN GET YOU TEN TIMES MORE EXPOSURE AND PRESS, A HEADLINE TOUR...
WELL, KIM AND DIANA MIGHT NOT BE AS SAVVY AS YOU GUYS, BUT THEY HAVE GOTTEN US THIS FAR!

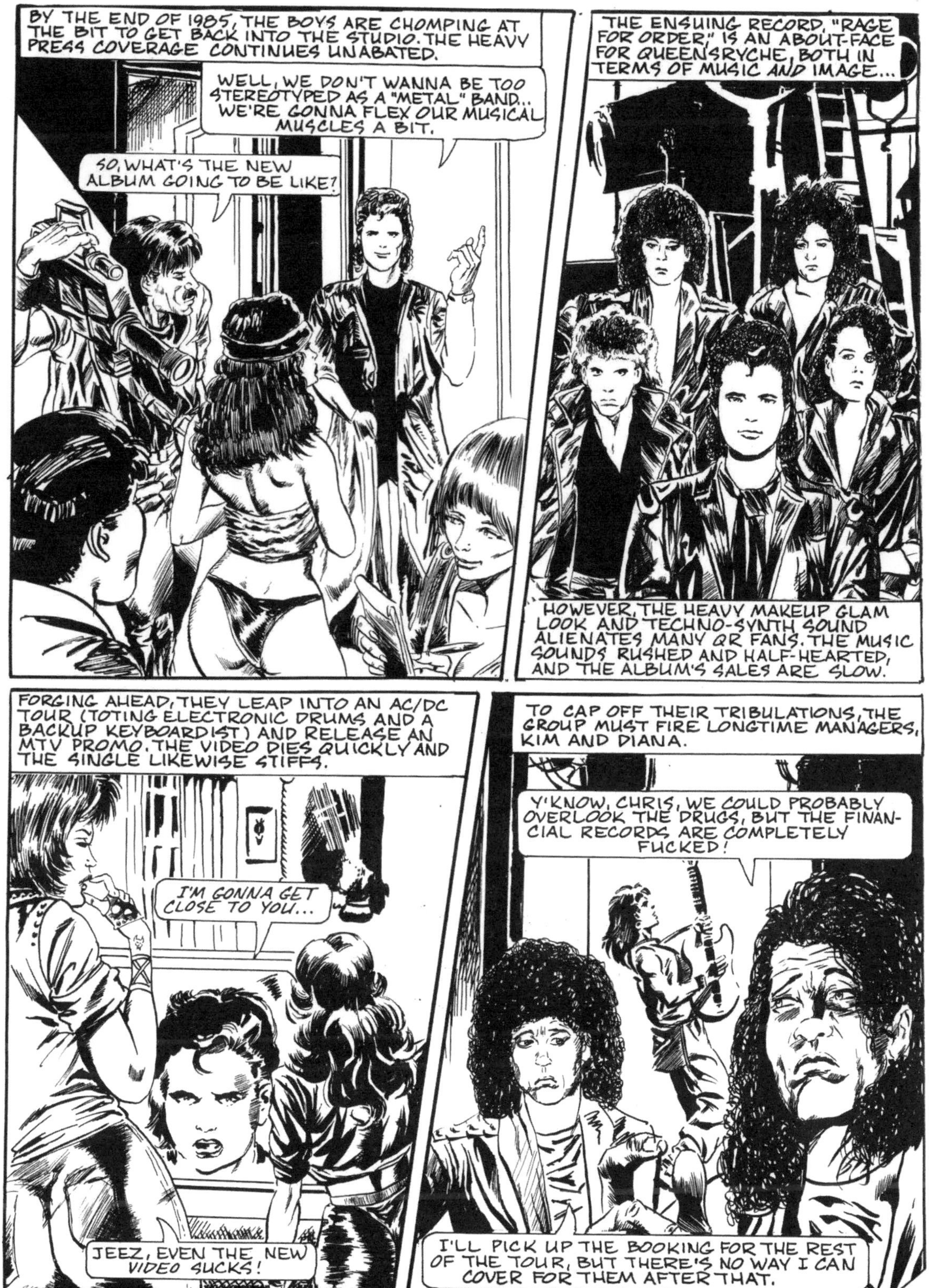
BY THE END OF 1985, THE BOYS ARE CHOMPING AT THE BIT TO GET BACK INTO THE STUDIO. THE HEAVY PRESS COVERAGE CONTINUES UNABATED.
WELL, WE DON'T WANNA BE TOO STEREOTYPED AS A "METAL" BAND... WE'RE GONNA FLEX OUR MUSICAL MUSCLES A BIT.
SO, WHAT'S THE NEW ALBUM GOING TO BE LIKE?
THE ENSUING RECORD, "RAGE FOR ORDER," IS AN ABOUT-FACE FOR QUEENSRYCHE, BOTH IN TERMS OF MUSIC AND IMAGE...
HOWEVER, THE HEAVY MAKEUP GLAM LOOK AND TECHNO-SYNTH SOUND ALIENATES MANY QR FANS. THE MUSIC SOUNDS RUSHED AND HALF-HEARTED, AND THE ALBUM'S SALES ARE SLOW.
FORGING AHEAD, THEY LEAP INTO AN AC/DC TOUR (TOTING ELECTRONIC DRUMS AND A BACKUP KEYBOARDIST) AND RELEASE AN MTV PROMO. THE VIDEO DIES QUICKLY AND THE SINGLE LIKEWISE STIFFS.
I'M GONNA GET CLOSE TO YOU...
JEEZ, EVEN THE NEW VIDEO SUCKS!
TO CAP OFF THEIR TRIBULATIONS, THE GROUP MUST FIRE LONGTIME MANAGERS, KIM AND DIANA.
Y'KNOW, CHRIS, WE COULD PROBABLY OVERLOOK THE DRUGS, BUT THE FINANCIAL RECORDS ARE COMPLETELY FUCKED!
I'LL PICK UP THE BOOKING FOR THE REST OF THE TOUR, BUT THERE'S NO WAY I CAN COVER FOR THEM AFTER THAT.

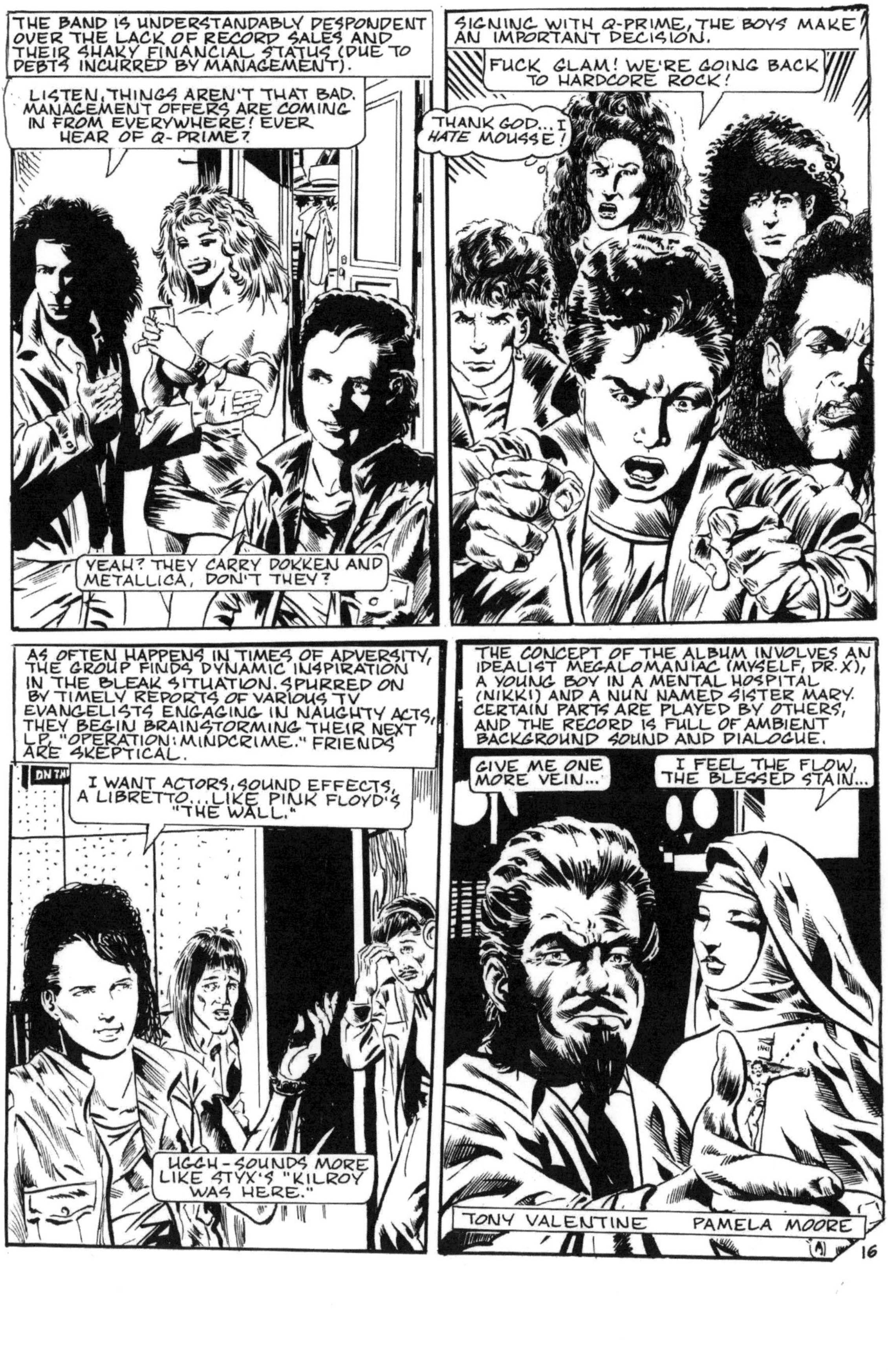
THE BAND IS UNDERSTANDABLY DESPONDENT OVER THE LACK OF RECORD SALES AND THEIR SHAKY FINANCIAL STATUS (DUE TO DEBTS INCURRED BY MANAGEMENT).
LISTEN, THINGS AREN'T THAT BAD. MANAGEMENT OFFERS ARE COMING IN FROM EVERYWHERE! EVER HEAR OF Q-PRIME?
YEAH? THEY CARRY DOKKEN AND METALLICA, DON'T THEY?
SIGNING WITH Q-PRIME, THE BOYS MAKE AN IMPORTANT DECISION.
FUCK GLAM! WE'RE GOING BACK TO HARDCORE ROCK!
THANK GOD... I HATE MOUSSE!
AS OFTEN HAPPENS IN TIMES OF ADVERSITY, THE GROUP FINDS DYNAMIC INSPIRATION IN THE BLEAK SITUATION. SPURRED ON BY TIMELY REPORTS OF VARIOUS TV EVANGELISTS ENGAGING IN NAUGHTY ACTS, THEY BEGIN BRAINSTORMING THEIR NEXT LP, "OPERATION: MINDCRIME." FRIENDS ARE SKEPTICAL.
I WANT ACTORS, SOUND EFFECTS, A LIBRETTO... LIKE PINK FLOYD'S "THE WALL."
UGGH-SOUNDS MORE LIKE STYX'S "KILROY WAS HERE."
THE CONCEPT OF THE ALBUM INVOLVES AN IDEALIST MEGALOMANIAC (MYSELF, DR. X), A YOUNG BOY IN A MENTAL HOSPITAL (NIKKI) AND A NUN NAMED SISTER MARY. CERTAIN PARTS ARE PLAYED BY OTHERS, AND THE RECORD IS FULL OF AMBIENT BACKGROUND SOUND AND DIALOGUE.
GIVE ME ONE MORE VEIN...
I FEEL THE FLOW, THE BLESSED STAIN...
TONY VALENTINE
PAMELA MOORE

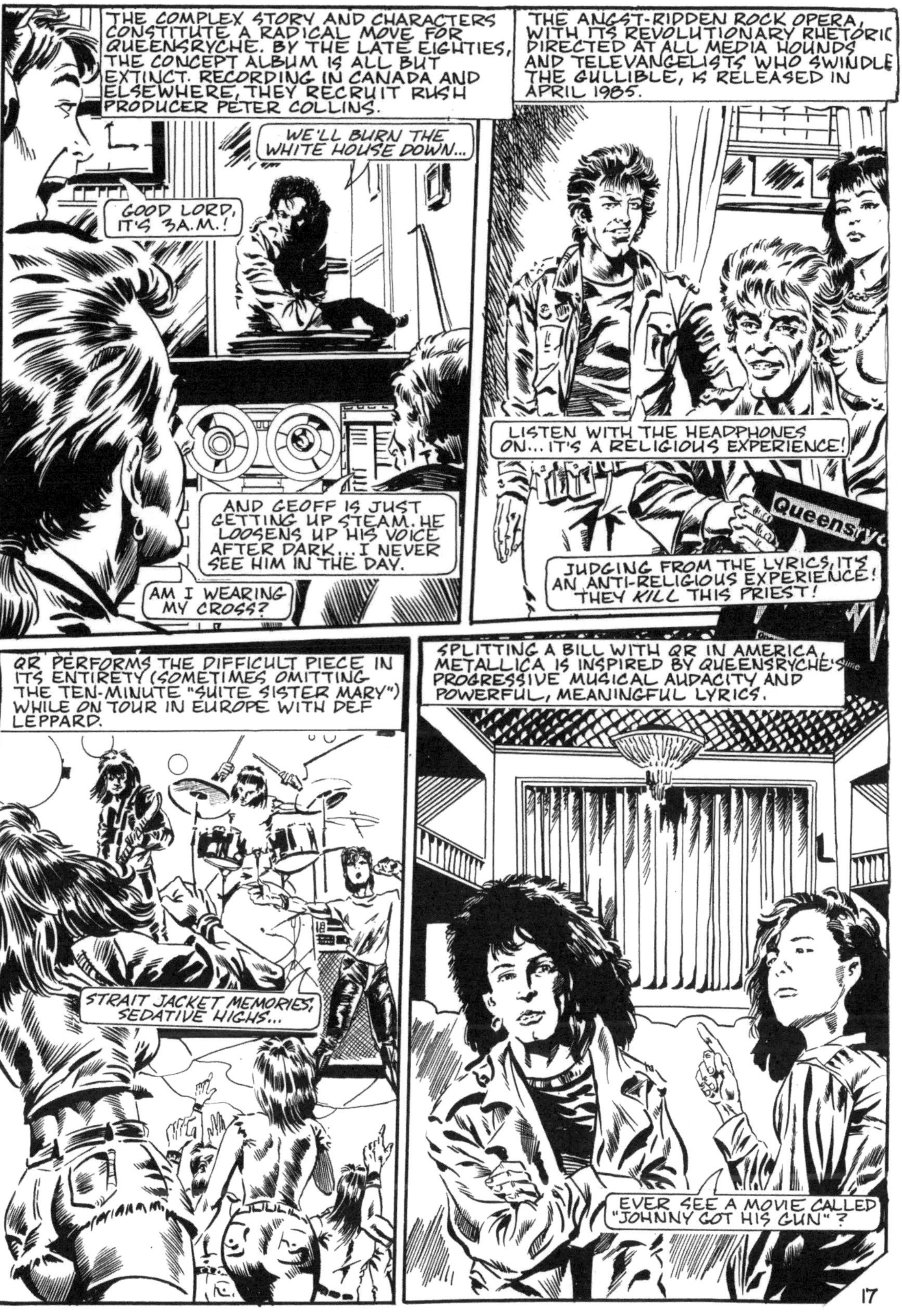
THE COMPLEX STORY AND CHARACTERS CONSTITUTE A RADICAL MOVE FOR QUEENSRYCHE. BY THE LATE EIGHTIES, THE CONCEPT ALBUM IS ALL BUT EXTINCT. RECORDING IN CANADA AND ELSEWHERE, THEY RECRUIT RUSH PRODUCER PETER COLLINS.
WE'LL BURN THE WHITE HOUSE DOWN...
GOOD LORD, IT'S 3A.M.!
AND GEOFF IS JUST GETTING UP STEAM. HE LOOSENS UP HIS VOICE AFTER DARK... I NEVER SEE HIM IN THE DAY.
AM I WEARING MY CROSS?
THE ANGST-RIDDEN ROCK OPERA, WITH ITS REVOLUTIONARY RHETORIC DIRECTED AT ALL MEDIA HOUNDS AND TELEVANGELISTS WHO SWINDLE THE GULLIBLE, IS RELEASED IN APRIL 1985.
LISTEN WITH THE HEADPHONES ON... IT'S A RELIGIOUS EXPERIENCE!
Queensryc
JUDGING FROM THE LYRICS, IT'S AN ANTI-RELIGIOUS EXPERIENCE! THEY KILL THIS PRIEST!
QR PERFORMS THE DIFFICULT PIECE IN ITS ENTIRETY (SOMETIMES OMITTING THE TEN-MINUTE "SUITE SISTER MARY") WHILE ON TOUR IN EUROPE WITH DEF LEPPARD.
STRAIT JACKET MEMORIES, SEDATIVE HIGHS...
SPLITTING A BILL WITH QR IN AMERICA, METALLICA IS INSPIRED BY QUEENSRYCHE'S PROGRESSIVE MUSICAL AUDACITY AND POWERFUL, MEANINGFUL LYRICS.
EVER SEE A MOVIE CALLED "JOHNNY GOT HIS GUN"?

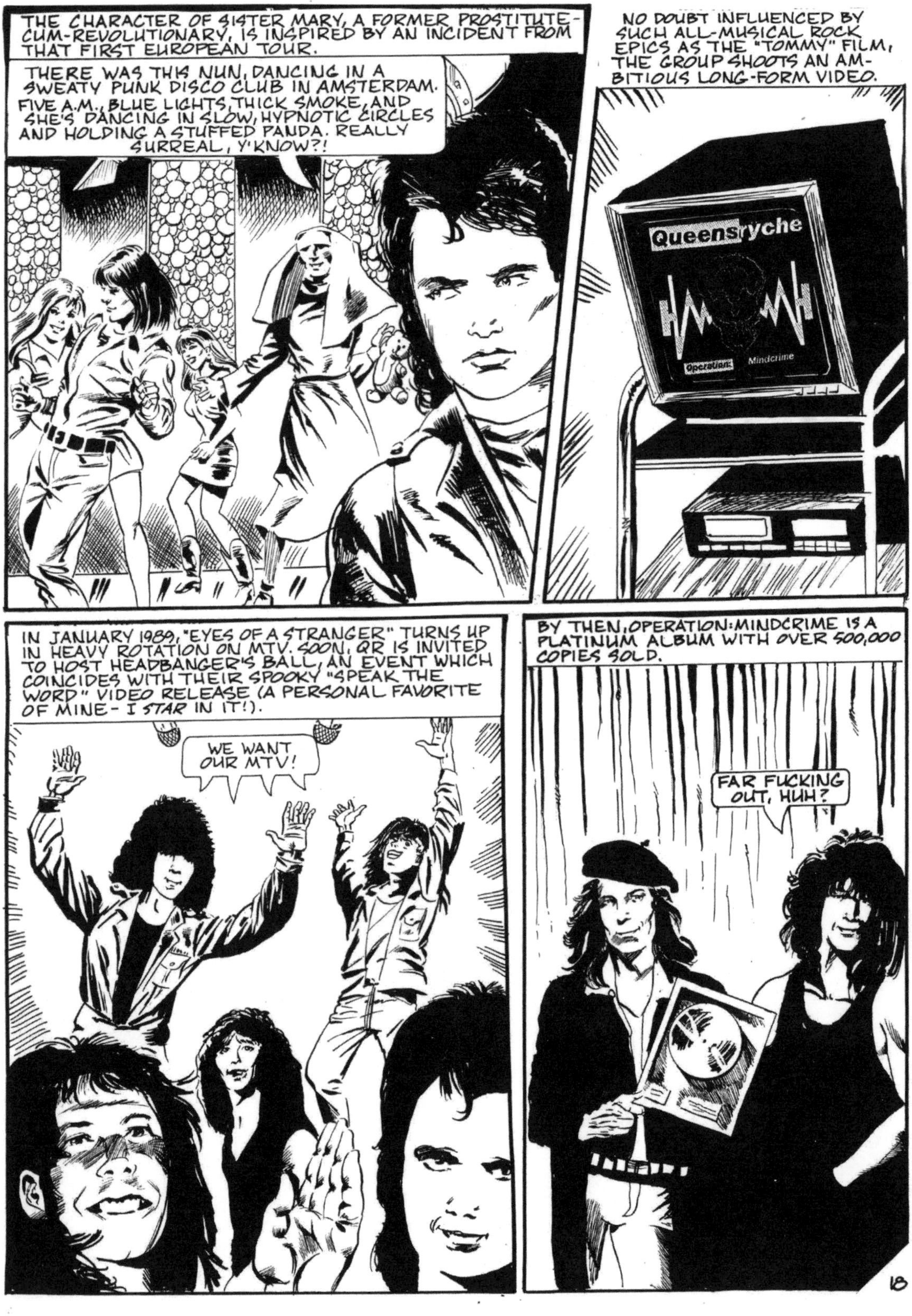
THE CHARACTER OF SISTER MARY, A FORMER PROSTITUTE-CUM-REVOLUTIONARY, IS INSPIRED BY AN INCIDENT FROM THAT FIRST EUROPEAN TOUR.
THERE WAS THIS NUN, DANCING IN A SWEATY PUNK DISCO CLUB IN AMSTERDAM. FIVE A.M., BLUE LIGHTS, THICK SMOKE, AND SHE'S DANCING IN SLOW, HYPNOTIC CIRCLES AND HOLDING A STUFFED PANDA. REALLY SURREAL, Y'KNOW?!
NO DOUBT INFLUENCED BY SUCH ALL-MUSICAL ROCK EPICS AS THE "TOMMY" FILM, THE GROUP SHOOTS AN AMBITIOUS LONG-FORM VIDEO.
Queensryche
Operation: Mindcrime
IN JANUARY 1989, "EYES OF A STRANGER" TURNS UP IN HEAVY ROTATION ON MTV. SOON, QR IS INVITED TO HOST HEADBANGER'S BALL, AN EVENT WHICH COINCIDES WITH THEIR SPOOKY "SPEAK THE WORD" VIDEO RELEASE (A PERSONAL FAVORITE OF MINE - I STAR IN IT!).
WE WANT OUR MTV!
BY THEN, OPERATION: MINDCRIME IS A PLATINUM ALBUM WITH OVER 500,000 COPIES SOLD.
FAR FUCKING OUT, HUH?

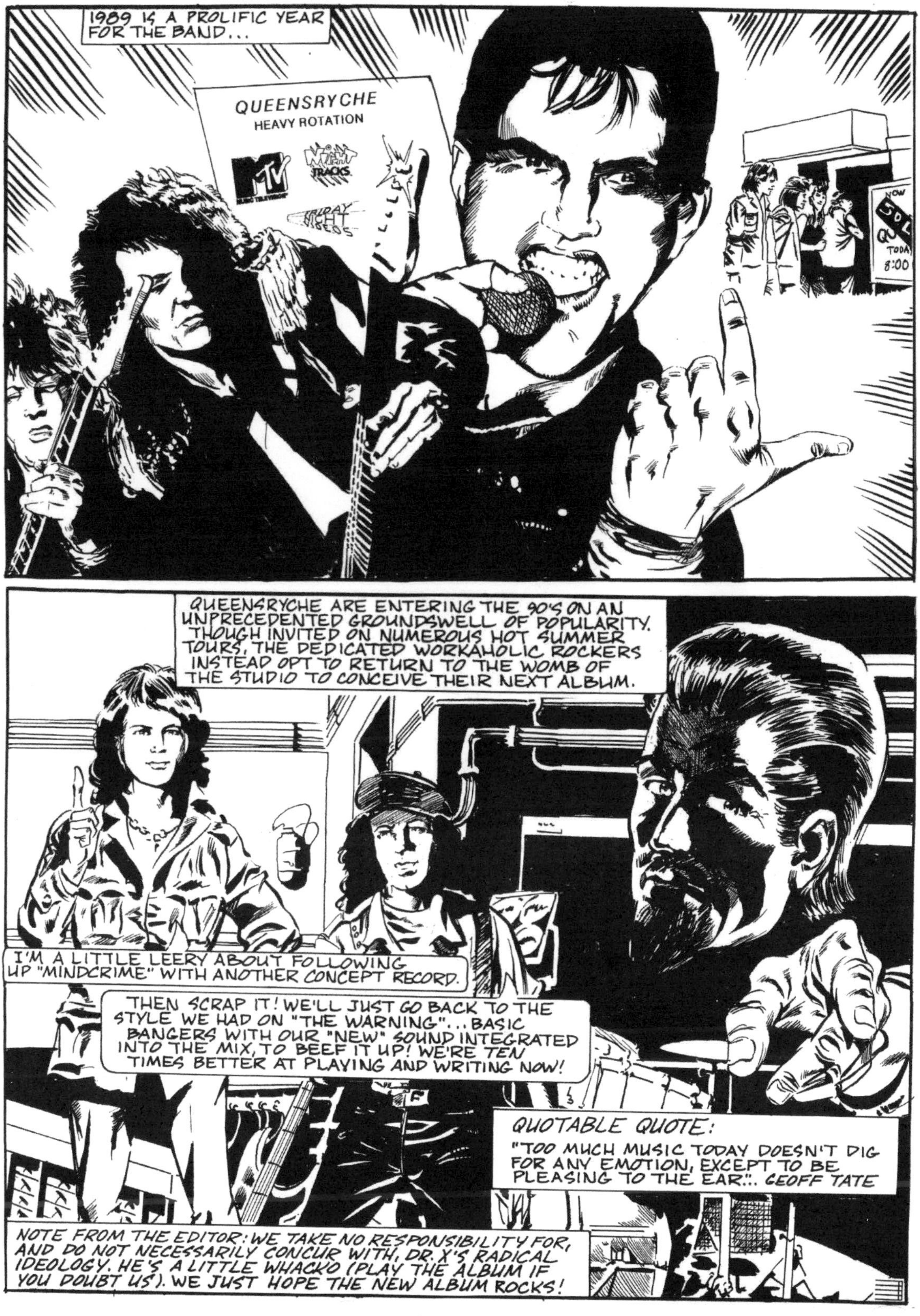

1989 IS A PROLIFIC YEAR FOR THE BAND...
QUEENSRYCHE
HEAVY ROTATION
MTV
NIGHT TRACKS
FRIDAY NIGHT VIDEOS
TODAY
8:00
QUEENSRYCHE ARE ENTERING THE 90'S ON AN UNPRECEDENTED GROUNDSWELL OF POPULARITY. THOUGH INVITED ON NUMEROUS HOT SUMMER TOURS, THE DEDICATED WORKAHOLIC ROCKERS INSTEAD OPT TO RETURN TO THE WOMB OF THE STUDIO TO CONCEIVE THEIR NEXT ALBUM.
I'M A LITTLE LEERY ABOUT FOLLOWING UP "MINDCRIME" WITH ANOTHER CONCEPT RECORD.
THEN SCRAP IT! WE'LL JUST GO BACK TO THE STYLE WE HAD ON "THE WARNING"... BASIC BANGERS WITH OUR "NEW" SOUND INTEGRATED INTO THE MIX, TO BEEF IT UP! WE'RE TEN TIMES BETTER AT PLAYING AND WRITING NOW!
QUOTABLE QUOTE:
"TOO MUCH MUSIC TODAY DOESN'T DIG FOR ANY EMOTION, EXCEPT TO BE PLEASING TO THE EAR." GEOFF TATE
NOTE FROM THE EDITOR: WE TAKE NO RESPONSIBILITY FOR, AND DO NOT NECESSARILY CONCUR WITH, DR. X'S RADICAL IDEOLOGY. HE'S A LITTLE WHACKO (PLAY THE ALBUM IF YOU DOUBT US). WE JUST HOPE THE NEW ALBUM ROCKS!

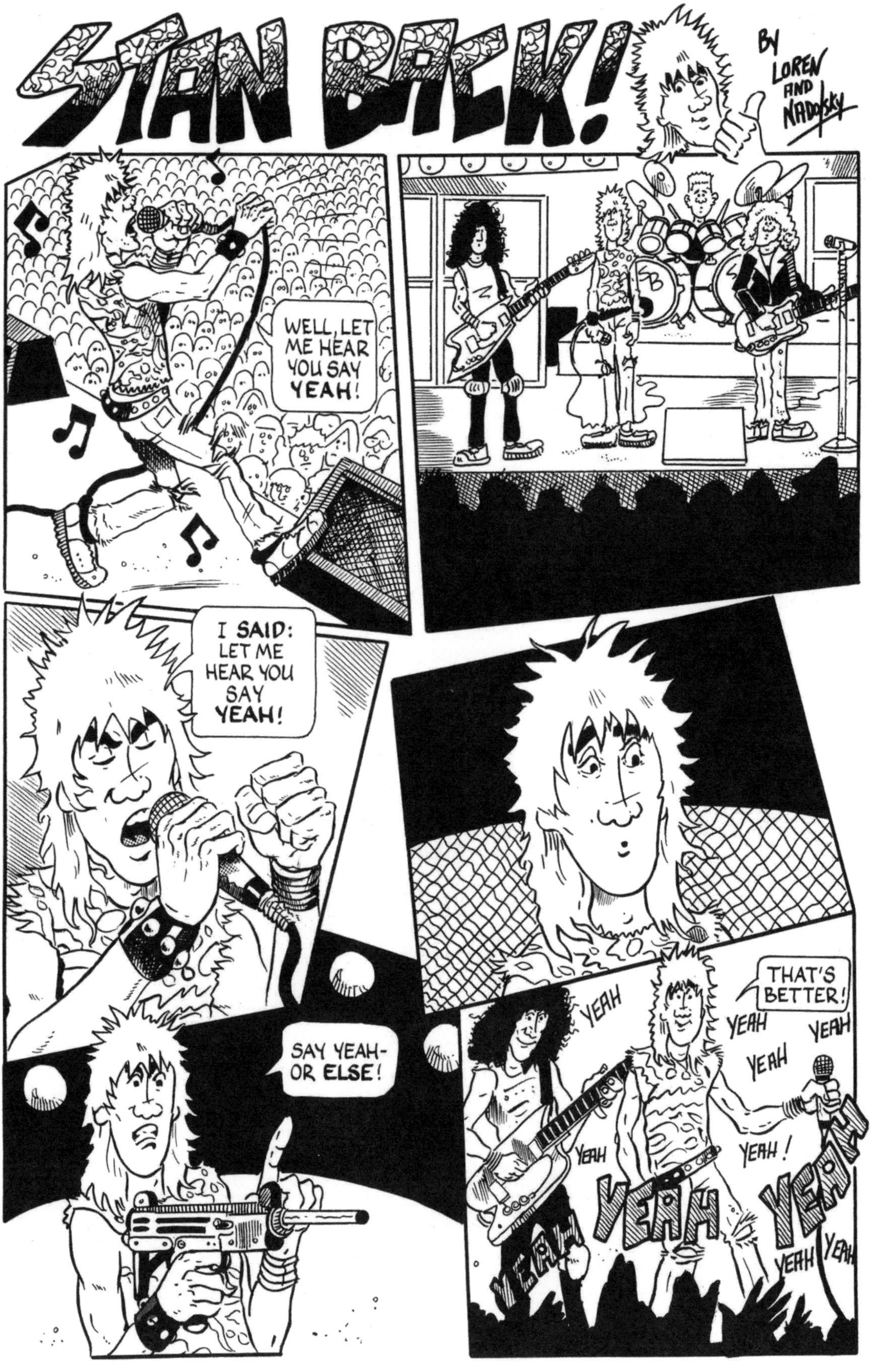
STAN BACK!
BY LOREN AND NADOLSKY
WELL, LET ME HEAR YOU SAY YEAH!
I SAID: LET ME HEAR YOU SAY YEAH!
SAY YEAH- OR ELSE!
THAT'S BETTER!
YEAH
YEAH
YEAH
YEAH
YEAH
YEAH!
YEAH YEAH YEAH YEAH
YEAH
YEAH

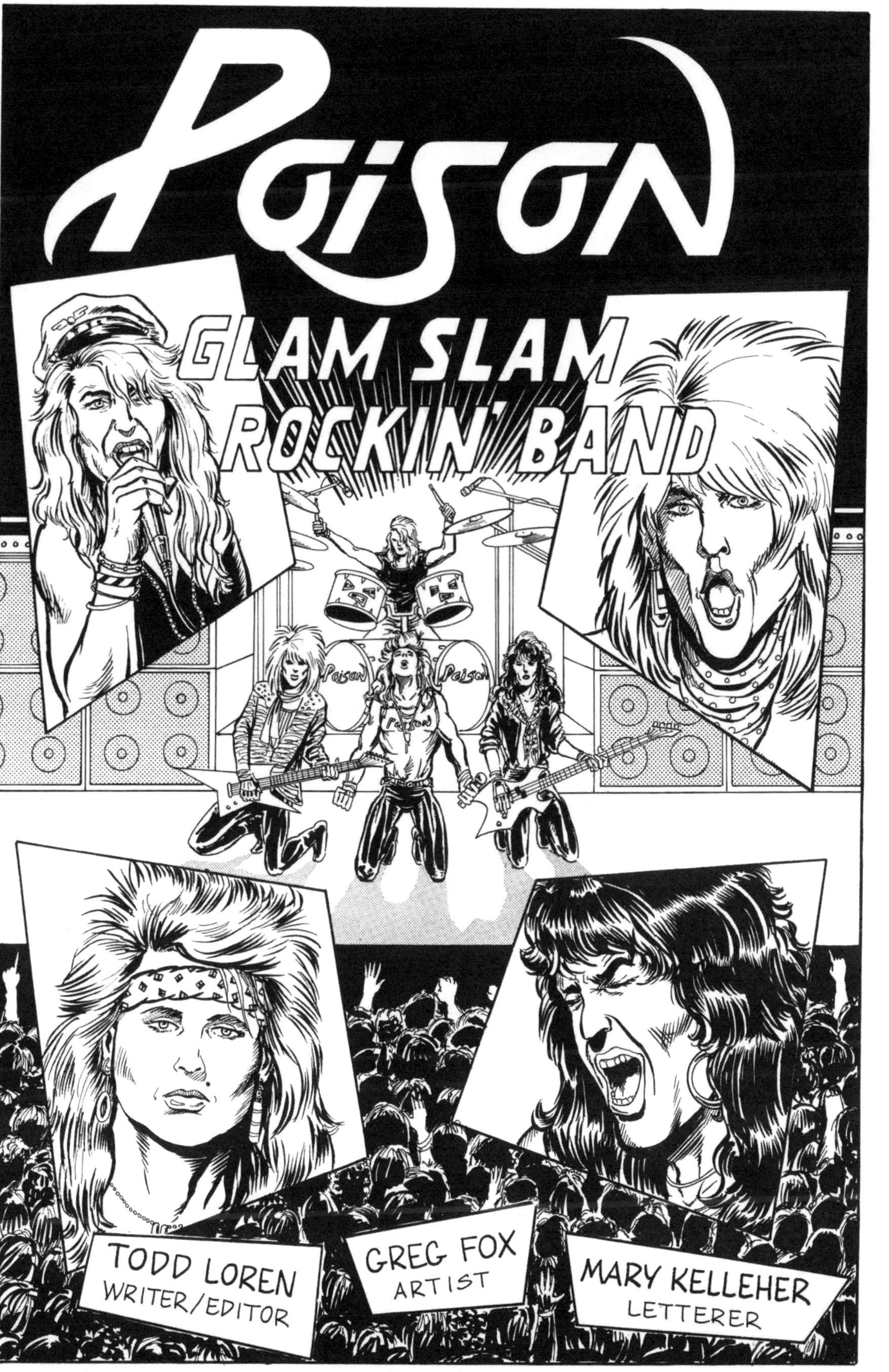
Poison
GLAM SLAM
ROCKIN' BAND
Poison
Poison
Poison
TODD LOREN
WRITER/EDITOR
GREG FOX
ARTIST
MARY KELLEHER
LETTERER

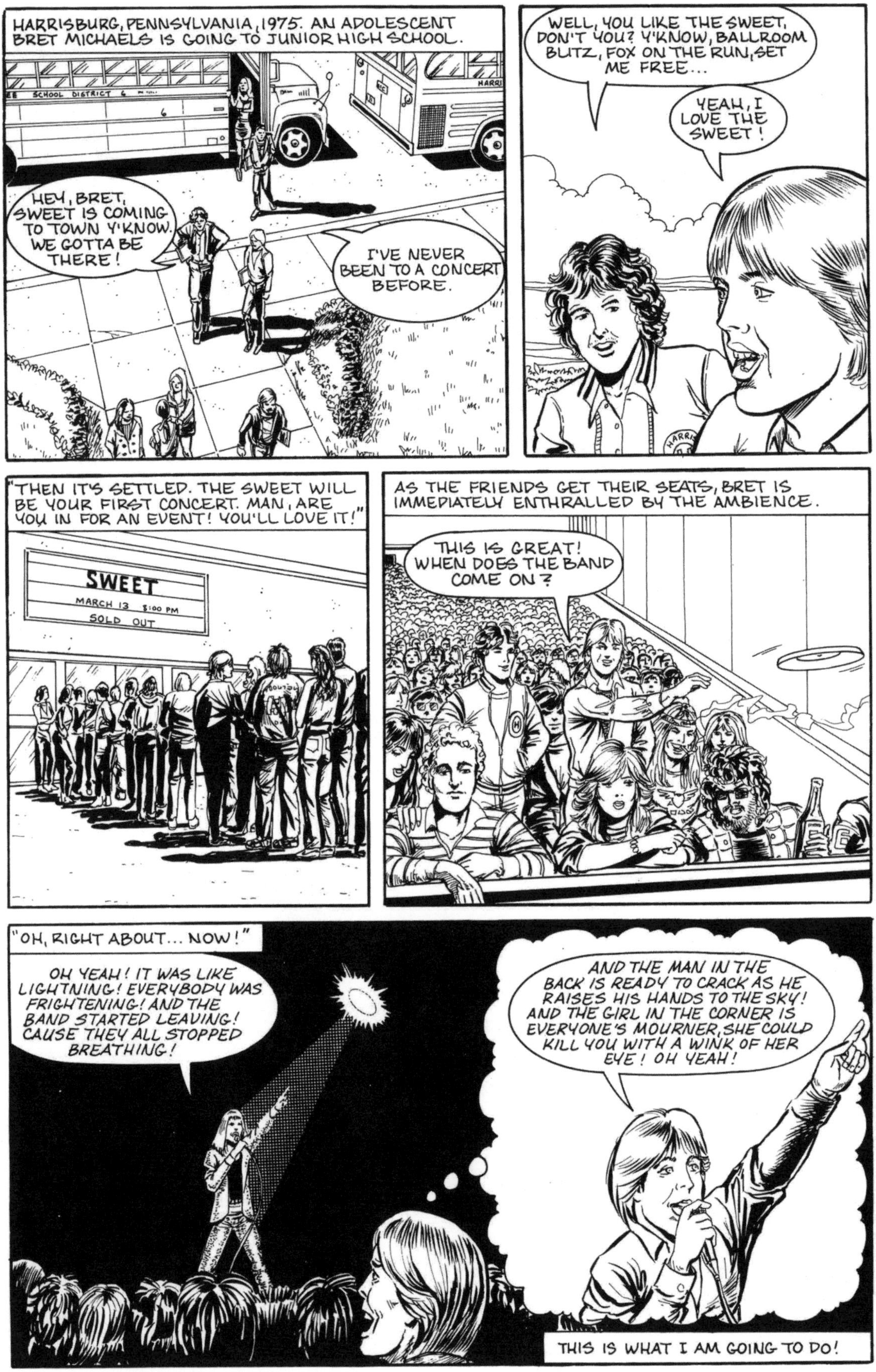
HARRISBURG, PENNSYLVANIA, 1975. AN ADOLESCENT BRET MICHAELS IS GOING TO JUNIOR HIGH SCHOOL.
SCHOOL DISTRICT
HEY, BRET, SWEET IS COMING TO TOWN Y'KNOW. WE GOTTA BE THERE!
I'VE NEVER BEEN TO A CONCERT BEFORE.
WELL, YOU LIKE THE SWEET, DON'T YOU? Y'KNOW, BALLROOM BLITZ, FOX ON THE RUN, SET ME FREE...
YEAH, I LOVE THE SWEET!
"THEN IT'S SETTLED. THE SWEET WILL BE YOUR FIRST CONCERT. MAN, ARE YOU IN FOR AN EVENT! YOU'LL LOVE IT!"
SWEET
MARCH 13 8:00 PM
SOLD OUT
AS THE FRIENDS GET THEIR SEATS, BRET IS IMMEDIATELY ENTHRALLED BY THE AMBIENCE.
THIS IS GREAT! WHEN DOES THE BAND COME ON?
"OH, RIGHT ABOUT... NOW!"
OH YEAH! IT WAS LIKE LIGHTNING! EVERYBODY WAS FRIGHTENING! AND THE BAND STARTED LEAVING! CAUSE THEY ALL STOPPED BREATHING!
AND THE MAN IN THE BACK IS READY TO CRACK AS HE RAISES HIS HANDS TO THE SKY! AND THE GIRL IN THE CORNER IS EVERYONE'S MOURNER, SHE COULD KILL YOU WITH A WINK OF HER EYE! OH YEAH!
THIS IS WHAT I AM GOING TO DO!

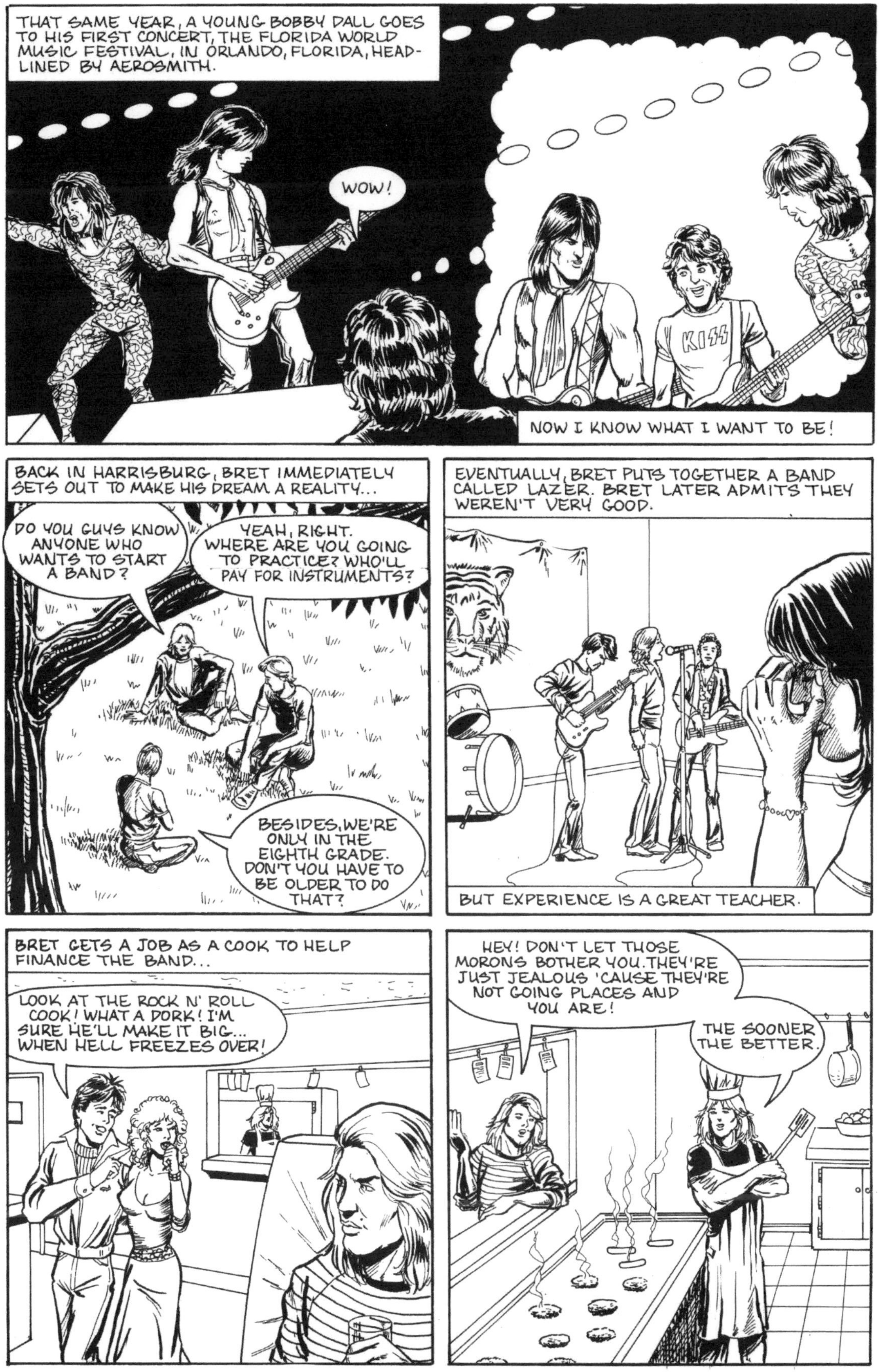
THAT SAME YEAR, A YOUNG BOBBY DALL GOES TO HIS FIRST CONCERT, THE FLORIDA WORLD MUSIC FESTIVAL, IN ORLANDO, FLORIDA, HEAD-LINED BY AEROSMITH.
WOW!
KISS
NOW I KNOW WHAT I WANT TO BE!
BACK IN HARRISBURG, BRET IMMEDIATELY SETS OUT TO MAKE HIS DREAM A REALITY...
DO YOU GUYS KNOW ANYONE WHO WANTS TO START A BAND?
YEAH, RIGHT. WHERE ARE YOU GOING TO PRACTICE? WHO'LL PAY FOR INSTRUMENTS?
BESIDES, WE'RE ONLY IN THE EIGHTH GRADE. DON'T YOU HAVE TO BE OLDER TO DO THAT?
EVENTUALLY, BRET PUTS TOGETHER A BAND CALLED LAZER. BRET LATER ADMITS THEY WEREN'T VERY GOOD.
BUT EXPERIENCE IS A GREAT TEACHER.
BRET GETS A JOB AS A COOK TO HELP FINANCE THE BAND...
LOOK AT THE ROCK N' ROLL COOK! WHAT A DORK! I'M SURE HE'LL MAKE IT BIG... WHEN HELL FREEZES OVER!
HEY! DON'T LET THOSE MORONS BOTHER YOU. THEY'RE JUST JEALOUS 'CAUSE THEY'RE NOT GOING PLACES AND YOU ARE!
THE SOONER THE BETTER.

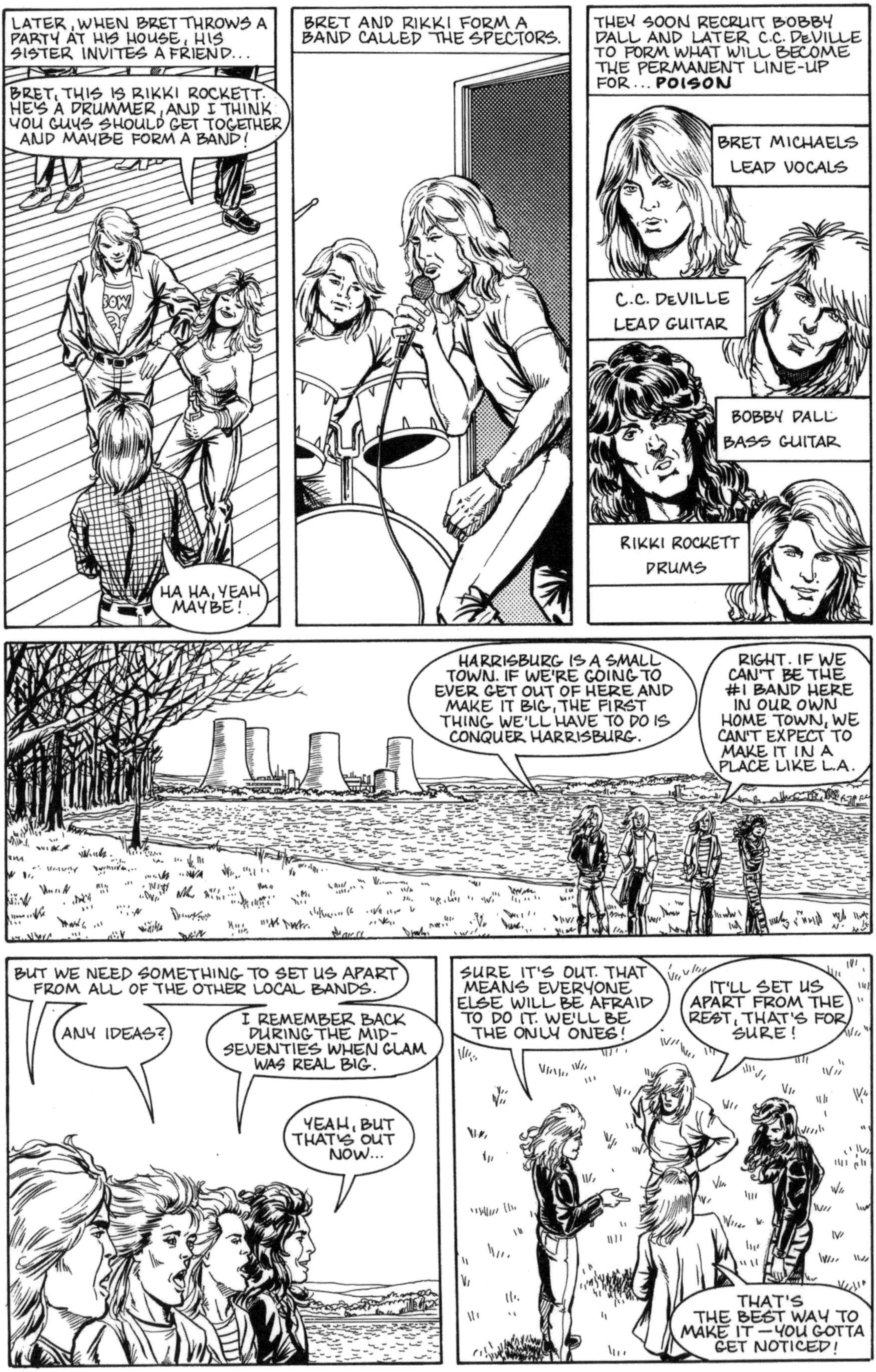

LATER, WHEN BRET THROWS A PARTY AT HIS HOUSE, HIS SISTER INVITES A FRIEND...
BRET, THIS IS RIKKI ROCKETT. HE'S A DRUMMER, AND I THINK YOU GUYS SHOULD GET TOGETHER AND MAYBE FORM A BAND!
HA HA, YEAH MAYBE!
BRET AND RIKKI FORM A BAND CALLED THE SPECTORS.
THEY SOON RECRUIT BOBBY DALL AND LATER C.C. DeVILLE TO FORM WHAT WILL BECOME THE PERMANENT LINE-UP FOR... POISON
BRET MICHAELS LEAD VOCALS
C.C. DeVILLE LEAD GUITAR
BOBBY DALL BASS GUITAR
RIKKI ROCKETT DRUMS
HARRISBURG IS A SMALL TOWN. IF WE'RE GOING TO EVER GET OUT OF HERE AND MAKE IT BIG, THE FIRST THING WE'LL HAVE TO DO IS CONQUER HARRISBURG.
RIGHT. IF WE CAN'T BE THE #1 BAND HERE IN OUR OWN HOME TOWN, WE CAN'T EXPECT TO MAKE IT IN A PLACE LIKE L.A.
BUT WE NEED SOMETHING TO SET US APART FROM ALL OF THE OTHER LOCAL BANDS.
ANY IDEAS?
I REMEMBER BACK DURING THE MID-SEVENTIES WHEN GLAM WAS REAL BIG.
YEAH, BUT THAT'S OUT NOW...
SURE IT'S OUT. THAT MEANS EVERYONE ELSE WILL BE AFRAID TO DO IT. WE'LL BE THE ONLY ONES!
IT'LL SET US APART FROM THE REST, THAT'S FOR SURE!
THAT'S THE BEST WAY TO MAKE IT — YOU GOTTA GET NOTICED!

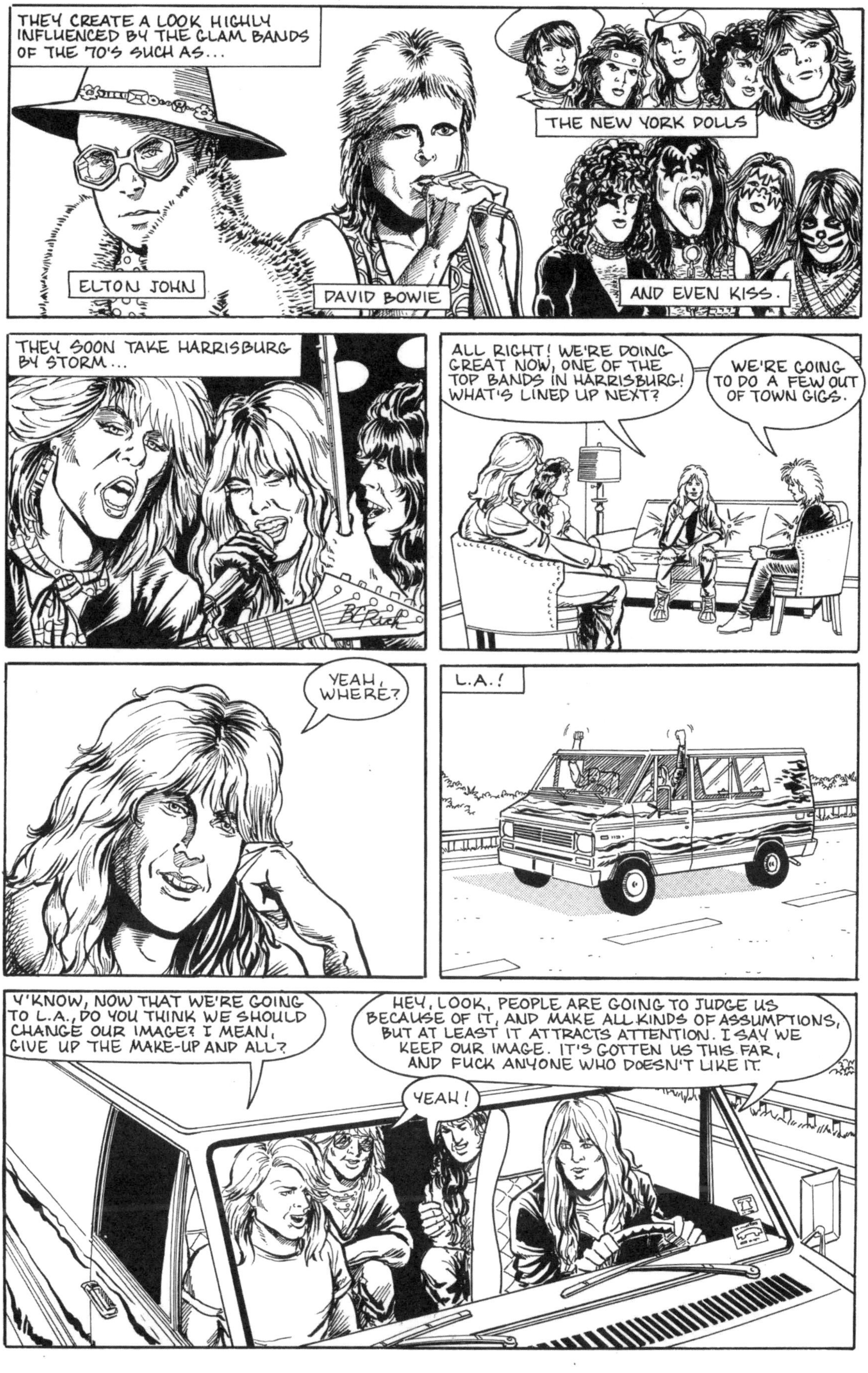

THEY CREATE A LOOK HIGHLY INFLUENCED BY THE GLAM BANDS OF THE '70'S SUCH AS...
ELTON JOHN
DAVID BOWIE
THE NEW YORK DOLLS
AND EVEN KISS.
THEY SOON TAKE HARRISBURG BY STORM...
BC Rich
ALL RIGHT! WE'RE DOING GREAT NOW, ONE OF THE TOP BANDS IN HARRISBURG! WHAT'S LINED UP NEXT?
WE'RE GOING TO DO A FEW OUT OF TOWN GIGS.
YEAH, WHERE?
L.A.!
Y'KNOW, NOW THAT WE'RE GOING TO L.A., DO YOU THINK WE SHOULD CHANGE OUR IMAGE? I MEAN, GIVE UP THE MAKE-UP AND ALL?
HEY, LOOK, PEOPLE ARE GOING TO JUDGE US BECAUSE OF IT, AND MAKE ALL KINDS OF ASSUMPTIONS, BUT AT LEAST IT ATTRACTS ATTENTION. I SAY WE KEEP OUR IMAGE. IT'S GOTTEN US THIS FAR, AND FUCK ANYONE WHO DOESN'T LIKE IT.
YEAH!

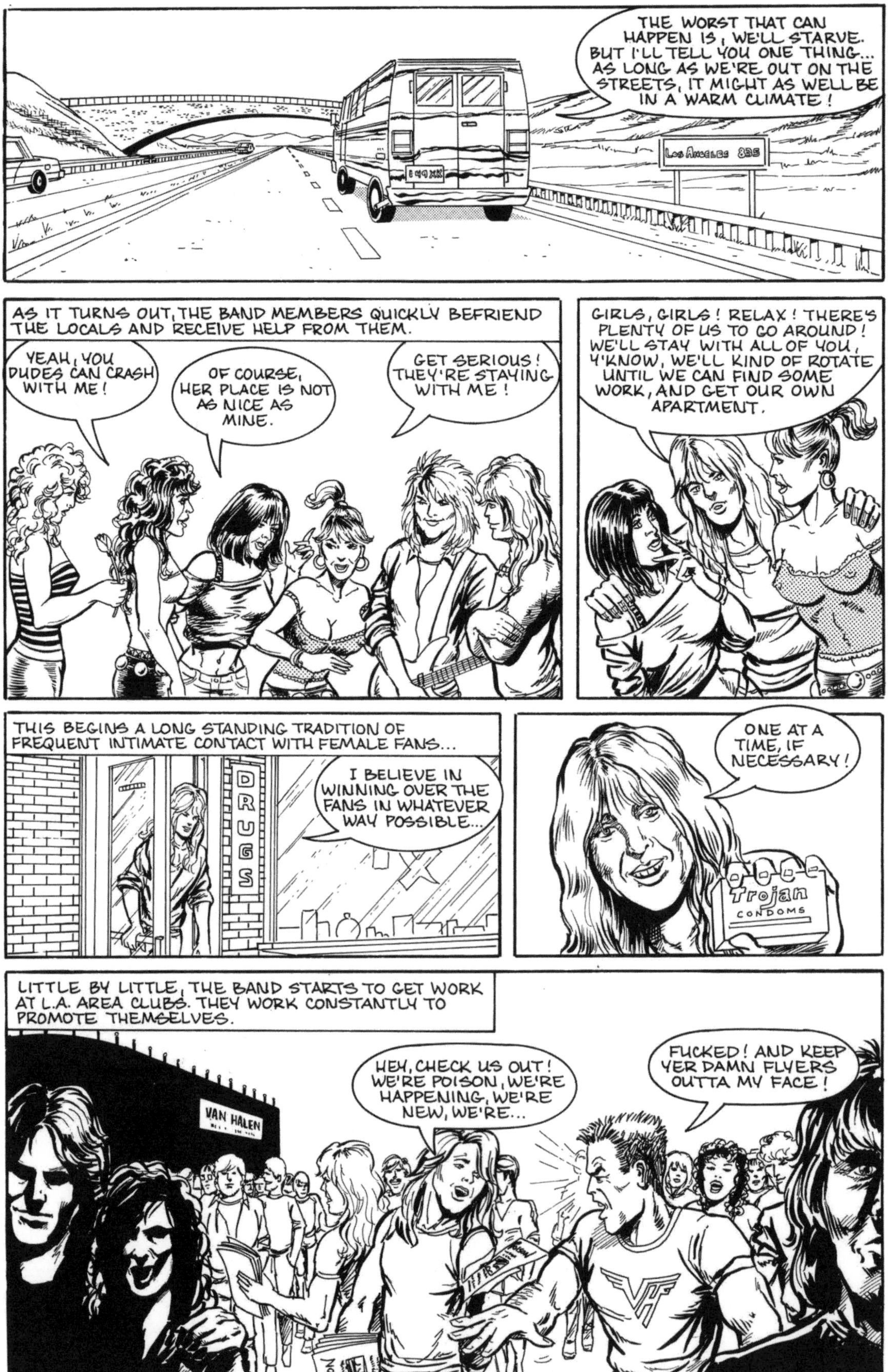
THE WORST THAT CAN HAPPEN IS, WE'LL STARVE. BUT I'LL TELL YOU ONE THING... AS LONG AS WE'RE OUT ON THE STREETS, IT MIGHT AS WELL BE IN A WARM CLIMATE!
LOS ANGELES 835
AS IT TURNS OUT, THE BAND MEMBERS QUICKLY BEFRIEND THE LOCALS AND RECEIVE HELP FROM THEM.
YEAH, YOU DUDES CAN CRASH WITH ME!
OF COURSE, HER PLACE IS NOT AS NICE AS MINE.
GET SERIOUS! THEY'RE STAYING WITH ME!
GIRLS, GIRLS! RELAX! THERE'S PLENTY OF US TO GO AROUND! WE'LL STAY WITH ALL OF YOU, Y'KNOW, WE'LL KIND OF ROTATE UNTIL WE CAN FIND SOME WORK, AND GET OUR OWN APARTMENT.
THIS BEGINS A LONG STANDING TRADITION OF FREQUENT INTIMATE CONTACT WITH FEMALE FANS...
DRUGS
I BELIEVE IN WINNING OVER THE FANS IN WHATEVER WAY POSSIBLE...
ONE AT A TIME, IF NECESSARY!
Trojan
CONDOMS
LITTLE BY LITTLE, THE BAND STARTS TO GET WORK AT L.A. AREA CLUBS. THEY WORK CONSTANTLY TO PROMOTE THEMSELVES.
VAN HALEN
HEY, CHECK US OUT! WE'RE POISON, WE'RE HAPPENING, WE'RE NEW, WE'RE...
FUCKED! AND KEEP YER DAMN FLYERS OUTTA MY FACE!

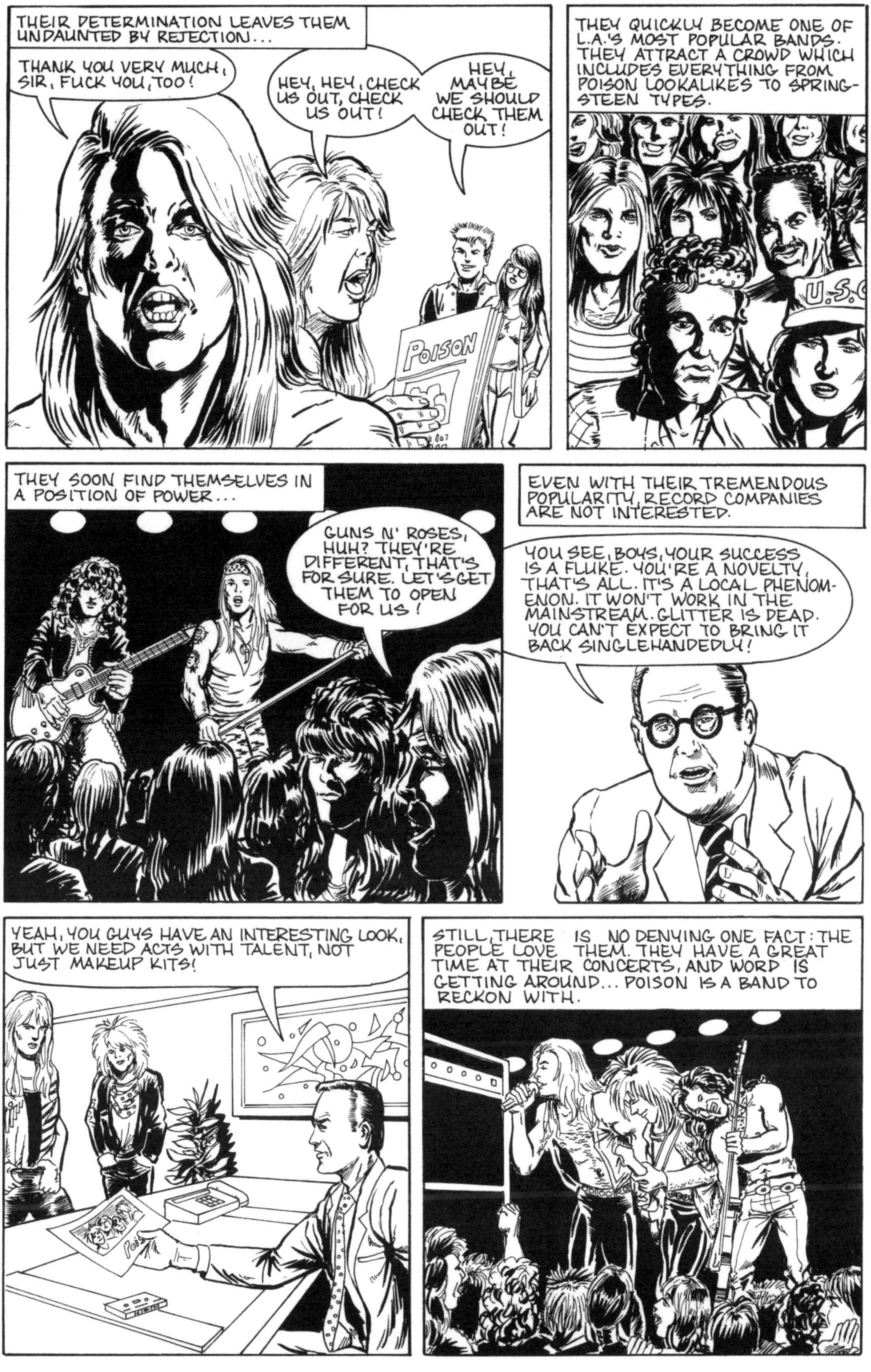
THEIR DETERMINATION LEAVES THEM UNDAUNTED BY REJECTION...
THANK YOU VERY MUCH, SIR, FUCK YOU, TOO!
HEY, HEY, CHECK US OUT, CHECK US OUT!
HEY, MAYBE WE SHOULD CHECK THEM OUT!
POISON
THEY QUICKLY BECOME ONE OF L.A.'S MOST POPULAR BANDS. THEY ATTRACT A CROWD WHICH INCLUDES EVERYTHING FROM POISON LOOKALIKES TO SPRING-STEEN TYPES.
THEY SOON FIND THEMSELVES IN A POSITION OF POWER...
GUNS N' ROSES, HUH? THEY'RE DIFFERENT, THAT'S FOR SURE. LET'S GET THEM TO OPEN FOR US!
EVEN WITH THEIR TREMENDOUS POPULARITY, RECORD COMPANIES ARE NOT INTERESTED.
YOU SEE, BOYS, YOUR SUCCESS IS A FLUKE. YOU'RE A NOVELTY, THAT'S ALL. IT'S A LOCAL PHENOM-ENON. IT WON'T WORK IN THE MAINSTREAM. GLITTER IS DEAD. YOU CAN'T EXPECT TO BRING IT BACK SINGLEHANDEDLY!
YEAH, YOU GUYS HAVE AN INTERESTING LOOK, BUT WE NEED ACTS WITH TALENT, NOT JUST MAKEUP KITS!
STILL, THERE IS NO DENYING ONE FACT: THE PEOPLE LOVE THEM. THEY HAVE A GREAT TIME AT THEIR CONCERTS, AND WORD IS GETTING AROUND... POISON IS A BAND TO RECKON WITH.

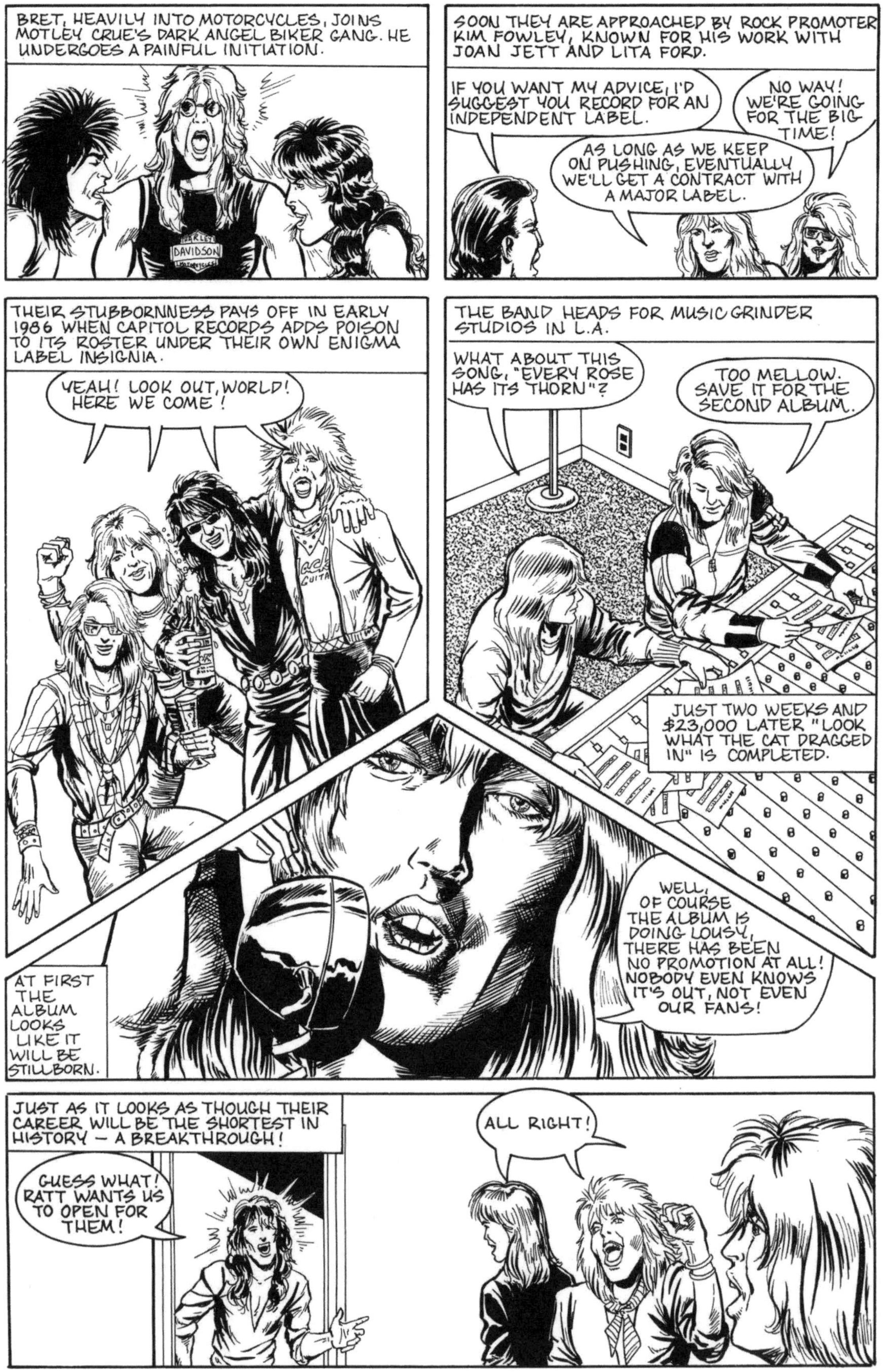
BRET, HEAVILY INTO MOTORCYCLES, JOINS MOTLEY CRUE'S DARK ANGEL BIKER GANG. HE UNDERGOES A PAINFUL INITIATION.
HARLEY DAVIDSON MOTORCYCLES
SOON THEY ARE APPROACHED BY ROCK PROMOTER KIM FOWLEY, KNOWN FOR HIS WORK WITH JOAN JETT AND LITA FORD.
IF YOU WANT MY ADVICE, I'D SUGGEST YOU RECORD FOR AN INDEPENDENT LABEL.
NO WAY! WE'RE GOING FOR THE BIG TIME!
AS LONG AS WE KEEP ON PUSHING, EVENTUALLY WE'LL GET A CONTRACT WITH A MAJOR LABEL.
THEIR STUBBORNNESS PAYS OFF IN EARLY 1986 WHEN CAPITOL RECORDS ADDS POISON TO ITS ROSTER UNDER THEIR OWN ENIGMA LABEL INSIGNIA.
YEAH! LOOK OUT, WORLD! HERE WE COME!
THE BAND HEADS FOR MUSIC GRINDER STUDIOS IN L.A.
WHAT ABOUT THIS SONG, "EVERY ROSE HAS ITS THORN"?
TOO MELLOW. SAVE IT FOR THE SECOND ALBUM.
JUST TWO WEEKS AND $23,000 LATER "LOOK WHAT THE CAT DRAGGED IN" IS COMPLETED.
AT FIRST THE ALBUM LOOKS LIKE IT WILL BE STILLBORN.
WELL, OF COURSE THE ALBUM IS DOING LOUSY, THERE HAS BEEN NO PROMOTION AT ALL! NOBODY EVEN KNOWS IT'S OUT, NOT EVEN OUR FANS!
JUST AS IT LOOKS AS THOUGH THEIR CAREER WILL BE THE SHORTEST IN HISTORY – A BREAKTHROUGH!
GUESS WHAT! RATT WANTS US TO OPEN FOR THEM!
ALL RIGHT!

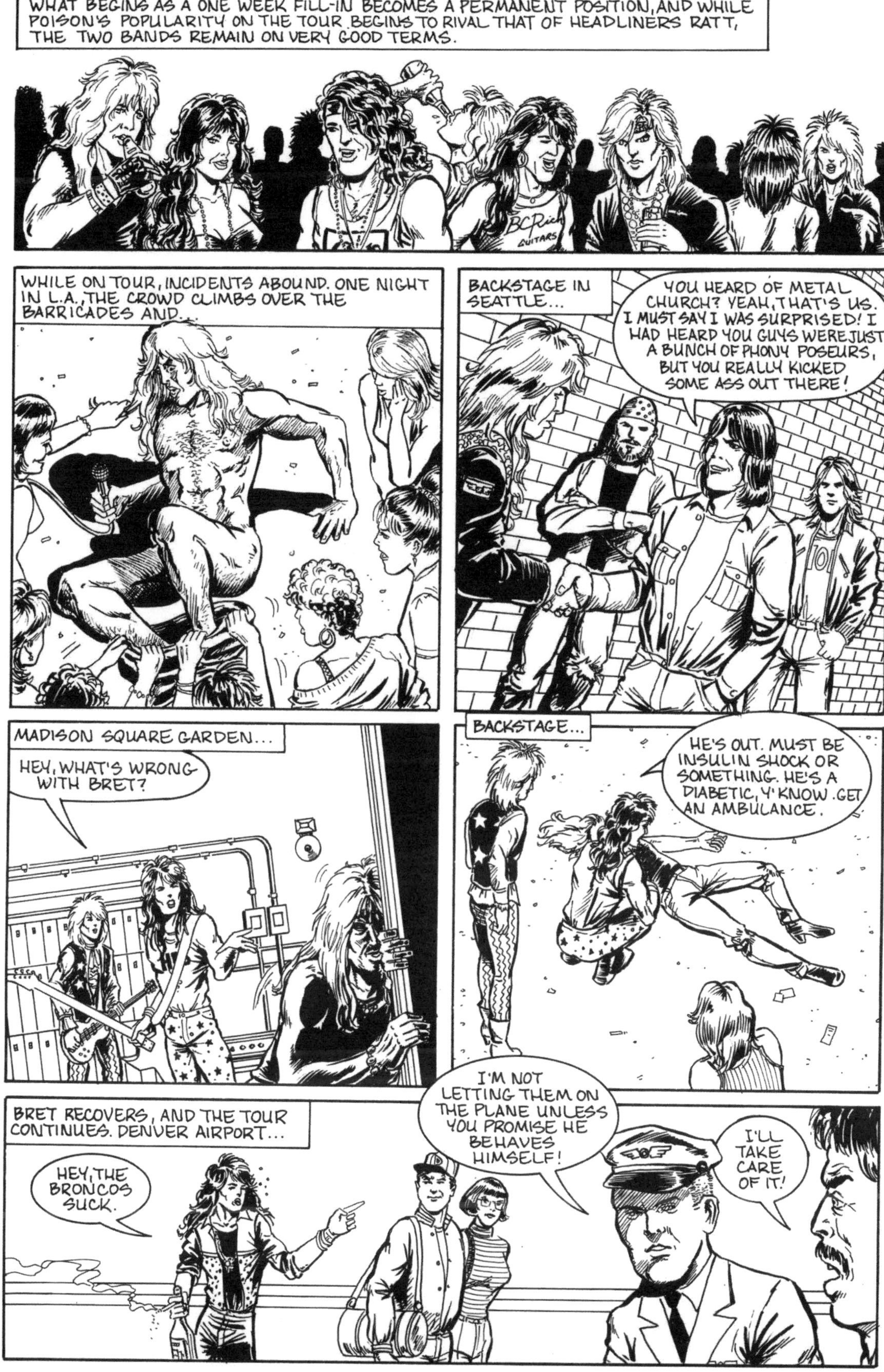
WHAT BEGINS AS A ONE WEEK FILL-IN BECOMES A PERMANENT POSITION, AND WHILE POISON'S POPULARITY ON THE TOUR BEGINS TO RIVAL THAT OF HEADLINERS RATT, THE TWO BANDS REMAIN ON VERY GOOD TERMS.
BC Rich GUITARS
WHILE ON TOUR, INCIDENTS ABOUND. ONE NIGHT IN L.A., THE CROWD CLIMBS OVER THE BARRICADES AND...
BACKSTAGE IN SEATTLE...
YOU HEARD OF METAL CHURCH? YEAH, THAT'S US. I MUST SAY I WAS SURPRISED! I HAD HEARD YOU GUYS WERE JUST A BUNCH OF PHONY POSEURS, BUT YOU REALLY KICKED SOME ASS OUT THERE!
MADISON SQUARE GARDEN...
HEY, WHAT'S WRONG WITH BRET?
BACKSTAGE...
HE'S OUT. MUST BE INSULIN SHOCK OR SOMETHING. HE'S A DIABETIC, Y'KNOW. GET AN AMBULANCE.
BRET RECOVERS, AND THE TOUR CONTINUES. DENVER AIRPORT...
HEY, THE BRONCOS SUCK.
I'M NOT LETTING THEM ON THE PLANE UNLESS YOU PROMISE HE BEHAVES HIMSELF!
I'LL TAKE CARE OF IT!

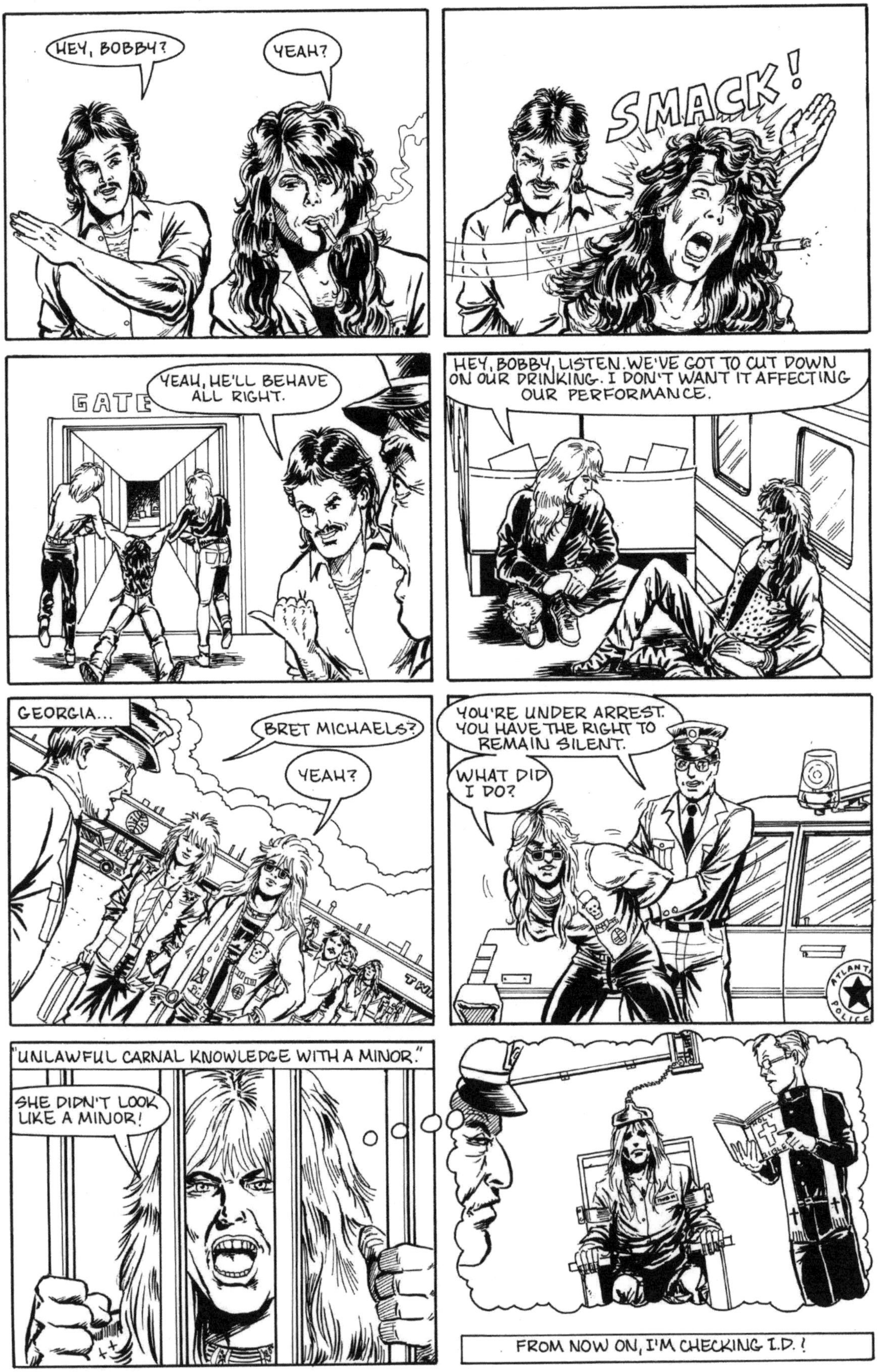
HEY, BOBBY?
YEAH?
SMACK!
YEAH, HE'LL BEHAVE ALL RIGHT.
GATE
HEY, BOBBY, LISTEN. WE'VE GOT TO CUT DOWN ON OUR DRINKING. I DON'T WANT IT AFFECTING OUR PERFORMANCE.
GEORGIA...
BRET MICHAELS?
YEAH?
YOU'RE UNDER ARREST. YOU HAVE THE RIGHT TO REMAIN SILENT.
WHAT DID I DO?
ATLANTA POLICE
"UNLAWFUL CARNAL KNOWLEDGE WITH A MINOR."
SHE DIDN'T LOOK LIKE A MINOR!
HOLY BIBLE
FROM NOW ON, I'M CHECKING I.D.!

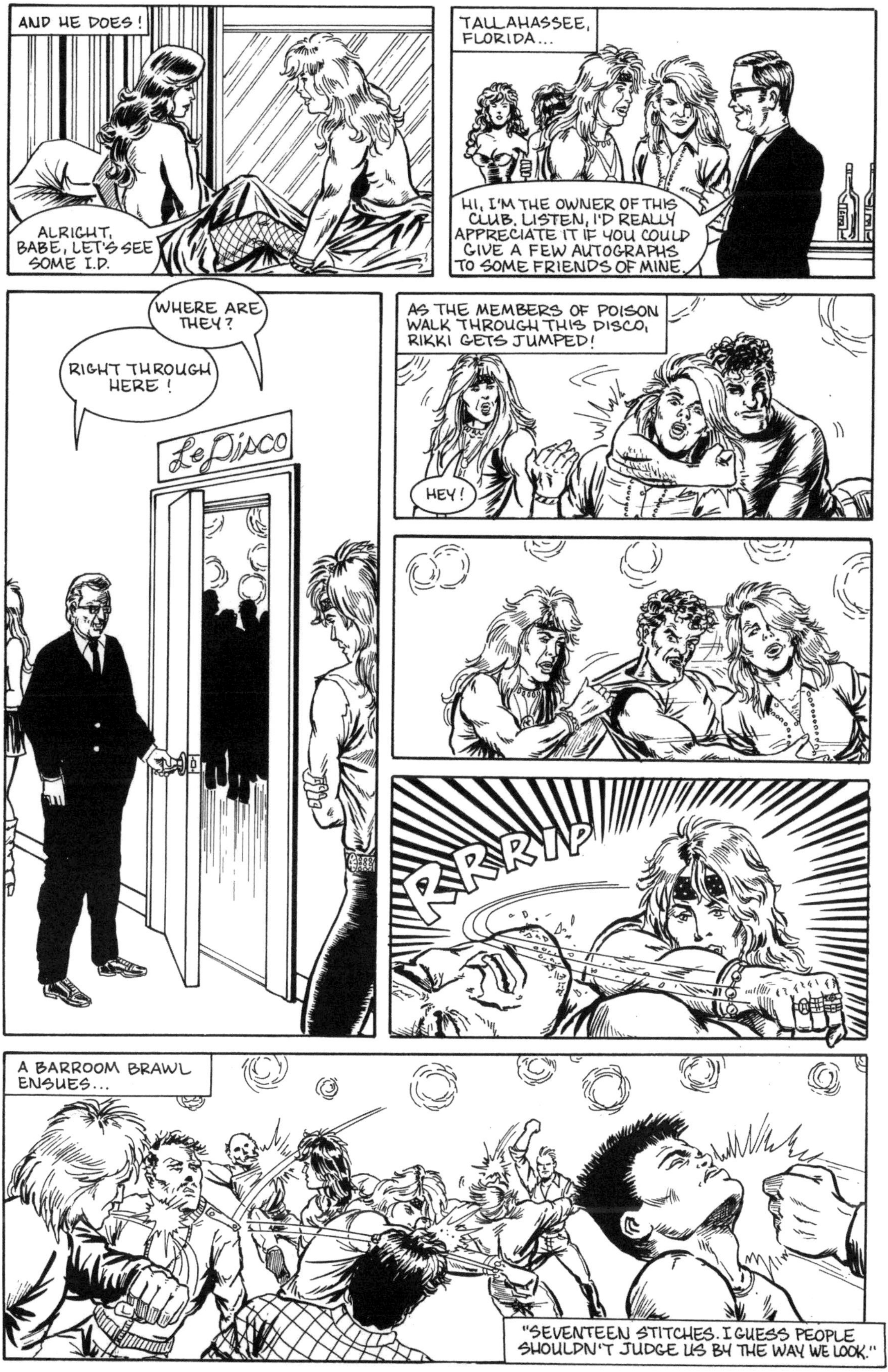
AND HE DOES!
ALRIGHT, BABE, LET'S SEE SOME I.D.
TALLAHASSEE, FLORIDA...
HI, I'M THE OWNER OF THIS CLUB. LISTEN, I'D REALLY APPRECIATE IT IF YOU COULD GIVE A FEW AUTOGRAPHS TO SOME FRIENDS OF MINE.
WHERE ARE THEY?
RIGHT THROUGH HERE!
Le Disco
AS THE MEMBERS OF POISON WALK THROUGH THIS DISCO, RIKKI GETS JUMPED!
HEY!
RRRIP
A BARROOM BRAWL ENSUES...
"SEVENTEEN STITCHES. I GUESS PEOPLE SHOULDN'T JUDGE US BY THE WAY WE LOOK."

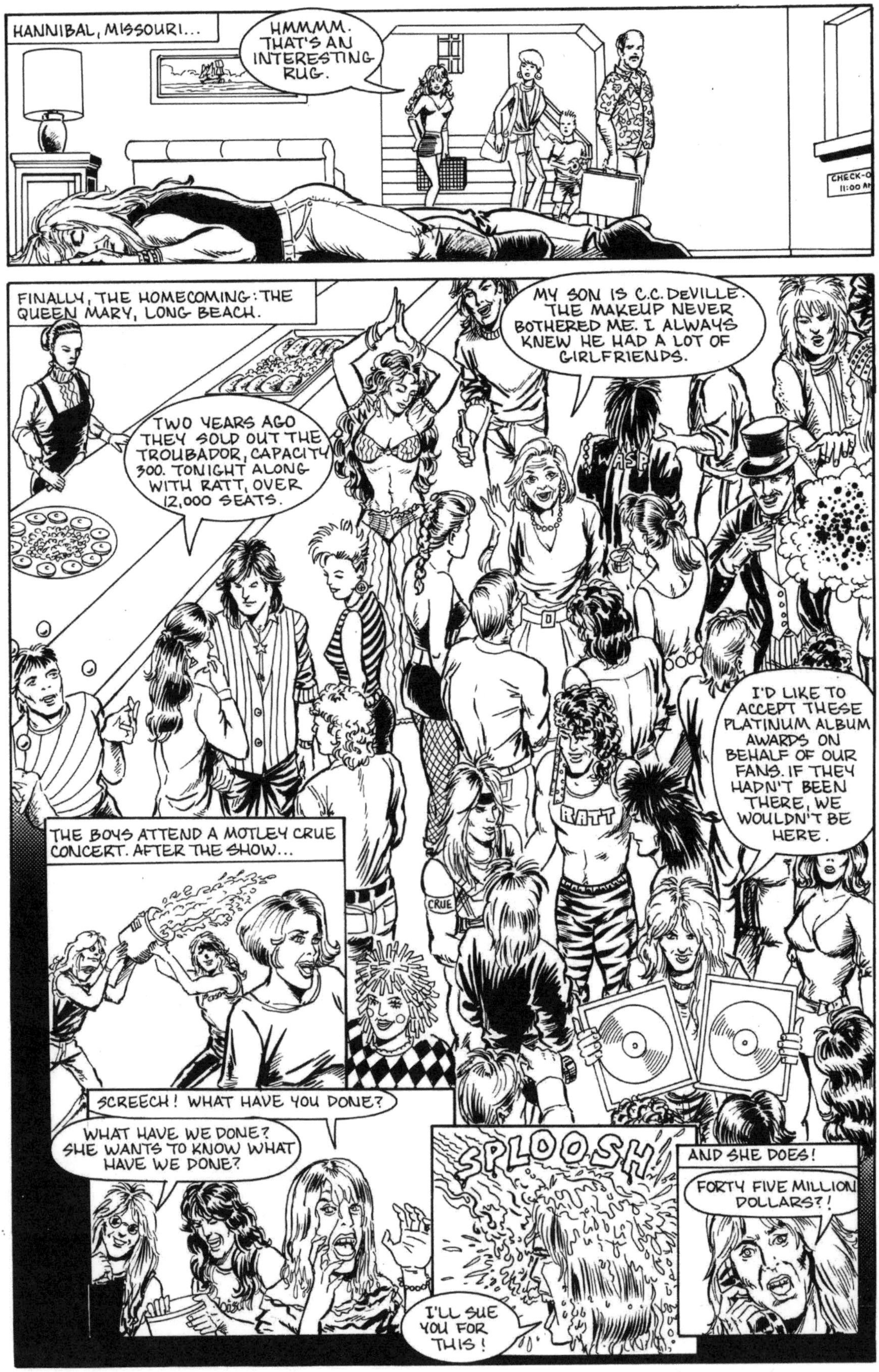
HANNIBAL, MISSOURI...
HMMMM. THAT'S AN INTERESTING RUG.
CHECK-O 11:00 AM
FINALLY, THE HOMECOMING: THE QUEEN MARY, LONG BEACH.
MY SON IS C.C. DeVILLE. THE MAKEUP NEVER BOTHERED ME. I ALWAYS KNEW HE HAD A LOT OF GIRLFRIENDS.
TWO YEARS AGO THEY SOLD OUT THE TROUBADOR, CAPACITY 300. TONIGHT ALONG WITH RATT, OVER 12,000 SEATS.
WASP
I'D LIKE TO ACCEPT THESE PLATINUM ALBUM AWARDS ON BEHALF OF OUR FANS. IF THEY HADN'T BEEN THERE, WE WOULDN'T BE HERE.
RATT
CRUE
THE BOYS ATTEND A MOTLEY CRUE CONCERT. AFTER THE SHOW...
SCREECH! WHAT HAVE YOU DONE?
WHAT HAVE WE DONE? SHE WANTS TO KNOW WHAT HAVE WE DONE?
SPLOOSH
I'LL SUE YOU FOR THIS!
AND SHE DOES!
FORTY FIVE MILLION DOLLARS?!

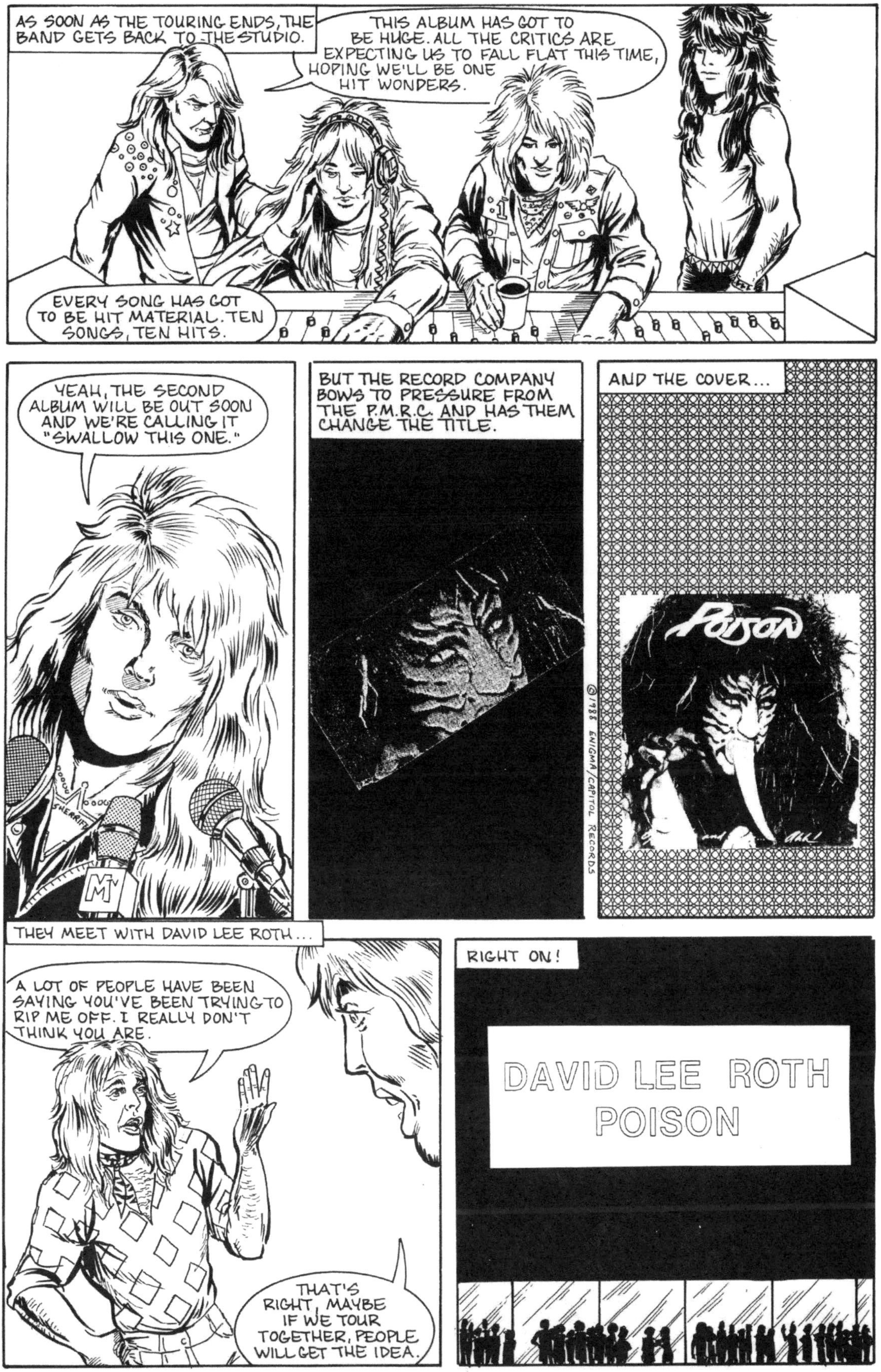

AS SOON AS THE TOURING ENDS, THE BAND GETS BACK TO THE STUDIO.
THIS ALBUM HAS GOT TO BE HUGE. ALL THE CRITICS ARE EXPECTING US TO FALL FLAT THIS TIME, HOPING WE'LL BE ONE HIT WONDERS.
EVERY SONG HAS GOT TO BE HIT MATERIAL. TEN SONGS, TEN HITS.
YEAH, THE SECOND ALBUM WILL BE OUT SOON AND WE'RE CALLING IT "SWALLOW THIS ONE."
SHERRITY
BUT THE RECORD COMPANY BOWS TO PRESSURE FROM THE P.M.R.C. AND HAS THEM CHANGE THE TITLE.
©1988 ENIGMA/CAPITOL RECORDS
AND THE COVER...
POISON
THEY MEET WITH DAVID LEE ROTH...
A LOT OF PEOPLE HAVE BEEN SAYING YOU'VE BEEN TRYING TO RIP ME OFF. I REALLY DON'T THINK YOU ARE.
THAT'S RIGHT, MAYBE IF WE TOUR TOGETHER, PEOPLE WILL GET THE IDEA.
RIGHT ON!
DAVID LEE ROTH
POISON

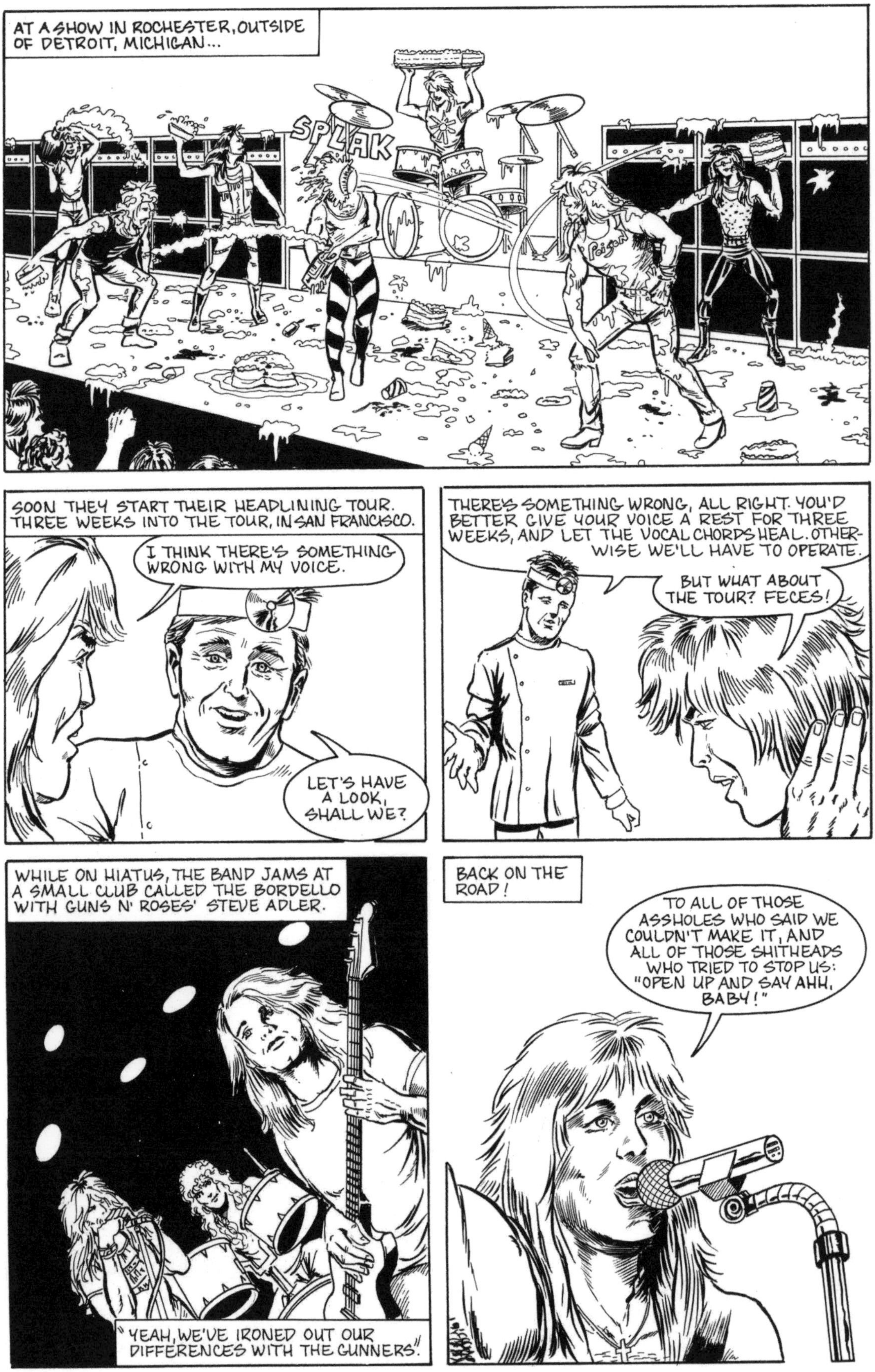
AT A SHOW IN ROCHESTER, OUTSIDE OF DETROIT, MICHIGAN...
SPLAK
SOON THEY START THEIR HEADLINING TOUR. THREE WEEKS INTO THE TOUR, IN SAN FRANCISCO.
I THINK THERE'S SOMETHING WRONG WITH MY VOICE.
LET'S HAVE A LOOK, SHALL WE?
THERE'S SOMETHING WRONG, ALL RIGHT. YOU'D BETTER GIVE YOUR VOICE A REST FOR THREE WEEKS, AND LET THE VOCAL CHORDS HEAL. OTHERWISE WE'LL HAVE TO OPERATE.
BUT WHAT ABOUT THE TOUR? FECES!
WHILE ON HIATUS, THE BAND JAMS AT A SMALL CLUB CALLED THE BORDELLO WITH GUNS N' ROSES' STEVE ADLER.
"YEAH, WE'VE IRONED OUT OUR DIFFERENCES WITH THE GUNNERS."
BACK ON THE ROAD!
TO ALL OF THOSE ASSHOLES WHO SAID WE COULDN'T MAKE IT, AND ALL OF THOSE SHITHEADS WHO TRIED TO STOP US: "OPEN UP AND SAY AHH, BABY!"

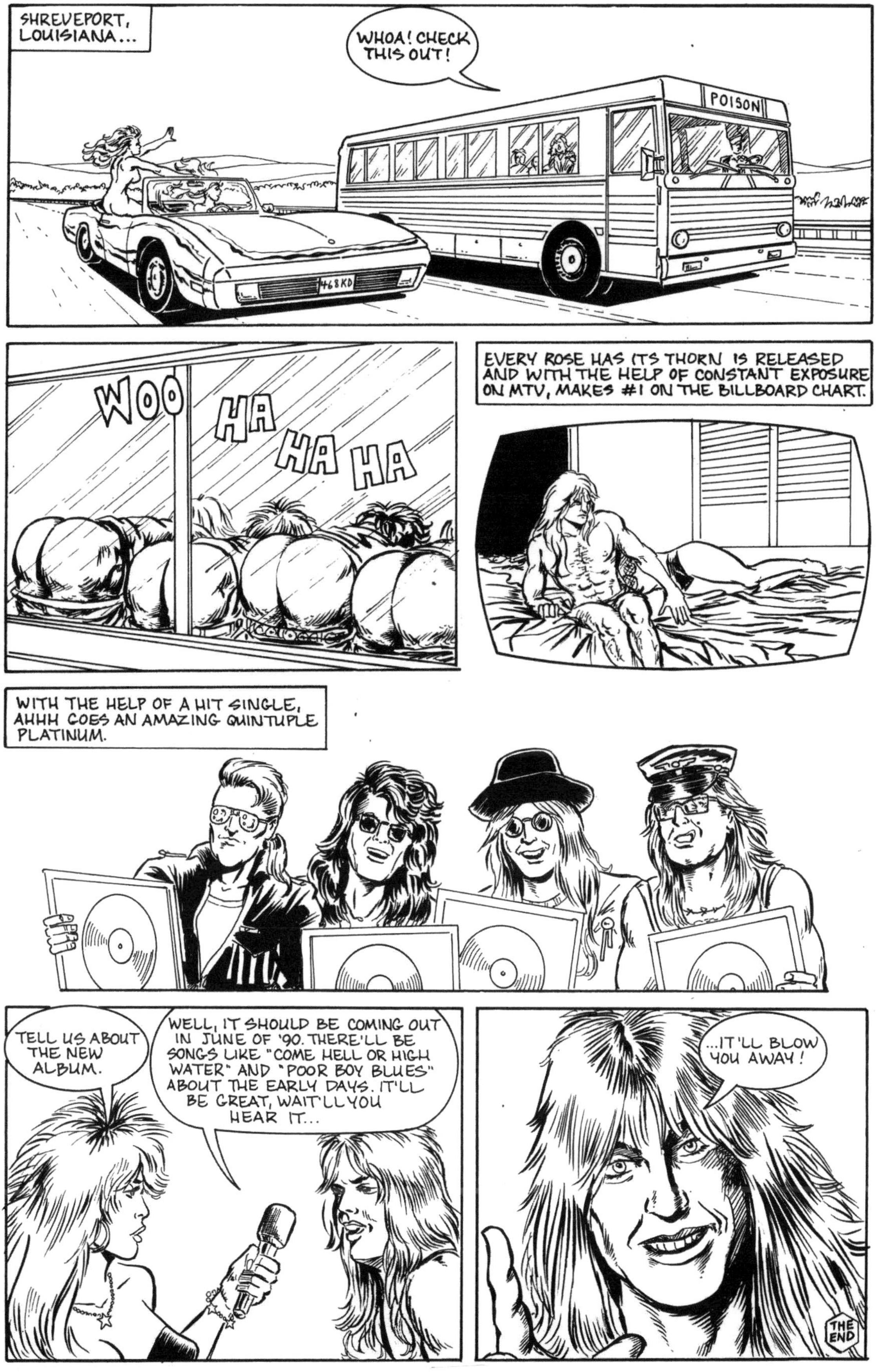
SHREVEPORT, LOUISIANA...
WHOA! CHECK THIS OUT!
POISON
468KD
WOO
HA
HA
HA
EVERY ROSE HAS ITS THORN IS RELEASED AND WITH THE HELP OF CONSTANT EXPOSURE ON MTV, MAKES #1 ON THE BILLBOARD CHART.
WITH THE HELP OF A HIT SINGLE, AHHH GOES AN AMAZING QUINTUPLE PLATINUM.
TELL US ABOUT THE NEW ALBUM.
WELL, IT SHOULD BE COMING OUT IN JUNE OF '90. THERE'LL BE SONGS LIKE "COME HELL OR HIGH WATER" AND "POOR BOY BLUES" ABOUT THE EARLY DAYS. IT'LL BE GREAT, WAIT'LL YOU HEAR IT...
...IT'LL BLOW YOU AWAY!
THE END

Tuneful Trivia

OKAY, SO YOU KNOW THE LYRICS TO ALL YOUR FAVORITE SONGS, FORWARD AND BACKWARDS, BUT WHY NOT TRY PUTTING YOUR MIND-FOR-MUSIC TO THE TEST!

1. PEARL JAM'S ORIGINAL NAME WAS:
   A. THE VIRGIN PRUNES
   B. THE SUBMERGED TENTH
   C. MOOKIE BLAYLOCK

2. BEFORE MARRYING "YOUNG GUN" EMILIO ESTEVEZ, PAULA ABDUL USED TO DATE:
   A. CHARLIE SHEEN
   B. JOHN STAMOS
   C. WARREN BEATTY

3. WHICH BAND HAD NOTHING TO DO WITH "BILL AND TED'S BOGUS JOURNEY"?
   A. PRIMUS
   B. FAITH NO MORE
   C. UGLY KID JOE

4. THE GUNS N' ROSES COVER SONG "KNOCKIN' ON HEAVEN'S DOOR" WAS WRITTEN BY:
   A. BOB DYLAN
   B. ELTON JOHN AND BERNIE TAUPIN
   C. JOHN LENNON

5. WHICH PUNK BAND DOES FLEA CLAIM HE ONCE WAS A MEMBER OF?
   A. FEAR
   B. BLACK FLAG
   C. THE GERMS

6. NELSON'S HIT "(CAN'T LIVE WITHOUT YOUR) LOVE AND AFFECTION" WAS INSPIRED BY WHAT WOMAN?
   A. ERIN EVERLY
   B. CHYNNA PHILLIPS
   C. CINDY CRAWFORD

7. COLOR ME BADD'S HIT "I WANNA SEX YOU UP" WAS FEATURED IN WHICH MOVIE?
   A. "NEW JACK CITY"
   B. "BOOMERANG"
   C. "BOYZ N THE HOOD"

8. WHO WAS BORN IN DETROIT ON AUG. 16, 1958?
   A. JON BON JOVI
   B. MADONNA
   C. MICHAEL STIPE

9. WHO ARE CHRISTOPHER MARTIN AND CHRISTOPHER REID?
   A. MILLI VANILLI
   B. KID N' PLAY
   C. KRIS KROSS

10. WHICH SEATTLE BAND ISN'T FEATURED IN THE "SINGLES" SOUNDTRACK?
    A. SOUNDGARDEN
    B. MUDHONEY
    C. NIRVANA

NADOLSKY

ANSWERS AND SCORING:
1.C 2.B 3.C 4.A 5.A 6.C 7.A 8.B 9.B 10.C
0-3 WHAT?? DON'T YOU WANT YOUR MTV??
4-7 NOT BAD, YOU CAN KEEP UP WITH MOST MUSICAL CHATTER THAT COMES YOUR WAY
8-10 YOU'RE TAPPING YOUR FINGERS RIGHT ON THE PULSE OF THE MUSIC BIZ!

13

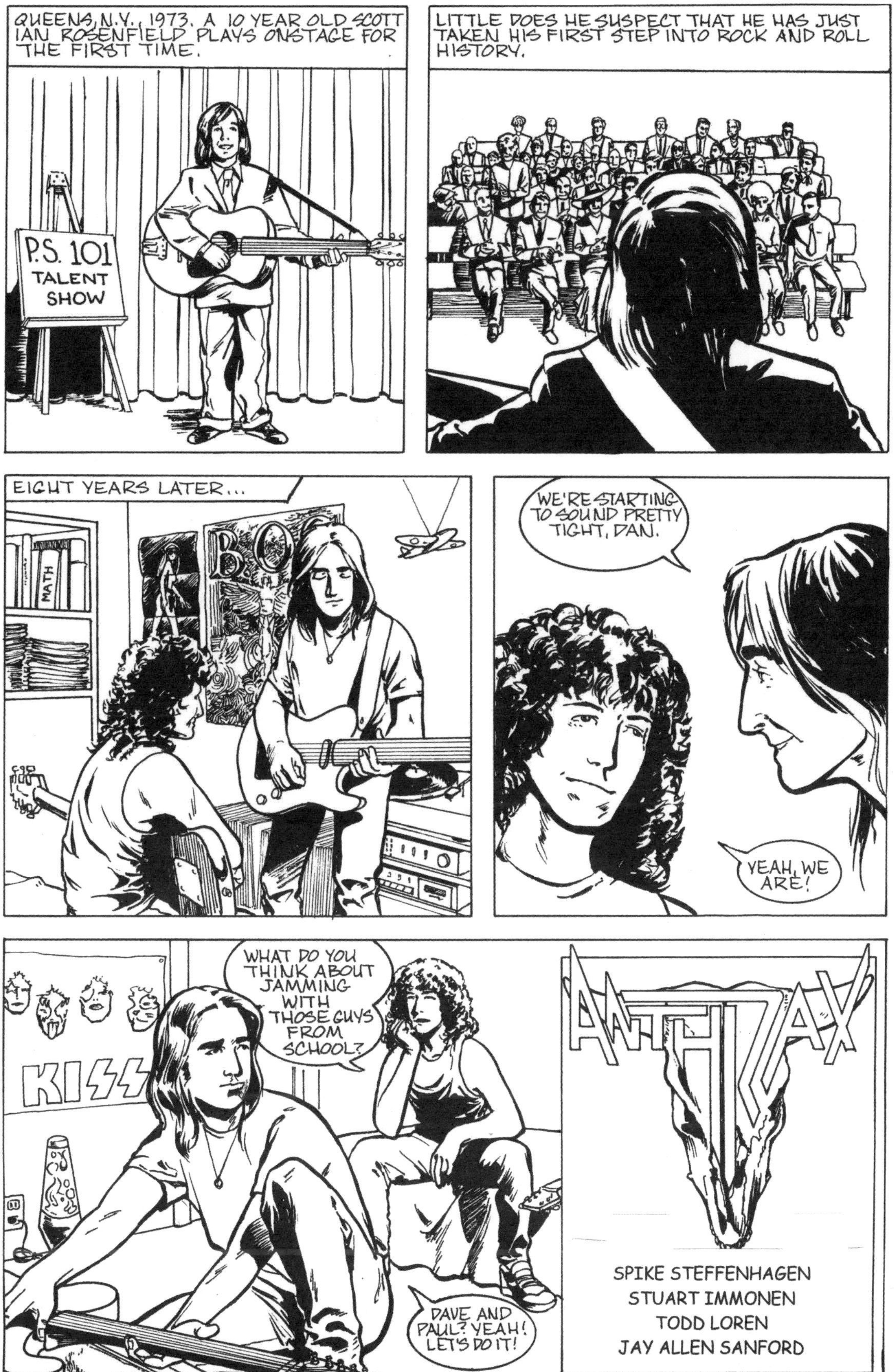
QUEENS, N.Y., 1973. A 10 YEAR OLD SCOTT IAN ROSENFIELD PLAYS ONSTAGE FOR THE FIRST TIME.
P.S. 101 TALENT SHOW
LITTLE DOES HE SUSPECT THAT HE HAS JUST TAKEN HIS FIRST STEP INTO ROCK AND ROLL HISTORY.
EIGHT YEARS LATER...
MATH
WE'RE STARTING TO SOUND PRETTY TIGHT, DAN.
YEAH, WE ARE!
KISS
WHAT DO YOU THINK ABOUT JAMMING WITH THOSE GUYS FROM SCHOOL?
DAVE AND PAUL? YEAH! LET'S DO IT!
ANTHRAX
SPIKE STEFFENHAGEN
STUART IMMONEN
TODD LOREN
JAY ALLEN SANFORD

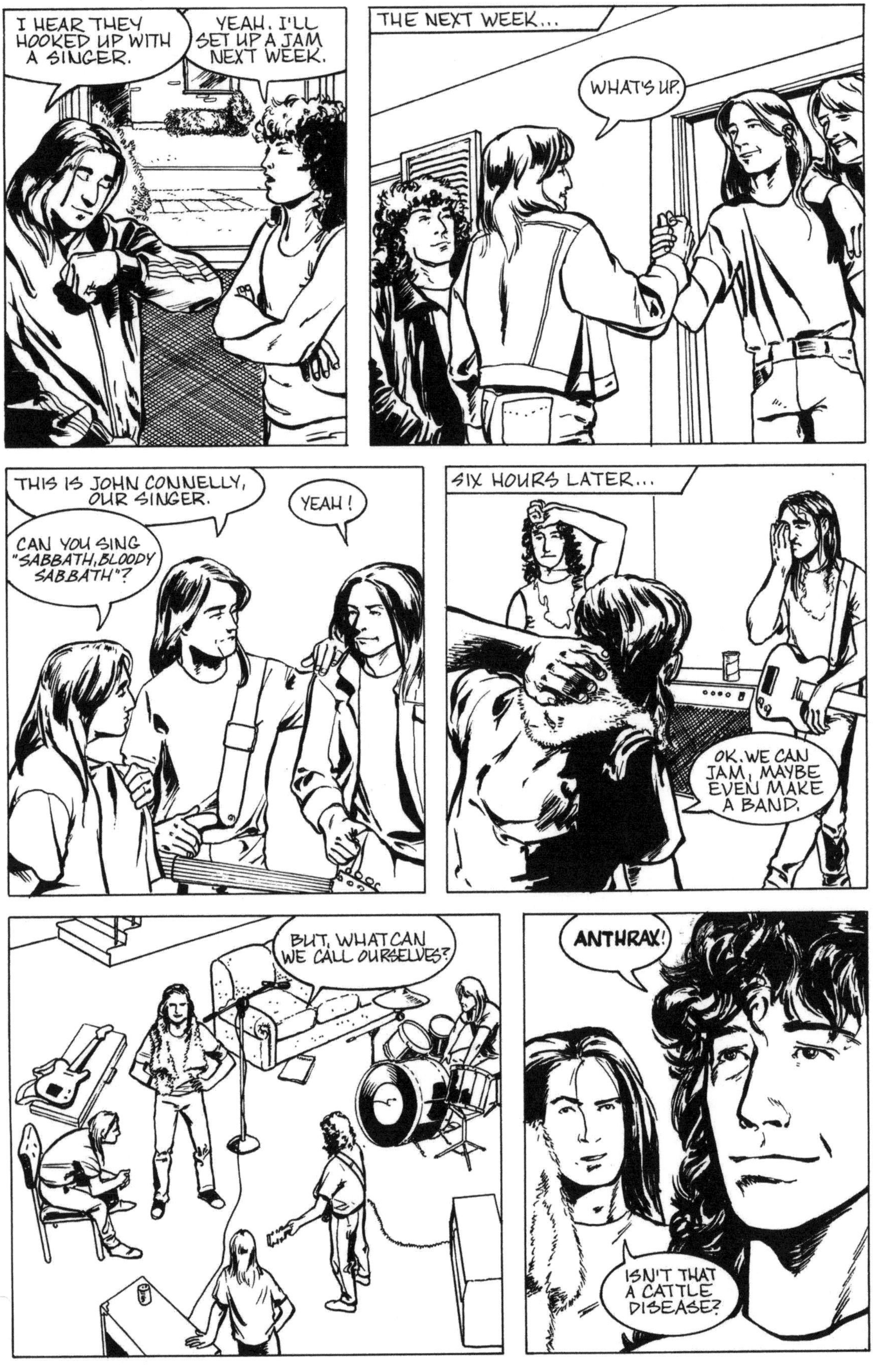
I HEAR THEY HOOKED UP WITH A SINGER.
YEAH. I'LL SET UP A JAM NEXT WEEK.
THE NEXT WEEK...
WHAT'S UP.
THIS IS JOHN CONNELLY, OUR SINGER.
YEAH!
CAN YOU SING "SABBATH, BLOODY SABBATH"?
SIX HOURS LATER...
OK. WE CAN JAM, MAYBE EVEN MAKE A BAND.
BUT, WHAT CAN WE CALL OURSELVES?
ANTHRAX!
ISN'T THAT A CATTLE DISEASE?

YEAH, A DEADLY ONE!

BATTLE of the BANDS
Bayside Lutheran Church
Sunday Sermon 8 a.m.

"ANTHRAX" MAKES THEIR LIVE DEBUT IN LATE 1981.

THE BAND WINS THE "BATTLE," BEATING OUT THE ONE OTHER CONTESTANT.

JOHN CONNELLY, DAVE WEISS AND PAUL KAHN DON'T WORK OUT.

NOW WHAT THE FUCK ARE WE GONNA DO?

WE CAN'T JUST GIVE UP, WE'LL REPLACE THEM.

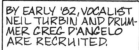

BY EARLY '82, VOCALIST NEIL TURBIN AND DRUMMER GREG D'ANGELO ARE RECRUITED.

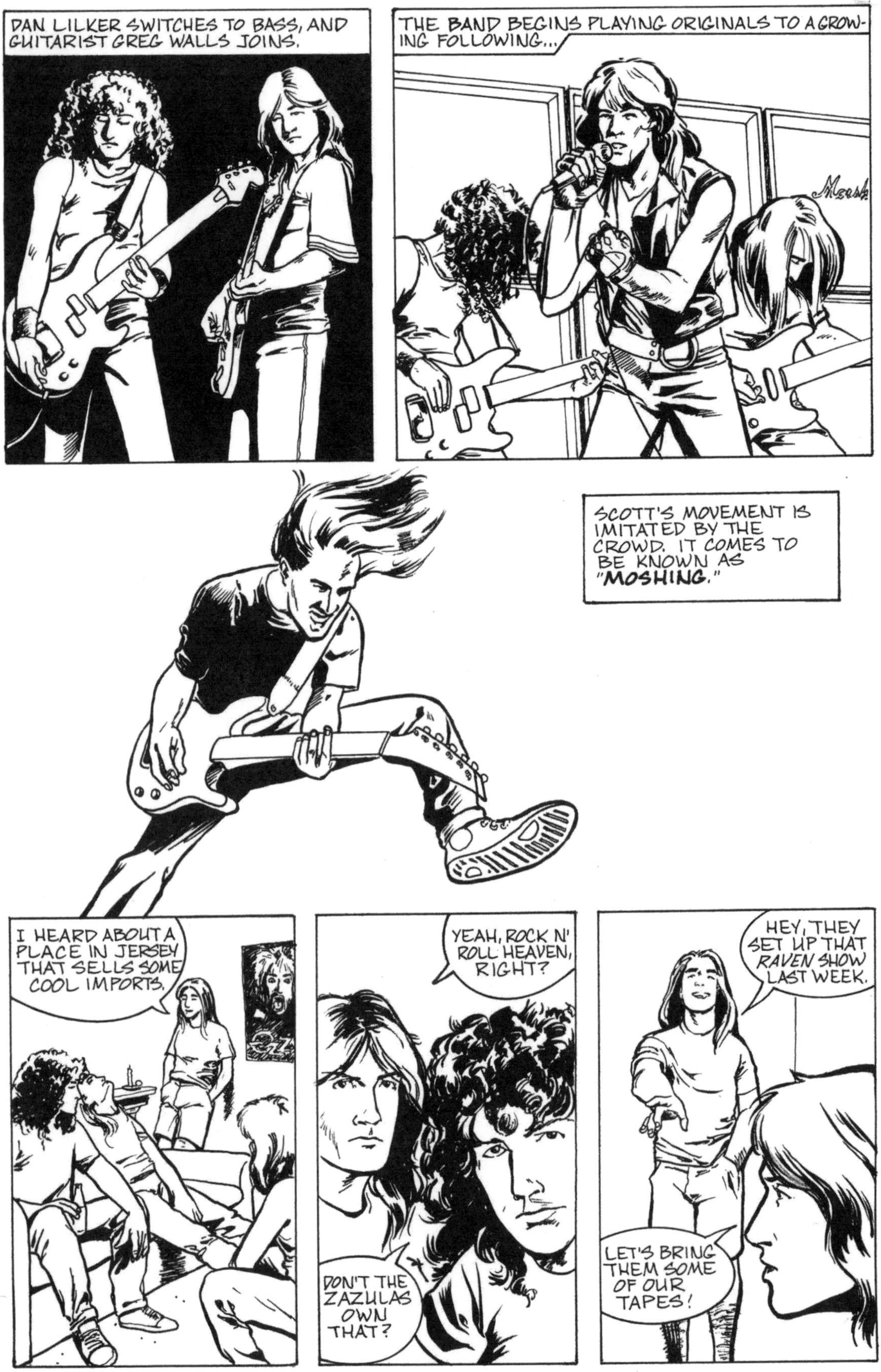

DAN LILKER SWITCHES TO BASS, AND GUITARIST GREG WALLS JOINS.
THE BAND BEGINS PLAYING ORIGINALS TO A GROWING FOLLOWING...
SCOTT'S MOVEMENT IS IMITATED BY THE CROWD. IT COMES TO BE KNOWN AS "**MOSHING**."
I HEARD ABOUT A PLACE IN JERSEY THAT SELLS SOME COOL IMPORTS.
YEAH, ROCK N' ROLL HEAVEN, RIGHT?
DON'T THE ZAZULAS OWN THAT?
HEY, THEY SET UP THAT *RAVEN* SHOW LAST WEEK.
LET'S BRING THEM SOME OF OUR TAPES!

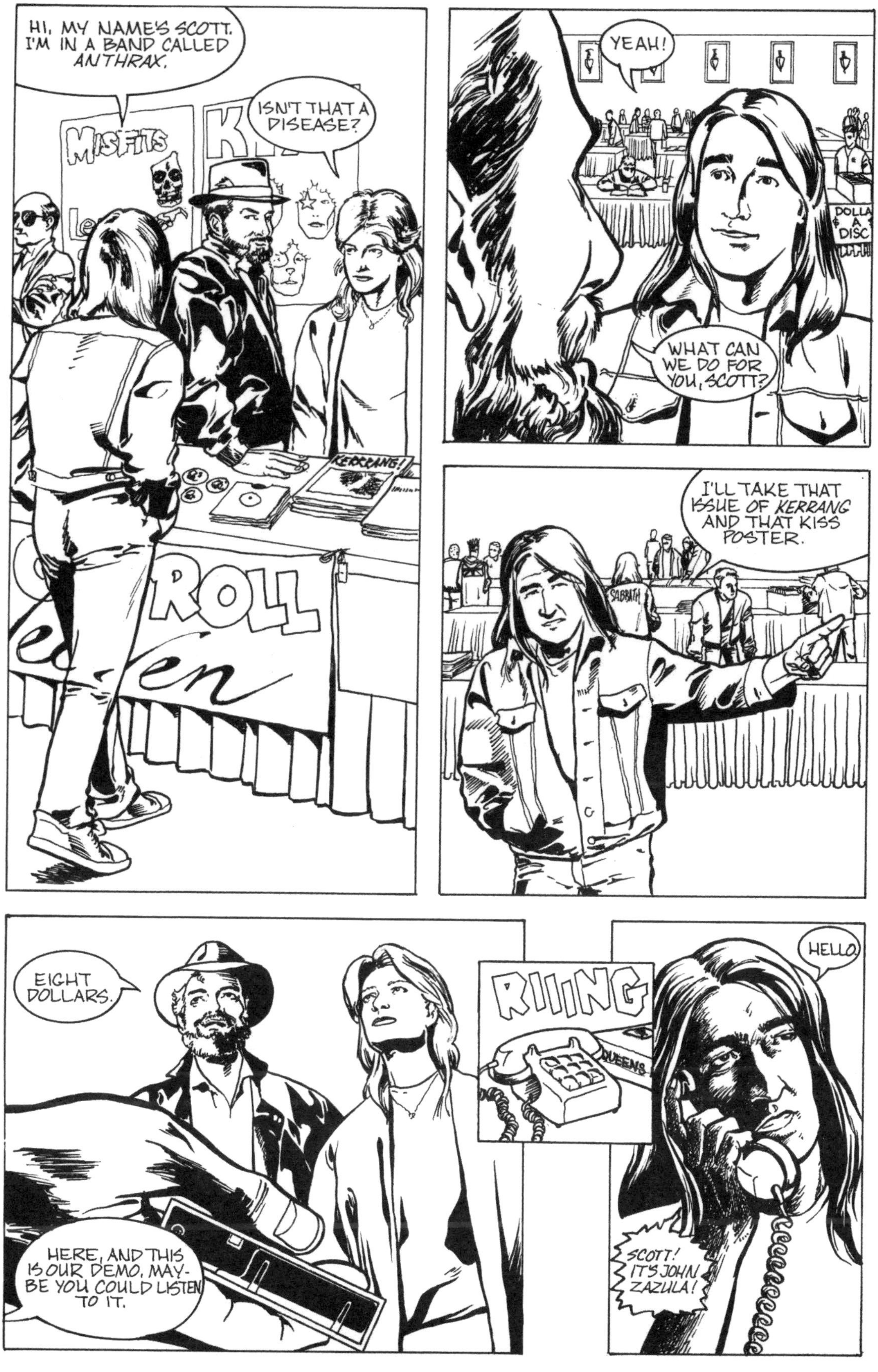
HI, MY NAME'S SCOTT. I'M IN A BAND CALLED ANTHRAX.
ISN'T THAT A DISEASE?
MISFITS
KERRANG!
ROLL
YEAH!
DOLLA A DISC
WHAT CAN WE DO FOR YOU, SCOTT?
I'LL TAKE THAT ISSUE OF KERRANG AND THAT KISS POSTER.
SABBATH
EIGHT DOLLARS.
HERE, AND THIS IS OUR DEMO. MAY-BE YOU COULD LISTEN TO IT.
RIIING
QUEENS
HELLO.
SCOTT! IT'S JOHN ZAZULA!

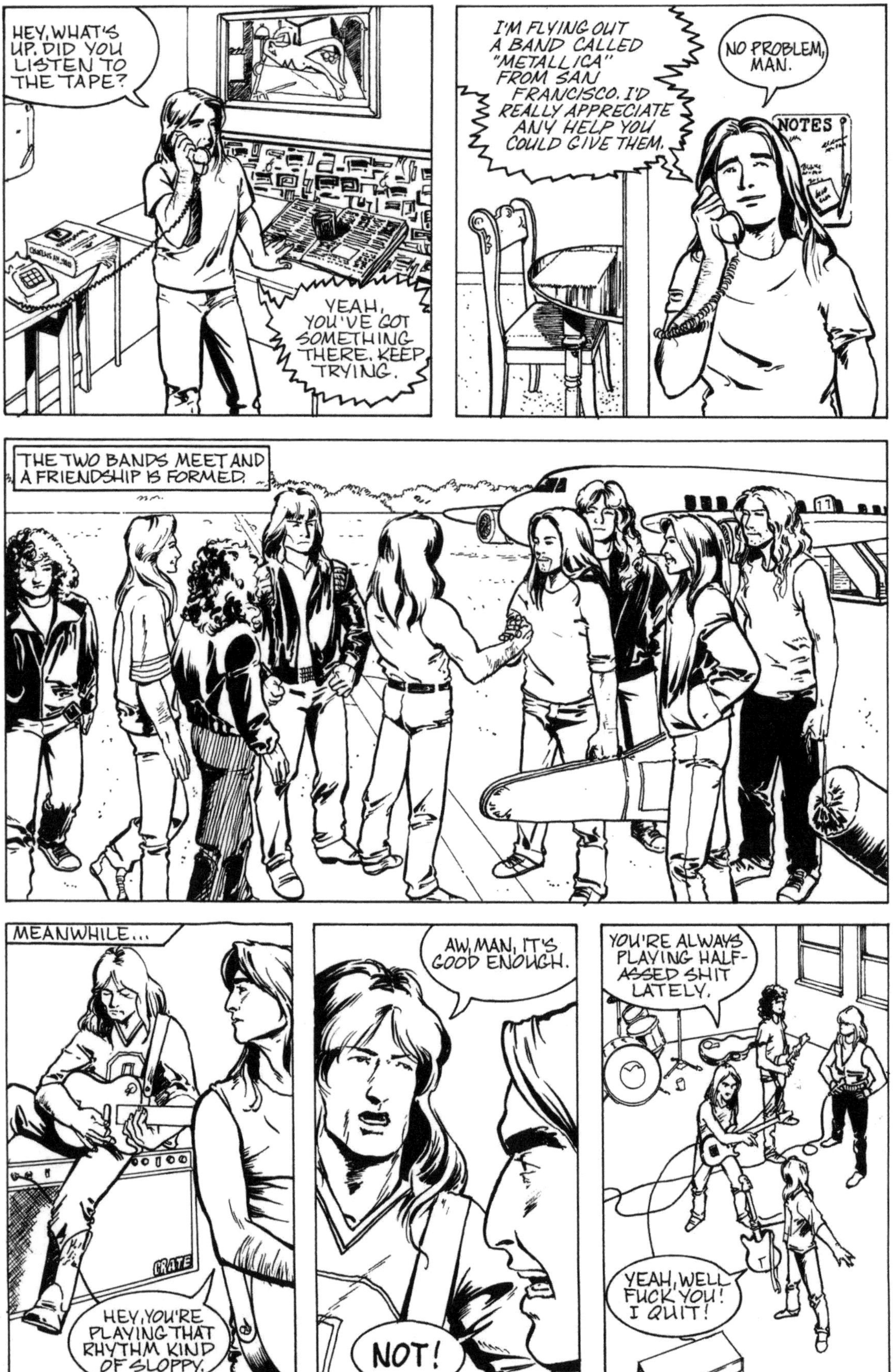
HEY, WHAT'S UP. DID YOU LISTEN TO THE TAPE?
YEAH, YOU'VE GOT SOMETHING THERE. KEEP TRYING.
I'M FLYING OUT A BAND CALLED "METALLICA" FROM SAN FRANCISCO. I'D REALLY APPRECIATE ANY HELP YOU COULD GIVE THEM.
NO PROBLEM, MAN.
NOTES
THE TWO BANDS MEET AND A FRIENDSHIP IS FORMED.
MEANWHILE...
CRATE
HEY, YOU'RE PLAYING THAT RHYTHM KIND OF SLOPPY.
AW, MAN, IT'S GOOD ENOUGH.
NOT!
YOU'RE ALWAYS PLAYING HALF-ASSED SHIT LATELY.
YEAH, WELL FUCK YOU! I QUIT!

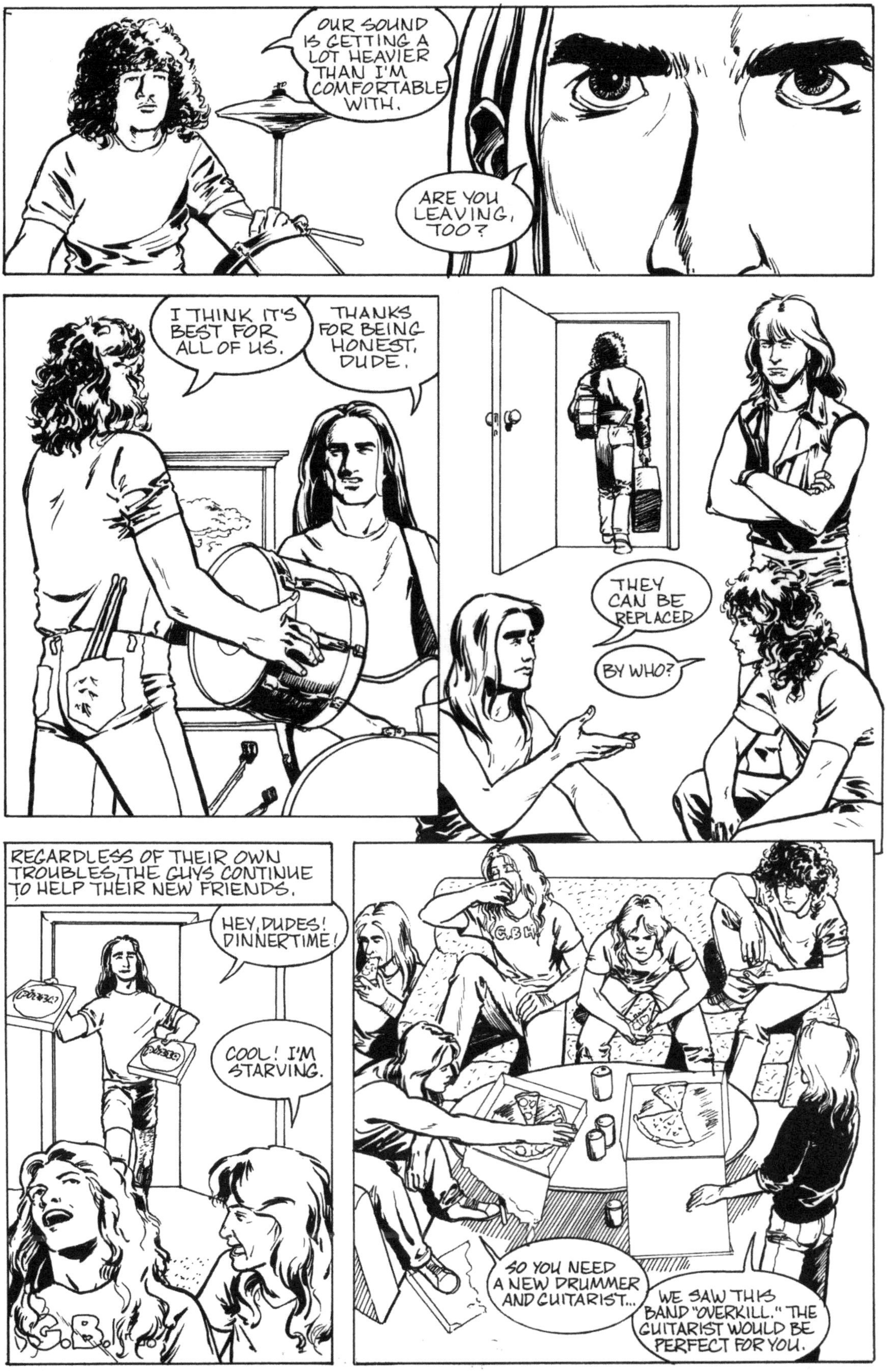
OUR SOUND IS GETTING A LOT HEAVIER THAN I'M COMFORTABLE WITH.
ARE YOU LEAVING, TOO?
I THINK IT'S BEST FOR ALL OF US.
THANKS FOR BEING HONEST, DUDE.
THEY CAN BE REPLACED.
BY WHO?
REGARDLESS OF THEIR OWN TROUBLES, THE GUYS CONTINUE TO HELP THEIR NEW FRIENDS.
HEY, DUDES! DINNERTIME!
COOL! I'M STARVING.
G.B.H.
SO YOU NEED A NEW DRUMMER AND GUITARIST...
WE SAW THIS BAND "OVERKILL." THE GUITARIST WOULD BE PERFECT FOR YOU.

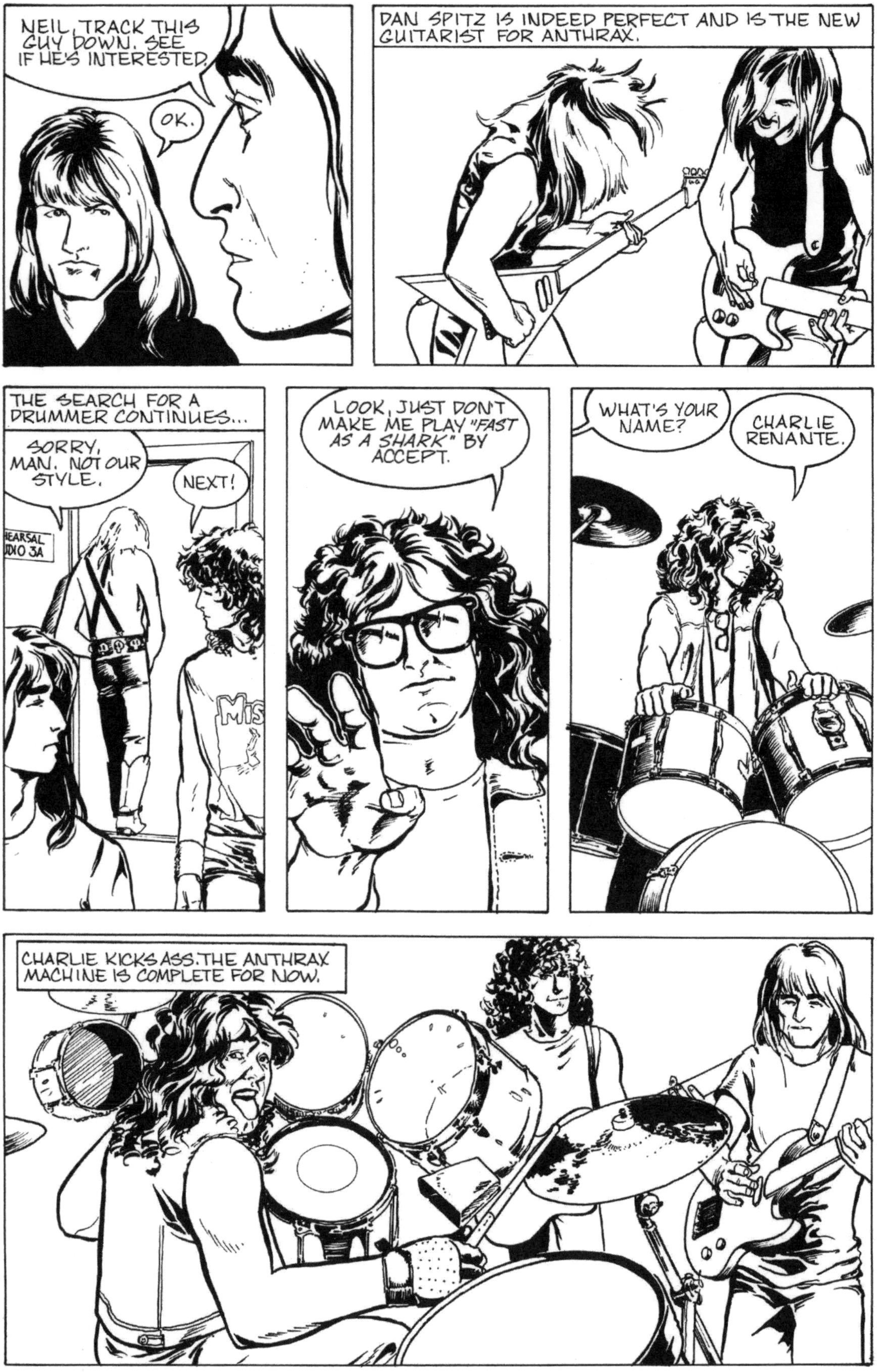
NEIL, TRACK THIS GUY DOWN. SEE IF HE'S INTERESTED.
OK.
DAN SPITZ IS INDEED PERFECT AND IS THE NEW GUITARIST FOR ANTHRAX.
THE SEARCH FOR A DRUMMER CONTINUES...
SORRY, MAN. NOT OUR STYLE.
NEXT!
LOOK, JUST DON'T MAKE ME PLAY "FAST AS A SHARK" BY ACCEPT.
WHAT'S YOUR NAME?
CHARLIE RENANTE.
CHARLIE KICKS ASS. THE ANTHRAX MACHINE IS COMPLETE FOR NOW.

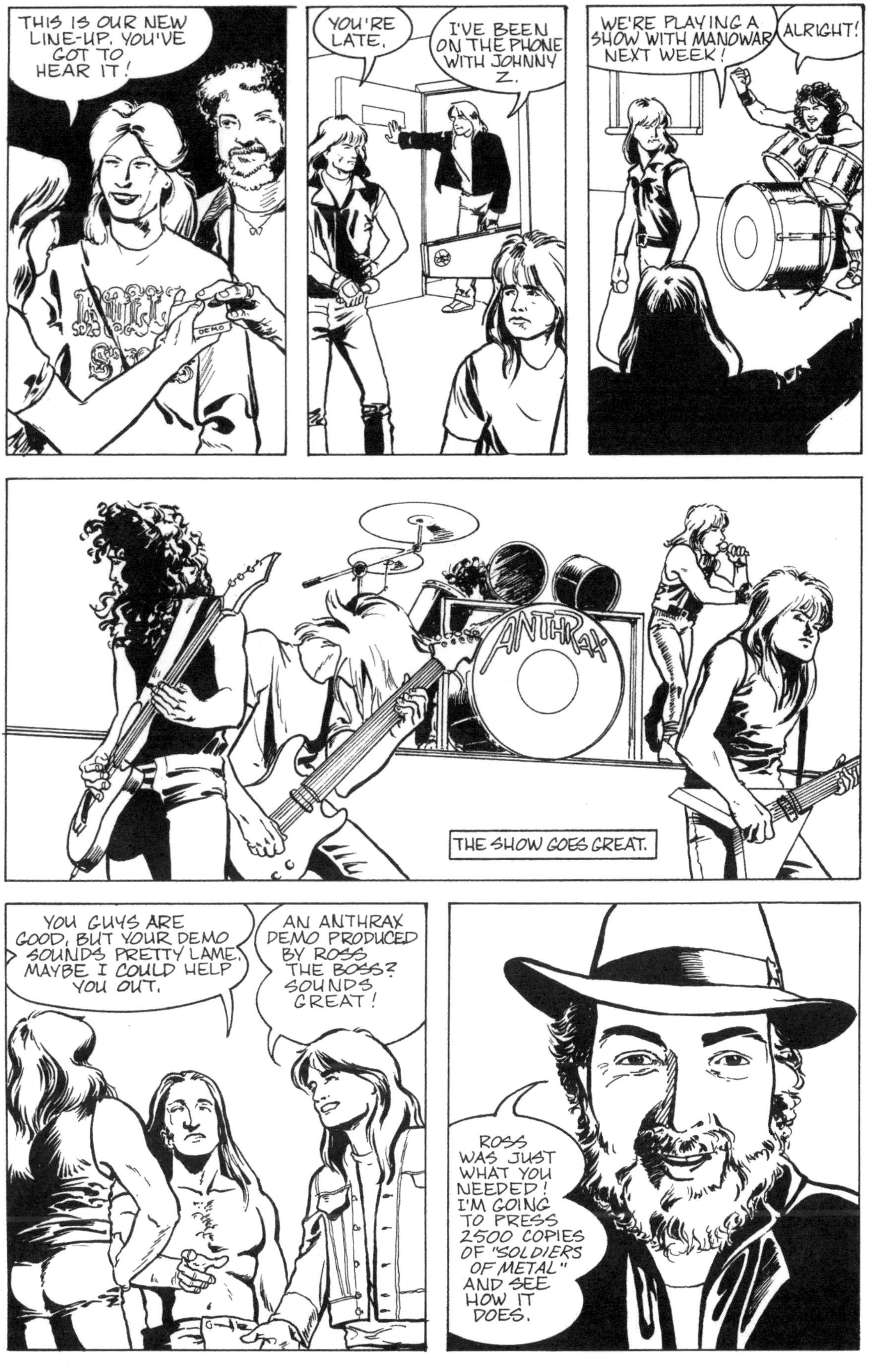
THIS IS OUR NEW LINE-UP. YOU'VE GOT TO HEAR IT!
DEMO
YOU'RE LATE.
I'VE BEEN ON THE PHONE WITH JOHNNY Z.
WE'RE PLAYING A SHOW WITH MANOWAR NEXT WEEK!
ALRIGHT!
ANTHRAX
THE SHOW GOES GREAT.
YOU GUYS ARE GOOD, BUT YOUR DEMO SOUNDS PRETTY LAME. MAYBE I COULD HELP YOU OUT.
AN ANTHRAX DEMO PRODUCED BY ROSS THE BOSS? SOUNDS GREAT!
ROSS WAS JUST WHAT YOU NEEDED! I'M GOING TO PRESS 2500 COPIES OF "SOLDIERS OF METAL" AND SEE HOW IT DOES.

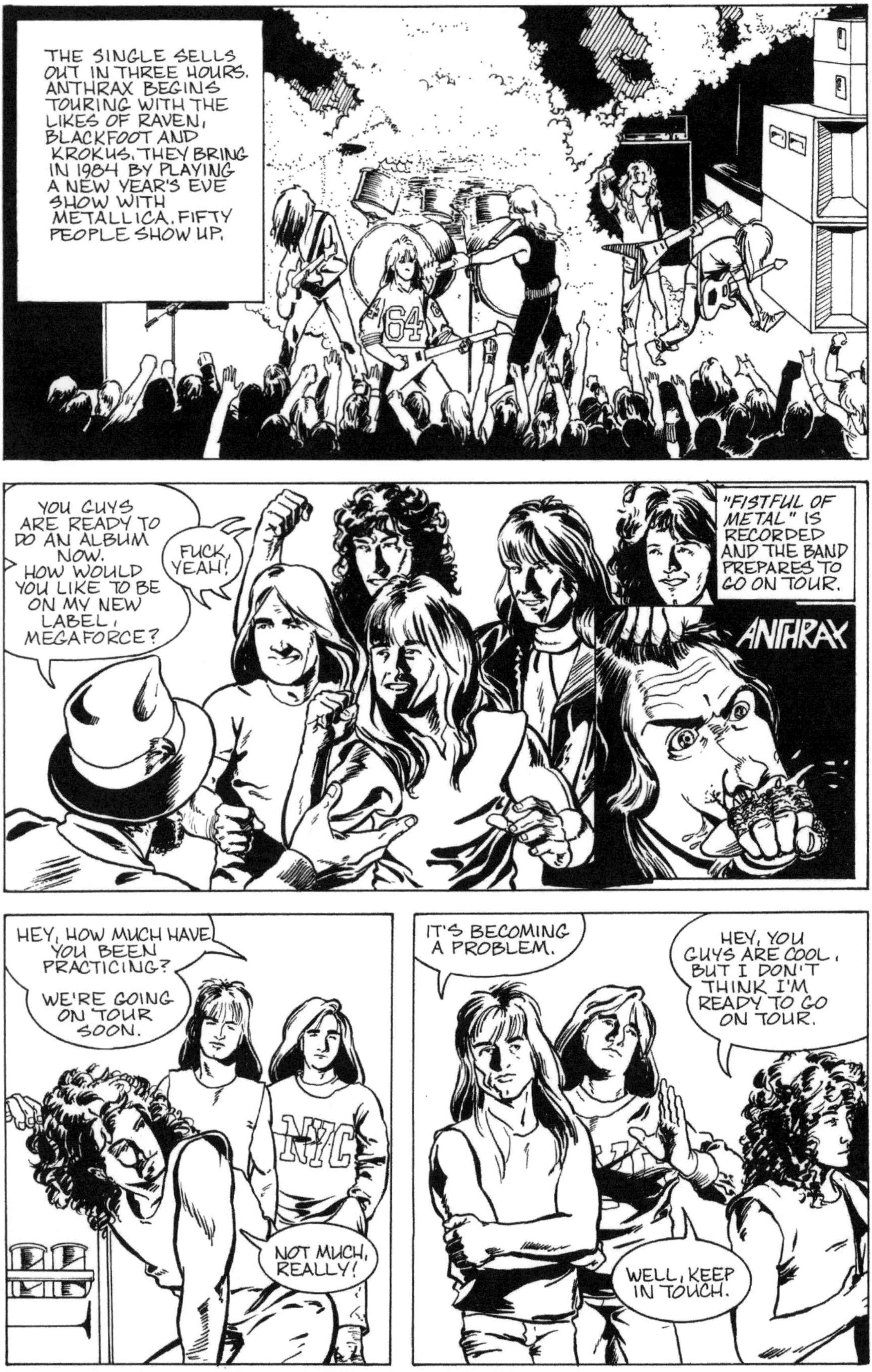
THE SINGLE SELLS OUT IN THREE HOURS. ANTHRAX BEGINS TOURING WITH THE LIKES OF RAVEN, BLACKFOOT AND KROKUS. THEY BRING IN 1984 BY PLAYING A NEW YEAR'S EVE SHOW WITH METALLICA. FIFTY PEOPLE SHOW UP.
YOU GUYS ARE READY TO DO AN ALBUM NOW. HOW WOULD YOU LIKE TO BE ON MY NEW LABEL, MEGAFORCE?
FUCK, YEAH!
"FISTFUL OF METAL" IS RECORDED AND THE BAND PREPARES TO GO ON TOUR.
ANTHRAX
HEY, HOW MUCH HAVE YOU BEEN PRACTICING?
WE'RE GOING ON TOUR SOON.
NOT MUCH, REALLY!
IT'S BECOMING A PROBLEM.
HEY, YOU GUYS ARE COOL, BUT I DON'T THINK I'M READY TO GO ON TOUR.
WELL, KEEP IN TOUCH.

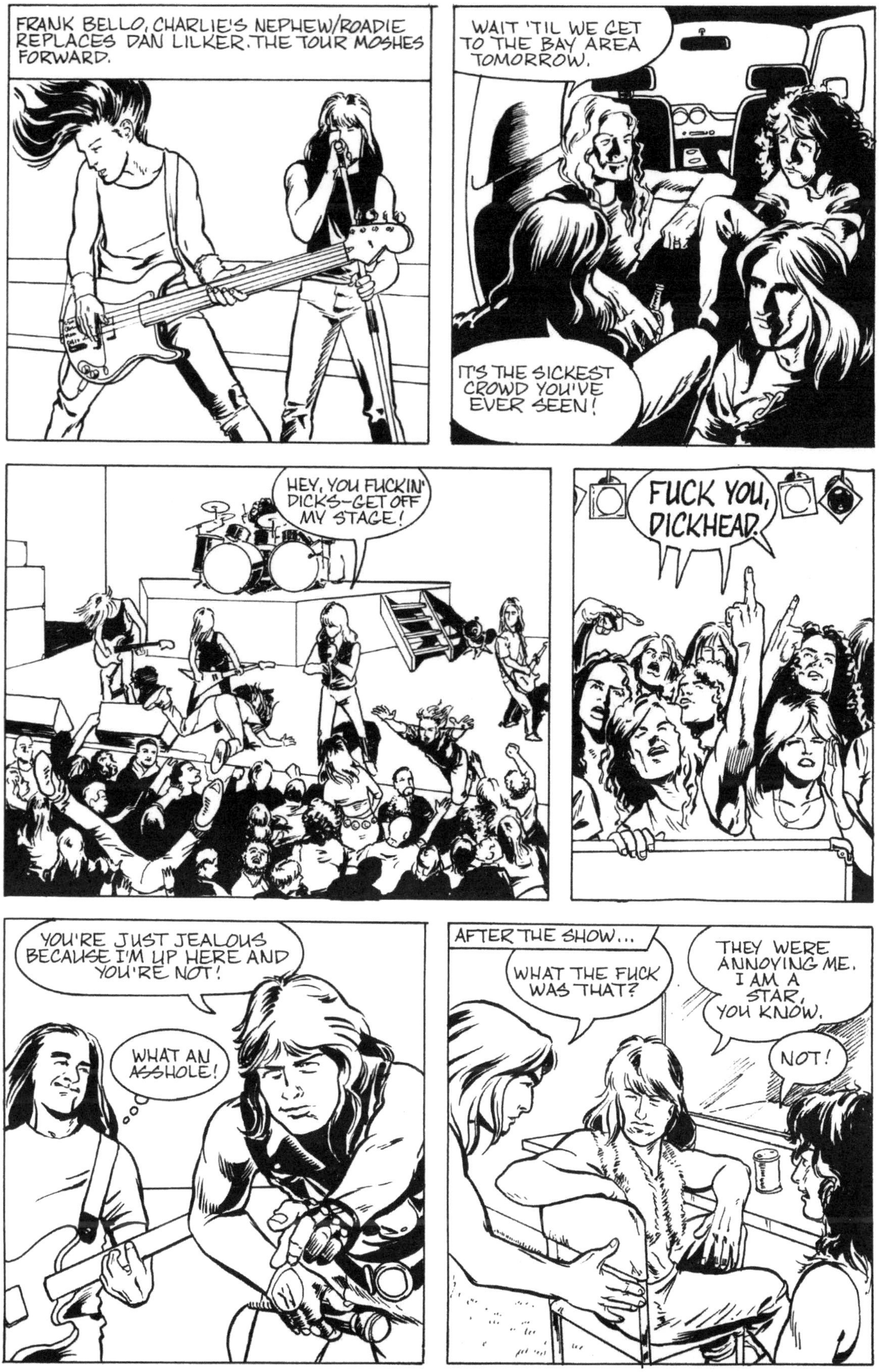
FRANK BELLO, CHARLIE'S NEPHEW/ROADIE REPLACES DAN LILKER. THE TOUR MOSHES FORWARD.
WAIT 'TIL WE GET TO THE BAY AREA TOMORROW.
IT'S THE SICKEST CROWD YOU'VE EVER SEEN!
HEY, YOU FUCKIN' DICKS—GET OFF MY STAGE!
FUCK YOU, DICKHEAD.
YOU'RE JUST JEALOUS BECAUSE I'M UP HERE AND YOU'RE NOT!
WHAT AN ASSHOLE!
AFTER THE SHOW...
WHAT THE FUCK WAS THAT?
THEY WERE ANNOYING ME. I AM A STAR, YOU KNOW.
NOT!

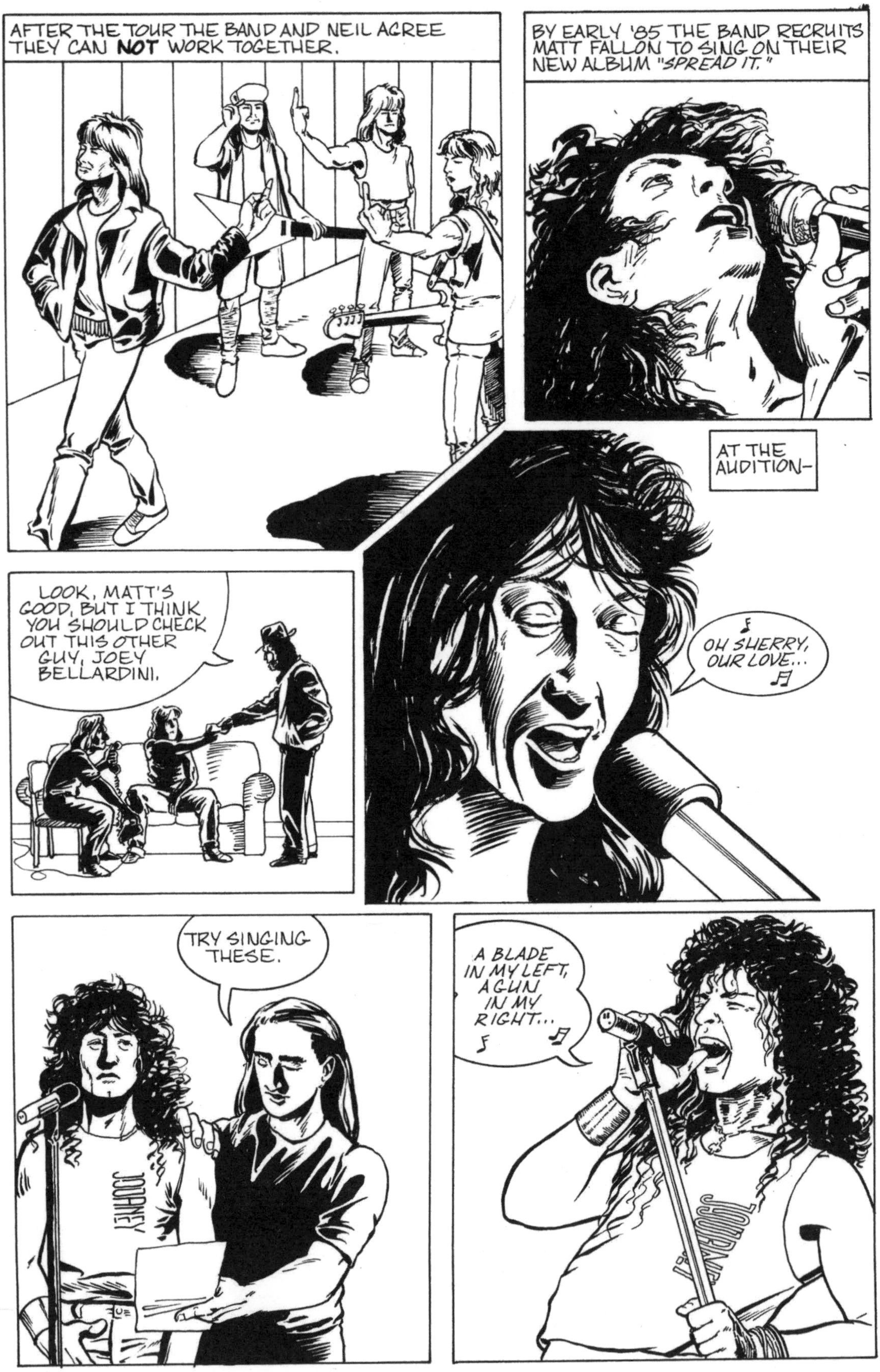
AFTER THE TOUR THE BAND AND NEIL AGREE THEY CAN NOT WORK TOGETHER.
BY EARLY '85 THE BAND RECRUITS MATT FALLON TO SING ON THEIR NEW ALBUM "SPREAD IT."
AT THE AUDITION-
LOOK, MATT'S GOOD, BUT I THINK YOU SHOULD CHECK OUT THIS OTHER GUY, JOEY BELLARDINI.
OH SHERRY, OUR LOVE...
TRY SINGING THESE.
A BLADE IN MY LEFT, A GUN IN MY RIGHT...
JOURNEY
JOURNEY

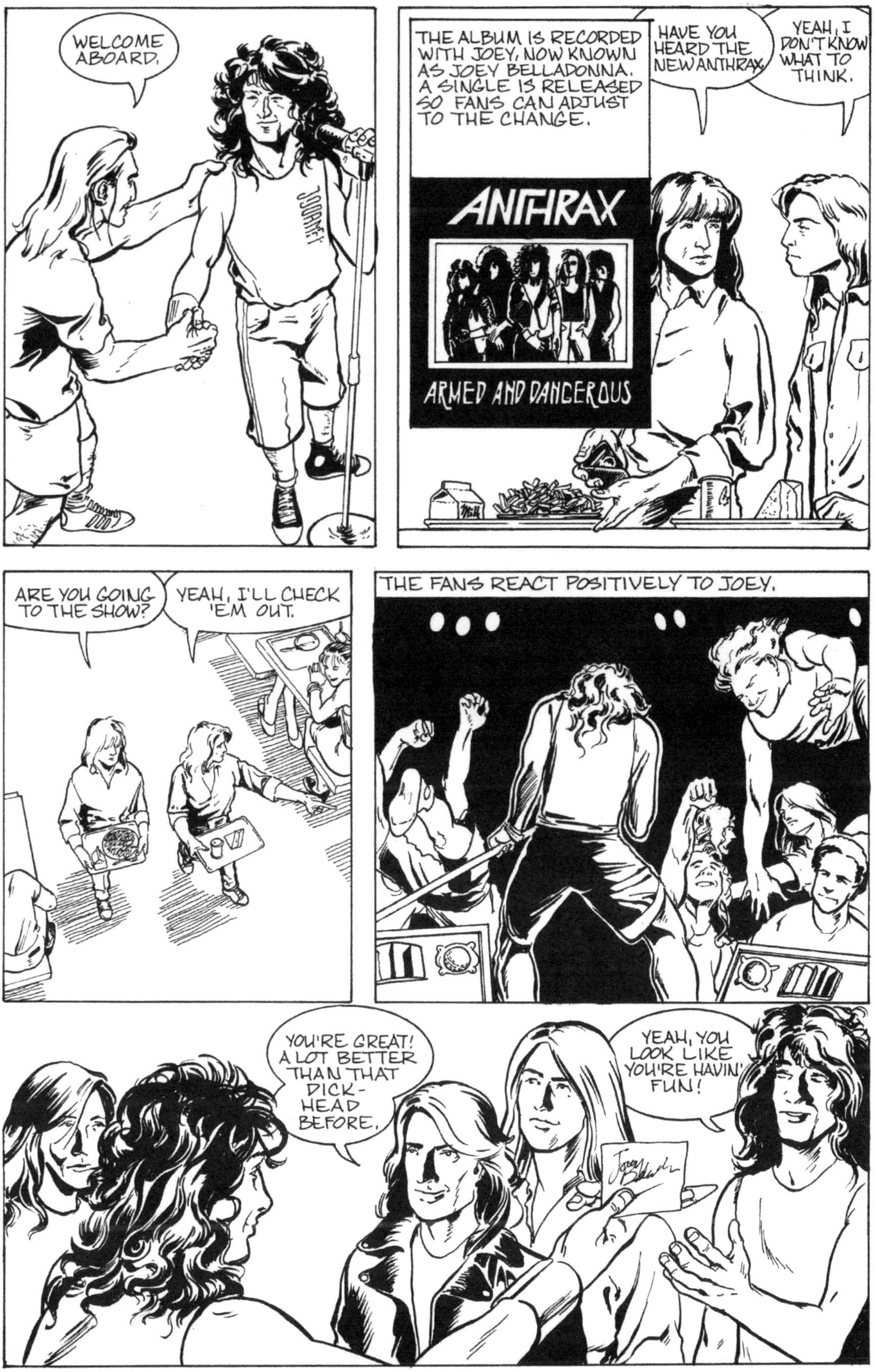
WELCOME ABOARD.
THE ALBUM IS RECORDED WITH JOEY, NOW KNOWN AS JOEY BELLADONNA. A SINGLE IS RELEASED SO FANS CAN ADJUST TO THE CHANGE.
HAVE YOU HEARD THE NEW ANTHRAX.
YEAH, I DON'T KNOW WHAT TO THINK.
ANTHRAX
ARMED AND DANGEROUS
ARE YOU GOING TO THE SHOW?
YEAH, I'LL CHECK 'EM OUT.
THE FANS REACT POSITIVELY TO JOEY.
YOU'RE GREAT! A LOT BETTER THAN THAT DICK-HEAD BEFORE.
YEAH, YOU LOOK LIKE YOU'RE HAVIN' FUN!

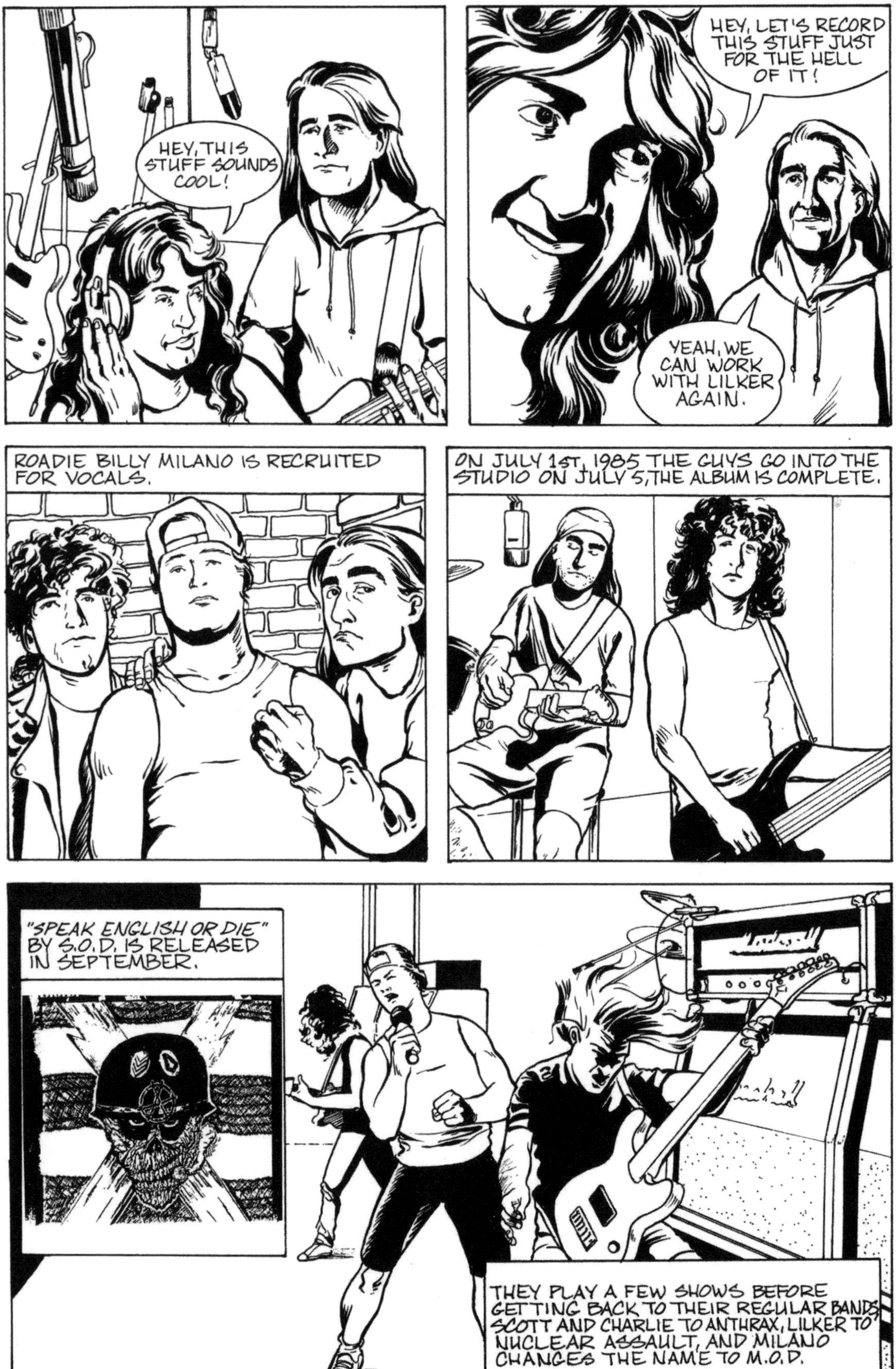
HEY, THIS STUFF SOUNDS COOL!
HEY, LET'S RECORD THIS STUFF JUST FOR THE HELL OF IT!
YEAH, WE CAN WORK WITH LILKER AGAIN.
ROADIE BILLY MILANO IS RECRUITED FOR VOCALS.
ON JULY 1ST, 1985 THE GUYS GO INTO THE STUDIO ON JULY 5, THE ALBUM IS COMPLETE.
"SPEAK ENGLISH OR DIE" BY S.O.D. IS RELEASED IN SEPTEMBER.
THEY PLAY A FEW SHOWS BEFORE GETTING BACK TO THEIR REGULAR BANDS, SCOTT AND CHARLIE TO ANTHRAX, LILKER TO NUCLEAR ASSAULT, AND MILANO CHANGES THE NAME TO M.O.D.

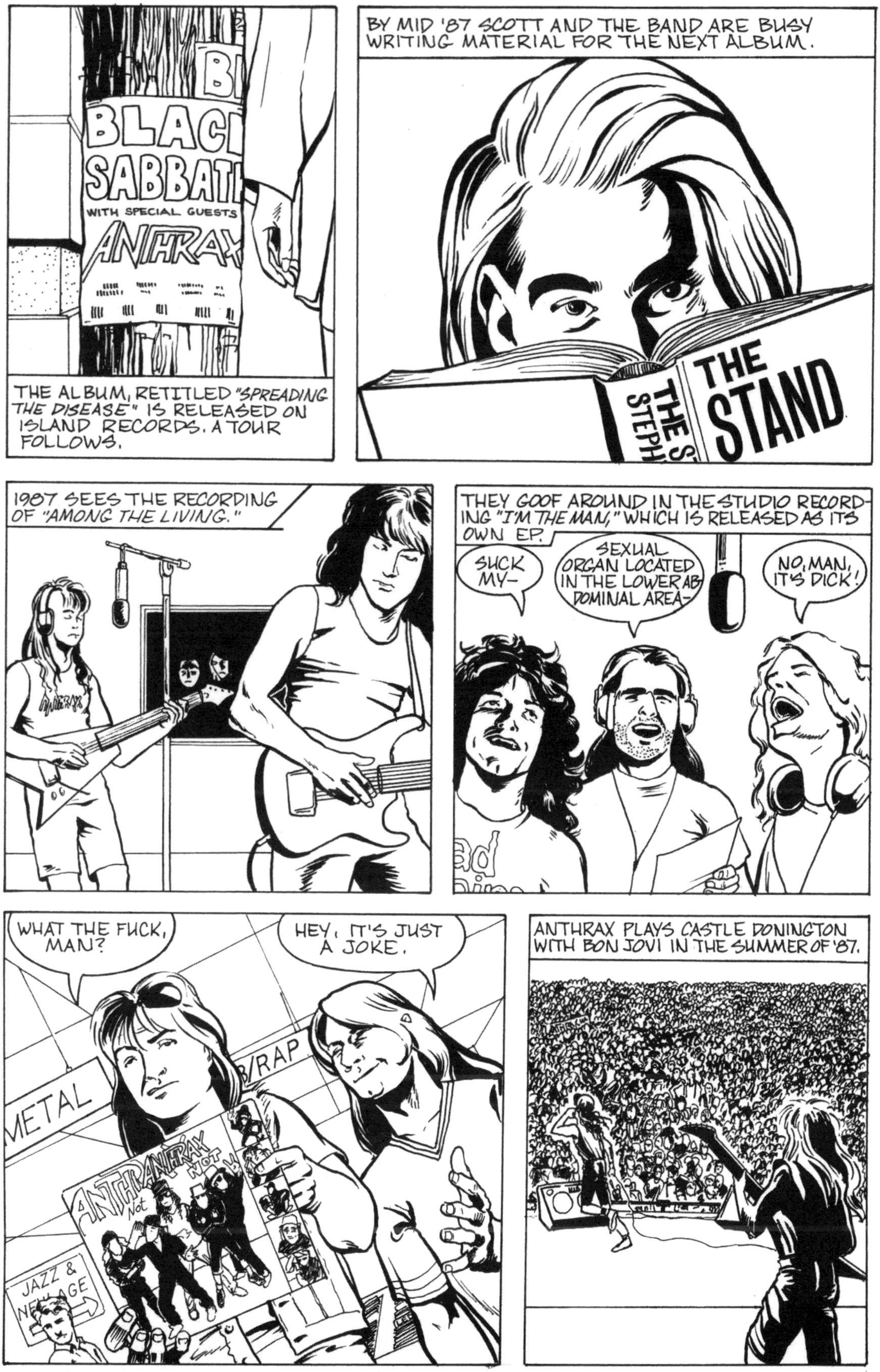
BLACK SABBATH
WITH SPECIAL GUESTS
ANTHRAX
THE ALBUM, RETITLED "SPREADING THE DISEASE" IS RELEASED ON ISLAND RECORDS. A TOUR FOLLOWS.
BY MID '87 SCOTT AND THE BAND ARE BUSY WRITING MATERIAL FOR THE NEXT ALBUM.
THE STAND
1987 SEES THE RECORDING OF "AMONG THE LIVING."
THEY GOOF AROUND IN THE STUDIO RECORDING "I'M THE MAN," WHICH IS RELEASED AS ITS OWN EP.
SUCK MY-
SEXUAL ORGAN LOCATED IN THE LOWER ABDOMINAL AREA-
NO, MAN, IT'S DICK!
WHAT THE FUCK, MAN?
HEY, IT'S JUST A JOKE.
METAL
/RAP
ANTHRAX
JAZZ & NEW AGE
ANTHRAX PLAYS CASTLE DONINGTON WITH BON JOVI IN THE SUMMER OF '87.

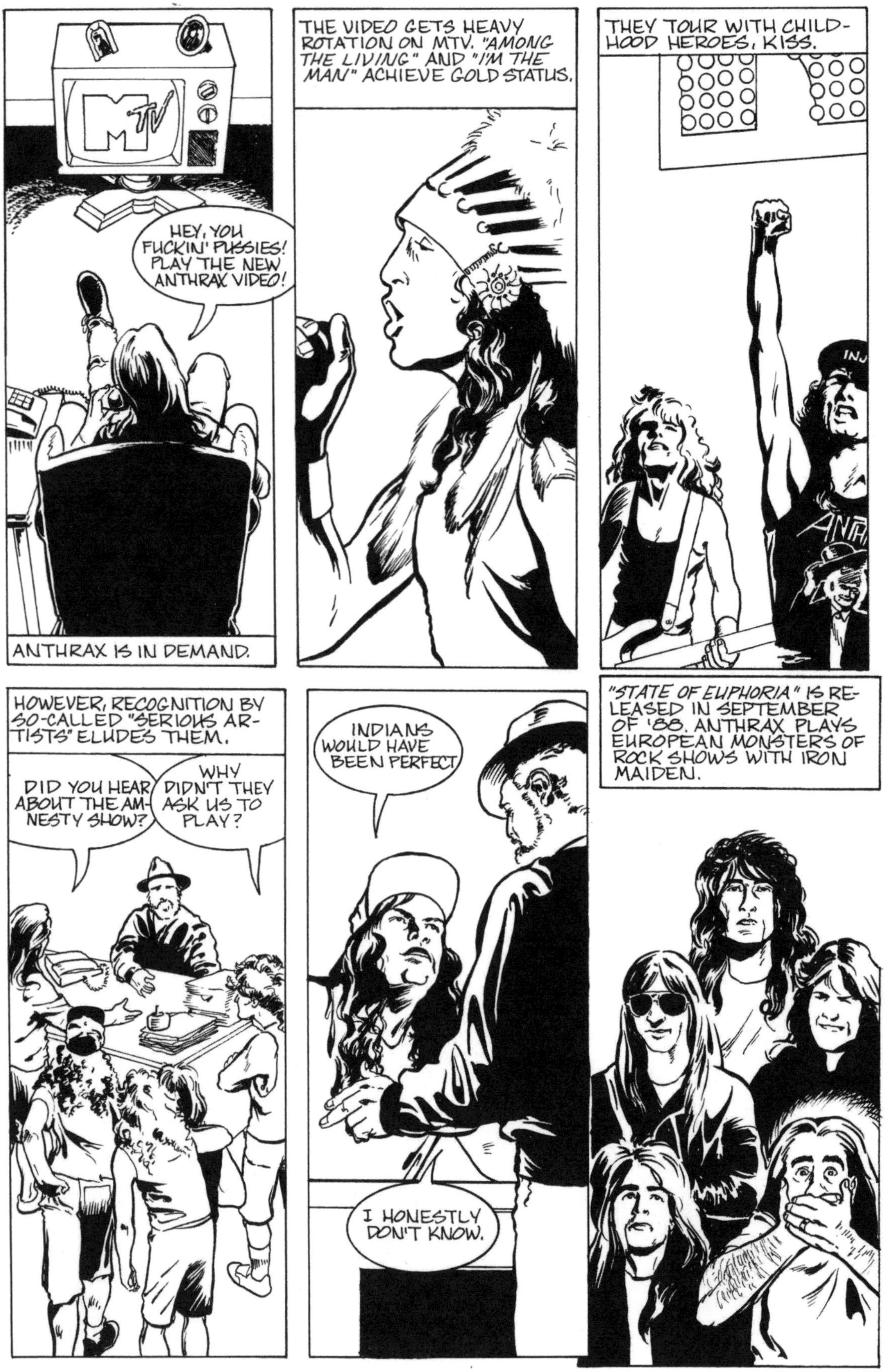
HEY, YOU FUCKIN' PUSSIES! PLAY THE NEW ANTHRAX VIDEO!
ANTHRAX IS IN DEMAND.
THE VIDEO GETS HEAVY ROTATION ON MTV. "AMONG THE LIVING" AND "I'M THE MAN" ACHIEVE GOLD STATUS.
THEY TOUR WITH CHILDHOOD HEROES, KISS.
HOWEVER, RECOGNITION BY SO-CALLED "SERIOUS ARTISTS" ELUDES THEM.
DID YOU HEAR ABOUT THE AMNESTY SHOW?
WHY DIDN'T THEY ASK US TO PLAY?
INDIANS WOULD HAVE BEEN PERFECT.
I HONESTLY DON'T KNOW.
"STATE OF EUPHORIA" IS RELEASED IN SEPTEMBER OF '88. ANTHRAX PLAYS EUROPEAN MONSTERS OF ROCK SHOWS WITH IRON MAIDEN.

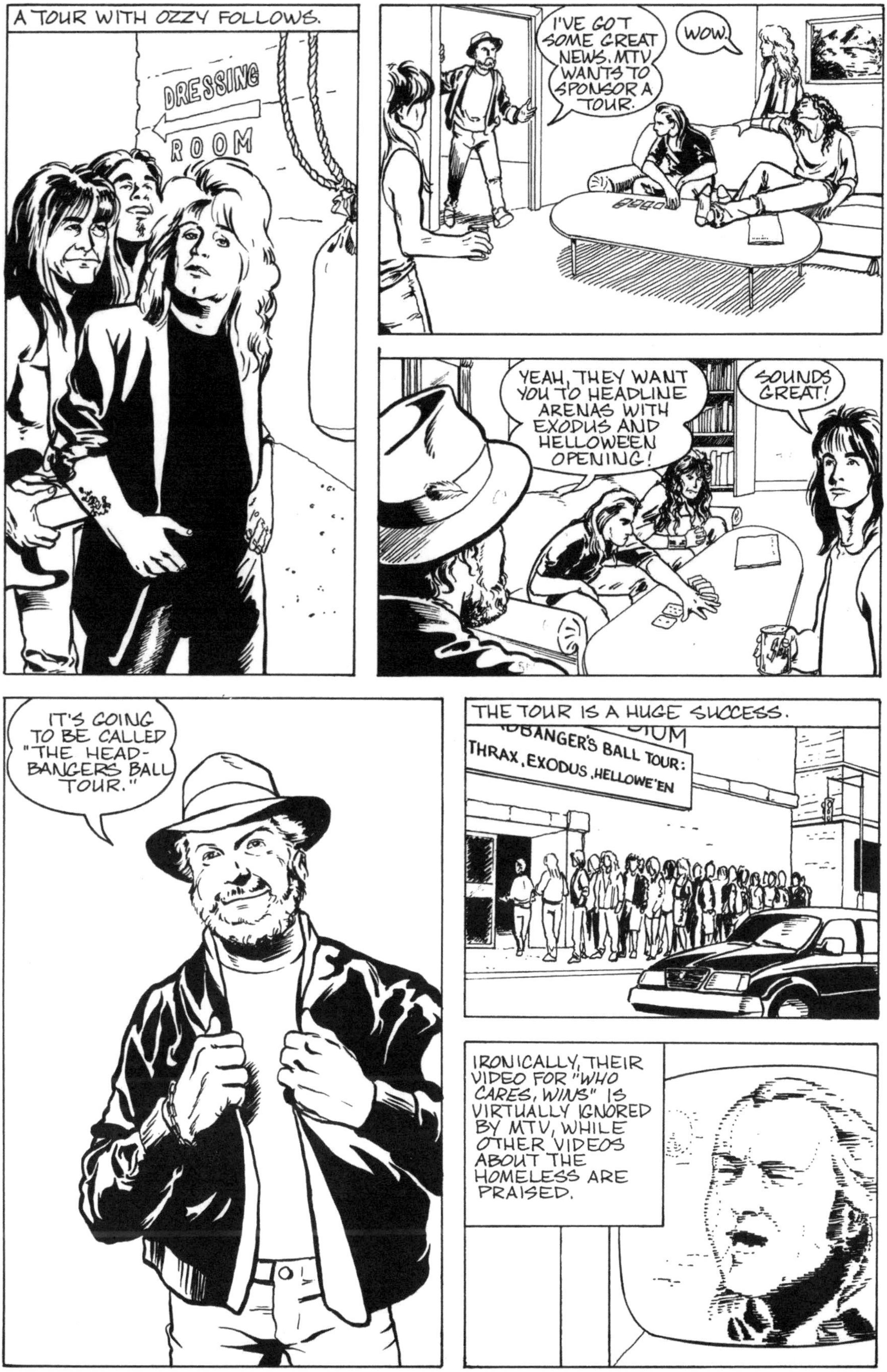
A TOUR WITH OZZY FOLLOWS.
DRESSING ROOM
I'VE GOT SOME GREAT NEWS. MTV WANTS TO SPONSOR A TOUR.
WOW.
YEAH, THEY WANT YOU TO HEADLINE ARENAS WITH EXODUS AND HELLOWEEN OPENING!
SOUNDS GREAT!
IT'S GOING TO BE CALLED "THE HEAD-BANGERS BALL TOUR."
THE TOUR IS A HUGE SUCCESS.
DBANGER'S BALL TOUR:
THRAX, EXODUS, HELLOWE'EN
IRONICALLY, THEIR VIDEO FOR "WHO CARES, WINS" IS VIRTUALLY IGNORED BY MTV, WHILE OTHER VIDEOS ABOUT THE HOMELESS ARE PRAISED.

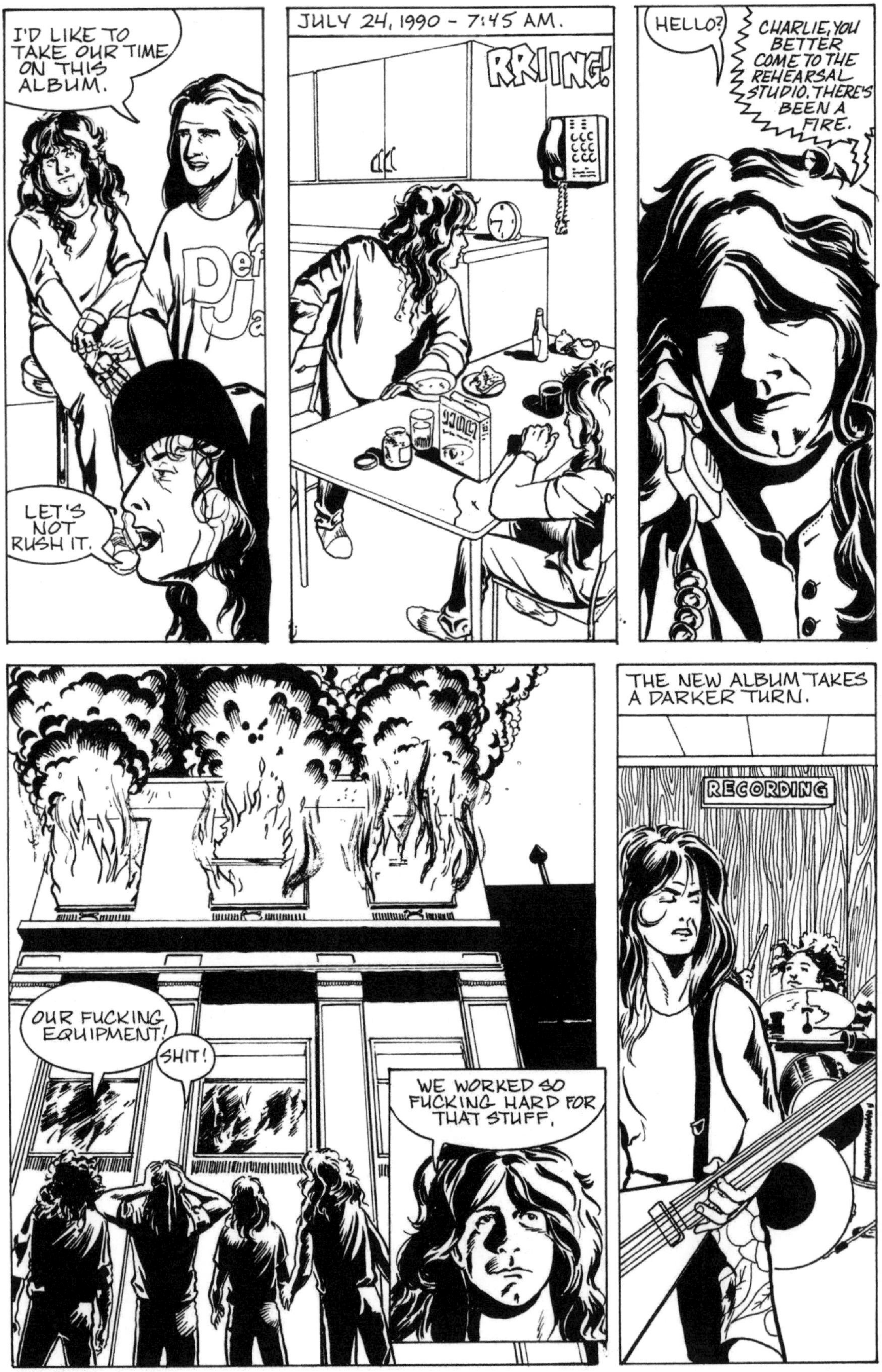
I'D LIKE TO TAKE OUR TIME ON THIS ALBUM.
LET'S NOT RUSH IT.
JULY 24, 1990 - 7:45 AM.
RRIING!
HELLO?
CHARLIE, YOU BETTER COME TO THE REHEARSAL STUDIO. THERE'S BEEN A FIRE.
OUR FUCKING EQUIPMENT!
SHIT!
WE WORKED SO FUCKING HARD FOR THAT STUFF.
THE NEW ALBUM TAKES A DARKER TURN.
RECORDING

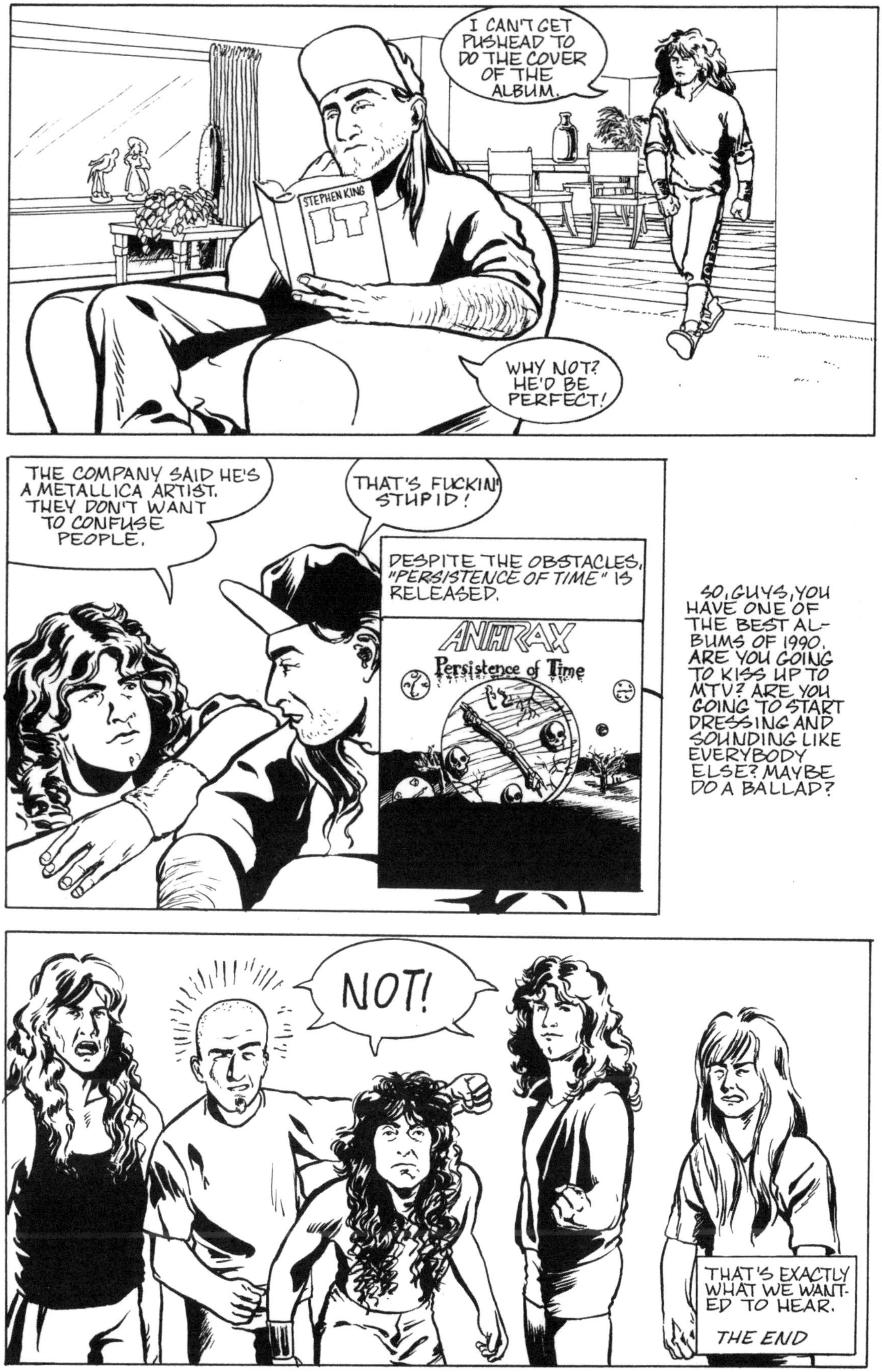
I CAN'T GET PUSHEAD TO DO THE COVER OF THE ALBUM.
STEPHEN KING
IT
WHY NOT? HE'D BE PERFECT!
THE COMPANY SAID HE'S A METALLICA ARTIST. THEY DON'T WANT TO CONFUSE PEOPLE.
THAT'S FUCKIN' STUPID!
DESPITE THE OBSTACLES, "PERSISTENCE OF TIME" IS RELEASED.
ANTHRAX
Persistence of Time
SO, GUYS, YOU HAVE ONE OF THE BEST AL-BUMS OF 1990. ARE YOU GOING TO KISS UP TO MTV? ARE YOU GOING TO START DRESSING AND SOUNDING LIKE EVERYBODY ELSE? MAYBE DO A BALLAD?
NOT!
THAT'S EXACTLY WHAT WE WANT-ED TO HEAR.
THE END

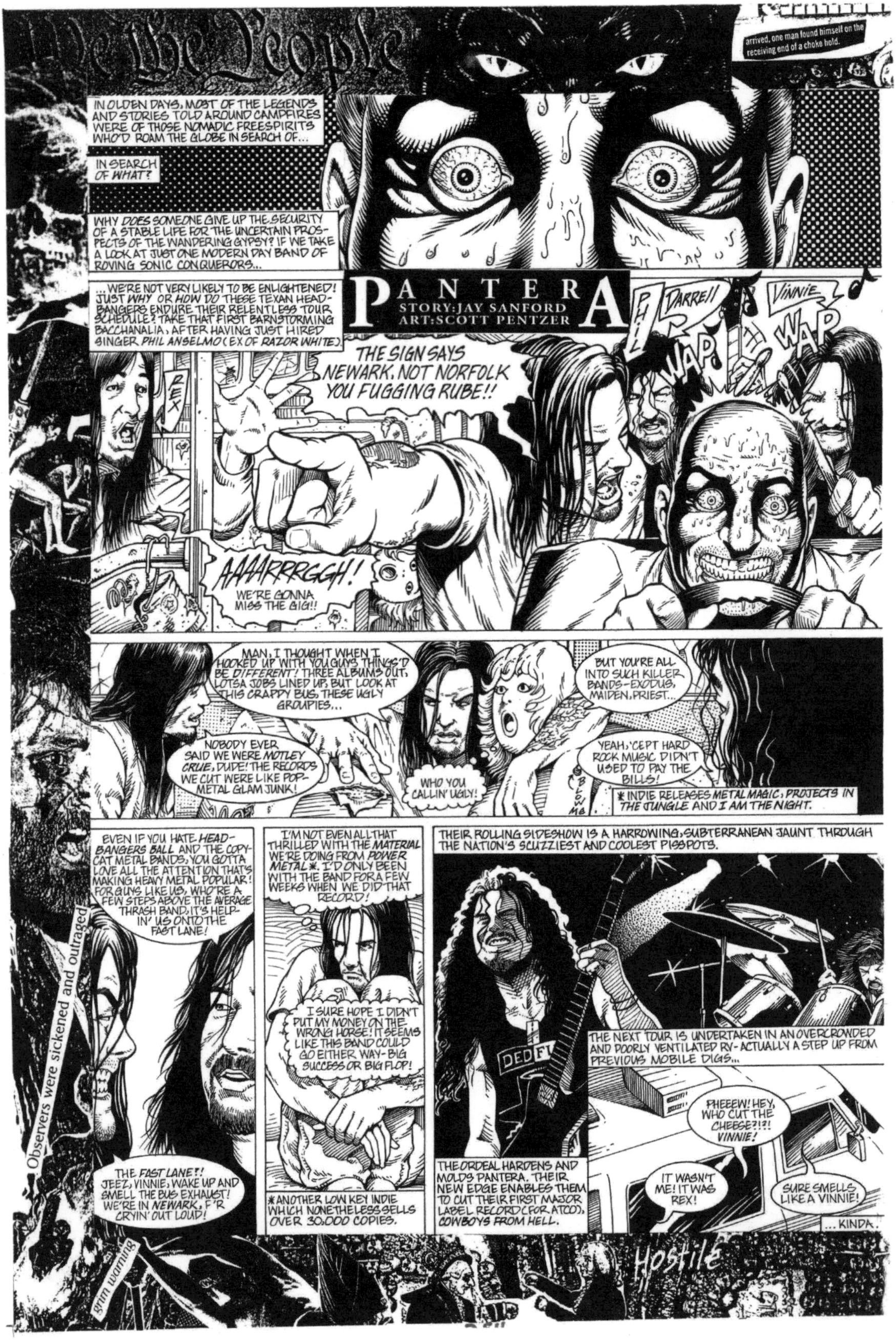

We the People
arrived, one man found himself on the receiving end of a choke hold.
IN OLDEN DAYS, MOST OF THE LEGENDS AND STORIES TOLD AROUND CAMPFIRES WERE OF THOSE NOMADIC FREESPIRITS WHO'D ROAM THE GLOBE IN SEARCH OF...
IN SEARCH OF WHAT?
WHY DOES SOMEONE GIVE UP THE SECURITY OF A STABLE LIFE FOR THE UNCERTAIN PROSPECTS OF THE WANDERING GYPSY? IF WE TAKE A LOOK AT JUST ONE MODERN DAY BAND OF ROVING SONIC CONQUERORS...
...WE'RE NOT VERY LIKELY TO BE ENLIGHTENED! JUST WHY OR HOW DO THESE TEXAN HEADBANGERS ENDURE THEIR RELENTLESS TOUR SCHEDULE? TAKE THAT FIRST BARNSTORMING BACCHANALIA, AFTER HAVING JUST HIRED SINGER PHIL ANSELMO (EX OF RAZOR WHITE).
PANTERA
STORY: JAY SANFORD
ART: SCOTT PENTZER
PHIL
DARRELL
VINNIE
WAP
WAP
REX
THE SIGN SAYS NEWARK, NOT NORFOLK YOU FUGGING RUBE!!
AAAARRRGGH!
WE'RE GONNA MISS THE GIG!!
MAN, I THOUGHT WHEN I HOOKED UP WITH YOU GUYS THINGS'D BE DIFFERENT! THREE ALBUMS OUT, LOTSA JOBS LINED UP, BUT LOOK AT THIS CRAPPY BUS, THESE UGLY GROUPIES...
NOBODY EVER SAID WE WERE MOTLEY CRUE, DUDE! THE RECORDS WE CUT WERE LIKE POP-METAL GLAM JUNK!
WHO YOU CALLIN' UGLY!
BUT YOU'RE ALL INTO SUCH KILLER BANDS- EXODUS, MAIDEN, PRIEST...
YEAH, 'CEPT HARD ROCK MUSIC DIDN'T USED TO PAY THE BILLS!
BLOW ME
* INDIE RELEASES METAL MAGIC, PROJECTS IN THE JUNGLE AND I AM THE NIGHT.
EVEN IF YOU HATE HEADBANGERS BALL AND THE COPYCAT METAL BANDS, YOU GOTTA LOVE ALL THE ATTENTION THAT'S MAKING HEAVY METAL POPULAR! FOR GUYS LIKE US, WHO'RE A FEW STEPS ABOVE THE AVERAGE THRASH BAND, IT'S HELPIN' US ONTO THE FAST LANE!
THE FAST LANE?! JEEZ, VINNIE, WAKE UP AND SMELL THE BUS EXHAUST! WE'RE IN NEWARK, F'R CRYIN' OUT LOUD!
I'M NOT EVEN ALL THAT THRILLED WITH THE MATERIAL WE'RE DOING FROM POWER METAL*. I'D ONLY BEEN WITH THE BAND FOR A FEW WEEKS WHEN WE DID THAT RECORD!
I SURE HOPE I DIDN'T PUT MY MONEY ON THE WRONG HORSE! IT SEEMS LIKE THIS BAND COULD GO EITHER WAY- BIG SUCCESS OR BIG FLOP!
* ANOTHER LOW KEY INDIE WHICH NONETHELESS SELLS OVER 30,000 COPIES.
THEIR ROLLING SIDESHOW IS A HARROWING, SUBTERRANEAN JAUNT THROUGH THE NATION'S SCUZZIEST AND COOLEST PISSPOTS.
DED FL
THE ORDEAL HARDENS AND MOLDS PANTERA. THEIR NEW EDGE ENABLES THEM TO CUT THEIR FIRST MAJOR LABEL RECORD (FOR ATCO), COWBOYS FROM HELL.
THE NEXT TOUR IS UNDERTAKEN IN AN OVERCROWDED AND POORLY VENTILATED RV- ACTUALLY A STEP UP FROM PREVIOUS MOBILE DIGS...
PHEEEW! HEY, WHO CUT THE CHEESE?!?! VINNIE!
IT WASN'T ME! IT WAS REX!
SURE SMELLS LIKE A VINNIE!
...KINDA.
Observers were sickened and outraged
grim warning
Hostile

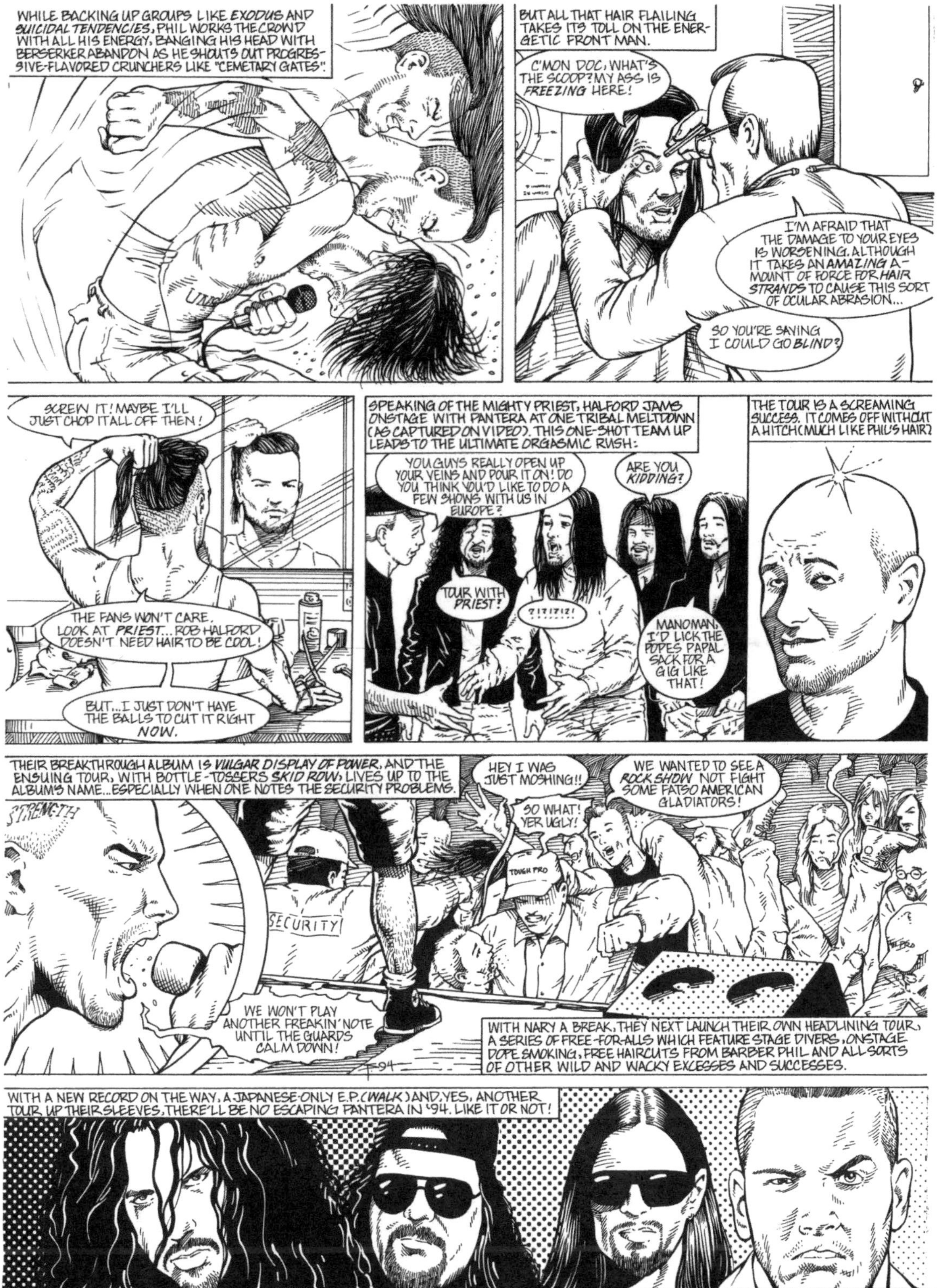
WHILE BACKING UP GROUPS LIKE EXODUS AND SUICIDAL TENDENCIES, PHIL WORKS THE CROWD WITH ALL HIS ENERGY, BANGING HIS HEAD WITH BERSERKER ABANDON AS HE SHOUTS OUT PROGRESSIVE-FLAVORED CRUNCHERS LIKE "CEMETARY GATES".
BUT ALL THAT HAIR FLAILING TAKES ITS TOLL ON THE ENERGETIC FRONT MAN.
C'MON DOC, WHAT'S THE SCOOP? MY ASS IS FREEZING HERE!
I'M AFRAID THAT THE DAMAGE TO YOUR EYES IS WORSENING. ALTHOUGH IT TAKES AN AMAZING AMOUNT OF FORCE FOR HAIR STRANDS TO CAUSE THIS SORT OF OCULAR ABRASION...
SO YOU'RE SAYING I COULD GO BLIND?
SCREW IT! MAYBE I'LL JUST CHOP IT ALL OFF THEN!
THE FANS WON'T CARE. LOOK AT PRIEST... ROB HALFORD DOESN'T NEED HAIR TO BE COOL!
BUT... I JUST DON'T HAVE THE BALLS TO CUT IT RIGHT NOW.
SPEAKING OF THE MIGHTY PRIEST, HALFORD JAMS ONSTAGE WITH PANTERA AT ONE TRIBAL MELTDOWN (AS CAPTURED ON VIDEO). THIS ONE-SHOT TEAM UP LEADS TO THE ULTIMATE ORGASMIC RUSH:
YOU GUYS REALLY OPEN UP YOUR VEINS AND POUR IT ON! DO YOU THINK YOU'D LIKE TO DO A FEW SHOWS WITH US IN EUROPE?
ARE YOU KIDDING?
TOUR WITH PRIEST!
?!?!?!?!
MAN O MAN, I'D LICK THE POPE'S PAPAL SACK FOR A GIG LIKE THAT!
THE TOUR IS A SCREAMING SUCCESS. IT COMES OFF WITHOUT A HITCH (MUCH LIKE PHIL'S HAIR)
THEIR BREAKTHROUGH ALBUM IS VULGAR DISPLAY OF POWER, AND THE ENSUING TOUR, WITH BOTTLE-TOSSERS SKID ROW, LIVES UP TO THE ALBUM'S NAME... ESPECIALLY WHEN ONE NOTES THE SECURITY PROBLEMS.
STRENGTH
HEY I WAS JUST MOSHING!!
SO WHAT! YER UGLY!
WE WANTED TO SEE A ROCK SHOW NOT FIGHT SOME FATSO AMERICAN GLADIATORS!
SECURITY
TOUGH PRO
WE WON'T PLAY ANOTHER FREAKIN' NOTE UNTIL THE GUARDS CALM DOWN!
WITH NARY A BREAK, THEY NEXT LAUNCH THEIR OWN HEADLINING TOUR, A SERIES OF FREE-FOR-ALLS WHICH FEATURE STAGE DIVERS, ONSTAGE DOPE SMOKING, FREE HAIRCUTS FROM BARBER PHIL AND ALL SORTS OF OTHER WILD AND WACKY EXCESSES AND SUCCESSES.
WITH A NEW RECORD ON THE WAY, A JAPANESE-ONLY E.P. (WALK) AND, YES, ANOTHER TOUR UP THEIR SLEEVES, THERE'LL BE NO ESCAPING PANTERA IN '94. LIKE IT OR NOT!

HEY!! IF YOU WOULD LIKE TO SEE MORE OF THESE ROCK COMICS IN RIP MAGAZINE THEN PLEASE WRITE IN AND DEMAND THEIR CONTINUANCE. WE NEED YER SUPPORT. THANX!

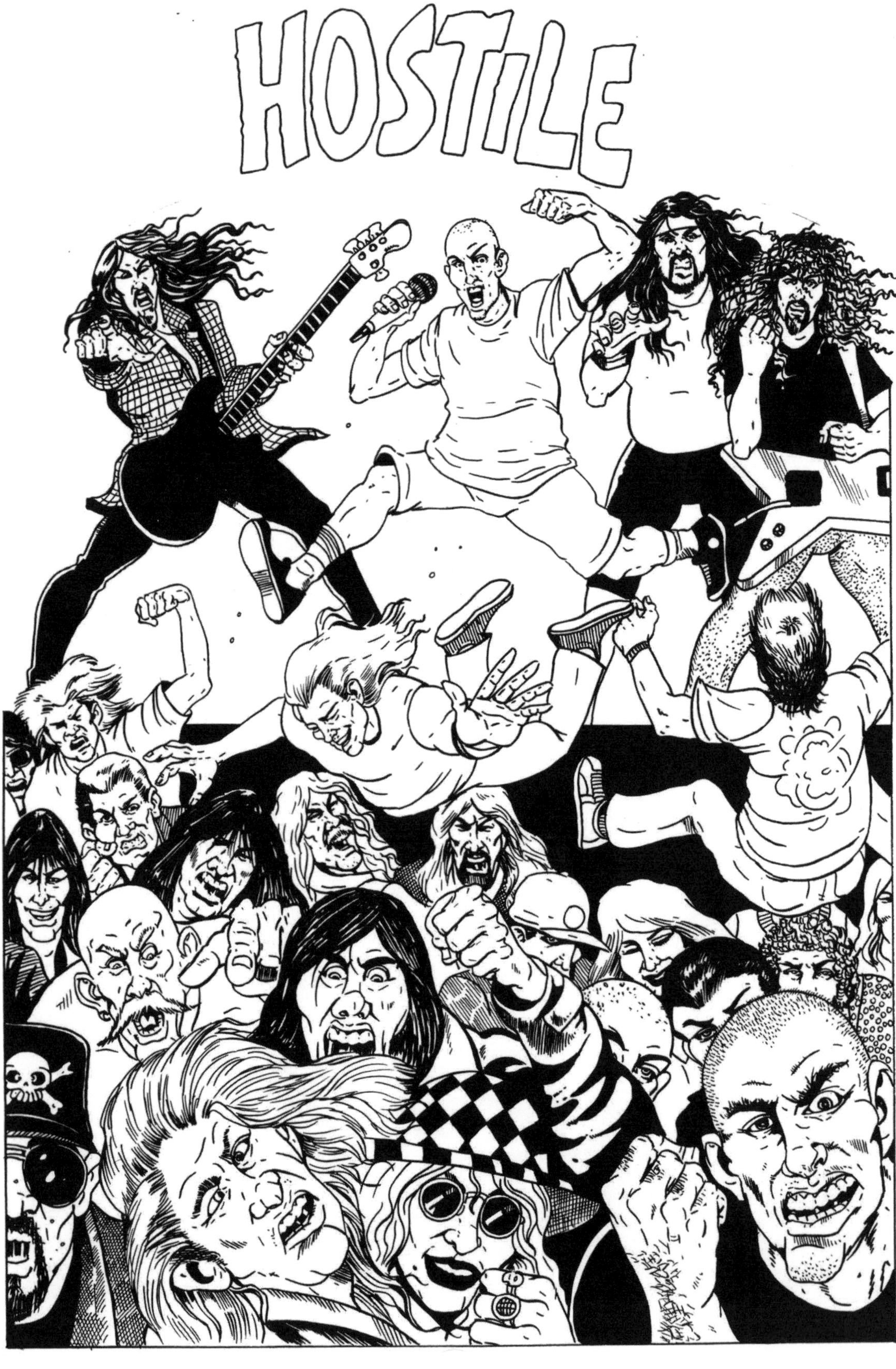
HOSTILE

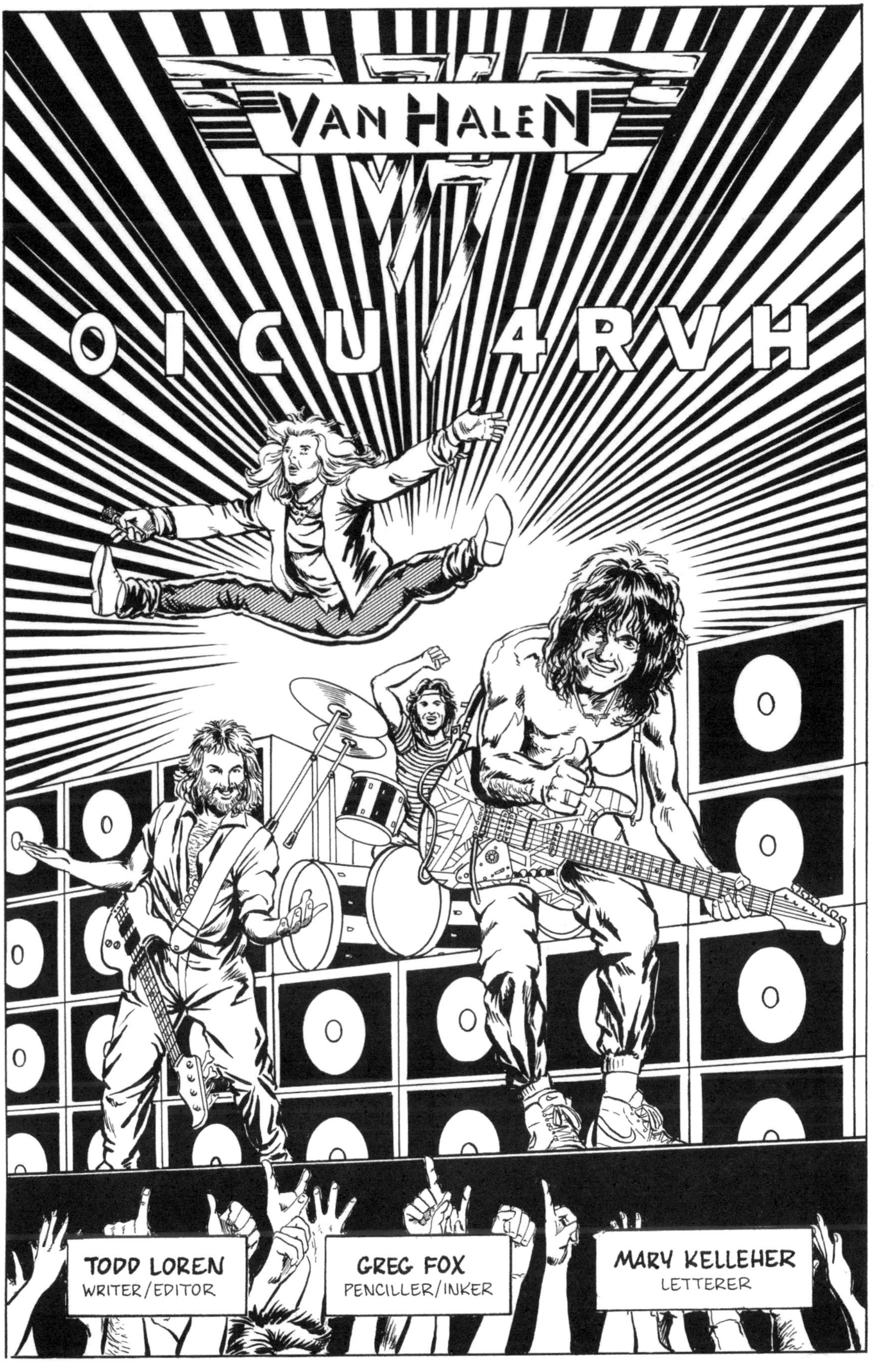
VAN HALEN
OICU 4RVH
TODD LOREN
WRITER/EDITOR
GREG FOX
PENCILLER/INKER
MARY KELLEHER
LETTERER

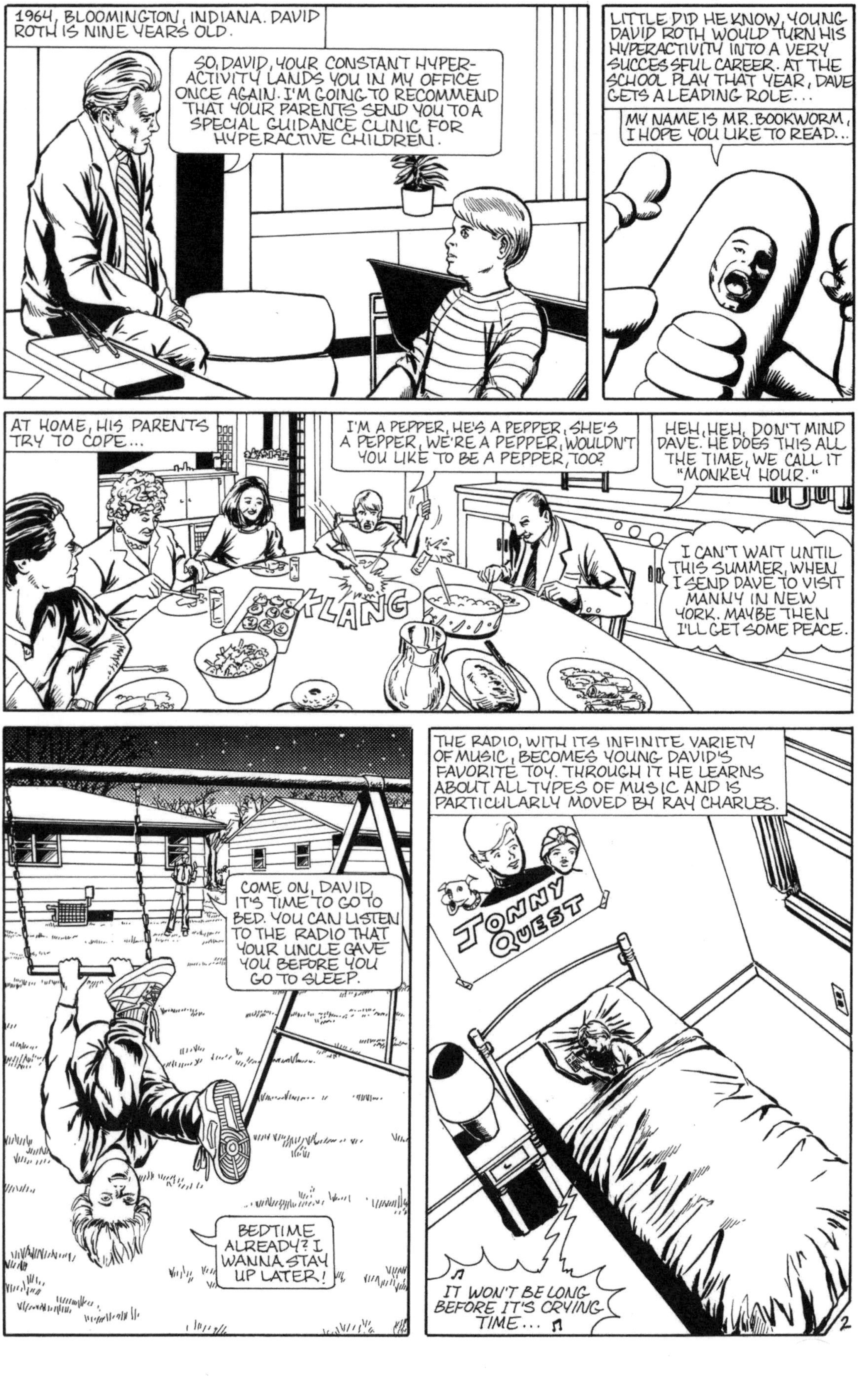

1964, BLOOMINGTON, INDIANA. DAVID ROTH IS NINE YEARS OLD.
SO, DAVID, YOUR CONSTANT HYPER-ACTIVITY LANDS YOU IN MY OFFICE ONCE AGAIN. I'M GOING TO RECOMMEND THAT YOUR PARENTS SEND YOU TO A SPECIAL GUIDANCE CLINIC FOR HYPERACTIVE CHILDREN.
LITTLE DID HE KNOW, YOUNG DAVID ROTH WOULD TURN HIS HYPERACTIVITY INTO A VERY SUCCESSFUL CAREER. AT THE SCHOOL PLAY THAT YEAR, DAVE GETS A LEADING ROLE...
MY NAME IS MR. BOOKWORM, I HOPE YOU LIKE TO READ...
AT HOME, HIS PARENTS TRY TO COPE...
I'M A PEPPER, HE'S A PEPPER, SHE'S A PEPPER, WE'RE A PEPPER, WOULDN'T YOU LIKE TO BE A PEPPER, TOO?
HEH, HEH, DON'T MIND DAVE. HE DOES THIS ALL THE TIME, WE CALL IT "MONKEY HOUR."
KLANG
I CAN'T WAIT UNTIL THIS SUMMER, WHEN I SEND DAVE TO VISIT MANNY IN NEW YORK. MAYBE THEN I'LL GET SOME PEACE.
COME ON, DAVID, IT'S TIME TO GO TO BED. YOU CAN LISTEN TO THE RADIO THAT YOUR UNCLE GAVE YOU BEFORE YOU GO TO SLEEP.
BEDTIME ALREADY? I WANNA STAY UP LATER!
THE RADIO, WITH ITS INFINITE VARIETY OF MUSIC, BECOMES YOUNG DAVID'S FAVORITE TOY. THROUGH IT HE LEARNS ABOUT ALL TYPES OF MUSIC AND IS PARTICULARLY MOVED BY RAY CHARLES.
TONNY QUEST
IT WON'T BE LONG BEFORE IT'S CRYING TIME...

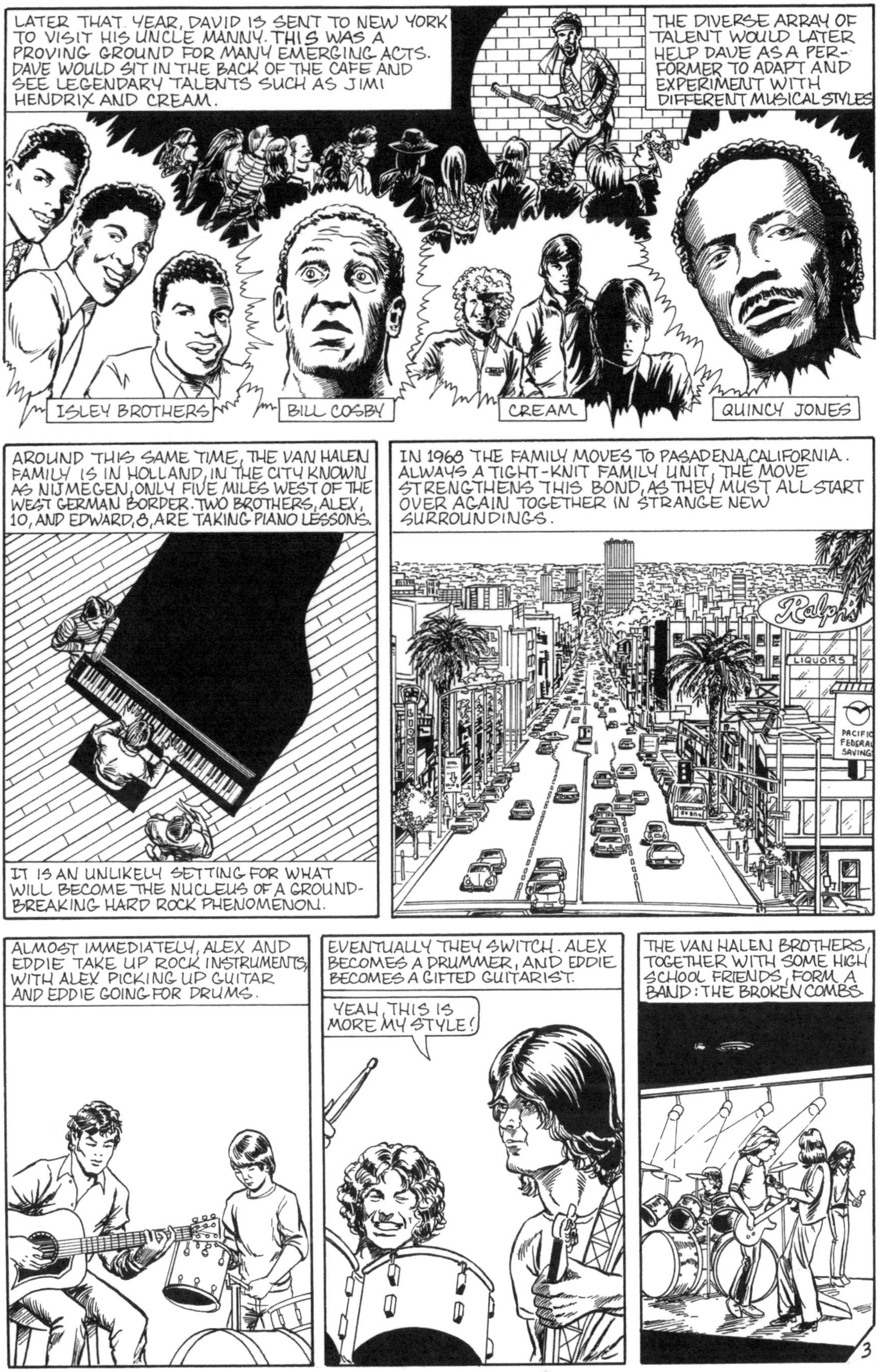
LATER THAT YEAR, DAVID IS SENT TO NEW YORK TO VISIT HIS UNCLE MANNY. THIS WAS A PROVING GROUND FOR MANY EMERGING ACTS. DAVE WOULD SIT IN THE BACK OF THE CAFE AND SEE LEGENDARY TALENTS SUCH AS JIMI HENDRIX AND CREAM.
THE DIVERSE ARRAY OF TALENT WOULD LATER HELP DAVE AS A PERFORMER TO ADAPT AND EXPERIMENT WITH DIFFERENT MUSICAL STYLES
ISLEY BROTHERS
BILL COSBY
CREAM
QUINCY JONES
AROUND THIS SAME TIME, THE VAN HALEN FAMILY IS IN HOLLAND, IN THE CITY KNOWN AS NIJMEGEN, ONLY FIVE MILES WEST OF THE WEST GERMAN BORDER. TWO BROTHERS, ALEX, 10, AND EDWARD, 8, ARE TAKING PIANO LESSONS.
IT IS AN UNLIKELY SETTING FOR WHAT WILL BECOME THE NUCLEUS OF A GROUND-BREAKING HARD ROCK PHENOMENON.
IN 1968 THE FAMILY MOVES TO PASADENA, CALIFORNIA. ALWAYS A TIGHT-KNIT FAMILY UNIT, THE MOVE STRENGTHENS THIS BOND, AS THEY MUST ALL START OVER AGAIN TOGETHER IN STRANGE NEW SURROUNDINGS.
Ralph's
LIQUORS
LIQUOR
PACIFIC FEDERAL SAVINGS
ALMOST IMMEDIATELY, ALEX AND EDDIE TAKE UP ROCK INSTRUMENTS, WITH ALEX PICKING UP GUITAR AND EDDIE GOING FOR DRUMS.
EVENTUALLY THEY SWITCH. ALEX BECOMES A DRUMMER, AND EDDIE BECOMES A GIFTED GUITARIST.
YEAH, THIS IS MORE MY STYLE!
THE VAN HALEN BROTHERS, TOGETHER WITH SOME HIGH SCHOOL FRIENDS, FORM A BAND: THE BROKEN COMBS.

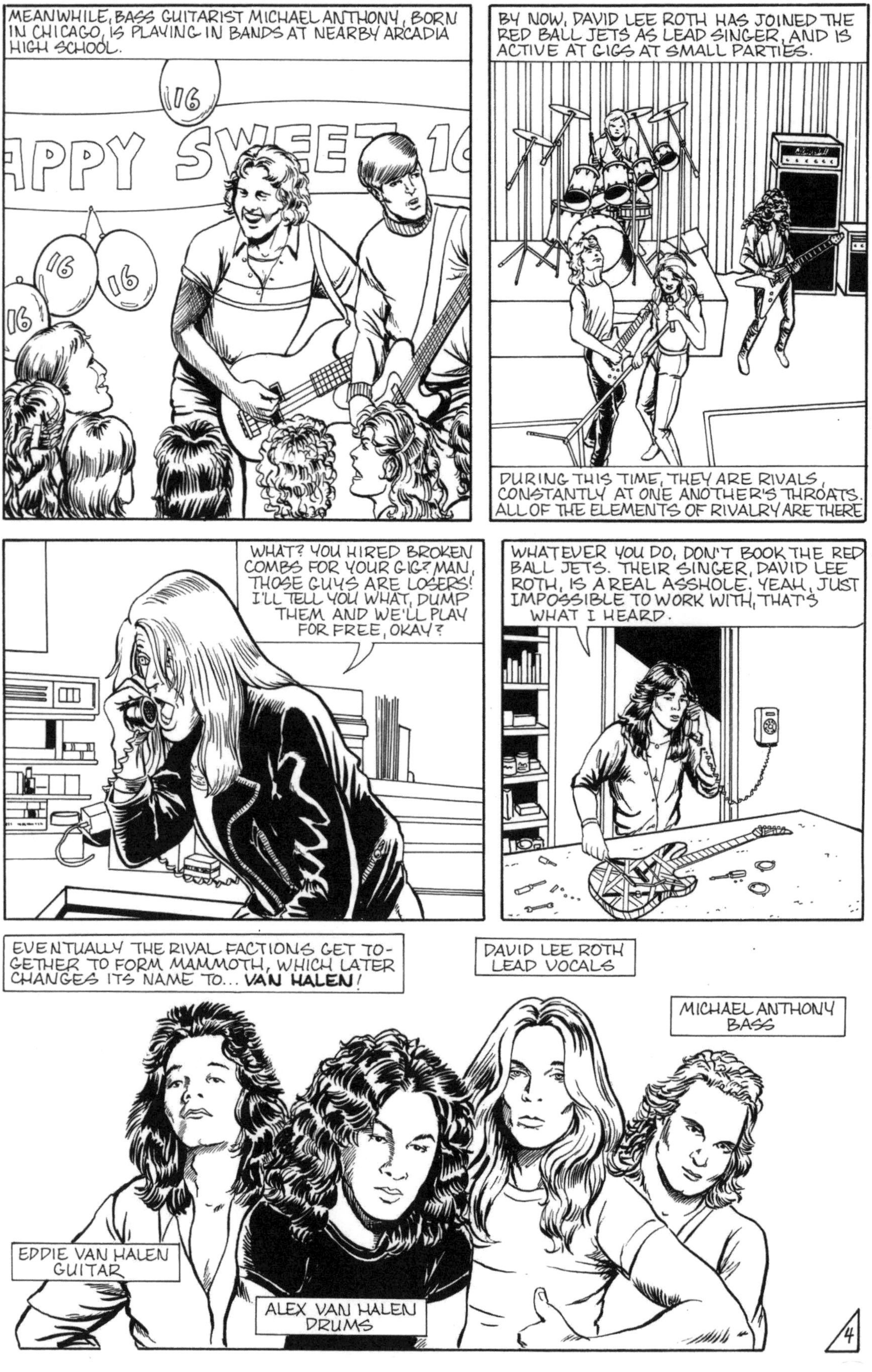
MEANWHILE, BASS GUITARIST MICHAEL ANTHONY, BORN IN CHICAGO, IS PLAYING IN BANDS AT NEARBY ARCADIA HIGH SCHOOL.
16
APPY SWEET 16
16
16
16
BY NOW, DAVID LEE ROTH HAS JOINED THE RED BALL JETS AS LEAD SINGER, AND IS ACTIVE AT GIGS AT SMALL PARTIES.
DURING THIS TIME, THEY ARE RIVALS, CONSTANTLY AT ONE ANOTHER'S THROATS. ALL OF THE ELEMENTS OF RIVALRY ARE THERE
WHAT? YOU HIRED BROKEN COMBS FOR YOUR GIG? MAN, THOSE GUYS ARE LOSERS! I'LL TELL YOU WHAT, DUMP THEM AND WE'LL PLAY FOR FREE, OKAY?
WHATEVER YOU DO, DON'T BOOK THE RED BALL JETS. THEIR SINGER, DAVID LEE ROTH, IS A REAL ASSHOLE. YEAH, JUST IMPOSSIBLE TO WORK WITH, THAT'S WHAT I HEARD.
EVENTUALLY THE RIVAL FACTIONS GET TOGETHER TO FORM MAMMOTH, WHICH LATER CHANGES ITS NAME TO... VAN HALEN!
DAVID LEE ROTH LEAD VOCALS
MICHAEL ANTHONY BASS
EDDIE VAN HALEN GUITAR
ALEX VAN HALEN DRUMS

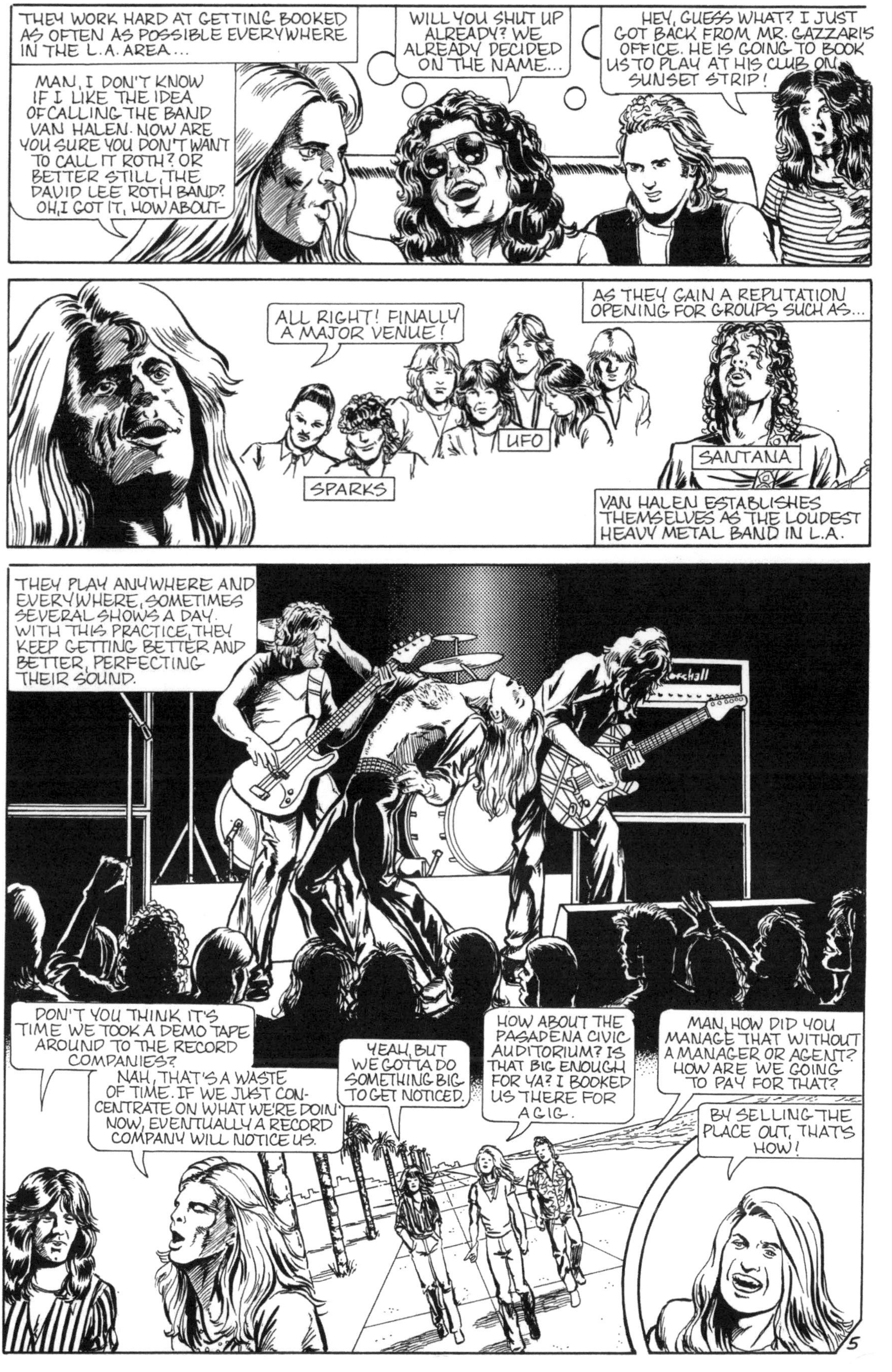
THEY WORK HARD AT GETTING BOOKED AS OFTEN AS POSSIBLE EVERYWHERE IN THE L.A. AREA...
MAN, I DON'T KNOW IF I LIKE THE IDEA OF CALLING THE BAND VAN HALEN. NOW ARE YOU SURE YOU DON'T WANT TO CALL IT ROTH? OR BETTER STILL, THE DAVID LEE ROTH BAND? OH, I GOT IT, HOW ABOUT-
WILL YOU SHUT UP ALREADY? WE ALREADY DECIDED ON THE NAME...
HEY, GUESS WHAT? I JUST GOT BACK FROM MR. GAZZARI'S OFFICE. HE IS GOING TO BOOK US TO PLAY AT HIS CLUB ON SUNSET STRIP!
ALL RIGHT! FINALLY A MAJOR VENUE!
AS THEY GAIN A REPUTATION OPENING FOR GROUPS SUCH AS...
SPARKS
UFO
SANTANA
VAN HALEN ESTABLISHES THEMSELVES AS THE LOUDEST HEAVY METAL BAND IN L.A.
THEY PLAY ANYWHERE AND EVERYWHERE, SOMETIMES SEVERAL SHOWS A DAY. WITH THIS PRACTICE, THEY KEEP GETTING BETTER AND BETTER, PERFECTING THEIR SOUND.
DON'T YOU THINK IT'S TIME WE TOOK A DEMO TAPE AROUND TO THE RECORD COMPANIES?
NAH, THAT'S A WASTE OF TIME. IF WE JUST CONCENTRATE ON WHAT WE'RE DOIN' NOW, EVENTUALLY A RECORD COMPANY WILL NOTICE US.
YEAH, BUT WE GOTTA DO SOMETHING BIG TO GET NOTICED.
HOW ABOUT THE PASADENA CIVIC AUDITORIUM? IS THAT BIG ENOUGH FOR YA? I BOOKED US THERE FOR A GIG.
MAN, HOW DID YOU MANAGE THAT WITHOUT A MANAGER OR AGENT? HOW ARE WE GOING TO PAY FOR THAT?
BY SELLING THE PLACE OUT, THAT'S HOW!

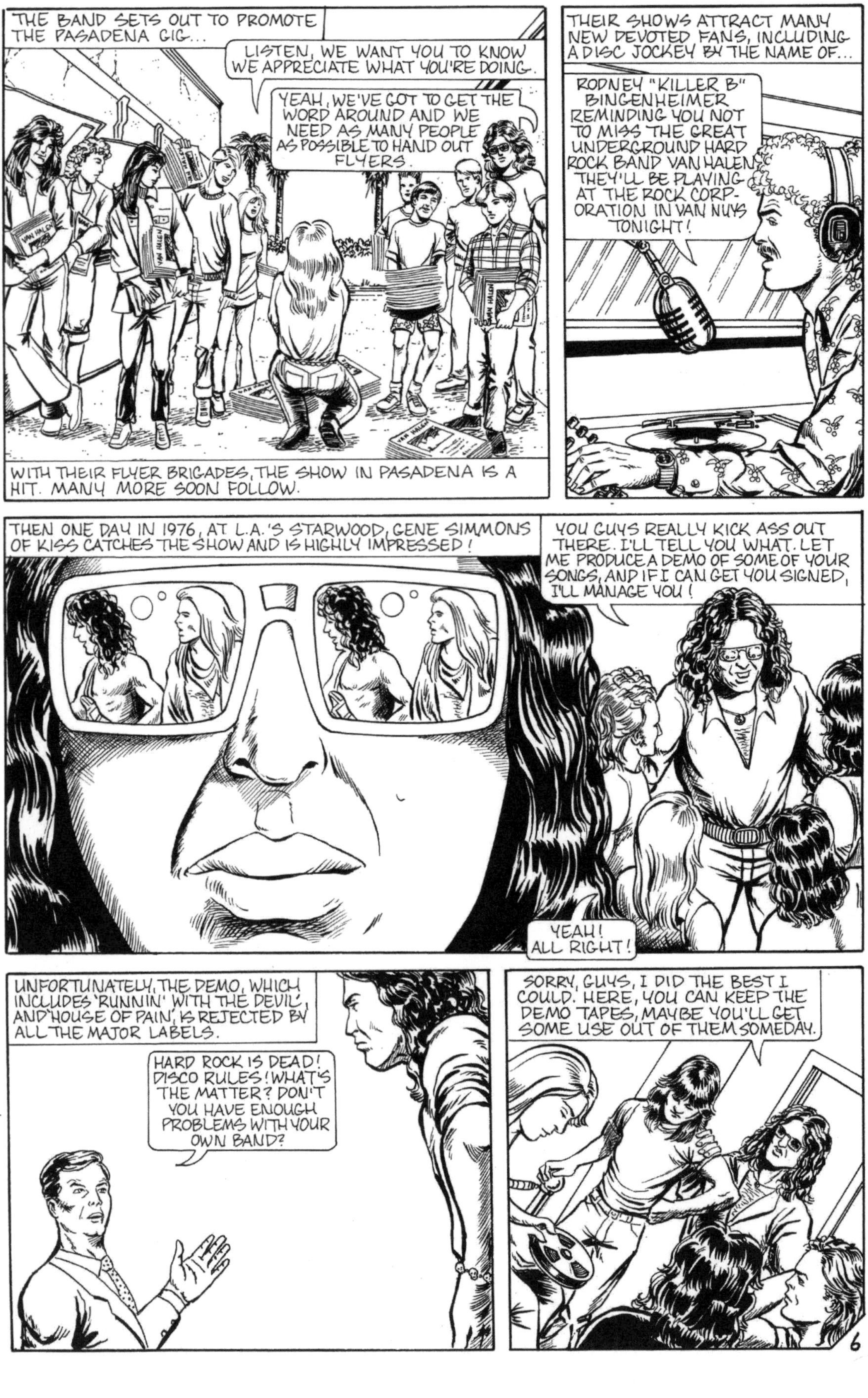
THE BAND SETS OUT TO PROMOTE THE PASADENA GIG...
LISTEN, WE WANT YOU TO KNOW WE APPRECIATE WHAT YOU'RE DOING.
YEAH, WE'VE GOT TO GET THE WORD AROUND AND WE NEED AS MANY PEOPLE AS POSSIBLE TO HAND OUT FLYERS.
VAN HALEN
WITH THEIR FLYER BRIGADES, THE SHOW IN PASADENA IS A HIT. MANY MORE SOON FOLLOW.
THEIR SHOWS ATTRACT MANY NEW DEVOTED FANS, INCLUDING A DISC JOCKEY BY THE NAME OF...
RODNEY "KILLER B" BINGENHEIMER REMINDING YOU NOT TO MISS THE GREAT UNDERGROUND HARD ROCK BAND VAN HALEN. THEY'LL BE PLAYING AT THE ROCK CORPORATION IN VAN NUYS TONIGHT!
THEN ONE DAY IN 1976, AT L.A.'S STARWOOD, GENE SIMMONS OF KISS CATCHES THE SHOW AND IS HIGHLY IMPRESSED!
YOU GUYS REALLY KICK ASS OUT THERE. I'LL TELL YOU WHAT. LET ME PRODUCE A DEMO OF SOME OF YOUR SONGS, AND IF I CAN GET YOU SIGNED, I'LL MANAGE YOU!
YEAH! ALL RIGHT!
UNFORTUNATELY, THE DEMO, WHICH INCLUDES 'RUNNIN' WITH THE DEVIL', AND 'HOUSE OF PAIN', IS REJECTED BY ALL THE MAJOR LABELS.
HARD ROCK IS DEAD! DISCO RULES! WHAT'S THE MATTER? DON'T YOU HAVE ENOUGH PROBLEMS WITH YOUR OWN BAND?
SORRY, GUYS, I DID THE BEST I COULD. HERE, YOU CAN KEEP THE DEMO TAPES, MAYBE YOU'LL GET SOME USE OUT OF THEM SOMEDAY.

VAN HALEN MOVES FORWARD UNDAUNTED. ROTH EVOLVES AS THE PRIMARY LYRICIST, WHILE OTHER MEMBERS CREATE THE MUSIC...

UH, LET'S SEE... MIGHT AS WELL JUMP. HMM. NAH!

NOW IT'S 1977, AT STARWOOD ONCE AGAIN. THE AUDIENCE IS GOING WILD.

TED TEMPLEMAN AND MO OSTIN OF WARNER ARE IN THE AUDIENCE. THEY LIKE WHAT THEY SEE... AND HEAR.

YOUR BAND IS LIVING PROOF THAT HARD ROCK N' ROLL IS NOT DEAD. I'M GOING BACK TO CONVINCE THEM TO SIGN YOU. HAVE YOU GOT A DEMO TAPE?

SURE DO!

WARNER WANTS TO SIGN VAN HALEN. THE USUAL CONTRACTUAL DIFFICULTIES ENSUE...

WE WANT TOTAL ARTISTIC CONTROL. VAN HALEN DOES NOT ANSWER TO ANYONE!

AND DON'T FORGET THE PATERNITY CLAUSE.

FEBRUARY 1978. THE SELF-TITLED ALBUM IS RELEASED.

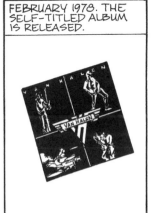

IT WILL REACH #19 ON THE BILLBOARD ALBUM CHARTS - EXCELLENT CONSIDERING THIS IS STILL THE PEAK OF THE DISCO AGE.

7

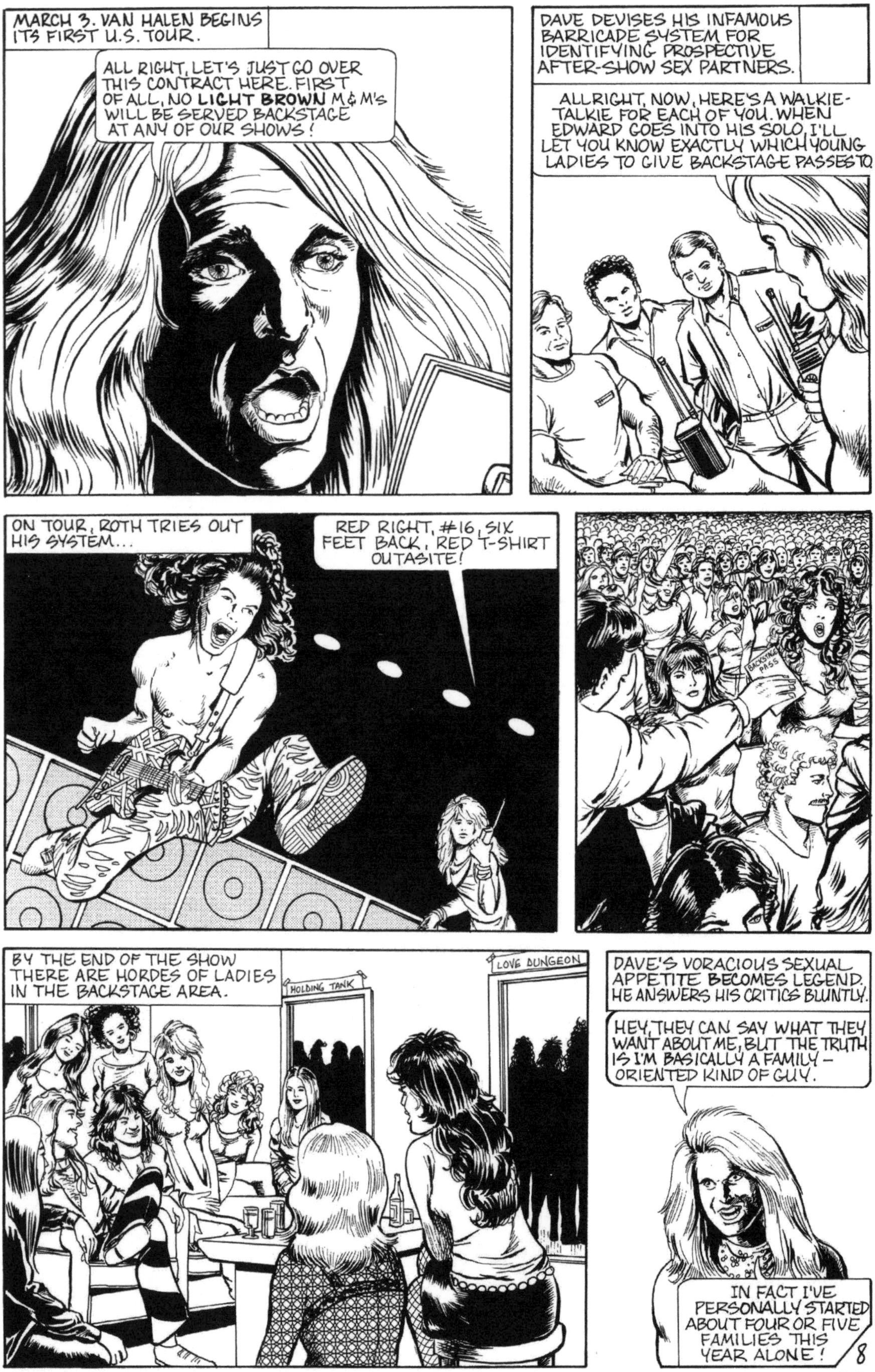
MARCH 3. VAN HALEN BEGINS ITS FIRST U.S. TOUR.
ALL RIGHT, LET'S JUST GO OVER THIS CONTRACT HERE. FIRST OF ALL, NO LIGHT BROWN M&M'S WILL BE SERVED BACKSTAGE AT ANY OF OUR SHOWS!
DAVE DEVISES HIS INFAMOUS BARRICADE SYSTEM FOR IDENTIFYING PROSPECTIVE AFTER-SHOW SEX PARTNERS.
ALL RIGHT, NOW, HERE'S A WALKIE-TALKIE FOR EACH OF YOU. WHEN EDWARD GOES INTO HIS SOLO, I'LL LET YOU KNOW EXACTLY WHICH YOUNG LADIES TO GIVE BACKSTAGE PASSES TO.
ON TOUR, ROTH TRIES OUT HIS SYSTEM...
RED RIGHT, #16, SIX FEET BACK, RED T-SHIRT OUTASITE!
BACKSTAGE PASS
BY THE END OF THE SHOW THERE ARE HORDES OF LADIES IN THE BACKSTAGE AREA.
HOLDING TANK
LOVE DUNGEON
DAVE'S VORACIOUS SEXUAL APPETITE BECOMES LEGEND. HE ANSWERS HIS CRITICS BLUNTLY.
HEY, THEY CAN SAY WHAT THEY WANT ABOUT ME, BUT THE TRUTH IS I'M BASICALLY A FAMILY-ORIENTED KIND OF GUY.
IN FACT I'VE PERSONALLY STARTED ABOUT FOUR OR FIVE FAMILIES THIS YEAR ALONE!

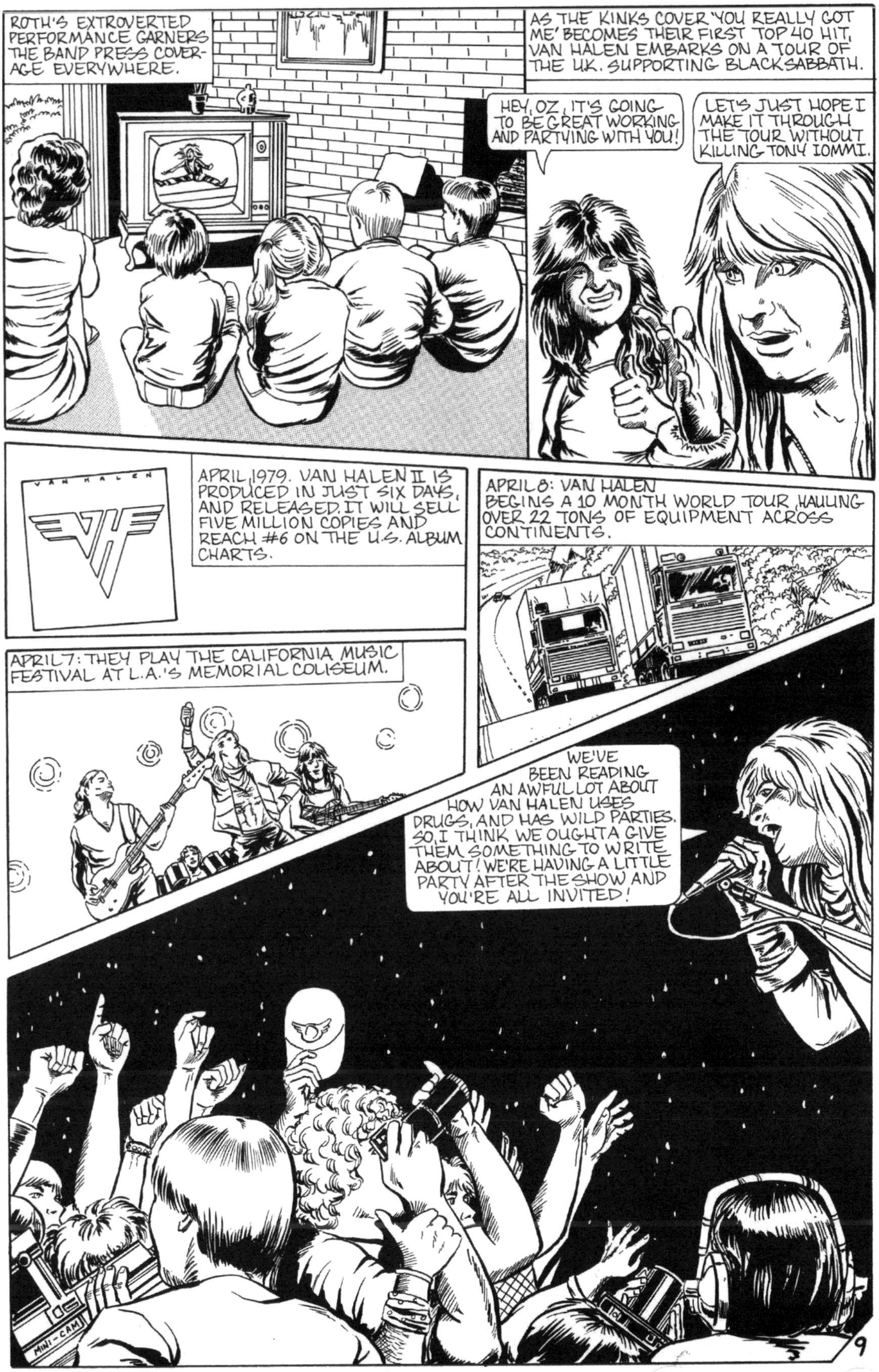
ROTH'S EXTROVERTED PERFORMANCE GARNERS THE BAND PRESS COVERAGE EVERYWHERE.
AS THE KINKS COVER 'YOU REALLY GOT ME' BECOMES THEIR FIRST TOP 40 HIT, VAN HALEN EMBARKS ON A TOUR OF THE U.K. SUPPORTING BLACK SABBATH.
HEY, OZ, IT'S GOING TO BE GREAT WORKING AND PARTYING WITH YOU!
LET'S JUST HOPE I MAKE IT THROUGH THE TOUR WITHOUT KILLING TONY IOMMI.
VAN HALEN
APRIL, 1979. VAN HALEN II IS PRODUCED IN JUST SIX DAYS, AND RELEASED. IT WILL SELL FIVE MILLION COPIES AND REACH #6 ON THE U.S. ALBUM CHARTS.
APRIL 8: VAN HALEN BEGINS A 10 MONTH WORLD TOUR, HAULING OVER 22 TONS OF EQUIPMENT ACROSS CONTINENTS.
APRIL 7: THEY PLAY THE CALIFORNIA MUSIC FESTIVAL AT L.A.'S MEMORIAL COLISEUM.
WE'VE BEEN READING AN AWFUL LOT ABOUT HOW VAN HALEN USES DRUGS, AND HAS WILD PARTIES. SO, I THINK WE OUGHTA GIVE THEM SOMETHING TO WRITE ABOUT! WE'RE HAVING A LITTLE PARTY AFTER THE SHOW AND YOU'RE ALL INVITED!
MINI-CAM

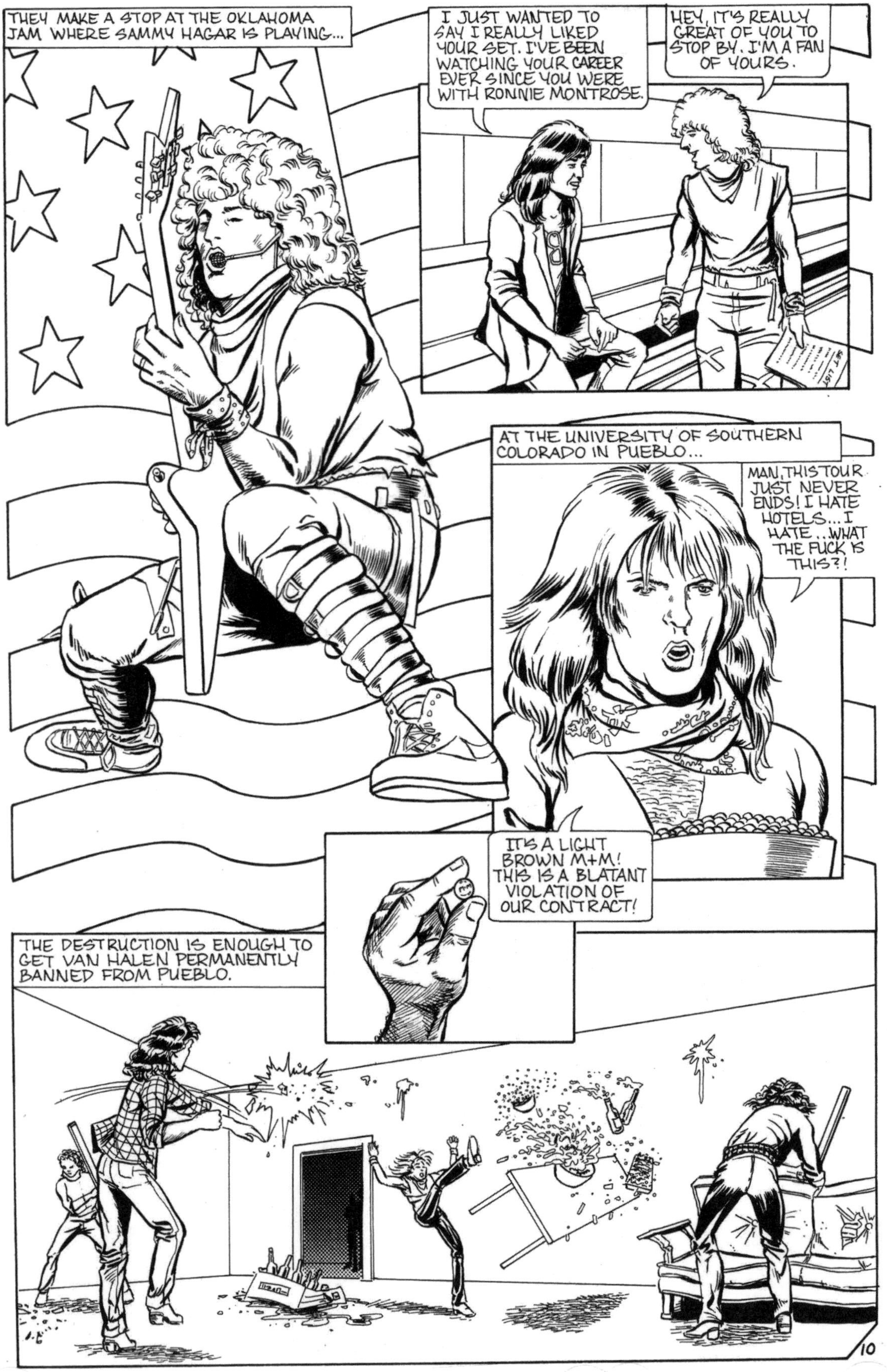
THEY MAKE A STOP AT THE OKLAHOMA JAM WHERE SAMMY HAGAR IS PLAYING...
I JUST WANTED TO SAY I REALLY LIKED YOUR SET. I'VE BEEN WATCHING YOUR CAREER EVER SINCE YOU WERE WITH RONNIE MONTROSE.
HEY, IT'S REALLY GREAT OF YOU TO STOP BY. I'M A FAN OF YOURS.
SET LIST
AT THE UNIVERSITY OF SOUTHERN COLORADO IN PUEBLO...
MAN, THIS TOUR JUST NEVER ENDS! I HATE HOTELS... I HATE... WHAT THE FUCK IS THIS?!
IT'S A LIGHT BROWN M+M! THIS IS A BLATANT VIOLATION OF OUR CONTRACT!
THE DESTRUCTION IS ENOUGH TO GET VAN HALEN PERMANENTLY BANNED FROM PUEBLO.

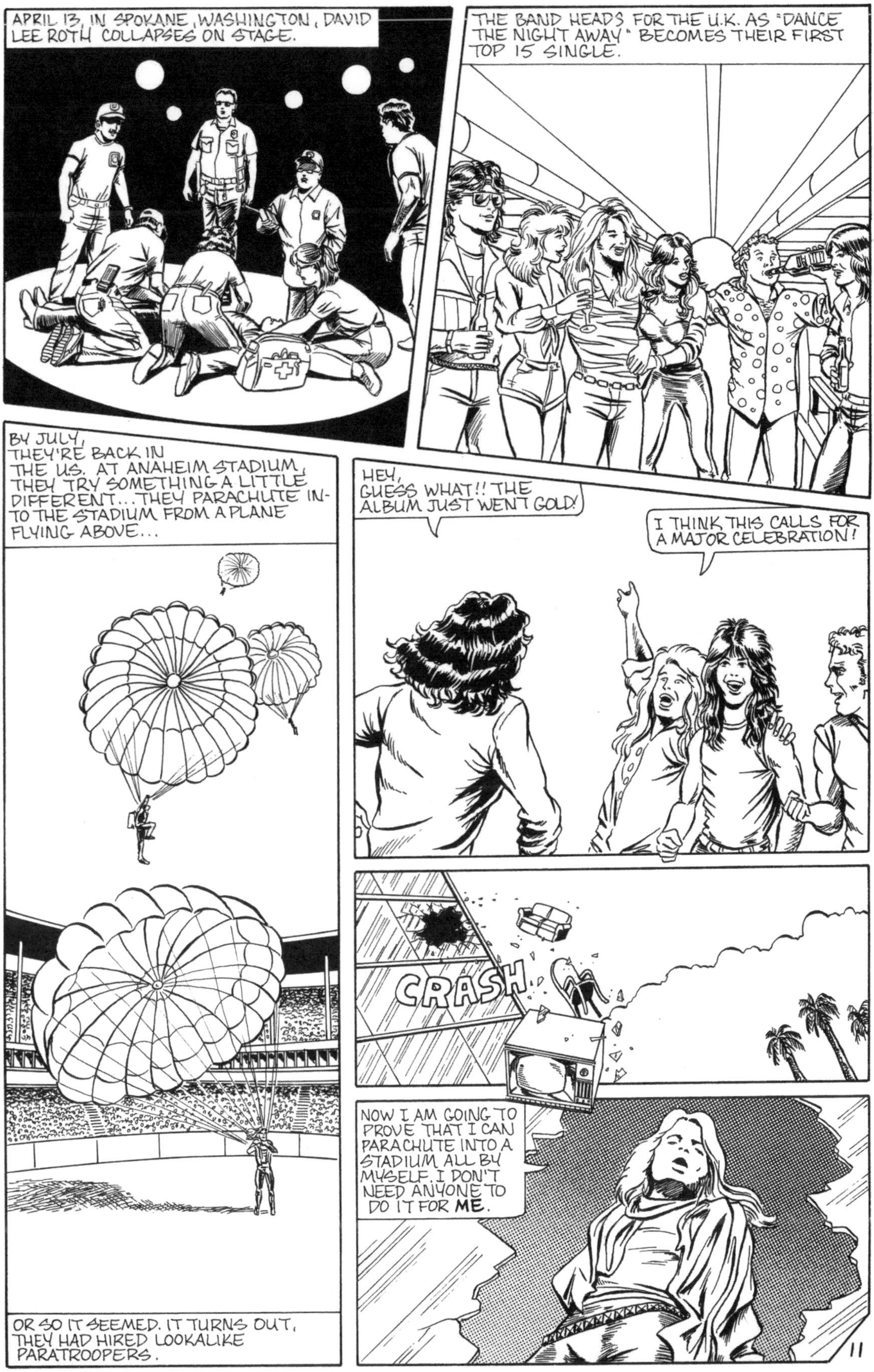
APRIL 13, IN SPOKANE, WASHINGTON, DAVID LEE ROTH COLLAPSES ON STAGE.
THE BAND HEADS FOR THE U.K. AS "DANCE THE NIGHT AWAY" BECOMES THEIR FIRST TOP 15 SINGLE.
BY JULY, THEY'RE BACK IN THE U.S. AT ANAHEIM STADIUM, THEY TRY SOMETHING A LITTLE DIFFERENT... THEY PARACHUTE INTO THE STADIUM FROM A PLANE FLYING ABOVE...
OR SO IT SEEMED. IT TURNS OUT, THEY HAD HIRED LOOKALIKE PARATROOPERS.
HEY, GUESS WHAT!! THE ALBUM JUST WENT GOLD!
I THINK THIS CALLS FOR A MAJOR CELEBRATION!
CRASH
NOW I AM GOING TO PROVE THAT I CAN PARACHUTE INTO A STADIUM ALL BY MYSELF. I DON'T NEED ANYONE TO DO IT FOR **ME**.

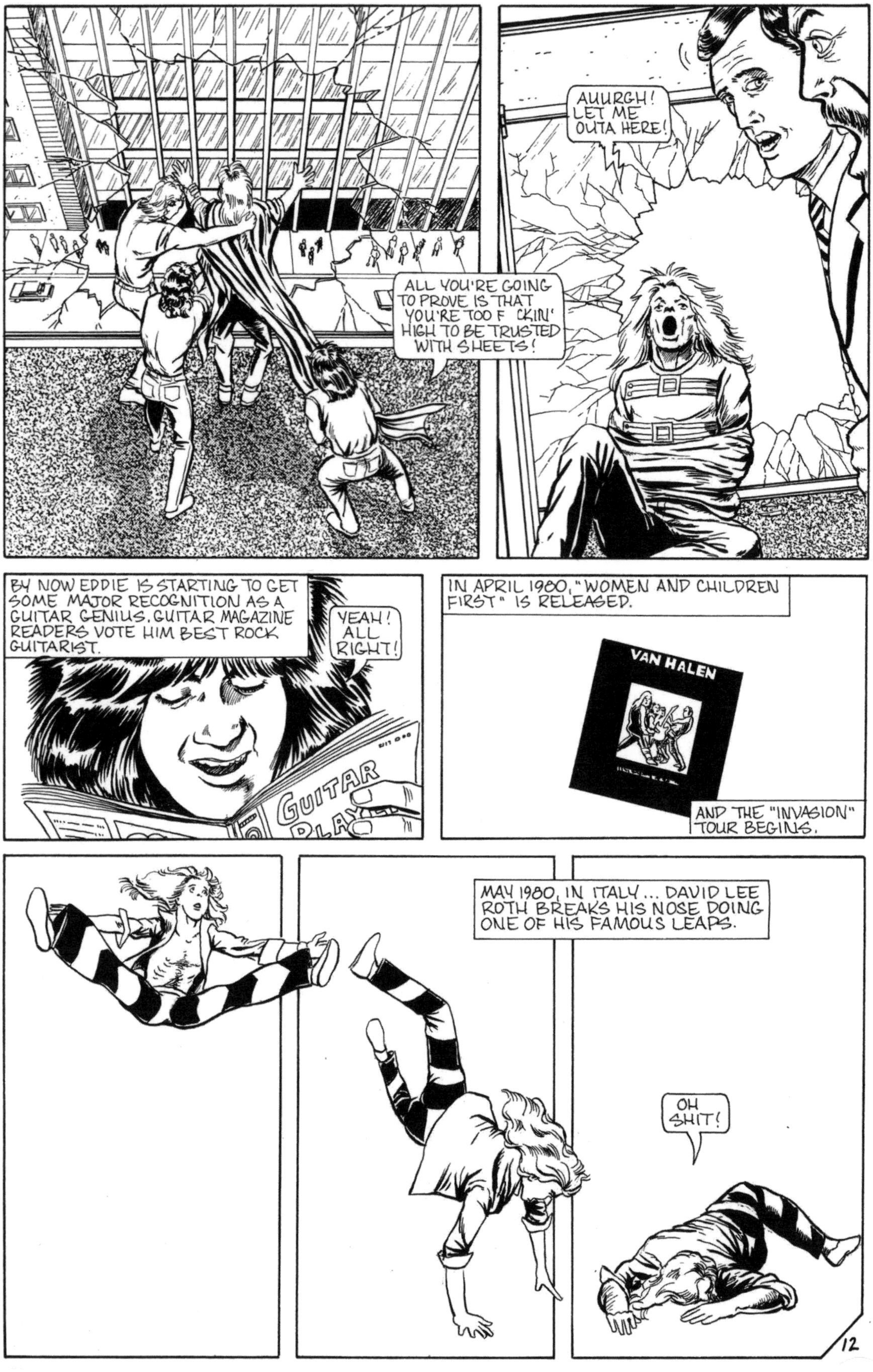
ALL YOU'RE GOING TO PROVE IS THAT YOU'RE TOO F CKIN' HIGH TO BE TRUSTED WITH SHEETS!
AUURGH! LET ME OUTA HERE!
BY NOW EDDIE IS STARTING TO GET SOME MAJOR RECOGNITION AS A GUITAR GENIUS. GUITAR MAGAZINE READERS VOTE HIM BEST ROCK GUITARIST.
YEAH! ALL RIGHT!
GUITAR PLAYER
IN APRIL 1980, "WOMEN AND CHILDREN FIRST" IS RELEASED.
VAN HALEN
AND THE "INVASION" TOUR BEGINS.
MAY 1980, IN ITALY... DAVID LEE ROTH BREAKS HIS NOSE DOING ONE OF HIS FAMOUS LEAPS.
OH SHIT!

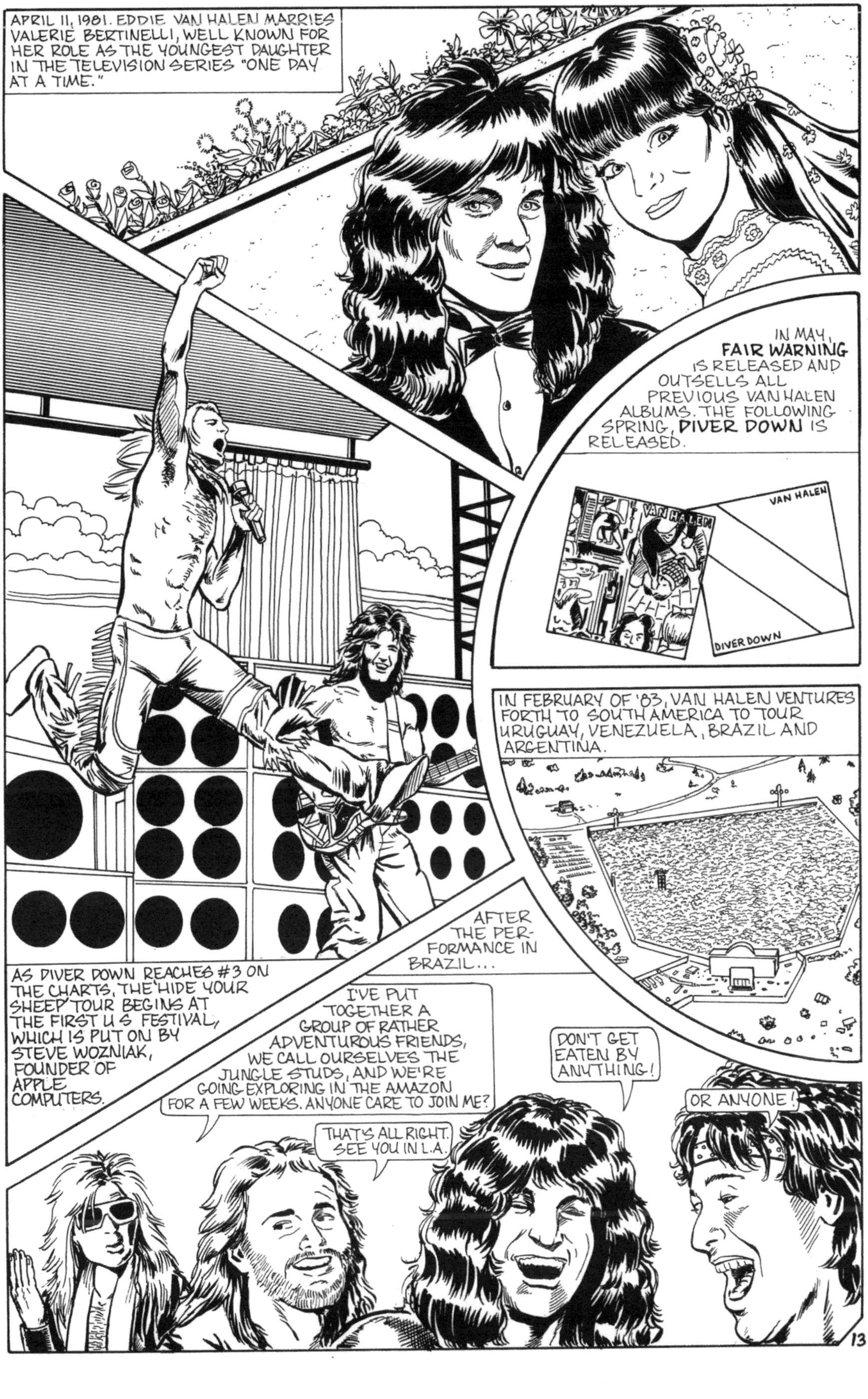
APRIL 11, 1981. EDDIE VAN HALEN MARRIES VALERIE BERTINELLI, WELL KNOWN FOR HER ROLE AS THE YOUNGEST DAUGHTER IN THE TELEVISION SERIES "ONE DAY AT A TIME."
IN MAY, FAIR WARNING IS RELEASED AND OUTSELLS ALL PREVIOUS VAN HALEN ALBUMS. THE FOLLOWING SPRING, DIVER DOWN IS RELEASED.
VAN HALEN
VAN HALEN
DIVER DOWN
IN FEBRUARY OF '83, VAN HALEN VENTURES FORTH TO SOUTH AMERICA TO TOUR URUGUAY, VENEZUELA, BRAZIL AND ARGENTINA.
AS DIVER DOWN REACHES #3 ON THE CHARTS, THE 'HIDE YOUR SHEEP' TOUR BEGINS AT THE FIRST U S FESTIVAL, WHICH IS PUT ON BY STEVE WOZNIAK, FOUNDER OF APPLE COMPUTERS.
AFTER THE PERFORMANCE IN BRAZIL...
I'VE PUT TOGETHER A GROUP OF RATHER ADVENTUROUS FRIENDS, WE CALL OURSELVES THE JUNGLE STUDS, AND WE'RE GOING EXPLORING IN THE AMAZON FOR A FEW WEEKS. ANYONE CARE TO JOIN ME?
THAT'S ALL RIGHT. SEE YOU IN L.A.
DON'T GET EATEN BY ANYTHING!
OR ANYONE!

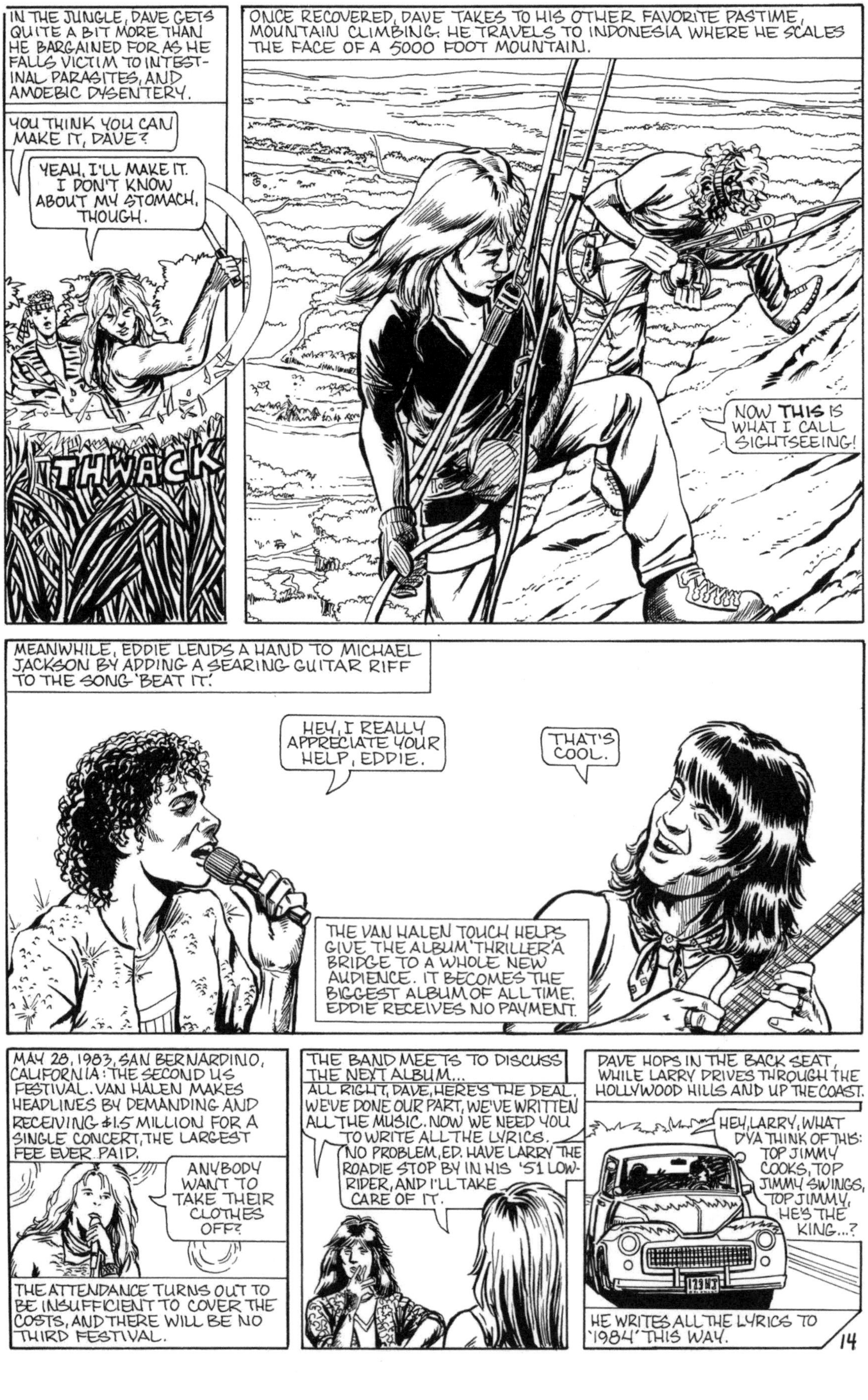
IN THE JUNGLE, DAVE GETS QUITE A BIT MORE THAN HE BARGAINED FOR AS HE FALLS VICTIM TO INTESTINAL PARASITES, AND AMOEBIC DYSENTERY.
YOU THINK YOU CAN MAKE IT, DAVE?
YEAH, I'LL MAKE IT. I DON'T KNOW ABOUT MY STOMACH, THOUGH.
THWACK
ONCE RECOVERED, DAVE TAKES TO HIS OTHER FAVORITE PASTIME, MOUNTAIN CLIMBING. HE TRAVELS TO INDONESIA WHERE HE SCALES THE FACE OF A 5000 FOOT MOUNTAIN.
NOW THIS IS WHAT I CALL SIGHTSEEING!
MEANWHILE, EDDIE LENDS A HAND TO MICHAEL JACKSON BY ADDING A SEARING GUITAR RIFF TO THE SONG 'BEAT IT.'
HEY, I REALLY APPRECIATE YOUR HELP, EDDIE.
THAT'S COOL.
THE VAN HALEN TOUCH HELPS GIVE THE ALBUM 'THRILLER' A BRIDGE TO A WHOLE NEW AUDIENCE. IT BECOMES THE BIGGEST ALBUM OF ALL TIME. EDDIE RECEIVES NO PAYMENT.
MAY 28, 1983, SAN BERNARDINO, CALIFORNIA: THE SECOND US FESTIVAL. VAN HALEN MAKES HEADLINES BY DEMANDING AND RECEIVING $1.5 MILLION FOR A SINGLE CONCERT, THE LARGEST FEE EVER PAID.
ANYBODY WANT TO TAKE THEIR CLOTHES OFF?
THE ATTENDANCE TURNS OUT TO BE INSUFFICIENT TO COVER THE COSTS, AND THERE WILL BE NO THIRD FESTIVAL.
THE BAND MEETS TO DISCUSS THE NEXT ALBUM...
ALL RIGHT, DAVE, HERE'S THE DEAL. WE'VE DONE OUR PART, WE'VE WRITTEN ALL THE MUSIC. NOW WE NEED YOU TO WRITE ALL THE LYRICS.
NO PROBLEM, ED. HAVE LARRY THE ROADIE STOP BY IN HIS '51 LOW-RIDER, AND I'LL TAKE CARE OF IT.
DAVE HOPS IN THE BACK SEAT, WHILE LARRY DRIVES THROUGH THE HOLLYWOOD HILLS AND UP THE COAST.
HEY, LARRY, WHAT D'YA THINK OF THIS: TOP JIMMY COOKS, TOP JIMMY SWINGS, TOP JIMMY, HE'S THE KING...?
HE WRITES ALL THE LYRICS TO '1984' THIS WAY.

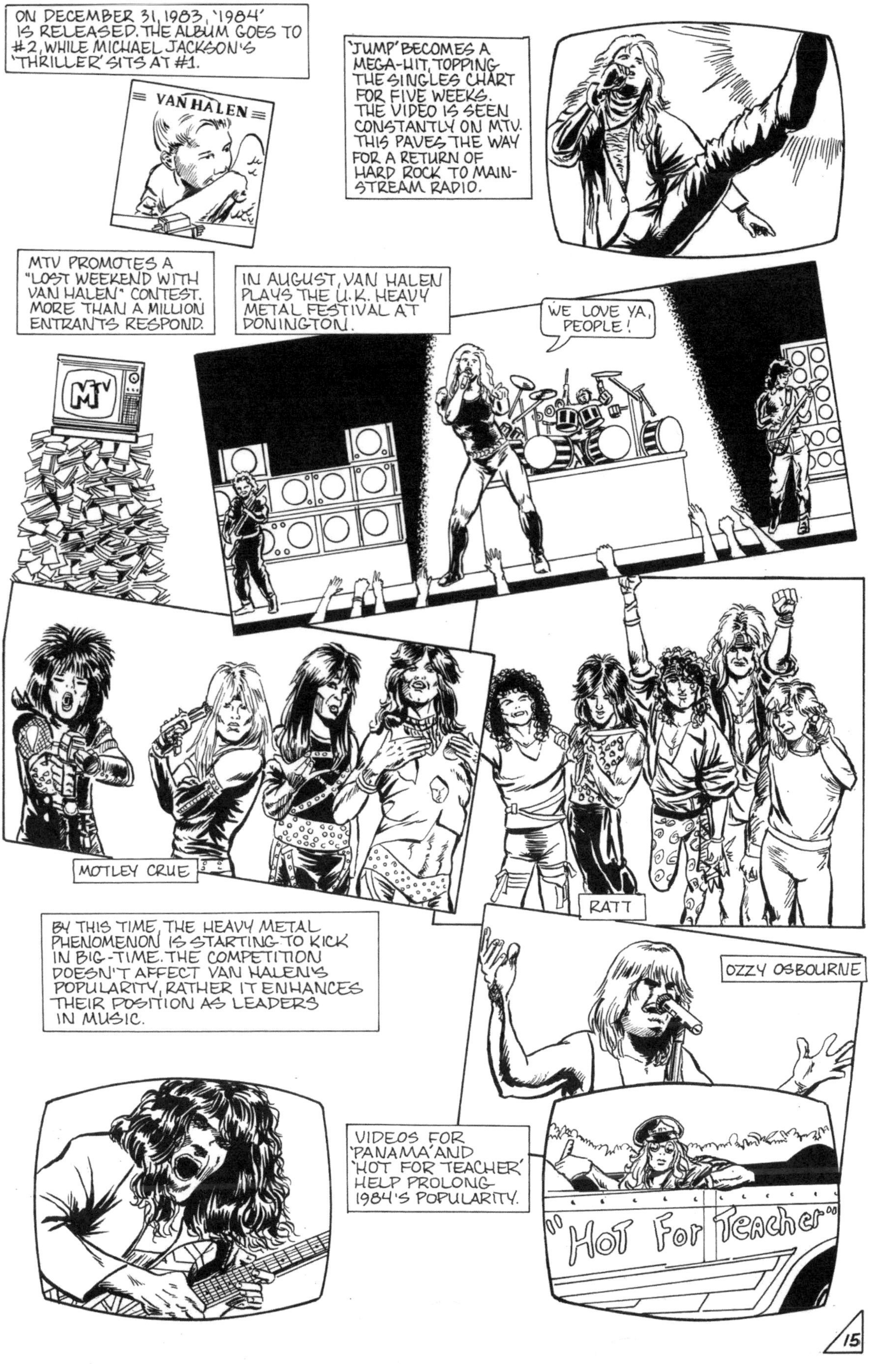

ON DECEMBER 31, 1983, '1984' IS RELEASED. THE ALBUM GOES TO #2, WHILE MICHAEL JACKSON'S 'THRILLER' SITS AT #1.
VAN HALEN
'JUMP' BECOMES A MEGA-HIT, TOPPING THE SINGLES CHART FOR FIVE WEEKS. THE VIDEO IS SEEN CONSTANTLY ON MTV. THIS PAVES THE WAY FOR A RETURN OF HARD ROCK TO MAIN-STREAM RADIO.
MTV PROMOTES A "LOST WEEKEND WITH VAN HALEN" CONTEST. MORE THAN A MILLION ENTRANTS RESPOND.
MTV
IN AUGUST, VAN HALEN PLAYS THE U.K. HEAVY METAL FESTIVAL AT DONINGTON.
WE LOVE YA, PEOPLE!
MOTLEY CRUE
RATT
BY THIS TIME, THE HEAVY METAL PHENOMENON IS STARTING TO KICK IN BIG-TIME. THE COMPETITION DOESN'T AFFECT VAN HALEN'S POPULARITY, RATHER IT ENHANCES THEIR POSITION AS LEADERS IN MUSIC.
OZZY OSBOURNE
VIDEOS FOR 'PANAMA' AND 'HOT FOR TEACHER' HELP PROLONG 1984'S POPULARITY.
"Hot For Teacher"

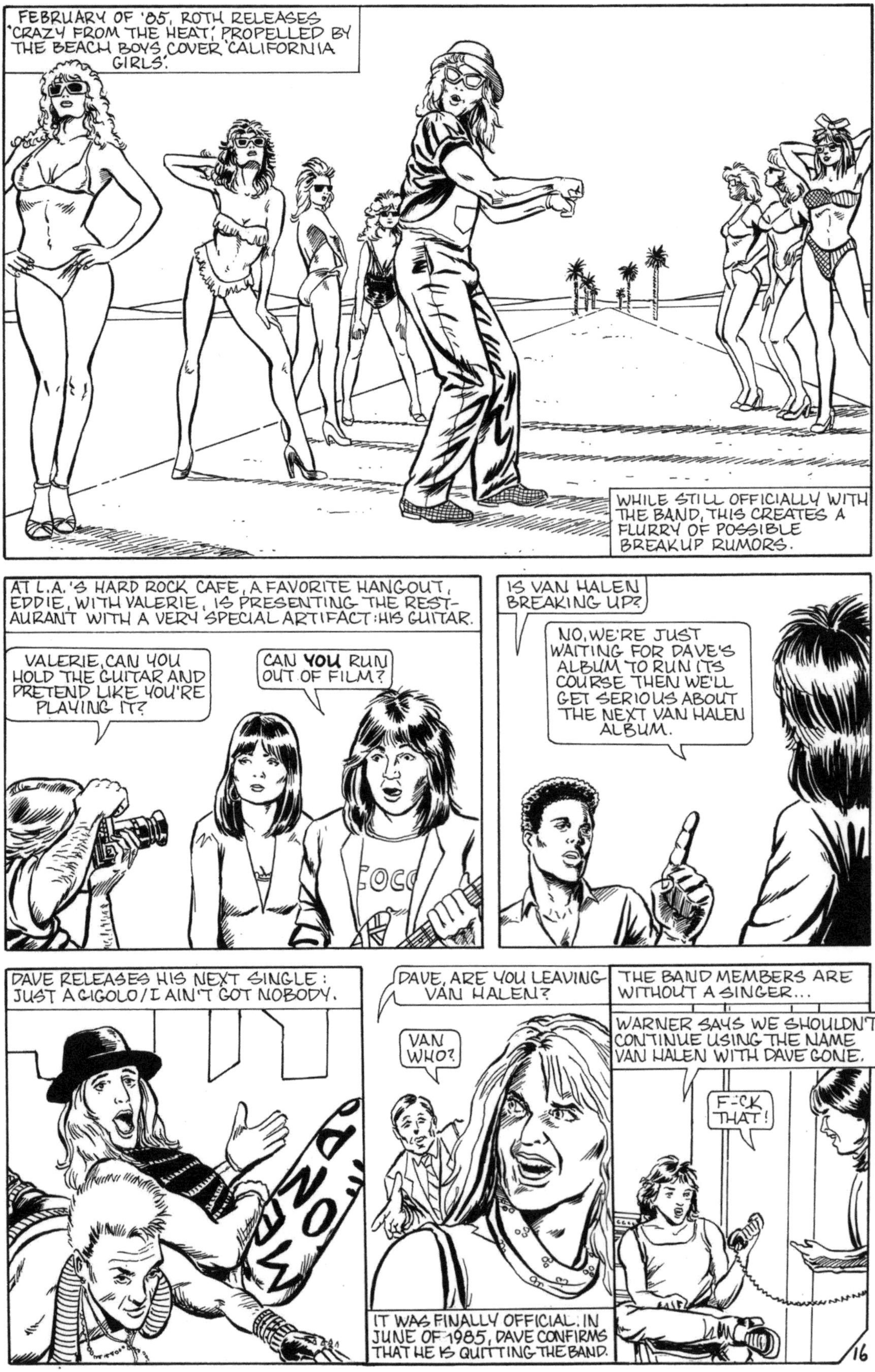

FEBRUARY OF '85, ROTH RELEASES 'CRAZY FROM THE HEAT,' PROPELLED BY THE BEACH BOYS COVER 'CALIFORNIA GIRLS'.
WHILE STILL OFFICIALLY WITH THE BAND, THIS CREATES A FLURRY OF POSSIBLE BREAKUP RUMORS.
AT L.A.'S HARD ROCK CAFE, A FAVORITE HANGOUT, EDDIE, WITH VALERIE, IS PRESENTING THE RESTAURANT WITH A VERY SPECIAL ARTIFACT: HIS GUITAR.
VALERIE, CAN YOU HOLD THE GUITAR AND PRETEND LIKE YOU'RE PLAYING IT?
CAN **YOU** RUN OUT OF FILM?
IS VAN HALEN BREAKING UP?
NO, WE'RE JUST WAITING FOR DAVE'S ALBUM TO RUN ITS COURSE THEN WE'LL GET SERIOUS ABOUT THE NEXT VAN HALEN ALBUM.
DAVE RELEASES HIS NEXT SINGLE: JUST A GIGOLO/I AIN'T GOT NOBODY.
DAVE, ARE YOU LEAVING VAN HALEN?
VAN WHO?
IT WAS FINALLY OFFICIAL. IN JUNE OF 1985, DAVE CONFIRMS THAT HE IS QUITTING THE BAND.
THE BAND MEMBERS ARE WITHOUT A SINGER...
WARNER SAYS WE SHOULDN'T CONTINUE USING THE NAME VAN HALEN WITH DAVE GONE.
F-CK THAT!

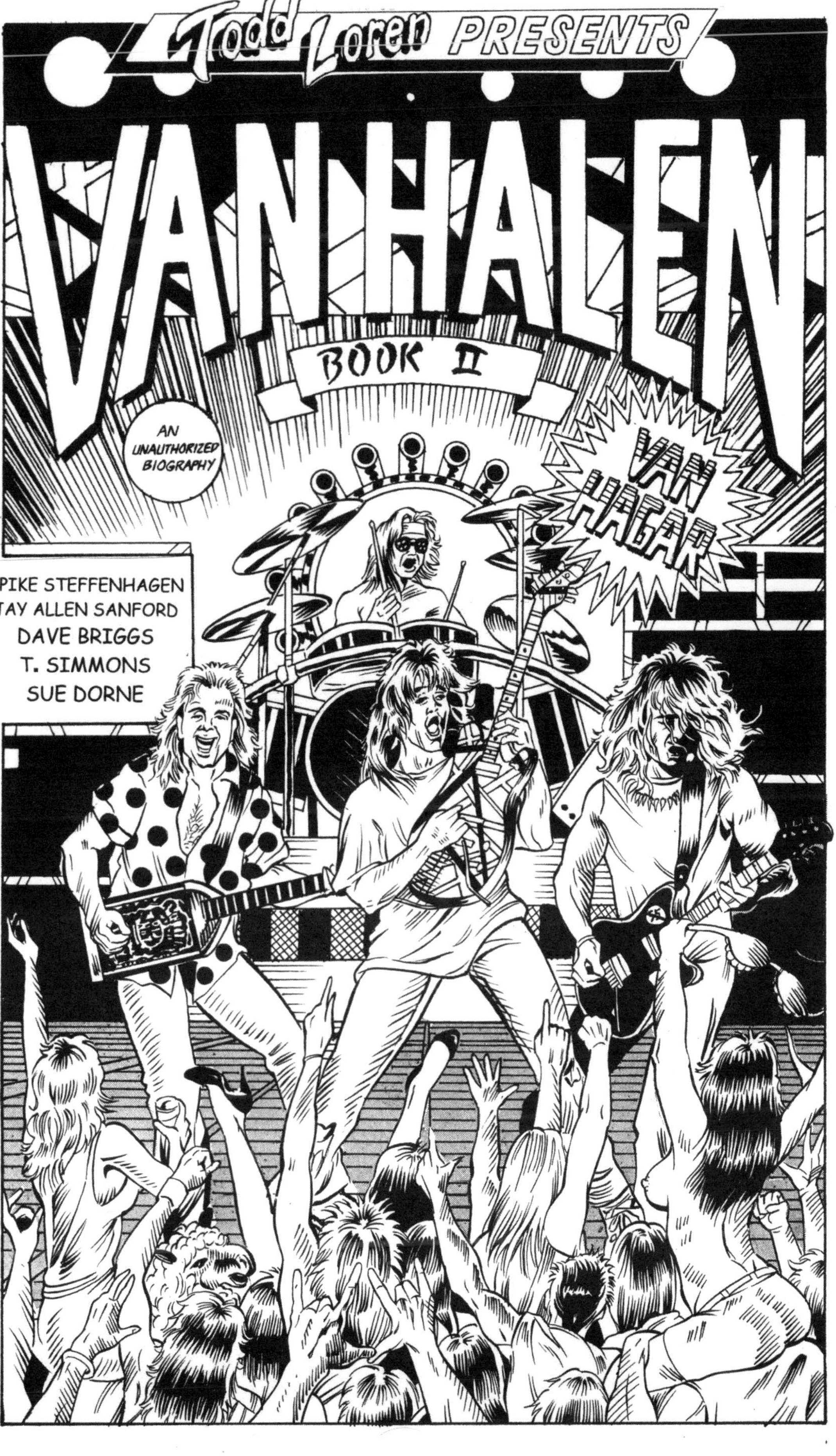
Todd Loren PRESENTS
VAN HALEN
BOOK II
AN UNAUTHORIZED BIOGRAPHY
VAN HAGAR
SPIKE STEFFENHAGEN
JAY ALLEN SANFORD
DAVE BRIGGS
T. SIMMONS
SUE DORNE

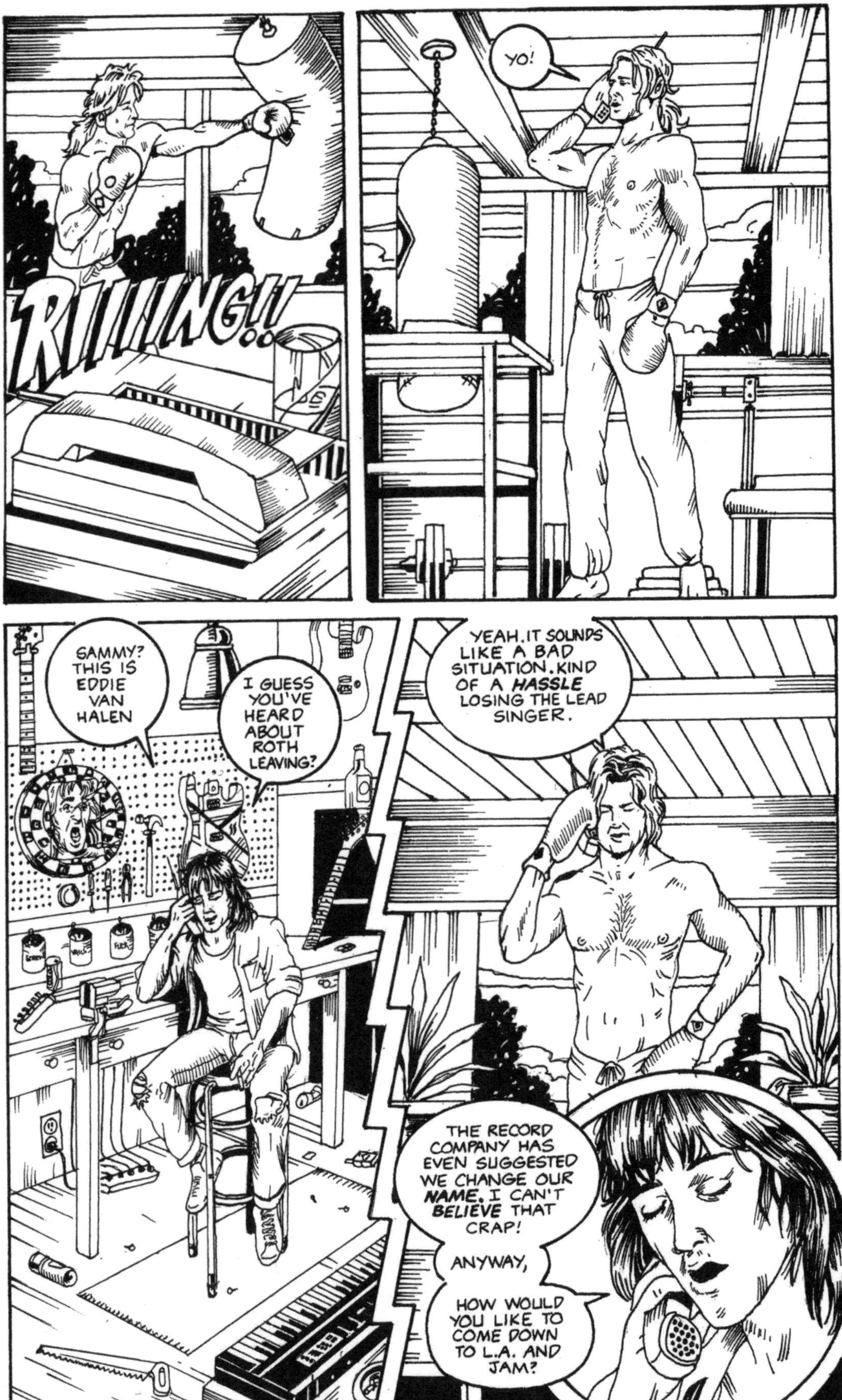
RIIIIING!!
YO!
SAMMY? THIS IS EDDIE VAN HALEN
I GUESS YOU'VE HEARD ABOUT ROTH LEAVING?
YEAH. IT SOUNDS LIKE A BAD SITUATION. KIND OF A HASSLE LOSING THE LEAD SINGER.
THE RECORD COMPANY HAS EVEN SUGGESTED WE CHANGE OUR NAME. I CAN'T BELIEVE THAT CRAP!
ANYWAY,
HOW WOULD YOU LIKE TO COME DOWN TO L.A. AND JAM?

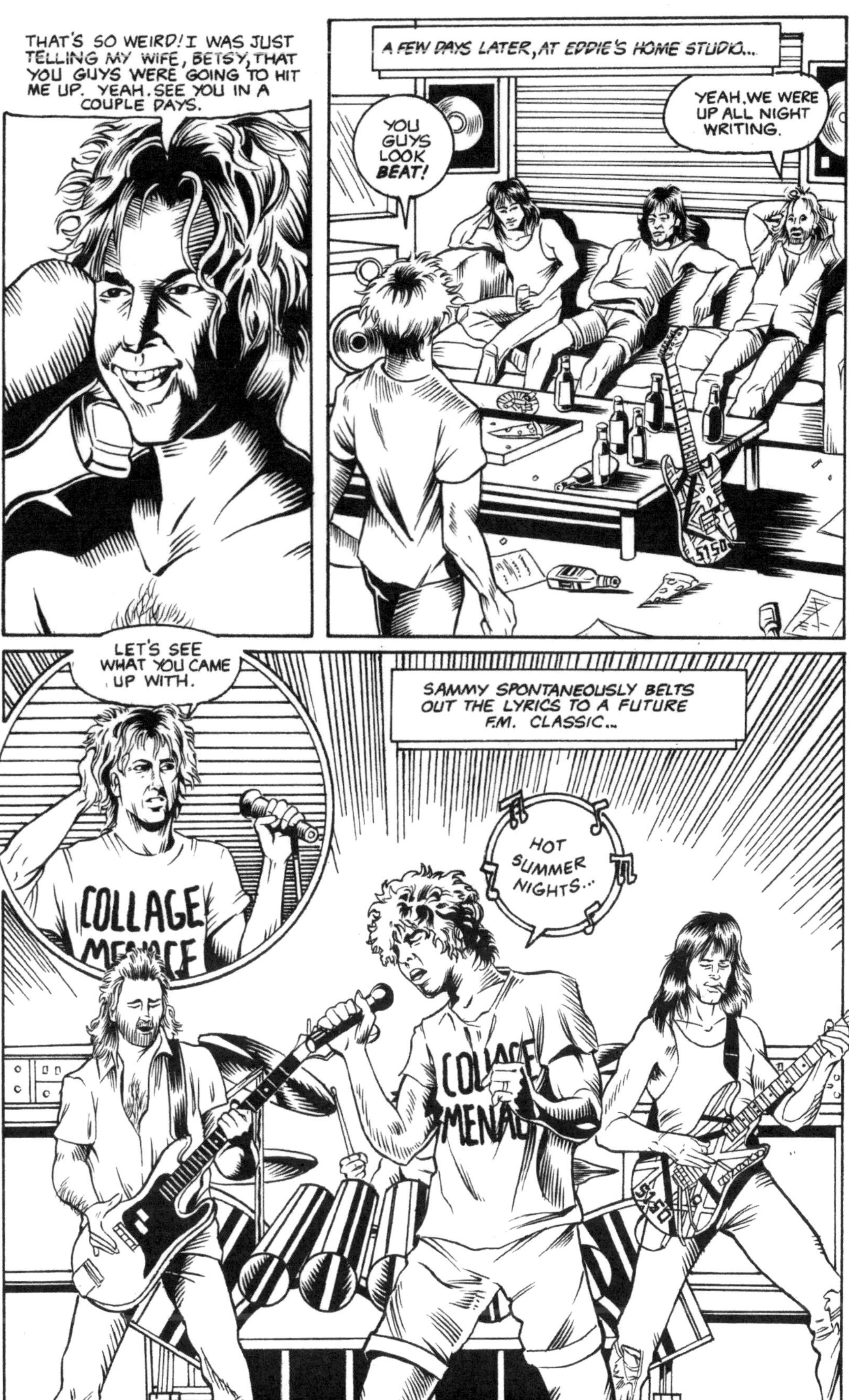
THAT'S SO WEIRD! I WAS JUST TELLING MY WIFE, BETSY, THAT YOU GUYS WERE GOING TO HIT ME UP. YEAH. SEE YOU IN A COUPLE DAYS.
A FEW DAYS LATER, AT EDDIE'S HOME STUDIO...
YOU GUYS LOOK BEAT!
YEAH, WE WERE UP ALL NIGHT WRITING.
5150
LET'S SEE WHAT YOU CAME UP WITH.
SAMMY SPONTANEOUSLY BELTS OUT THE LYRICS TO A FUTURE F.M. CLASSIC...
COLLAGE MENACE
HOT SUMMER NIGHTS...
5150

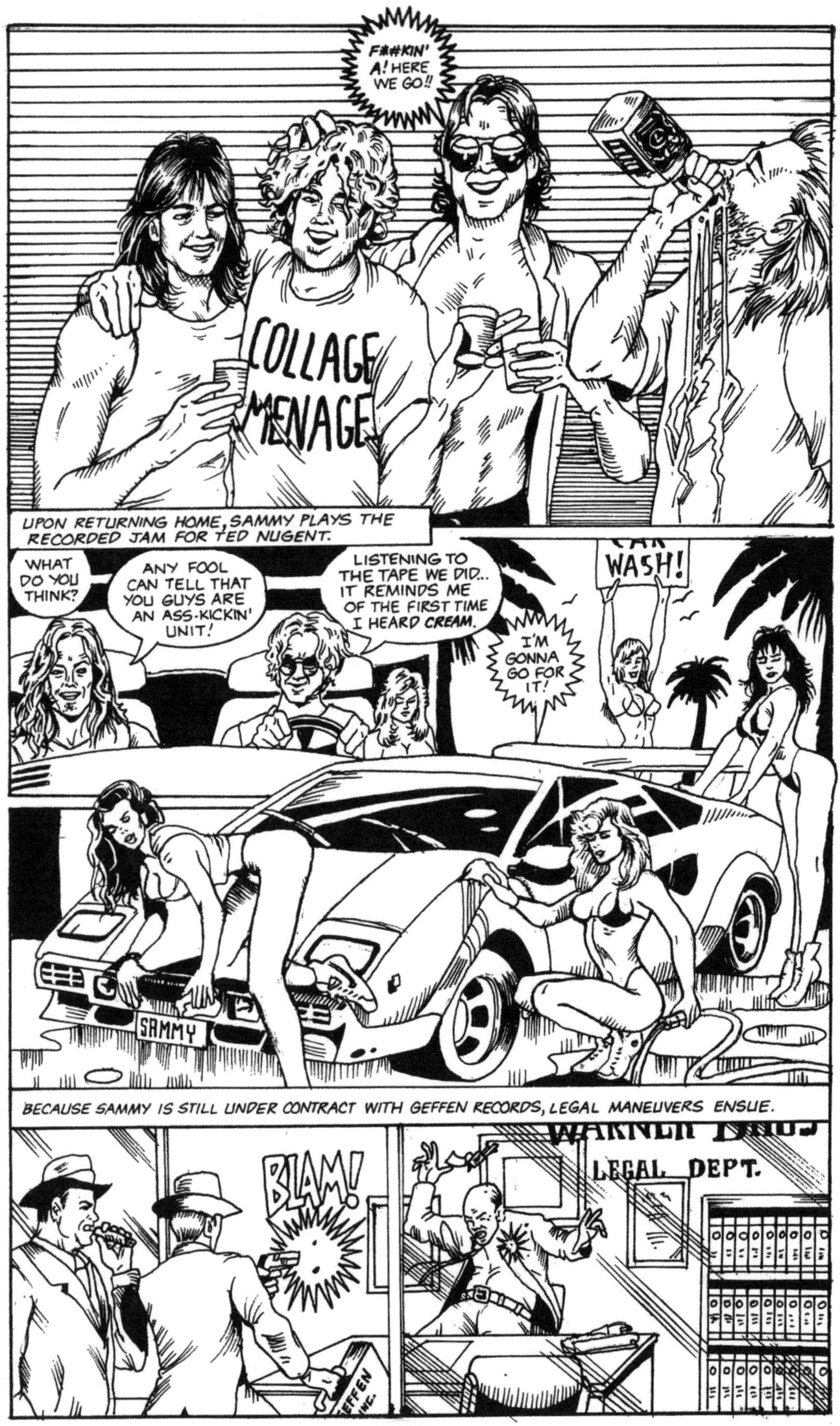
F*#KIN' A! HERE WE GO!!
UPON RETURNING HOME, SAMMY PLAYS THE RECORDED JAM FOR TED NUGENT.
WHAT DO YOU THINK?
ANY FOOL CAN TELL THAT YOU GUYS ARE AN ASS-KICKIN' UNIT!
LISTENING TO THE TAPE WE DID... IT REMINDS ME OF THE FIRST TIME I HEARD CREAM.
WASH!
I'M GONNA GO FOR IT!
COLLAGE MENAGE
SAMMY
BECAUSE SAMMY IS STILL UNDER CONTRACT WITH GEFFEN RECORDS, LEGAL MANEUVERS ENSUE.
BLAM!
LEGAL DEPT.
GEFFEN INC.

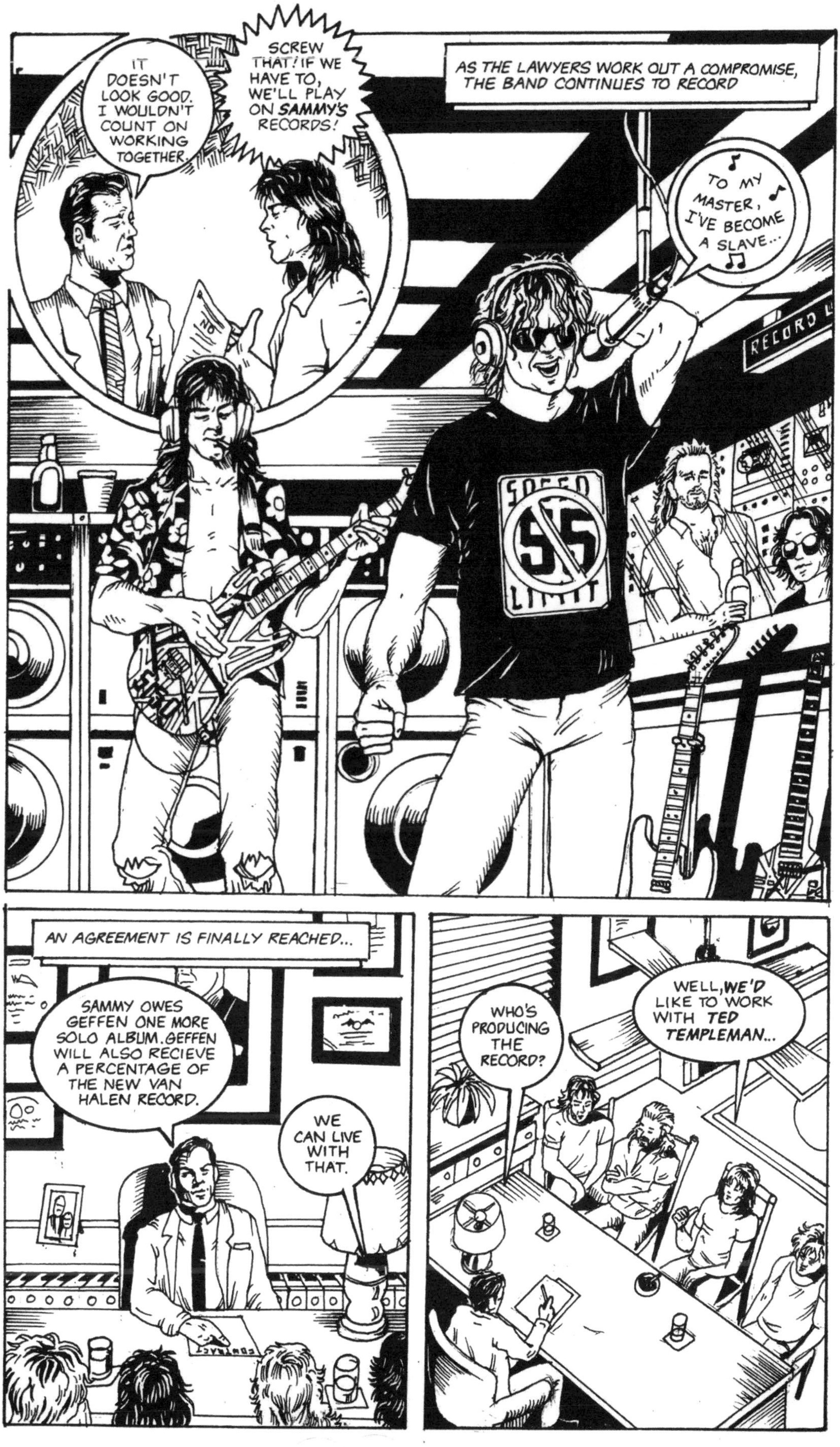
IT DOESN'T LOOK GOOD. I WOULDN'T COUNT ON WORKING TOGETHER.
SCREW THAT! IF WE HAVE TO, WE'LL PLAY ON SAMMY'S RECORDS!
AS THE LAWYERS WORK OUT A COMPROMISE, THE BAND CONTINUES TO RECORD
TO MY MASTER, I'VE BECOME A SLAVE...
AN AGREEMENT IS FINALLY REACHED...
SAMMY OWES GEFFEN ONE MORE SOLO ALBUM. GEFFEN WILL ALSO RECIEVE A PERCENTAGE OF THE NEW VAN HALEN RECORD.
WE CAN LIVE WITH THAT.
WHO'S PRODUCING THE RECORD?
WELL, WE'D LIKE TO WORK WITH TED TEMPLEMAN...

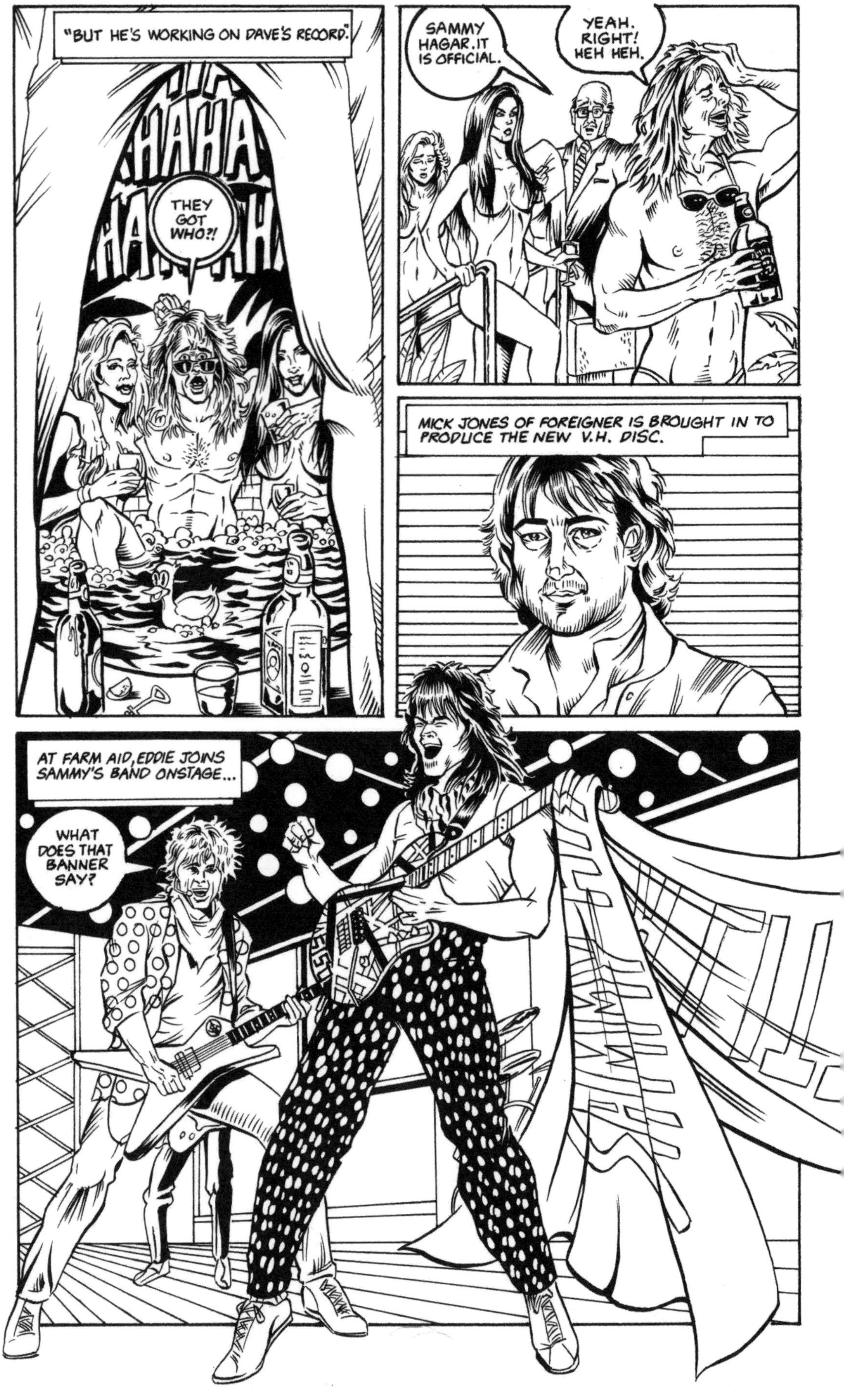
"BUT HE'S WORKING ON DAVE'S RECORD."
HAHA HA HA
THEY GOT WHO?!
SAMMY HAGAR. IT IS OFFICIAL.
YEAH. RIGHT! HEH HEH.
MICK JONES OF FOREIGNER IS BROUGHT IN TO PRODUCE THE NEW V.H. DISC.
AT FARM AID, EDDIE JOINS SAMMY'S BAND ONSTAGE...
WHAT DOES THAT BANNER SAY?

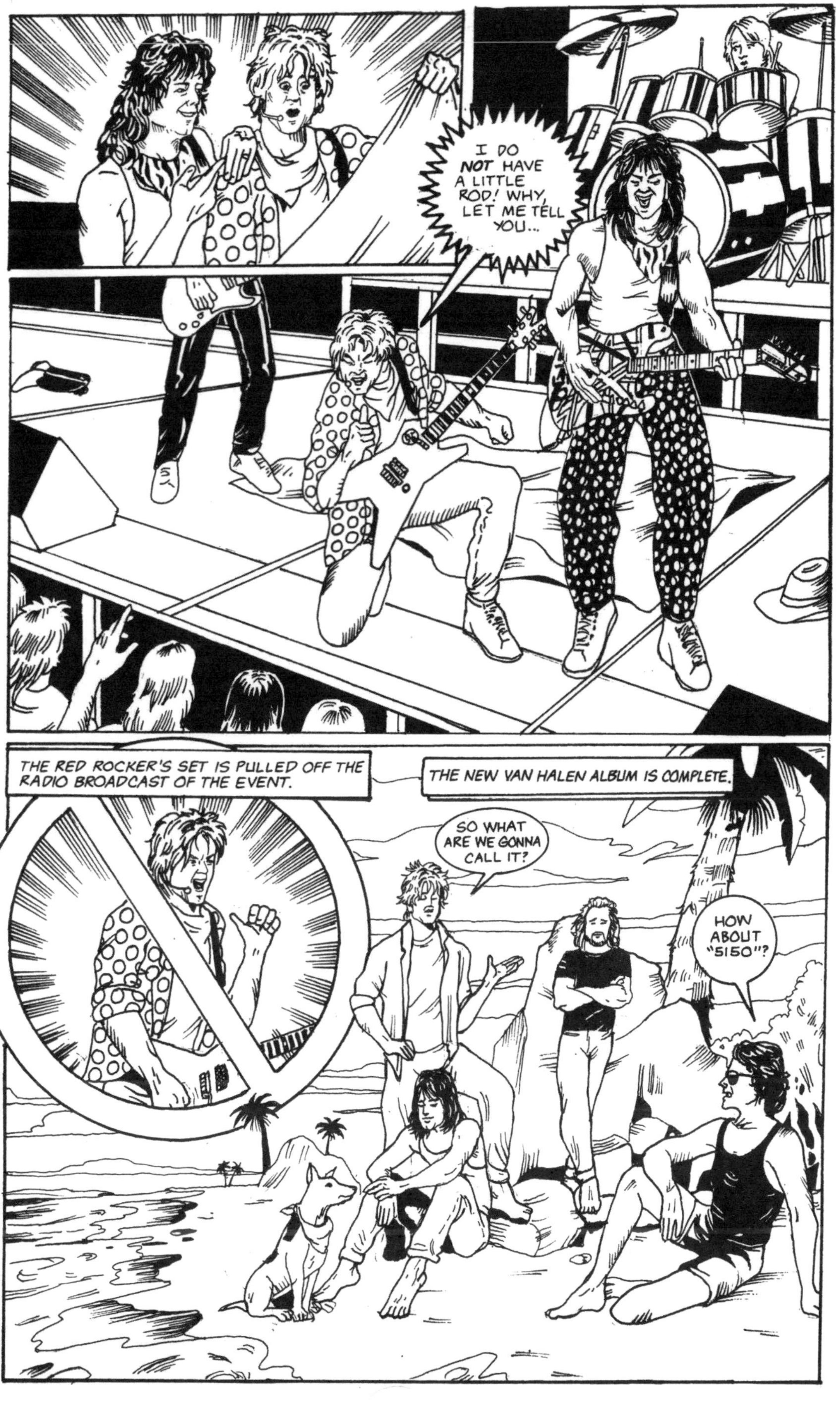
I DO NOT HAVE A LITTLE ROD! WHY, LET ME TELL YOU...
THE RED ROCKER'S SET IS PULLED OFF THE RADIO BROADCAST OF THE EVENT.
THE NEW VAN HALEN ALBUM IS COMPLETE.
SO WHAT ARE WE GONNA CALL IT?
HOW ABOUT "5150"?

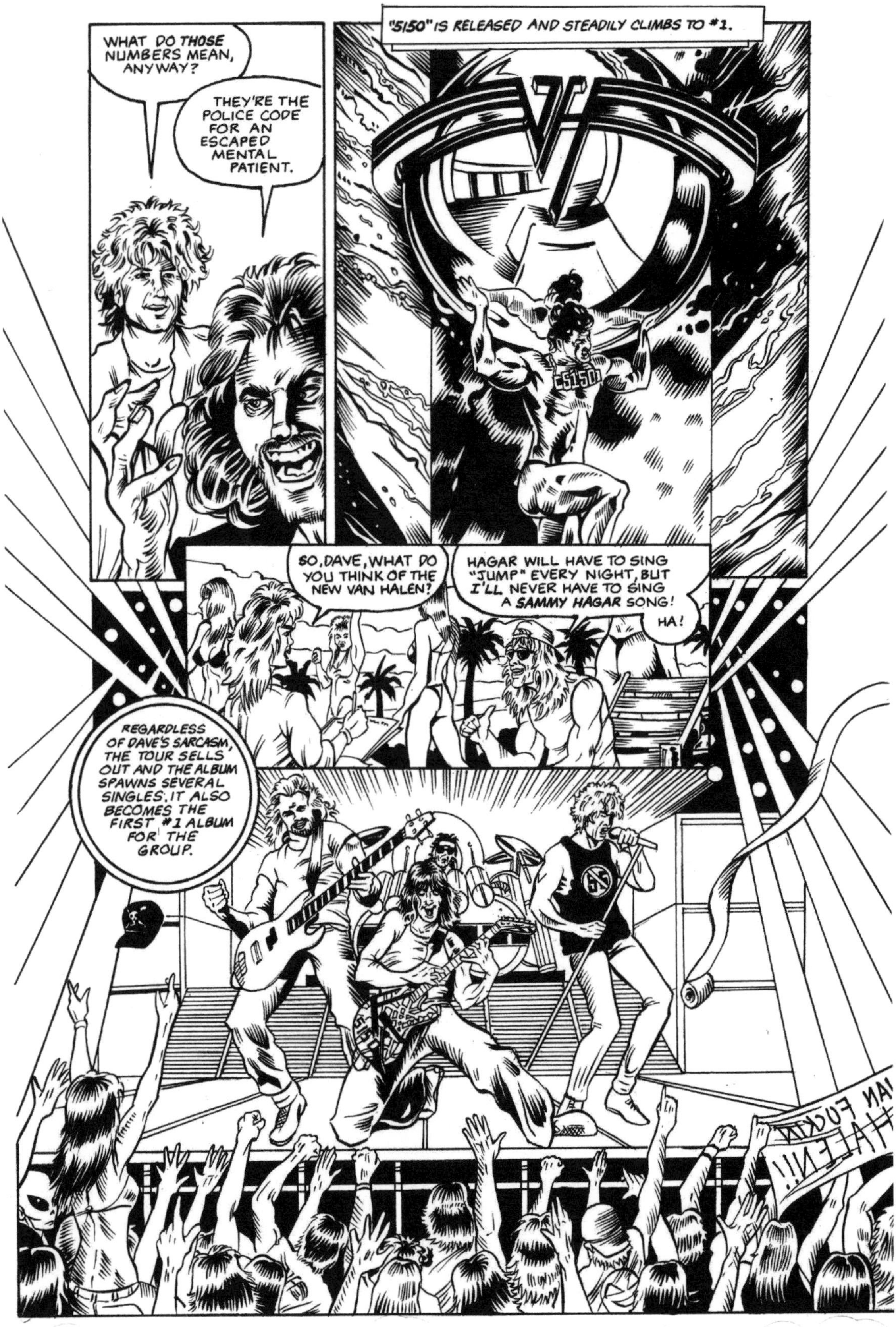
WHAT DO THOSE NUMBERS MEAN, ANYWAY?
THEY'RE THE POLICE CODE FOR AN ESCAPED MENTAL PATIENT.
"5150" IS RELEASED AND STEADILY CLIMBS TO #1.
SO, DAVE, WHAT DO YOU THINK OF THE NEW VAN HALEN?
HAGAR WILL HAVE TO SING "JUMP" EVERY NIGHT, BUT I'LL NEVER HAVE TO SING A SAMMY HAGAR SONG!
HA!
REGARDLESS OF DAVE'S SARCASM, THE TOUR SELLS OUT AND THE ALBUM SPAWNS SEVERAL SINGLES. IT ALSO BECOMES THE FIRST #1 ALBUM FOR THE GROUP.

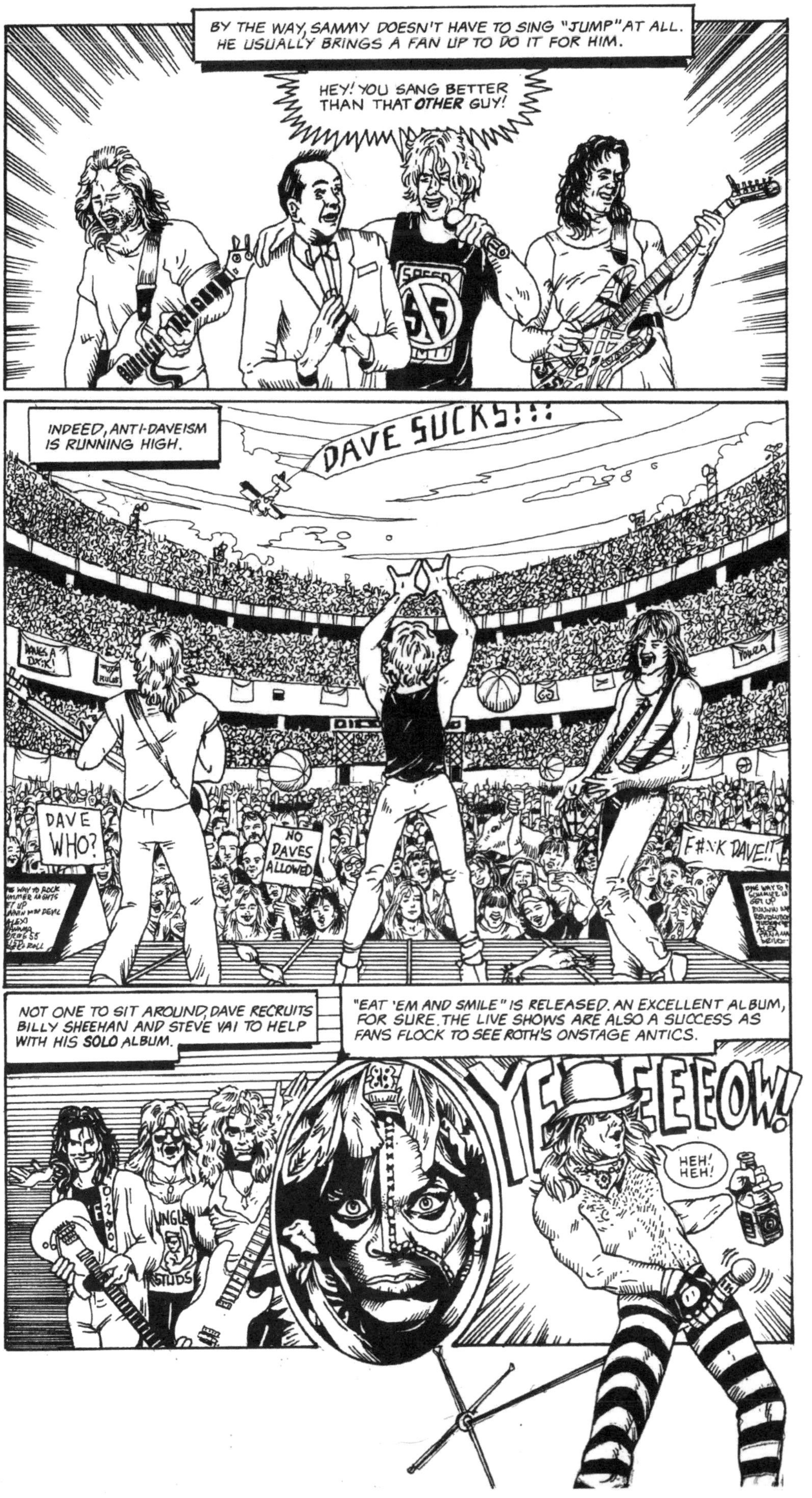
BY THE WAY, SAMMY DOESN'T HAVE TO SING "JUMP" AT ALL. HE USUALLY BRINGS A FAN UP TO DO IT FOR HIM.
HEY! YOU SANG BETTER THAN THAT OTHER GUY!
INDEED, ANTI-DAVEISM IS RUNNING HIGH.
DAVE SUCKS!!!
DAVE WHO?
NO DAVES ALLOWED
F#!K DAVE!!
NOT ONE TO SIT AROUND, DAVE RECRUITS BILLY SHEEHAN AND STEVE VAI TO HELP WITH HIS SOLO ALBUM.
"EAT 'EM AND SMILE" IS RELEASED. AN EXCELLENT ALBUM, FOR SURE. THE LIVE SHOWS ARE ALSO A SUCCESS AS FANS FLOCK TO SEE ROTH'S ONSTAGE ANTICS.
STUDS
YE EEEOW!
HEH! HEH!

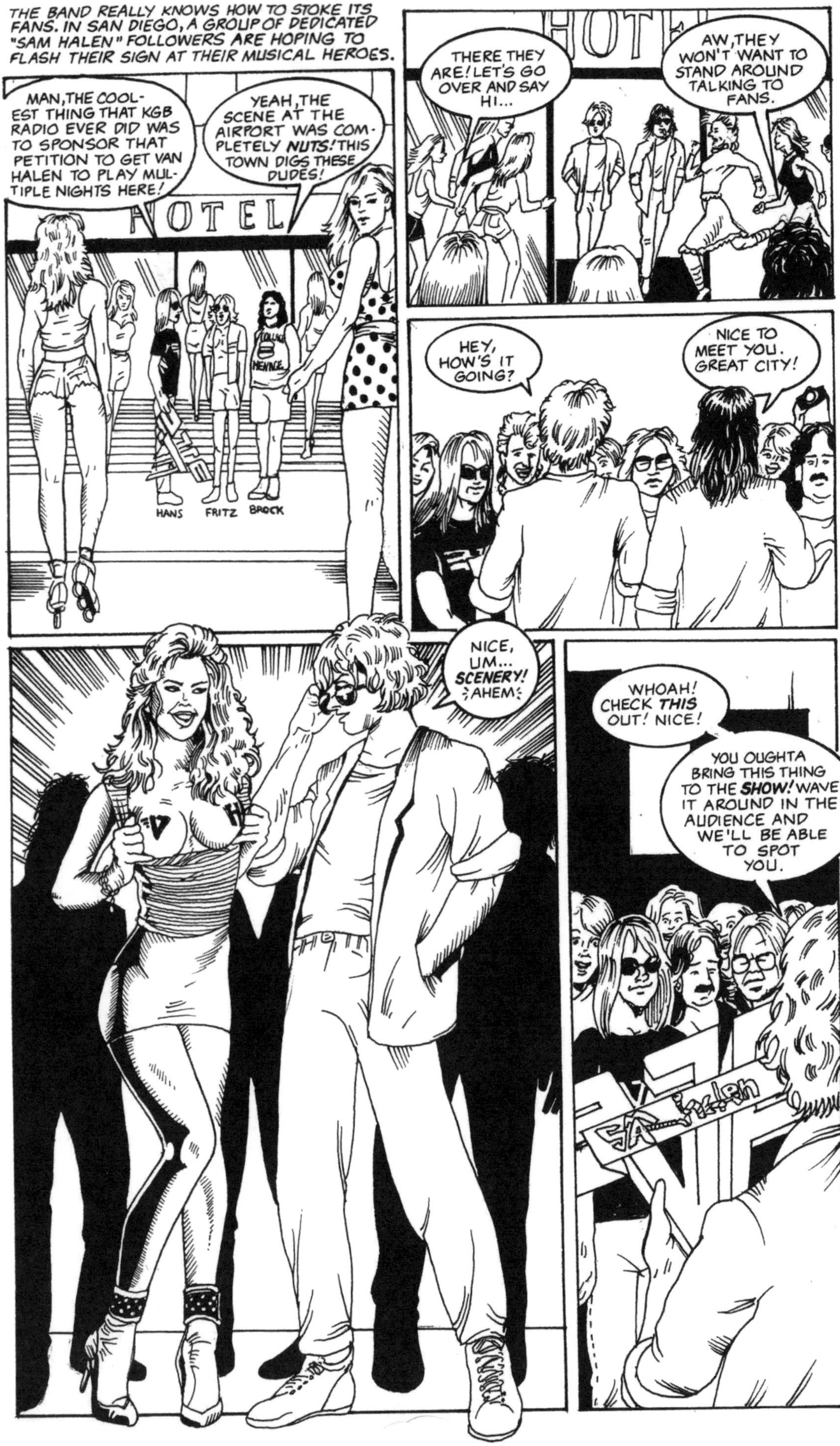
THE BAND REALLY KNOWS HOW TO STOKE ITS FANS. IN SAN DIEGO, A GROUP OF DEDICATED "SAM HALEN" FOLLOWERS ARE HOPING TO FLASH THEIR SIGN AT THEIR MUSICAL HEROES.
MAN, THE COOLEST THING THAT KGB RADIO EVER DID WAS TO SPONSOR THAT PETITION TO GET VAN HALEN TO PLAY MULTIPLE NIGHTS HERE!
YEAH, THE SCENE AT THE AIRPORT WAS COMPLETELY NUTS! THIS TOWN DIGS THESE DUDES!
HOTEL
HANS
FRITZ
BROCK
THERE THEY ARE! LET'S GO OVER AND SAY HI...
AW, THEY WON'T WANT TO STAND AROUND TALKING TO FANS.
HEY, HOW'S IT GOING?
NICE TO MEET YOU. GREAT CITY!
NICE, UM... SCENERY! AHEM
WHOAH! CHECK THIS OUT! NICE!
YOU OUGHTA BRING THIS THING TO THE SHOW! WAVE IT AROUND IN THE AUDIENCE AND WE'LL BE ABLE TO SPOT YOU.

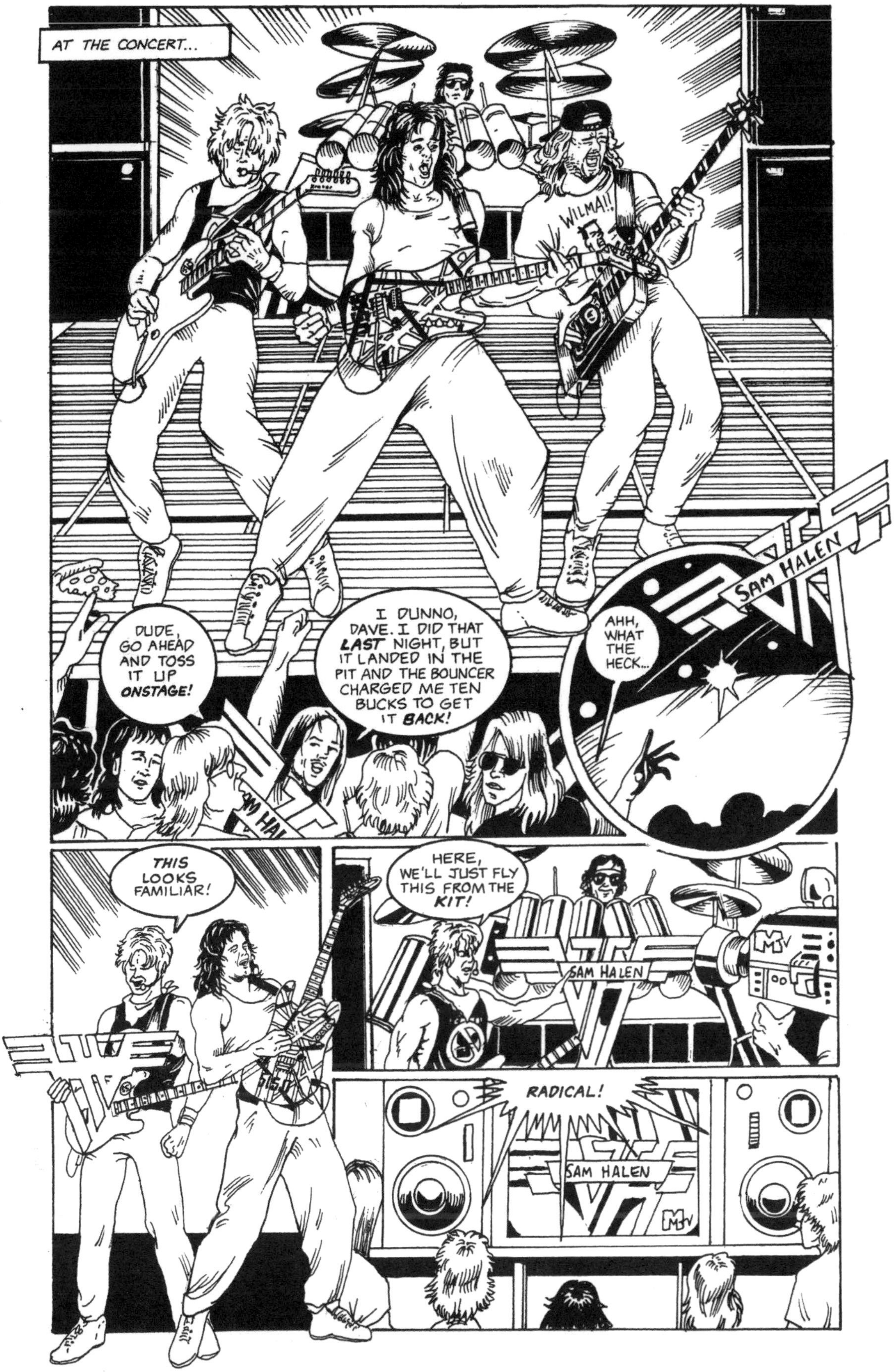

AT THE CONCERT...
WILMA!!
DUDE, GO AHEAD AND TOSS IT UP ONSTAGE!
I DUNNO, DAVE. I DID THAT LAST NIGHT, BUT IT LANDED IN THE PIT AND THE BOUNCER CHARGED ME TEN BUCKS TO GET IT BACK!
AHH, WHAT THE HECK...
SAM HALEN
THIS LOOKS FAMILIAR!
HERE, WE'LL JUST FLY THIS FROM THE KIT!
SAM HALEN
RADICAL!
SAM HALEN

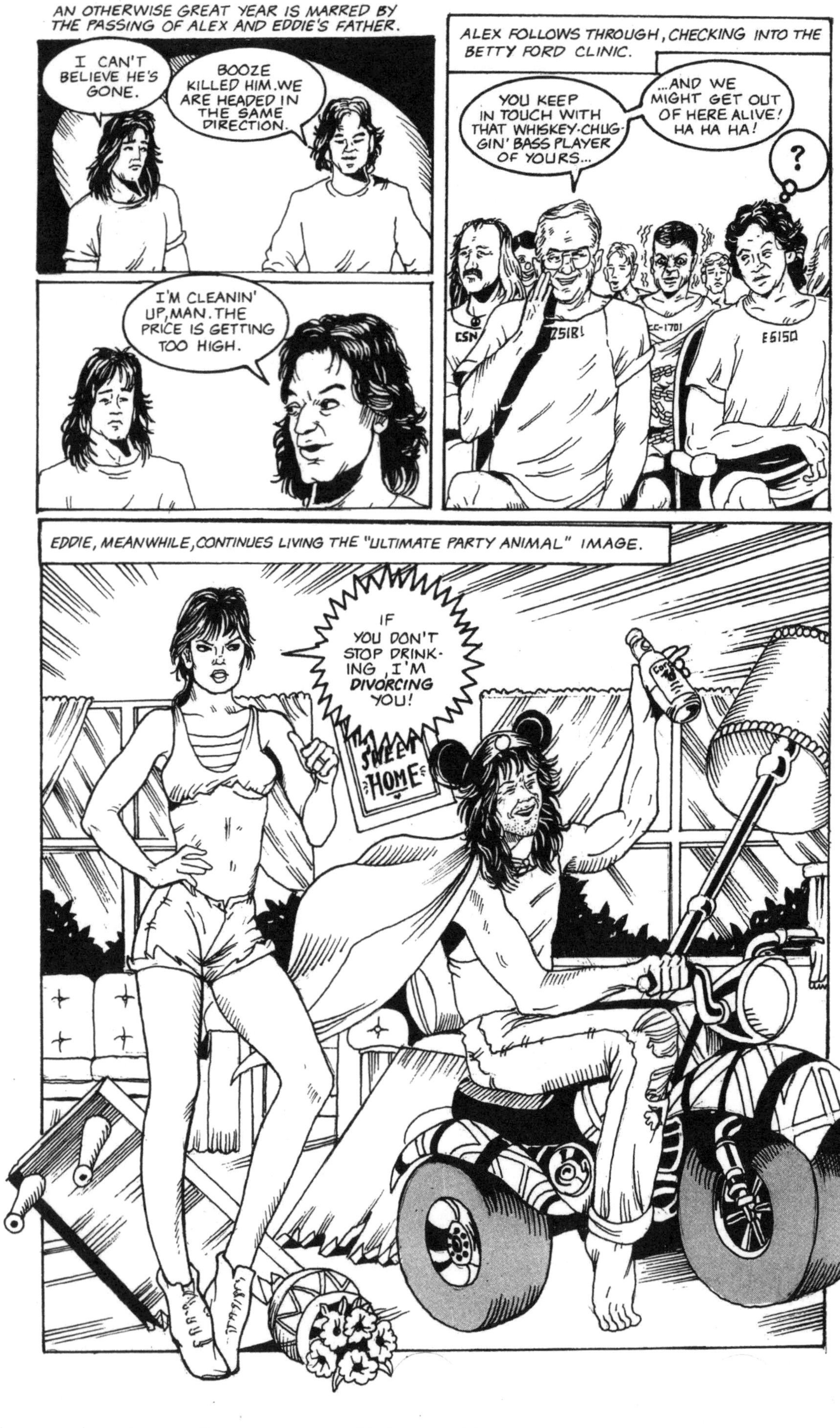
AN OTHERWISE GREAT YEAR IS MARRED BY THE PASSING OF ALEX AND EDDIE'S FATHER.
I CAN'T BELIEVE HE'S GONE.
BOOZE KILLED HIM. WE ARE HEADED IN THE SAME DIRECTION.
I'M CLEANIN' UP, MAN. THE PRICE IS GETTING TOO HIGH.
ALEX FOLLOWS THROUGH, CHECKING INTO THE BETTY FORD CLINIC.
YOU KEEP IN TOUCH WITH THAT WHISKEY-CHUG-GIN' BASS PLAYER OF YOURS...
...AND WE MIGHT GET OUT OF HERE ALIVE! HA HA HA!
?
CSN
2518!
CC-1701
E6150
EDDIE, MEANWHILE, CONTINUES LIVING THE "ULTIMATE PARTY ANIMAL" IMAGE.
IF YOU DON'T STOP DRINK-ING, I'M DIVORCING YOU!
SWEET HOME

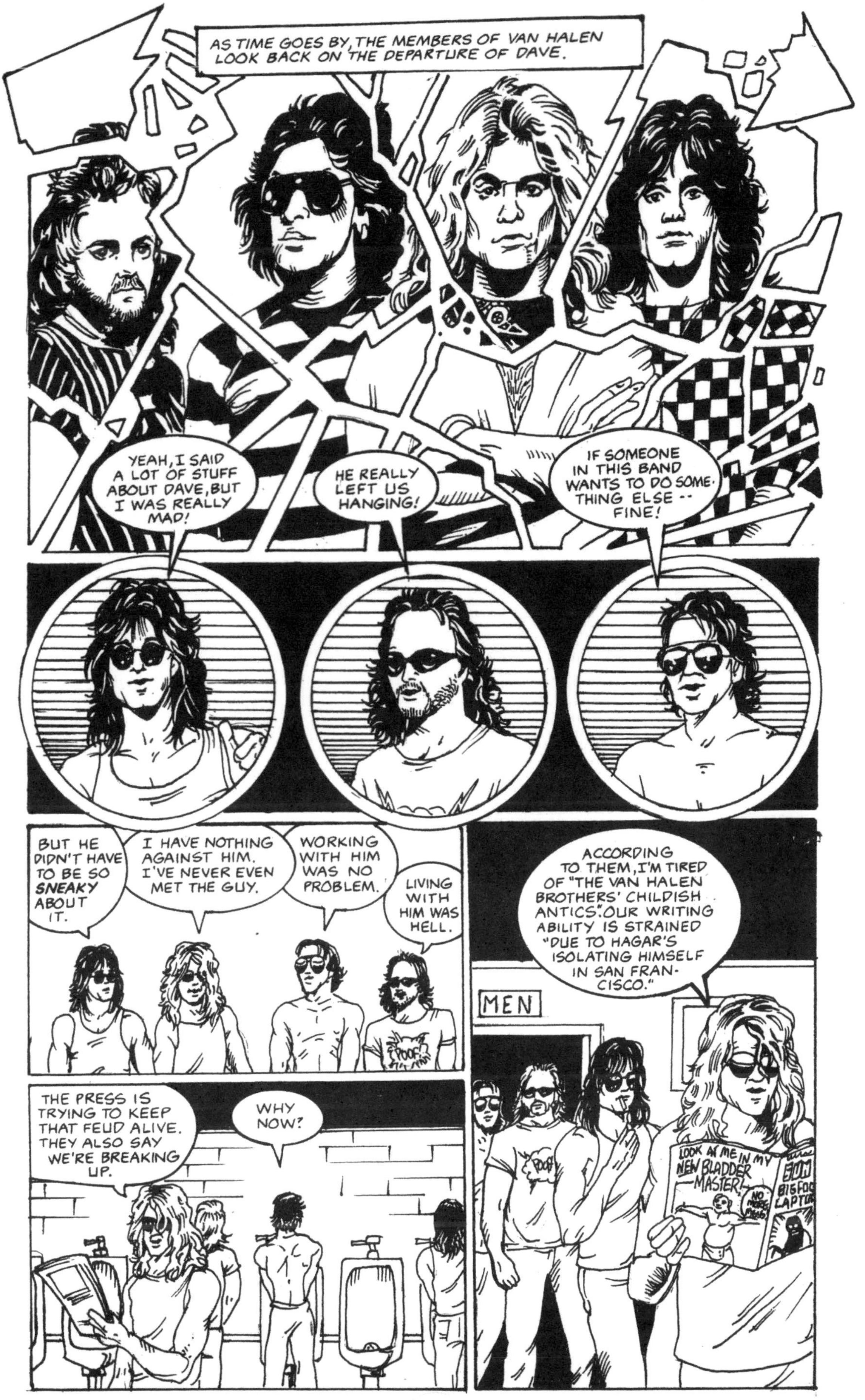
AS TIME GOES BY, THE MEMBERS OF VAN HALEN LOOK BACK ON THE DEPARTURE OF DAVE.
YEAH, I SAID A LOT OF STUFF ABOUT DAVE, BUT I WAS REALLY MAD!
HE REALLY LEFT US HANGING!
IF SOMEONE IN THIS BAND WANTS TO DO SOMETHING ELSE -- FINE!
BUT HE DIDN'T HAVE TO BE SO SNEAKY ABOUT IT.
I HAVE NOTHING AGAINST HIM. I'VE NEVER EVEN MET THE GUY.
WORKING WITH HIM WAS NO PROBLEM.
LIVING WITH HIM WAS HELL.
POOF
THE PRESS IS TRYING TO KEEP THAT FEUD ALIVE. THEY ALSO SAY WE'RE BREAKING UP.
WHY NOW?
ACCORDING TO THEM, I'M TIRED OF "THE VAN HALEN BROTHERS' CHILDISH ANTICS." OUR WRITING ABILITY IS STRAINED "DUE TO HAGAR'S ISOLATING HIMSELF IN SAN FRANCISCO."
MEN
POOF
LOOK AT ME IN MY NEW BLADDER MASTER!
NO MORE PADS

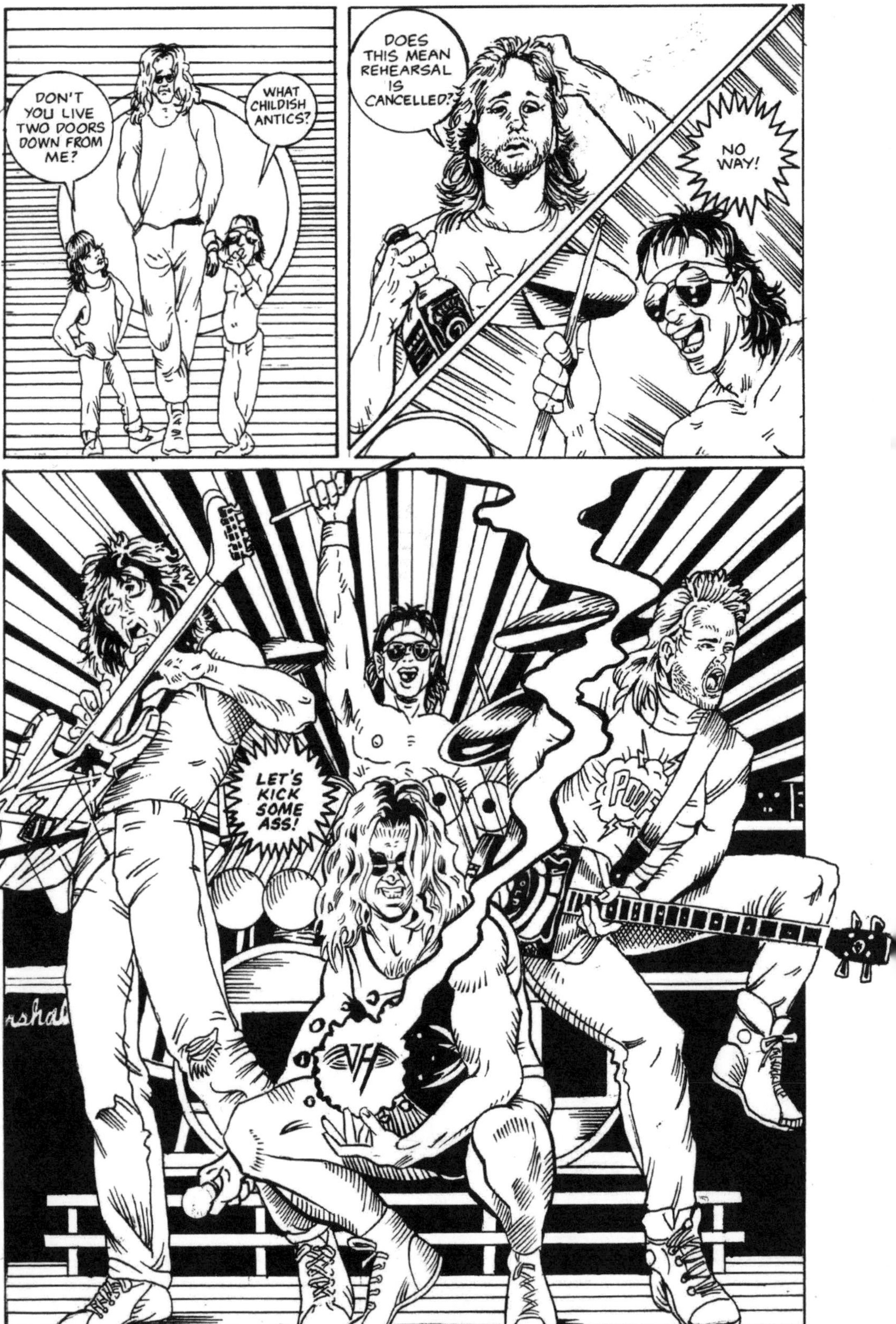
DON'T YOU LIVE TWO DOORS DOWN FROM ME?
WHAT CHILDISH ANTICS?
DOES THIS MEAN REHEARSAL IS CANCELLED?
NO WAY!
LET'S KICK SOME ASS!

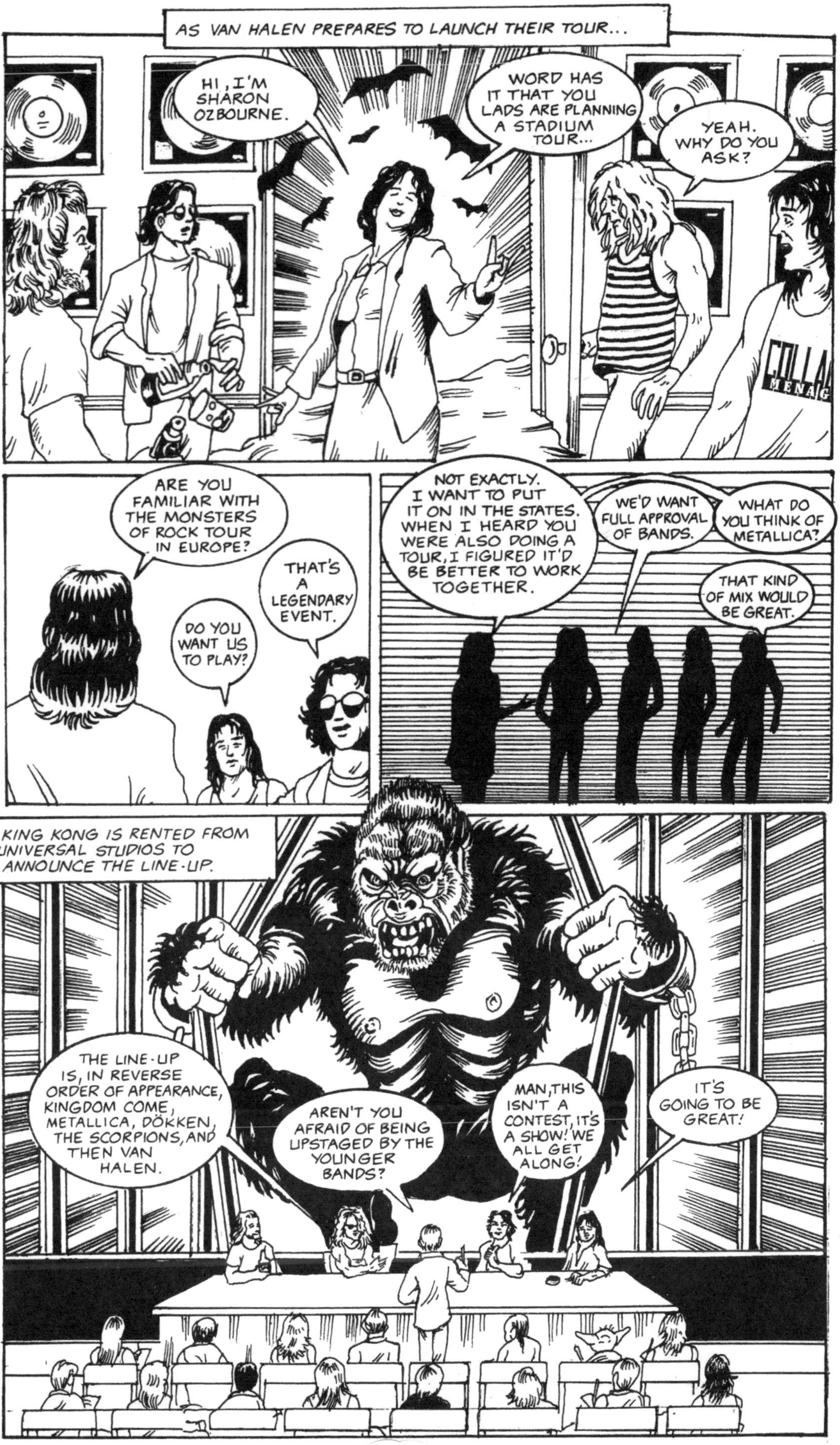

AS VAN HALEN PREPARES TO LAUNCH THEIR TOUR...
HI, I'M SHARON OZBOURNE.
WORD HAS IT THAT YOU LADS ARE PLANNING A STADIUM TOUR...
YEAH. WHY DO YOU ASK?
ARE YOU FAMILIAR WITH THE MONSTERS OF ROCK TOUR IN EUROPE?
THAT'S A LEGENDARY EVENT.
DO YOU WANT US TO PLAY?
NOT EXACTLY. I WANT TO PUT IT ON IN THE STATES. WHEN I HEARD YOU WERE ALSO DOING A TOUR, I FIGURED IT'D BE BETTER TO WORK TOGETHER.
WE'D WANT FULL APPROVAL OF BANDS.
WHAT DO YOU THINK OF METALLICA?
THAT KIND OF MIX WOULD BE GREAT.
KING KONG IS RENTED FROM UNIVERSAL STUDIOS TO ANNOUNCE THE LINE-UP.
THE LINE-UP IS, IN REVERSE ORDER OF APPEARANCE, KINGDOM COME, METALLICA, DÖKKEN, THE SCORPIONS, AND THEN VAN HALEN.
AREN'T YOU AFRAID OF BEING UPSTAGED BY THE YOUNGER BANDS?
MAN, THIS ISN'T A CONTEST, IT'S A SHOW! WE ALL GET ALONG!
IT'S GOING TO BE GREAT!

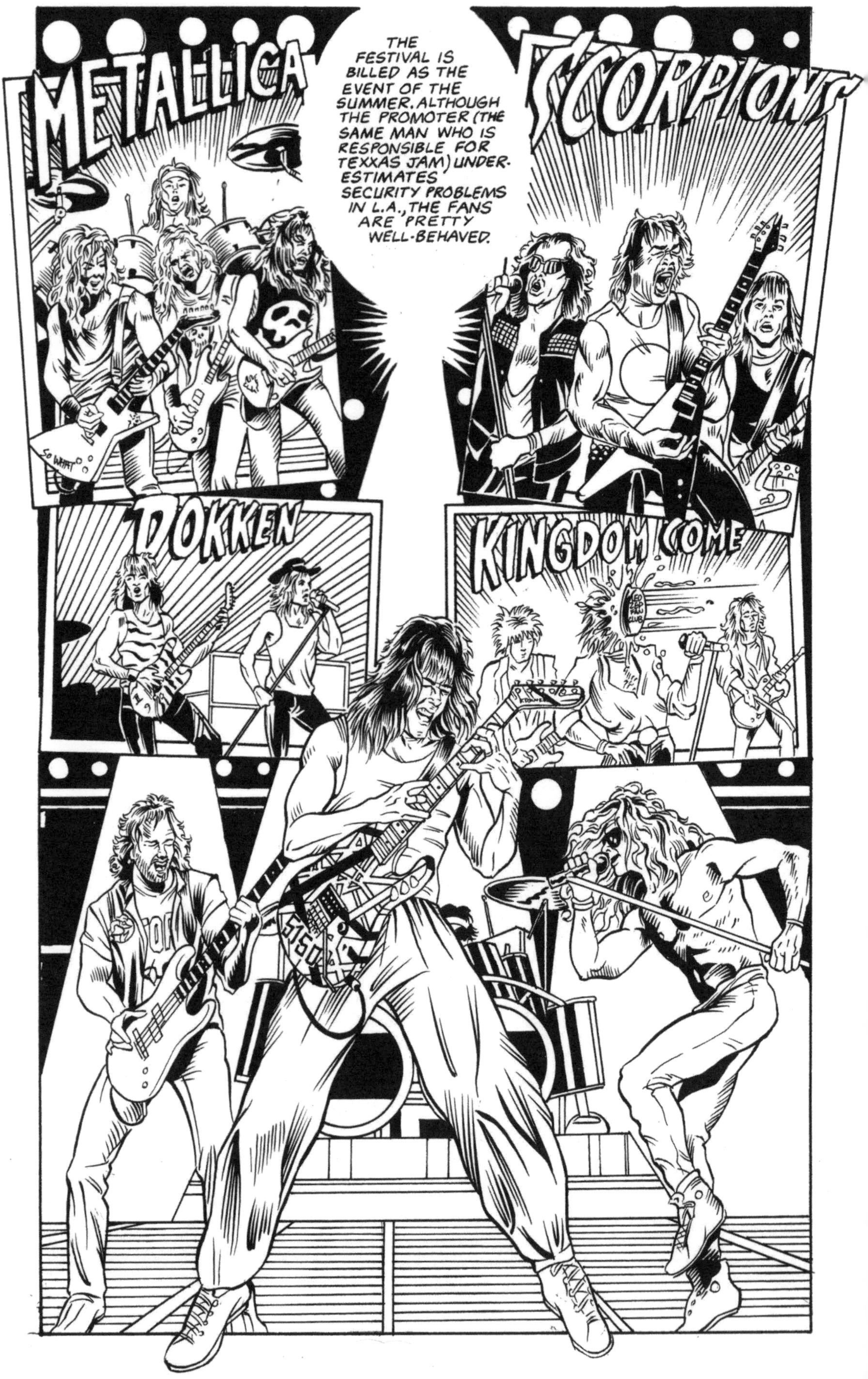
METALLICA
SCORPIONS
THE FESTIVAL IS BILLED AS THE EVENT OF THE SUMMER. ALTHOUGH THE PROMOTER (THE SAME MAN WHO IS RESPONSIBLE FOR TEXXAS JAM) UNDER-ESTIMATES SECURITY PROBLEMS IN L.A., THE FANS ARE PRETTY WELL-BEHAVED.
SO WHAT
DOKKEN
KINGDOM COME
5150

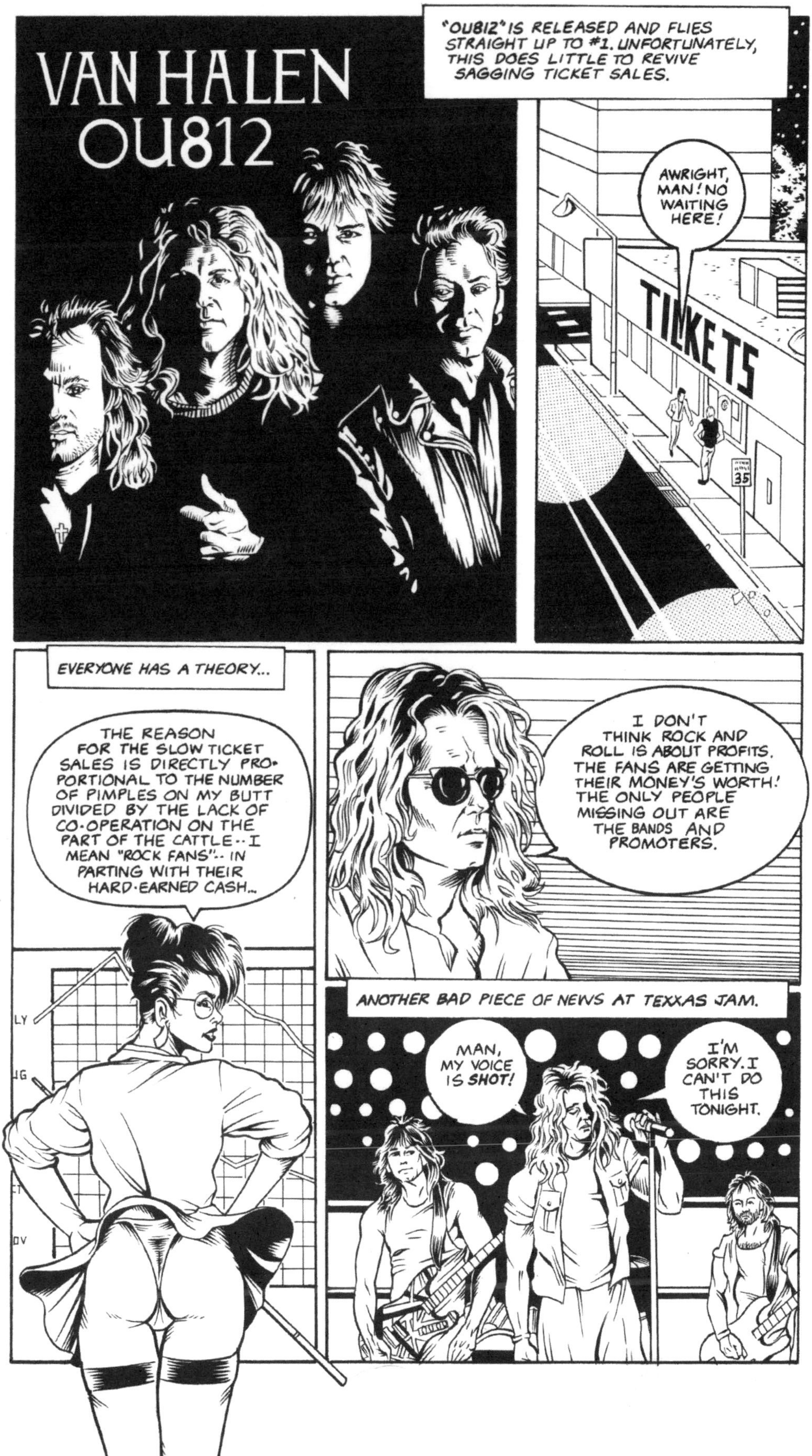
VAN HALEN
OU812
"OU812" IS RELEASED AND FLIES STRAIGHT UP TO #1. UNFORTUNATELY, THIS DOES LITTLE TO REVIVE SAGGING TICKET SALES.
AWRIGHT, MAN! NO WAITING HERE!
TICKETS
35
EVERYONE HAS A THEORY...
THE REASON FOR THE SLOW TICKET SALES IS DIRECTLY PROPORTIONAL TO THE NUMBER OF PIMPLES ON MY BUTT DIVIDED BY THE LACK OF CO-OPERATION ON THE PART OF THE CATTLE-- I MEAN "ROCK FANS"-- IN PARTING WITH THEIR HARD-EARNED CASH...
I DON'T THINK ROCK AND ROLL IS ABOUT PROFITS. THE FANS ARE GETTING THEIR MONEY'S WORTH! THE ONLY PEOPLE MISSING OUT ARE THE BANDS AND PROMOTERS.
ANOTHER BAD PIECE OF NEWS AT TEXXAS JAM.
MAN, MY VOICE IS **SHOT!**
I'M SORRY. I CAN'T DO THIS TONIGHT.

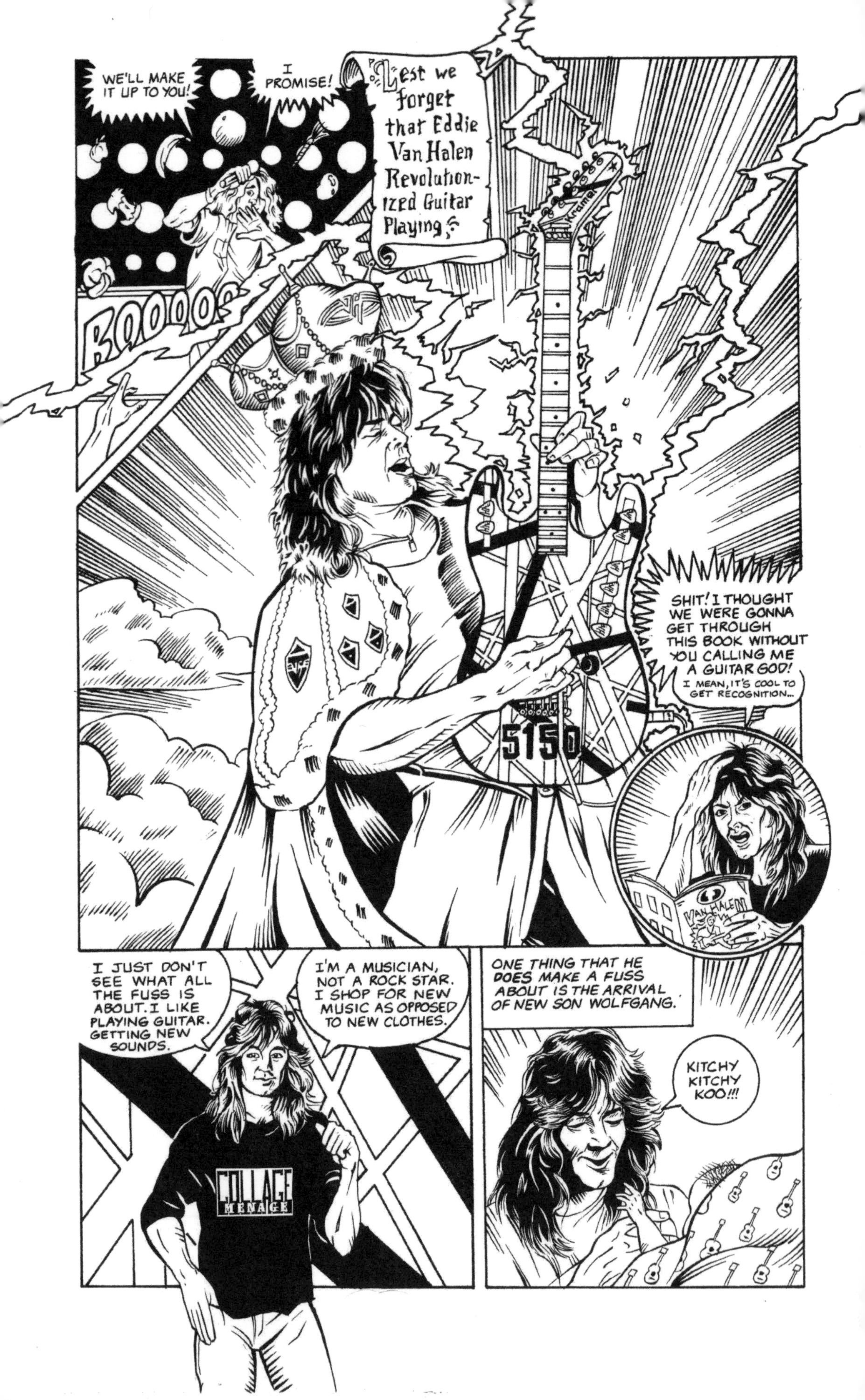
WE'LL MAKE IT UP TO YOU!
I PROMISE!
Lest we Forget that Eddie Van Halen Revolutionized Guitar Playing
BOOOOS
5150
SHIT! I THOUGHT WE WERE GONNA GET THROUGH THIS BOOK WITHOUT YOU CALLING ME A GUITAR GOD!
I MEAN, IT'S COOL TO GET RECOGNITION...
VAN HALEN
I JUST DON'T SEE WHAT ALL THE FUSS IS ABOUT. I LIKE PLAYING GUITAR. GETTING NEW SOUNDS.
I'M A MUSICIAN, NOT A ROCK STAR. I SHOP FOR NEW MUSIC AS OPPOSED TO NEW CLOTHES.
COLLAGE MENAGE
ONE THING THAT HE DOES MAKE A FUSS ABOUT IS THE ARRIVAL OF NEW SON WOLFGANG.
KITCHY KITCHY KOO!!!

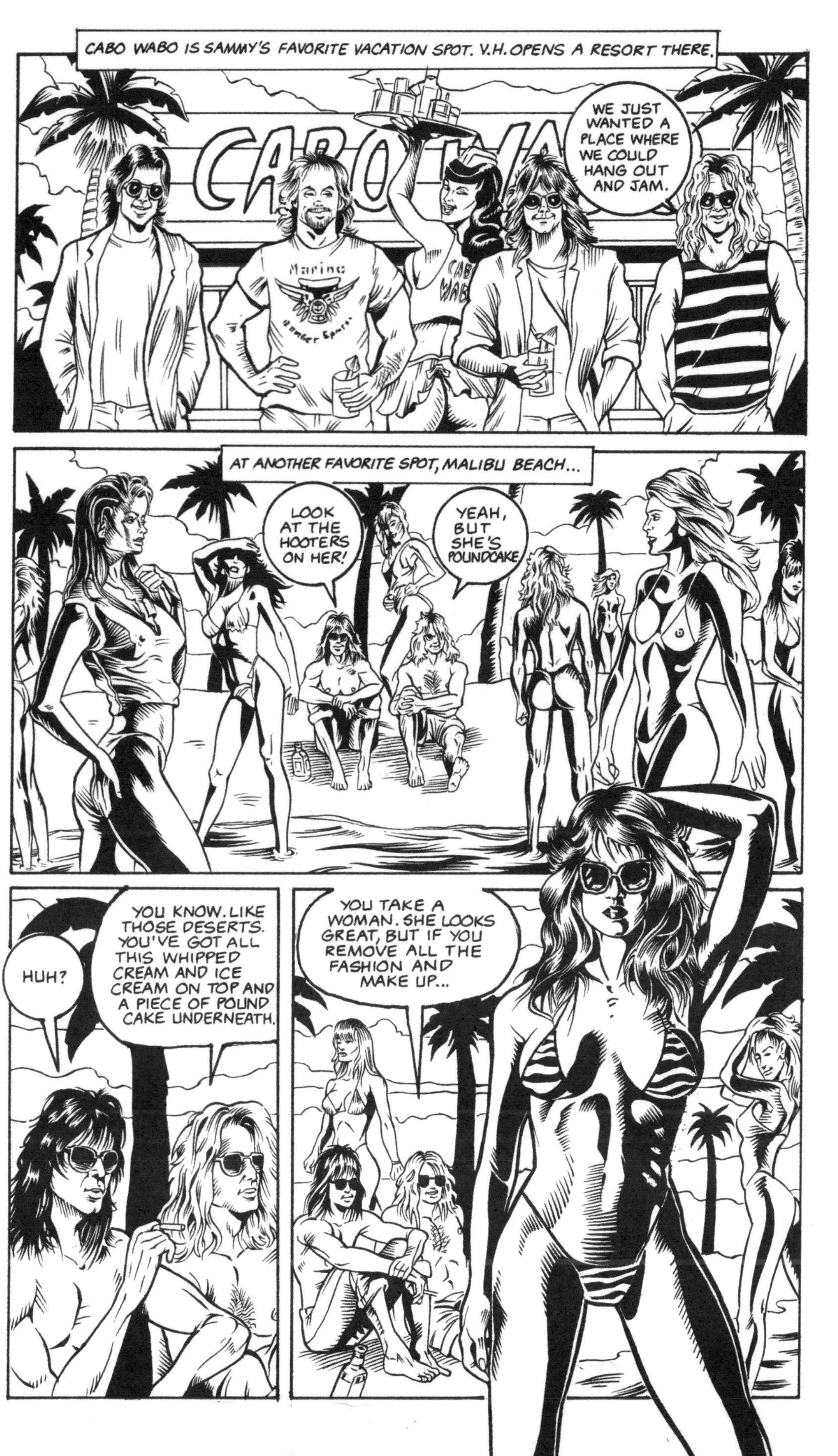
CABO WABO IS SAMMY'S FAVORITE VACATION SPOT. V.H. OPENS A RESORT THERE.
WE JUST WANTED A PLACE WHERE WE COULD HANG OUT AND JAM.
AT ANOTHER FAVORITE SPOT, MALIBU BEACH...
LOOK AT THE HOOTERS ON HER!
YEAH, BUT SHE'S POUNDCAKE
HUH?
YOU KNOW. LIKE THOSE DESERTS. YOU'VE GOT ALL THIS WHIPPED CREAM AND ICE CREAM ON TOP AND A PIECE OF POUND CAKE UNDERNEATH.
YOU TAKE A WOMAN. SHE LOOKS GREAT, BUT IF YOU REMOVE ALL THE FASHION AND MAKE UP...

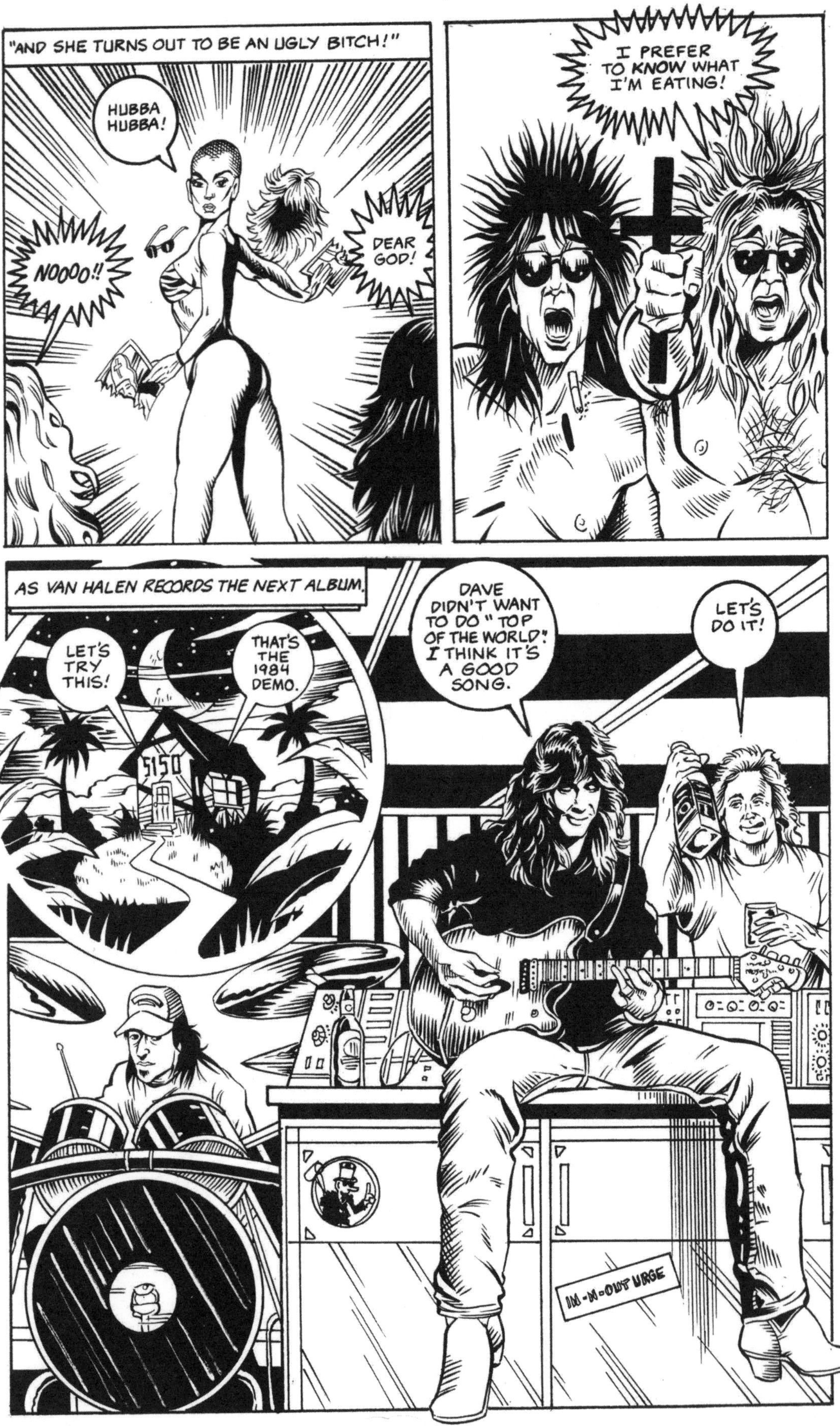
"AND SHE TURNS OUT TO BE AN UGLY BITCH!"
HUBBA HUBBA!
NOOOO!!
DEAR GOD!
I PREFER TO KNOW WHAT I'M EATING!
AS VAN HALEN RECORDS THE NEXT ALBUM.
LET'S TRY THIS!
THAT'S THE 1984 DEMO.
5150
DAVE DIDN'T WANT TO DO "TOP OF THE WORLD". I THINK IT'S A GOOD SONG.
LET'S DO IT!
IN-N-OUT URGE

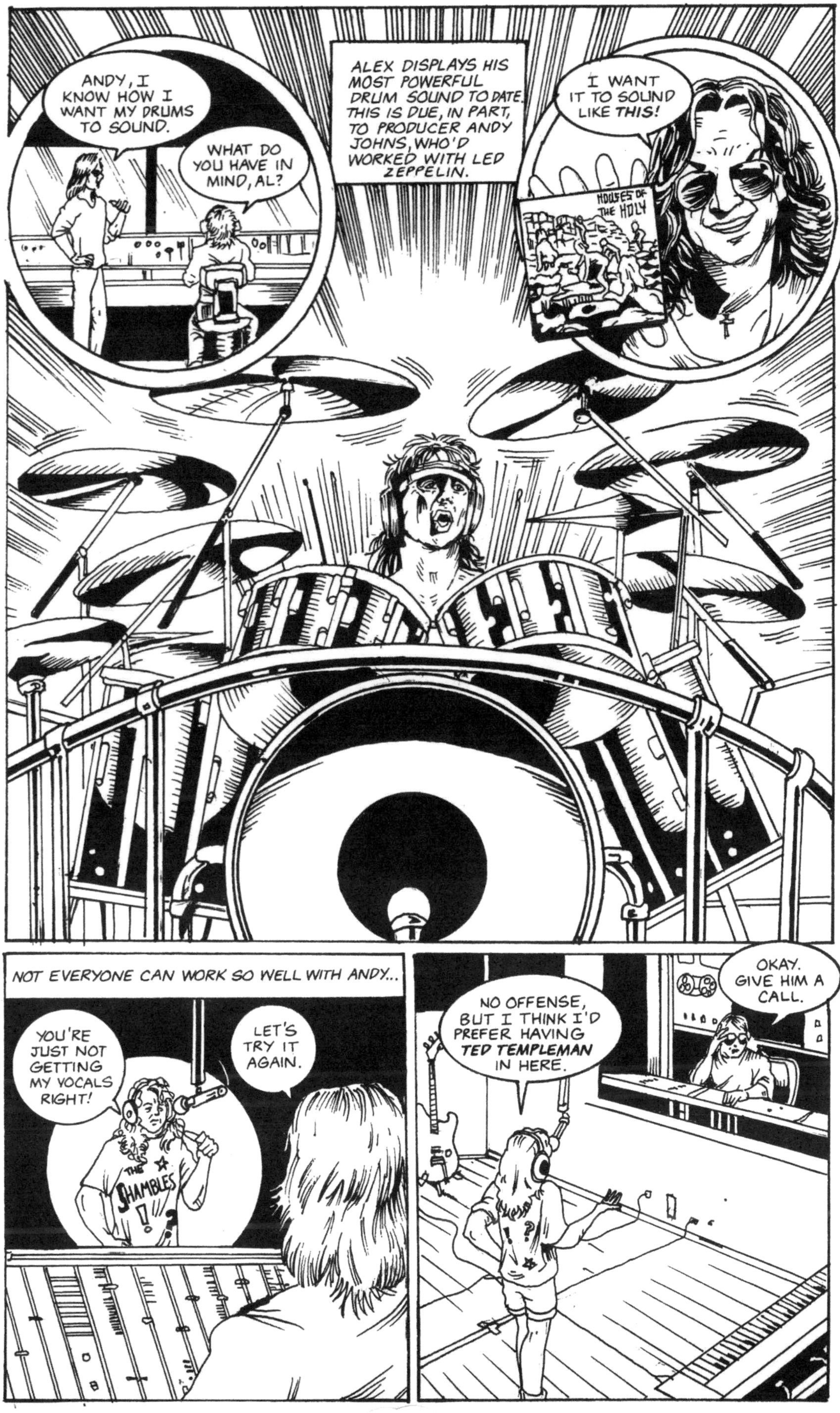
ANDY, I KNOW HOW I WANT MY DRUMS TO SOUND.
WHAT DO YOU HAVE IN MIND, AL?
ALEX DISPLAYS HIS MOST POWERFUL DRUM SOUND TO DATE. THIS IS DUE, IN PART, TO PRODUCER ANDY JOHNS, WHO'D WORKED WITH LED ZEPPELIN.
I WANT IT TO SOUND LIKE THIS!
HOUSES OF THE HOLY
NOT EVERYONE CAN WORK SO WELL WITH ANDY...
YOU'RE JUST NOT GETTING MY VOCALS RIGHT!
LET'S TRY IT AGAIN.
THE SHAMBLES
NO OFFENSE, BUT I THINK I'D PREFER HAVING TED TEMPLEMAN IN HERE.
OKAY. GIVE HIM A CALL.

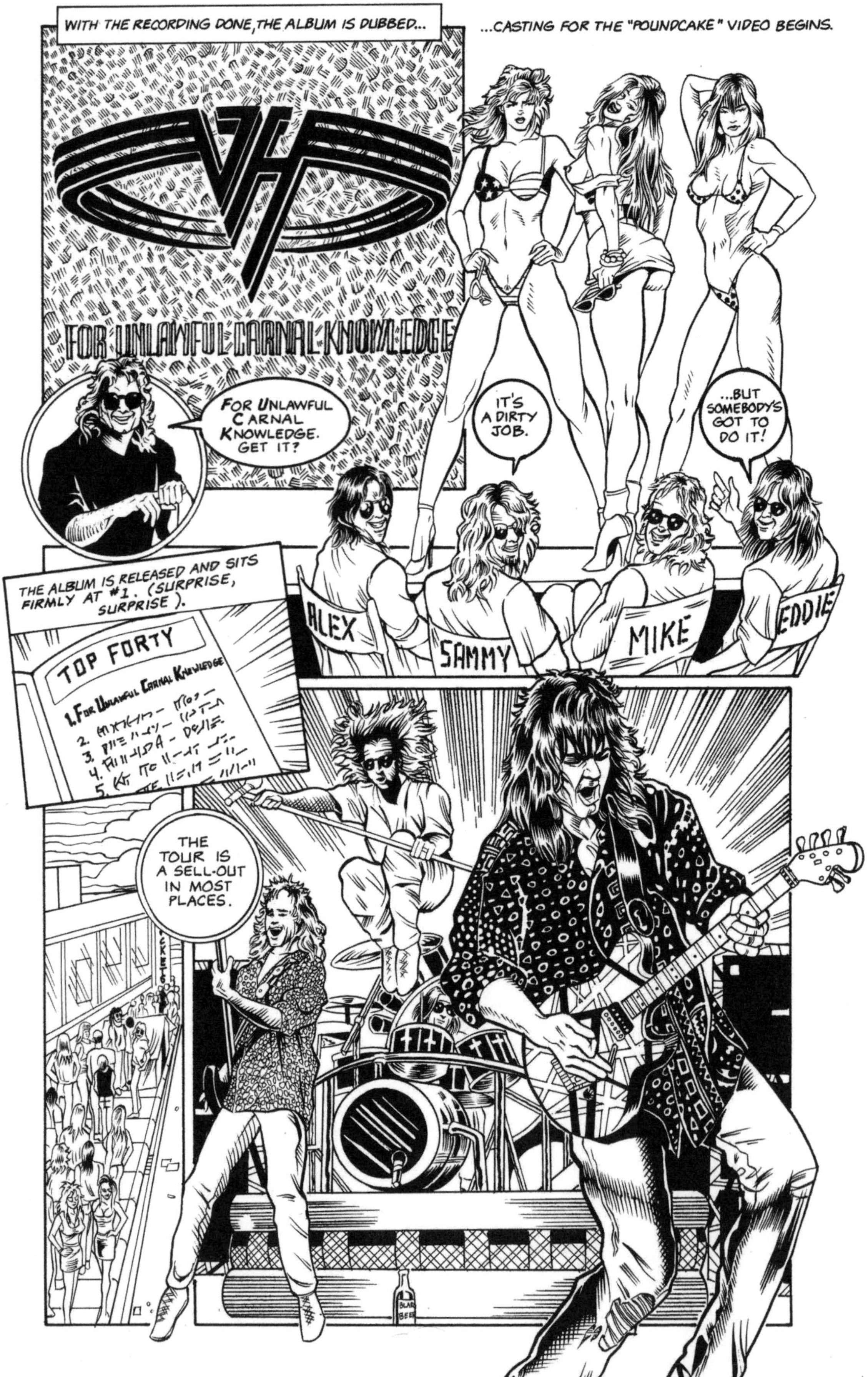
WITH THE RECORDING DONE, THE ALBUM IS DUBBED...
FOR UNLAWFUL CARNAL KNOWLEDGE
FOR UNLAWFUL CARNAL KNOWLEDGE. GET IT?
...CASTING FOR THE "POUNDCAKE" VIDEO BEGINS.
IT'S A DIRTY JOB.
...BUT SOMEBODY'S GOT TO DO IT!
ALEX
SAMMY
MIKE
EDDIE
THE ALBUM IS RELEASED AND SITS FIRMLY AT #1. (SURPRISE, SURPRISE).
TOP FORTY
1. FOR UNLAWFUL CARNAL KNOWLEDGE
THE TOUR IS A SELL-OUT IN MOST PLACES.

THE NINETIES ARE OFF TO A PROFITABLE START FOR THE BAND AS ED UNVEILS HIS OWN LINE OF GUITARS AND AMPS.

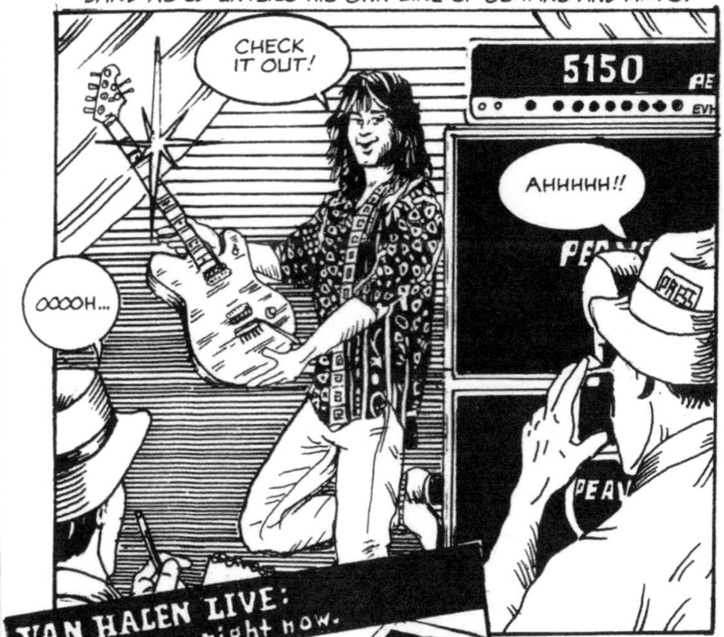
CHECK IT OUT!
AHHHHH!!
OOOOH...
5150

SAMMY EVEN PRODUCES HIS OWN ARRAY OF CASUAL CLOTHING.

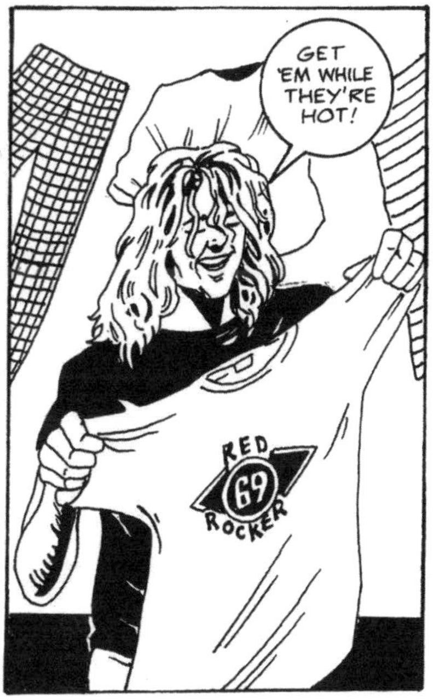
GET 'EM WHILE THEY'RE HOT!
RED 69 ROCKER

THEY ALSO RELEASE THEIR VERY FIRST LIVE ALBUM, "**RIGHT HERE, RIGHT NOW**". A LIVE VIDEO SOON FOLLOWS.

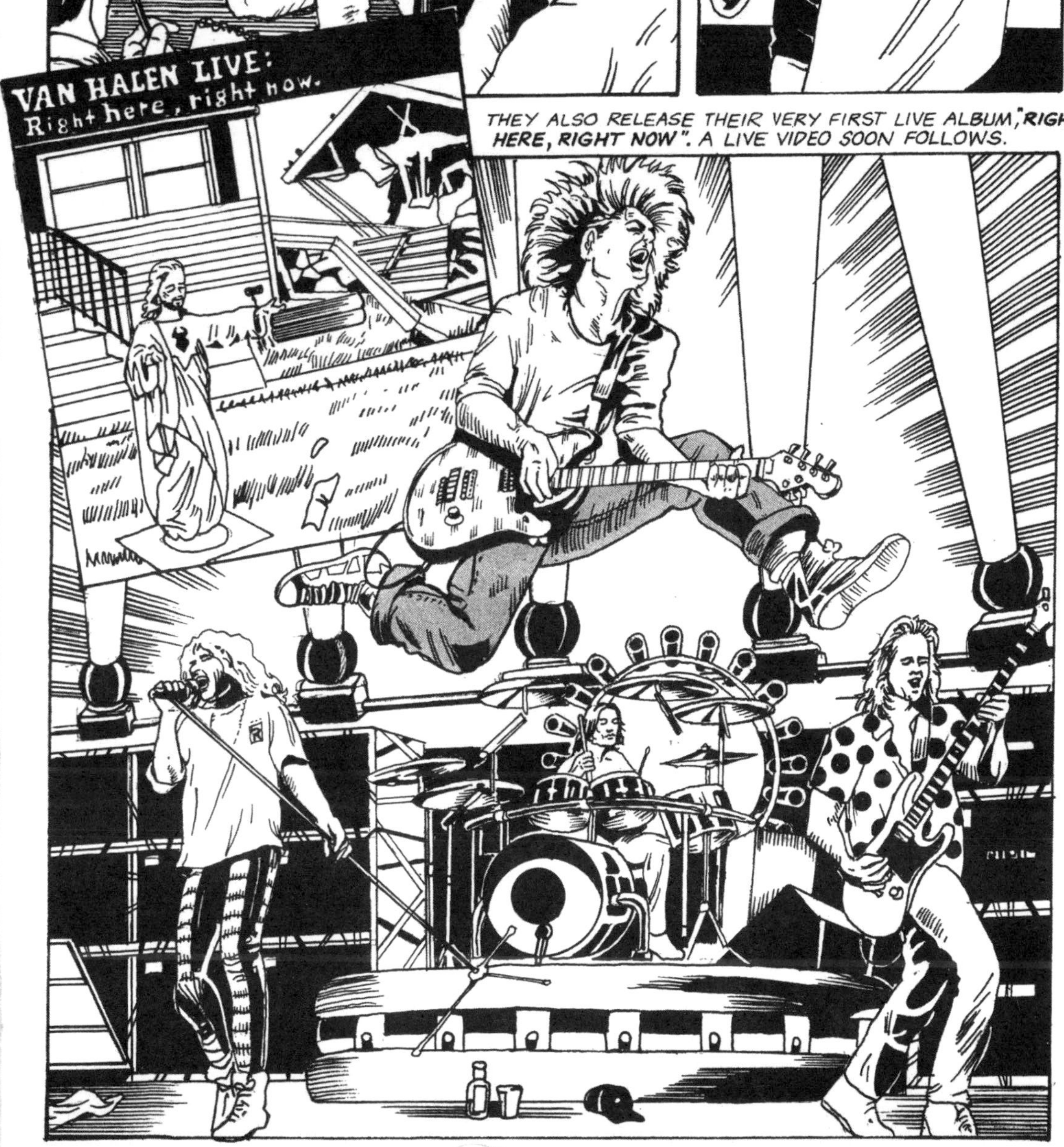
VAN HALEN LIVE:
Right here, right now.

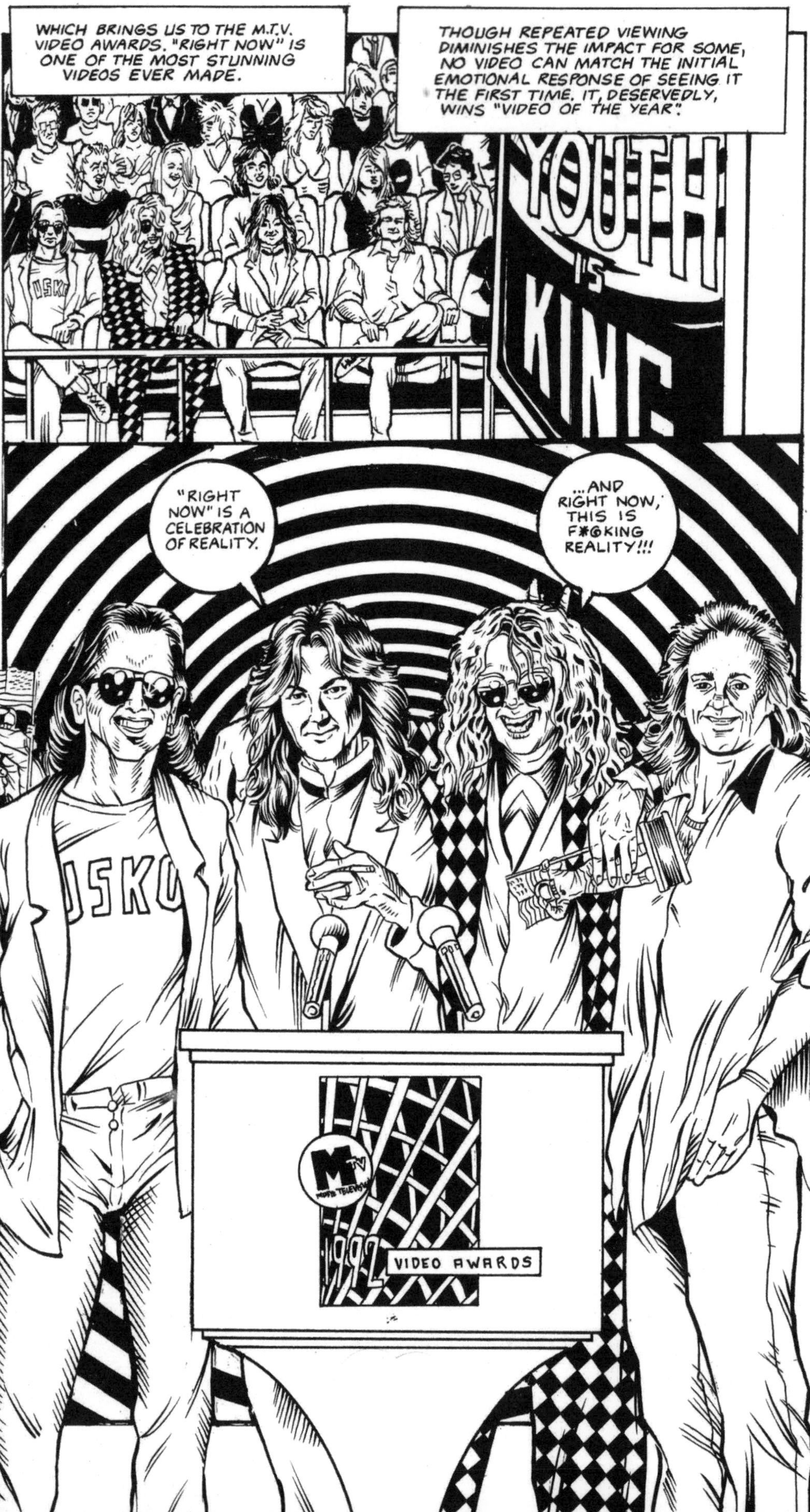
WHICH BRINGS US TO THE M.T.V. VIDEO AWARDS. "RIGHT NOW" IS ONE OF THE MOST STUNNING VIDEOS EVER MADE.
THOUGH REPEATED VIEWING DIMINISHES THE IMPACT FOR SOME, NO VIDEO CAN MATCH THE INITIAL EMOTIONAL RESPONSE OF SEEING IT THE FIRST TIME. IT, DESERVEDLY, WINS "VIDEO OF THE YEAR".
YOUTH IS KING
"RIGHT NOW" IS A CELEBRATION OF REALITY.
...AND RIGHT NOW, THIS IS F*@KING REALITY!!!
USKO
USKO
1992
VIDEO AWARDS